# 1001 MUFFINS

# 1001 MUFFINS,

## BISCUITS, DOUGHNUTS, PANCAKES, WAFFLES, POPOVERS, FRITTERS, SCONES AND OTHER QUICK BREADS

GREGG R. GILLESPIE

PHOTOGRAPHS BY CLAIRE YOUNG, WILD BILL STUDIOS

BLACK DOG
& LEVENTHAL
PUBLISHERS
NEW YORK

Copyright © 1998 by Gregg R. Gillespie

Photographs copyright © 1998 by Black Dog & Leventhal, Inc.

Published by
Black Dog & Leventhal Publishers, Inc.
151 West 19th Street
New York, NY 10011

Distributed by
Workman Publishing Company
708 Broadway
New York, NY 10003

Designed by Martin Lubin Design

Typesetting by Brad Walrod/High Text Graphics

Manufactured in the United States of America

ISBN: 1-57912-042-3

h   g   f   e   d

**Library of Congress Cataloging-in-Publication Data**

Gillespie. Gregg R., 1934–
    1001 muffins, biscuits, doughnuts, pancakes, waffles, popovers, fritters, scones, and other quick breads/Gregg R. Gillespie.
        p.     cm.
    Includes index.
    ISBN 1-57912-042-3
    1. Bread.   2. Biscuits.   3. Muffins.   4. Pancakes, waffles, etc.   I. Title.
TX769.G55   1998
641.8′15—dc21                                          98-23243
                                                                CIP

# ACKNOWLEDGMENTS

As always, I am at a loss for words when it comes to all of those who must be thanked for helping me with this project. The first naturally will be my publisher, J.P. Leventhal, who has had enough confidence in my work to do a fourth book. And many thanks to Pamela Horn, my editor (I don't know how she puts up with me). Then there is a special thanks to Gordon Allan, who has worked as hard and as long on this projects as I have; without his memory I would be lost.

I would also like to thank John Darack at the Dirigo Corporation of Massachusetts, the processor of Cunningham Spice®, who was of great assistance to me at the beginning of this project.

A special thanks also goes out to the employees of the Reno, Nevada, SPCA; the employees of the Reno, Nevada, Animal Control facility; the Reno, Nevada, St. Vincent de Paul; the Washoe County, Nevada, Senior Citizen Center; the employees of the Washoe County, Nevada, Library, North Hills Branch; and of course to the gang at the office of Dr. Marvin Altom.

# CONTENTS

# INTRODUCTION

Since the early 1970s, I have had a fascination with quick breads in general and with muffins specifically. The fascination started with my relocation from Roseville, California, to Portsmouth, New Hampshire. At that time in California, quick breads were almost nonexistent, muffins nowhere to be seen. I discovered these treats back East in New Hampshire. I thought, however, if muffins were as great as people declared—why were they being offered only as a breakfast item? Why wasn't there more variety? Why were some bite-size, while others were huge? When I asked these questions, I always obtained the same answer: "...because that's the way it had always been done."

So I returned to my baking studies, read and baked, baked and read. What I learned surprised me. Almost all muffins and quick breads have only five basic ingredients: flour, baking powder (and/or baking soda), eggs, fat (butter, margarine, shortening, or oil), and milk (or another liquid). Everything beyond these basic ingredients are for variation in flavor or texture, and can be modified and changed to produce a world of new tastes.

So I went back to the kitchen and started to create a multitude of recipes simply by varying flavoring and adjusting the basic ingredients. The results can be found in the pages of this book, and are the product of many years of research and baking.

I have tried to give you, the reader, the widest possible range of recipes from which to choose. Where I did not have, nor could not find, a recipe for a specific category, then I created one anew. I have also tried to make the instructions in this book as simple as possible. I know, because of the kitchen testing by others, that if you follow the instructions as directed, you should have no problem preparing any of these recipes. (One note about the testing process: As each new recipe was tested, the finished product was distributed to senior-citizens' groups, needy families, soup kitchens, and others who were always willing to taste something new.)

Finally, most recipes in this collection suggest various sauces, glazes, or toppings that might be used or served with each baked good. These are serving suggestions only, and the choice of whether to use that specific addition (or to omit it all together) is left up to the baker—or, perhaps, those lucky enough to enjoy the fruits of his or her labor!

Gregg Gillespie
1998

# Chapter 1

# THE BAKER'S KITCHEN

## Basic Ingredients

There are only a few basic ingredients required to make quick breads.

**Baking powder** A leavening agent added to batters that causes them to rise during baking. Baking powder is a combination of baking soda and cream of tartar. It is usually added to mixtures that contain some acid, and reacts with the liquids in the batter, producing gas bubbles. Double-acting baking powder, the most common type, produces this bubbling effect twice: First during mixing, and then in the heat of the oven. Baking powder gets old and loses its leavening power, so it should be replaced at least once a year.

It is very important to accurately measure the amout of baking powder or baking soda used in a recipe. If more is added than necessary it will adversely affect the taste of the end product and may give it a very crumbly texture that will cause it to fall apart when you remove it from the pan.

Too much leavening in a recipe is usually the cause of baked goods falling during and immediately after baking. If an item has too little baking powder in it, it will be dense.

**Baking soda** Baking soda, or bicarbonate of soda, is a leavening agent used alone or in combination with baking powder. Dough and batter containing baking soda should be baked as soon as they are mixed because the soda starts reacting and creating gas bubbles as soon as it comes in contact with acid and liquid. Baking soda should be replaced about once every six to eight months.

**Butter and margarine** Butter and margarine are the most common kind of fat called for in the recipes of this book, although shortening, oils, and even bacon drippings or lard are sometimes used. Butter and margarine can be purchased salted or sweet. Baking with sweet butter and adding your own salt according to the recipe give the baker more control over the amount of salt used. Always use the stick-type butter or margarine—never substitute

whipped or tub-style–for baking.

**Eggs** In all cases, the eggs called for in the recipes of this book are large grade-A eggs. Unless directed otherwise, all eggs will be cold, although eggs at room temperature will beat to a higher degree of volume.

**Flour** In all cases unless otherwise stated, the flour referred to in this book will be bleached, all-purpose flour. For those who are so inclined, unbleached all-purpose flour may be used. Also listed in some recipes is whole-wheat flour, buckwheat flour, corn flour, graham flour, rice flour, rye flour, and soy flour. These flours can be found in health-food and specialty-food stores.

**Milk** Unless otherwise stated, you should use whole, fresh milk for the recipes in this book that call for milk.

**Sugar** There are several types of sugar used in this book. Most commonly, white, granulated sugar is called for. Brown sugar, meaning light-brown sugar unless dark-brown is specifically called for, is also used extensively. Powdered sugar, also called confectioners' sugar or icing sugar, is used when sugar crystals would effect the end product.

## Secondary Ingredients

Following are ingredients commonly called for in the recipes of this book in order to vary flavor and texture. They are added in addition to, and sometimes as substitutions for, the basic ingredients listed above.

**Buttermilk** Although readily available in anything but the smallest grocery store, sour milk (see below) can usually be used as a substitution.

**Canola Oil** A rapeseed oil that is commonly used because of the low saturated fat content (about 6% lower than other oils). By choice I have used canola extensively, but other neutral-flavored vegetable oils, such as safflower and soy can be substituted.

**Heavy cream** Heavy cream is sometimes used in place of milk to add richness. It is sometimes called for whipped in order to add lightness to a recipe or to be used as a topping or garnish. When whipping cream, for best results have it well-chilled and chill the bowl and beaters and whisk as well. Whip cream only until it forms soft, light peaks—over whipping will

produce a heavy product and will eventually result in butter.

**Honey** Honey acts as a sweetener, but also adds a distinctive flavor to baked goods. Because of this, and because of its high water content, honey and sugar should not be used interchangeably.

**Hot Sauce** Many commercial hot sauces are available, with brands varying regionally. Recipes calling for hot sauce in this book are referring specifically to the Tabasco®-type sauce, and not to salsa or pepper relish.

**Maple syrup** In addition to being used on pancakes and waffles, maple syrup is also called for as a sweetener in some baked goods. Maple-flavored syrup can be used as a substitute, but it is not recommended as these syrups cannot replicate the flavor of pure maple syrup. If your syrup crystallizes, place the jar or bottle in hot water for a few minutes and it will be smooth again.

**Molasses** This thick, flavorful syrup is a by-product of sugar processing. Sulfured, unsulfured, and black-strap are commonly available, and any of these may be used in the recipes in this book unless a specific variety is called for. If you do not have molasses at hand, dark corn syrup can be used as a substitution, although it will not impart the same distinctive flavor.

**Sour cream and yogurt** Sour cream and yogurt are used to impart a richness and mild

acidity or tang to baked goods. They may usually be used interchangeably in the recipes. Yogurt, in addition to the plain, unflavored variety, comes in many flavors, and a specific flavor is sometimes called for in order to complement the other flavors in a recipe. For example, in a plum-based bread, plum-flavored yogurt may be called for.

**Sour milk** If you do not have sour milk on hand, add one tablespoon of cider vinegar to one cup of fresh milk and you will have a substitute.

## Equipment

With the right tools, the making of any of the quick breads, muffins, or other recipes in this book should be one of the simplest baking experiences. Chances are good you will have every one of the items listed below.

**Blender** Blenders can perform a number of jobs in the kitchen, from pureeing fruits and vegetables to grinding nuts. A heavy-duty blender with a glass container is recommended.

**Food processor** Food processors usually have a clear plastic container with a cover, and a very sharp blade inserted into the container which can chop or puree foods. Most also come with a number of additional blades for shredding, slicing, or mixing dough. While not an absolute essential, the food processor can accomplish some tasks extremely well and rapidly and so is called for in a number of recipes in this book.

**Loaf or bread pans** Loaf pans used for making quick breads are usually metal, although there is a full variety made of glass, universally referred to as Pyrex®, that work as well as the metal (although baking times should be extended slightly because of the thickness of the glass). The size of the pan called for in each recipe represents the size used during the testing processes. Other sizes may be substituted, as long as baking times are adjusted accordingly.

**Measuring cups** There is nothing more important to the baker than a good set of measuring cups. If the cups that you use are inaccurate, you will not get good results. You need both a set of dry measuring cups (the type in which the rim of the cup is equal to the quantity stated) and at least a 1-cup glass measuring cup for liquids. Do not use liquid measuring cups for dry ingredients or vice-versa—the measurements will not be accurate.

**Measuring spoons** Like measuring cups, good measuring spoons are extremely important to the baker. Sets of spoons usually include ¼, ½ and 1 teaspoon spoons as well as 1 tablespoon. Do not purchase plastic spoons or flimsy metal ones as they will become worn and bent

enough over time to make measurement inaccurate.

**Mixing bowls** You should have at least three mixing bowls: one large, one medium, and one small. Invest in a good set of mixing bowls, either ceramic, heavy glass, or stainless steel. (Plastic is not recommended as it tends to absorb odors and flavors over time and becomes difficult to clean. Also, if exposed to heat they can melt or warp.) Most professional bakers prefer stainless-steel bowls: they don't rust, they are easy to clean, and they don't break.

**Mixing spoons** There are those who think a wooden spoon is an absolute necessity for baking. I do not. A good large metal mixing spoon will do as well, the only requisite is that the bowl of the spoon be large enough to do the job and that the handle be sturdy.

**Muffin tins or pans** Although commercial bakers use large-size muffin pans, those available to the home baker are usually of a smaller size. For this book, the measurements used to identify the sizes of the muffin baking cups were taken by measuring across the top of the cup. The smallest size is 1½-inches and ¾-inch deep, and there are usually 24 baking cups in each pan of this size. Then there is the 2-inch size with a cup depth of 1-inch, and 6 or 12 cups per pan. The next size

is 2¾-inches across and 1¼-inches deep, and can be found with 6, 8, and 12 cups per pan; this size is the most standard for the home. The largest size is a 3½-inch cup with a depth of 1⅝ inches, with pans generally holding 6 cups. Remember that the sizes called for in a specific recipe are recommendations only; the batter may be baked in other-size cups as long as the baking time is adjusted.

**Pastry brush** A fine-bristled pastry brush is an absolute must for spreading on egg washes, glazes, or melted butter. Avoid using brushes with nylon bristles, as they can melt when used with hot liquids.

**Potholders and oven mitts** For baking, oven mitts are recommended because of the added protection they offer to the wrists and arms. This is particularly important when reaching into a hot oven. Replace any potholder or mitt that has worn spots or rips, and never use a damp mitt or holder.

**Rubber spatulas** If you are purchasing them new, purchase the ones with wooden handles. Two spatulas are recommended: one should be at least 4 inches long, and another should be small enough to fit into small cans and jars.

**Wire cooling racks** Wire racks allow for circulation of air around the sides of cooling baked goods. This allows for faster cooling, and also prevents condensation from forming on the bottom of the items.

**Wire whisks** There are those who prefer the round wire whisk, and some prefer the flat. They both work equally as well. I suggest that you have at least three of varied sizes: a small 8-inch, a medium 10-inch, and a large 12-inch. These three sizes were used in the testing of the recipes in this book.

## Muffin and Quick Bread Preparation and Baking

Quick breads and muffins are extremely easy to make if you are willing to follow the six simple steps outlined below. With a very few variations, these steps are followed in almost every recipe in this book. Those variations are little more than letting something sit for a time, or baking the muffins or bread before adding or brushing with a final ingredient. Hopefully, the texture and flavor of your finished products will be as tasty and inviting as I have tried to make them.

**Step one** Position a rack in the center of the oven and preheat to the temperature called for in the recipe.

**Step two** Prepare the baking pan or pans as directed. For both the breads and muffins, lightly grease and flour the bottom of the pan or, in the case of muffins, you may use baking cups to paper-line the pan. (Paper cups are not usually available for very large or very small muffins.)

**Step three** In a large bowl, using a fork or a wire whisk, blend together the dry ingredients. A large bowl is used so that all final blending can be accomplished in this bowl.

**Step four** In a medium bowl, using a fork or electric mixer on medium speed, mix, blend, or beat together the moist ingredients called for in the recipe.

**Step five** Using a large spoon or spatula, combine the two mixtures (the moist ingredients and the dry ingredients), blending until the dry ingredients are just moistened. This step is the most important. When the two mixes are being blended, you must be sure not to overmix. Overmixing will result in tough muffins and breads; a few lumps in the batter is normal.

**Step six** Bake according to the recipe directions, and use the method of testing for doneness as indicated. Remove the pan from the oven and cool on a wire rack for 5 minutes before removing the item from the pan. (While this isn't always necessary when paper liners are used with muffins, it should always be followed when paper liners are not used.)

While some of the recipes direct that a particular syrup, glaze, or other topping be

used on the finished product, it isn't necessary to do this. While preparing the items to be photographed, I tried to stay away from the glazes and various other decorations that were not an integral part of the recipe. To assist you, I have tried to show you the items as they would appear coming out of the oven.

## A Note on Ingredients

Every recipe listed has an addition in one form or another, it is the thing that gives each muffin a distinctive taste. It may be as simple as sprinkling granulated sugar over the top of the mixture before baking; or filling with chili and bean, or sausage meat.

I try to place most of the heavy items into the dry mixture, (i.e. raisins, etc.) in this way the ingredient will become coated with the dry flour mixture, and will not sink to the bottom during baking. It is simple, just blend it in with the flour and baking powder. If on the other hand, something like onions that will impart a distinctive taste to the muffin, then I will ask for it to be placed in the liquid mixture.

There are recipes where a single spoonful of the mixture is dropped into a muffin cup, a spoonful of filling is pressed into the first spoonful in the pan, and a second spoonful of the mixture in dropped on top of filling. This is done so the filling is completely covered. Another method of filling is to press a small cube of cream cheese or fruit into the mixture in the pan, just before baking. When the batter rises during baking, most of the cube or filling will be covered.

When something is to be placed on top, just loosely scatter it over the top of the muffin, and let it bake as directed. This is called the crumble method and is widely used in baking.

A very old and popular way to coat muffins with sugar, is to bake the muffin, cool it on a wire rack for 5 minutes, and when it is cool to the touch, roll it in a still warm liquefied clarified butter, and immediately roll it in granulated sugar. This same method can be used for coating the muffins with nuts, or with sesame seeds.

One very unique way to add flavor to a muffin is in the Passover Recipe (see page 215). In this case the baking pan is greased with schmaltz, a kind of flavored chicken fat. When the muffin mixture is dropped into the pans, and baked, the chicken-fat coating melts and spreads around the muffin.

## Hints for Baking

**1** Always read a recipe over at least once before starting.

**2** Since oven temperatures vary, most recipes offer a range of baking times.

Always test for doneness at the minimum baking time stated; for instance, if the recipe suggests a baking time of 12 to 15 minutes, use 12 minutes as the first time to check the item for doneness.

**3** Be sure to allow adequate time for the oven to preheat before you begin baking.

**4** A dark metal pan or baking sheet will bake faster than a shiny metal pan.

**5** If baking in batches, always allow the pans to cool to room temperature before reusing.

**6** To keep breads and muffins from sticking, grease your pans with a fat that does not contain salt and then lightly dust with flour. Do not assume that nonstick pans will not stick; grease them lightly also.

**7** If using older muffin baking pans, fill as many cups as you have batter for, and fill any remaining empty cups half full with water. This will prevent the pan from warping.

**8** Muffins may be reheated by very lightly sprinkling them with water before placing them in a paper bag. Close the bag and place in an oven preheated to 400 degrees F and turn off the oven. Do not disturb for 10 to 15 minutes. Muffins may also be reheated by placing them in a microwave for 4 to 5 seconds;

place a paper towel over the top of the muffins before reheating them in this way.

**9** Allow baked goods to cool completely on a wire rack before wrapping or storing them. This prevents condensation from spoiling the texture of the item and decreases the chance of rapid molding.

**10** When measuring liquids, use glass measuring cups and read the measure at eye level.

**11** When measuring dry ingredients, use measuring cups that have rims level with the designated amount and use a knife or spatula as a straight edge to level off the top.

**12** When measuring sticky products like honey, molasses, and corn syrup, lightly grease or oil the measuring utensil first; the liquid will run out of the cup easily, making the measurement more accurate. If oil or shortening are used in the recipe, measure these first; this will automatically oil the utensil.

**13** If a recipe calls for "½ cup of almonds, ground," measure out a ½ cup of whole almonds first, and then grind them. If a recipe calls for "½ cup ground almonds," grind the nuts before measuring them.

**14** Since flour is the primary ingredient in most baked goods, you should always have good quality, fresh flour on hand. Store flour in an airtight container for best results.

15 Unless otherwise stated, you should use double-acting baking powder when baking powder is called for in the recipes in this book.

16 If a recipe calls for sour milk or buttermilk, and you do not have any at hand, simply place a tablespoon of cider vinegar into a cup of milk and let set for 2 to 3 minutes before using.

17 A slice of fresh bread placed in an airtight container with hard brown sugar will loosen the sugar within several hours.

18 Egg whites will beat up lighter when they are at a temperature, between 60 and 70 degrees F.

19 For best results when beating egg whites, be sure the bowl and beaters or whisk are clean and free of any grease or fat.

20 To determine if an egg is fresh, place it in a small pot of cool salted water. If it sinks it is fresh, if it floats it is not. Also, the shells of fresh eggs are usually rough and chalky while old eggs have a smooth shell.

21 Never wash fresh eggs before storing them in the refrigerator. Washing destroys the protective coating on the egg shell that helps to keep it fresh.

22 If you have problems separating eggs, try breaking the eggs into a small funnel. The yolk will stay in the top and the white can ooze down into a cup or bowl.

23 When making hard-cooked eggs, never boil the eggs. For best results they should be simmered.

24 To make shelling hard-cooked eggs easier, cook them in salted water and immediately rinse in cold water after cooking.

25 Evaporated milk can be used to make a substitute for whipped cream if prepared properly. Have the milk, bowl, and beater chilled as cold as possible without freezing prior to whipping the milk and it will whip up similarly to heavy cream.

26 To get more juice out of a lemon, soak it first in hot water for several minutes and then use the palm of your hand to roll it back and forth a few times on a flat surface.

27 To easily remove the skin from peaches and apricots, blanch the fruit in a solution of 2 gallons water and ½ cup baking soda. Bring it to a boil and place each fruit in the liquid until the skin is loosened. Remove the fruit, immerse it in cold water until cooled, and slip the skins off.

28 An alternate method for plumping raisins is to thoroughly rinse the raisins and strain in a colander. Cover and place the colander over a pot of boiling water for about 5 to 10 minutes.

29 When stewing rhubarb, add ⅛ teaspoonful of baking soda for each 2 cups of rhubarb. This will reduce the amount of sugar needed to sweeten the rhubarb.

30 If a recipe calls for snipped parsley or other fresh herbs, wash them, shake them dry, and snip them into small pieces with kitchen shears just before incorporating them into the preparation.

31 Bacon will curl less if dipped in ice-cold water prior to frying.

32 An easy way to remove unwanted fat from sausages, including hot dogs and frankfurters, is to boil them in water before cooking them by another method.

33 Most people throw away meat fat and renderings, but they can be saved in the refrigerator or freezer and added to stews and soups for additional flavor.

34 If a recipe calls for drained canned fruit and does not include the liquid, save the juices. They can be used for making gelatin desserts, combined with ginger ale to make a drink, or thickened with cornstarch or arrowroot to form sauces.

35 When cooked chopped meat or poultry is needed in a muffin recipe, consider using leftovers from a previous meal.

# Substitutions

| INGREDIENT | AMOUNT | SUBSTITUTE |
|---|---|---|
| Allspice | 1 teaspoon | ½ teaspoon cinnamon plus ½ teaspoon cloves |
| Arrowroot | 1½ teaspoons | 1 tablespoon flour plus 1½ teaspoons corn starch |
| Baking powder | 1 teaspoon | ⅓ teaspoon baking soda plus ½ teaspoon cream of tartar |
| | | ¼ teaspoon baking soda plus ½ cup milk (decrease the liquid in the recipe by ½ cup) |
| Butter | 1 cup | 1 cup shortening plus ½ teaspoon salt |
| | | ¾ cup plus 2 tablespoons lard plus ½ teaspoon salt |
| | | 1 cup margarine |
| Buttermilk | 1 cup | 1 cup plain yogurt |
| | | 1 cup minus 1 tablespoon milk plus 1 tablespoon fresh lemon juice or vinegar |
| Chocolate (semisweet) | 1⅔ ounces | 1 ounce unsweetened chocolate plus 4 teaspoons sugar |
| Chocolate chips | 6 ounces | 2 squares unsweetened chocolate plus 2 tablespoons shortening and ½ cup sugar |
| Chocolate (unsweetened) | 1 ounce | 3 tablespoons cocoa plus 1 tablespoon fat |
| Cocoa (semisweet) | ¼ cup | 1 ounce chocolate (reduce the amount of fat in the recipe by 1½ teaspoons) |
| Corn syrup | 1 cup | 1 cup honey |
| | | 1 cup sugar (increase the liquid in the recipe by ½ cup) |
| Egg | 1 large | 2 large egg yolks plus 1 tablespoon water |
| Fine Herbs | 4 teaspoons | 1 teaspoon chervil, 1 teaspoon chives, 1 teaspoon tarragon, 1 teaspoon parsley |
| Flour, all-purpose | 1 cup | 1 cup plus 2 tablespoons cake flour |
| | | 1 cup minus 2 tablespoons unsifted flour |
| | | 1½ cups bread crumbs |
| | | 1 cup rolled oats |
| Lemon extract | 1 teaspoon | 2 teaspoons grated lemon zest |
| Maple sugar | ½ cup | 1 cup maple syrup |
| | | 1 cup brown sugar |
| Milk, whole | 1 cup | 1 cup reconstituted nonfat dry milk plus 2 teaspoons melted butter or margarine |
| | | ½ cup evaporated milk plus ½ cup water |
| | | 1 cup buttermilk plus ½ teaspoon baking soda |
| Molasses | 1 cup | 1 cup honey |
| Pumpkin-pie spice | 1 teaspoon | ½ teaspoon ground cinnamon, ¼ teaspoon ground nutmeg, ⅛ teaspoon ground ginger, ⅛ teaspoon ground cloves |
| Prepared mustard | 1 tablespoon | 1 teaspoon dry mustard plus 2 teaspoons red wine vinegar |
| Sour cream | 1 cup | 1 cup plain yogurt |
| | | ¾ cup plus 2 tablespoons sour milk plus ⅓ cup butter |
| Sour milk | 1 cup | 1 cup plain yogurt |
| | | 1 cup minus 1 tablespoon milk plus 1 tablespoon fresh lemon juice or vinegar |
| Sugar, granulated | 1 cup | 1 cup corn syrup (decrease liquid in recipe by ¼ cup) |
| | | 1⅓ cups molasses (decrease the liquid in the recipe by ⅓ cup) |
| | | 1 cup brown sugar |
| | | 1 cup honey (decrease the liquid in the recipe by ¼ cup) |
| | | 1¾ cups packed powdered sugar |
| Vegetable shortening, melted | 1 cup | 1 cup cooking oil |
| Yogurt, plain | 1 cup | 1 cup buttermilk |
| | | 1 cup pureed cottage cheese |
| | | 1 cup sour cream |

## EGGS

| | |
|---|---|
| 1 egg | 2 egg yolks |
| 1 cup egg yolks | yolks of 12 to 14 large eggs |
| 1 cup egg whites | whites of 8 large eggs |

## MILK & DAIRY

| | |
|---|---|
| 1 cup heavy cream | 2 cups whipped cream |
| ⅓ cup evaporated milk | ⅓ cup dry milk plus 6 tablespoons water |
| One 14-ounce can evaporated milk | 1⅔ cups |
| 8 ounces sour cream | 1 cup |
| 1 pound cheese | 4 cup grated cheese |
| 8 ounces cream cheese | 6 tablespoons |

# Chapter 2

# MUFFINS

Muffins are no longer for breakfast anymore, and the recipes in this collection prove that statement to be true. These muffin recipes were created with the idea in mind that sweet or savory muffins are good any time of day. In this collection you will find the traditional, tried-and-true recipes that go back one hundred or so years; as well as about one hundred muffin recipes that have never before been published. The recipes have been thoroughly tested. While some titles sound new and different—try all of them, you'll love them.

## 100-YEAR-OLD MUFFINS

*MAKES: 5 to 6 muffins*

1 cup cornmeal
1 tablespoon baking powder
¼ teaspoon ground nutmeg
½ teaspoon salt
2 tablespoons butter or margarine
1 tablespoon granulated sugar
2 large eggs
¾ cup milk
1 cup cooked mashed potatoes

**1** Position the rack in the center of the oven and preheat to 400 degrees F. Lightly grease or line with paper baking cups six 2¾-inch muffin cups.

**2** In a large bowl, blend together the cornmeal, baking powder, nutmeg, and salt. In a medium bowl, cut the butter into the sugar. Stir in the eggs, milk, and potatoes. Combine the two mixtures, blending until the dry ingredients are just moistened.

**3** Spoon the batter into the prepared muffin cups, filling each about three-quarters full. Bake for 15 to 20 minutes, or until the tops start to turn a light golden and a cake tester or wooden toothpick inserted into the center of a muffin comes out clean. Cool in the pan on a wire rack for 5 to 7 minutes. Serve warm, or invert onto the rack to cool completely.

**SERVING SUGGESTION: Serve with seedless jam or preserves.**

## ALL-SEASON MUFFINS

*MAKES: 11 to 12 muffins*

2¼ cups all-purpose flour
2½ teaspoons baking powder
1 teaspoon baking soda
2 large eggs
⅓ cup butter or margarine, melted
½ cup granulated sugar
1 teaspoon vanilla extract
1 cup plus 3 tablespoons plain
    yogurt or sour cream
Fresh Fruit Sauce (see recipe below)

**1** Position the rack in the center of the oven and preheat to 375 degrees F. Lightly grease or line with paper baking cups twelve 2¾-inch muffin cups.

**2** In a large bowl, blend together the flour, baking powder, and baking soda. In a medium bowl, beat the eggs until foamy. Beat in the butter, sugar, vanilla extract, and yogurt. Combine the two mixtures, blending until the dry ingredients are just moistened.

**3** Spoon the batter into the prepared muffin cups, filling each about three-quarters full. Bake for 15 to 20 minutes, or until a cake tester or wooden toothpick inserted into the center of a muffin comes out clean. Cool in the pan on a wire rack for 5 to 7 minutes. Serve warm, or invert onto the rack to cool completely. Top with Fresh Fruit Sauce.

## FRESH FRUIT SAUCE

*MAKES: 1¼ cup*

½ cup light corn syrup
2 cups any chopped fresh fruit in
    season
1 teaspoon lemon juice
¼ teaspoon almond extract

In the container of a blender or food processor, combine the corn syrup, fruit, and lemon juice. Process on high speed until the mixture is smooth. Pour into a serving bowl and stir in the almond extract.

## ALMOND-FLAVORED APRICOT MUFFINS

MAKES: *9 to 10 muffins*

1 cup diced dried apricots
¼ cup boiling water
1 teaspoon baking soda
1 cup plain yogurt or sour cream
1¼ cups all-purpose flour
1 cup whole-wheat flour
1 tablespoon baking powder
½ cup granulated sugar
4 large egg whites
2 tablespoons butter or margarine, melted
1½ teaspoons almond extract

1  Position the rack in the center of the oven and preheat to 375 degrees F. Lightly grease or line with paper baking cups twelve 2¾-inch muffin cups.

2  In a small bowl, soak the apricots in the boiling water for 5 to 7 minutes. In another small bowl, stir the baking soda into the yogurt. Drain the apricots and pat dry between two layers of paper towel. In a large bowl, blend together the flours, apricots, baking powder, and sugar. In a medium bowl, beat the egg whites until foamy. Beat in the yogurt, butter, and almond extract. Combine the two mixtures, blending until the dry ingredients are just moistened.

3  Spoon the batter into the prepared muffin cups, filling each about three-quarters full. Bake for 15 to 20 minutes, or until a cake tester or wooden toothpick inserted into the center of a muffin comes out clean. Remove from the oven and immediately brush the tops of the muffins with glaze. Cool on a wire rack for 5 to 7 minutes. Serve warm, or invert onto the rack to cool completely.

SERVING SUGGESTION: **Serve with a marmalade-type jam.**

## ALMOND-FLAVORED BLACKBERRY MUFFINS

MAKES: *11 to 12 muffins*

2 cups all-purpose flour
2 teaspoons baking powder
½ teaspoon salt
2 cups fresh blackberries, rinsed and dried
½ cup butter or margarine
1¼ cups powdered sugar
2 teaspoons Amaretto liqueur or almond extract
2 large eggs
½ cup heavy cream
Ginger Cream (see recipe below)

1  Position the rack in the center of the oven and preheat to 400 degrees F. Lightly grease or line with paper baking cups twelve 2¾-size muffin cups.

2  In a large bowl, blend together the flour, baking powder, and salt. Fold in the blackberries. In a medium bowl, cream the butter and sugar until smooth. Beat in the Amaretto. Beat in the eggs, one at a time, beating vigorously after each addition. Beat in the heavy cream. Combine the two mixtures, blending until the dry ingredients are just moistened.

3  Spoon the batter into the prepared muffin cups, filling each about three-quarters full. Bake for 15 to 20 minutes, or until a wooden toothpick is removed clean. Cool in the pan on a wire rack for 5 to 7 minutes. Serve warm, or invert onto the rack to cool completely. Top with Ginger Cream.

## GINGER CREAM

MAKES: *2 cups*

1 cup heavy cream
2 teaspoons granulated sugar
2 teaspoons ground ginger

In a medium bowl, using a whisk or an electric mixer on high speed, beat the cream foamy before adding the sugar and ginger. Continue beating until soft peaks form. Cover and chill until ready to use.

# ALMOST ICE CREAM MUFFINS

MAKES: *12 to 14 muffins*

1½ cups all-purpose flour
1 teaspoon baking powder
1 large egg
2 tablespoons canola oil
2 cups (1 pint) flavored ice cream of choice
Orange Marshmallow Sauce (see recipe below)

**1** Position the rack in the center of the oven and preheat to 400 degrees F. Lightly grease or line with paper baking cups fourteen 2¾-inch muffin cups.

**2** In a large bowl, blend together the flour and baking powder. In a medium bowl, beat the egg, oil, and ice cream until smooth. (Do not overbeat as this will melt the ice cream.) Combine the two mixtures, blending until the dry ingredients are just moistened.

**3** Spoon the batter into the prepared muffin cups, filling each about three-quarters full. Bake for 15 to 20 minutes, or until a cake tester or wooden toothpick inserted into the center of a muffin comes out clean. Cool in the pan on a wire rack for 5 to 7 minutes. Serve warm, or invert onto the rack to cool completely. Top with Orange Marshmallow Sauce.

## ORANGE MARSHMALLOW SAUCE

MAKES: *About ⅓ to ½ cup*

16 large marshmallows, each cut into quarters
2 teaspoons grated orange zest
2 tablespoons fresh orange juice

In the top of a double boiler set over simmering water, melt the marshmallows, stirring, until smooth. Remove from the heat and stir in the orange zest and orange juice. Serve at once.

2 cups all-purpose flour
2 teaspoons baking powder
½ teaspoon baking soda
½ cup granulated sugar
1 cup sliced almonds
1 large egg
⅔ cup sour milk or buttermilk
3 tablespoons butter or margarine, melted
½ cup Amaretto liqueur
Jelly Sauce (see recipe below)

1  Position the rack in the center of the oven and preheat to 375 degrees F. Lightly grease or line with paper baking cups twelve 2¾-inch muffin cups.

2  In a large bowl, blend together the flour, baking powder, baking soda, sugar, and almonds. In a medium bowl, beat the egg, milk, butter, and Amaretto until smooth. Combine the two mixtures, blending until the dry ingredients are just moistened.

3  Spoon the batter into the prepared muffin cups, filling each about three-quarters full. Bake for 15 to 20 minutes, or until a cake tester or wooden toothpick inserted into the center of a muffin comes out clean. Cool in the pan on a wire rack for 5 to 7 minutes. Serve warm, or invert onto the rack to cool completely. Top with Jelly Sauce.

# AMARETTO-AND-ALMOND MUFFINS

MAKES: *11 to 12 muffins*

## JELLY SAUCE

MAKES: *1 cup*

1¼ cups grape jelly or jelly of choice
3 tablespoons hot water

In a small saucepan set over medium heat, combine the jelly and water. Cook, stirring, until the mixture is smooth. Remove from the heat and pour into a bowl.

---

1½ cups all-purpose flour
½ cup yellow cornmeal
1 tablespoon baking powder
½ teaspoon baking soda
½ teaspoon salt
1 large egg
¼ cup packed light-brown sugar
3 tablespoons molasses
1 cup sour milk or buttermilk
¼ teaspoon butter or margarine, melted
Whipped Butter (see recipe below)

1  Position the rack in the center of the oven and preheat to 425 degrees F. Lightly grease or line with paper baking cups twelve 2¾-inch muffin cups.

2  In a large bowl, blend together the flour, cornmeal, baking powder, baking soda, and salt. In a medium bowl, beat the egg, sugar, molasses, milk, and butter until smooth. Combine the two mixtures, blending until the dry ingredients are just moistened.

3  Spoon the batter into the prepared muffin cups, filling each about three-quarters full. Bake for 15 to 20 minutes, or until a cake tester or wooden toothpick inserted into the center of a muffin comes out clean. Cool in the pan on a wire rack for 5 to 7 minutes. Serve warm, or invert onto the rack to cool completely. Serve with Whipped Buter.

# ANADAMA MUFFINS

MAKES: *7 to 8 muffins*

## WHIPPED BUTTER

MAKES: *½ cup*

½ cup butter, at room temperature
2 tablespoons milk or half-and-half

In a small bowl, using an electric mixer on high speed, beat the butter and milk until light and smooth.

# APPLE-AND-DATE MUFFINS

MAKES: *10 muffins*

1½ cups whole-wheat flour
¾ cup All-Bran cereal
2 teaspoons baking powder
½ teaspoon ground cinnamon
¼ teaspoon salt
¾ cup peeled, cored, diced apple
¼ cup chopped dates
2 large eggs
¾ cup milk
½ cup warm honey
Sweet Red Sauce (see recipe below)

**1** Position the rack in the center of the oven and preheat to 375 degrees F. Lightly grease or line with paper baking cups twelve 2¾-inch muffin cups.

**2** In a large bowl, blend together the flour, cereal, baking powder, cinnamon, salt, apples, and dates. In a medium bowl, beat the eggs until foamy. Beat in the milk and honey. Combine the two mixtures, blending until the dry ingredients are just moistened.

**3** Spoon the batter into the prepared muffin cups, filling each about three-quarters full. Bake for 15 to 20 minutes, or until a cake tester or wooden toothpick inserted into the center of a muffin comes out clean. Cool on a wire rack for 5 to 7 minutes. Top with Sweet Red Sauce.

## SWEET RED SAUCE

MAKES: *About 1 cup*

¼ cup granulated sugar
¼ cup ketchup
¼ cup cider vinegar
¼ cup canola oil
¼ teaspoon onion powder
Pinch cayenne
1 tablespoon fresh snipped tarragon

In a small bowl, combine all of the ingredients except the tarragon. Cover and refrigerate for at least 30 minutes. Stir in the tarragon just before serving.

1¼ cups whole-wheat flour
1 cup oat bran
2½ teaspoons baking powder
¼ teaspoon baking soda
¼ teaspoon ground cinnamon
¾ cup finely chopped apple
¼ teaspoon salt
2 large egg whites
1 cup buttermilk or sour milk
⅓ cup packed light-brown sugar
2 tablespoons canola oil
Blender Apricot Sauce (see recipe
    below)

1  Position the rack in the center
of the oven and preheat to 375
degrees F. Lightly grease or line
with paper baking cups twelve
2¾-inch muffin cups.

2  In a large bowl, blend together
the flour, oat bran, baking powder, baking soda, cinnamon,
apples, and salt. In a medium
bowl, beat the egg whites until
foamy. Beat in the buttermilk,
sugar, and oil. Combine the two
mixtures, blending until the dry
ingredients are just moistened.

3  Spoon the batter into the prepared muffin cups, filling each
about three-quarters full. Bake
for 15 to 20 minutes, or until a
cake tester or wooden toothpick
inserted into the center of a muffin comes out clean. Cool in the
pan on a wire rack for 5 to 7 minutes. Serve warm, or invert onto
the rack to cool completely. Top
with Blender Apricot Sauce.

# APPLE-AND-OAT BRAN MUFFINS

MAKES: *11 to 12 muffins*

# BLENDER APRICOT SAUCE

MAKES: *1¼ cups*

One 16-ounce can apricot halves in
    light syrup, drained
⅓ cup orange juice
2 teaspoons lemon juice

In the container of a blender or
food processor, combine the
apricots, orange juice, and
lemon juice. Processs on high
speed until the mixture is
smooth. Transfer to a small
bowl and refrigerate for 1 hour
before serving.

---

2½ cups all-purpose flour
1 teaspoon baking soda
1½ cups peeled, cored, and diced
    apple
½ cup chopped pecans
1 teaspoon salt
1 large egg
1 cup buttermilk or sour milk
1½ cups packed light-brown sugar
¼ cup canola oil
1 teaspoon vanilla extract

1  Position the rack in the center
of the oven and preheat to 375
degrees F. Lightly grease or line
with paper baking cups fourteen
2¾-inch muffin cups.

2  In a large bowl, blend together
the flour, baking soda, apples,
pecans, and salt. In a medium

bowl, beat the egg until foamy.
Beat in the buttermilk, brown
sugar, oil, and vanilla extract.
Combine the two mixtures,
blending until the dry ingredients are just moistened.

3  Spoon the batter into the prepared muffin cups, filling each
about three-quarters full. Bake
for 20 to 25 minutes, or until a
cake tester or wooden toothpick
inserted into the center of a muffin comes out clean. Cool in the
pan on a wire rack for 5 to 7 minutes. Serve warm, or invert onto
the rack to cool completely.

SERVING SUGGESTIONS: **Serve
with apple butter.**

# APPLE-AND-PECAN MUFFINS

MAKES: *12 to 14 muffins*

# APPLE-AND-SPICY PECAN MUFFINS

MAKES: *5 to 6 muffins*

2½ cups all-purpose flour
1 tablespoon baking powder
½ cup granulated sugar
⅓ cup chopped pecans
¾ teaspoon ground cinnamon
Pinch ground nutmeg
Pinch ground cloves
Pinch curry powder
½ teaspoon salt
2 large eggs
¾ cup milk
¼ cup packed light-brown sugar
⅓ cup butter or margarine, melted
1½ cups peeled, finely diced apple
Chocolate Sauce (see recipe below)

**1** Position the rack in the center of the oven and preheat to 375 degrees F. Lightly grease or line with paper baking cups six 3-inch muffin cups.

**2** In a large bowl, blend together the flour, baking powder, granulated sugar, pecans, cinnamon, nutmeg, cloves, curry powder, and salt. In a medium bowl, beat the eggs until foamy. Beat in the milk, brown sugar, and butter. Stir in the apples. Combine the two mixtures, blending until the dry ingredients are just moistened. (Although this mixture will be very moist, do not overmix.)

**3** Spoon the batter into the prepared muffin cups, filling each about three-quarters full. Bake for about 25 to 30 minutes, or until a cake tester or wooden toothpick inserted into the center of a muffin comes out clean. Cool in the pan on a wire rack for 5 to 7 minutes. Serve warm, or invert onto the rack to cool completely. Top with Chocolate Sauce.

## CHOCOLATE SAUCE

MAKES: *1¾ cups*

½ cup heavy cream
⅓ cup powdered sugar
3 squares (1 ounce each) semisweet
  chocolate, chopped
1 square (1 ounce) unsweetened
  chocolate, chopped
½ teaspoon vanilla extract

In a medium saucepan set over medium heat, blend together the cream and sugar. Cook, stirring constantly, until the mixture just comes to a boil. Reduce the heat and add the chocolate. Stir until the chocolate is melted and the mixture is smooth, 3 to 5 minutes. Remove from the heat, stir in the vanilla extract and pour into a serving bowl.

1 cup peeled, diced apple
1 tablespoon fresh lemon juice
1½ cups all-purpose flour
1 cup whole-wheat flour
2 tablespoons granulated sugar
1 tablespoon baking powder
½ teaspoon ground cinnamon
½ teaspoon salt
1 large egg
1 cup milk
½ cup packed dark-brown sugar
¼ cup butter or margarine, melted
Coffee Custard Sauce (see recipe
   below)

1  Position the rack in the center of the oven and preheat to 400 degrees F. Lightly grease or line with paper baking cups ten 2¾-inch muffins cups.

2  Place the apples in a small bowl and sprinkle them with lemon juice; set aside. In a large bowl, blend together the two flours, granulated sugar, baking powder, cinnamon, and salt. In a medium bowl, beat the egg until foamy. Beat in the milk, brown sugar, and butter. Stir in the apples. Combine the two mixtures, blending until the dry ingredients are just moistened.

3  Spoon the batter into the prepared muffin cups, filling each about three-quarters full. Sprinkle with crumbly topping. Bake for about 20 to 25 minutes, or until the tops are golden and a cake tester or wooden toothpick inserted into the center of a muffin comes out clean. Cool in the pan on a wire rack for 5 to 7 minutes. Serve warm, or invert onto the rack to cool completely. Top with Coffee Custard Sauce.

# APPLE CRUMB MUFFINS

MAKES: *9 to 10 muffins*

# COFFEE CUSTARD SAUCE

MAKES: *About 1¼ cups*

2 large eggs
2 teaspoons granulated sugar
1 cup milk
2 teaspoons powdered instant
   coffee crystals
¼ teaspoon vanilla extract

1  In a small bowl, blend together the eggs, sugar, and 3 tablespoons of the milk. In a small saucepan set over medium heat, warm the milk and coffee together until lukewarm. Beat the egg mixture into the warm milk and pour into the top of a double boiler set over simmering water. Cook, stirring, until the custard thickens enough to coat the back of a wooden spoon.

2  Remove from the heat and stir in the vanilla extract. Serve hot or cold.

# APPLE MUFFINS WITH CINNAMON

MAKES: *5 to 6 muffins*

¾ cup all-purpose flour
1 cup whole-wheat flour
2 tablespoons granulated sugar, plus more for sugarcoating the muffins
2 teaspoons baking powder
½ teaspoon salt
1¼ teaspoons ground cinnamon
½ teaspoon ground nutmeg
1 large egg
1 cup skim milk
6 tablespoons canola oil
½ cup frozen apple-juice concentrate, thawed
¼ teaspoon lemon extract
1 large apple, peeled, cored and finely chopped
Mint Jelly (see recipe below)

**1** Position the rack in the center of the oven and preheat to 400 degrees F. Lightly grease or line with paper baking cups six 3-inch muffin cups.

**2** In a large bowl, blend together the two flours, 2 tablespoons sugar, baking powder, salt, cinnamon, and nutmeg. In a medium bowl, beat the egg, milk, oil, apple juice, and lemon extract until smooth. Stir in the apple. Combine the two mixtures, blending until the dry ingredients are just moistened.

**3** Spoon the batter into the prepared muffin cups, filling each about three-quarters full. Bake for 20 to 25 minutes, or until the tops are golden and a cake tester or wooden toothpick inserted into the center of a muffin comes out clean. Cool in the pan on a wire rack for 5 to 7 minutes. Serve warm, or invert onto the rack to cool completely. While still warm, coat the muffins with sugar. Serve with Mint Jelly.

## MINT JELLY

MAKES: *3 cups*

1½ cups granulated sugar
2 tablespoons water
2 cups apple juice
¼ cup fresh snipped mint leaves
Green food coloring

In a medium saucepan set over medium heat, combine the sugar, water, and apple juice. Cook, stirring constantly, until the sugar is dissolved. Continue to cook until bubbles form around the edges of the pan. Reduce the heat to low, insert a candy thermometer, and continue to cook until the thermometer registers 235 degrees F. (This is the soft-ball stage for those who don't have thermometers.) Remove from the heat, stir in the mint leaves and the food coloring, and pour into a serving bowl or into small jars for storage.

2 medium apples, peeled, cored and
 diced
1 tablespoon fresh lemon juice
1¼ cups all-purpose flour
1¼ cups oat bran
1 tablespoon baking powder
1 teaspoon ground cinnamon
½ teaspoon ground nutmeg
2 teaspoons nonfat dry milk powder
¼ cup chopped pecans
¼ cup seedless raisins
½ teaspoon salt
3 large eggs
½ cup packed light-brown sugar
¾ cup milk
¼ cup corn oil
1 teaspoon almond or vanilla extract
Custard Sauce (see recipe below)

**1** Position the rack in the center
of the oven and preheat to 400
degrees F. Lightly grease or line
with paper baking cups fourteen
2¾-inch muffin cups.

**2** Place the apples in a small
bowl and sprinkle with the
lemon juice; set aside. In a large
bowl, blend together the flour,

oat bran, baking powder, cinnamon, nutmeg, milk powder,
pecans, raisins, and salt. In
another large bowl, beat the eggs
until foamy. Beat in the sugar,
milk, oil, and almond extract. Stir
in the apples. Combine the two
mixtures, blending until the dry
ingredients are just moistened.

**3** Spoon the batter into the prepared muffin cups, filling each
about three-quarters full. Bake
for 20 to 25 minutes, or until the
tops are golden brown and a cake
tester or wooden toothpick
inserted in the center of a muffin
comes out clean. Cool in the pan
on a wire rack for 5 to 7 minutes.
Serve warm, or invert onto the
rack to cool completely. Top with
Custard Sauce.

# APPLE–OAT BRAN MUFFINS I

MAKES: *12 to 14 muffins*

# CUSTARD SAUCE

MAKES: *2 cups*

2 cups milk
2 large eggs
½ cup granulated sugar
1 teaspoon vanilla extract

**1** In a medium saucepan set
over medium heat, warm 1¾
cups of the milk until bubbles
appear around the edges of the
pan (do not allow it to boil) and
immediately remove the pan
from the heat.

**2** In a small bowl, beat the eggs
until foamy before beating in
the remaining ¼ cup milk. Beat
in the sugar. Slowly whisk the
egg mixture into the hot milk in
the saucepan. Set the saucepan
over low heat and cook, stirring
constantly with a wooden
spoon, until the custard thickens just enough to coat the back
of the spoon.

**3** Remove from the heat and
stir in the vanilla. Pour the custard through a fine-mesh sieve
into a serving bowl.

# APPLE–OAT BRAN MUFFINS II

MAKES: *6 to 8 muffins*

½ cup all-purpose flour
¾ cup rolled oats
¼ cup oat bran
2 teaspoons baking powder
½ teaspoon ground nutmeg
Pinch ground cloves
1 medium apple, cored and grated
   with peel
2 tablespoons golden raisins
½ teaspoon salt
1 large egg
3 tablespoons packed light-brown
   sugar
2 tablespoons canola oil
¼ cup skim milk
½ cup apple juice
Chocolate–Honey Sauce (see recipe
   below)

**1** Position the rack in the center of the oven and preheat to 400 degrees F. Lightly grease or line with paper baking cups twelve 2¾-inch muffin cups.

**2** In a large bowl, blend together the flour, oats, oat bran, baking powder, nutmeg, cloves, apple, raisins, and salt. In a medium bowl, beat the egg until foamy. Beat in the sugar, oil, milk, and apple juice. Combine the two mixtures, blending until the dry ingredients are incorporated. (The mixture will be very moist.)

**3** Spoon the batter into the prepared muffin cups, filling each about three-quarters full. Bake for 15 to 20 minutes, or until the tops are a golden and a cake tester or wooden toothpick inserted into the center of a muffin comes out clean. Cool in the pan on a wire rack for 5 to 7 minutes. Serve warm, or invert onto the rack to cool completely. Top with Chocolate–Honey Sauce.

## CHOCOLATE–HONEY SAUCE

MAKES: *1¼ cups*

¼ cup butter or margarine
1 tablespoon cornstarch or
   arrowroot
¼ cup Dutch-processed cocoa
   powder
½ cup honey
½ cup water
1 teaspoon vanilla extract

In the top of a double boiler set over simmering water, combine the butter, cornstarch, cocoa, honey, and water. Cook, stirring constantly, for 3 to 4 minutes or until the mixture is very hot. Remove from the heat, stir in the vanilla extract, and pour into a serving bowl.

2 cups all-purpose flour
1 tablespoon baking powder
¼ teaspoon baking soda
½ cup granulated sugar
1 teaspoon ground cinnamon
½ cup chopped walnuts
2 cups grated, cored apples, with
  peel
¼ teaspoon salt
2 large eggs
¾ cup sour milk or buttermilk
¼ cup butter or margarine, melted
Chocolate Coffee Sauce (see recipe
  below)

**1** Position the rack in the center of the oven and preheat to 375 degrees F. Lightly grease or line with paper baking cups twenty-four 2¾-inch muffin cups.

**2** In a large bowl, blend together the flour, baking powder, baking soda, sugar, cinnamon, walnuts, apples, and salt. In a medium bowl, beat the eggs until foamy. Beat in the milk and butter. Combine the two mixtures, blending until the dry ingredients are just moistened.

**3** Spoon the batter into the prepared muffin cups, filling each about three-quarters full. Bake for 18 to 22 minutes, or until the tops are golden and a cake tester or wooden toothpick inserted into a muffin is removed clean. Cool in the pan on a wire rack for 5 to 7 minutes before coating with cinnamon sugar. Top with Chocolate Coffee Sauce.

# APPLE–WALNUT MUFFINS

MAKES: *14 to 16 muffins*

# CHOCOLATE COFFEE SAUCE

MAKES: *1¾ cups*

1 cup (6 ounces) semisweet
  chocolate chips
¾ cup corn syrup
¼ cup milk
1 tablespoon instant coffee crystals
2 tablespoons butter or margarine

In the top of a double boiler set over simmering water, combine the chocolate and corn syrup. Cook, stirring, until the chocolate chips are melted and the mixture is smooth. Stir in the milk, coffee crystals, and butter. Continue to cook, stirring frequently, until the mixture is smooth. Remove from the heat and cool to room temperature before serving.

# APPLE–YOGURT MUFFINS

MAKES: *11 to 12 muffins*

**1½ cups all-purpose flour**
**¾ cup granulated sugar**
**2 teaspoons baking powder**
**1 teaspoon baking soda**
**1 medium apple, peeled and grated**
**½ teaspoon salt**
**⅔ cup sour milk or buttermilk**
**⅔ cup plain yogurt or sour cream**
**Caramel Sauce (see recipe below)**

**1** Position the rack in the center of the oven and preheat to 400 degrees F. Lightly grease or line with paper baking cups twelve 2¾-inch muffin cups.

**2** In a large bowl, blend together the flour, sugar, baking powder, baking soda, apple, and salt. In a medium bowl, blend the milk and yogurt until smooth. Combine the two mixtures, blending until the dry ingredients are just moistened.

**3** Spoon the batter into the prepared muffin cups, filling each about three-quarters full. Bake for 15 to 20 minutes, or until the tops are golden and a cake tester or wooden toothpick inserted into the center of a muffin comes out clean. Cool in the pan on a wire rack for 5 to 7 minutes. Serve warm, or invert onto the rack to cool completely. Top with Caramel Sauce.

## CARAMEL SAUCE

MAKES: *1 to 1¼ cups*

**½ cup light or dark corn syrup**
**6 ounces caramel candies**
**¼ cup unsweetened evaporated milk**
**½ cup toasted nuts or semisweet chocolate chips**

In a small saucepan, combine the corn syrup, caramel candy, and milk. Set the pan over medium heat and stir constantly until the candy has melted and the sauce is very smooth. Stir in the nuts and serve warm or at room temperature (do not chill before serving).

2 cups all-purpose flour
1 tablespoon baking powder
1 teaspoon ground cinnamon
¼ teaspoon ground nutmeg
¼ teaspoon ground cloves
½ cup chopped, unsalted peanuts
½ teaspoon salt
2 large eggs
1 cup packed light-brown sugar
½ cup milk
⅓ cup butter or margarine, melted
½ cup unsweetened applesauce
Orange Sauce (see recipe below)

**1** Position the rack in the center of the oven and preheat to 400 degrees F. Lightly grease or line with paper baking cups twelve 2¾-inch muffin cups.

**2** In a large bowl, blend together the flour, baking powder, cinnamon, nutmeg, cloves, peanuts, and salt. In a medium bowl, beat the eggs until foamy. Beat in the sugar. Beat in the milk, butter, and applesauce. Combine the two mixtures, blending until the dry ingredients are just moistened.

**3** Spoon the batter into the prepared muffin cups, filling each about three-quarters full. Bake for about 25 to 30 minutes, or until the tops are golden and a cake tester or wooden toothpick inserted into the center of a muffin comes out clean. Cool in the pan on a wire rack for 5 to 7 minutes. Serve warm, or invert onto the rack to cool completely. Top with Orange Sauce.

# APPLESAUCE-AND-PEANUT MUFFINS

MAKES: *11 to 12 muffins*

# ORANGE SAUCE

MAKES: *About 1 cup*

½ cup granulated sugar
1 tablespoon cornstarch
Pinch ground cinnamon
¾ cup boiling water
1 tablespoon canola oil
¼ cup fresh orange juice
1 teaspoon grated orange zest
1 teaspoon lemon juice

In a small saucepan, combine the sugar, cornstarch, cinnamon, and water. Set over medium heat and bring to a boil. Cook, stirring constantly, for about 5 minutes. Remove from the heat and add the oil, orange juice, and orange zest. Cool to room temperature and serve.

# APPLESAUCE-AND-BRAN-CEREAL MUFFINS

MAKES: *5 to 6 muffins*

3 cups All-Bran cereal
2 cups skim milk
2½ cups all-purpose flour
4 teaspoons baking powder
1 cup packed dark-brown sugar
1 teaspoon ground cinnamon
1 teaspoon dried grated lemon zest
¼ teaspoon salt
2 large eggs
⅓ cup canola oil
1 cup applesauce
1 tablespoon chilled butter or margarine for topping
Fluffy Cream Dressing (see recipe below)

**1** Position the rack in the center of the oven and preheat to 375 degrees F. Lightly grease or line with paper baking cups six 3-inch muffin cups.

**2** In a medium bowl, combine the cereal and milk and let stand for 3 to 5 minutes. In a large bowl, blend together the flour, baking powder, ¾ cup of the brown sugar, the cinnamon, lemon zest, and salt. In a medium bowl, beat the eggs until foamy. Beat in the oil and applesauce. Stir in the cereal mixture. Combine the two mixtures, blending until the dry ingredients are just moistened.

**3** Spoon the batter into the prepared muffin cups, filling each about three-quarters full. In a cup, combine the butter and remaining ¼ cup of brown sugar and stir until smooth. Sprinkle it over the tops of the muffins. Bake for 20 to 25 minutes, or until a cake tester or wooden toothpick inserted into the center of a muffin comes out clean. Cool in the pan on a wire rack for 5 to 7 minutes. Serve warm, or invert onto the rack to cool completely. Top with Fluffy Cream Dressing.

## FLUFFY CREAM DRESSING

MAKES: *About 1½ cups*

1 large egg, separated
¾ cup powdered sugar
½ cup heavy cream, whipped until soft peaks form
3 tablespoons brandy

In a medium bowl, beat the egg whites until stiff but not dry before beating in the sugar. Beat in the egg yolk, and fold in the whipped cream and brandy. Cover and refrigerate until ready to serve.

**WARNING: This dish contains uncooked eggs and must be used at once. It will not keep.**

½ cup butter or margarine, at room
  temperature
⅓ cup granulated sugar
2 large eggs
1 cup unsweetened applesauce
1 cup all-purpose flour
¾ cup graham flour
1 tablespoon baking powder
½ cup chopped walnuts
½ teaspoon salt

**1** Position the rack in the center
of the oven and preheat to 400
degrees F. Lightly grease or line
with paper baking cups ten 2¾-
inch muffin cups.

**2** In a large bowl, beat the butter
and sugar until light and fluffy.
Beat in the eggs, one at a time,
beating vigorously after each
addition. Stir in the applesauce.

In a medium bowl, blend together the two flours, baking powder,
walnuts, and salt. Combine the
two mixtures, blending until the
dry ingredients are just
moistened.

**3** Spoon the batter into the prepared muffin cups, filling each
about three-quarters full. Bake
for 20 to 25 minutes, or until the
tops are golden and a cake tester
or wooden toothpick inserted
into a muffin comes out clean.
Cool in the pan on a wire rack for
5 to 7 minutes. Serve warm, or
invert onto the rack to cool
completely.

**SERVING SUGGESTION: Serve
with apple butter.**

# APPLESAUCE MUFFINS

MAKES: *9 to 10 muffins*

---

1¼ cups all-purpose flour
1½ cups quick-cooking oats
½ teaspoon baking powder
½ teaspoon baking soda
1 teaspoon ground nutmeg
1 teaspoon ground cinnamon
1 teaspoon ground allspice
1 cup finely chopped pecans
4 large egg whites
⅓ cups butter or margarine, melted
½ cup packed light-brown sugar
1 cup applesauce
Maple Butter (see recipe below)

**1** Position the rack in the center
of the oven and preheat to 400
degrees F. Lightly grease or line
with paper baking cups twelve
2¾-inch muffin cups.

**2** In a large bowl, blend together
the flour, oats, baking powder,
baking soda, nutmeg, cinnamon,

allspice, and pecans. In a medium bowl, beat the egg whites
until foamy. Beat in the butter
and sugar. Stir in the applesauce.
Combine the two mixtures,
blending until the dry ingredients are just moistened.

**3** Spoon the batter into the prepared muffin cups, filling each
about three-quarters full. Bake
for 18 to 20 minutes, or until the
tops are golden and a cake tester
or wooden toothpick inserted
into the center of a muffin comes
out clean. Cool in the pan on a
wire rack for 5 to 7 minutes.
Serve warm, or invert onto the
rack to cool completely. Serve
with Maple Butter.

# APPLESAUCE–
OATMEAL MUFFINS
WITH A BITE

MAKES: *11 to 12 muffins*

---

# MAPLE BUTTER

MAKES: *1½ cups*

½ cup butter, at room temperature
¾ cup plus 3 tablespoons pure
  maple syrup
⅔ cup finely chopped almonds or
  walnuts

In a small bowl, combine all of
the ingredients and blend until
smooth. Cover and refrigerate
for at least 30 minutes before
serving.

## APPLESAUCE–RAISIN MUFFINS

MAKES: *11 to 12 muffins*

1½ cups all-purpose flour
½ cup graham flour
2 teaspoons baking powder
½ teaspoon baking soda
½ teaspoon ground cinnamon
½ teaspoon salt
½ cup golden raisins
1 large egg
¼ cup canola oil
⅓ cup milk
⅔ cup unsweetened applesauce
¼ cup granulated sugar
Brown sugar for sprinkling

**1** Position the rack in the center of the oven and preheat to 400 degrees F. Lightly grease or line with paper baking cups twelve 2¾-inch muffin cups.

**2** In a large bowl, blend together the flours, baking powder, baking soda, cinnamon, salt, and raisins. In a medium bowl, beat the egg until foamy. Beat in the oil, milk, applesauce, and sugar. Combine the two mixtures, blending until the dry ingredients are just moistened.

**3** Spoon the batter into the prepared muffin cups, filling each about three-quarters full. Sprinkle a little of the brown sugar over each muffin and bake for 18 to 20 minutes, or until a cake tester or wooden toothpick inserted into the center of a muffin comes out clean. Cool in the pan on a wire rack for 5 to 7 minutes. Serve warm, or invert onto the rack to cool completely.

**SERVING SUGGESTION: Serve with grape jelly.**

## APPLESAUCE MUFFINS WITH WALNUTS AND RAISINS

MAKES: *11 to 12 muffins*

1 cup all-purpose flour
1 cup whole-wheat flour
1 teaspoon baking powder
1 teaspoon baking soda
1½ cups granulated sugar
½ teaspoon ground cinnamon
¼ teaspoon ground nutmeg
½ cup chopped walnuts
1 cup seedless raisins
3 large egg whites
3 tablespoons buttermilk or sour milk
¼ cup canola oil
1 cup unsweetened applesauce
Whipped Hot Chocolate (see recipe below)

**1** Position the rack in the center of the oven and preheat to 375 degrees F. Lightly grease or line with paper baking cups twelve 2¾-inch muffin cups.

**2** In a large bowl, blend together the flours, baking powder, baking soda, sugar, cinnamon, nutmeg, walnuts, and raisins. In a medium bowl, beat the egg whites until stiff but not dry. Stir in the milk, oil, and applesauce. Fold in the dry ingredients, folding until the dry ingredients are just moistened.

**3** Spoon the batter into the prepared muffin cups, filling each about three-quarters full. Bake for 20 to 25 minutes, or until the tops are golden and a cake tester or wooden toothpick inserted into the center of a muffin comes out clean. Cool in the pan on a wire rack for 5 to 7 minutes. Serve warm, or invert onto the rack to cool completely. Serve with Whipped Hot chocolate.

## WHIPPED HOT CHOCOLATE

MAKES: *1¼ cups*

1 cup milk or half-and-half
3 heaping tablespoons Dutch processed cocoa powder
1 tablespoon granulated sugar

In a small saucepan, over medium heat scald the milk until just below boiling point. Remove from the heat. Using an electric mixer on high speed, beat in the cocoa powder and sugar, continuing to beat until sugar is dissolved. Pour into a warm mug and serve.

1⅔ cups all-purpose flour
2 teaspoons baking powder
½ cup granulated sugar
¼ teaspoon ground cinnamon
½ teaspoon salt
1 large egg
¾ cup milk
⅓ cup butter or margarine, melted
½ cup apricot jam
½ cup chopped walnuts
Hot Buttered Rum Sauce (see recipe
    below)

1  Position the rack in the center of the oven and preheat to 400 degrees F. Lightly grease or line with paper baking cups twelve 2¾-inch muffin cups.

2  In a large bowl, blend together the flour, baking powder, sugar, cinnamon, and salt. In a medium bowl, beat the egg until foamy. Beat in the milk and butter. Combine the two mixtures, blending until the dry ingredients are just moistened.

3  Spoon the batter into the prepared muffin cups, filling each about three-quarters full. Lightly press 1 teaspoon of apricot jam into the center of each muffin. Sprinkle each with chopped walnuts. Bake for 20 to 25 minutes, or until a wooden toothpick inserted near the edge of a muffin (not into the jam filling) is removed clean. Cool in the pan on a wire rack for 5 to 7 minutes. Serve warm, or invert onto the rack to cool completely. Top with Hot Buttered Rum Sauce.

# APRICOT-AND-WALNUT MUFFINS

MAKES: *5 to 6 muffins*

## HOT BUTTERED RUM SAUCE

MAKES: *2 cups*

1 cup firmly packed brown sugar
¼ cup dark corn syrup
½ cup heavy cream
2 tablespoons butter
Pinch salt
1 tablespoon rum or 1 teaspoon
    rum extract
½ cup chopped pecans

In a medium saucepan set over medium heat, combine the brown sugar, corn syrup, cream, butter, and salt. Cook, stirring constantly, until the mixture boils and thickens. Reduce the heat to low and simmer, stirring frequently, for 5 minutes. Remove from the heat and stir in the rum and pecans.

# APRICOT TEA MUFFINS

MAKES: *11 to 12 muffins*

12 dried apricot halves
¼ cup boiling water or hot brandy
¼ cup packed light-brown sugar
2 tablespoons butter or margarine
2 cups all-purpose flour
4 teaspoons baking powder
¼ cup granulated sugar
½ teaspoon salt
2 large eggs
⅔ cup milk
1 teaspoon almond extract
Berry Sauce (see recipe below)

**1** Thoroughly wash the apricots and place them in a small bowl. Pour in the water or brandy and allow to soak for 10 minutes. Meanwhile, position the rack in the center of the oven and preheat to 400 degrees F. Lightly grease or line with paper baking cups twelve 2¾-inch muffin cups.

**2** Drain the apricots and pat them dry between paper towels. Place one apricot in the bottom of each muffin cup, rounded-side down. Sprinkle each with 1 teaspoon of brown sugar and dot each with a ½ teaspoon of butter. In a large bowl, blend together the flour, baking powder, granulated sugar, and salt. In a medium bowl, beat the eggs, buttermilk, and almond extract until smooth. Combine the two mixtures, blending until the dry ingredients are just moistened.

**3** Spoon the batter into the prepared muffin cups, filling each about three-quarters full. Bake for 15 to 20 minutes, or until the tops are golden and a cake tester or wooden toothpick inserted into the center of a muffin comes out clean. Cool in the pan on a wire rack for 5 to 7 minutes. Serve warm, or invert onto the rack to cool completely. Top with Berry Sauce.

## BERRY SAUCE

MAKES: *1½ cups*

One 10-ounce package red raspberries in light syrup, thawed
½ cup red currant jelly
4 teaspoons cornstarch

In the container of a blender or food processor, process the raspberries and jelly until smooth. Add the cornstarch and process until blended. Pour into a small saucepan and cook over medium heat for 3 to 5 minutes, or until the mixture thickens. Remove from the heat and cool slightly before transferring to a serving bowl.

25 dried apricot halves
¼ cup boiling water
1¼ cups all-purpose flour
1 cup whole-wheat flour
1 tablespoon baking powder
1 teaspoon baking soda
2 tablespoons butter or margarine, melted
½ cup granulated sugar
4 large egg whites
1 cup plain yogurt or sour cream
1½ teaspoons almond or vanilla extract
Sugarless Apricot Sauce (see recipe below)

**1** Position the rack in the center of the oven and preheat to 375 degrees F. Lightly grease or line with paper baking cups twenty-six 2-inch muffin cups.

**2** In a small bowl, combine the apricots and water and allow to soak for 10 minutes. In a large bowl, blend together the two flours, baking powder, and baking soda. In a medium bowl, beat the butter and sugar fluffy. Beat in the egg whites, yogurt, and almond extract. Combine the two mixtures, blending until the dry ingredients are just moistened.

3 Drain the apricots and pat dry between paper towels. Place one half, round side up, into the bottom of each muffin cup. Spoon 1 tablespoon of the mixture into each cup and bake for about 12 to 15 minutes, or until the tops are golden and a cake tester or wooden toothpick inserted into the center of a muffin comes out clean. Cool in the pan on a wire rack for 5 minutes to 7 minutes. Top with Sugarless Apricot Sauce.

## Apricot Muffins

Makes: *25 to 26 muffins*

## Sugarless Apricot Sauce

Makes: *About 1⅓ cups*

One 12-ounce can apricot nectar
1 tablespoon cornstarch
2 teaspoons prepared mustard
1 teaspoon lemon zest
1 tablespoon fresh lemon juice
2 packets Equal® artificial sweetener

In a medium saucepan set over medium-low heat, combine the nectar, cornstarch, mustard, lemon zest, and juice. Cook, stirring frequently, until the mixture bubbles and thickens. Remove from the heat, stir in the Equal. Serve hot.

# ARROZ CON POLLO MUFFINS

MAKES: *11 to 12 muffins*

2 cups all-purpose flour
1 tablespoon baking powder
2 cups chopped, cooked chicken
  meat
1 cup cooked rice
1 teaspoon garlic powder
1 teaspoon salt
Pinch ground black pepper
2 large eggs
¼ cup butter-flavored vegetable
  shortening
¾ cup sour cream or plain yogurt
2 tablespoons tomato catsup
Mustard–Pepper Butter (see recipe
  below)

**1** Position the rack in the center of the oven and preheat 400 degrees F. Lightly grease or line with paper baking cups twelve 2¾-inch muffin cups.

**2** In a large bowl, blend together the flour, baking powder, chicken, rice, garlic powder, salt, and pepper. In a medium bowl, beat the eggs foamy. Beat in the shortening, sour cream, and catsup. Combine the two mixtures, blending until the dry ingredients are just moistened.

**3** Spoon the batter into the prepared muffin cups, filling each about three-quarters full. Bake for 18 to 22 minutes, or until the tops are golden and a cake tester or wooden toothpick inserted into the center of a muffin comes out clean. Cool in the pan on a wire rack for 5 to 7 minutes. Serve warm, or invert onto the rack to cool completely. Serve with Mustard–Pepper Butter.

# MUSTARD–PEPPER BUTTER

MAKES: *⅔ cup*

½ cup cream cheese
2 tablespoons butter
2 teaspoons prepared mustard
1 teaspoon crushed green
  peppercorns

In a small bowl, combine the cream cheese, butter, mustard, and peppercorns and beat until smooth. Transfer to a serving bowl and refrigerate for 30 minutes before serving.

2 cups all-purpose flour
2 teaspoons baking powder
¼ cup granulated sugar
½ teaspoon salt
1 cup toasted, slivered almonds
1 large egg
¼ cup butter or margarine, melted
1 cup milk
1 medium ripe avocado, peeled, seeded and pureed
Peach Sauce (see recipe below)

**1** Position the rack in the center of the oven and preheat to 375 degrees F. Lightly grease or line with paper baking cups twelve 2¾-inch muffin cups.

**2** In a large bowl, blend together the flour, baking powder, sugar, salt, and almonds. In a small bowl, beat the egg until foamy. Beat in the butter, milk, and pureed avocado. Combine the two mixtures, blending until the dry ingredients are just moistened.

**3** Spoon the batter into the prepared muffin cups, filling each about three-quarters full. Bake for 15 to 20 minutes, or until a cake tester or wooden toothpick inserted into the center of a muffin comes out clean. Cool in the pan on a wire rack for 5 to 7 minutes. Serve warm, or invert onto the rack to cool completely. Top with Peach Sauce.

# AVOCADO MUFFINS

MAKES: *11 to 12 muffins*

# PEACH SAUCE

MAKES: *2½ to 3 cups*

½ pound finely chopped dried peaches, soaked overnight in peach-flavored brandy
2 cups water
1 cup sugar
1 tablespoon grated lemon zest
1 tablespoon brandy from soaking peaches

**1** Drain the peaches, reserving 1 tablespoon of the brandy they soaked in. Set aside.

**2** In a small saucepan, combine the sugar, water, and lemon zest. Cook over medium-low heat, stirring constantly, for 2 to 3 minutes before stirring in the peaches. Continue to cook for about 8 minutes. Strain the mix through a sieve, add the brandy, and serve warm or cold.

# BACON MUFFINS

MAKES: *11 to 12 muffins*

1⅓ cups all-purpose flour
1 tablespoon baking powder
8 slices crisply cooked bacon,
   crumbled
1 teaspoon salt
1 large egg
1 tablespoon granulated sugar
¾ cup milk
1 tablespoon bacon drippings
Mustard Butter (see recipe below)

**1** Position the rack in the center of the oven and preheat to 425 degrees F. Lightly grease or line with paper baking cups twelve 2¾-inch muffin cups.

**2** In a large bowl, blend together the flour, baking powder, crumbled bacon, and salt. In a medium bowl, beat the egg until foamy. Beat in the sugar, milk, and drippings. Combine the two mixtures, blending until the dry ingredients are just moistened.

**3** Spoon the batter into the prepared muffin cups, filling each about three-quarters full. Bake for 15 to 20 minutes, or until a cake tester or wooden toothpick inserted into the center of a muffin comes out clean. Cool in the pan on a wire rack for 5 to 7 minutes. Serve warm, or invert onto the rack to cool completely. Serve with Mustard Butter.

## MUSTARD BUTTER

MAKES: *¾ cups*

½ cup chilled butter
¼ cup prepared mustard

In a small bowl, beat together the butter and mustard until smooth. Transfer to a serving bowl and refrigerate for 30 minutes before serving.

1¾ cups all-purpose flour
1 tablespoon baking powder
½ cup (3 ounces) semisweet
  chocolate chips
½ teaspoon salt
2 tablespoons packed light-brown
  sugar
2 tablespoons granulated sugar
⅓ cup butter or margarine, melted
1 large, ripe banana, mashed
1 large egg
¾ cup milk
Blueberry Syrup (see recipe below)

**1** Position the rack in the center
of the oven and preheat to 400
degrees F. Lightly grease or line
with paper baking cups ten 2¾-
inch muffin cups.

**2** In a large bowl, blend the flour,
baking powder, chocolate chips,
and salt. In a medium bowl, beat
together the sugars, butter, and
banana until smooth. Beat in the
egg and milk. Combine the two
mixtures, blending until the dry
ingredients are just moistened.

**3** Spoon the batter into the prepared muffin cups, filling each
about three-quarters full. Bake
for 15 to 20 minutes, or until the
tops are golden and a cake tester
or wooden toothpick inserted
into the center of a muffin comes
out clean. Cool in the pan on a
wire rack for 5 to 7 minutes.
Serve warm, or invert onto the
rack to cool completely. Top with
Blueberry Syrup.

# BANANA-AND-CHOCOLATE-CHIP MUFFINS

MAKES: *9 to 10 muffins*

## BLUEBERRY SYRUP

MAKES: *About 1 cup*

1 cup blueberries
½ cup unsweetened apple juice
1½ teaspoons cornstarch
3 packets Equal® artificial
  sweetener
½ teaspoon grated lemon zest
1 tablespoon fresh lemon juice
1 tablespoon butter or margarine

In the container of a blender,
combine the berries and apple
juice and blend until smooth.
Pour into a medium saucepan
and stir in the cornstarch. Cook
for 2 minutes on medium to
low heat, stirring frequently
until the mixture thickens.
Remove from the heat and stir
in the sweetener, lemon zest,
lemon juice, and butter. Serve
warm or cold.

# BANANA-AND-WHEAT-GERM MUFFINS

MAKES: *11 to 12 muffins*

1½ cups all-purpose flour
1 tablespoon baking powder
¾ cup granulated sugar
½ teaspoon salt
¾ cup wheat germ
2 large eggs
⅓ cup canola oil
½ cup milk
1½ cups (about 3 medium) mashed ripe banana
1 teaspoon vanilla extract
Orange Marshmallow Sauce (see recipe below)

1  Position the rack in the center of the oven and preheat to 400 degrees F. Lightly grease or line with paper baking cups twelve 2¾-inch muffin cups.

2  In a large bowl, blend together the flour, baking powder, sugar, and salt. Stir in the wheat germ.

In a medium bowl, beat together the eggs, oil, milk, bananas, and vanilla extract. Combine the two mixtures, blending until the dry ingredients are just moistened.

3  Spoon the batter into the prepared muffin cups, filling each about three-quarters full. Bake for 20 to 25 minutes, or until the tops of the muffins are golden and a cake tester or wooden toothpick inserted into the center of a muffin comes out clean. Cool in the pan on a wire rack for 5 to 7 minutes. Serve warm, or invert onto the rack to cool completely. Top with Orange Marshmallow Sauce.

## ORANGE MARSHMALLOW SAUCE

MAKES: *About ⅓ to ½ cup*

16 large marshmallows, each cut into quarters
2 teaspoons grated orange zest
2 tablespoons fresh orange juice

In the top of a double boiler set over simmering water, melt the marshmallows, stirring, until smooth. Remove from the heat and stir in the orange zest and orange juice. Serve at once.

1 cup all-purpose flour
½ cup whole bran
2 teaspoons baking powder
¼ teaspoon salt
1 large egg
½ cup granulated sugar
¼ cup canola oil
¼ cup milk
1 medium ripe banana, mashed
Cherry–Almond–Rum Sauce (see
  recipe below)

1  Position the rack in the center of the oven and preheat to 400 degrees F. Lightly grease or line with paper baking cups twelve 2¾-inch muffin cups.

2  In a large bowl, blend together the flour, bran, baking powder, and salt. In a medium bowl, beat the egg, sugar, oil, milk, and banana until smooth. Combine the two mixtures, blending until the dry ingredients are just moistened.

3  Spoon the batter into the prepared muffin cups, filling each about three-quarters full. Bake for 15 to 20 minutes, or until a cake tester or wooden toothpick inserted into the middle of a muffin comes out clean. Cool in the pan on a wire rack for 5 to 7 minutes. Serve warm, or invert onto the rack to cool completely. Top with Cherry-Almond-Rum Sauce.

# BANANA–BRAN MUFFINS

MAKES: *11 to 12 muffins*

## CHERRY–ALMOND– RUM SAUCE

MAKES: *1½ cups*

¼ cup butter or margarine
One 14-ounce can sweetened
  condensed milk
1 tablespoon rum or 2 teaspoons
  rum extract
¼ cup chopped almonds
½ cup canned cherry-pie filling

In a medium saucepan set over medium heat, melt the butter. Stir in the milk, rum, and almonds. Cook for 1 to 2 minutes, stirring constantly, until bubbles start to form around the edges of the pan. Remove from the heat and stir in the pie filling. Transferring to a serving bowl and serve warm or at room temperature.

1 cup all-purpose flour
½ cup whole-wheat flour
½ cup oat bran
2 tablespoons chopped pecans
½ cup (2¾ ounces) miniature
  chocolate chips
½ teaspoon baking soda
1 large egg
½ cup granulated sugar
½ cup water
½ cup canola oil
1 cup (about 2 medium ) mashed
  ripe banana
Chocolate Sauce (see recipe page 26)

1  Position a rack in the center of the oven and preheat to 375 degrees F. Lightly grease or line with paper baking cups twelve 2¾-inch muffin cups.

2  In a large bowl, blend together the flours, oat bran, pecans, chocolate chips, and baking soda. In a medium bowl, beat the egg, sugar, water, oil, and bananas until smooth. Combine the two mixtures, blending until the dry ingredients are just moistened.

3  Spoon the batter into the prepared muffin cups, filling each about three-quarters full. Bake for 15 to 20 minutes, or until a cake tester or wooden toothpick inserted into the center of a muffin comes out clean. Cool in the pan on a wire rack for 5 to 7 minutes. Serve warm, or invert onto the rack to cool completely. Top with Chocolate Sauce.

# BANANA-AND- CHOCOLATE-BIT MUFFINS

MAKES: *11 to 12 muffins*

# Banana–Chocolate Muffins

Makes: *11 to 12 muffins*

2 cups all-purpose flour
2 teaspoons baking soda
¼ teaspoon salt
4 ounces unsweetened chocolate, grated
½ cup pistachio nuts, chopped
6 tablespoons butter or margarine
⅔ cup granulated sugar
2 large eggs
1 cup (about 2 medium) mashed ripe banana
1 teaspoon crème de cacao
¼ cup sour milk or buttermilk
Pineapple Syrup (see recipe below)

**1** Position a rack in the center of the oven and preheat to 375 degrees F. Lightly grease or line with paper baking cups ten 2¾-inch muffin cups.

**2** In a large bowl, blend together the flour, baking soda, salt, chocolate, and pistachios. In a medium bowl, cream the butter and sugar together. Beat in the eggs, bananas, crème de cacao, and milk. Combine the two mixtures, blending until the dry ingredients are just moistened.

**3** Spoon the batter into the prepared muffin cups, filling each about three-quarters full. Bake for 20 to 25 minutes, or until a cake tester or wooden toothpick inserted into the center of a muffin comes out clean. Cool in the pan on a wire rack for 5 to 7 minutes. Serve warm, or invert onto the rack to cool completely. Top with Pineapple Syrup.

## Pineapple Syrup

Makes: *¾ cup*

1 cup granulated sugar
½ cup crushed canned pineapple, drained
1 teaspoon pineapple juice

In a small saucepan set over low heat, blend together the sugar, pineapple, and pineapple juice. Cook for 1 to 2 minutes, or until the sugar is dissolved. Transfer to a serving bowl.

1¾ cups plus 2 tablespoons all-purpose flour
⅓ cup granulated sugar
2 tablespoons Dutch-process cocoa powder
1 tablespoon baking powder
1 cup (6 ounces) semisweet miniature chocolate chips
1 cup (about 2 medium) mashed ripe bananas
⅔ cup canola oil
1 large egg
Plum Butter (see recipe below)

**1** Position a rack in the center of the oven and preheat to 400 degrees F. Lightly grease or line with paper baking cups four 3-inch muffin cups.

**2** In a large bowl, blend together the flour, sugar, cocoa powder, baking powder, and chocolate chips. In a medium bowl, beat the bananas, oil, and egg until smooth. Combine the two mixtures, blending until the dry ingredients are just moistened.

**3** Spoon the batter into the prepared muffin cups, filling each about three-quarters full. Bake for 15 to 20 minutes, or until the tops are golden brown and a cake tester or wooden toothpick inserted into the center of a muffin comes out clean. Cool in the pan on a wire rack for 5 to 7 minutes. Serve warm, or invert onto the rack to cool completely. Serve with Plum Butter.

# BANANA–COCOA MUFFINS

MAKES: *3 to 4 muffins*

## PLUM BUTTER

MAKES: *1½ cups*

½ cup chopped fresh plums
1 cup honey

In the container of a blender or small food processor, combine the plums and honey and process on high until smooth. Transfer to a serving bowl and refrigerate for 30 minutes before serving.

# BANANA CROWNS

MAKES: *11 to 12 muffins*

2 cups all-purpose flour
¾ cup granulated sugar
1 teaspoon baking soda
½ cup chopped walnuts
1 teaspoon salt
2 large eggs
1½ cups (about 3 medium) mashed
  bananas
2 to 4 tablespoons mango jam or
  preserves
1 large banana, sliced into 24 pieces
Raspberry Sauce (see recipe below)

**1** Position the rack in the center of the oven and preheat to 375 degrees F. Lightly grease or line with paper baking cups twelve 2¾-inch muffin cups.

**2** In a large bowl, blend together the flour, sugar, baking soda, walnuts, and salt. In a small bowl, beat the eggs and mashed bananas until smooth. Combine the two mixtures, blending until the dry ingredients are just moistened.

**3** Spoon the batter into the prepared muffin cups, filling each about three-quarters full. Press ¼ teaspoon of the mango jam and a banana slice into the center of each cup. Bake for 15 to 20 minutes, or until a cake tester or wooden toothpick inserted into a muffin (not into the jam) comes out clean. Cool in the pan on a wire rack for 5 to 7 minutes. Remove the muffins from the pan and brush the tops with the dessert syrup. Allow to cool to room temperature. Top with Raspberry Sauce.

## RASPBERRY SAUCE

MAKES: *1⅓ cups*

One 10-ounce package frozen
  raspberries, thawed, strain to
  remove seeds
⅓ cup light corn syrup

In the container of a food processor or blender, combine the raspberries and corn syrup. Process on high speed until the mixture is smooth. Pour into a serving bowl and chill until ready to use.

1¾ cups all-purpose flour
2 teaspoons baking powder
¼ teaspoon baking soda
½ cup semisweet miniature
  chocolate chips
¼ teaspoon plus one pinch salt
2 large egg whites
⅓ cup granulated sugar
2 tablespoons canola oil
1 cup (about 2 medium) mashed ripe
  bananas
1 teaspoon banana extract
Vanilla Cream Sauce (see recipe
  below)

1  Position the rack in the center of the oven and preheat to 400 degrees F. Lightly grease or line with paper baking cups four 3-inch muffin cups.

2  In a large bowl, blend together the flour, baking powder, baking soda, chocolate chips, and ¼ tea-spoon salt. In a medium bowl, beat the egg whites with the remaining pinch of salt until stiff but not dry. Beat in the sugar, canola oil, bananas, and banana extract. Combine the two mixtures, blending until the dry ingredients are just moistened.

3  Spoon the batter into the prepared muffin cups, filling each about three-quarters full. Bake 20 to 25 minutes, or until the tops are golden brown color and a cake tester or wooden toothpick inserted into the center of a muffin comes out clean. Cool in the pan on a wire rack for 5 to 7 minutes. Serve warm, or invert onto the rack to cool completely. Top with Vanilla Cream Sauce.

## BANANA MUFFINS

*MAKES: 3 to 4 muffins*

## VANILLA CREAM SAUCE

*MAKES: 1¼ cups*

1½ tablespoons butter or
  margarine
1½ tablespoons cornstarch
1 cup boiling water
2 tablespoons granulated sugar
½ teaspoon salt
1 teaspoon vanilla

In a small saucepan set over medium heat, melt the butter. Stir in the cornstarch. Stir in the boiling water, sugar, and salt. Cook, stirring constantly, until the mixture thickens. Remove from the heat and stir in the vanilla. Pour the sauce into a serving bowl and refrigerate for 30 minutes before using.

# BANANA–NUT MUFFINS

MAKES: *11 to 12 muffins*

2 cups all-purpose flour
¾ cup granulated sugar
1 teaspoon baking soda
½ cup chopped pecans
1 teaspoon salt
2 large eggs, beaten
1½ cups (about 3 medium) mashed bananas
Honey–Ginger Sauce (see recipe below)

1  Position the rack in the center of the oven and preheat to 375 degrees F. Lightly grease or line with paper baking cups ten 2¾-inch muffin cups.

2  In a large bowl, blend together the flour, sugar, baking soda, pecans, and salt. In a medium bowl, beat together the eggs and bananas. Combine the two mixes, blending until the dry ingredients are just moistened.

3  Spoon the batter into the prepared muffin cups, filling each about three-quarters full. Bake for 12 to 18 minutes, or until the tops are golden brown and a cake tester or wooden toothpick inserted into the center of a muffin comes out clean. Cool in the pan on a wire rack for 5 to 7 minutes. Serve warm, or invert onto the rack to cool completely. Top with Honey–Ginger Sauce.

## HONEY–GINGER SAUCE

MAKES: *About ⅔ cup*

½ cup plain yogurt
2 tablespoons mayonnaise
2 teaspoons honey
½ teaspoon ground ginger

In a small bowl, combine all of the ingredients, blending until smooth. Cover and refrigerate until ready to serve.

2 cups all-purpose flour
1 teaspoon baking powder
1½ teaspoons baking soda
1 teaspoon ground cinnamon
¼ teaspoon ground cloves
¼ teaspoon ground nutmeg
¼ teaspoon salt
¼ cup seedless raisins
2 tablespoons dried grated orange zest
2 large eggs
¾ cup Triple Sec liqueur
2 large ripe bananas, mashed
10 orange sections
Brown Sugar Topping (see recipe below)

**1** Position the rack in the center of the oven and preheat to 375 degrees F. Lightly grease or line with paper baking cups ten 2¾-inch muffin cups.

**2** In a large bowl, combine the flour, baking powder, baking soda, cinnamon, cloves, nutmeg, salt, raisins, and orange zest. In a medium bowl, beat together the eggs until foamy. Beat in the Triple Sec and bananas. Combine the two mixtures, blending until the dry ingredients are just moistened.

**3** Spoon the batter into the prepared muffin cups, filling each about three-quarters full. Press an orange section into each muffin and bake for 15 to 20 minutes, or until a cake tester or wooden toothpick inserted into the center of a muffin comes out clean. Cool in the pan on a wire rack for 5 to 7 minutes. Serve warm, or invert onto the rack to cool completely. Top with Brown Sugar Topping.

## BANANA–ORANGE– RAISIN MUFFINS

MAKES: *9 to 10 muffins*

## BROWN SUGAR TOPPING

MAKES: *½ cup*

¼ cup all-purpose flour
¼ cup packed light-brown sugar
2 tablespoons butter or margarine

In a medium bowl, combine the flour and sugar until thoroughly blended. Using a pastry blender or two knives scissor-fashion, cut the butter into the sugar mixture until it forms coarse crumbs. Cover and refrigerate until ready to use.

---

1½ cups all-purpose flour
2 teaspoons baking powder
¼ teaspoon ground nutmeg
½ teaspoon salt
1 large banana, diced
½ cup chopped pecans
2 large eggs
½ cup granulated sugar
½ cup milk
¼ cup butter or margarine
Whipped Cream Topping (see recipe page 208)

**1** Position the rack in the center of the oven and preheat to 400 degrees F. Lightly grease or line with paper baking cups ten 2¾-inch muffin cups.

**2** In a large bowl, blend together the flour, baking powder, nutmeg, and salt. Fold in the banana

and pecans. In a medium bowl, beat the eggs until foamy. Beat in the sugar, milk, and butter. Combine the two mixtures, blending until the dry ingredients are just moistened.

**3** Spoon the batter into the prepared muffin cups, filling each about three-quarters full. Bake for 15 to 20 minutes, or until a cake tester or wooden toothpick inserted into the center of a muffin comes out clean. Cool in the pan on a wire rack for 5 to 7 minutes. Serve warm, or invert onto the rack to cool completely. Top with Whipped Cream Topping.

## BANANA–PECAN MUFFINS

MAKES: *9 to 10 muffins*

# BANANA–PRALINE MUFFINS

MAKES: *9 to 10 muffins*

1¼ cups all-purpose flour
½ cup plus 2 tablespoons
  granulated sugar
2 teaspoons baking powder
½ teaspoon salt
1 large egg
1 tablespoon sour cream or plain
  yogurt
3 tablespoons packed light-brown
  sugar
⅓ cup chopped pecans
3 large ripe bananas, mashed
⅓ cup canola oil
Coarsely crushed pecans for garnish
Cherry Sauce (see recipe below)

**1** Position the rack in the center of the oven and preheat to 400 degrees F. Lightly grease or line with paper baking cups ten 2¾-inch muffin cups.

**2** In a large bowl, blend together the flour, granulated sugar, baking powder, and salt. In a medium bowl, beat the egg foamy. Beat in the sour cream, brown sugar, pecans, bananas, and oil. Combine the two mixes, blending until the dry ingredients are just moistened.

**3** Spoon the batter into the prepared muffin cups, filling each three-quarters full. Sprinkle pecans over the top of each. Bake for about 12 to 15 minutes, or until a cake tester or wooden toothpick inserted into the center of a muffin comes out clean. Cool in the pan on a wire rack for 5 to 7 minutes. Serve warm, or invert onto the rack to cool completely. Serve with Cherry Sauce.

## CHERRY SAUCE

MAKES: *1½ cups*

One 21-ounce can cherry-pie filling
1 tablespoon grated lemon zest
1 tablespoon lemon juice

In a medium bowl using a fork or wire whisk, blend together the filling, zest, and lemon juice. Transfer to a serving bowl and serve at room temperature.

1¾ cups all-purpose flour
2 teaspoons baking powder
¼ teaspoon baking soda
¾ teaspoon salt
1 large egg
⅓ cup canola oil
½ cup granulated sugar
2 large bananas, mashed
Honey Glaze (see recipe below)

**1** Position the rack in the center of the oven and preheat to 400 degrees F. Lightly grease or line with paper baking cups twelve 2¾-inch muffin cups.

**2** In a large bowl, blend together the flour, baking powder, baking soda, and salt. In a medium bowl, beat the egg until foamy. Beat in the oil, sugar, and banana. Combine the two mixtures, blending until the dry ingredients are just moistened.

**3** Spoon 1 heaping tablespoon of the batter into the prepared muffin cups and bake 10 to 15 minutes, or until a cake tester or wooden toothpick inserted into the center of a muffin comes out clean. Remove from the oven and immediately brush the tops of the muffins with the glaze. Cool in the pan on a wire rack for 5 to 7 minutes. Brush with Honey Glaze. Serve warm, or transfer to the rack to cool completely.

# Banana Tea Muffins

MAKES: *11 to 12 muffins*

# Honey Glaze

MAKES: *1 to 1¼ cups*

**1 tablespoon butter or margarine**
**¾ cup honey**
**⅓ cup light corn syrup**

In a small saucepan set over medium heat, combine the butter and honey and cook, stirring, until smooth. Stir in the corn syrup. Remove from heat and pour into a bowl.

# BANANA–WALNUT MUFFINS

MAKES: *3 to 4 muffins*

1 cup all-purpose flour
⅔ cup wheat bran
1 teaspoon baking powder
½ teaspoon baking soda
¼ cup dry milk powder
¼ teaspoon salt
¼ cup chopped walnuts
1 large egg
2 large egg whites
3 large ripe bananas, mashed
Coffee Hard Sauce (see recipe
   below)

**1** Position the rack in the center of the oven and preheat to 375 degrees F. Lightly grease or line with paper baking cups four 3-inch muffin cups.

**2** In a large bowl, blend together the flour, bran, baking powder, baking soda, milk powder, salt, and walnuts. In a medium bowl, beat the egg foamy. Beat in the egg whites and bananas, beating until smooth. Combine the two mixtures, blending until the dry ingredients are just moistened.

**3** Spoon the batter into the prepared muffin cups, filling each about three-quarters full. Bake for 20 to 25 minutes, or until the tops are golden and a cake tester or wooden toothpick inserted into the center of a muffin comes out clean. Cool in the pan on a wire rack for 5 to 7 minutes. Serve warm, or invert onto the rack to cool completely. Serve with Coffee Hard Sauce.

## COFFEE HARD SAUCE

MAKES: *1 cup*

½ cup butter or margarine, at room
   temperature
1¼ cups sifted powdered sugar
1 tablespoon extra-strong brewed
   coffee or coffee liqueur
1 teaspoon chocolate extract

In a small bowl, beat the butter and sugar until fluffy. Stir in the coffee and chocolate extract. Pour into a serving bowl and serve at room temperature.

1½ cups all-purpose flour
2 teaspoons baking powder
1 teaspoon baking soda
½ teaspoon ground allspice
½ teaspoon salt
⅔ cup plain yogurt or sour cream
⅔ cup skim milk
¼ cup packed light-brown sugar
1 small ripe banana, mashed
Yogurt Cream (see recipe below)

**1** Position the rack in the center of the oven and preheat to 375 degrees F. Lightly grease or line with paper baking cups twenty-four 2¾-inch muffin cups. In a large bowl, blend together the flour, baking powder, baking soda, allspice, and salt. In a medium bowl, beat together the yogurt, milk, brown sugar, and banana until smooth. Combine the two mixtures, blending until the dry ingredients are just moistened.

**3** Spoon the batter into the prepared muffin cups, filling each about three-quarters full. Bake for 15 to 20 minutes, or until a cake tester or wooden toothpick inserted into the center of a muffin comes out clean. Cool in the pan on a wire rack for 5 to 7 minutes. Serve warm, or invert onto the rack to cool completely. Serve with Yogurt Cream.

# BANANA–YOGURT MUFFINS

MAKES: *17 to 18 muffins*

# YOGURT CREAM

MAKES: *1 cup*

½ cup cream, at room temperature
½ plain yogurt, at room temperature
1 teaspoon freshly grated orange zest
1 tablespoon passion-fruit pulp

In a small bowl, using an electric mixer on high speed, beat the cream until it forms soft peaks. Beat in the yogurt, orange zest, and fruit pulp. Cover and refrigerate for 30 minutes, or until ready to serve. Just before serving, use a wire whisk to fluff the mixture before transferring it to a serving bowl.

**BAKING NOTES: Vary this recipe by substituting different fruits, or by using flavored yogurts instead of plain.**

2 cups all-purpose flour
2 teaspoons baking powder
1½ tablespoons poppy seeds
½ teaspoon salt
1 large egg
¾ cup granulated sugar
¼ cup canola oil
2 teaspoons dried grated orange zest
1 medium ripe banana, mashed

**1** Position the rack in the center of the oven and preheat to 375 degrees F. Lightly grease or line with paper baking cups twelve 2¾-inch muffin cups.

**2** In a large bowl, blend together the flour, baking powder, poppy seeds, and salt. In a medium bowl, beat the egg foamy. Beat in the sugar, oil, orange zest, and banana. Combine the two mixtures, blending until the dry ingredients are just moistened.

**3** Spoon 1 heaping tablespoon of the batter into the prepared muffin cups. Bake for 15 to 20 minutes, or until a cake tester or wooden toothpick inserted into the center of a muffin comes out clean. Remove from the oven and immediately brush the tops of the muffins with the topping. Cool in the pan on a wire rack for 5 to 7 minutes. Serve warm, or invert onto the rack to cool completely.

# BANANA–POPPY SEED MUFFINS

MAKES: *11 to 12 muffins*

# BANGKOK GINGER MUFFINS

MAKES: *44 to 48 muffins*

3 cups all-purpose flour
2 teaspoons baking powder
1 teaspoon baking soda
3 tablespoons finely chopped fresh ginger root
½ teaspoon five-star powder
¼ teaspoon salt
1 cup vegetable shortening
1 cup turbinado sugar (see Note)
3 large eggs
1 cup buttermilk or sour milk
1 cup honey
Banana Cream (see recipe below)

**1** Position the rack in the center of the oven and preheat to 375 degrees F. Lightly grease or line with paper baking cups forty-eight 2¾-inch muffin cups.

**2** In a large bowl, blend together the flour, baking powder, baking soda, ginger, spice powder, and salt. In a medium bowl, cream together the shortening and sugar. Beat in the eggs, buttermilk, and honey. Combine the two mixtures, blending until the dry ingredients are just moistened.

**3** Spoon 1 heaping tablespoon of the batter into the prepared muffin cups, filling each about three-quarters full. Bake for 15 to 20 minutes, or until and cake tester or wooden toothpick inserted into the center of a muffin comes out clean. Remove from the oven and brush with the glaze. Cool in the pan on a wire rack for 5 to 7 minutes. Serve warm, or transfer to the rack to cool completely. Top with Banana Cream.

NOTE: **Turbinado sugar is available in Asian or specialty-food stores.**

## BANANA CREAM

MAKES: *About 1 cup*

1 medium banana, mashed
¼ cup nonfat banana-flavored yogurt
1 teaspoon honey
½ teaspoon vanilla extract

In a medium bowl, using the back of a spoon, blend all of the ingredients together until smooth. Cover and refrigerate until ready to serve.

2 cups all-purpose flour
½ cup whole-wheat flour
1 tablespoon baking powder
2 large eggs
⅔ cup milk
1 cup Progresso® Beef Barley soup
Cheese Sauce (see recipe below)

**1** Position the rack in the center of the oven and preheat to 375 degrees F. Lightly grease or line with paper baking cups twelve 2¾-inch muffin cups.

**2** In a large bowl, blend together the two flours and baking powder. In a medium bowl, beat the eggs foamy. Beat in the milk and soup. Combine the two mixtures, blending until the dry ingredients are just moistened.

**3** Spoon the batter into the prepared muffin cups, filling each about three-quarters full. Bake for 15 to 20 minutes, or until a cake tester or wooden toothpick inserted into the center of a muffin comes out clean. Cool in the pan on a wire rack for 5 to 7 minutes. Serve warm, or invert onto the rack to cool completely. Top with Cheese Sauce.

# BEEF-BARLEY MUFFINS

MAKES: *11 to 12 muffins*

## CHEESE SAUCE

MAKES: *2 cups*

2 tablespoons butter
1½ tablespoons all-purpose flour
½ teaspoon salt
¼ teaspoon ground pepper
¼ teaspoon paprika
½ pound American cheese, diced
1½ cups milk

In the top of a double boiler, melt the butter. Add the flour, salt, pepper, and paprika. Blend thoroughly. Add the milk gradually, stirring constantly, until the mixture is thick. Continue to cook on low heat and add the cheese, a little at a time, until all the cheese is melted and the mixture is smooth.

**NOTE: Various soft and semi-soft cheeses can be substituted for American cheese in this recipe.**

---

4 cups Bisquick® baking mix
3 tablespoons granulated sugar
One 12-ounce can beer
Ham Spread (see recipe below)

**1** Position the rack in the center of the oven and preheat to 375 degrees F. Lightly grease or line with paper baking cups fourteen 2¾-inch muffin cups.

**2** In a large bowl, combine the baking mix, sugar, and beer, blending until the dry ingredients are just moistened.

**3** Spoon the batter into the prepared muffin cups, filling each about three-quarters full. Bake for 15 to 20 minutes, or until a cake tester or wooden toothpick inserted into the center of a muffin comes out clean. Cool in the pan on a wire rack for 5 to 7 minutes. Serve warm, or invert onto the rack to cool completely. Serve with Ham Spread.

# BEER MUFFINS

MAKES: *13 to 14 muffins*

## HAM SPREAD

MAKES: *About 1½ cups*

½ cup mayonnaise
⅓ cup sour cream
Two 2¼-ounce cans deviled ham, flaked or chopped
1 tablespoon finely chopped onion
¼ teaspoon Worcestershire sauce

In a small bowl, combine all of the ingredients and stir until smooth. Refrigerate until ready to serve.

# BLACK CURRANT MUFFINS

MAKES: *11 to 12 muffins*

2 cups all-purpose flour
1 tablespoons baking powder
¼ cup granulated sugar
½ cup black currants
1 teaspoon salt
1 cup milk
1 large egg
¼ cup butter or margarine, melted
Whipped Cream Topping (see recipe page 208)

**1** Position the rack in the center of the oven and preheat to 400 degrees F. Lightly grease or line with paper baking cups twelve 2¾-inch muffin cups.

**2** In a large bowl, blend together the flour, baking powder, sugar currants, and salt. In medium bowl, beat together the milk, egg and melted butter. Combine the two mixtures, blending until the dry ingredients are just moistened.

**3** Spoon the batter into the prepared muffin cups, filling each about three-quarters full. Bake for 15 to 20 minutes, or until the tops are golden brown and a cake tester or wooden toothpick inserted into the center of a muffin comes out clean. Cool in the pan on a wire rack for 5 to 7 minutes. Serve warm, or invert onto the rack to cool completely. Top with Whipped Cream Topping.

# BLACKBERRY MUFFINS

MAKES: *5 to 6 muffins*

2½ cups all-purpose flour
1 tablespoon baking powder
½ teaspoon salt
3 large eggs, separated
½ cup granulated sugar
¼ cup canola oil
⅔ cup milk
1 cup blackberries, rinsed and dried
Caramel Topping (see recipe below)

**1** Position the rack in the center of the oven and preheat to 400 degrees F. Lightly grease or line with paper baking cups six 3-inch muffin cups.

**2** In a large bowl, blend together the flour, baking powder, and salt. In a medium bowl, beat together the egg yolks, sugar, oil, and milk. In a small bowl, beat the egg whites until stiff but not dry. Fold the blackberries into the egg whites. Combine the dry ingredients and the egg yolk mixture, blending until just moistened. Gently fold in the egg whites. Spoon the batter into the prepared muffin cups, filling each about three-quarters full.

**3** Bake for 20 to 25 minutes, or until the tops are golden brown and a cake tester or wooden toothpick inserted into the center of a muffin comes out clean. Cool in the pan on a wire rack for 5 to 7 minutes. Serve warm, or invert onto the rack to cool completely. Top with Caramel Topping.

## CARAMEL TOPPING

MAKES: *1 to 1¼ cups*

½ cup light or dark corn syrup
6 ounces caramel candies
¼ cup evaporated milk
½ cup toasted nuts or semisweet chocolate chips

In a small saucepan, combine the corn syrup, caramel candy, and milk. Set the pan over medium heat and stir constantly, until the candy has melted and the sauce is very smooth. Stir in the nuts and serve warm or at room temperature (do not chill before serving).

½ cup whole-wheat flour
2 tablespoons wheat germ
2 tablespoons lecithin granules (see Note)
½ teaspoon ground nutmeg
¼ teaspoon salt
1 tablespoon freshly grated lemon zest
3 large eggs
3 tablespoons sour cream or plain yogurt
1 cup large-curd cottage cheese
2 tablespoons honey
1 teaspoon almond extract
Chicken Liver Spread (see recipe below)

**1** Position the rack in the center of the oven and preheat to 375 degrees F. Lightly grease or line with paper baking cups twelve 2¾-inch muffin cups.

**2** In a large bowl, blend together the flour, wheat germ, lecithin, nutmeg, salt, and lemon zest. In a medium bowl, beat the eggs thick and light colored before beating in the sour cream, cheese, honey, and almond extract. Combine the two mixtures, blending until the dry ingredients are just moistened.

**3** Spoon the batter into the prepared muffin cups, filling each about three-quarters full. Bake for 15 to 20 minutes, or until a cake tester or wooden toothpick inserted into the center of a muffin comes out clean. Cool in the pan on a wire rack for 5 to 7 minutes. Serve warm, or invert onto the rack to cool completely. Serve with Chicken Liver Spread.

NOTE: **Lecithin granules may be found in health-food stores.**

# BLINTZ SUBSTITUTE MUFFINS

MAKES: *11 to 12 muffins*

# CHICKEN LIVER SPREAD

MAKES: *About 1½ cups*

8 ounces cooked chicken livers
One 8-ounce package cream cheese, at room temperature
1 tablespoon tomato ketchup
1½ teaspoons lemon juice

In the container of a blender, combine all of the ingredients and process on medium speed until smooth. Transfer the spread to a bowl and refrigerate until ready to serve.

# BLUE CHEESE MUFFINS

MAKES: *11 to 12 muffins*

½ cup all-purpose flour
1 cup rye flour
1 tablespoon baking powder
1 teaspoon baking soda
3½ ounces crumbled blue cheese
Pinch white pepper
2 large eggs
2 tablespoons butter or margarine, melted
½ cup milk
2 teaspoon horseradish
¼ cup finely chopped shallots (green onions)
Black Treacle Sauce (see recipe below)

1  Position the rack in the center of the oven and preheat to 400 degrees F. Lightly grease or line with paper baking cups twelve 2¾-inch muffin cups. In a large bowl, blend together the two flours, baking powder, baking soda, cheese and pepper. In a medium bowl, beat the eggs until foamy. Beat in the butter, milk, and horseradish. Stir in the shallots. Combine the two mixtures, blending until the dry ingredients are just moistened.

3  Spoon the batter into the prepared muffin cups, filling each about three-quarters full. Bake for 15 to 20 minutes, or until a cake tester or wooden toothpick inserted into the center of a muffin comes out clean. Cool in the pan on a wire rack for 5 to 7 minutes. Serve warm, or invert onto the rack to cool completely. Serve with Black Treacle Sauce.

## BLACK TREACLE SAUCE

MAKES: *About 1 cup*

½ cup black treacle or molasses
2 tablespoons soy flour
1½ tablespoons canola oil
2 tablespoons fresh lemon juice

In a small microwave-proof bowl, heat the treacle on ½ power for 1 minute. Pour into the container of a blender, add all the remaining ingredients, and process on medium speed until smooth. Serve hot.

2½ cups all-purpose flour
2½ teaspoons baking powder
¼ teaspoon salt
2 large eggs
1 cup granulated sugar
1 cup buttermilk or sour milk
¼ cup butter or margarine, melted
1½ cups blueberries, rinsed and
    drained
Lemon Sauce (see recipe below)

**1** Position the rack in the center of the oven and preheat to 400 degrees F. Lightly grease or line with paper baking cups six 3-inch muffin cups.

**2** In a large bowl, blend together the flour, baking powder, and salt. In a medium bowl, beat the eggs until foamy. Beat in the sugar, buttermilk, and melted butter until smooth. Fold in the blueberries. Combine the two mixtures, blending until the dry ingredients are just moistened.

**3** Spoon the batter into the prepared muffin cups, filling each about three-quarters full. Bake for 15 to 20 minutes, or until the tops are golden and a cake tester or wooden toothpick inserted into the center of a muffin comes out clean. Cool in the pan on a wire rack for 5 to 7 minutes. Serve warm, or invert onto the rack to cool completely. Top with Lemon Sauce.

# BLUEBERRY–BUTTERMILK MUFFINS

MAKES: *5 to 6 muffins*

# LEMON SAUCE

MAKES: *About ½ cup*

2 teaspoons cornstarch
½ cup water, at room temperature
Pinch sea salt
1 tablespoon fresh lemon juice
Pinch ground nutmeg

In a cup, blend the cornstarch and 1 tablespoon of the water together to form a smooth paste. In small saucepan, combine the remaining water, the salt, lemon juice, and nutmeg. Stir in the cornstarch. Place the pan over medium-low heat and cook, stirring, until the mixture just starts to boil and thickens. Remove from the heat and serve hot.

## BLUEBERRY MUFFINS

MAKES: *11 to 12 muffins*

2½ cups all-purpose flour
1 tablespoon baking powder
1½ cups blueberries, rinsed and
    dried
½ teaspoon salt
2 large eggs
½ cup granulated sugar
1 cup milk
3 tablespoons butter or vegetable
    shortening, melted
Blueberry Spread (see recipe below)

1  Position the rack in the center
of the oven and preheat to 375
degrees F. Lightly grease or line
with paper baking cups twelve
2¾-inch muffin cups.

2  In a large bowl, blend together
the flour, baking powder, blueberries, and salt. In a medium
bowl, beat the eggs until foamy.
Beat in the sugar, milk, and butter. Combine the two mixtures,
blending until the dry ingredients are just moistened.

3  Spoon the batter into the prepared muffin cups, filling each
about three-quarters full. Bake
for 15 to 20 minutes, or until a
cake tester or wooden toothpick
inserted into the center of a muffin comes out clean. Cool in the
pan on a wire rack for 5 to 7 minutes. Serve warm, or invert onto
the rack to cool completely. Serve
with Blueberry Spread.

## BLUEBERRY SPREAD

MAKES: *2 cups*

⅓ cup cold water
1 package unflavored gelatin (¼
    ounce)
3 cups blueberries
½ teaspoon ground ginger
2 tablespoons granulated sugar
4 teaspoons lemon juice
1 teaspoon grated lemon zest

Place the water in a medium
saucepan and sprinkle in the
gelatin. Set the pan over
medium-low heat and stir gently until the gelatin has dissolved. Using a large spoon, stir
in the blueberries, ginger, sugar,
lemon juice, and zest. Raise the
heat and bring the mixture to a
boil. Reduce to a simmer, cover
the pan, and cook for 3 to 5
minutes, or until the fruit is tender. Remove from the heat and
cool for 5 minutes before transferring to a serving bowl. Serve
warm or cold.

2 cups oat-bran cereal, uncooked
2 teaspoons baking powder
¼ teaspoon salt
2 large egg whites
¼ cup skim milk
2 tablespoons canola oil
¼ cup packed light-brown sugar
¼ cup honey
1 teaspoon grated lemon zest
1 cup (8 ounces) plain yogurt or sour cream
½ cup fresh or frozen blueberries, rinsed and dried
Yogurt Cream (see recipe page 55)

**1** Position the rack in the center of the oven and preheat to 425 degrees F. Lightly grease or line with paper baking cups twelve 2¾-inch muffin cups.

**2** In a large bowl, blend together the cereal, baking powder, and salt. In a medium bowl, beat the egg whites until stiff but not dry. Stir in the milk, oil, sugar, honey, lemon zest, and yogurt. Fold in the blueberries. Combine the two mixtures, blending until the dry ingredients are just moistened.

**2** Spoon the batter into the prepared muffin cups, filling each about three-quarters full. Bake for 15 to 20 minutes, or until a cake tester or wooden toothpick inserted into the center of a muffin comes out clean. Cool in the pan on a wire rack for 5 to 7 minutes. Serve warm, or invert onto the rack to cool completely. Serve with Yogurt Cream.

**BAKING NOTES: These muffins are very delicate and will not rise as high as most other muffins.**

## BLUEBERRY–YOGURT MUFFINS

MAKES: *15 to 16 muffins*

---

2 large eggs
⅓ cup canola oil
½ cup pineapple juice concentrate
1 cup (about 2 medium) mashed ripe bananas
1 tablespoon Triple Sec or concentrated orange juice
2 teaspoons baking soda
¼ teaspoon salt
2 cups all-purpose flour
1 cup fresh blueberries, rinsed and dried
Dieter's Butter (see recipe below)

**1** Position the rack in the center of the oven and preheat to 375 degrees F. Lightly grease or line with paper baking cups eighteen 2¾-inch muffin cups.

**2** In a large bowl, beat the eggs until thick and light-colored. Beat in the oil, pineapple juice, bananas, Triple Sec, baking soda, and salt. Stir in the flour, blending until the flour is just moistened. Gently fold in the blueberries.

**3** Spoon the batter into the prepared muffin cups, filling each about three-quarters full. Bake for 15 to 20 minutes, or until the tops are a light golden-brown and a cake tester or wooden toothpick inserted into the center of a muffin comes out clean. Cool in the pan on a wire rack for 5 to 7 minutes. Serve warm, or invert onto the rack to cool completely. Serve with Dieter's Butter.

## BLUEBERRY–BANANA MUFFINS

MAKES: *17 to 18 muffins*

## DIETER'S BUTTER

MAKES: *About 2 cups*

½ teaspoon unflavored Knox® gelatin
1 cup unsalted butter, at room temperature
1 cup chilled skim milk
½ teaspoon powdered butter flavoring

**1** Soften the gelatin in a microwave-proof glass bowl. Microwave on medium heat until the gelatin is dissolved. Cool slightly.

**2** In a small bowl, beat the gelatin and butter together until smooth. Very slowly beat in the milk a very little at a time (it should take a full 5 minutes to beat in all of the milk). Beat in the butter flavoring, cover and refrigerate until hard. Use as a spread only.

# BRAN CEREAL MUFFINS

MAKES: *15 muffins*

2 cups all-purpose flour
2½ cups bran flake cereal or raisin
   bran cereal, crushed
2 tablespoons baking powder
¼ cup semisweet miniature
   chocolate chips
1½ teaspoons salt
2 large eggs
¼ cup granulated sugar
⅔ cup canola oil
1½ cups milk
Carrot Butter (see recipe below)

1  Position the rack in the center of the oven and preheat to 400 degrees F. Lightly grease or line with paper baking cups eighteen 2¾-inch muffin cups.

2  In a large bowl, blend together the flour, cereal, baking powder, chocolate chips, and salt. In a medium bowl, beat the eggs, sugar, oil, and milk until smooth. Combine the two mixtures, blending until the dry ingredients are just moistened.

3 Spoon the batter into the prepared muffin cups, filling each about three-quarters full. Bake for 15 to 20 minutes, or until a cake tester or wooden toothpick inserted into the center of a muffin is removed clean. Cool in the pan on a wire rack for 5 to 7 minutes. Serve warm, or invert onto the rack to cool completely. Serve with Carrot Butter.

## CARROT BUTTER

MAKES: *About 1½ cups*

½ cup cooked diced carrots
1 cup butter or margarine, at room
   temperature
½ cup finely chopped seedless
   raisins

In a medium bowl, whip together the carrots, butter, and raisins until smooth. Cover and refrigerate until ready to serve.

1 cup all-purpose flour
1 cup wheat bran
1 teaspoon baking powder
1 teaspoon ground cinnamon
¼ teaspoon salt
1 large egg
½ cup packed light-brown sugar
1 cup buttermilk or sour milk
½ teaspoon baking soda
⅓ cup butter or margarine, melted
½ cup molasses
⅓ cup seedless raisins
Honey Glaze (see recipe page 53)
Coconut Chutney (see recipe below)

1  Position the rack in the center of the oven and preheat to 400 degrees F. Lightly grease or line with paper baking cups twelve 2¾-inch muffin cups.

2  In a large bowl, blend together the flour, bran, baking powder, cinnamon, and salt. In a medium bowl, beat the egg, brown sugar, buttermilk, baking soda, butter, molasses, and raisins until smooth. Combine the two mixtures, blending until the dry ingredients are just moistened.

3  Spoon the batter into the prepared muffin cups, filling each about three-quarters full. Bake for 15 to 20 minutes, or until the tops are golden brown and a cake tester or wooden toothpick inserted into the center of a muffin comes out clean. Cool in the pan on a wire rack for 5 to 7 minutes. Invert onto the rack to cool completely. Drizzle Honey Glaze over the tops of the muffins and serve with Coconut Chutney.

# BRAN MUFFINS WITH HONEY GLAZE

MAKES: *11 to 12 muffins*

## COCONUT CHUTNEY

MAKES: *About 2½ cups*

1 cup sweetened flaked coconut
½ cup plain yogurt
2 small green sweet Bell peppers, stemmed, seeded and finely chopped
2 small red sweet Bell peppers, stemmed, seeded and finely chopped
2 tablespoons boiling water
¼ cup canola oil
½ teaspoon prepared mustard
¼ teaspoon salt

In the container of a blender, combine all of the ingredients and process on medium speed until smooth. Pour into a small skillet and cook over medium heat, stirring constantly, until the mixture starts to sputter. Remove from the heat and serve.

## BRAN MUFFINS WITH NUTS AND RAISINS

MAKES: *17 to 18 muffins*

2 cups graham flour
1½ cups oat bran
1¼ teaspoons baking soda
1 cup chopped walnuts
1 cup seedless raisins
¼ teaspoon salt
1 large egg
2 cups buttermilk or sour milk
2 tablespoons packed light-brown sugar
½ cup molasses
2 tablespoons butter or margarine, melted
Brown Sugar Glaze (see recipe below)
Jam or jelly

1 Position the rack in the center of the oven and preheat to 375 degrees F. Lightly grease or line with paper baking cups eighteen 2¾-inch muffin cups.

2 In a large bowl, blend together the graham flour, bran, baking soda, walnuts, raisins, and salt. In medium bowl, beat together the egg, buttermilk, brown sugar, molasses, and butter. Combine the two mixtures, blending until the dry ingredients are just moistened.

3 Spoon the batter into the prepared muffin cups, filling each about three-quarters full. Bake for 15 to 20 minutes, or until a cake tester or wooden toothpick inserted into the center of a muffin comes out clean. Remove from the oven and immediately brush the tops of the muffins with Brown Sugar Glaze. Cool in the pan on a wire rack for 5 to 7 minutes. Serve warm, or transfer to the rack to cool completely.

## BROWN SUGAR GLAZE

MAKES: *½ cup*

¼ cup all-purpose flour
¼ cup packed light-brown sugar
2 tablespoons butter or margarine

In a medium bowl, combine the flour and sugar until thoroughly blended. Using a pastry blender or two knives scissor-fashion, cut the butter into the sugar mixture until it forms coarse crumbs. Cover and refrigerate until ready to use. Sprinkle on top of muffins just before baking.

SERVING SUGGESTION: **Serve with jam or jelly.**

1¼ cups all-purpose flour
2 cups All-Bran® cereal
2 tablespoons baking powder
1 cup golden raisins
¼ teaspoon salt
1 large egg
1¼ cups milk
½ cup granulated sugar
¼ cup canola oil
Orange Glaze (see recipe below)
Jam or jelly

**1** Position the rack in the center of the oven and preheat to 400 degrees F. Lightly grease or line with paper baking cups twelve 2¾-inch muffin cups.

**2** In a large bowl, blend together the flour, cereal, baking powder, raisins, and salt. In a medium bowl, beat the egg and milk together until smooth Beat in the sugar and oil. Combine the two mixtures, blending until the dry ingredients are just moistened.

**3** Spoon the batter into the prepared muffin cups, filling each about three-quarters full. Bake for 15 to 20 minutes, or until the tops are golden brown and a cake tester or wooden toothpick inserted into the center of a muffin comes out clean. Remove from the oven and immediately brush the tops of the muffins with Orange Glaze. Cool in the pan on a wire rack for 5 to 7 minutes. Serve warm, or transfer to the rack to cool completely.

# BRAN MUFFINS WITH RAISINS

MAKES: *11 to 12 muffins*

# ORANGE GLAZE

MAKES: *¾ cup*

¾ cup fresh orange juice
1 tablespoon cornstarch
1 teaspoon orange extract or Triple Sec
1 teaspoon orange zest

In a small saucepan, combine the orange juice and corn starch and stir until smooth. Place the pan over medium-high heat and bring to a full boil. Remove from the heat and stir in the orange extract and orange zest.

# BRAN MUFFINS

MAKES: *23 to 24 muffins*

1 cup all-purpose flour
½ cup whole-wheat flour
1 cup All-Bran® cereal, crushed
1 tablespoon baking powder
¼ teaspoon salt
1 cup milk
2 tablespoons granulated sugar
1 large egg
3 tablespoons canola oil
Cinnamon–Rhubarb Sauce (see
   recipe below)

1  Position the rack in the center of the oven and preheat to 400 degrees F. Lightly grease or line with paper baking cups twenty-four 2-inch muffin cups.

2  In a large bowl, blend together the two flours, cereal, baking powder, and salt. In a medium bowl, beat together the milk, sugar, egg, and oil. Combine the two mixtures, blending until the dry ingredients are just moistened.

3  Spoon the batter into the prepared muffin cups, filling each about three-quarters full. Bake for 12 to 15 minutes, or until a cake tester or wooden toothpick inserted into the center of a muffin comes out clean. Remove from the oven and immediately spread the tops of the muffins with Cinnamon–Rhubarb Sauce. Cool in the pan on a wire rack for 5 to 7 minutes. Serve warm, or transfer to the rack to cool completely.

## CINNAMON– RHUBARB SAUCE

MAKES: *About 2 cups*

2 cups finely diced fresh rhubarb
5 tablespoons granulated sugar
¼ teaspoon ground cinnamon
⅛ teaspoon lemon extract

1  In a medium saucepan set over medium-low heat, combine the rhubarb, sugar, and cinnamon. Cover and cook for about 20 minutes, or until the rhubarb is tender.

2  Remove from the heat, cool slightly, and pour into the container of a blender. Add the lemon extract and process on medium speed until smooth. Serve warm.

2 cups all-purpose flour
1 cup whole-wheat flour
½ cup graham flour
1½ cups granulated sugar
2½ tablespoons baking powder
1½ tablespoons fresh grated orange zest
½ teaspoon salt
4 large egg whites
¾ cup canola oil
1¼ cups cranberry juice
¼ cup brandy
2 cups dried cranberries, finely chopped
Fluffy Brandy Sauce (see recipe below)

**1** Position the rack in the center of the oven and preheat to 375 degrees F. Lightly grease or line with paper baking cups thirty 2¾-inch muffin cups.

**2** In a large bowl, combine the three flours, sugar, baking powder, orange zest, and salt. In another large bowl, beat the egg whites until stiff but not dry. Beat in the oil, cranberry juice, brandy, and cranberries. Combine the two mixtures, blending until the dry ingredients are just moistened.

**3** Spoon the batter into the prepared muffin cups, filling each about three-quarters full. Bake for 15 to 20 minutes, or until the tops are a light golden-brown and a cake tester or wooden toothpick inserted into the center of a muffin comes out clean. Cool in the pan on a wire rack for 5 to 7 minutes. Serve warm, or invert onto the rack to cool completely. Serve with Fluffy Brandy Sauce.

# BRANDY–CRANBERRY MUFFINS

MAKES: *29 to 30 muffins*

# FLUFFY BRANDY SAUCE

MAKES: *About 1½ cups*

1 large egg, separated
¾ cup powdered sugar
½ cup heavy cream, whipped until soft peaks form
3 tablespoons brandy

In a medium bowl, beat the egg whites until stiff but not dry before beating in the sugar. Beat in the egg yolk, and fold in the whipped cream and brandy. Cover and refrigerate until ready to serve.

**WARNING: This dish contains uncooked eggs and must be used at once. It will not keep.**

# BREAKFAST MUFFINS

MAKES: *16 to 20 muffins*

1 cup seedless raisins
½ cup boiling water
4 large egg whites
1 cup yogurt or sour cream
1 teaspoon baking soda
7 tablespoons orange juice
  concentrate
1 cup rolled oats
1 cup all-purpose flour
1 teaspoon cinnamon
¼ teaspoon salt
Brazil Nut Cream Sauce (see recipe
  below)

**1** Position the rack in the center of the oven and preheat to 375 degrees F. Lightly grease or line with paper baking cups twenty 2¾-inch muffin cups.

**2** In a small bowl, combine the raisins and boiling water and set aside. In a medium bowl, beat the egg whites until stiff but not dry. Beat in the yogurt, baking soda, and orange juice. In a large bowl, blend together the oats, flour, cinnamon, and salt. Combine the two mixtures, blending until the dry ingredients are just moistened. Drain the raisins and pat dry between paper towels before folding them into the batter.

**3** Spoon the batter into the prepared muffin cups, filling each cup three-quarters full. Bake for 15 to 20 minutes, or until a cake tester or wooden toothpick inserted into the muffins comes out clean. Cool in the pan on a wire rack for 5 to 7 minutes. Serve warm, or invert onto the rack to cool completely. Top with Brazil Nut Cream Sauce.

## BRAZIL NUT CREAM SAUCE

MAKES: *About 1 cup*

2 large egg yolks
1 cup powdered sugar
½ cup finely ground Brazil nuts
1 tablespoon sherry or rum

In a small bowl, beat the egg yolks until light colored. Beat in the sugar, nuts, and sherry. Cover with plastic wrap and refrigerate until ready to serve.

**WARNING: This must be used at once it will not keep. The egg yolks are not cooked.**

# BRITISH BANANA- AND-CURRY MUFFINS

MAKES: *11 to 12 muffins*

2 cups all-purpose flour
1½ cups oat bran
2 teaspoons baking powder
½ teaspoon baking soda
1 teaspoon curry powder
¼ teaspoon salt
1 cup milk
2 tablespoons butter or margarine,
  melted
1 tablespoon molasses
3 tablespoons sweetened condensed
  milk
3 medium bananas, mashed

**1** Position the rack in the center of the oven and preheat to 375 degrees F. Lightly grease or line with paper baking cups twelve 2¾-inch muffin cups.

**2** In a large bowl, blend together the flour, oat bran, baking powder, baking soda, curry powder, and salt. In a medium bowl, beat the milk, butter, molasses, and bananas until smooth. Combine the two mixtures, blending until the dry ingredients are just moistened.

**3** Spoon the batter into the prepared muffin cups, filling each about three-quarters full. Bake for 15 to 20 minutes, or until a cake tester or wooden toothpick inserted into the center of a muffin comes out clean. Cool in the pan on a wire rack for 5 to 7 minutes. Serve warm, or invert onto the rack to cool completely.

**SERVING SUGGESTION: Serve with black currant preserves.**

# BROCCOLI MUFFINS

MAKES: *14 to 15 muffins*

1 cup all-purpose flour
1 cup graham flour
1 tablespoon baking powder
¼ cup granulated sugar
1 cup finely chopped broccoli
　flowerettes
1 teaspoon ground nutmeg
1 teaspoon salt
1 large egg
½ cup mayonnaise
1 cup milk
1 teaspoon lemon juice
¼ cup warmed honey
¼ cup finely shredded sharp cheese
Cheese Sauce (see recipe page 57)

1 Position the rack in the center of the oven and preheat to 375 degrees F. Lightly grease or line with paper baking cups twelve 2¾-inch muffin cups.

2 In a large bowl, blend together the two flours, baking powder, sugar, broccoli, nutmeg, and salt. In a medium bowl, beat together the egg, mayonnaise, milk, lemon juice, and honey. Combine the two mixtures, blending until the dry ingredients are just moistened.

3 Spoon the batter into the prepared muffin cups, filling each about three-quarters full. Sprinkle the cheese over the tops of the muffins. Bake for 15 to 20 minutes, or until a cake tester or wooden toothpick inserted into the center of a muffin comes out clean. Cool in the pan on a wire rack for 5 to 7 minutes. Serve warm, or invert onto the rack to cool completely. Serve with Cheese Sauce.

# BROWN BREAD MUFFINS

MAKES: *5 to 6 muffins*

2 cups whole-wheat flour
⅔ cup all-purpose flour
2 teaspoons baking soda
1 teaspoon pumpkin-pie spice
¼ teaspoon salt
¾ cup seedless raisins
⅔ cup packed brown sugar
2 cups buttermilk or sour milk
Creamy Dill Sauce (see recipe
　below)

1 Position the rack in the center of the oven and preheat to 375 degrees F. Lightly grease or line with paper baking cups six 3-inch muffin cups.

2 In a large bowl, blend together the two flours, baking soda, pumpkin-pie spice, salt, and raisins. In a small bowl, beat the sugar and milk until smooth. Combine the two mixtures, blending until the dry ingredients are just moistened.

3 Spoon the batter into the prepared muffin cups, filling each about three-quarters full. Bake for 15 to 20 minutes, or until the tops are golden and a cake tester or wooden toothpick inserted into the center of a muffin comes out clean. Cool in the pan on a wire rack for 5 to 7 minutes. Serve warm, or invert onto the rack to cool completely. Serve with Creamy Dill Sauce.

# CREAMY DILL SAUCE

MAKES: *About 1¼ cups*

½ cup mayonnaise
½ cup sour cream
⅓ cup drained, finely chopped
　Kosher pickles
½ teaspoon crushed dried dill

In a small bowl, combine all of the ingredients and refrigerate until ready to serve.

# BROWN RICE MUFFINS

MAKES: *5 to 6 muffins*

1¼ cups whole-wheat flour
2 teaspoons baking powder
¼ teaspoon salt
2 large eggs
⅔ cup milk
¼ cup canola oil
2 tablespoons packed brown sugar
¼ teaspoon almond extract
1 cup cooked brown rice
Crab Spread (see recipe below)

**1** Position the rack in the center of the oven and preheat to 400 degrees F. Lightly grease or line with paper baking cups six 2¾-inch muffin cups.

**2** In a large bowl, blend together the flour, baking powder, and salt. In a medium bowl, beat together the eggs and milk. Beat in the oil, brown sugar, and almond extract. Stir in the cooked rice. Combine the two mixtures, blending until the dry ingredients are just moistened.

**3** Spoon the batter into the prepared muffin cups, filling each cup almost to the top. Bake for 15 to 20 minutes, or until a cake tester or wooden toothpick inserted into the center of a muffin comes out clean. Cool in the pan on a wire rack for 5 to 7 minutes. Serve warm, or invert onto the rack to cool completely. Serve with Crab Spread.

## CRAB SPREAD

MAKES: *About 1½ cups*

One 3-ounce package cream
    cheese, at room temperature
One 6½-ounce can crabmeat,
    undrained
⅔ cup mayonnaise
⅛ teaspoon bottled hot sauce
Paprika for sprinkling

**1** Position the rack to the center of the oven and preheat the oven to 325 degrees F. Lightly grease a small oven-proof baking dish or pan.

**2** In a medium bowl, blend all the ingredients together until smooth. Spread into the prepared baking dish, sprinkle with paprika and bake for about 20 minutes, or until the mixture bubbles. Remove from the oven and serve hot.

2 cups all-purpose flour
1 teaspoon baking powder
1 teaspoon baking soda
¼ cup chopped pecans
¼ teaspoon salt
1 large egg
1 cup packed light-brown sugar
½ cup butter or margarine, melted
1 cup milk
2 teaspoons vanilla extract
Peach Melba Sauce (see recipe
   below)

**1** Position the rack in the center of the oven and preheat to 400 degrees F. Lightly grease or line with paper baking cups twelve 2¾-inch muffin cups.

**2** In a large bowl, blend together the flour, baking powder, baking soda, pecans, and salt. In a medi-um bowl, beat the egg and brown sugar together until thick. Beat in the butter, milk, and vanilla extract. Combine the two mixtures, blending until the dry ingredients are just moistened.

**3** Spoon the batter into the prepared muffin cups, filling each about three-quarters full. Sprinkle the topping over the tops of the muffins. Bake for 15 to 20 minutes, or until a cake tester or wooden toothpick inserted into the center of a muffin comes out clean. Cool in the pan on a wire rack for 5 to 7 minutes. Serve warm, or transfer to the rack to cool completely. Serve with Peach Melba Sauce.

# BROWN SUGAR MUFFINS

MAKES: *11 to 12 muffins*

# PEACH MELBA SAUCE

MAKES: *3½ cups*

2 cups raspberries
2 peaches, peeled, stoned, and
   thinly sliced
¾ cup granulated sugar
1 tablespoon cornstarch

**1** In a large bowl, combine the raspberries and peaches. Sprinkle with ½ cup of the sugar, cover, and refrigerate for at least 2 hours.

**2** Remove the peaches and raspberries from the refrigerator and drain the juice from the mixture. Add enough water to the juices to equal 1 cup.

**3** In a medium saucepan, combine the remaining ¼ cup sugar and the cornstarch. Add the 1 cup fruit juice and set the pan over medium heat. Cook, stirring constantly, for 4 to 5 minutes, or until the mixture thickens. Remove from the heat and cool slightly before pouring the mixture into the container of a blender. Add the reserved raspberries and peaches and process on high until smooth. Pour into a serving bowl and cool to room temperature before serving.

# BUCKWHEAT MUFFINS WITH APPLE

MAKES: *11 to 12 muffins*

1½ cups all-purpose flour
½ cup buckwheat flour
1 tablespoon baking powder
1 large apple, peeled, cored and chopped
1 cup chopped walnuts or almonds
¼ teaspoon salt
1 large egg
½ cup granulated sugar
¼ cup butter or margarine, melted
¾ cup apple juice
Peppery Lemon Butter (see recipe below)

1 Position the rack in the center of the oven and preheat to 400 degrees F. Lightly grease or line with paper baking cups twelve 2¾-inch muffin cups.

2 In a large bowl, blend together the two flours, baking powder, apple, walnuts and salt. In a medium bowl, beat the egg, sugar, butter, and apple juice until smooth. Combine the two mixtures, blending until the dry ingredients are just moistened.

3 Spoon the batter into the prepared muffin cups, filling each about three-quarters full. Bake for 15 to 20 minutes, or until a cake tester or wooden toothpick inserted into the center of a muffin comes out clean. Cool in the pan on a wire rack for 5 to 7 minutes. Serve warm, or invert onto the rack to cool completely. Serve with Peppery Lemon Butter.

## PEPPERY LEMON BUTTER

MAKES: *About ⅔ cup*

½ cup butter or margarine, at room temperature
¼ cup fresh lemon juice
¼ teaspoon onion powder
¼ teaspoon fresh ground black pepper

In a small bowl, beat all of the ingredients together until smooth. Refrigerate until serving.

2½ cups wheat bran
1½ cups all-purpose flour
1½ teaspoons baking soda
½ cup chopped seedless raisins
1 teaspoon salt
2 large eggs
½ cup granulated sugar
¼ cup molasses
1½ cups sour milk or buttermilk, at room temperature
2½ tablespoons vegetable shortening
Sesame Sauce (see recipe below)

**1** Position the rack in the center of the oven and preheat to 400 degrees F. Lightly grease or line with paper baking cups sixteen 2¾-inch muffin cups.

**2** In a large bowl, blend together the bran, flour, baking soda, raisins, and salt. In a medium bowl, beat together the eggs, sugar, molasses, sour milk, and shortening. Combine the two mixtures, blending until the dry ingredients are just moistened.

**3** Spoon the batter into the prepared muffin cups, filling each about three-quarters full. Bake for 15 to 20 minutes, or until a cake tester or wooden toothpick inserted into the center of a muffin comes out clean. Cool in the pan on a wire rack for 5 to 7 minutes. Serve warm, or invert onto the rack to cool completely. Serve with Sesame Sauce.

## BUTTERMILK–BRAN MUFFINS

MAKES: *15 to 16 muffins*

## SESAME SAUCE

MAKES: *About 1½ cups*

½ cup water
½ cup fresh lemon juice
1 cup sesame seeds
2 tablespoons canola oil
Salt to taste

In the container of a blender, combine all of the ingredients except the salt and process on medium speed until smooth. Serve cold.

---

4 cups all-purpose flour
2 tablespoons cornmeal
1 teaspoon baking soda
1 teaspoon salt
2 large eggs
1 tablespoon granulated sugar
3½ cups buttermilk or sour milk, at room temperature
Peach Melba Sauce (see recipe page 73)

**1** Position the rack in the center of the oven and preheat to 400 degrees F. Lightly grease or line with paper baking cups twenty 2¾-inch muffin cups.

**2** In a large bowl, blend together the flour, cornmeal, baking soda, and salt. In a medium bowl, beat the eggs, sugar, and buttermilk until smooth. Combine the two mixtures, blending until the dry ingredients are just moistened.

**3** Spoon the batter into the prepared muffin cups, filling each about three-quarters full. Bake for 15 to 20 minutes, or until a cake tester or wooden toothpick inserted into the center of a muffin comes out clean. Cool in the pan on a wire rack for 5 to 7 minutes. Serve warm, or invert onto the rack to cool completely. Serve with Peach Melba Sauce.

## BUTTERMILK MUFFINS

MAKES: *19 to 20 muffins*

## BUTTERMILK–
## BLUEBERRY MUFFINS

MAKES: *11 to 12 muffins*

2 cups all-purpose flour
½ cup granulated sugar
2½ teaspoons baking powder
¼ teaspoon baking soda
1 cup fresh blueberries, rinsed and
  dried
1 teaspoon salt
1 large egg, separated
¾ cup buttermilk or sour milk
¼ cup butter or margarine, melted
Pineapple Syrup (see recipe page 46)

**1** Position the rack in the center of the oven and preheat to 400 degrees F. Lightly grease or line with paper baking cups twelve 2¾-inch muffin cups.

**2** In a large bowl, blend the flour, sugar, baking powder, baking soda, blueberries, and salt until smooth. In a small bowl, beat the egg white until stiff but not dry. In a medium bowl, beat together the egg yolk, buttermilk, and butter. Stir in the egg white. Combine the two mixtures, blending until the dry ingredients are just moistened.

**3** Spoon the batter into the prepared muffin cups, filling each about three-quarters full. Bake for 15 to 20 minutes, or until a cake tester or wooden toothpick inserted into the center of a muffin comes out clean. Cool in the pan on a wire rack for 5 to 7 minutes. Serve warm, or invert onto the rack to cool completely. Serve with Pineapple Syrup.

## BUTTERNUT
## SQUASH MUFFINS

MAKES: *15 to 16 muffins*

2 cups all-purpose flour
2 tablespoons granulated sugar
1 tablespoon baking powder
1 teaspoon salt
1 large egg
1 cup milk
¼ cup butter or margarine, melted
⅔ cup mashed cooked butternut
  squash
Onion-and-Pepper Relish (see
  recipe below)

**1** Position the rack in the center of the oven and preheat to 400 degrees F. Lightly grease or line with paper baking cups sixteen 2¾-inch muffin cups.

**2** In a large bowl, blend together the flour, sugar, baking powder, and salt. In a medium bowl, beat the egg, milk, butter, and mashed squash until smooth. Combine the two mixtures, blending until the dry ingredients are just moistened.

**3** Spoon the batter into the prepared muffin cups, filling each about three-quarters full. Bake for 15 to 20 minutes, or until a cake tester or wooden toothpick inserted into the center of a muffin comes out clean. Cool in the pan on a wire rack for 5 to 7 minutes. Serve warm, or invert onto the rack to cool completely. Serve with Onion-and-Pepper Relish.

## ONION-AND-
## PEPPER RELISH

MAKES: *About 1½ cups*

2 medium red onions, peeled and
  finely chopped
1 medium green bell pepper,
  stemmed, seeded, and finely
  chopped
1 small green sweet bell pepper,
  stemmed, seeded, and finely
  chopped
1 medium ripe tomato, peeled and
  finely chopped
½ cup fresh snipped parsley
2 teaspoons fresh snipped tarragon
1 teaspoon honey vinegar
1 tablespoon lemon juice
2 tablespoons honey
Salt to taste

In a small bowl, combine all of the ingredients except the salt and stir until well mixed. Season to taste with salt. Cover and refrigerate until ready to use.

1½ cups cornmeal
1½ cups all-purpose flour
3 tablespoons granulated sugar
1 tablespoon plus 1½ teaspoons
   baking powder
1 teaspoon cayenne pepper
1½ teaspoons ground black pepper
½ cup seeded and diced red bell
   pepper
¼ cup seeded and diced green bell
   pepper
¼ cup finely minced yellow onion
1½ teaspoons salt
2 large eggs
¼ cup canola oil
1 tablespoon butter or margarine,
   melted
Mexican Sauce (see recipe below)

**1** Position the rack in the center of the oven and preheat to 400 degrees F. Lightly grease or line with paper baking cups twelve 2¾-inch muffin cups.

**2** In a large bowl, blend together the cornmeal, flour, sugar, baking powder, cayenne pepper, black pepper, bell peppers, onions, and salt. In a medium bowl, beat together the eggs, oil, and butter. Combine the two mixtures, blending until the dry ingredients are just moistened.

**3** Spoon the batter into the prepared muffin cups, filling each about three-quarters full. Bake for 15 to 20 minutes, or until a cake tester or wooden toothpick inserted into the center of a muffin comes out clean. Cool in the pan on a wire rack for 5 to 7 minutes. Serve warm, or invert onto the rack to cool completely. Serve with Mexican Sauce.

# Cajun Corn Muffins

Makes: *11 to 12 muffins*

# Mexican Sauce

Makes: *2 cups*

1 teaspoon instant-coffee crystals
2 tablespoons hot water
1 cup (6 ounces) semisweet
   chocolate chips
2 tablespoons butter or margarine
One 14-ounce can sweetened
   condensed milk
1 teaspoon ground cinnamon or
   allspice
1 teaspoon vanilla extract

**1** In a cup, combine the coffee and water. Set aside.

**2** In the top of a double boiler set over simmering water, combine the chocolate chips, butter, condensed milk, and cinnamon. Cook, stirring constantly, until smooth. Continue to cook, stirring occasionally, for another 5 minutes, or until the mixture thickens. Remove from the heat and stir in the vanilla extract and coffee. Pour into a serving bowl.

# CARAWAY SEED MUFFINS

MAKES: *6 to 7 muffins*

2 cups all-purpose flour
1 tablespoon baking powder
1 tablespoon caraway seeds
½ teaspoon salt
1 large egg
2 tablespoons granulated sugar
1 cup milk
¼ cup canola oil
Fresh Blueberry Sauce (see recipe below)

1  Position the rack in the center of the oven and preheat to 425 degrees F. Lightly grease or line with paper baking cups seven 2¾-inch muffin cups.

2  In a large bowl, blend together the flour, baking powder, caraway seeds, and salt. In a medi-um bowl, beat the egg until foamy. Beating in the sugar, milk, and oil. Combine the two mixtures, blending until just moistened.

3  Spoon the batter into the prepared muffin cups, filling each almost to the top. Bake for 15 to 20 minutes, or until a cake tester or wooden toothpick inserted into the center of a muffin comes out clean. Cool in the pan on a wire rack for 5 to 7 minutes. Serve warm, or invert onto the rack to cool completely. Serve with Fresh Blueberry Sauce.

## FRESH BLUEBERRY SAUCE

MAKES: *¾ cup*

1 cup water
1 pint blueberries
¾ cup granulated sugar
1 tablespoon cornstarch
⅛ teaspoon salt
1 teaspoon lemon juice

1  In a medium saucepan set over medium heat, bring the water to a boil. Add the blueberries. Return to a boil.

2  Meanwhile, in a small bowl, blend together the sugar, cornstarch, and salt and stir the mixture into the boiling blueberries. Cook, stirring constantly, until the mixture thickens. Remove from the heat and stir in the lemon juice. Pour the sauce into a serving bowl.

# CARDAMOM ALMOND MUFFINS

MAKES: *11 to 12 muffins*

1 cup whole-wheat flour
½ cup graham flour
2 teaspoons baking powder
1 teaspoon baking soda
1 teaspoon ground cardamom
½ cup cornstarch
½ teaspoon salt
¾ cup soy milk
½ cup chopped almonds
Whipped Cream Topping (see recipe page 208)

1  Position the rack in the center of the oven and preheat to 375 degrees F. Lightly grease or line with paper baking cups twelve 2¾-inch muffin cups.

2  In a large bowl, blend together the two flours, baking powder, baking soda, cardamom, corn-starch, and salt. Stir in the milk, all at one time, blending until the dry ingredients are just moistened. Add almonds.

3  Spoon the batter into the prepared muffin cups, filling each about one-half full. Bake for 15 to 20 minutes, or until the tops are a golden brown and a cake tester or wooden toothpick inserted into a muffin comes out clean. Cool in the pan on a wire rack for 5 to 7 minutes. Serve warm, or invert onto the rack to cool completely. Serve with Whipped Cream Topping.

1 cup whole-wheat flour
½ cup all-purpose flour
1 teaspoon baking powder
½ teaspoon baking soda
1¾ cups carob powder
½ cup butter or margarine, melted
¼ cup honey
3 large eggs
½ cup milk
1 cup ricotta or cottage cheese
Coffee Cream Sauce (see recipe
 below)

**1** Position the rack in the center of the oven and preheat to 375 degrees F. Lightly grease or line with paper baking cups fourteen 2¾-inch muffin cups.

**2** In a large bowl, blend together the two flours, baking powder, baking soda, and carob. In a medium bowl, beat the butter and honey until smooth. Beat in two of the eggs and the milk. Combine the two mixtures, blending until the dry ingredients are just blended.

**3** Spoon the batter into the prepared baking pan, filling each about three-quarters full. In a small bowl, beat the cheese and remaining egg until smooth. Using a tablespoon, press a spoonful of the cheese mixture into the center of each muffin. Bake for 15 to 20 minutes, or until a cake tester or wooden toothpick inserted into the edge of a muffin (not into the cheese) comes out clean. Cool in the pan on a wire rack for 5 to 7 minutes. Serve warm, or invert onto the rack to cool completely. Serve with Coffee Cream Sauce.

# CAROB–CHEESE MUFFINS

MAKES: *12 to 14 muffins*

# COFFEE CREAM SAUCE

MAKES: *About 1 to 1½ cups*

2 large eggs
6 tablespoons double-strength,
 brewed coffee
2 tablespoons granulated sugar
½ cup heavy cream

**1** In a small bowl, beat the eggs until thick and light colored. Beat in the coffee and pour the mixture into the top of a double boiler set over simmering water. Stir in the sugar and cook, stirring, until the sauce thickens enough to coat the back of a wooden spoon. Remove from the heat, transfer to a bowl, and refrigerate until chilled.

**2** When ready to serve, place the cream in a medium bowl and beat until soft peaks form. Fold the cream into the chilled coffee sauce.

# CARROT-AND-OAT-BRAN MUFFINS

MAKES: *7 to 8 muffins*

1¼ cups oat bran
¾ cup all-purpose flour
2 teaspoons baking powder
1 teaspoon ground cinnamon
½ cup golden raisins
1 cup (about 3 medium) finely
    chopped carrots
½ teaspoon salt
2 large egg whites
¼ cup packed light-brown sugar
¼ cup milk
¼ cup warmed honey
2 tablespoons canola oil
Citrus Frosting (see recipe below)

**1** Position the rack in the center of the oven and preheat to 400 degrees F. Lightly grease or line with paper baking cups eight 2¾-inch muffin cups.

**2** In a large bowl, blend together the oat bran, flour, baking powder, cinnamon, raisins, carrots, and salt. In a medium bowl, beat together the egg whites, brown sugar, milk, honey, and oil. Combine the two mixtures, blending until the dry ingredients are just moistened.

**3** Spoon the batter into the prepared muffin cups, filling each about three-quarters full. Bake for 15 to 20 minutes, or until a cake tester or wooden toothpick inserted into the center of a muffin comes out clean. Brush tops of muffins with Citrus Frosting. Cool in the pan on a wire rack for 5 to 7 minutes. Serve warm, or invert onto the rack to cool completely.

## CITRUS FROSTING

MAKES: *½ cup*

1¼ cups powdered sugar
¼ cup orange juice
1 teaspoon orange zest
1 teaspoon orange extract
2 to 3 drops orange food coloring

In a medium bowl, beat together all the ingredients until smooth. As soon as the muffins are removed from the pan, brush the top of each muffin with this frosting.

2 cups whole-wheat flour
1 tablespoon baking powder
½ teaspoon ground cinnamon
¼ teaspoon salt
3 medium-size carrots, peeled and grated
One 8¾-ounce can crushed pineapple, drained
1 large egg
1⅓ cups packed dark-brown sugar
¾ cup milk
⅓ cup canola oil
½ teaspoon coconut or almond extract
Tropical Sauce (see recipe below)

**1** Position the rack in the center of the oven and preheat to 375 degrees F. Lightly grease or line with paper baking cups fourteen 2¾-inch muffin cups.

**2** In a large bowl, blend together the flour, baking powder, cinnamon, salt, carrots, and pineapple. In a medium bowl, beat together the egg and brown sugar until smooth. Beat in the milk, oil, and coconut extract. Combine the two mixtures, blending until the dry ingredients are just moistened.

**3** Spoon the batter into the prepared muffin cups, filling each two-thirds full. Bake for 15 to 20 minutes, or until a cake tester or wooden toothpick inserted into the center of a muffin comes out clean. Cool in the pan on a wire rack for 5 to 7 minutes. Serve warm, or invert onto the rack to cool completely. Serve with Tropical Sauce.

# CARROT-AND-PINEAPPLE MUFFINS

MAKES: *12 to 14 muffins*

## TROPICAL SAUCE

MAKES: *About 1⅓ cups*

1 cup crushed pineapple, undrained
¼ cup water
2 teaspoons coconut dessert pudding mix
Pinch ground allspice

In the container of a blender, combine all of the ingredients and process on medium speed until smooth. Pour into a small saucepan and cook, stirring constantly, until the mixture comes to a boil. Remove from the heat, pour into a bowl, and serve warm.

# CARROT–APPLE MUFFINS

MAKES: *11 to 12 muffins*

1 cup whole-wheat flour
1 cup all-purpose flour
1 tablespoon baking powder
½ teaspoon baking soda
1 teaspoon ground cinnamon
¼ teaspoon salt
1 medium apple, peeled, cored, and diced
1 cup grated carrot
2 large eggs
2 large egg whites
¾ cup granulated sugar
½ cup canola oil
1 teaspoon vanilla extract
Amaretto–Apricot Cream (see recipe below)

**1** Position the rack in the center of the oven and preheat to 375 degrees F. Lightly grease or line with paper baking cups twelve 2¾-inch muffin cups.

**2** In a large bowl, blend together the two flours, baking powder, baking soda, cinnamon, salt, apple, and carrots. In a medium bowl, beat the eggs until thick and foamy. Beat in the egg whites, sugar, oil, and vanilla extract. Combine the two mixtures, blending until the dry ingredients are just moistened.

**3** Spoon the batter into the prepared muffin cups, filling each about three-quarters full. Bake for 15 to 20 minutes, or until a cake tester or wooden toothpick inserted into the center of a muffin is removed clean. Cool in the pan on a wire rack for 5 to 7 minutes. Serve warm, or invert onto the rack to cool completely. Serve with Amaretto–Apricot Cream.

## AMARETTO– APRICOT CREAM

MAKES: *3 cups*

2 tablespoons Amaretto liqueur
¼ cup chopped dried apricots
3 cups frozen nondairy whipped topping, thawed

**1** In a small bowl, combine the liqueur and apricots and allow to soak for 2 hours.

**2** In a medium bowl using a wire whisk or electric mixer on high speed, beat the topping until it is thick. Stir in the apricots. Chill until ready to use.

1 cup all-purpose flour
1 cup Ralston® Multi-Bran Chex
  cereal, crushed
2 teaspoons baking powder
½ teaspoon baking soda
¾ teaspoon ground cinnamon
¼ cup seedless raisins
¼ cup chopped pecans or walnuts
1 cup (about 3 medium) finely
  chopped carrot
½ teaspoon salt
1 large egg
¼ cup packed brown sugar
3 tablespoons canola oil
1 cup milk
Two-Tone Sauce (see recipe below)

**1** Position the rack in the center of the oven and preheat to 400 degrees F. Lightly grease or line with paper baking cups twelve 2¾-inch muffin cups.

**2** In a large bowl, blend together the flour, cereal, baking powder, baking soda, cinnamon, raisins, walnuts, carrots, and salt. In a medium bowl, beat together the egg, brown sugar, oil, and milk. Combine the two mixtures, blending until the dry ingredients are just moistened.

**3** Spoon the batter into the prepared muffin cups, filling each about three-quarters full. Bake for 15 to 20 minutes, or until the tops are golden and a cake tester or wooden toothpick inserted into the center of a muffin comes out clean. Cool in the pan on a wire rack for 5 to 7 minutes. Serve warm, or invert onto the rack to cool completely. Serve with Two-Tone Sauce.

# CARROT–BRAN MUFFINS

MAKES: *11 to 12 muffins*

## TWO-TONE SAUCE

MAKES: *About ½ cup*

⅓ cup canola oil
1 tablespoon fresh orange juice
1 tablespoon fresh lemon juice
1 teaspoon granulated sugar
½ teaspoon salt
½ teaspoon grated orange zest
¼ teaspoon dry mustard
¼ teaspoon Hungarian paprika
Pinch white pepper

In a small bowl, beat all of the ingredients together until smooth. Cover and refrigerate until ready to serve.

# CARROT–MACADAMIA MUFFINS

MAKES: *36 to 40 muffins*

1 cup boiling water
1½ cups shredded wheat cereal
2¼ cups all-purpose flour
1½ cups wheat-bran flakes
3½ teaspoons baking soda
1⅓ cups shredded carrot
One 7-ounce package chopped
    pitted dates
One 3½ ounce jar macadamia nuts,
    finely chopped
1 teaspoon salt
3 large eggs
1 cup packed light-brown sugar
2 cups sour milk or buttermilk
¼ cup molasses
½ cup canola oil
Yogurt Cream (see recipe page 55)

1 In a small bowl, combine the water and shredded-wheat cereal and let sit 10 minutes. Meanwhile, in a large bowl, blend together the flour, wheat-bran flakes, baking soda, carrots, dates, macadamia nuts, and salt. In another medium bowl, beat the eggs until thick and light-colored before beating in the brown sugar, milk, molasses, and oil. Stir in the shredded-wheat cereal. Combine the two mixtures, blending until the dry ingredients are just moistened. Cover the bowl with plastic wrap and refrigerate for 1 to 2 hours, or overnight.

2 When ready to bake, position the racks towards the center of the oven and preheat to 375 degrees F. Lightly grease or line with paper baking cups forty 2¾-inch muffin cups. Spoon 2 heaping tablespoons of the batter into the prepared muffins cups. Bake for 15 to 20 minutes, or until a cake tester or wooden toothpick inserted into the center of a muffin comes out clean. Brush tops of muffins with Yogurt Cream. Cool in the pan on a wire rack for 5 to 7 minutes. Serve warm, or invert onto the rack to cool completely.

# CARROT–MOLASSES MUFFINS

MAKES: *11 to 12 muffins*

1½ cups whole-wheat flour
1 cup all-purpose flour
1½ teaspoons baking soda
1 teaspoon ground nutmeg
¼ teaspoon salt
1 cup (2 medium) grated carrot
½ cup seedless raisins
½ cup chopped pecans or almonds
2 large eggs
1½ cups milk
¼ cup molasses
⅓ cup honey
¼ cup canola oil

1 Position the rack in the center of the oven and preheat to 375 degrees F. Lightly grease or line with paper baking cups twelve 2¾-inch muffin cups.

2 In a large bowl, blend together the flours, baking soda, nutmeg, salt, carrots, raisins, and pecans. In a medium bowl, beat the eggs, milk, molasses, honey, and oil until smooth. Combine the two mixtures, blending until the dry ingredients are just moistened.

3 Spoon the batter into the prepared muffin cups, filling each about three-quarters full. Bake for 15 to 20 minutes, or until a cake tester or wooden toothpick inserted into the center of a muffin comes out clean. Cool in the pan on a wire rack for 5 to 7 minutes. Serve warm, or invert onto the rack to cool completely.

SERVING SUGGESTION: **Serve with jam or jelly.**

2 cups all-purpose flour
2 teaspoons baking powder
1 teaspoon baking soda
½ teaspoon crushed dried tarragon
1 cup finely chopped cooked
  cauliflower
½ teaspoon salt
1 large egg
6 tablespoons milk
¼ cup butter or margarine, melted
1 teaspoon vanilla extract
3 tablespoons lemon juice
1 cup shredded Cheddar cheese
¼ cup chopped walnuts
Sweet Mustard Sauce (see recipe
  below)

1  Position the rack in the center of the oven and preheat to 375 degrees F. Lightly grease or line with paper baking cups twelve 2¾-inch muffin cups.

2  In a large bowl, blend together the flour, baking powder, baking soda, tarragon, cauliflower, and salt. In a medium bowl, beat the egg until foamy. Beat in the milk, butter, vanilla extract, and lemon juice. Combine the two mixtures, blending until the dry ingredients are just moistened.

3  Spoon the batter into the prepared muffin cups, filling each two-thirds full. Sprinkle the cheese and nuts over the tops. Bake for 15 to 20 minutes, or until a cake tester or wooden toothpick inserted into the center of a muffin comes out clean. Cool in the pan on a wire rack for 5 to 7 minutes. Serve warm, or invert onto the rack to cool completely. Serve with Sweet Mustard Sauce.

# CAULIFLOWER-AND-CHEESE MUFFINS

MAKES: *11 to 12 muffins*

## SWEET MUSTARD SAUCE

MAKES: *About 1½ cups*

½ cup spicy mustard
2 tablespoons dry mustard
5 tablespoons light-brown sugar
¼ cup rice wine vinegar
½ teaspoon ground cinnamon
¼ teaspoon ground nutmeg
¼ teaspoon ground cloves
⅔ cup canola oil
1 teaspoon crushed dried dill

In the container of a blender or food processor, combine all the ingredients and process on low speed for 3 to 5 seconds. Pour into a small bowl and serve.

# CEREAL MUFFINS

MAKES: *11 to 12 muffins*

1½ cups all-purpose flour
¼ cup granulated sugar
1 tablespoon plus 1 teaspoon baking powder
½ teaspoon salt
½ cup cooked oatmeal
1 large egg
½ cup milk
2 tablespoons butter or margarine, melted
Sugarless Cranberry Sauce (see recipe below)

**1** Position the rack in the center of the oven and preheat to 400 degrees F. Lightly grease or line with paper baking cups twelve 2¾-inch muffin cups.

**2** In a large bowl, blend together the flour, sugar, baking powder, and salt. Stir in the cooked oatmeal. In a medium bowl, beat the egg, milk, and butter until smooth. Combine the two mixtures, blending until the dry ingredients are just moistened.

**3** Spoon the batter into the prepared muffin cups, filling each about three-quarters full, and let sit, uncovered, for about 7 minutes.

**4** Press ½ teaspoon of the custard filling into the center of each muffin. Bake for 15 to 20 minutes, or until a cake tester or wooden toothpick inserted into the edge of a muffin (not into the filling) is removed clean. Remove from the oven and immediately brush the tops of the muffins with citrus glaze. Cool in the pan on a wire rack for 5 to 7 minutes. Serve warm, or invert onto the rack to cool completely. Serve with Sugarless Cranberry Sauce.

## SUGARLESS CRANBERRY SAUCE

MAKES: *About 1½ cups*

⅔ cup water
2 cups cranberries
23 packets Equal® artificial sweetener

In a medium saucepan set over medium heat, combine the water and berries and cook until the mixture just comes to a boil. Reduce the heat to low and simmer, uncovered, for an additional 8 minutes, stirring occasionally. (The skins on the cranberries will pop open.) Remove from the heat, mash lightly, and stir in the Equal until dissolved. Cover and refrigerate until ready to serve.

1½ cups (8 ounces) pitted chopped prunes
¾ cup boiling water
2 cups all-purpose flour
¼ cup granulated sugar
1 teaspoon baking powder
1 teaspoon baking soda
2 cups (8 ounces) grated Cheddar cheese
½ cup chopped pecans
2 large eggs
½ cup milk
2 tablespoons butter or margarine
¼ cup molasses
Plum Butter (see recipe page 47)

1  Position the rack in the center of the oven and preheat to 375 degrees F. Lightly grease or line with paper baking cups sixteen 2¾-inch muffin cups.

2  In a small bowl, combine the prunes and boiling water. In a large bowl, blend together the flour, sugar, baking powder, baking soda, cheese, and pecans. In a medium bowl, beat the eggs, milk, butter, and molasses until smooth. Drain the prunes, discarding the water, and stir the prunes into the egg mixture. Combine the two mixtures, blending until the dry ingredients are just moistened.

3  Spoon the batter into the prepared muffin cups, filling each about three-quarters full. Bake for 15 to 20 minutes, or until a cake tester or wooden toothpick inserted into the center of a muffin is removed clean. Cool in the pan on a wire rack for 5 to 7 minutes. Serve warm, or invert onto the rack to cool completely. Serve with Plum Butter.

# CHEDDAR CHEESE-AND-PRUNE MUFFINS

MAKES: *15 to 16 muffins*

---

2 cups all-purpose flour
3½ teaspoons baking powder
1 cup grated Cheddar cheese
⅔ cup seedless raisins
1 teaspoon salt
1 large egg
¼ cup butter or margarine, melted
1 cup milk
1 tablespoon paprika
Raspberry–Rhubarb Blend (see recipe below)

1  Position the rack in the center of the oven and preheat to 425 degrees F. Lightly grease or line with paper baking cups twelve 2¾-inch muffin cups.

2  In a large bowl, blend together the flour, baking powder, cheese, raisins, and salt. In a medium bowl, beat the egg, butter, and milk until smooth. Combine the two mixtures, blending until the dry ingredients are just moistened.

3  Spoon the batter into the prepared muffin cups, filling each about three-quarters full, and sprinkle the tops lightly with the paprika. Bake for 10 to 15 minutes, or until a cake tester or wooden toothpick inserted into the muffins is removed clean. Cool in the pan on a wire rack for 5 to 7 minutes. Serve warm, or invert onto the rack to cool completely. Serve with Raspberry–Rhubarb Blend.

# CHEDDAR CHEESE-AND-RAISIN MUFFINS

MAKES: *11 to 12 muffins*

# RASPBERRY–RHUBARB BLEND

MAKES: *About 1½ cups*

1½ cups finely diced fresh rhubarb
½ cup raspberries
2 cups granulated sugar

In a medium saucepan set over medium heat, combine the rhubarb, berries, and sugar. Bring to a boil, reduce the heat to low, and simmer until the mixture thickens. Pour into a bowl and serve.

# CHEDDAR CHEESE-AND-PEPPER MUFFINS

MAKES: *11 to 12 muffins*

2 cups all-purpose flour
1 cup (4 ounces) shredded sharp
  Cheddar cheese
1 tablespoon granulated sugar
1 tablespoon baking powder
1½ teaspoons ground white pepper
½ teaspoon salt
1 large egg
¼ cup canola oil
1¼ cups milk
Sweet Butter Sauce (see recipe
  below)

**1** Position the rack in the center of the oven and preheat to 400 degrees F. Lightly grease or line with paper baking cups twelve 2¾-inch muffin cups.

**2** In a large bowl, blend together the flour, ¾ cup of the cheese, sugar, baking powder, pepper, and salt. In a medium bowl, beat the egg, oil, and milk until smooth. Combine the two mixtures, blending until the dry ingredients are just moistened.

**3** Spoon the batter into the prepared muffin cups, filling each about three-quarters full. Bake for 10 minutes. Sprinkle the remaining ¼ cup of cheese over the tops of the muffins and continue to bake for 5 to 10 minutes more, or until a cake tester or wooden toothpick inserted into the center of a muffin comes out clean. Cool in the pan on a wire rack for 5 to 7 minutes. Serve warm, or transfer to the rack to cool completely. Serve with Sweet Butter Sauce.

## SWEET BUTTER SAUCE

MAKES: *1¼ cups*

½ cup granulated sugar
1 teaspoon cornstarch
½ cup heavy cream
¼ cup butter or margarine, melted
½ teaspoon vanilla extract

In a 4-cup microwave-safe bowl, combine the sugar and cornstarch. Stir in the cream and butter. Microwave on high for about 1½ to 2 minutes, or until the mixture just starts to boil, stirring once halfway through the cooking time. Microwave on high for 1more minute. Remove from the microwave and stir in the vanilla.

1 cup yellow cornmeal
1 cup all-purpose flour
1½ cups grated Cheddar cheese
1 cup whole-kernel corn, drained
2 teaspoons dried savory
1 tablespoon baking powder
¼ teaspoon salt
1 large egg
⅓ cup granulated sugar
1 cup butter or margarine, melted
Sweet Onion Relish (see recipe
    below)

1 Position the rack in the center of the oven and preheat to 400 degrees F. Lightly grease or line with paper baking cups thirty-six 2-inch muffin cups.

2 In a large bowl, blend together the cornmeal, flour, cheese, corn, savory, baking powder, and salt. In a medium bowl, beat the egg, sugar, and butter until smooth. Combine the two mixtures, blending until the dry ingredients are just moistened.

3 Spoon the batter into the prepared muffin cups, filling each about three-quarters full. Bake for 10 to 15 minutes, or until a cake tester or wooden toothpick inserted into the center of a muffin comes out clean. Cool in the pan on a wire rack for 5 to 7 minutes. Serve warm, or invert onto the rack to cool completely. Serve with Sweet Onion Relish.

# CHEESE-AND-CORN MUFFINS

MAKES: *32 to 36 muffins*

# SWEET ONION RELISH

MAKES: *About 1½ cups*

3 medium-size Bermuda onions,
    peeled and chopped
1 medium chili, stemmed, seeded,
    and finely chopped
2 teaspoons cider vinegar
3 tablespoons honey
Salt to taste

In a small bowl, combine all of the ingredients except the salt and stir until combined. Season to taste with salt. Cover and refrigerate until ready to use.

½ pound American cheese, chopped
    very fine
2 cups all-purpose flour
1 tablespoon baking powder
½ teaspoon baking soda
1 tablespoon granulated sugar
½ teaspoon salt
1 large egg
⅓ cup butter or margarine, melted
⅔ cup sour milk or buttermilk
¼ cup bacon bits
Cherry–Almond–Rum Sauce (see
    recipe page 45)

1 Position the rack in the center of the oven and preheat to 400 degrees F. Lightly grease or line with paper baking cups sixteen 2¾-inch muffin cups.

2 In a large bowl, blend together the cheese, flour, baking powder, baking soda, sugar, and salt. In a medium bowl, beat the egg, butter, and milk until smooth. Combine the two mixes, blending until the dry ingredients are just moistened.

3 Spoon the batter into the prepared muffin cups, filling each about three-quarters full. Sprinkle each muffin with bacon bits and bake for 15 to 20 minutes, or until a cake tester or wooden toothpick inserted into the center of a muffin comes out clean. Cool in the pan on a wire rack for 5 to 7 minutes. Serve warm, or invert onto the rack to cool completely. Serve with Cherry–Almond–Rum Sauce.

# CHEESE MUFFINS

MAKES: *14 to 16 muffins*

## CHEESY BACON-N'-APPLE MUFFINS

MAKES: *11 to 12 muffins*

1 medium apple, peeled, cored, and grated
¼ cup granulated sugar
2 cups all-purpose flour
1 tablespoon baking powder
⅔ cup crumbled cooked bacon or bacon bits
¾ cup shredded Cheddar cheese
½ teaspoon salt
1 large egg
1 cup sour milk or butter milk
½ teaspoon baking soda
½ cup butter or margarine, melted
Cheese Sauce (see recipe page 57)

1 Position the rack in the center of the oven and preheat to 375 degrees F. Lightly grease or line with paper baking cups twelve 2¾-inch muffin cups.

2 Place the apple in a small bowl and sprinkle with the sugar. In a large bowl, blend together the flour, baking powder, bacon, cheese, and salt. In a medium bowl, beat the egg until thick and light-colored before beating in the milk, baking soda, and butter. Stir in the apple. Combine the two mixtures, blending until the dry ingredients are just moistened.

3 Spoon the batter into the prepared muffin cups, filling each about three-quarters full. Bake for 15 to 20 minutes, or until a cake tester or wooden toothpick inserted into the center of a muffin comes out clean. Cool in the pan on a wire rack for 5 to 7 minutes. Serve warm, or invert onto the rack to cool completely. Serve with Cheese Sauce.

## CHERRY MUFFINS

MAKES: *5 to 6 muffins*

2 cups all-purpose flour
1 tablespoon baking powder
1 cup (16 ounces) pitted sweet black cherry halves
¼ teaspoon salt
2 large eggs
⅔ cup granulated sugar
6 tablespoons butter or margarine, melted
½ cup milk
1 teaspoon vanilla extract
Cherry–Almond–Rum Sauce (see recipe page 45)

1 Position the rack in the center of the oven and preheat to 400 degrees F. Lightly grease or line with paper baking cups six 3-inch muffin cups.

2 In a large bowl, blend together the flour, baking powder, cherries, and salt. In a medium bowl, beat the eggs, butter, sugar, milk, and vanilla extract until smooth. Combine the two mixtures, blending until the dry ingredients are just moistened.

3 Spoon the batter into the prepared muffin cups, filling each about three-quarters full. Bake for 15 to 20 minutes, or until a cake tester or wooden toothpick inserted into the center of a muffin comes out clean. Remove from the oven and immediately spread the tops of the muffins with the cherry sauce. Cool in the pan on a wire rack for 5 to 7 minutes. Serve warm, or transfer to the rack to cool completely. Serve with Cherry–Almond–Rum Sauce.

½ cup dried cherries
2 cups all-purpose flour
½ cup granulated sugar
1 tablespoon baking powder
½ cup slivered almonds
¾ cup semisweet miniature
  chocolate chips
1 tablespoon dried orange zest
½ teaspoon salt
1 cup heavy cream or evaporated
  milk
⅓ cup canola oil
⅓ cup butter or margarine, melted
1 large egg
Chocolate–Honey Sauce (see recipe
  page 30)

**1** Place the dried cherries in a cup or small bowl and add boiling water or brandy to cover. Set aside for 1 hour. Drain, discard the liquid, and chop the cherries into small pieces.

**2** When ready to bake, position the rack in the center of the oven and preheat to 400 degrees F.

Lightly grease or line with paper baking cups twelve 2¾-inch muffin cups.

**3** In a large bowl, blend together the flour, sugar, baking powder, almonds, chocolate chips, orange zest, cherries, and salt. In a medium bowl, beat the heavy cream, oil, butter, and egg until smooth. Combine the two mixtures, blending until the dry ingredients are just moistened.

**4** Spoon the batter into the prepared muffin cups, filling each about three-quarters full. Bake for 15 to 20 minutes, or until a cake tester or wooden toothpick inserted into the center of a muffin comes out clean. Cool in the pan on a wire rack for 5 to 7 minutes. Serve warm, or invert onto the rack to cool completely. Serve with Chocolate–Honey Sauce.

# CHERRY–NUT MUFFINS WITH CHOCOLATE CHIPS

MAKES: *11 to 12 muffins*

2½ cups all-purpose flour
1 tablespoon baking powder
2 large eggs
⅔ cup milk
1 cup Progresso® Chicken Rice Soup
  with Vegetables
Cucumber Dill Sauce (see recipe
  below)

**1** Position the rack in the center of the oven and preheat to 375 degrees F. Lightly grease or line with paper baking cups twelve 2¾-inch muffin cups.

**2** In a large bowl, blend together the flour and baking powder. In a medium bowl, beat the eggs until

foamy. Beat in the milk and soup. Combine the two mixtures, blending until the dry ingredients are just moistened.

**3** Spoon the batter into the prepared muffin cups, filling each about three-quarters full. Bake for 15 to 20 minutes, or until a cake tester or wooden toothpick inserted into the center of a muffin comes out clean. Cool in the pan on a wire rack for 5 to 7 minutes. Serve warm, or invert onto the rack to cool completely. Serve with Cucumber Dill Sauce.

# CHICKEN–RICE MUFFINS WITH VEGETABLES

MAKES: *12 to 14 muffins*

# CUCUMBER DILL SAUCE

MAKES: *About 2½ cups*

One 8-ounce package cream
  cheese, at room temperature
1 cup mayonnaise
2 medium cucumbers, peeled,
  seeded, and finely chopped
2 tablespoons finely chopped
  scallion (green onion)

1 tablespoon fresh lemon juice
½ teaspoon dried crushed dill
½ teaspoon Tabasco® sauce

In a bowl, beat the cream cheese until smooth before beating in the remaining ingredients. Cover with plastic wrap and refrigerate for at least one hour before serving.

## CHILI–CHEESE MUFFINS

MAKES: *8 to 10 muffins*

2 cups Bisquick® baking mix
½ teaspoon baking powder
1 teaspoon chili con carne seasoning
½ teaspoon dried oregano
2 teaspoons dried chervil
1 cup grated Cheddar cheese
1 large egg
¾ cup milk
Artichoke Spread (see recipe page 139)

**1** Position the rack in the center of the oven and preheat to 400 degrees F. Lightly grease or line with paper baking cups twelve 2¾-inch muffin cups.

**2** In a large bowl, blend together the baking mix, baking powder, chili seasoning, oregano, chervil, and cheese. In a small bowl, beat the egg and milk until smooth. Combine the two mixtures, blending until the dry ingredients are just moistened.

**3** Spoon the batter into the prepared muffin cups, filling each about three-quarters full. Bake for 10 to 15 minutes, or until a cake tester or wooden toothpick inserted into the center of a muffin comes out clean. Cool in the pan on a wire rack for 5 to 7 minutes. Serve warm, or invert onto the rack to cool completely. Serve with Artichoke Spread.

## CHIVE DINNER MUFFINS

MAKES: *11 to 12 muffins*

2 cups all-purpose flour
2 teaspoons baking powder
¼ teaspoon baking soda
¼ cup snipped fresh chives
1 teaspoon salt
2 tablespoons butter or margarine, melted
1 large egg
⅔ cup sour milk or buttermilk
Bean Salad (see recipe below)

**1** Position the rack in the center of the oven and preheat to 400 degrees F. Lightly grease or line with paper baking cups twelve 2¾-inch muffin cups.

**2** In a large bowl, blend together the flour, baking powder, baking soda, chives, and salt. In a medium bowl, beat the butter, egg, and milk until smooth. Combine the two mixtures, blending until the dry ingredients are just moistened.

**3** Spoon the batter into the prepared muffin cups, filling each about three-quarters full. Bake for 15 to 20 minutes, or until a cake tester or wooden toothpick inserted into the center of a muffin comes out clean. Cool in the pan on a wire rack for 5 to 7 minutes. Serve warm, or invert onto the rack to cool completely. Serve with Bean Salad.

## BEAN SALAD

MAKES: *About 2½ to 3 cups*

One 16-ounce can pork and beans
½ cup diced Cheddar cheese
1 medium green bell pepper, stemmed, seeded, and diced
1 teaspoon prepared mustard

In a large bowl, combine all of the ingredients and stir. Cover and refrigerate until ready to serve. Serve on a bed of lettuce.

1¾ cups all-purpose flour
2 teaspoons baking powder
½ teaspoon baking soda
⅓ cup Dutch-process cocoa powder
2 large eggs
1 cup granulated sugar
½ cup canola oil
⅓ cup buttermilk or sour milk
1⅓ cups cooked, mashed beets
Vanilla Cream Sauce (see recipe
    page 49)

**1** Position the rack in the center of the oven and preheat to 375 degrees F. Lightly grease or line with paper baking cups fourteen 2¾-inch muffin cups.

**2** In a large bowl, blend together the flour, baking powder, baking soda, and cocoa powder. In a medium bowl, beat the egg until foamy. Beat in the sugar, oil, and buttermilk. Stir in the beets. Combine the two mixtures, blending until the dry ingredients are just moistened.

**3** Spoon the batter into the prepared muffin cups, filling each about three-quarters full. Bake for 15 to 20 minutes, or until a cake tester or wooden toothpick inserted into the center of a muffin comes out clean. Cool in the pan on a wire rack for 5 to 7 minutes. Serve warm, or invert onto the rack to cool completely. Serve with Vanilla Cream Sauce.

# CHOCOLATE-AND-BEET MUFFINS

MAKES: *12 to 14 muffins*

---

1½ cups all-purpose flour
1 cup uncooked rolled oats
½ cup granulated sugar
1 teaspoon baking powder
1 teaspoon ground cinnamon
¼ cup Dutch-process cocoa powder
¼ teaspoon salt
½ cup seedless raisins
1 cup shredded carrots
1 cup milk
¼ cup canola oil
1 large egg
2 teaspoons strong brewed coffee
Coffee Hard Sauce (see recipe page
    54)

**1** Position a rack in the center of the oven and preheat to 400 degrees F. Lightly grease or line with paper baking cups twelve 2¾-inch muffin cups.

**2** In a large bowl, blend together the flour, oats, sugar, baking powder, cinnamon, cocoa powder, salt, raisins, and carrots. In a medium bowl, beat together the milk, oil, egg, and coffee. Combine the two mixtures, blending until the dry ingredients are just moistened.

**3** Spoon the batter into the prepared muffin cups, filling each about three-quarters full. Bake for 15 to 20 minutes, or until a cake tester or wooden toothpick inserted into the center of a muffin comes out clean. Cool in the pan on a wire rack for 5 to 7 minutes. Serve warm, or invert onto the rack to cool completely. Serve with Coffee Hard Sauce.

# CHOCOLATE CARROT MUFFINS

MAKES: *15 to 16 muffins*

## CHOCOLATE–CHERRY–ALMOND MUFFINS

MAKES: *5 to 6 muffins*

2 cups all-purpose flour
½ cup granulated sugar
1 tablespoon baking powder
1 tablespoon grated lemon zest
¾ cup semisweet chocolate chips
½ cup slivered almonds
1 cup pitted, chopped dark sweet
    cherries
½ teaspoon salt
1 large egg
⅓ cup butter or margarine, melted
⅓ cup canola oil
1 cup milk
12 whole pitted cherries
Chocolate Sauce (see recipe page 26)

1  Position the rack in the center of the oven and preheat to 400 degrees F. Lightly grease or line with paper baking cups six 3-inch size muffin cups.

2  In a large bowl, blend together the flour, sugar, baking powder, lemon zest, chocolate chips, almonds, chopped cherries, and salt. In a medium bowl, beat the egg, butter, oil, and milk until smooth. Combine the two mixtures, blending until the dry ingredients are just moistened.

3  Spoon the batter into the prepared muffin cups, filling each about three-quarters full. Press a whole cherry into the center of each muffin, and bake for 15 to 20 minutes, or until a cake tester or wooden toothpick inserted into the center of a muffin comes out clean. Cool in the pan on a wire rack for 5 to 7 minutes. Serve warm, or invert onto the rack to cool completely. Top with Chocolate Sauce.

## CHOCOLATE–CHERRY MUFFINS

MAKES: *23 to 24 muffins*

2 cups all-purpose flour
½ cup graham flour
½ cup granulated sugar
5 teaspoons baking powder
1 cup semisweet miniature chocolate
    chips
One 16-ounce can pitted sweet
    cherries, drained and chopped
½ cup chopped almonds
½ teaspoon salt
2 large eggs
1 cup plus 1½ tablespoons sour
    cream or cherry-flavored yogurt
½ cup butter or margarine, melted
Maple-Flavored Whipped Cream
    (see recipe below)

1  Position the rack in the center of the oven and preheat to 375 degrees F. Lightly grease or line with paper baking cups twenty-four 2¾-inch muffin cups.

2  In a large bowl, blend together the two flours, sugar, baking powder, chocolate chips, cherries almonds, and salt. In a medium bowl, beat the eggs, sour cream, and butter until smooth. Combine the two mixtures, blending until the dry ingredients are just moistened.

3  Spoon the batter into the prepared muffin cups, filling each about three-quarters full. Bake for 15 to 20 minutes, or until a cake tester or wooden toothpick inserted into the center of a muffin comes out clean. Cool in the pan on a wire rack for 5 to 7 minutes. Serve warm, or invert onto the rack to cool completely. Serve with Maple-Flavored Whipped Cream.

## MAPLE-FLAVORED WHIPPED CREAM

MAKES: *About 2 cups*

1 cup chilled cream
¼ teaspoon maple flavoring

In a bowl, whip the cream until soft peaks form. Sprinkle the flavoring over the top and gently fold in. Refrigerate until ready to serve.

2 cups all-purpose flour
2 teaspoons baking powder
⅔ cup miniature chocolate chips
2 tablespoons dried grated orange
   zest
½ teaspoon salt
¾ cup heavy cream
½ cup canola oil
1 large egg
2 teaspoons Triple Sec liqueur
⅓ cup packed dark-brown sugar
Orange Butter (see recipe below)

1  Position the rack in the center of the oven and preheat to 400 degrees F. Lightly grease or line with paper baking cups twelve 2¾-inch muffin cups.

2  In a large bowl, blend together the flour, baking powder, chocolate chips, orange zest, and salt.

In a large bowl, beat the cream, oil, egg, Triple Sec, and brown sugar until smooth. Combine the two mixtures, blending until the dry ingredients are just moistened.

3  Spoon the batter into the prepared muffin cups, filling each about three-quarters full. Bake for 15 to 20 minutes, or until a cake tester or wooden toothpick inserted into the center of a muffin comes out clean. Cool in the pan on a wire rack for 5 to 7 minutes. Invert onto the rack to cool completely. When cool, spread the tops with a layer of orange frosting. Serve with Orange Butter.

# CHOCOLATE CHIP-AND-ORANGE MUFFINS

MAKES: *11 to 12 muffins*

# ORANGE BUTTER

MAKES: *½ cup*

½ cup butter or margarine, at room
   temperature
2 tablespoons orange juice
1 tablespoon grated orange zest

In a small bowl, beat together the butter, orange juice, and orange zest until smooth. Transfer to a serving bowl and refrigerate for 30 minutes before serving.

# CHOCOLATE CHIP– BRAN MUFFINS

MAKES: *31 to 32 muffins*

3 cups whole-bran cereal
1 cup boiling water
2½ cups all-purpose flour
¾ cup packed brown sugar
1 tablespoon baking powder
2 tablespoons miniature chocolate chips
½ teaspoon salt
3 large eggs
½ teaspoon baking soda
2 cups buttermilk or sour milk
½ cup butter or margarine, melted
Poppy Seed Butter (see recipe below)

1  Position the rack in the center of the oven and preheat to 400 degrees F. Lightly grease or line with paper baking cups thirty-two 2¾-inch muffin cups.

2  In a medium bowl, combine the cereal and water and set aside. In a large bowl, blend together the flour, sugar, baking powder, chocolate chips, and salt. In a medium bowl, beat the eggs, baking soda, buttermilk, and butter until smooth. Combine the three mixes, blending until the dry ingredients are just moistened and the cereal is well distributed.

3  Spoon 1 heaping tablespoon of the mixture into each of the prepared muffin cups. Bake for 15 to 20 minutes, or until a cake tester or wooden toothpick inserted into the center of a muffin comes out clean. Cool in the pan on a wire rack for 5 to 7 minutes. Serve warm, or invert onto the rack to cool completely. Serve with Poppy Seed Butter.

## POPPY SEED BUTTER

MAKES: *½ cup*

½ cup butter, at room temperature
½ cup toasted poppy seeds

In a small bowl, blend together the butter and poppy seeds, blending until the mixture is smooth and the poppy seeds are evenly distributed throughout the butter. Refrigerate until ready to serve.

2 cups all-purpose flour
2 teaspoons baking powder
½ cup seedless raisins
½ cup chocolate chips
1 large egg
⅔ cup packed brown sugar
¼ cup canola oil
¾ cup milk
Hard Sauce (see recipe below)
1½ teaspoons strong brewed coffee
    or coffee-flavored liqueur
1 teaspoon instant-coffee granules

**1** Position the rack in the center of the oven and preheat to 375 degrees F. Lightly grease or line with paper baking cups twelve 2¾-inch muffin cups.

**2** In a large bowl, blend together the flour, baking powder, raisins, and chocolate chips. In a medium bowl, beat the egg until foamy. Beat in the brown sugar, oil, milk, and coffee. Combine the two mixes, blending until the dry ingredients are just moistened.

**3** Spoon the batter into the prepared muffin cups, filling each about three-quarters full. Sprinkle a few grains of instant coffee on top of each. Bake for 15 to 20 minutes, or until a cake tester or wooden toothpick inserted into the center of a muffin comes out clean. Cool in the pan on a wire rack for 5 to 7 minutes. Serve warm, or invert onto the rack to cool completely. Serve with Hard Sauce.

# CHOCOLATE CHIP MUFFINS WITH RAISINS

MAKES: *11 to 12 muffins*

# HARD SAUCE

MAKES: *⅓ cup*

1 cup powdered sugar
¼ cup butter or margarine,
    softened
1½ teaspoons hot water

In a small bowl, beat the sugar, butter, and water until smooth. Cover and refrigerate for at least one hour before serving.

# CHOCOLATE CHIP MUFFINS

MAKES: *3 to 4 muffins*

⅓ cup plus 1 tablespoon all-purpose flour
1 teaspoon baking powder
⅓ cup (2 ounces) semisweet miniature chocolate chips
Pinch salt
1 large egg
2 tablespoons butter or margarine, melted
¼ cup granulated sugar
½ teaspoon vanilla or chocolate extract
Grand Marnier Sauce (see recipe below)

**1** Position a rack in the center of the oven and preheat to 375 degrees F. Lightly grease or line with paper baking cups four 2¾-inch muffin cups.

**2** In a medium bowl, blend together the flour, baking powder, chocolate chips, and salt. In another medium bowl, beat the egg until thick and light-colored before beating in the butter, sugar, and vanilla extract. Combine the two mixtures, blending until the dry ingredients are just moistened.

**3** Spoon the batter into the prepared muffin cups, filling each about three-quarters full. Bake for 15 to 20 minutes, or until a cake tester or wooden toothpick inserted into the center of a muffin comes out clean. Cool in the pan on a wire rack for 5 to 7 minutes. Serve warm, or invert onto the rack to cool completely. Serve with Grand Marnier Sauce.

## GRAND MARNIER SAUCE

MAKES: *2 cups*

4 large egg yolks
¾ cup heavy cream
1 cup scalded milk
½ cup granulated sugar
¼ teaspoon salt
½ teaspoon vanilla extract
3 tablespoons Grand Marnier

**1** In the top of a double boiler set over medium heat, whisk the egg yolks until they are thick and light-colored. Whisk in the cream, milk, sugar, and salt. Cook, stirring constantly with a wooden spoon, until the mixture thickens enough to coat the back of the spoon.

**2** Remove from the heat and whisk in the vanilla extract and Grand Marnier. Pour the sauce into a bowl and serve at room temperature.

1½ cups all-purpose flour
2 teaspoons baking powder
1 teaspoon nutmeg
¼ cup miniature semisweet chocolate chips
¼ cup chopped walnuts or pecans
1 large egg
¾ cup granulated sugar
¼ cup milk
½ cup canola oil
1 teaspoon vanilla extract
1 cup shredded zucchini

**1** Position the rack in the center of the oven and preheat to 375 degrees F. Lightly grease or line with paper baking cups twelve 2¾-inch muffin cups.

**2** In a large bowl, blend together the flour, baking powder, nutmeg, chocolate chips, and walnuts. In a medium bowl, beat the egg until foamy. Beat in the sugar, milk, oil, and vanilla extract. Stir in the zucchini. Combine the two mixtures, blending until the dry ingredients are just moistened.

**3** Spoon the batter into the prepared muffin cups, filling each about three-quarters full. Bake for 15 to 20 minutes, or until a cake tester or wooden toothpick inserted into the center of a muffin comes out clean. Cool in the pan on a wire rack for 5 to 7 minutes. Serve warm, or invert onto the rack to cool completely.

# CHOCOLATE CHIP–ZUCCHINI MUFFINS

MAKES: *11 to 12 muffins*

---

1 cup butter or margarine
1½ cups granulated sugar
Four 1-ounce squares semisweet chocolate
2 cups all-purpose flour
½ teaspoon salt
4 large eggs
1 teaspoon vanilla extract
Chocolate Sauce (see recipe page 26)

**1** Position the rack in the center of the oven and preheat to 300 degrees F. Lightly grease or line with paper baking cups twenty-four 2¾-inch muffin cups.

**2** In the top of a double boiler set over simmering water, combine the butter and sugar. Cook, stirring occasionally, until smooth. Add the chocolate all at one time and stir constantly until just melted. Remove from the heat.

**3** In a large bowl, blend together the flour and salt. In a medium bowl, beat the eggs until thick and light-colored. Beat in the vanilla extract. Combine the three mixtures, blending until smooth. (The mixture will be very moist.)

**4** Spoon the batter into the prepared muffin cups, filling each about three-quarters full. Bake for 15 to 20 minutes, or until a cake tester or wooden toothpick inserted into the center of a muffin comes out clean. Cool in the pan on a wire rack for 5 to 7 minutes. Serve warm, or invert onto the rack to cool completely. Serve with Chocolate Sauce.

# CHOCOLATE FUDGE MUFFINS

MAKES: *23 to 24 muffins*

# CHOCOLATE MUFFINS

MAKES: *11 to 12 muffins*

1½ cups all-purpose flour
1 cup uncooked oats
⅔ cup granulated sugar
1 tablespoon baking powder
¼ cup unsweetened cocoa powder
¼ teaspoon salt
1 large egg
1 cup milk
¼ cup canola oil
1 teaspoon almond extract
Chocolate Sauce (see recipe page 26)

**1** Position the rack in the center of the oven and preheat to 400 degrees F. Lightly grease or line with paper baking cups twelve 2¾-inch muffin cups.

**2** In a large bowl, blend together the flour, oats, sugar, baking powder, cocoa, and salt. In a medium bowl, beat the egg, milk, oil, and almond extract until smooth. Combine the two mixtures, blending until the dry ingredients are just moistened.

**3** Spoon the batter into the prepared muffin cups, filling each about three-quarters full. Bake for 15 to 20 minutes, or until a cake tester or wooden toothpick inserted into the center of a muffin comes out clean. Cool in the pan on a wire rack for 5 to 7 minutes. Serve warm, or invert onto the rack to cool completely. Serve with Chocolate Sauce.

# CHOCOLATE– RASPBERRY MUFFINS

MAKES: *12 to 14 muffins*

2 cups all-purpose flour
2 teaspoons baking powder
½ teaspoon baking soda
½ cup granulated sugar
6 ounces semisweet chocolate, finely chopped
1 large egg
2 tablespoons butter or margarine, melted
¾ cup buttermilk or sour milk
1 cup raspberries preserves
finely chopped pecans for sprinkling
Raspberry Sauce (see recipe page 48)

**1** Position the rack in the center of the oven and preheat to 375 degrees F. Lightly grease or line with paper baking cups fourteen 2¾-inch muffin cups.

**2** In a large bowl, blend together the flour, baking powder, baking soda, sugar, and chocolate. In a medium bowl, beat the egg, butter, and buttermilk until smooth. Combine the two mixtures, blending until the dry ingredients are just moistened. Using a rubber spatula, gently fold in the raspberry preserves.

**3** Spoon the batter into the prepared muffin cups, filling each about three-quarters full. Sprinkle with chopped pecans and bake for about 12 to 15 minutes, or until a cake tester or wooden toothpick inserted into the center of a muffin comes out clean. Cool in the pan on a wire rack for 5 to 7 minutes. Serve warm, or invert onto the rack to cool completely. Serve with Raspberry Sauce.

2 cups all-purpose flour
1 tablespoon baking powder
2 tablespoons granulated sugar
¾ cup miniature semisweet
   chocolate chips
1 large egg
1 cup milk
⅓ cup canola oil
1 tablespoon crème de cacao
Chocolate Sauce (see recipe page 26)

**1** Position the rack in the center of the oven and preheat to 425 degrees F. Lightly grease or line with paper baking cups twelve 2¾-inch muffin cups.

**2** In a large bowl, blend together the flour, baking powder, sugar, and chocolate chips. In a medium bowl, beat the egg foamy. Beat in the milk, oil, and crème de cacao. Combine the two mixtures, blending until the dry ingredients are just moistened.

**3** Spoon the batter into the prepared muffin cups, filling each about three-quarters full. Bake for 15 to 20 minutes, or until a cake tester or wooden toothpick inserted into the center of a muffin comes out clean. Cool in the pan on a wire rack for 5 to 7 minutes. Serve warm, or invert onto the rack to cool completely. Serve with Chocolate Sauce.

# CHOCOLATE SPECK MUFFINS

MAKES: *11 to 12 muffins*

---

1 cup seedless raisins, chopped fine
½ cup granulated sugar
¼ cup dark rum
1⅔ cups all-purpose flour
1 tablespoon baking powder
⅓ cup Dutch-processed cocoa
   powder
1 cup (6 ounces) semisweet
   chocolate chips
1 large egg
3 tablespoons butter or margarine,
   melted
Plum Topping (see recipe below)

**1** In a cup or small bowl, combine the raisins, sugar, and rum and stir until the sugar is dissolved. Set aside for 30 minutes.

**2** Position the rack in the center of the oven and preheat to 375 degrees F. Lightly grease or line with paper baking cups twelve 2¾-inch size muffin cups.

**3** In a large bowl, blend together the flour, baking powder, cocoa, and chocolate chips. In a medium bowl, beat the egg until foamy. Beat in the butter. Stir in the raisins. Combine the two mixtures, blending until the dry ingredients are just moistened.

**4** Spoon the batter into the prepared muffin cups, filling each about three-quarters full. Bake for 15 to 20 minutes, or until a cake tester or wooden toothpick inserted into the center of a muffin comes out clean. Cool in the pan on a wire rack for 5 to 7 minutes. Serve warm, or invert onto the rack to cool completely. Serve with Plum Topping.

# CHOCOLATE–RUM MUFFINS

MAKES: *11 to 12 muffins*

---

# PLUM TOPPING

MAKES: *2¾ cups*

6 large plums, pitted and thinly
   sliced
¼ cup granulated sugar
6 tablespoons orange juice
1 tablespoon cornstarch or
   arrowroot
½ teaspoon grated orange zest

**1** Combine the plums and sugar in a medium saucepan. Let stand for 30 minutes.

**2** In a cup, combine 2 tablespoons of the orange juice and the cornstarch, blending until smooth. Set aside.

**3** Add the orange zest and remaining 4 tablespoons of the orange juice to the saucepan with the plums. Place the pan over medium heat and cook, stirring frequently, for about 5 minutes, or until the plums are just tender. Stir in the cornstarch and cook for 2 to 3 minutes longer, or until the mixture thickens and is clear. Transfer to a serving bowl.

# CHORIZO–AND– CORN MUFFINS

MAKES: *10 to 12 muffins*

¾ cup chorizo sausage
1¾ cups all-purpose flour
2 teaspoons baking powder
1 teaspoon baking soda
½ teaspoon ground cumin
½ teaspoon ground coriander
1 teaspoon hot Hungarian paprika
1 tablespoon finely chopped jalapeño pepper
1 bell pepper, washed, seeded, and chopped fine
½ teaspoon garlic powder
½ teaspoon onion powder
2 large eggs
3 tablespoons butter or margarine, melted
1 cup buttermilk or sour milk
One 15-ounce can cream-style corn
3 drops Tabasco®
Dill Butter (see recipe below)

**1** Position the rack in the center of the oven and preheat to 375 degrees F. Lightly grease or line with paper baking cups six 2¾-inch muffin cups. Using a sharp knife, remove the meat from the sausage casing and chop into small pieces. Set aside.

**2** In a large bowl, blend together the flour, baking powder, baking soda, cumin, coriander, paprika, jalapeño, bell pepper, garlic powder, and onion powder. In a medium bowl, beat the eggs, butter, and buttermilk until smooth. Stir in the corn and Tabasco. Combine the two mixtures, blending until the dry ingredients are just moistened.

**3** Spoon the batter into the prepared muffin cups, filling each about three-quarters full. Bake for 15 to 20 minutes, or until a cake tester or wooden toothpick inserted into the center of a muffin comes out clean. Cool in the pan on a wire rack for 5 to 7 minutes. Serve warm, or invert onto the rack to cool completely. Serve with Dill Butter.

## DILL BUTTER

MAKES: *About 1 cup*

1 cup butter, at room temperature
½ cup fresh snipped dill sprigs
1 tablespoon fresh lemon or lime juice
1 medium garlic, peeled and smashed
Salt and pepper to taste

In a medium bowl, using an electric mixer on medium speed, beat all of the ingredients together until smooth. Cover and refrigerate until ready to serve.

1¼ cups all-purpose flour
¾ cup cornmeal
2 tablespoons granulated sugar
1 tablespoon baking powder
¼ teaspoon salt
1 large egg
1 cup milk
2 tablespoons butter or margarine, melted
6 to 7 teaspoons prepared chili with beans
crushed tortilla chips for sprinkling
Mexican Sauce (see recipe page 77)

**1** Position the rack in the center of the oven and preheat to 400 degrees F. Lightly grease or line with paper baking cups twelve 2¾-inch muffin cups.

**2** In a large bowl, blend together the flour, cornmeal, sugar, baking powder, and salt. In a medium bowl, beat the egg, milk, and butter until smooth. Combine the two mixtures, blending until the dry ingredients are just moistened.

**3** Spoon 1 heaping tablespoon of the batter into each of the prepared muffin cups. Place ½ teaspoon of chili onto the center of each muffin. Spoon a second heaping tablespoon of the batter on top of the chili. Sprinkle the tops of the muffins with crushed tortilla chips and bake for 15 to 20 minutes, or until a cake tester or wooden toothpick inserted into the edge of a muffin (not into the chili) comes out clean. Cool in the pan on a wire rack for 5 to 7 minutes. Serve warm, or invert onto the rack to cool completely. Serve with Mexican Sauce.

# CINCO DE MAYO MUFFINS

MAKES: *12 to 14 muffins*

---

1½ cups all-purpose flour
2 teaspoons baking powder
1½ teaspoons ground cinnamon
½ cup seedless raisins
¼ teaspoon salt
½ cup packed brown sugar
1 large egg
¼ cup vegetable shortening, melted
½ cup milk

**1** Position the rack in the center of the oven and preheat to 375 degrees F. Lightly grease or line with paper baking cups ten 2¾-inch muffin cups.

**2** In a large bowl, blend together the flour, baking powder, cinnamon, raisins, and salt. In a medium bowl, beat the sugar, egg, shortening, and milk until smooth. Combine the two mixtures, blending until the dry ingredients are just moistened.

**3** Spoon the batter into the prepared muffins cups, filling each about three-quarters full. Bake for 15 to 20 minutes, or until a cake tester or wooden toothpick inserted into the center of a muffin comes out clean. Cool in the pan on a wire rack for 5 to 7 minutes. Serve warm, or invert onto the rack to cool completely.

**SERVING SUGGESTION: Serve with jam or jelly.**

# CINNAMON-AND-RAISIN MUFFINS

MAKES: *9 to 10 muffins*

# CINNAMON MUFFINS

MAKES: *7 to 8 muffins*

1½ cups all-purpose flour
½ cup granulated sugar
2 teaspoons baking powder
½ teaspoon ground cinnamon
¼ teaspoon salt
2 large eggs
½ cup applesauce
½ cup milk
Mandarin Orange Gelatin Salad (see recipe below)

1  Position the rack in the center of the oven and preheat to 375 degrees F. Lightly grease or line with paper baking cups eight 2¾-inch muffin cups.

2  In a large bowl, blend together the flour, sugar, baking powder, cinnamon, and salt. In a medium bowl, beat the eggs, applesauce, and milk until smooth. Combine the two mixtures, blending until the dry ingredients are just moistened.

3  Spoon the batter into the prepared muffin cups, filling each about three-quarters full, and sprinkle some of the topping over each muffin. Bake for 15 to 20 minutes, or until a cake tester or wooden toothpick inserted into the center of a muffin comes out clean. Cool in the pan on a wire rack for 5 to 7 minutes. Serve warm, or invert onto the rack to cool completely. Serve with Mandarin Orange Gelatin Salad.

# MANDARIN ORANGE GELATIN SALAD

MAKES: *4 to 6 servings*

2 packages orange-flavored gelatin
1 small can frozen orange juice
2½ cups hot water
1 small (4-ounce) can crushed pineapple, drained
One 4-ounce can Mandarin orange sections, drained
2 medium bananas, sliced

In a small bowl, combine the gelatin, orange juice, and water and stir until dissolved. Cool slightly. Stir in the pineapple, orange sections, and bananas. Pour into a large bowl and refrigerate until set.

1¾ cups all-purpose flour
1 tablespoon baking powder
3 tablespoons granulated sugar
¼ teaspoon salt
1 tablespoon dried grated orange zest
1 tablespoon fresh grated lime zest
1 large egg
¾ cup milk
⅓ cup butter or margarine, melted, plus more for brushing the muffins
Citrus Glaze (see recipe below)

**1** Position the rack in the center of the oven and preheat to 400 degrees F. Lightly grease or line with paper baking cups twelve 2¾-inch muffin cups.

**2** In a large bowl, blend together the flour, baking powder, sugar, salt, orange zest, and lime zest. In a medium bowl, beat the egg, milk, and butter until smooth. Combine the two mixtures, blending until the dry ingredients are just moistened.

**3** Spoon the batter into the prepared muffin cups, filling each about three-quarters full. Bake for 10 minutes. Remove from the oven and brush the tops of the muffins lightly with melted butter. Bake for an additional 5 to 10 minutes, or until a cake tester or wooden toothpick inserted into the center of a muffin comes out clean. Cool in the pan on a wire rack for 5 to 7 minutes. Invert onto the rack to cool completely. When cooled, brush with Citrus Glaze.

# CITRUS MUFFINS
MAKES: *11 to 12 muffins*

# CITRUS GLAZE
MAKES: ¾ *cup*

**1 tablespoon granulated sugar**
**2 teaspoons cornstarch**
**½ cup orange juice**
**¼ cup water**
**1 tablespoon lemon juice**
**¼ teaspoon grated lemon zest**

In a small saucepan, combine the sugar and cornstarch. Stir in the orange juice and water. Place the pan over medium heat and bring the mixture to a boil, stirring constantly. Remove from the heat and stir in the lemon juice and zest. Cool slightly before brushing on muffins.

# COCOA MUFFINS WITH BANANAS

MAKES: *11 to 12 muffins*

**1¼ cups all-purpose flour**
**1 tablespoon baking powder**
**¼ teaspoon baking soda**
**1 cup rolled oats**
**⅓ cup Dutch-processed cocoa powder**
**1 cup (about 2 medium) mashed bananas**
**½ cup packed light-brown sugar**
**½ cup milk**
**⅓ cup butter or margarine, melted**
**1 large egg**
**1 teaspoon chocolate extract**
**Chocolate Frosting (see recipe below)**

**1** Position the rack in the center of the oven and preheat to 400 degrees F. Lightly grease or line with paper baking cups twelve 2¾-inch muffin cups.

**2** In a large bowl, blend together the flour, baking powder, baking soda, oats, and cocoa powder. In a medium bowl, beat the banana, brown sugar, milk, butter, egg, and chocolate extract until smooth. Combine the two mixtures, blending until the dry ingredients are just moistened.

**3** Spoon the batter into the prepared muffin cups, filling each about three-quarters full. Bake for 15 to 20 minutes, or until a cake tester or wooden toothpick inserted into the center of a muffin comes out clean. Cool in the pan on a wire rack for 5 to 7 minutes. Serve warm, or invert onto the rack to cool completely. Brush with Chocolate Frosting.

## CHOCOLATE FROSTING

MAKES: *2 to 2½ cups*

**1 cup (6 ounces) semisweet chocolate chips**
**¾ cup butter**
**½ cup finely chopped almonds**

In the top of a double boiler set over simmering water, combine the chocolate chips and butter and cook, stirring, until the chocolate chips are melted and the mixture is smooth. Remove from the heat and stir in the almonds. Refrigerate for 25 to 30 minutes, or until thick enough to spread.

1 cup all-purpose flour
⅔ cup granulated sugar
1 tablespoon baking powder
¼ cup Dutch-processed cocoa
    powder
½ cup chopped walnuts
1 cup raisins
¼ teaspoon salt
1 egg
½ cup milk
¼ cup canola oil
Chocolate Glaze (see recipe below)

**1** Position the rack in the center of the oven and preheat to 375 degrees F. Lightly grease or line with paper baking cups fourteen 2¾-inch muffin cups.

**2** In a large bowl, blend together the flour, sugar, baking powder, cocoa, walnuts, raisins, and salt. In a medium bowl, beat the egg until foamy. Beat in the milk and oil. Combine the two mixtures, blending until the dry ingredients are just moistened.

**3** Spoon the batter into the prepared muffin cups, filling each about three-quarters full. Bake for 15 to 20 minutes, or until a cake tester or wooden toothpick inserted into the center of a muffin comes out clean. Cool in the pan on a wire rack for 5 to 7 minutes. Serve warm, or invert onto the rack to cool completely. Brush with Chocolate Glaze.

# COCOA MUFFINS

MAKES: *12 to 14 muffins*

# CHOCOLATE GLAZE

MAKES: *½ to ¾ cup*

**2 ounces unsweetened chocolate**
**3 tablespoons butter**
**1 cup powdered sugar**
**¾ teaspoon vanilla extract**
**1 to 2 tablespoons hot water**

In the top of a double boiler set over simmering water, melt the chocolate and butter, stirring constantly, until smooth. Remove from the heat and stir in the sugar and vanilla. Stir in the hot water, a teaspoon at a time, until the mixture is the right consistency to brush over muffins.

## COCOA–RAISIN–WALNUT MUFFINS

MAKES: *14 to 16 muffins*

**2¼ cups all-purpose flour**
**¾ cup granulated sugar**
**1 tablespoon baking powder**
**½ cup Dutch-processed cocoa**
**⅓ cup chopped walnuts**
**1 cup seedless raisins**
**½ teaspoon salt**
**2 large eggs**
**½ cup butter or margarine, melted**
**1¼ cups milk**
**Cranberry Sauce (see recipe below)**

**1** Position the rack in the center of the oven and preheat to 400 degrees F. Lightly grease or line with paper baking cups sixteen 2¾-inch muffin cups.

**2** In a large bowl, blend together the flour, sugar, baking powder, cocoa, walnuts, raisins, and salt.

In a medium bowl, beat the eggs, butter, and milk until smooth. Combine the two mixtures, blending until the dry ingredients are just moistened.

**3** Spoon the batter into the prepared muffin cups, filling each about three-quarters full. Bake for 15 to 20 minutes, or until a cake tester or wooden toothpick inserted into the center of a muffin comes out clean. Cool in the pan on a wire rack for 5 to 7 minutes. Serve warm, or invert onto the rack to cool completely. Serve with Cranberry Sauce.

## CRANBERRY SAUCE

MAKES: *3½ cups*

**1 pound raw cranberries, rinsed**
**¾ cup water or orange juice**
**1½ cups granulated sugar**

Place the cranberries in a medium saucepan and add enough water to just cover them. Cover the pan and cook over a medium heat for 8 to 10 minutes, or until the skins of the cranberries start to burst open. Remove from the heat and stir in the sugar. Pour into a serving bowl and cool to room temperature before serving.

1¼ cups all-purpose flour
¾ teaspoon baking soda
1 cup granulated sugar
½ cup Dutch-processed cocoa
    powder
½ cup chopped walnuts
½ teaspoon ground cinnamon
¼ teaspoon ground nutmeg
¼ teaspoon ground cloves
¼ teaspoon salt
1 large egg
¾ cup applesauce
¾ cup milk
¼ cup butter or margarine, melted
Cream Cheese Spread (see recipe
    below)

**1** Position the rack in the center of the oven and preheat to 375 degrees F. Lightly grease or line with paper baking cups twenty-four 2¾-inch muffin cups.

**2** In a large bowl, blend together the flour, baking soda, sugar, cocoa, walnuts, cinnamon, nutmeg, cloves, and salt. In a medium bowl, beat the egg, applesauce, milk, and butter until smooth. Combine the two mixtures, blending until the dry ingredients are just moistened.

**3** Spoon the mixture into the prepared muffin cups, filling each about three-quarters full. Bake for 15 to 20 minutes, or until a cake tester or wooden toothpick inserted into the center of a muffin comes out clean. Cool in the pan on a wire rack for 5 to 7 minutes. Serve warm, or invert onto the rack to cool completely. Serve with Cream Cheese Spread.

# Cocoa Spice Muffins

Makes: *23 to 24 muffins*

# Cream Cheese Spread

Makes: *1 to 1¼ cups*

2 tablespoons butter or margarine,
    at room temperature
4 ounces cream cheese, at room
    temperature
½ cup ricotta cheese, at room
    temperature
1 teaspoon vanilla extract
2 cups powdered sugar

In a large bowl, beat together the butter, cream cheese, and ricotta until smooth. Beat in the vanilla and sugar, beating until the mixture is smooth and creamy.

# COCONUT, APPLE AND CARROT MUFFINS

MAKES: *35 to 36 muffins*

4 cups all-purpose flour
2 cups granulated sugar
4 teaspoons baking soda
1 tablespoon ground cinnamon
½ teaspoon ground nutmeg
4 cups (about 1 pound) grated carrot
2 large apples, peeled, cored, and grated
1 cup unsweetened flaked coconut
½ cup seedless raisins
½ cup chopped pitted dates
1 cup sliced almonds
1 tablespoon fresh grated orange zest
1 teaspoon salt
6 large eggs
1⅓ cups canola oil
1 tablespoon almond extract
Coconut-and-Whipped-Cream Sauce (see recipe below)

1  Position the rack in the center of the oven and preheat to 375 degrees F. Lightly grease or line with paper baking cups thirty-six 2¾-inch muffin cups.

2  In a very large bowl, blend together the flour, sugar, baking soda, cinnamon, nutmeg, carrots, apples, coconut, raisins, dates, almonds, orange zest, and salt. In a medium bowl, beat the eggs, oil, and almond extract until smooth. Combine the two mixtures, blending until the dry ingredients are just moistened. (The mixture will be very thin.)

3  Spoon the batter into the prepared muffin cups, filling each with one tablespoon of batter. Bake for 15 to 20 minutes, or until a cake tester or wooden toothpick inserted into the center of a muffin comes out clean. Cool in the pan on a wire rack for 5 to 7 minutes. Serve warm, or invert onto the rack to cool completely. Top with Coconut-and-Whipped-Cream Sauce.

## COCONUT-AND-WHIPPED-CREAM SAUCE

MAKES: *2 cups*

1 cup heavy cream
¼ cup powdered sugar
1 teaspoon coconut extract
¼ cup sweetened flaked coconut

In a medium bowl, beat the heavy cream until foamy. Add the sugar and extract and continue to beat until the mixture forms soft peaks. Fold in the coconut and pour into a serving bowl. Chill until ready to serve.

2 cups all-purpose flour
¼ cup granulated sugar
4 teaspoons baking powder
1 cup flaked coconut
½ teaspoon salt
1 large egg
3 tablespoons margarine, melted
1 cup unsweetened coconut milk
Alcohol-Free Hard Sauce (see recipe below)

**1** Position the rack in the center of the oven and preheat to 450 degrees F. Lightly grease or line with paper baking cups twelve 2¾-inch muffin cups.

**2** In a large bowl, blend together the flour, sugar, baking powder, coconut, and salt. In a medium

bowl, beat the egg, margarine, and coconut milk until smooth. Combine the two mixtures, blending until the dry ingredients are just moistened.

**3** Spoon the batter into the prepared muffin cups, filling each about three-quarters full. Bake for 15 to 20 minutes, or until a cake tester or wooden toothpick inserted into the center of a muffin comes out clean. Cool in the pan on a wire rack for 5 to 7 minutes. Serve warm, or invert onto the rack to cool completely. Serve with Alcohol-Free Hard Sauce.

# Coconut Muffins

MAKES: *11 to 12 muffins*

# Alcohol-Free Hard Sauce

MAKES: *About 1 cup*

¼ cup honey
½ cup soy flour
3 tablespoons fresh lemon juice
¼ cup butter or margarine, melted

In a small bowl, blend together the honey and soy flour until smooth. Stir in the lemon juice and butter. Cover and refrigerate until ready to serve.

# COFFEE–GINGER MUFFINS

MAKES: *23 to 24 muffins*

1¾ cups all-purpose flour
½ cup granulated sugar
1 teaspoon baking soda
¼ teaspoon ground ginger
½ teaspoon ground cardamom
¼ teaspoon salt
1 large egg
½ cup molasses
½ cup strong brewed coffee
¼ cup butter or margarine, melted
Almond–Apple Topping (see recipe below)

**1** Position the rack in the center of the oven and preheat to 375 degrees F. Lightly grease or line with paper baking cups twenty-four 2¾-inch muffin cups.

**2** In a large bowl, blend together the flour, sugar, baking soda, ginger, cardamom, and salt. In a medium bowl, beat the egg, molasses, coffee, and butter until smooth. Combine the two mixtures, blending until the dry ingredients are just moistened.

**3** Spoon the batter into the prepared muffin cups, filling each about three-quarters full. Bake for 15 to 20 minutes, or until a cake tester or wooden toothpick inserted into the center of a muffin comes out clean. Cool in the pan on a wire rack for 5 to 7 minutes. Serve warm, or invert onto the rack to cool completely. Top with Almond–Apple Topping.

# ALMOND–APPLE TOPPING

MAKES: *About 1 cup*

1 cup unsweetened applesauce
2 tablespoons finely chopped almonds
¼ teaspoon almond extract

In a small bowl, combine all of the ingredients and stir until blended. Cover and refrigerate until ready to serve.

2 cups all-purpose flour
2 teaspoons baking powder
½ teaspoon salt
1 cup cold, strong brewed coffee
1 cup granulated sugar
2 large eggs
1 cup sour cream or plain yogurt
Spiced Cherry Sauce (see recipe
  below)

**1** Position the rack in the center of the oven and preheat to 400 degrees F. Lightly grease or line with paper baking cups eighteen 2¾-inch muffin cups.

**2** In a large bowl, blend together the flour, baking powder, and salt. In a medium bowl, beat the coffee, sugar, eggs, and sour cream until smooth. Combine the two mixtures, blending until the dry ingredients are just moistened.

**3** Spoon the batter into the prepared muffin cups, filling each about three-quarters full. Bake for 15 to 20 minutes, or until a cake tester or wooden toothpick inserted into the center of a muffin comes out clean. Cool in the pan on a wire rack for 5 to 7 minutes. Serve warm, or invert onto the rack to cool completely. Top with Spiced Cherry Sauce.

# COFFEE MUFFINS

MAKES: *17 to 18 muffins*

# SPICED CHERRY SAUCE

MAKES: *2 to 2½ cups*

¾ cup granulated sugar
3 tablespoons cornstarch
¼ teaspoon ground cinnamon
¼ teaspoon ground nutmeg
1 cup chopped cherries
1 teaspoon fresh lemon juice
1 cup kirsch or cherry-flavored
  brandy

In a medium saucepan set over medium-low heat, combine the sugar, cornstarch, cinnamon, nutmeg, and cherries. Bring the mixture to boil, stirring constantly, and continue to cook for no more than one minute. Remove from the heat and stir in the lemon juice and kirsch. Serve warm.

# COLOMBIAN TINY COCOA MUFFINS

MAKES: *27 to 28 muffins*

1½ cups all-purpose flour
1½ cups granulated sugar
1 tablespoon baking powder
¼ cup Dutch-processed cocoa powder
½ teaspoon salt
3 large eggs
⅔ cup milk
½ cups butter or margarine, melted
1 teaspoon vanilla extract
Cappuccino (see recipe below)

1  Position the rack in the center of the oven and preheat to 375 degrees F. Lightly grease or line with paper baking cups twenty-eight 2¼-inch muffin cups.

2  In a large bowl, blend together the flour, sugar, baking powder, cocoa, and salt. In a medium bowl, beat the eggs, milk, butter and vanilla extract until smooth. Combine the two mixtures, blending until the dry ingredients are just moistened.

3  Spoon 1 heaping tablespoon of the mixture into the prepared muffin cups and bake for 12 to 15 minutes, or until a cake tester or wooden toothpick inserted into the center of a muffin comes out clean. Cool in the pan on a wire rack for 5 to 7 minutes. Serve warm, or invert onto the rack to cool completely. Serve with a Capuccino.

## CAPPUCCINO

MAKES: *About 2 cups*

½ cup nonfat dry milk powder
¼ cup instant decaffeinated coffee crystals
2 tablespoons sugar
1 teaspoon ground cinnamon

Combine all of the ingredients and store in an airtight container. To serve, stir 1 tablespoon of the mix into ¾ cup of boiling water. Top with a daub of whipped cream.

1 cup all-purpose flour
½ cup whole-wheat flour
½ cup graham flour
1 tablespoon baking powder
½ teaspoon salt
1 teaspoon garlic powder
½ cup shredded zucchini
½ cup whole-kernel corn
2 large egg whites
1¼ cups milk
2 tablespoons butter or margarine, melted
Vegetable and Beans with Franks (see recipe below)

1  Position the rack in the center of the oven and preheat to 375 degrees F. Lightly grease or line with paper baking cups twelve 2¾-inch muffin cups.

2  In a large bowl, blend together the three flours, baking powder, garlic powder, salt, zucchini, and corn. In a medium bowl, beat the egg whites until stiff but not dry before beating in the milk and butter. Combine the two mixtures, blending until the dry ingredients are just moistened.

3  Spoon the batter into the prepared muffin cups, filling each about three-quarters full. Bake for 15 to 20 minutes, or until a cake tester or wooden toothpick inserted into the center of a muffin comes out clean. Cool in the pan on a wire rack for 5 to 7 minutes. Serve warm, or invert onto the rack to cool completely. Serve with Vegetable and Beans with Franks.

# CORN-AND-ZUCCHINI MUFFINS

MAKES: *11 to 12 muffins*

# VEGETABLE AND BEANS WITH FRANKS

MAKES: *About 2½ to 3 cups*

2 tablespoons butter or margarine
½ cup julienned carrots, partially cooked
3 stalks celery, finely chopped
1 small onion, peeled and finely chopped
One 10½-ounce can pork and beans
½ pound chicken franks, sliced
1 tablespoon molasses

In a large skillet set over medium-low heat, melt the butter and saute the carrots, celery, and onion until tender. Stir in the pork and beans, franks, and molasses, and heat through. Pour into a bowl and serve.

# CORN DOG MUFFINS

MAKES: *17 to 18 muffins*

**2½ cups all-purpose flour**
**1 cup yellow cornmeal**
**¼ cup corn**
**5 teaspoons baking powder**
**½ teaspoon salt**
**½ cup chopped onion**
**2 large eggs**
**1½ teaspoons prepared mustard**
**⅔ cup canola oil**
**1½ cups milk**
**18 canned Vienna sausage links**
**Chili–Tomato Sauce (see recipe below)**

**1** Position the rack in the center of the oven and preheat to 400 degrees F. Lightly grease or line with paper baking cups eighteen 2¾-inch muffin cups.

**2** In a large bowl, blend together the flour, cornmeal, corn flour, baking powder, salt, and onions.

In a medium bowl, beat the eggs until foamy. Beat in the mustard, oil, and milk. Combine the two mixtures, blending until the dry ingredients are just moistened.

**3** Spoon the batter into the prepared muffin cups, filling each about three-quarters full. Lay a sausage on top of each muffin and gently press them into the muffins until completely covered. Bake for 15 to 20 minutes, or until a cake tester or wooden toothpick inserted at the edge of a muffin comes out clean. Cool in the pan on a wire rack for 5 to 7 minutes. Serve warm, or invert onto the rack to cool completely. Serve with Chili–Tomato Sauce.

## CHILI–TOMATO SAUCE

MAKES: *About 2 cups*

**2 cups tomato sauce**
**1 tablespoon instant minced onions**
**1 teaspoon crushed dried oregano**
**1 teaspoon crushed dried basil**
**1 teaspoon chili powder**

In a small saucepan set over medium-low heat, combine all of the ingredients and cook, stirring occasionally, for 10 minutes. Remove from the heat and serve hot or cold.

1 cup all-purpose flour
1 tablespoon baking powder
2 tablespoons granulated sugar
½ teaspoon ground allspice
½ cup chopped pecans
1 cup cornflakes
½ teaspoon salt
1 large egg
⅔ cup milk
3 tablespoons butter or margarine, melted
Prune Spread (see recipe below)

**1** Position the rack in the center of the oven and preheat to 425 degrees F. Lightly grease or line with paper baking cups twelve 2¾-inch muffin cups.

**2** In a large bowl, blend together the flour, baking powder, sugar, allspice, pecans, cornflakes, and salt. In a medium bowl, beat the egg, milk, and butter until smooth. Combine the two mixtures, blending until the dry ingredients are just moistened.

**3** Spoon the batter into the prepared muffin cups, filling each about three-quarters full. Bake for 15 to 20 minutes, or until a cake tester or wooden toothpick inserted into the center of a muffin comes out clean. Cool in the pan on a wire rack for 5 to 7 minutes. Serve warm, or invert onto the rack to cool completely. Serve with Prune Spread.

# CORNFLAKE–PECAN MUFFINS

MAKES: *11 to 12 muffins*

# PRUNE SPREAD

MAKES: *About ½ cup*

½ cup finely chopped pitted dried prunes
2 tablespoons heavy cream
½ teaspoon ground cinnamon
1–2 tablespoons granulated sugar

In the container of a blender, combine all of the ingredients and process on medium speed until smooth. Chill before serving.

# CORN–PINEAPPLE MUFFINS

*MAKES: 29 to 30 muffins*

1½ cups all-purpose flour
4 teaspoons baking powder
2 tablespoons granulated sugar
1 cup yellow cornmeal
¼ teaspoon salt
2 large eggs
1¼ cups milk
½ cup butter or margarine, melted
1 small can (8 ounces) crushed
    pineapple, drained
Pineapple–Cream Cheese Spread
    (see recipe below)

**1** Position the rack in the center of the oven and preheat to 425 degrees F. Lightly grease or line with paper baking cups thirty 2¾-inch muffin cups.

**2** In a large bowl, blend together the flour, baking powder, sugar, cornmeal, and salt. In a medium bowl, beat the eggs, milk, and butter until smooth. Stir in the drained pineapple. Combine the two mixtures, blending until the dry ingredients are just moistened.

**3** Spoon 1 heaping tablespoon of the mixture into the prepared muffin cups and press ¼ to ½ teaspoon of the pineapple preserves into the center of each muffin. Bake for about 12 to 15 minutes, or until a cake tester or wooden toothpick inserted into the edge of a muffin (not into the preserves) comes out clean. Cool in the pan on a wire rack for 5 to 7 minutes. Serve warm, or invert onto the rack to cool completely. Serve with Pineapple–Cream Cheese Spread.

## PINEAPPLE–CREAM CHEESE SPREAD

*MAKES: 3 to 3½ cups*

1 large package (8 ounces) cream
    cheese, at room temperature
½ cup butter or margarine, at room
    temperature
One 8-ounce can crushed
    pineapple, drained
4½ cups powdered sugar

In a large bowl, beat together the cream cheese and butter, beating until the mixture is smooth. Beat in the pineapple. Beat in the sugar, a little at a time, until the mixture reaches a spreadable consistency. Using a small spatula, spread an even coating over each muffin.

1 cup yellow cornmeal
2 tablespoons all-purpose flour
1 tablespoon granulated sugar
2 teaspoons baking powder
½ teaspoon salt
1 large egg
1 tablespoon butter or margarine, melted
½ cup milk
Chili Butter (see recipe below)

**1** Position the rack in the center of the oven and preheat to 425 degrees F. Lightly grease or line with paper baking cups sixteen 2¾-inch muffin cups.

**2** In a large bowl, blend together the cornmeal, flour, sugar, baking powder, and salt. In a medium bowl, beat the egg until thick and light-colored before beating in the butter and milk. Combine the two mixtures, blending until the dry ingredients are just moistened.

**3** Spoon 1 heaping tablespoon of the mixture into the prepared baking pan. Bake for 15 to 20 minutes, or until a cake tester or wooden toothpick inserted into the center of a muffin comes out clean. Cool in the pan on a wire rack for 5 to 7 minutes. Serve warm from pan, or invert onto the rack to cool completely. Serve with Chili Butter.

# CORNBREAD MUFFINS

MAKES: *10 muffins*

## CHILI BUTTER

MAKES: *¼ cup*

¼ cup butter, at room temperature
2 tablespoons salsa

In a small bowl, using a fork or wire whisk, beat together the butter and salsa, blending until smooth. Refrigerate for 30 minutes to blend the flavors. Serve at room temperature.

---

1 cup all-purpose flour
1 cup coarse cornmeal
2 tablespoons granulated sugar
1 teaspoon baking powder
¼ teaspoon salt
1 large egg
1 cup skim milk
1 tablespoon butter or margarine, melted
1 cup fresh blueberries
Tartar Sauce (see recipe below)

**1** Position the rack in the center of the oven and preheat to 425 degrees F. Lightly grease or line with paper baking cups twelve 2¾-inch muffin cups.

**2** In a large bowl, blend together the flour, cornmeal, sugar, baking powder, and salt. In a medium bowl, beat the egg, milk, and butter until smooth. Stir in the blueberries. Combine the two mixtures, blending until the dry ingredients are just moistened.

**3** Spoon the mixture into the prepared muffin cups, filling each about three-quarters full. Bake for 15 to 20 minutes, or until the tops are golden and a cake tester or wooden toothpick inserted into the center of a muffin is removed clean. Cool in the pan on a wire rack for 5 to 7 minutes. Serve warm, or invert onto the rack to cool completely. Serve with Tartar Sauce.

# CORNMEAL MUFFINS WITH BERRIES

MAKES: *11 to 12 muffins*

## TARTAR SAUCE

MAKES: *About 2 cups*

2 cups mayonnaise
2 tablespoons white vinegar
3 sweet pickles, minced
2 scallions (green onions), minced
¼ cup capers, drained

In a small bowl, combine all of the ingredients. Cover and refrigerate for at least 30 minutes before serving.

# CORNMEAL MUFFINS

MAKES: *11 to 12 muffins*

1¼ cups all-purpose flour
¾ cup cornmeal
2 tablespoons granulated sugar
4 teaspoons baking powder
½ teaspoon salt
1 large egg
1 cup milk
2 tablespoons butter or margarine, melted
Tomato–Onion Fried Relish (see recipe below)

**1** Position the rack in the center of the oven and preheat to 400 degrees F. Lightly grease or line with paper baking cups twelve 2¾-inch muffin cups.

**2** In a large bowl, blend together the flour, cornmeal, sugar, baking powder, and salt. In a medium bowl, beat the egg, milk, and butter until smooth. Combine the two mixtures, blending until the dry ingredients are just moistened.

**3** Spoon the batter into the prepared muffin cups, filling each about three-quarters full. Bake for 15 to 20 minutes, or until a cake tester or wooden toothpick inserted into the center of a muffin comes out clean. Cool in the pan on a wire rack for 5 to 7 minutes. Serve warm, or invert onto the rack to cool completely. Serve with Tomato–Onion Fried Relish.

## TOMATO–ONION FRIED RELISH

MAKES: *About 1½ cups*

2 tablespoons olive oil
2 medium tomatoes, peeled and finely chopped
2 medium red onions, peeled and finely chopped
1 clove garlic, mashed
2 strips crisply cooked bacon, crumbled

In a medium skillet set over medium-high heat, heat the oil until hot. Add the tomatoes, onion, and garlic and cook, stirring constantly, until the onions are translucent. Remove from the heat, stir in the bacon, and serve hot.

2 cups all-purpose flour
2½ teaspoons baking powder
½ teaspoon baking soda
2 cups thinly sliced fresh okra
½ cup finely chopped onions
½ teaspoon salt
2 large eggs
1 tablespoon brown sugar
½ cup butter or margarine, melted
1¼ cups milk
1 teaspoon steak sauce of choice
¼ teaspoon bottled hot sauce
Grated Swiss cheese for sprinkling
Nut Spread (see recipe below)

1  Position the rack in the center of the oven and preheat to 375 degrees F. Lightly grease or line with paper baking cups twelve 2¾-inch muffin cups.

2  In a large bowl, blend together the flour, baking powder, baking soda, okra, onions, and salt. In a medium bowl, beat the eggs until thick and light-colored. Beat in the sugar, butter, milk, steak sauce, and hot sauce. Combine the two mixtures, blending until the dry ingredients are just moistened.

3  Spoon the batter into the prepared muffin cups, filling each three-quarters full. Sprinkle cheese over the top of each and bake for 15 to 20 minutes, or until a cake tester or wooden toothpick inserted into the center of a muffin comes out clean. Cool in the pan on a wire rack for 5 to 7 minutes. Serve warm, or invert onto the rack to cool completely. Serve with Nut Spread.

# COUNTRY-TIME OKRA MUFFINS
MAKES: *12 to 14 muffins*

## NUT SPREAD
MAKES: *About ½ cup*

½ cup blanched almonds
2 tablespoons heavy cream
¼ teaspoon curry paste
Salt to taste

In the container of a blender, finely chop the almonds twice. Add the cream and curry, and process on medium until smooth. Transfer to a bowl, add salt to taste, and serve.

3 cups all-purpose flour
5 teaspoons baking powder
1 tablespoon granulated sugar
½ cup finely chopped crabmeat
½ teaspoon dry mustard powder
½ teaspoon ground white pepper
1½ cups milk
½ cup brandy
Grated Gruyère cheese for topping

1  Position the rack in the center of the oven and preheat to 375 degrees F. Lightly grease or line with paper baking cups eighteen 2¾-inch muffin cups.

2  In a large bowl, blend together the flour, baking powder, sugar, crabmeat, mustard, and pepper. Make a well in the center of the mixture and pour in the milk and brandy. Combine the ingredients, blending until the dry ingredients are just moistened.

3  Spoon the mixture into the prepared muffin cups, filling each about three-quarters full, and sprinkle a little Gruyère cheese over the top of each. Bake for 15 to 20 minutes, or until a cake tester or wooden toothpick inserted into the center of a muffin comes out clean. Cool in the pan on a wire rack for 5 to 7 minutes. Serve warm, or invert onto the rack to cool completely.

SERVING SUGGESTION: **Serve with a cheese of choice and a dry white wine.**

# CRAB MUFFINS
MAKES: *16 to 18 muffins*

# CRACKED-WHEAT MUFFINS

MAKES: *11 to 12 muffins*

1 cup all-purpose flour
¾ cup cracked wheat
1 tablespoon baking powder
1 teaspoon salt
1 large egg
1¼ cups milk
¼ cup butter or margarine, melted
Pumpkin Butter (see recipe below)

**1** Position the rack in the center of the oven and preheat to 400 degrees F. Lightly grease or line with paper baking cups twelve 2¾-inch muffin cups.

**2** In a large bowl, blend together the flour, wheat, baking powder, and salt. In a medium bowl, beat the egg until thick and light-colored before beating in the milk and butter. Combine the two mixtures, blending until the dry ingredients are just moistened.

**3** Spoon the batter into the pre-pared muffin cups, filling each about three-quarters full. Bake for 15 to 20 minutes, or until a cake tester or wooden toothpick inserted into the center of a muf-fin comes out clean. Cool in the pan on a wire rack for 5 to 7 min-utes. Serve warm, or invert onto the rack to cool completely. Serve with Pumpkin Butter.

## PUMPKIN BUTTER

MAKES: *About 1½ cups*

1½ cups pumpkin puree
2 tablespoons molasses
1 tablespoon granulated sugar
1 teaspoon ground allspice
1 teaspoon ground cinnamon
1 teaspoon ground cloves

In a saucepan, combine all of the ingredients, and cook, stir-ring frequently, until the mix-ture is thick. Pour into a bowl and refrigerate until ready to use.

2 cups all-purpose flour
¾ cup granulated sugar
1 tablespoon baking powder
½ teaspoon salt
1 large egg
1 cup milk
¼ cup butter or margarine, melted
1 cup chopped dried cranberries
Peach Butter (see recipe below)

**1** Position the rack in the center of the oven and preheat to 400 degrees F. Lightly grease or line with paper baking cups sixteen 2¾-inch muffin cups.

**2** In a large bowl, blend together the flour, sugar, baking powder, and salt. In a medium bowl, beat the egg, milk, and butter until smooth. Fold in the cranberries. Combine the two mixtures, blending until the dry ingredients are just moistened.

**3** Spoon the batter into the prepared muffin cups, filling each about three-quarters full. Bake for 15 to 20 minutes, or until a cake tester or wooden toothpick inserted into the center of a muffin comes out clean. Remove from the oven an cool in the pan on a wire rack for 5 to 7 minutes. Serve warm, or invert onto the rack to cool completely. Serve with Peach Butter.

## PEACH BUTTER
MAKES: *1 to 1¼ cups*

½ cup butter, at room temperature
½ cup canned diced peaches, drained and finely chopped
½ cup granulated sugar
1 teaspoon ground cinnamon
¼ teaspoon ground cloves

In a small bowl, beat the butter and peaches until thoroughly combined. Beat in the sugar, cinnamon, and cloves. Transfer the mixture to a serving bowl and refrigerate for 30 minutes before serving.

## CRANBERRY MUFFINS WITH CHEESE

MAKES: *12 to 14 muffins*

1½ cups all-purpose flour
½ cup whole-wheat flour
1 tablespoon baking powder
⅓ cup granulated sugar
1 cup chopped fresh cranberries
1 teaspoon dried grated orange zest
½ teaspoon salt
1 large egg
1 cup milk, sour milk, or buttermilk
¼ cup canola oil
½ cup grated Swiss cheese
Grated Romano cheese for topping
 (optional)
Papaya Salsa (see recipe below)

1 Position the rack in the center of the oven and preheat 425 degrees F. Lightly grease or line with paper baking cups twelve 2¾-inch muffin cups.

2 In a large bowl, blend together the two flours, baking powder, sugar, cranberries, orange zest, and salt. In a medium bowl, beat the egg until foamy. Beat in the milk and oil. Fold in the Swiss cheese. Combine the two mixtures, blending until the dry ingredients are just moistened.

3 Spoon the batter into the prepared muffin cups, filling each about three-quarters full. Srinkle the top of each with the Romano cheese. Bake for 15 to 20 minutes, or until a cake tester or wooden toothpick inserted into the center of a muffin comes out clean. Cool in the pan on a wire rack for 5 to 7 minutes. Serve warm, or invert onto the rack to cool completely. Serve with Papaya Salsa.

## PAPAYA SALSA

MAKES: *About 2 cups*

2 cups peeled, seeded, and finely
 diced papaya
4 cloves garlic, peeled and mashed
¼ cup snipped fresh cilantro
2 tablespoons lemon juice

In the container of a blender or food processor, combine all the ingredients and process on low for 3 to 5 seconds. Pour into a small bowl and serve.

## CRANBERRY–ORANGE MUFFINS

MAKES: *12 to 14 muffins*

2 cups all-purpose flour
⅔ cup granulated sugar
1 tablespoon baking powder
2 tablespoons dried grated orange
 zest
½ teaspoon salt
1 large egg
1 cup milk
3 tablespoons butter or margarine,
 melted
1 cup dried cranberries

1 Position the rack in the center of the oven and preheat 400 degrees F. Lightly grease or line with paper baking cups fourteen 2¾-inch muffin cups.

2 In a large bowl, blend together the flour, sugar, baking powder, orange zest, and salt. In a medium bowl, beat the egg, milk, and butter until smooth. Fold in the cranberries. Combine the two mixtures, blending until the dry ingredients are just moistened.

3 Spoon the batter into the prepared muffin cups, filling each about three-quarters full. Bake for 15 to 20 minutes, or until a cake tester or wooden toothpick inserted into the center of a muffin comes out clean. Remove from the oven and brush with Citrus Glaze. Cool in the pan on a wire rack for 5 to 7 minutes. Serve warm, or transfer to the rack to cool completely.

SERVING SUGGESTION: **Serve with orange marmalade.**

1½ cups all-purpose flour
1 cup rolled oats
½ cup granulated sugar
1 tablespoon baking powder
½ cup chopped walnuts or pecans
¼ teaspoon salt
1 large egg
1 cup milk
¼ cup canola oil
1 cup dried cranberries
Molasses Sauce (see recipe below)

**1** Position the rack in the center of the oven and preheat to 400 degrees F. Lightly grease or line with paper baking cups fourteen 2¾-inch muffin cups.

**2** In a large bowl, blend together the flour, oats, sugar, baking powder, walnuts, and salt. In a medium bowl, beat the egg, milk, and oil until smooth. Stir in the cranberries. Combine the two mixtures, blending until the dry ingredients are just moistened.

**3** Spoon the batter into the prepared muffin cups, filling each about three-quarters full. Bake for 15 to 20 minutes, or until a cake tester or wooden toothpick inserted into the center of a muffin comes out clean. Cool in the pan on a wire rack for 5 to 7 minutes. Invert onto the rack to cool completely. When cool, brush the tops with Molasses Sauce.

# CRANBERRY–ORANGE MUFFINS WITH WALNUTS

MAKES: *12 to 14 muffins*

# MOLASSES SAUCE

MAKES: *About 1½ cups*

1½ cups water
½ cup sugar
Pinch salt
2 tablespoons molasses
½ cup milk
2 tablespoons cornstarch
2 tablespoons butter or margarine
1 tablespoon vanilla extract

**1** In a small saucepan set over medium heat, combine the water, sugar, salt, and molasses. Cook, stirring constantly, until the sugar is dissolved. Remove from the heat.

**2** In a cup, combine the milk and cornstarch and stir until the cornstarch is dissolved. Slowly stir into the hot syrup, stirring constantly until the mixture thickens. Stir in the vanilla, and serve warm or cold.

## CRANBERRY–PECAN MUFFINS

MAKES: *21 to 22 muffins*

2 cups all-purpose flour
2 teaspoons baking powder
½ teaspoon
1 cup chopped pecans
2 large eggs
⅔ cup orange juice
⅓ cup canola oil
¾ cup packed brown sugar
1 cup chopped cranberries, fresh or dried
Ginger–Lime Sauce (see recipe below)

1  Position the rack in the center of the oven and preheat to 375 degrees F. Lightly grease or line with paper baking cups twenty-two 2¼-inch muffin cups.

2  In a large bowl, blend together the flour, baking powder, salt, and pecans. In a medium bowl, beat the egg, orange juice, oil, and brown sugar until smooth. Stir in the cranberries. Combine the two mixtures, blending until the dry ingredients are just moistened.

3  Spoon the batter into the prepared muffin cups, filling each about three-quarters full. Bake for 15 to 20 minutes, or until a cake tester or wooden toothpick inserted into the center of a muffin comes out clean. Cool in the pan on a wire rack for 5 to 7 minutes. Serve warm, or invert onto the rack to cool completely. Serve with Ginger–Lime Sauce.

## GINGER–LIME SAUCE

MAKES: *About 1 cup*

½ cup mayonnaise
½ cup sour cream or yogurt
2 teaspoons grated lime zest
1 tablespoon fresh lime juice
1 tablespoon honey
1 teaspoon ground ginger
1 tablespoon finely chopped crystallized ginger

In a small bowl, combine all of the ingredients together and whisk until smooth. Cover with plastic wrap and refrigerate until ready to use.

## CRANBERRY– PUMPKIN MUFFINS

MAKES: *9 to 10 muffins*

2 cups fresh cranberries, washed, stemmed, and halved
2½ cups all-purpose flour
½ cup whole-wheat flour
1 cup granulated sugar
2 teaspoons baking powder
1 teaspoon baking soda
1½ teaspoons ground cinnamon
¾ teaspoon ground allspice
¼ teaspoon salt
2 large eggs
½ cup butter or margarine, melted
2½ cups canned pumpkin puree
Pumpkin Butter (see recipe page 122)

1  Position the rack in the center of the oven and preheat to 375 degrees F. Lightly grease or line with paper baking cups ten 2¾-inch muffin cups.

2  In a large bowl, blend together the cranberries, two flours, sugar, baking powder, baking soda, cinnamon, allspice, and salt. In a medium bowl, beat the eggs until foamy. Beat in the butter and pumpkin. Combine the two mixtures, blending until the dry ingredients are just moistened.

3  Spoon the batter into the prepared muffin cups, filling each about three-quarters full. Bake for 15 to 20 minutes or until a cake tester or wooden toothpick inserted into the center of a muffin comes out clean. Cool in the pan on a wire rack for 5 to 7 minutes. Serve warm, or invert onto the rack to cool completely. Serve with Pumpkin Butter.

½ cup packed light-brown sugar

1 cup fresh cranberries, cleaned, stemmed, and halved

½ cup butter or margarine, melted

2 cups all-purpose flour

2 tablespoons granulated sugar

1 tablespoon baking powder

½ teaspoon salt

1 large egg

1 cup milk

5 teaspoons Amaretto liqueur

Crab Spread (see recipe below)

**1** Position the rack in the center of the oven and preheat to 400 degrees F. Lightly grease or line with paper baking cups twelve 2¾-inch muffin cups. Divide the brown sugar between the prepared cups. Place an equal amount of the cranberries into each cup, and drizzle 1 teaspoon of the melted butter over the cranberries in each cup. Set aside.

**2** In a large bowl, blend together the flour, granulated sugar, baking powder, and salt. In a medium bowl, beat the egg, milk, Amaretto, and remaining ¼ cup of butter until smooth. Combine the two mixtures, blending until the dry ingredients are just moistened.

**3** Spoon the batter over the cranberries in the prepared muffin cups, filling each about three-quarters full. Bake for 15 to 20 minutes, or until a cake tester or wooden toothpick inserted into the center of a muffin comes out clean. Cool in the pan on a wire rack for about 5 to 7 minutes. Serve warm, or invert onto the rack to cool completely. Serve with Crab Spread.

# CRANBERRY UPSIDE-DOWN MUFFINS

MAKES: *11 to 12 muffins*

# CRAB SPREAD

MAKES: *About 1½ cups*

One 3-ounce package cream cheese, at room temperature

One 6½-ounce can crabmeat, undrained

⅔ cup mayonnaise

⅛ teaspoon bottled hot sauce

Paprika for sprinkling

**1** Position the rack to the center of the oven and preheat the oven to 325 degrees F. Lightly grease a small oven-proof baking dish or pan.

**2** In a medium bowl, blend all the ingredients together until smooth. Spread into the prepared baking dish, sprinkle with paprika and bake for about 20 minutes, or until the mixture bubbles. Remove from the oven and serve hot.

## CRANBERRY-AND-WHEAT-BERRY MUFFINS

MAKES: *9 to 10 muffins*

1 cup all-purpose flour
1 cup whole-wheat flour
½ cup wheat berries
1 teaspoon baking soda
½ teaspoon salt
½ cup butter
1 cup packed brown sugar
2 large eggs
¾ cup sour cream
2 cups fresh chopped cranberries
Coconut-and-Whipped-Cream Sauce
  (see recipe page 110)

1  Position the rack in the center of the oven and preheat to 375 degrees F. Lightly grease or line with paper baking cups twelve 2¾-inch muffin cups.

2  In a large bowl, blend together the two flours, wheat berries, baking soda, and salt. In a medium bowl, cream together the butter and sugar before beating in the eggs and sour cream. Fold in the cranberries. Combine the two mixtures, blending until the dry ingredients are just moistened.

3  Spoon the batter into the prepared muffin cups, filling each about three-quarters full. Bake for 15 to 20 minutes, or until a cake tester or wooden toothpick inserted into the center of a muffin comes out clean. Cool in the pan on a wire rack for 5 to 7 minutes. Serve warm, or invert onto the rack to cool completely. Top with Coconut-and-Whipped-Cream Sauce.

## CREAM CHEESE-AND-PUMPKIN MUFFINS

MAKES: *11 to 12 muffins*

1 small (3-ounce) package cream
  cheese, at room temperature
1 tablespoon milk
⅓ cup plus 1 tablespoon granulated
  sugar
1½ cups all-purpose flour
1 tablespoon baking powder
1¼ teaspoons pumpkin-pie spice
½ teaspoon salt
2 large eggs
½ cup canned pumpkin puree
½ cup milk
¼ cup canola oil
Sausage Skillet (see recipe below)

1  Position the rack in the center of the oven and preheat to 400 degrees F. Lightly grease or line with paper baking cups twelve 2¾-inch muffin cups.

2  In a small bowl, beat the cream cheese, milk, and 1 tablespoon of the sugar until smooth. Set aside. In a large bowl, blend together the flour, baking powder, remaining ⅓ cup sugar, pumpkin-pie spice, and salt. In a medium bowl, beat the eggs until thick and light-colored before beating in the pumpkin, milk, and oil. Combine the two mixtures, blending until the dry ingredients are just moistened.

3  Spoon 1 heaping tablespoon of the batter into the prepared baking pan. Spoon the cream-cheese mix evenly between the cups, and top each with a second tablespoon of the remaining batter. Bake for 15 to 20 minutes, or until a cake tester or wooden toothpick inserted into the edge of a muffin (not into the cream cheese) comes out clean. Cool in the pan on a wire rack for 5 to 7 minutes. Serve warm, or invert onto the rack to cool completely. Serve with Sausage Skillet.

## SAUSAGE SKILLET

MAKES: *About 1½ to 2 cups*

¼ cup pork sausage links
One 16-ounce can pork and beans
½ cup finely chopped dried
  apricots, plumped in hot water

1  In a small saucepan set over low heat, cover the sausage with boiling water, and let sit for about 5 minutes. Drain the sausages and transfer them to a skillet set over medium heat. Cook, turning, until the sausage is well browned.

2  Pour off the fat, add the beans and apricots to the skillet, and cook, stirring occasionally, for 5 minutes. Remove from the heat and serve.

2 cups all-purpose flour
1 tablespoon baking powder
2 tablespoons granulated sugar
½ teaspoon salt
1 large egg
1 cup milk
¼ cup canola oil
1 package (8 ounces) cream cheese, cut into 12 chunks
28 to 32 raspberries
Brazil Nut Cream Sauce (see recipe page 70)

**1** Position the rack in the center of the oven and preheat to 425 degrees F. Lightly grease or line with paper baking cups twelve 2¾-inch muffin cups.

**2** In a large bowl, blend together the flour, baking powder, sugar, and salt. In a small bowl, beat the egg until foamy. Beat in the milk and oil. Combine the two mixtures, blending until the dry ingredients are just moistened.

**3** Spoon 1 heaping tablespoon of the batter into the prepared muffin cups. Press a cube of cream cheese into the center of each and top with two raspberries. Spoon a second tablespoon of the remaining batter on top of the raspberries. Bake for 15 to 20 minutes, or until a cake tester or wooden toothpick inserted near the edge of a muffin (not into the cream cheese) comes out clean. Cool in the pan on a wire rack for 5 to 7 minutes. Serve warm, or invert onto the rack to cool completely. Serve with Brazil Nut Cream Sauce.

## CREAM CHEESE-FILLED MUFFINS WITH RASPBERRIES

MAKES: *12 muffins*

½ cup all-purpose flour
1 cup cornmeal
2 teaspoons baking powder
½ teaspoon baking soda
2 tablespoons wheat germ
¼ teaspoon salt
2 tablespoons molasses
¼ cup canola oil
1 cup plain yogurt
1 cup canned cream-style corn
¾ cup chopped pitted prunes
Plum Butter (see recipe page 47)

**1** Position the rack in the center of the oven and preheat to 400 degrees F. Lightly grease or line with paper baking cups twenty-four 2¾-inch muffin cups.

**2** In a large bowl, blend together the flour, cornmeal, baking powder, baking soda, wheat germ, and salt. In a medium bowl, blend the molasses, oil, yogurt, and corn until smooth. Combine the two mixtures, blending until the dry ingredients are just moistened. Fold in the prunes.

**3** Spoon 1 heaping tablespoon of the mixture into the prepared muffin cups and bake for 15 to 20 minutes, or until a cake tester or wooden toothpick inserted into the center of a muffin comes out clean. Cool in the pan on a wire rack for 5 to 7 minutes. Serve warm, or invert onto the rack to cool completely. Serve with Plum Butter.

## CREAM CORN-AND-PRUNE MUFFINS

MAKES: *23 to 24 muffins*

## CREAM OF TOMATO MUFFINS

MAKES: *23 to 24 muffins*

¾ cup all-purpose flour
1 cup whole-wheat flour
1 tablespoon baking powder
¼ cup granulated sugar
1 large egg
¼ cup canola oil
¼ cup milk
One 10¼-ounce can condensed
   tomato soup
3 tablespoons grated Parmesan or
   Romano cheese
Tomato–Basil Dip (see recipe below)

**1** Position the rack in the center of the oven and preheat to 375 degrees F. Lightly grease or line with paper baking cups twenty-four 2¾-inch size muffin cups.

**2** In a large bowl, blend together the two flours, baking powder, and sugar. In a medium bowl, beat the egg until foamy. Beat in the oil, milk, and tomato soup. Combine the two mixtures, blending until the dry ingredients are just moistened.

**3** Spoon one tablespoon of the batter into the prepared muffin cups, filling each about three-quarters full, and sprinkle the cheese over the tops. Bake for 15 to 20 minutes, or until a cake tester or wooden toothpick inserted into the center of a muffin comes out clean. Cool in the pan on a wire rack for 5 to 7 minutes. Serve warm, or invert onto the rack to cool completely. Serve with Tomato–Basil Dip.

## TOMATO–BASIL DIP

MAKES: *About 1½ cups*

1 cup tomato sauce
½ cup fresh snipped basil
3 medium cloves garlic, peeled and
   mashed
2 tablespoons tomato paste
1 tablespoon lemon juice
¼ cup olive oil
Salt and pepper to taste

In the container of a blender or food processor, combine all of the ingredients except the salt and pepper; process on low for 3 to 5 seconds. Pour into a small bowl, season to taste with salt and pepper, and serve.

1 cup dry cracked-wheat bread crumbs
½ cup seedless raisins
¾ cup sour milk or buttermilk
½ cup all-purpose flour
2 teaspoons caraway seeds
2 teaspoons baking powder
½ teaspoon salt
1 large egg
½ tablespoon butter or margarine, melted
Marshmallow Sauce (see recipe below)

**1** Position the rack in the center of the oven and preheat to 425 degrees F. Lightly grease or line with paper baking cups ten 2¾-inch muffin cups.

**2** In a medium bowl, blend the bread crumbs, raisins, and sour milk together. Set aside. In a large bowl, blend together the flour, caraway seeds, baking powder, and salt. In a small bowl, beat the egg until thick and light-colored. Beat in the butter. Fold in the bread-crumbs mixture. Combine the two mixtures, blending until the dry ingredients are just moistened.

**3** Spoon the batter into the prepared muffin cups, filling each about three-quarters full. Bake for 15 to 20 minutes, or until a cake tester or wooden toothpick inserted into the center of a muffin comes out clean. Cool in the pan on a wire rack for 5 to 7 minutes. Serve warm, or invert onto the rack to cool completely. Top with Marshmallow Sauce.

# CRUMB MUFFINS WITH RAISINS

MAKES: *9 to 10 muffins*

# MARSHMALLOW SAUCE

MAKES: *About 2½ cups*

1 cup granulated sugar
½ cup water
16 large marshmallows, each cut into eighths
2 large egg whites

**1** In a medium saucepan set over medium heat, combine the sugar and water and boil for 5 minutes. Add the marshmallows to the hot syrup and stir until dissolved.

**2** In a medium bowl, beat the egg whites until stiff but not dry. Slowly pour the hot liquid over the egg whites, beating constantly. Continue to beat until smooth and well blended.

# CRUMB MUFFINS

MAKES: *6 to 8 muffins*

1 cup dry honey whole-wheat bread crumbs
1 cup dry white-bread crumbs
¼ cup finely chopped pitted green olives
1¼ cups milk
1 cup all-purpose flour
2 teaspoons baking powder
¼ teaspoon salt
2 large eggs
1 tablespoon butter or margarine, melted
Romano cheese for sprinkling
Mint Salsa (see recipe below)

**1** Position the rack in the center of the oven and preheat to 400 degrees F. Lightly grease or line with paper baking cups ten 2¾-inch muffin cups.

**2** In a large bowl, blend the two bread crumbs, olives, and milk together. Set aside for 10 minutes.

In a large bowl, blend together the flour, baking powder, and salt. In a medium bowl, beat the eggs until foamy. Beat in the butter. Fold in the bread-crumb mix. Combine the two mixtures, blending until the dry ingredients are just moistened.

**3** Drop 1 heaping tablespoon of the mixture into the prepared muffin cups and sprinkle the cheese lightly over the top. Bake for 15 to 20 minutes, or until a cake tester or wooden toothpick inserted into the center of a muffin comes out clean. Cool in the pan on a wire rack for 5 to 7 minutes. Serve warm, or invert onto the rack to cool completely. Serve with Mint Salsa.

# MINT SALSA

MAKES: *About 2 cups*

2 cups snipped fresh mint leaves
⅔ cup finely chopped ripe tomatoes
2 medium cloves garlic, peeled and finely chopped
1 jalapeño pepper, stemmed, seeded, and finely chopped
1 tablespoon finely chopped onion
2 tablespoons lemon juice
Salt and ground black pepper to taste

In the container of a blender or food processor, combine all the ingredients except the salt and pepper and process on low for 3 to 5 seconds. Pour into a small bowl, season to taste with salt and pepper, and serve.

2 cups all-purpose flour
⅓ cup granulated sugar
⅓ cup instant nonfat dry milk powder
4 teaspoons baking powder
1 cup (about 2 medium) peeled, cored, and finely chopped apples
1 teaspoon ground cinnamon
1 teaspoon salt
1 large egg
¼ cup canola oil
¾ cup water
Brandy Hard Sauce (see recipe page 135)

**1** Position the rack in the center of the oven and preheat to 400 degrees F. Lightly grease or line with paper baking cups six 3-inch muffin cups.

**2** In a large bowl, blend together the flour, sugar, milk powder, baking powder, apples, cinnamon, and salt. In a medium bowl, beat the egg, oil, and water until smooth. Combine the two mixtures, blending until the dry ingredients are just moistened.

**3** Spoon the batter into the prepared muffin cups, filling each about three-quarters full. Bake for 17 to 22 minutes, or until a cake tester or wooden toothpick inserted into a muffin is removed clean. Cool in the pan on a wire rack for 5 to 7 minutes. Serve warm, or invert onto the rack to cool completely. Top with Brandy Hard Sauce.

# CRUNCH-APPLE MUFFINS

MAKES: *5 to 6 muffins*

---

2 cups all-purpose flour
1 tablespoon granulated sugar
1 tablespoon baking powder
One 3½-ounce can French's® fried onions, crumbled
½ teaspoon salt
1 large egg
¼ cup canola oil
½ cup milk
One 10½-ounce can cream of chicken soup, condensed
½ cup crushed potato chips
½ cup grated Cheddar cheese
Cottage Cheese and Bacon (see recipe below)

**1** Position the rack in the center of the oven and preheat to 400 degrees F. Lightly grease or line with paper baking cups twelve 2¾-inch muffin cups.

**2** In a large bowl, blend together the flour, sugar, baking powder, onions, and salt. In a medium bowl, beat the egg, oil, milk, and soup until smooth. Combine the two mixtures, blending until the dry ingredients are just moistened.

**3** Spoon the batter into the prepared muffin cups, filling each about three-quarters full. In a small-size bowl, blend together the potato chips and cheese, sprinkling it evenly over the top of the mixture in the baking pan. Bake for 15 to 20 minutes, or until a cake tester or wooden toothpick inserted into the center of a muffin comes out clean. Cool in the pan on a wire rack for 5 to 7 minutes. Serve warm, or transfer to the rack to cool completely. Serve with Cottage Cheese and Bacon.

# CRUNCHY BRUNCH MUFFINS

MAKES: *11 to 12 muffins*

---

# COTTAGE CHEESE AND BACON

MAKES: *About 1 cup*

¼ cup bacon bits
1 cup cottage cheese
2 teaspoons finely chopped scallion (green onion)

In a small bowl, combine all of the ingredients and stir until smooth.

## CURAÇAO MUFFINS

MAKES: *7 to 8 muffins*

1¾ cups all-purpose flour
2 teaspoons baking powder
¼ teaspoon salt
½ cup grated Swiss cheese
2 large eggs
¾ cup granulated sugar
¼ cup unsweetened apple juice
½ cup butter or margarine, melted
½ cup Curaçao liqueur
Coffee Custard Sauce (see recipe page 27)

1  Position the rack in the center of the oven and preheat to 375 degrees F. Lightly grease or line with paper baking cups twelve 2¾-inch muffin cups.

2  In a large bowl, blend together the flour, baking powder, salt, and cheese. In a medium bowl, beat the eggs and sugar until smooth before beating in the apple juice, butter, and liqueur. Combine the two mixtures, blending until the dry ingredients are just moistened.

3  Spoon the batter into the prepared muffin cups, filling each about three-quarters full. Bake for 15 to 20 minutes, or until a cake tester or wooden toothpick inserted into the center of a muffin comes out clean. Cool in the pan on a wire rack for 5 to 7 minutes. Serve warm, or invert onto the rack to cool completely. Serve with Coffee Custard Sauce.

## CURRIED-CHICKEN MUFFINS

MAKES: *11 to 12 muffins*

2¼ cups all-purpose flour
2 teaspoons baking powder
2 tablespoons chopped fresh cilantro (coriander)
½ pound cooked chicken, chopped fine
1 tablespoon curry powder
¼ teaspoon salt
2 large eggs
2 tablespoons fresh lemon juice
1 cup plain yogurt
½ cup canola oil
Paprika for sprinkling
Chicken 'N Cheese Spread

1  Position the rack in the center of the oven and preheat to 375 degrees F. Lightly grease or line with paper baking cups twelve 2¾-inch muffin cups.

2  In a large bowl, blend together the flour, baking powder, cilantro, chicken, curry powder, and salt. In a medium bowl, beat the eggs, lemon juice, yogurt, and oil until smooth. Combine the two mixtures, blending until the dry ingredients are just moistened.

3  Spoon the batter into the prepared muffin cups, filling each about three-quarters full. Lightly sprinkle the tops of the muffins with paprika. Bake for 15 to 20 minutes, or until a cake tester or wooden toothpick inserted into the center of a muffin comes out clean. Cool in the pan on a wire rack for 5 to 7 minutes. Serve warm, or invert onto the rack to cool completely. Serve with Chicken 'N Cheese Spread.

### CHICKEN 'N CHEESE SPREAD

MAKES: *About 1½ cups*

One 5-ounce can prepared chicken spread
One 3-ounce package cream cheese, at room temperature
2 tablespoons finely chopped onions
2 stalks celery, finely chopped
¼ teaspoon curry powder

In a small bowl, combine all of the ingredients and blend until smooth. Cover and refrigerate until ready to use.

1½ cups whole-wheat flour
½ cup all-purpose flour
1½ cups bran flakes
2 tablespoons granulated sugar
1¼ teaspoons baking soda
¼ teaspoon salt
1 large egg
2 cups buttermilk or sour milk
½ cup dark molasses
2 tablespoons butter or margarine, melted
Brandy Hard Sauce (see recipe below)

**1** Position the rack in the center of the oven and preheat to 375 degrees F. Lightly grease or line with paper baking cups thirty-two 2¾-inch muffin cups.

**2** In a large bowl, blend together the two flours, bran flakes, sugar, baking soda, and salt. In a medium bowl, beat the egg, buttermilk, molasses, and butter until smooth. Combine the two mixtures, blending until the dry ingredients are just moistened.

**3** Drop 1 heaping tablespoon of the mixture into the prepared muffin cups and bake for 15 to 20 minutes, or until a cake tester or wooden toothpick inserted into the center of a muffin comes out clean. Cool in the pan on a wire rack for 5 to 7 minutes. Serve warm, or invert onto the rack to cool completely. Serve with Brandy Hard Sauce.

# DARK-AND-MOIST BRAN MUFFINS

MAKES: *30 to 32 muffins*

# BRANDY HARD SAUCE

MAKES: *About 1 cup*

1 tablespoon cornstarch
1 cup milk
1 tablespoon butter
1 tablespoon granulated sugar
2 tablespoons brandy

In a cup, combine the cornstarch and 1 tablespoon of the milk and stir to form a smooth paste. In a small saucepan set over medium heat, warm the remaining milk slightly before adding the cornstarch. Cook, stirring, until the mixture boils and thickens. Reduce the heat to low and simmer for 2 minutes, stirring constantly. Remove from the heat and stir in the butter, sugar, and brandy.

# DATE-AND-BANANA–BUTTERMILK MUFFINS

MAKES: *14 to 16 muffins*

1¼ cups all-purpose flour
½ cup shredded-bran cereal
1 teaspoon baking powder
½ teaspoon baking soda
1 teaspoon ground cinnamon
½ cup chopped pitted dates
¼ cup chopped walnuts
½ teaspoon salt
1 large egg
¾ cup buttermilk
¼ cup canola oil
⅓ cup honey
½ cup (about 2 medium) mashed
  bananas
Date Sauce (see recipe below)

**1** Position the rack in the center of the oven and preheat to 400 degrees F. Lightly grease or line with paper baking cups sixteen 2¾-inch muffin cups.

**2** In a large bowl, blend together the flour, cereal, baking powder, baking soda, cinnamon, dates, walnuts, and salt. In a medium bowl, beat the egg, buttermilk, oil, honey, and banana until smooth. Combine the two mixtures, blending until the dry ingredients are just moistened.

**3** Spoon the batter into the prepared muffin cups, filling each about three-quarters full. Bake for 15 to 20 minutes, or until a cake tester or wooden toothpick inserted into the center of a muffin comes out clean. Cool in the pan on a wire rack for 5 to 7 minutes. Serve warm, or invert onto the rack to cool completely. Serve with Date Sauce.

## DATE SAUCE

MAKES: *About 1½ cups*

1 cup water
1 tablespoon oil
8 pitted dates, finely chopped

In the container of a blender, combine all of the ingredients and process on medium speed until smooth. Pour into a small saucepan and cook over medium heat until the mixture just starts to boil. Remove from the heat and serve.

1 cup all-purpose flour
1½ cups shredded bran cereal
¼ cup packed light-brown sugar
2½ teaspoons baking powder
½ cup finely chopped dates
2 large egg whites
3 tablespoons canola oil
1 cup milk
Creamy Glaze (see recipe below)

**1** Position the rack in the center of the oven and preheat to 400 degrees F. Lightly grease or line with paper baking cups sixteen 2¾-inch muffin cups.

**2** In a large bowl, blend together the flour, cereal, sugar, baking powder, and dates. In a medium bowl, beat the egg whites until stiff but not dry. Beat in the oil and milk. Combine the two mixtures, blending until the dry ingredients are just moistened.

**3** Drop 1 heaping tablespoon of the batter into each of the prepared muffin cups and bake for 15 to 20 minutes, or until a cake tester or wooden toothpick inserted into the center of a muffin comes out clean. Cool in the pan on a wire rack for 5 to 7 minutes. Invert onto the rack to cool completely and brush with Creamy Glaze.

# DATE-AND-BRAN MUFFINS
MAKES: *14 to 16 muffins*

# CREAMY GLAZE
MAKES: *½ cup*

1 small (3-ounce) package cream cheese, at room temperature
¾ cup powdered sugar
2 tablespoons milk

In a small bowl, beat together the cream cheese, sugar, and milk until smooth.

---

2 cups all-purpose flour
¼ cup granulated sugar
4 teaspoons baking powder
½ package (7¼ ounces) pitted dates, chopped
¼ cup chopped walnuts or pecans
½ teaspoon salt
1 large egg
¼ cup butter or margarine, melted
1 cup hot milk

**1** Position the rack in the center of the oven and preheat to 400 degrees F. Lightly grease or line with paper baking cups sixteen 2¾-inch muffin cups.

**2** In a large bowl, blend together the flour, sugar, baking powder, dates, walnuts, and salt. In a medium bowl, beat the egg until thick and light-colored before beating in the butter. Beat in the hot milk a little at a time. Combine the two mixtures, blending until the dry ingredients are just blended.

**3** Spoon the batter into the prepared muffin cups, filling each about three-quarters full. Bake for 15 to 20 minutes, or until a cake tester or wooden toothpick inserted into the center of a muffin comes out clean. Cool in the pan on a wire rack for 5 to 7 minutes. Serve warm, or invert onto the rack to cool completely.

# DATE-AND-NUT MUFFINS
MAKES: *14 to 16 muffins*

# DATE LOVERS' MUFFINS

MAKES: *11 to 12 muffins*

2 cups all-purpose flour
¼ cup granulated sugar
2 teaspoons baking powder
½ pound dates, pitted and chopped
½ teaspoon salt
1 large egg
⅓ cup butter or margarine, melted
¾ cup milk

**1** Position the rack in the center of the oven and preheat to 400 degrees F. Lightly grease or line with paper baking cups twelve 2¾-inch muffin cups.

**2** In a large bowl, blend together the flour, sugar, baking powder, dates, and salt. In a medium bowl, beat the egg, butter, and milk until smooth. Combine the two mixtures, blending until the dry ingredients are just moistened.

**3** Spoon the batter into the prepared muffin cups, filling each about three-quarters full. Bake for 15 to 20 minutes, or until a cake tester or wooden toothpick inserted into the center of a muffin comes out clean. Cool in the pan on a wire rack for 5 to 7 minutes. Serve warm, or invert onto the rack to cool completely.

**SERVING SUGGESTION: Roll in butter and sugar.**

# DATE MUFFINS

MAKES: *20 to 24 muffins*

2 cups all-purpose flour
1 tablespoon baking powder
¼ cup pitted dates, chopped fine
½ cup chopped walnuts
½ teaspoon salt
2 tablespoons granulated sugar
1 large egg
1 cup milk
¼ cup canola oil
Applesauce (see recipe below)

**1** Position the rack in the center of the oven and preheat to 425 degrees F. Lightly grease or line with paper baking cups twenty-four 2¾-inch muffin cups.

**2** In a large bowl, blend together the flour, baking powder, dates, walnuts, and salt. In a medium bowl, beat the sugar, egg, milk, and oil until smooth. Combine the two mixtures, blending until the dry ingredients are just moistened.

**3** Drop 1 heaping tablespoon of the mixture into each prepared muffin cup and bake for 15 to 20 minutes, or until a cake tester or wooden toothpick inserted into the center of a muffin comes out clean. Cool in the pan on a wire rack for 5 to 7 minutes. Serve warm, or invert onto the rack to cool completely. Serve with Applesauce.

# APPLESAUCE

MAKES: *2 cups*

**5 teaspoons cornstarch**
**1 cup water**
**One 6-ounce can frozen apple juice concentrate, thawed**
**¼ cup firmly packed brown sugar**
**½ teaspoon ground allspice**
**½ teaspoon vanilla extract**

In a small saucepan using a fork or the back of a spoon, combine the cornstarch and water until smooth. Add the apple juice, sugar, and allspice. Set the pan over low heat and cook, stirring constantly, until the mixture is very thick, about 2 to 3 minutes. Remove from the heat and stir in the vanilla extract. Pour into a bowl and serve at room temperature.

2 cups all-purpose flour
1 tablespoon baking powder
¾ teaspoon salt
1 large egg
⅓ cup granulated sugar
¼ cup canola oil
¼ cup Triple Sec
½ cup orange juice
1 tablespoon grated orange zest
Honey Glaze (see recipe page 53)

**1** Position the rack in the center of the oven and preheat to 400 degrees F. Lightly grease or line with paper baking cups eighteen 2¾-inch muffin cups.

**2** In a large bowl, blend together the flour, baking powder, and salt. In a medium bowl, beat the egg until foamy. Beat in the sugar. Beat in the oil, Triple Sec, juice, and orange zest. Combine the two mixtures, blending until the dry ingredients are just moistened.

**3** Drop 1 heaping tablespoon of the batter into the prepared muffin cups. Bake for 15 to 20 minutes, or until a cake tester or wooden toothpick inserted into the center of a muffin comes out clean. Cool in the pan for 5 minutes before transferring the muffins to a wire rack to cool completely. Serve with Honey Glaze.

## DELUXE ORANGE MUFFINS

MAKES: *16 to 18 muffins*

---

⅔ cup oat bran
⅔ cup all-purpose flour
⅔ cup whole-wheat flour
1 tablespoon baking powder
1½ teaspoons dried dill, crushed
½ teaspoon dried thyme, crushed
¼ teaspoon garlic powder
1 teaspoon nonfat dry milk powder
½ teaspoon salt
1 cup milk
½ cup cottage cheese or ricotta cheese
¼ cup butter or margarine, melted
2 large egg whites
1 teaspoon canola oil
Artichoke Spread (see recipe below)

**1** Position the rack in the center of the oven and preheat to 425 degrees F. Lightly grease or line with paper baking cups fourteen 2¾-inch muffin cups.

**2** In a large bowl, blend together the oat bran, two flours, baking powder, dill, thyme, garlic powder, milk powder, and salt. In a medium bowl, beat the milk, cheese, butter, egg whites, and oil until smooth. Combine the two mixtures, blending until the dry ingredients are just moistened.

**3** Spoon the batter into the prepared muffin cups, filling each about three-quarters full. Bake for 15 to 20 minutes, or until a cake tester or wooden toothpick inserted into the center of a muffin comes out clean. Cool in the pan on a wire rack for 5 to 7 minutes. Serve warm, or invert onto the rack to cool completely. Serve with Artichoke Spread.

## DILL-AND-THYME MUFFINS

MAKES: *12 to 14 muffins*

---

## ARTICHOKE SPREAD

MAKES: *About 2½ cups*

1 package frozen artichoke hearts, thawed and drained
1 cup mayonnaise
1 cup grated Romano cheese

**1** Position a rack in the center of the oven and preheat to 325 degrees F. Lightly grease a ½-quart casserole dish.

**2** In a medium bowl, mash the artichoke hearts. Blend in the mayonnaise and cheese. Pour into the prepared casserole dish and bake for about 20 minutes, or until the mixture bubbles. Remove from the oven and serve at once.

## DOUBLE CHOCOLATE MUFFINS

MAKES: *11 to 12 muffins*

2 cups all-purpose flour
1 tablespoon baking powder
¾ cup Dutch-processed cocoa powder
½ teaspoon salt
1½ cups (7¾ ounces) miniature semisweet chocolate chips
½ cup vegetable shortening
1 cup granulated sugar
1 large egg
1 cup warm milk

1  Position a rack in the center of the oven and preheat to 400 degrees F. Lightly grease or line with paper baking cups twelve 2¾-inch muffin cups.

2  In a large bowl, blend together the flour, baking powder, cocoa, salt, and chocolate chips. In a medium bowl, beat the shortening and sugar until fluffy. Beat in the egg and milk. Combine the two mixtures, blending until the dry ingredients are just moistened.

3  Spoon the batter into the prepared muffin cups, filling each about three-quarters full. Bake for 15 to 20 minutes or until a cake tester or wooden toothpick inserted into the center of a muffin comes out clean. Cool in the pan on a wire rack for 5 to 7 minutes. Serve warm, or invert onto the rack to cool completely.

SERVING SUGGESTION: **Serve with chocolate ice cream.**

## DOUBLE CHOCOLATE-AND-SOUR CREAM MUFFINS

MAKES: *11 to 12 muffins*

¼ cup butter-flavored vegetable shortening
3 ounces unsweetened chocolate, grated
2 cups all-purpose flour
1 teaspoon baking soda
¼ teaspoon salt
1 cup granulated sugar
1 large egg
1 cup buttermilk or sour milk
2 teaspoons chocolate extract
1 cup (6 ounces) semisweet chocolate chips
Whipped Hot Chocolate (see recipe page 36)

1  Position the rack in the center of the oven and preheat to 375 degrees F. Lightly grease or line with paper baking cups twelve 2¾-inch muffin cups.

2  In a small saucepan set over low heat, melt the shortening and chocolate, stirring constantly, until melted and smooth. Remove from the heat and set aside. In a small bowl, blend together the flour, baking soda, and salt. In a medium bowl, beat the sugar, egg, buttermilk, and chocolate extract until smooth. Combine the two mixtures, blending until the dry ingredients are just moistened. Stir in the melted chocolate and fold in the chocolate chips.

3  Spoon the batter into the prepared muffin cups, filling each about three-quarters full. Bake for 15 to 20 minutes, or until a cake tester or wooden toothpick inserted into the center of a muffin comes out clean. Cool in the pan on a wire rack for 5 to 7 minutes. Serve warm, or invert onto the rack to cool completely. Serve with Whipped Hot Chocolate.

2 cups all-purpose flour
1 tablespoon baking powder
½ cup chopped mixed dried fruits
½ teaspoon salt
2 large eggs
¼ cup packed light-brown sugar
½ cup butter or margarine, melted
¾ cup milk
¼ teaspoon raspberry flavoring
Honey Butter (see recipe page 146)

1  Position the rack in the center of the oven and preheat to 400 degrees F. Lightly grease or line with paper baking cups twelve 2¾-inch muffin cups.

2  In a large bowl, blend together the flour, baking powder, dried fruits, and salt. In a medium bowl, beat the egg until thick and light-colored. Beat in the brown sugar, butter, milk, and flavoring until smooth. Combine the two mixtures, blending until the dry ingredients are just moistened.

3  Spoon the batter into the prepared muffin cups, filling each about three-quarters full. Bake for 15 to 20 minutes, or until a cake tester or wooden toothpick inserted into the center of a muffin comes out clean. Cool in the pan on a wire rack for 5 to 7 minutes. Serve warm, or transfer the muffins to the rack to cool completely. Serve with Honey Butter.

# DRIED-FRUIT MUFFINS

MAKES: *11 to 12 muffins*

---

1½ cups all-purpose flour
2 teaspoons baking powder
1½ tablespoons packed brown sugar
⅛ teaspoon salt
¾ cup milk
¼ cup butter or margarine, melted
12 slices crisp, cooked bacon, crumbled
4 large eggs
¾ cup shredded Cheddar cheese
Pinch freshly ground black pepper
Mint Butter (see recipe below)

1  Position the rack in the center of the over and preheat to 375 degrees F. Lightly grease or line with paper baking cups ten 2¾-inch muffin cups.

2  In a large bowl, blend together the flour, baking powder, brown sugar, and salt. In a medium bowl, blend the milk and butter together before stirring in the bacon. Combine the two mixtures, blending until the dry ingredients are just moistened.

3  Drop 1½ heaping tablespoons of the batter into each of the prepared muffin cups. In a medium bowl, beat the eggs until thick and light-colored. Beat in the cheese and pepper. Spoon this mixture evenly over the tops of the muffins in the pan and bake for 15 to 20 minutes, or until a cake tester or wooden toothpick inserted into the center of a muffin comes out clean. Cool in the pan on a wire rack for 5 to 7 minutes. Serve warm and with Mint Butter.

# EARLY-MORNING BREAKFAST MUFFINS

MAKES: *8 to 10 muffins*

---

# MINT BUTTER

MAKES: *About 1¾ cups*

1 cup butter, at room temperature
1 cup fresh snipped mint leaves
5 small shallots
1 small clove garlic, peeled and smashed
1 tablespoon granulated sugar
¼ cup fresh lemon or lime juice
1 teaspoon Worcestershire sauce
Salt and pepper to taste

In the container of a blender or food processor, combine all of the ingredients and process until smooth. Pour into a bowl, cover, and refrigerate until ready to serve.

## EASY CHERRY MUFFINS

MAKES: *11 to 12 muffins*

1 cup biscuit mix (such as Bisquick®)
½ cup granulated sugar
1 large egg
2 tablespoons margarine, at room temperature
¾ cup milk
½ cup cottage cheese
1 cup tart canned cherries, drained
Cherry Sauce (see recipe page 52)

**1** Position the rack in the center of the oven and preheat to 425 degrees F. Lightly grease or line with paper baking cups twelve 2½-inch muffin cups.

**2** In a medium bowl, blend together the biscuit mix and sugar. In a large bowl, beat the egg, margarine, and milk until smooth. Fold in the cottage cheese and cherries. Combine the two mixtures, blending until the dry ingredients are just moistened.

**3** Spoon the batter into the prepared muffin cups, filling each about three-quarters full. Bake for 15 to 20 minutes, or until a cake tester or wooden toothpick inserted into the center of a muffin comes out clean. Cool in the pan on a wire rack for 5 to 7 minutes. Serve warm, or invert onto the rack to cool completely. Serve with Cherry Sauce.

## EGGLESS GRAHAM MUFFINS

MAKES: *19 to 20 muffins*

1 cup all-purpose flour
1½ cups graham flour
¾ teaspoon baking powder
1 teaspoon baking soda
¼ cup granulated sugar
½ teaspoon salt
3 tablespoons butter or margarine, melted
1½ cups buttermilk or sour milk
Mincemeat Sauce (see recipe below)

**1** Position the rack in the center of the oven and preheat to 400 degrees F. Lightly grease or line with paper baking cups twenty 2¾-inch muffin cups.

**2** In a large bowl, blend together the two flours, baking powder, baking soda, sugar, and salt. In a medium bowl, blend the butter and buttermilk until smooth. Combine the two mixtures, blending until the dry ingredients are just moistened.

**3** Drop 1 heaping tablespoon of the mixture into the prepared muffin cups and bake for 15 to 20 minutes, or until a cake tester or wooden toothpick inserted into the center of a muffin comes out clean. Cool in the pan on a wire rack for 5 to 7 minutes. Serve warm, or invert onto the rack to cool completely. Serve with Mincemeat Sauce.

## MINCEMEAT SAUCE

MAKES: *About ½ cup*

6 tablespoons prepared mincemeat
1 teaspoon unsweetened prune juice
1 teaspoon rum

In a small bowl, blend all of the ingredients together. Cover and refrigerate until ready to serve.

2 cups all-purpose flour
4 teaspoons baking powder
2 tablespoons rainbow sprinkles
½ teaspoon salt
¾ cup milk
¼ cup butter or margarine, melted
Orange Butter (see recipe page 95)

**1** Position the rack in the center of the oven and preheat to 400 degrees F. Lightly grease or line with paper baking cups twelve 2¾-inch muffin cups.

**2** In a large bowl, blend together the flour, baking powder, sprinkles, and salt. In a small bowl, beat the milk and margarine until smooth. Combine the two mixtures, blending until the dry ingredients are just moistened.

**3** Spoon the batter into the prepared muffin cups, filling each about three-quarters full. Bake for 15 to 20 minutes, or until a cake tester or wooden toothpick inserted into the center of a muffin comes out clean. Cool in the pan on a wire rack for 5 to 7 minutes. Serve warm, or invert onto the rack to cool completely. Serve with Orange Butter.

# EGGLESS RAINBOW MUFFINS

MAKES: *11 to 12 muffins*

# EGGNOG–SPICE MUFFINS

MAKES: *11 to 12 muffins*

**BATTER**

2 cups all-purpose flour
1 tablespoon baking powder
⅔ cup granulated sugar
¾ teaspoon ground nutmeg
1 large egg, beaten
5 tablespoons butter or margarine, melted
¾ cup commercially prepared eggnog
½ cup dark rum or brandy

**TOPPING**

2 tablespoons butter or margarine, melted
1 teaspoon ground cinnamon
½ cup packed light-brown sugar
¼ cup all-purpose flour
½ cup chopped pecans
Sweet Potato-and-Apple Salad (see recipe below)

**1** Position the rack in the center of the oven and preheat to 375 degrees. Lightly grease or line with paper baking cups twelve 2¾-inch size muffin cups.

**2** To make the batter, in a large bowl, blend together the flour, baking powder, sugar, and nutmeg. In a medium bowl, beat the egg, butter, eggnog, and rum until smooth. Combine the two mixtures, blending until the dry ingredients are just moistened. Spoon the mixture into the prepared muffin cups, filling each about three-quarters full.

**3** To make the topping, in a small bowl, blend together all of the ingredients. Sprinkle this evenly over the tops of the muffins.

**4** Bake for 15 to 20 minutes, or until a cake tester or wooden toothpick inserted into the center of a muffin comes out clean. Cool in the pan on a wire rack for 5 to 7 minutes. Serve warm, or transfer to the rack to cool completely. Serve with Sweet Potato-and-Apple Salad.

# SWEET POTATO-AND-APPLE SALAD

MAKES: *About 1½ cups*

1½ pounds boiled sweet potatoes, peeled and finely diced
1 large apple, peeled, cored, and finely diced
2 stalks celery, finely chopped
1 teaspoon salt
½ cup mayonnaise

In a bowl, combine the potatoes, apple, and celery. Sprinkle with salt and stir in the mayonnaise. Cover and refrigerate before serving.

# EMPIRE STATE MUFFINS

MAKES: *11 to 12 muffins*

2½ cups all-purpose flour
1 tablespoon baking powder
2 teaspoons baking soda
2 teaspoons ground cinnamon
1⅓ cups granulated sugar
2 cups shredded apples
1 cup chopped cranberries
1 cup shredded carrots
1 cup chopped almonds
½ teaspoon salt
2 large eggs
½ cup canola oil
Strawberry Sauce (see recipe below)

**1** Position the rack in the center of the oven and preheat to 375 degrees F. Lightly grease or line with paper baking cups twelve 2¾-inch muffin cups.

**2** In a large bowl, blend together the flour, baking powder, baking soda, cinnamon, sugar, apples, cranberries, carrots, almonds, and salt. In a small bowl, beat the eggs until thick and light-colored. Beat in the oil. Combine the two mixtures, blending until the dry ingredients are just moistened.

**3** Spoon the batter into the prepared muffin cups, filling each about three-quarters full. Bake for 15 to 20 minutes, or until a cake tester or wooden toothpick inserted into the center of a muffin comes out clean. Cool in the pan on a wire rack for 5 to 7 minutes. Serve warm, or invert onto the rack to cool completely. Serve with Strawberry Sauce.

## STRAWBERRY SAUCE

MAKES: *1 cup*

One 10-ounce package frozen strawberries in syrup, thawed and drained (reserve the liquid)
1 tablespoon Triple Sec or orange juice
2 teaspoons cornstarch
2 to 3 drops red food coloring

In a small saucepan, blend together the reserved strawberry liquid, liqueur, and cornstarch. Place the pan over medium heat and cook, stirring, until the mixture boils and starts to thicken. Remove from the heat and immediately add the thawed strawberries and food coloring. Pour into a serving bowl and cool to room temperature before serving.

## FETA CHEESE SURPRISE MUFFINS

MAKES: *11 to 12 muffins*

2 cups all-purpose flour
1½ teaspoons baking powder
2 tablespoons granulated sugar
½ cup finely chopped feta cheese
2 large eggs
½ cup plain yogurt
¼ cup skim milk
2 tablespoons butter or margarine, melted
⅓ cup jellied cranberry sauce
½ cup whole cranberry sauce for filling
⅓ cup chopped pecans for topping
Shrimp Spread (see recipe below)

1  Position the rack in the center of the oven and preheat to 375 degrees F. Lightly grease or line with paper baking cups twelve 2¾-inch muffin cups.

2  In a large bowl, blend together the flour, baking powder, sugar, and cheese. In a medium bowl, beat the eggs, yogurt, milk, butter, and jellied cranberry sauce until smooth. Combine the two mixtures, blending until the dry ingredients are just moistened.

3  Drop one heaping tablespoon of the batter into each of the prepared muffin cups. Divide the cranberry sauce between the cups placing it in the center before dropping a second tablespoon of batter into each cup. Sprinkle the chopped pecans over the tops of the muffins and bake for 15 to 20 minutes, or until a cake tester or wooden toothpick inserted into the edge of a muffin (not into the cranberry sauce) comes out clean. Cool in the pan on a wire rack for 5 to 7 minutes. Serve warm, or invert onto the rack to cool completely. Serve with Shrimp Spread.

## SHRIMP SPREAD

MAKES: *About 1½ cups*

One 8-ounce package cream cheese, at room temperature
One 5½-ounce can broken shrimp
½ teaspoon lemon juice

In a small bowl, blend together the cream cheese, shrimp, and lemon juice until smooth. Refrigerate until ready to use.

# FIG–ALL-BRAN MUFFINS

MAKES: *23 to 24 muffins*

¾ cup all-purpose flour
1 tablespoon baking powder
¼ teaspoon baking soda
1 cup dried figs, washed, trimmed,
    and chopped
2 large eggs
3 tablespoons butter or margarine,
    melted
2 tablespoons dark molasses
1 cup milk
2¼ cups All-Bran® cereal
Honey Butter (see recipe below)

**1** Position the rack in the center of the oven and preheat to 425 degrees F. Lightly grease or line with paper baking cups twenty-four 2-inch muffin cups.

**2** In a large bowl, blend together the flour, baking powder, baking soda, and figs. In a medium bowl, beat the eggs until thick and light-colored before beating in the butter, molasses, and milk. Stir in the All-Bran. Combine the two mixtures, blending until the dry ingredients are just moistened.

**3** Drop 1 heaping tablespoon of the batter into each of the prepared muffin cups. Bake for 12 to 15 minutes, or until a cake tester or wooden toothpick inserted into the center of a muffin comes out clean. Cool in the pan on a wire rack for 5 to 7 minutes. Serve warm, or invert onto the rack to cool completely. Serve with Honey Butter.

## HONEY BUTTER

MAKES: *1½ cups*

½ cup butter
1 cup honey

In a small bowl, blend together the butter and honey until smooth. Cover and refrigerate for 30 minutes before serving.

1 cup dried figs, washed, trimmed, and chopped
1½ cups all-purpose flour
2 tablespoon granulated sugar
5 teaspoons baking powder
3 cups bran flakes
1 teaspoon salt
2 large eggs
1 cup milk
4 tablespoons butter or margarine, melted
Creamy Pecan–Rum Sauce (see recipe below)

**1** Position the rack in the center of the oven and preheat to 400 degrees F. Lightly grease or line with paper baking cups fourteen 2¼-inch muffin cups.

**2** Place the figs in a small bowl and add boiling water to cover. Let soak for 10 minutes. Drain and set aside.

**3** In a large bowl, blend together the flour, sugar, baking powder, bran flakes, and salt. In a medium bowl, beat the eggs until thick and light-colored before beating in the milk and butter. Stir in the figs. Combine the two mixtures, blending until the dry ingredients are just moistened.

**4** Spoon the batter into the prepared muffin cups, filling each cup two-thirds full. Bake for 15 to 20 minutes, or until a cake tester or wooden toothpick inserted into the center of a muffin comes out clean. Cool in the pan on a wire rack for 5 to 7 minutes. Serve warm, or invert onto the rack to cool completely. Serve with Creamy Pecan–Rum Sauce.

# FIG–BRAN MUFFINS

MAKES: *12 to 14 muffins*

## CREAMY PECAN–RUM SAUCE

MAKES: *1½ cups*

¼ cup butter or margarine
One 14-ounce can sweetened condensed milk
1 tablespoon rum or ½ teaspoon rum flavoring
¼ cup finely chopped pecans

In a small saucepan set over medium heat, melt the butter. Stir in the milk and rum. Cook, stirring frequently, for 10 to 12 minutes, or until the mixture thickens. Remove from the heat and immediately stir in the pecans. Pour into a serving bowl and cool to room temperature.

# FIG-AND-ORANGE MUFFINS

MAKES: *14 to 18 muffins*

2 cups all-purpose flour
1 tablespoon baking powder
3 tablespoons granulated sugar
½ teaspoon salt
½ cup dried figs, washed, trimmed, and chopped
¾ teaspoon finely chopped orange zest
1 large egg
4 tablespoons butter or margarine, melted
1 cup milk
Honey–Orange Marmalade Sauce (see recipe below)

**1** Position the rack in the center of the oven and preheat to 425 degrees F. Lightly grease or line with paper baking cups eighteen 2¾-inch muffin cups.

**2** In a large bowl, blend together the flour, baking powder, sugar, salt, figs, and orange zest. In a medium bowl, beat the egg until thick and light-colored. Beat in the butter and milk. Combine the two mixtures, blending until the dry ingredients are just moistened.

**3** Spoon the batter into the prepared muffin cups, filling each about three-quarters full. Bake for 15 to 20 minutes, or until a cake tester or wooden toothpick inserted into the center of a muffin comes out clean. Cool in the pan on a wire rack for 5 to 7 minutes. Serve warm, or invert onto the rack to cool completely. Serve with Honey–Orange Marmalade Sauce.

## HONEY–ORANGE MARMALADE SAUCE

MAKES: *1½ cups*

½ cup butter or margarine
½ cup honey
½ cup marmalade
1 teaspoon Triple Sec liqueur

In a small saucepan set over medium heat, combine the butter and honey and cook, stirring, until the mixture is smooth. Stir in the marmalade. Cook, stirring frequently, for 1 to 2 minutes more. Remove from the heat and stir in the Triple Sec. Pour the sauce into a serving bowl.

# FIG MUFFINS

MAKES: *12 to 14 muffins*

3 cups all-purpose flour
2 tablespoons granulated sugar
4 teaspoons baking powder
1 cup dried figs, washed, trimmed, and chopped
1 teaspoon salt
1 large egg
1¼ cups milk
5 tablespoons butter or margarine, melted
Yogurt Cream (see recipe page 55)

**1** Position the rack in the center of the oven and preheat to 450 degrees F. Lightly grease or line with paper baking cups fourteen 2¾-inch muffin cups.

**2** In a large bowl, blend together the flour, sugar, baking powder, figs, and salt. In a medium bowl, beat the egg until thick and light-colored. Beat in the milk and butter. Combine the two mixtures, blending until the dry ingredients are just moistened.

**3** Spoon the batter into the prepared muffin cups, filling each about three-quarters full. Bake for 15 to 20 minutes, or until a cake tester or wooden toothpick inserted into the center of a muffin comes out clean. Cool in the pan on a wire rack for 5 to 7 minutes. Serve warm, or invert onto the rack to cool completely. Serve with Creamy Yogurt.

1 cup all-purpose flour
1 cup cornmeal
1 teaspoon baking powder
1 teaspoon baking soda
1 teaspoon salt
2 large eggs
1 cup sour milk
2 tablespoons butter or margarine,
    melted
¼ cup molasses
Herb Butter (see recipe below)

**1** Position the rack in the center of the oven and preheat to 375 degrees F. Lightly grease or line with paper baking cups fourteen 2¾-inch muffin cups.

**2** In a large bowl, blend together the flour, cornmeal, baking powder, baking soda, and salt. In a medium bowl, beat the eggs until thick and light-colored. Beat in the sour milk, butter, and molasses until smooth. Combine the two mixtures, blending until the dry ingredients are just moistened.

**3** Spoon the batter into the prepared muffin cups, filling each about three-quarters full. Bake for 15 to 20 minutes, or until a cake tester or wooden toothpick inserted into the center of a muffin comes out clean. Remove from the oven and immediately brush the tops of the muffins with the glaze. Cool in the pan on a wire rack for 5 to 7 minutes. Serve warm, or transfer the muffins to the rack to cool completely. Serve with Herb Butter.

# FLAVORED CORNMEAL MUFFINS

MAKES: *12 to 14 muffins*

# HERB BUTTER

MAKES: *About 1 cup*

1 cup butter, at room temperature
1 teaspoon fresh snipped parsley
1 teaspoon fresh snipped chives
2 teaspoons fresh snipped cilantro
1 teaspoon crushed basil
½ teaspoon fresh snipped tarragon
4 teaspoons fresh lime juice
Pinch cayenne pepper
Salt to taste

In a medium bowl, using an electric mixer on medium speed, beat all of the ingredients together until smooth. Cover and refrigerate until ready to serve.

## FOURTH OF JULY MUFFINS

MAKES: *23 to 24 muffins*

1¾ cups all-purpose flour
1 tablespoon baking powder
¼ cup granulated sugar
1 large egg
1 tablespoon molasses
1 cup milk
3 tablespoons butter or margarine, melted
1 cup canned pork and beans
Maple Syrup Glaze (see recipe below)

**1** Position the rack in the center of the oven and preheat to 375 degrees F. Lightly grease or line with paper baking cups twenty-four 2¾-inch muffin cups.

**2** In a large bowl, blend together the flour, baking powder, and sugar. In a medium bowl, beat the egg until foamy. Beat in the molasses, milk, and butter. Stir in the pork and beans. Combine the two mixtures, blending until the dry ingredients are just moistened.

**3** Drop 1 heaping tablespoon of the batter into the prepared muffin cups. Bake for 15 to 20 minutes, or until a cake tester or wooden toothpick inserted into the center of a muffin comes out clean. Cool in the pan on a wire rack for 5 to 7 minutes. Serve warm, or invert onto the rack to cool completely. Brush the tops of the muffins with Maple Syrup Glaze.

### MAPLE SYRUP GLAZE

MAKES: ⅔ *cup*

½ cup powdered sugar
1 tablespoon maple syrup
1 tablespoon butter or margarine, melted

In a small bowl, combine the sugar, syrup, and butter, blending until smooth. Brush over muffins hot from the oven.

## FRESH BLUEBERRY MUFFINS

MAKES: *5 to 6 muffins*

1 cup all-purpose flour
1½ teaspoons baking powder
¼ teaspoon salt
3 tablespoons powdered sugar
⅓ cup fresh blueberries, rinsed and dried
1 large egg
½ cup milk
1 tablespoon butter or margarine, melted
Blueberry Syrup (see recipe page 43)

**1** Position the rack in the center of the oven and preheat to 425 degrees F. Lightly grease or line with paper baking cups six 2¾-inch muffin cups.

**2** In a large bowl, blend together the flour, baking powder, and salt. In a small bowl, sprinkle the sugar over the blueberries and stir until they are coated. In a medium bowl, beat the egg until thick and light-colored. Beat in the milk and butter. Stir in the blueberries. Combine the two mixtures, blending until the dry ingredients are just moistened.

**3** Spoon the batter into the prepared muffin cups, filling each about three-quarters full. Bake for 15 to 20 minutes, or until a cake tester or wooden toothpick inserted into the center of a muffin comes out clean. Cool in the pan on a wire rack for 5 to 7 minutes. Serve warm, or invert onto the rack to cool completely. Serve with Blueberry Syrup.

2 cups whole-wheat flour
1 cup rolled oats
½ cup unprocessed wheat bran
½ cup packed brown sugar
1½ teaspoons baking soda
1½ teaspoons ground cinnamon
1 teaspoon salt
2 large eggs
1½ cups buttermilk
¼ cup canola oil
1 tablespoon orange juice
3 cups finely chopped peaches
Golden Sauce (see recipe below)

**1** Position the rack in the center of the oven and preheat to 400 degrees F. Lightly grease or line with paper baking cups twenty-four 2¾-inch muffin cups.

**2** In a large bowl, blend together the flour, oats, wheat bran, brown sugar, baking soda, cinna- mon, and salt. In a medium bowl, beat the eggs until foamy. Beat in the buttermilk, oil, and orange juice. Stir in the chopped peach-es. Combine the two mixtures, blending until the dry ingredi-ents are just moistened.

**3** Drop 1 heaping tablespoon of the batter into each of the pre-pared muffin cups. Bake for 15 to 20 minutes, or until a cake tester or wooden toothpick inserted into the center of a muffin comes out clean. Cool in the pan on a wire rack for 5 to 7 minutes. Serve warm, or invert onto the rack to cool completely. Serve with Golden Sauce.

# FRESH FRUIT, OAT, AND BRAN MUFFINS

MAKES: *23 to 24 muffins*

# GOLDEN SAUCE

MAKES: *About ½ cup*

1 large egg yolk
Pinch sea salt
½ cup hot soy milk
Pinch fresh snipped parsley
Pinch fresh snipped chives

In a small bowl, beat the egg and salt together until light-colored. Place the bowl in a larger bowl or pan of hot (not boiling) water. Gradually beat in the hot soy milk. Continue to beat until the mixture thickens. Stir in the parsley and chives and serve hot.

## FRESH PEACH MUFFINS

MAKES: *11 to 12 muffins*

1 cup chopped fresh peaches or
  fresh apricots
1 teaspoon lemon juice
⅔ cup granulated sugar
2 cups all-purpose flour
1 tablespoon baking powder
½ teaspoon ground cinnamon
1 large egg
1 cup milk
¼ cup margarine, melted
Amaretto–Peach Sauce (see recipe
  below)

1  Position the rack in the center of the oven and preheat to 450 degrees F. Lightly grease or line with paper baking cups twelve 2¾-inch muffin cups.

2  Place the peaches in a small bowl and sprinkle them with lemon juice and 1 tablespoon of the sugar. Set aside. In a large bowl, blend together the flour, remaining sugar, baking powder, and cinnamon. In a medium bowl, beat the egg until thick and light-colored. Beat in the milk and margarine. Stir in the peaches. Combine the two mixtures, blending until the dry ingredients are just moistened.

3  Spoon the batter into the prepared muffin cups, filling each about three-quarters full. Bake for 15 to 20 minutes, or until a cake tester or wooden toothpick inserted into the center of a muffin comes out clean. Cool in the pan on a wire rack for 5 to 7 minutes. Serve warm, or invert onto the rack to cool completely. Serve with Amaretto–Peach Sauce.

### AMARETTO– PEACH SAUCE

MAKES: *¼ cup*

¼ cup peach preserves
2 tablespoons Amaretto liqueur

In a small saucepan set over low heat, warm the peach preserve for 3 to 4 minutes before stirring in the Amaretto. Remove from the heat, transfer to a small bowl, and serve at room temperature.

## FRESH PUMPKIN– BUTTERMILK MUFFINS

MAKES: *12 to 14 muffins*

1 cup all-purpose flour
½ cup whole-wheat flour
½ cup granulated sugar
1 teaspoon baking powder
1 teaspoon Cunningham® English
  Mixture (see Note)
½ cup finely chopped pecans or
  hazelnuts
½ teaspoon salt
1 large egg
¼ cup butter, at room temperature
½ cup buttermilk
1 tablespoon Amaretto liqueur or 1
  teaspoon almond extract
1 cup grated fresh pumpkin, with
  rind
Herb Salsa (see recipe page 197)

1  Position the rack in the center of the oven and preheat to 400 degrees F. Lightly grease or line with paper baking cups twelve 2¾-inch muffin cups.

2  In a large bowl, blend together the two flours, sugar, baking powder, spice, nuts, and salt. In a medium bowl, beat the egg until thick and light-colored. Beat in the butter, buttermilk, and Amaretto. Stir in the pumpkin. Combine the two mixtures, blending until the drying ingredients are just moistened.

3  Spoon the batter into the prepared muffin cups, filling each about three-quarters full. Bake for 15 to 20 minutes, or until a cake tester or wooden toothpick inserted into a muffin comes out clean. Cool in the pan on a wire rack for 5 to 7 minutes. Serve warm, or invert onto the rack to cool completely. Serve with Herb Salsa.

NOTE: If you can't find the Cunningham® English mixture use ¾ teaspoon cinnamon and ¼ teaspoon nutmeg.

1 cup all-purpose flour
1 cup All-Bran® cereal
2 tablespoons granulated sugar
1 tablespoon baking powder
1½ cups finely chopped fresh fruit
    of choice (apples, berries,
    peaches, pineapples)
½ teaspoon salt
2 large eggs
1 cup milk
1 teaspoon orange or banana extract
Creamy Raspberry Sauce (see recipe
    below)

1  Position the rack in the center of the oven and preheat to 400 degrees F. Lightly grease or line with paper baking cups twelve 2¾-inch muffin cups.

2  In a large bowl, blend together the flour, cereal, sugar, baking powder, fruit, and salt. In a medium bowl, beat the eggs until thick and light-colored. Beat in the milk and extract. Combine the two mixtures, blending until the dry ingredients are just moistened.

3  Spoon the batter into the prepared muffin cups, filling each about three-quarters full. Bake for 15 to 20 minutes, or until a cake tester or wooden toothpick inserted into the center of a muffin comes out clean. Cool in the pan on a wire rack for 5 to 7 minutes. Serve warm, or invert onto the rack to cool completely. Top with Creamy Raspberry Sauce.

# FRUIT-AND-BRAN MUFFINS
MAKES: *11 to 12 muffins*

# CREAMY RASPBERRY SAUCE
MAKES: *1 to 1¼ cups*

One 10-ounce package frozen red
    raspberries in light syrup,
    thawed
3 tablespoons heavy cream

Place the raspberries in the container of a blender or food processor and process until smooth. Pour into a serving bowl and stir in the cream.

# FRUIT-FILLED MUFFINS

MAKES: *6 to 8 muffins*

2 cups Bisquick® baking mix
2 tablespoons granulated sugar
⅔ cup skim milk
1 tablespoon canola oil
¼ cup cholesterol-free egg product
1 tablespoon Amaretto liqueur
¼ cup fruit preserves
Dutch-Style Hard Sauce (see recipe
  below)

**1** Position the rack in the center of the oven and preheat to 400 degrees F. Lightly grease or line with paper baking cups eight 2¾-inch muffin cups.

**2** In a large bowl, blend together the Bisquick, and sugar. In a medium bowl, beat the milk, oil, Amaretto, and egg product until smooth. Combine the two mixtures, blending until the dry ingredients are just moistened.

**3** Spoon the batter into the prepared muffin cups, filling each about three-quarters full. Using a small spoon, divide the fruit preserves evenly between the cups into the center of each muffin. Bake for 15 to 20 minutes, or until a cake tester or wooden toothpick inserted at the edge of a muffin (not into the preserves) comes out clean. Cool in the pan on a wire rack for 5 to 7 minutes. Serve warm, or invert onto the rack to cool completely. Serve with Dutch-Style Hard Sauce.

## DUTCH-STYLE HARD SAUCE

MAKES: *About ⅔ cup*

¼ cup butter or margarine, at room
  temperature
1 cup powdered sugar
2 tablespoons sour cream or yogurt
¼ teaspoon vanilla extract
Pinch nutmeg

In a small bowl, cream the butter and ½ cup of the powdered sugar together. Stir in the sour cream and vanilla extract before stirring in the remaining sugar, a little at a time, until smooth. Stir in the nutmeg and serve.

# FRUIT-NUT MUFFINS

MAKES: *5 to 6 muffins*

1 cup pitted dates, chopped
1 cup pitted prunes, chopped
½ cup chopped seedless raisins
1 cup water
1 cup all-purpose flour
1 teaspoon baking powder
1 cup chopped walnuts or pecans
½ teaspoon ground nutmeg
¼ teaspoon salt
2 large eggs
½ cup butter or margarine, melted
1 teaspoon vanilla or almond extract
Blender Apricot Sauce (see recipe
  page 25)

**1** Position the rack in the center of the oven and preheat to 375 degrees F. Lightly grease or line with paper baking cups six 3-inch muffin cups.

**2** In a saucepan over a medium heat, combine the dates, prunes, raisins, and water. Bring to a boil and cook, stirring, until the fruit is very soft. Remove from the heat and set aside.

**3** In a large bowl, blend together the flour, baking powder, walnuts, nutmeg, and salt. In a medium bowl, beat the eggs until foamy. Beat in the butter and vanilla extract. Stir in the fruit. Combine the two mixtures, blending until the dry ingredients are just moistened.

**4** Spoon 3 heaping tablespoons of the mixture into the prepared muffin cups, filling each about three-quarters full. Bake 18 to 20 minutes, or until a cake tester or wooden toothpick inserted into the center of a muffin comes out clean. Cool in the pan on a wire rack for 5 to 7 minutes. Serve warm, or invert onto the rack to cool completely. Serve with Blender Apricot Sauce.

1 cup all-purpose flour
¾ cup buckwheat flour
1½ teaspoons baking powder
¼ teaspoon baking soda
⅓ cup granulated sugar
1 cup finely diced Granny Smith
    apples, peeled and cored
¼ cup finely diced dates
¾ cup buttermilk or sour milk
2 tablespoons canola oil
1 large egg
Creamy Glaze (see recipe page 137)

**1** Position the rack in the center of the oven and preheat to 375 degrees F. Lightly grease or line with paper baking cups twelve 2¾-inch muffin cups.

**2** In a large bowl, blend together the flour, buckwheat, baking powder, baking soda, sugar, apples, and dates. In a medium bowl, beat the buttermilk, oil, and egg until smooth. Combine the two mixtures, blending until the dry ingredients are just moistened.

**3** Spoon the batter into the prepared muffin cups, filling each about three-quarters full. Bake for about 18 to 20 minutes, or until a cake tester or wooden toothpick inserted into the center of a muffin comes out clean. Cool in the pan on a wire rack for 5 to 7 minutes. Serve warm, or invert onto the rack to cool completely. Serve with Creamy Glaze.

# FRUITY BUCKWHEAT MUFFINS

MAKES: *11 to 12 muffins*

---

¼ cup chopped dried apricots
¼ cup chopped dried cranberries
warmed brandy
1 cup white corn flour
¼ cup granulated sugar
2 teaspoons baking powder
¼ teaspoon baking soda
¼ teaspoon salt
2 large eggs
2 tablespoons butter or margarine,
    melted
¾ cup milk
Lime Glaze (see recipe page 190)

**1** Place the apricots and cranberries in a small bowl or cup and add the warmed brandy. Set aside for 20 minutes. Meanwhile, position the rack in the center of the oven and preheat to 375 degrees F. Lightly grease or line with paper baking cups twelve 2¾-inch muffin cups.

**2** In a large bowl, blend together the flour, sugar, baking powder, baking soda, and salt. In a medium bowl, beat the eggs until foamy. Beat in the butter and milk. Drain the fruit, saving the brandy for another use, and stir in the fruit. Combine the two mixtures, blending until the dry ingredients are just moistened.

**3** Spoon the batter into the prepared muffin cups, filling each about three-quarters full. Bake for 15 to 20 minutes, or until a cake tester or wooden toothpick inserted into the center of a muffin comes out clean. Cool in the pan on a wire rack for 5 to 7 minutes. Serve warm, or invert onto the rack to cool completely. Brush tops of muffins with Lime Glaze.

# FRUITY MUFFINS

MAKES: *11 to 12 muffins*

# FUDGE MUFFINS

MAKES: *23 to 24 muffins*

4 ounces unsweetened chocolate, grated
1 cup butter or margarine
1 cup all-purpose flour
¼ teaspoon salt
2 cups pecans, finely chopped
1¾ cups granulated sugar
4 large eggs
1 teaspoon chocolate or almond extract
Peanut Butter Sauce (see recipe below)

**1** Position a rack in the center of the oven and preheat to 300 degrees F. Lightly grease or line with paper baking cups twenty-four 2-inch muffin cups.

**2** In the top of a double boiler set over simmering water, combine the chocolate and butter and cook, stirring occasionally, until the mixture is smooth and melted. Remove from the heat and set aside. In a large bowl, blend together the flour, salt, and pecans. Pour the chocolate and butter into another large bowl and beat in the eggs, one at a time, beating vigorously after each addition. Beat in the sugar and almond extract. Combine the two mixtures, blending until the dry ingredients are just moistened.

**3** Spoon 1 heaping tablespoon of the batter into each of the prepared muffin cups. Bake for 12 to 15 minutes, or until a cake tester or wooden toothpick inserted into the center of a muffin comes out clean. Cool in the pan on a wire rack for 5 to 7 minutes. Serve warm, or invert onto the rack to cool completely. Top with Peanut Butter Sauce.

## PEANUT BUTTER SAUCE

MAKES: *1¾ to 2 cups*

1 cup (6 ounces) semisweet chocolate chips
½ cup smooth peanut butter
¾ cup granulated sugar
2 tablespoons all-purpose flour

**1** Place the chocolate chips in the top of a double boiler set over simmering water and cook, stirring, until the chips are melted. Set aside.

**2** In a medium bowl, beat together the peanut butter, sugar, and flour until smooth. Beat in the melted chocolate chips and continue beating until the mixture is smooth. Transfer to a serving bowl.

2 cups all-purpose flour
2 teaspoons baking powder
1 teaspoon garlic powder
1 teaspoon dry mustard powder
¼ cup chopped fresh scallions (green onions)
¼ cup grated fresh carrots (save the greens)
1 teaspoon dried crushed tarragon
½ teaspoon dried crushed thyme
½ teaspoon dried chervil
¼ teaspoon salt
2 large egg whites
1 cup skim milk
2 tablespoons butter or margarine, melted
2 tablespoons sour cream or plain yogurt
Grated Romano cheese for sprinkling
Mustard–Anchovy Spread (see recipe below)

**1** Position the rack in the center of the oven and preheat to 375 degrees F. Lightly grease or line with paper baking cups fourteen 2¾-inch muffin cups.

**2** In a large bowl, blend together the flour, baking powder, garlic powder, mustard, scallions, carrots, thyme, chervil, and salt. In a medium bowl, beat the egg whites until stiff but not dry. Beat in the milk, butter, and sour cream. Combine the two mixtures, blending until the dry ingredients are just moistened.

**3** Spoon the batter into the prepared muffin cups, filling each about three-quarters full. Sprinkle Romano cheese over the tops of the muffins. Bake for 15 to 20 minutes, or until a cake tester or wooden toothpick inserted into the center of a muffin comes out clean. Cool in the pan on a wire rack for 5 to 7 minutes. Serve warm, or invert onto the rack to cool completely. Serve with Mustard–Anchovy Spread.

# GARDEN HERB MUFFINS

MAKES: *12 to 14 muffins*

# MUSTARD–ANCHOVY SPREAD

MAKES: *About 1 cup*

1 cup butter, at room temperature
2 tablespoons anchovy paste
5 teaspoons dry mustard powder
½ teaspoon Worcestershire sauce

In a small bowl, using an electric mixer on medium speed, beat all of the ingredients together until smooth. Cover with plastic wrap and refrigerate until ready to serve.

---

1½ cups all-purpose flour
⅔ cup yellow cornmeal
4 teaspoons granulated sugar
1 tablespoon baking powder
½ teaspoon baking soda
1½ teaspoons garlic powder
1¼ teaspoons salt
2 large eggs
½ cup butter or margarine, melted
1 cup buttermilk or sour milk
1 cup whole-kernel corn
Herb Butter (see recipe page 149)

**1** Position the rack in the center of the oven and preheat to 425 degrees F. Lightly grease or line with paper baking cups fourteen 2¾-inch muffin cups.

**2** In a large bowl, blend together the flour, cornmeal, sugar, baking powder, baking soda, garlic powder, and salt. In a medium bowl, beat the eggs until thick and light-colored. Beat in the butter and buttermilk. Stir in the corn. Combine the two mixtures, blending until the dry ingredients are just moistened.

**3** Spoon the batter into the prepared muffin cups, filling each about three-quarters full. Bake for 15 to 20 minutes, or until a cake tester or wooden toothpick inserted into the center of a muffin comes out clean. Cool in the pan on a wire rack for 5 to 7 minutes. Serve warm, or invert onto the rack to cool completely. Top with Herb Butter.

# GARLIC-AND-CORN MUFFINS

MAKES: *12 to 14 muffins*

# GARLIC MUFFINS

MAKES: *12 to 14 muffins*

2 cups all-purpose flour
4 teaspoons baking powder
2 teaspoons granulated sugar
1 tablespoon garlic powder
¼ teaspoon salt
2 tablespoons freshly snipped
    chives
1 large egg
1 cup milk
3 tablespoons butter or margarine,
    melted
Garlic Sauce (see recipe below)

**1** Position the rack in the center of the oven and preheat to 375 degrees F. Lightly grease or line with paper baking cups fourteen 2¾-inch muffin cups.

**2** In a large bowl, blend together the flour, baking powder, sugar, garlic powder, salt, and chives. In a medium bowl, beat the egg until thick and light-colored. Beat in the milk and butter. Combine the two mixtures, blending until the dry ingredients are just moistened.

**3** Spoon the batter into the prepared muffin cups, filling each about three-quarters full. Bake for 15 to 20 minutes, or until a cake tester or wooden toothpick inserted into the center of a muffin comes out clean. Cool in the pan on a wire rack for 5 to 7 minutes. Serve warm, or invert onto the rack to cool completely. Serve with Garlic Sauce.

## GARLIC SAUCE

MAKES: *About 2 cups*

3 medium heads of garlic, cloves
    separated, peeled, and mashed
1½ cups fresh chicken broth

**1** In a medium saucepan, combine the garlic and chicken broth and set over medium-high heat. Bring to a boil, cover, reduce heat to low, and let simmer undisturbed for at least 25 minutes.

**2** Remove from the heat, cool to room temperature, and pour into the container of a blender. Process on low speed until smooth. Pour into a bowl and serve.

# GERMAN CABBAGE MUFFINS

MAKES: *12 to 14 muffins*

1¾ cups all-purpose flour
1 tablespoon baking powder
2 cups finely grated cabbage
2 teaspoons celery seeds
2 tablespoons finely minced onion
1 teaspoon salt
2 large eggs
1 tablespoon granulated sugar
¾ cup skim milk
6 tablespoons butter or margarine,
    melted
Olive Spread (see recipe page 164)

**1** Position the rack in the center of the oven and preheat to 400 degrees F. Lightly grease or line with paper baking cups fourteen 2¾-inch muffin cups.

**2** In a large bowl, blend together the flour, baking powder, cabbage, celery seeds, onions, and salt. In a medium bowl, beat the eggs until foamy. Beat in the sugar, milk, and butter. Combine the two mixtures, blending until the dry ingredients are just moistened.

**3** Spoon the batter into the prepared muffin cups, filling each about three-quarters full. Bake for 18 to 20 minutes, or until a cake tester or wooden toothpick inserted into the center of a muffin comes out clean. Cool in the pan on a wire rack for 5 to 7 minutes. Serve warm, or invert onto the rack to cool completely. Serve with Olive Spread.

¾ cup butter or margarine, at room temperature
½ cup granulated sugar
2 large eggs
4 teaspoons rum
1 teaspoon vanilla extract
3 tablespoons milk
2¼ cups all-purpose flour
2 teaspoons baking powder
½ teaspoon ground cinnamon
¼ teaspoon salt
¼ cup finely ground hazelnuts
1 tablespoon grated orange zest
¼ cup seedless raisins

**1** Position the rack in the center of the oven and preheat to 375 degrees F. Lightly grease or line with paper baking cups sixteen 2-inch muffin cups.

**2** In a medium bowl, beat the butter and sugar light and fluffy before beating in the eggs, rum, vanilla, and milk. In a large bowl, blend together the flour, baking powder, cinnamon, salt, hazelnuts, orange zest, and raisins. Combine the two mixtures, blending until the dry ingredients are just moistened.

**3** Spoon the batter into the prepared muffin cups, filling each about three-quarters full. Bake for 15 to 20 minutes, or until a cake tester or wooden toothpick inserted into the center of a muffin comes out clean. Cool in the pan on a wire rack for 5 to 7 minutes. Serve warm, or invert onto the rack to cool completely.

# GERMAN MUFFINS
MAKES: *15 to 16 muffins*

---

2 cups all-purpose flour
1 tablespoon baking powder
½ teaspoon baking soda
One 2-inch-long piece fresh ginger root, peeled and finely chopped
¼ teaspoon salt
¾ cup grated Muenster cheese
1 large egg
½ cup milk
½ cup molasses
¼ cup butter or shortening, melted
Golden Cheese Sauce (see recipe below)

**1** Position the rack in the center of the oven and preheat to 375 degrees F. Lightly grease or line with paper baking cups fourteen 2¾-inch muffin cups.

**2** In a large bowl, blend together the flour, baking powder, baking soda, ginger, and ½ cup of cheese. In a medium bowl, beat the egg until thick and light-colored. Beat in the milk, molasses, and butter. Combine the two mixtures, blending until the dry ingredients are just moistened.

**3** Spoon the batter into the prepared muffin cups, filling each about three-quarters full. Sprinkle the remaining cheese over the tops of the muffins. Bake for 15 to 20 minutes, or until the tops are golden brown and a cake tester or wooden toothpick inserted into the center of a muffin comes out clean. Cool in the pan on a wire rack for 5 to 7 minutes. Serve warm, or invert onto the rack to cool completely. Serve with Golden Cheese Sauce.

# GINGER-AND-CHEESE MUFFINS
MAKES: *12 to 14 muffins*

## GOLDEN CHEESE SAUCE
MAKES: *About 1 cup*

½ pound Velveeta® processed cheese, diced
¼ cup heavy cream
1 tablespoon finely chopped pitted ripe olives

In the top of a double boiler set over simmering water, combine all of the ingredients. Cook, stirring occasionally, until smooth. Remove from the heat and serve.

# GINGER-AND-MOLASSES MUFFINS

MAKES: *29 to 30 muffins*

3 cups all-purpose flour
½ cup graham flour
1½ teaspoons baking powder
1 teaspoon baking soda
2 teaspoons ground allspice
¼ cup finely chopped fresh, peeled ginger root
¼ teaspoon salt
¼ cup finely chopped pecans
1 cup golden raisins (optional)
4 large eggs, separated
1 cup granulated sugar
½ cup butter or margarine, melted
1 cup molasses
1 cup sour milk or buttermilk
Molasses Sauce (see recipe page 125)

**1** Position the rack in the center of the oven and preheat to 375 degrees F. Lightly grease or line with paper baking cups thirty 2¾-inch muffin cups.

**2** In a large bowl, blend together the two flours, baking powder, baking soda, allspice, ginger, salt, pecans, and raisins. In a medium bowl, beat the egg whites until stiff but not dry. Beating in the sugar, butter, molasses, and buttermilk. Combine the two mixtures, blending until the dry ingredients are just moistened.

**3** Spoon the batter into the prepared muffin cups, filling each about three-quarters full. Bake for 15 to 20 minutes, or until the tops are golden brown and a cake tester or wooden toothpick inserted into the center of a muffin comes out clean. Cool in the pan on a wire rack for 5 to 7 minutes. Serve warm, or invert onto the rack to cool completely. Serve with Molasses Sauce.

# GINGER–APRICOT MUFFINS

MAKES: *14 to 16 muffins*

1¾ cups all-purpose flour
2½ teaspoons baking powder
1½ teaspoons ground ginger
3 tablespoons granulated sugar
¼ teaspoon salt
¾ cup finely chopped dried apricots
1½ teaspoons fresh grated lemon zest
1 large egg
¾ cup milk
⅓ cup butter or margarine, melted
Amaretto–Apricot Cream (see recipe page 82)

**1** Position the rack in the center of the oven and preheat to 400 degrees F. Lightly grease or line with paper baking cups sixteen 2¾-inch muffin cups.

**2** In a large bowl, blend together the flour, baking powder, ginger, sugar, salt, apricots, and lemon zest. In a medium bowl, beat the egg until foamy. Beat in the milk and butter. Combine the two mixtures, blending until the dry ingredients are just moistened.

**3** Drop 1 heaping tablespoon of the mixture into each of the prepared muffin cups. Bake for 15 to 20 minutes, or until a cake tester or wooden toothpick inserted into the center of a muffin comes out clean. Cool in the pan on a wire rack for 5 to 7 minutes. Serve warm, or invert onto the rack to cool completely. Serve with Amaretto–Apricot Cream.

1 cup all-purpose flour
½ cup whole-wheat flour
2 tablespoons granulated sugar
2 teaspoons baking powder
2 teaspoons ground ginger
1 teaspoon ground cinnamon
¼ teaspoon ground cloves
¼ teaspoon salt
½ cup seedless raisins
1 large egg
¼ cup molasses
¼ cup water
¼ cup canola oil
¼ teaspoon cider vinegar
Ginger Cream (see recipe page 21)

1 Position the rack in the center of the oven and preheat to 375 degrees F. Lightly grease or line with paper baking cups twelve 2¾-inch muffin cups.

2 In a large bowl, blend together the two flours, sugar, baking powder, ginger, cinnamon, cloves, salt, and raisins. In a medium bowl, beat the egg until foamy. Beat in the molasses, water, oil, and vinegar. Combine the two mixtures, blending until the dry ingredients are just moistened.

3 Spoon the batter into the prepared muffin cups, filling each about three-quarters full. Bake for 15 to 20 minutes or until a cake tester or wooden toothpick inserted into the center of a muffin comes out clean. Cool in the pan on a wire rack for 5 to 7 minutes. Serve warm, or invert onto the rack to cool completely. Serve with Ginger Cream.

# GINGER MUFFINS

MAKES: *11 to 12 muffins*

1½ cups all-purpose flour
1 cup oat bran
1 teaspoon baking powder
1 teaspoon baking soda
1 teaspoon ground ginger
½ teaspoon ground cinnamon
⅛ teaspoon ground cardamom
3 tablespoons packed light-brown sugar
1 teaspoon nonfat dry milk powder
½ cup golden raisins
½ teaspoon salt
2 large egg whites
¼ cup molasses
¼ cup butter or margarine, melted
¾ cup sour milk or buttermilk
1 teaspoon canola oil
1 teaspoon vanilla extract
Marshmallow Sauce (see recipe page 131)

1 Position the rack in the center of the oven and preheat to 400 degrees F. Lightly grease or line with paper baking cups twelve 2¾-inch muffin cups.

2 In a large bowl, blend together the flour, oat bran, baking powder, baking soda, ginger, cinnamon, cardamom, brown sugar, milk powder, raisins, and salt. In a medium bowl, beat the egg whites until stiff but not dry. Beat in the molasses, butter, milk, oil, and vanilla extract. Combine the two mixtures, blending until the dry ingredients are just moistened.

3 Spoon the batter into the prepared muffin cups, filling each about three-quarters full. Bake for 15 to 20 minutes, or until a cake tester or wooden toothpick inserted into the center of a muffin comes out clean. Cool in the pan on a wire rack for 5 to 7 minutes. Serve warm, or invert onto the rack to cool completely. Top with Marshmallow Sauce.

# GINGERBREAD MUFFINS

MAKES: *11 to 12 muffins*

# GOOD MORNING MUFFINS

MAKES: *9 to 10 muffins*

1½ cups all-purpose flour
2 teaspoons baking powder
12 slices crisply cooked bacon, crumbled
¾ cup shredded Cheddar cheese
pinch freshly ground black pepper
⅛ teaspoon salt
4 large eggs
¾ cup milk
1½ tablespoons packed brown sugar
¼ cup butter or margarine, melted
Lemon Butter (see recipe page 236)

1  Position the rack in the center of the over and preheat to 375 degrees F. Lightly grease or line with paper baking cups ten 2¾-inch muffin cups.

2  In a large bowl, blend together the flour, baking powder, bacon, cheese, pepper, and salt. In a medium bowl, beat the eggs, milk, sugar, and butter until smooth. Combine the two mixtures, blending until the dry ingredients are just moistened.

3  Spoon the mixture into the prepared muffin cups, filling each about three-quarters full. Bake for 15 to 20 minutes, or until a cake tester or wooden toothpick inserted into the center of a muffin comes out clean. Cool in the pan on a wire rack for 5 to 7 minutes. Serve warm, or invert onto the rack to cool completely. Serve with Lemon Butter.

# GRAHAM MUFFINS

MAKES: *11 to 12 muffins*

2 cups graham flour
1 cup all-purpose flour
2 tablespoons granulated sugar
2 teaspoons baking powder
¾ teaspoon baking soda
½ teaspoon salt
1 large egg
1½ cups sour milk or buttermilk
2 tablespoons vegetable shortening, melted
Hot Artichoke Sauce (see recipe below)

1  Position the rack in the center of the oven and preheat to 400 degrees F. Lightly grease or line with paper baking cups twelve 2¾-inch muffin cups.

2  In a large bowl, blend together the two flours, sugar, baking powder, baking soda, and salt. In a medium bowl, beat the egg until foamy. Beat in the milk and shortening. Combine the two mixtures, blending until the dry ingredients are just moistened.

3  Spoon the batter into the prepared muffin cups, filling each about three-quarters full. Bake for 15 to 20 minutes, or until a cake tester or wooden toothpick inserted into the center of a muffin comes out clean. Cool in the pan on a wire rack for 5 to 7 minutes. Serve warm, or invert onto the rack to cool completely. Serve with Hot Artichoke Sauce.

## HOT ARTICHOKE SAUCE

MAKES: *About 2 cups*

½ cup mayonnaise
½ cup sour cream or yogurt
One 14-ounce can artichoke hearts, drained and finely chopped
⅓ cup grated Parmesan or Romano cheese
⅛ teaspoon Tabasco® sauce

In a medium saucepan, combine all of the ingredients and stir until combined. Place the pan over low heat and cook, stirring frequently, until the mixture comes to a slow boil. Remove from the heat and serve warm.

## GRANOLA MUFFINS

MAKES: *11 to 12 muffins*

1 cup all-purpose flour
1¾ cups granola cereal
¼ cup granulated sugar
2½ teaspoons baking powder
½ cup seedless raisins
1 large egg
1 cup milk
¼ cup canola oil
Caramel Sauce (see recipe page 32)

**1** Position the rack in the center of the oven and preheat to 375 degrees F. Lightly grease or line with paper baking cups twelve 2¾-inch muffin cups.

**2** In a large bowl, blend together the flour, cereal, sugar, baking powder, and raisins. In a medium bowl, beat the egg until thick and light-colored. Beat in the milk and oil. Combine the two mixtures, blending until the dry ingredients are just moistened.

**3** Spoon the batter into the prepared muffin cups, filling each about three-quarters full. Bake for 15 to 20 minutes, or until a cake tester or wooden toothpick inserted into the center of a muffin comes out clean. Cool in the pan on a wire rack for 5 to 7 minutes. Serve warm, or invert onto the rack to cool completely. Top with hot Caramel Sauce.

## GRAPE MUFFINS

MAKES: *11 to 12 muffins*

1 cup whole-wheat flour
1 cup cornmeal
1 tablespoon baking powder
¼ teaspoon salt
¼ teaspoon ground allspice
½ cup finely chopped pecans, plus more for topping the muffins
1 large egg
1 tablespoon canola oil
¼ cup grape-flavored yogurt (or berry-flavored yogurt)
1¼ cups grape-juice concentrate
1 teaspoon lemon juice
Herbed Orange Sauce (see recipe below)

**1** Position the rack in the center of oven and preheat to 375 degrees F. Lightly grease or line with paper baking cups twelve 2¾-inch muffin cups.

**2** In a large bowl, blend together the flour, cornmeal, baking powder, salt, allspice, and pecans. In a medium bowl, beat the egg until foamy. Beat in the oil, yogurt, grape juice, and lemon juice. Combine the two mixtures, blending until the dry ingredients are just moistened.

**3** Spoon the batter into the prepared muffin cups, filling each about three-quarters full. Sprinkle the tops of the muffins lightly with pecans. Bake for 15 to 20 minutes, or until a cake tester or wooden toothpick inserted into the center of a muffin comes out clean. Cool in the pan on a wire rack for 5 to 7 minutes. Serve warm, or invert onto the rack to cool completely. Top with Herbed Orange Sauce.

## HERBED ORANGE SAUCE

MAKES: *About 1 cup*

½ teaspoon grated orange zest
½ cup fresh orange juice
⅓ cup chicken broth
¼ cup sliced scallions (green onions)
2 teaspoons cornstarch
½ teaspoon dried crushed basil
2 packets Equal® artificial sweetener
Salt and pepper to taste

In a medium saucepan set over medium heat, combine the orange zest, orange juice, broth, scallions, cornstarch, and basil and cook, stirring frequently, until the mixture boils and thickens. Remove from the heat and stir in the Equal. Season to taste with salt and pepper and serve hot.

# GRATED CHEESE MUFFINS WITH CHIVES

MAKES: *9 to 10 muffins*

1¾ cups all-purpose flour
1 tablespoon granulated sugar
1 tablespoon baking powder
½ cup grated Cheddar cheese
½ teaspoon salt
1 large egg
3 tablespoons butter, melted
1 cup milk
Olive Spread (see recipe below)

**1** Position the rack in the center of the oven and preheat to 375 degrees F. Lightly grease or line with paper baking cups ten 2¾-inch muffin cups.

**2** In a large bowl, blend together the flour, sugar, baking powder, cheese, and salt. In a medium bowl, beat the egg, butter, and milk until smooth. Combine the two mixtures, blending until the dry ingredients are just moistened.

**3** Spoon the batter into the prepared muffin cups, filling each about three-quarters full. Bake for 15 to 20 minutes, or until a cake tester or wooden toothpick inserted into the center of a muffin comes out clean. Cool in the pan on a wire rack for 5 to 7 minutes. Serve warm, or invert onto the rack to cool completely. Serve with Olive Spread.

## OLIVE SPREAD

MAKES: *About 2 cups*

**3 cups pitted black olives**
**⅓ cup extra-virgin olive oil**

In the container of a blender or food processor, combine the olives and oil and process until smooth. Pour into a small bowl and serve.

# GREEN PEA SOUP MUFFINS

MAKES: *12 to 14 muffins*

2 cups all-purpose flour
½ cup oats
4 teaspoons baking powder
½ teaspoon onion powder
2 large eggs
One 16-ounce can Progresso® split-pea soup
3 tablespoons butter or shortening, melted
Soupy Sauce (see recipe below)

**1** Position the rack in the center of the oven and preheat to 375 degrees F. Lightly grease or line with paper baking cups fourteen 2¾-inch muffin cups.

**2** In a large bowl, blend together the flour, oats, baking powder, and onion powder. In a medium bowl, beat the eggs foamy before beating in the soup and butter. Combine the two mixtures, blending until the dry ingredients are just moistened.

**3** Spoon the batter into the prepared muffin cups, filling each about three-quarters full. Bake for 15 to 20 minutes, or until a cake tester or wooden toothpick inserted into the center of a muffin comes out clean. Cool in the pan on a wire rack for 5 to 7 minutes. Serve warm, or invert onto the rack to cool completely. Top with Soupy Sauce.

## SOUPY SAUCE

MAKES: *About 2 cups*

**One 5-ounce package Knorr®**
**vegetable soup mix**
**One 16-ounce container sour cream**

In a medium bowl, blend the soup mix and sour cream together until smooth. Refrigerate until ready to serve.

One 14.5-ounce can cut green beans
2 cups all-purpose flour
½ cup graham flour
1 tablespoon granulated sugar
1 tablespoon baking powder
½ cup crumbled feta cheese
¼ teaspoon ground nutmeg
½ teaspoon salt
2 large eggs
1 cup milk
2 tablespoons butter or margarine, melted
¼ teaspoon prepared mustard
Energy Drink (see recipe below)

1  Position the rack in the center of the oven and preheat to 375 degrees F. Lightly grease or line with paper baking cups fourteen 2¾-inch muffin cups.

2  Drain the can of beans and finely chop them. Set aside. In a large bowl, blend together the two flours, sugar, baking powder, cheese, nutmeg, and salt. In a medium bowl, beat the egg, milk, butter, and mustard until smooth. Sir in the beans. Combine the two mixtures, blending until the dry ingredients are just moistened.

3  Spoon the batter into the prepared muffin cups, filling each about three-quarters full. Bake for 15 to 20 minutes, or until a cake tester or wooden toothpick inserted into the center of a muffin comes out clean. Cool in the pan on a wire rack for 5 to 7 minutes. Serve warm, or invert onto the rack to cool completely. Serve with an Energy Drink.

# GREEN BEAN MUFFINS

MAKES: *12 to 14 muffins*

# ENERGY DRINK

MAKES: *About 2 cups*

½ cup prune juice
½ cup skim milk
1 large egg
1 small banana, sliced
1 tablespoon wheat germ
1 teaspoon orange-juice concentrate
1 teaspoon vanilla or almond extract

In the container of a blender, combine all of the ingredients and process on medium speed until smooth. Pour over several ice cubes in a tall glass.

# HASH MUFFINS

MAKES: *11 to 12 muffins*

2 cups all-purpose flour
1 cup whole-wheat flour
2 teaspoons baking powder
½ teaspoon baking soda
½ teaspoon dry mustard
3 large eggs
1½ cups milk
⅓ cup canola oil
One 15-ounce can corned beef hash
Sabayon Sauce (see recipe below)

1  Position the rack in the center of the oven and preheat to 375 degrees F. Lightly grease or line with paper baking cups twelve 2¾-inch muffin cups.

2  In a large bowl, blend together the two flours, baking powder, baking soda, and mustard. In a medium bowl, beat the eggs until foamy. Beat in the milk, oil, and hash. Combine the two mixtures, blending until the dry ingredients are just moistened.

3  Spoon the batter into the prepared muffin cups, filling each about three-quarters full. Bake for 15 to 20 minutes, or until a cake tester or wooden toothpick inserted into the center of a muffin comes out clean. Cool in the pan on a wire rack for 5 to 7 minutes. Serve warm, or invert onto the rack to cool completely. Top with Sabayon Sauce.

## SABAYON SAUCE

MAKES: *1⅔ cups*

4 large egg yolks
⅔ cup granulated sugar
1 cup white wine or Marsala wine
1 tablespoon Kirsch or rum

In the top of a double boiler set over simmering water, add the egg yolks and sugar and cook, whisking constantly, until they are thick and light-colored. Gradually whisk in the white wine. Continue whisking until the mixture is thick and creamy. (Do not overcook or the sauce will curdle.) Remove from the heat and beat in the Kirsch.

2 cups all-purpose flour
2 teaspoons baking powder
½ teaspoon baking soda
½ cup chopped macadamia nuts
½ cup crushed pineapple, canned
  and drained
½ teaspoon salt
2 large eggs
¼ cup packed light-brown sugar
¼ cup butter or margarine, melted
¾ cup milk
Ham Salad (see recipe below)

**1** Position the rack in the center of the oven and preheat to 400 degrees F. Lightly grease or line with paper baking cups twelve 2¾-inch muffin cups.

**2** In a large bowl, blend together the flour, baking powder, baking soda, nuts, pineapple, and salt. In a medium bowl, beat the eggs until foamy. Beat in the sugar, butter, and milk. Combine the two mixtures, blending until the dry ingredients are just moistened.

**3** Spoon the batter into the prepared muffin cups, filling each about three-quarters full. Bake for 15 to 20 minutes, or until a cake tester or wooden toothpick inserted into the center of a muffin comes out clean. Cool in the pan on a wire rack for 5 to 7 minutes. Serve warm, or invert onto the rack to cool completely. Serve with Ham Salad.

# HAWAIIAN NUT MUFFINS

MAKES: *11 to 12 muffins*

# HAM SALAD

MAKES: *About 2½ cups*

1½ cups ground cooked ham
2 hard cooked eggs, chopped
½ cup minced green bell pepper
½ cup minced celery
½ cup mayonnaise
2 tablespoons vinegar
2 tablespoons snipped chives

In a bowl, blend together the ham, eggs, pepper, and celery. Stir in the mayonnaise and vinegar. Sprinkle with chives and serve.

# HEIRLOOM RAISIN MUFFINS

MAKES: *5 to 6 muffins*

1 cup raisins
½ cup warmed brandy
1½ cups all-purpose flour
1 teaspoon baking powder
¼ cup granulated sugar
½ cup butter or margarine, at room temperature
2 large eggs, at room temperature
Apple–Cinnamon Syrup (see recipe below)

**1** Place the raisins in a cup or small bowl and pour in the brandy. Set aside for 20 minutes. Meanwhile, position the rack in the center of the oven and preheat to 400 degrees F. Lightly grease or line with paper baking cups six 3-inch muffin cups.

**2** Drain the raisins, discarding the brandy or saving it for another use. In a large bowl, blend together the flour, baking powder, and drained raisins. In a small bowl, cream the sugar and butter together. Beat in the eggs, one at a time, beating well after each addition. Combine the two mixtures, blending until the dry ingredients are just moistened.

**3** Drop 3 heaping tablespoons of the batter into each of the prepared muffin cups, filling each about three-quarters full. Bake for about 18 to 22 minutes, or until a cake tester or wooden toothpick inserted into the center of a muffin comes out clean. Cool in the pan on a wire rack for 5 to 7 minutes. Serve warm, or invert onto the rack to cool completely. Top with Apple–Cinnamon Syrup.

## APPLE–CINNAMON SYRUP

MAKES: *About 1 cup*

1 cup unsweetened apple juice
1½ tablespoons tapioca dessert mix
½ teaspoon ground cinnamon

In a small saucepan, combine all of the ingredients and let stand at room temperature for 5 minutes. Place the pan over medium heat and, stirring constantly, bring to a boil. Remove from the heat, cover and refrigerate until ready to use.

3 tablespoons olive oil
¼ cup packed light-brown sugar
2 cups coarsely chopped onions
3 cups all-purpose flour
¼ cup baking powder
1 teaspoon crushed cumin seeds
1 teaspoon crushed red-pepper
  flakes
¼ cup chopped fresh parsley
1 tablespoon chopped fresh tarragon
2 large eggs
6 tablespoons butter or margarine,
  melted
1⅓ cups milk
2 cups finely chopped pre-cooked
  polenta
Pesto Cream (see recipe below)

**1** Position the rack in the center of the oven and preheat to 375 degrees F. Lightly grease or line with paper baking cups twenty 2¾-inch muffin cups.

**2** In a medium skillet set over a medium heat, combine the olive oil and brown sugar. As soon as the sugar has melted, add the chopped onion and cook, stirring frequently, until the onions have turned a dark golden color. Remove from the heat and set aside to cool.

**3** In a large bowl, blend together the flour, baking powder, cumin, red-pepper flakes, parsley, and tarragon. In a medium bowl, combine the eggs, butter, and milk and beat until smooth. Stir in the polenta, stirring until combined but still slightly lumpy. Combine the two mixtures with three strokes. Add the onions and continue to stir until the dry ingredients are just moistened and the onions are well incorporated.

**4** Spoon the batter into the prepared muffin cups, filling each about three-quarters full. Bake for about 20 to 25 minutes, or until a cake tester or wooden toothpick inserted into the center of a muffin comes out clean. Cool in the pan on a wire rack for 5 to 7 minutes. Serve warm, or invert onto the rack to cool completely. Serve with Pesto Cream.

# Herbal Muffins with Polenta

Makes: *18 to 20 muffins*

## Pesto Cream

Makes: *½ cup*

½ cup sour cream
2 tablespoons bottled pesto sauce

In a small bowl or cup, blend together the sour cream and pesto until smooth.

---

1 cup all-purpose flour
1 tablespoon baking powder
3 cups canola cereal
½ teaspoon ground cinnamon
Pinch salt
1 large egg
⅓ cup packed light-brown sugar
1 cup milk
⅓ cup canola oil
Energy Drink (see recipe page 165)

**1** Position the rack in the center of the oven and preheat to 400 degrees F. Lightly grease or line with paper baking cups twelve 2¾-inch muffin cups.

**2** In a large bowl, blend together the flour, baking powder, cereal, cinnamon, and salt. In a medium bowl, beat the egg until foamy. Beat in the brown sugar, milk, and oil. Combine the two mixtures, blending until the dry ingredients are just moistened.

**3** Spoon the batter into the prepared muffin cups, filling each about three-quarters full. Bake for 15 to 20 minutes, or until a cake tester or wooden toothpick inserted into the center of a muffin comes out clean. Cool in the pan on a wire rack for 5 to 7 minutes. Serve warm, or invert onto the rack to cool completely. Serve with Energy Drink.

# High-Fiber Muffins

Makes: *11 to 12 muffins*

# HIGH-PROTEIN MUFFINS

MAKES: *9 to 10 muffins*

**1½ cups seedless raisins**
**½ cup warmed brandy**
**1 cup soy flour**
**1 cup whole-wheat flour**
**4 teaspoons baking powder**
**1 cup toasted wheat germ**
**1 teaspoon ground nutmeg**
**½ teaspoon ground cinnamon**
**¼ teaspoon salt**
**2½ cups 40% Bran Flakes®**
**1¾ cups milk**
**⅔ cup honey**
**¼ cup dark molasses**
**4 large eggs**
**⅔ cup canola oil**
**Yogurt Cream (see recipe page 55)**

**1** Place the raisins in a small bowl and add the warmed brandy. Set aside for 20 minutes. Meanwhile, position the rack in the center of the oven and preheat to 375 degrees F. Lightly grease or line with paper baking cups ten 3-inch muffin cups.

**2** In a large bowl, blend together the two flours, baking powder, wheat germ, nutmeg, cinnamon, salt, and cereal. In a medium bowl, beat the milk, honey, molasses, eggs, and oil until smooth. Combine the two mixes until the dry ingredients are just moistened. Drain the raisins, discarding the brandy or saving it for another use. Fold the drained raisins into the batter.

**3** Drop 3 heaping tablespoons of the mixture into each of the prepared muffin cups, filling each about three-quarters full. Sprinkle with the topping and bake for 20 to 25 minutes, or until a cake tester or wooden toothpick inserted into the center of a muffin comes out clean. Remove from oven and cool in the pan on a wire rack for 5 to 7 minutes. Serve warm, or invert onto the rack to cool completely. Serve with Yogurt Cream.

# HONEY–ALL-BRAN MUFFINS

MAKES: *5 to 6 muffins*

**2 cups all-purpose flour**
**2 cups All-Bran® cereal**
**1½ teaspoons baking powder**
**1 teaspoon baking soda**
**⅓ cup chopped walnuts**
**1 teaspoon salt**
**1 large egg**
**⅓ cup honey**
**1¾ cups sour milk or buttermilk**
**3 tablespoons butter or margarine, melted**
**Zucchini Spread (see recipe below)**

**1** Position the rack in the center of the oven and preheat to 400 degrees F. Lightly grease or line with paper baking cups six 3-inch muffin cups.

**2** In a large bowl, blend together the flour, cereal, baking powder, baking soda, walnuts, and salt. In a medium bowl, beat the egg, honey, milk, and butter until smooth. Combine the two mixtures, blending until the dry ingredients are just moistened.

**3** Drop 3 heaping tablespoons of the batter into the prepared muffin cups, filling each about three-quarters full. Bake for 15 to 20 minutes, or until a cake tester or wooden toothpick inserted into the center of a muffin comes out clean. Remove from the oven and brush the tops of the muffins with the honey glaze before cooling on a wire rack for 5 to 7 minutes. Serve warm, or transfer to the rack to cool completely. Serve with Zucchini Spread.

## ZUCCHINI SPREAD

MAKES: *About 1½ cups*

**1 cup chopped zucchini**
**½ cup mayonnaise**
**1 tablespoon honey**
**¼ cup seedless raisins, finely chopped**

In the container of a blender, combine the zucchini, mayonnaise, honey and raisins and process on medium speed until smooth. Pour into a small bowl and serve.

1 cup all-purpose flour
½ cup whole-wheat flour
2 teaspoons baking powder
1 teaspoon fresh grated orange zest
½ teaspoon salt
1 large egg
½ cup milk
½ cup honey
¼ cup butter or margarine, melted
½ cup chopped cooked prunes
Apple–Cinnamon Glaze (see recipe
    below)

**1** Position the rack in the center of the oven and preheat to 400 degrees F. Lightly grease or line with paper baking cups ten 2¾-inch muffin cups.

**2** In a large bowl, blend together the two flours, baking powder, orange zest, and salt. In a medi-um bowl, beat the egg, milk, honey, and butter until smooth. Stir in the prunes. Combine the two mixtures, blending until the dry ingredients are just moistened.

**3** Spoon the batter into the pre-pared muffin cups, filling each about three-quarters full. Bake for 15 to 20 minutes, or until a cake tester or wooden toothpick inserted into the center of a muffin comes out clean. Cool on the wire rack for 5 to 7 minutes. Serve warm, or invert onto the rack to cool completely. Brush with Apple–Cinnamon Glaze.

# Honey-and-Prune Muffins

MAKES: *8 to 10 muffins*

# Apple–Cinnamon Glaze

MAKES: *¼ cup*

¼ cup frozen apple-juice
    concentrate, thawed
1 teaspoon cornstarch
¼ teaspoon ground cinnamon

In a small cup, using a fork or the back of a spoon, combine the apple juice and cornstarch. Pour the mixture into a small saucepan, stir in the cinnamon, and set the saucepan over low heat. Stir constantly until thickened.

2 cups all-purpose flour
1 tablespoon baking powder
1 teaspoon salt
1 large egg
1 cup milk
¼ cup honey
¼ cup butter or margarine, melted
½ cup blueberries
Whipped Hot Chocolate (see recipe
    page 36)

**1** Position the rack in the center of the oven and preheat to 400 degrees F. Lightly grease or line with paper baking cups fourteen 2¾-inch muffin cups.

**2** In a large bowl, blend together the flour, baking powder, and salt. In a medium bowl, beat the egg, milk, honey, and butter until smooth. Combine the two mixtures, blending until the dry ingredients are just moistened. Stir in the blueberries.

**3** Spoon the batter into the pre-pared muffin cups, filling each about three-quarters full. Bake for 15 to 20 minutes, or until a cake tester or wooden toothpick inserted into the center of a muffin comes out clean. Cool in the pan on a wire rack for 5 to 7 minutes. Serve warm, or invert onto the rack to cool completely. Serve with Whipped Hot Chocolate.

# Honey–Blueberry Muffins

MAKES: *12 to 14 muffins*

# HONEY–BRAN MUFFINS

MAKES: *7 to 8 muffins*

1 cup all-purpose flour
1 cup bran
2 teaspoons baking powder
¼ cup finely chopped dates
¼ cup chopped walnuts
½ teaspoon salt
1 large egg
½ cup milk
¼ cup honey
1 tablespoon butter or margarine, melted

**1** Position the rack in the center of the oven and preheat to 400 degrees F. Lightly grease or line with paper baking cups eight 2¾-inch muffin cups.

**2** In a large bowl, blend together the flour, bran, baking powder, dates, walnuts, and salt. In a medium bowl, beat the egg, milk, honey, and butter until smooth. Combine the two mixtures, blending until the dry ingredients are just moistened.

**3** Spoon the batter into the prepared muffin cups, filling each about three-quarters full. Bake for 15 to 20 minutes, or until a cake tester or wooden toothpick inserted into the center of a muffin comes out clean. Cool in the pan on a wire rack for 5 to 7 minutes. Serve warm, or invert onto the rack to cool completely.

**SERVING SUGGESTION: Serve with fruit preserves.**

# HONEY–CRUNCH MUFFINS

MAKES: *12 to 14 muffins*

2¼ cups all-purpose flour
¼ cup crumbled cornflakes
4 teaspoons baking powder
½ teaspoon salt
1 large egg
¼ cup butter or margarine, melted
¼ cup honey
1 cup milk
Holiday Sauce (see recipe below)

**1** Position the rack in the center of the oven and preheat to 425 degrees F. Lightly grease or line with paper baking cups fourteen 2¾-inch muffin cups.

**2** In a large bowl, blend together the flour, cornflakes, baking powder, and salt. In a medium bowl, beat the egg, butter, honey, and milk until smooth. Combine the two mixtures, blending until the dry ingredients are just moistened.

**3** Spoon the batter into the prepared muffin cups, filling each about three-quarters full. Sprinkle the tops of the muffins with the topping. Bake for 15 to 20 minutes, or until a cake tester or wooden toothpick inserted into the center of a muffin comes out clean. Cool in the pan on a wire rack for 5 to 7 minutes. Serve warm, or invert onto the rack to cool completely. Top with Holiday Sauce.

# HOLIDAY SAUCE

MAKES: *About 1½ cups*

1 cup ready-made mincemeat
½ cup marmalade
¼ cup butter or margarine

In a small saucepan set over low heat, combine all of the ingredients. Cook, stirring frequently, until smooth. Remove from the heat and serve warm.

1¾ cups all-purpose flour
¼ cup graham flour
1 tablespoon baking powder
½ cup currants
1 teaspoon salt
1 large egg
1 cup milk
¼ cup honey
2 tablespoons Amaretto liqueur
¼ cup butter or margarine, melted
Apricot Frosting (see recipe below)

**1** Position the rack in the center of the oven and preheat to 400 degrees F. Lightly grease or line with paper baking cups twelve 2¾-inch muffin cups.

**2** In a large bowl, blend together the two flours, baking powder, currants, and salt. In a medium bowl, beat the egg, milk, honey, Amaretto, and butter until smooth. Combine the two mixtures, blending until the dry ingredients are just moistened.

**3** Spoon the batter into the prepared muffin cups, filling each about three-quarters full. Bake for 15 to 20 minutes, or until a cake tester or wooden toothpick inserted into the center of a muffin comes out clean. Cool in the pan on a wire rack for 5 to 7 minutes. Brush with Apricot Frosting. Serve warm, or invert onto the rack to cool completely.

# HONEY-CURRANT MUFFINS

MAKES: *11 to 12 muffins*

# APRICOT FROSTING

MAKES: *¾ cup*

1 cup powdered sugar
¼ cup apricot preserves
1 tablespoon butter or margarine, at room temperature
1 teaspoon almond extract

In a medium bowl, using a fork or electric mixer on slow speed, beat the sugar, preserves, butter, and almond extract until smooth.

---

1 cup all-purpose flour
1 cup bran
2 teaspoons baking powder
½ cup chopped dates
¼ cup chopped walnuts
½ teaspoon salt
1 large egg
¼ cup honey
1 tablespoon butter or margarine, melted
½ cup milk
Carrot Butter (see recipe page 64)

**1** Position the rack in the center of the oven and preheat to 400 degrees F. Lightly grease or line with paper baking cups four 3-inch muffin cups.

**2** In a large bowl, blend together the flour, bran, baking powder, dates, walnuts, and salt. In a medium bowl, beat the egg, honey, butter, and milk until smooth. Combine the two mixtures, blending until the dry ingredients are just moistened.

**3** Drop 3 heaping tablespoons of the batter into the prepared muffin cups, filling each about three-quarters full. Bake for 15 to 20 minutes, or until a cake tester or wooden toothpick inserted into the center of a muffin comes out clean. Cool in the pan on a wire rack for 5 to 7 minutes. Serve warm, or invert onto the rack to cool completely.

# HONEY–DATE– BRAN MUFFINS

MAKES: *3 to 4 muffins*

## HONEY–OATMEAL MUFFINS WITH FRUIT

MAKES: *5 to 6 muffins*

1 cup all-purpose flour
1½ cups rolled oats
⅓ cup packed brown sugar
1 tablespoon baking powder
1 cup chopped mixed dried fruit
½ teaspoon salt
1 large egg
¼ cup canola oil
½ cup milk
¼ cup honey
Blender Apricot Sauce (see recipe page 25)

1  Position the rack in the center of the oven and preheat to 400 degrees F. Lightly grease or line with paper baking cups six 3-inch muffin cups.

2  In a large bowl, blend together the flour, oats, brown sugar, baking powder, mixed fruit, and salt.

In a medium bowl, beat the egg, oil, milk, and honey until smooth. Combine the two mixtures, blending until the dry ingredients are just moistened.

3  Drop 3 heaping tablespoons of the mixture into the prepared muffin cups, filling each about three-quarters full. Bake for 15 to 20 minutes, or until a cake tester or wooden toothpick inserted into the center of a muffin comes out clean. Cool in the pan on a wire rack for 5 to 7 minutes. Serve warm, or invert onto the rack to cool completely. Top with Blender Apricot Sauce.

## HONEY–PRUNE MUFFINS

MAKES: *5 to 6 muffins*

1 cup all-purpose flour
½ cup whole-wheat flour
2 teaspoons baking powder
½ teaspoon baking soda
½ teaspoon salt
1 large egg
¼ cup butter or margarine, melted
¼ cup sour milk or buttermilk
½ cup honey
½ cup finely chopped cooked prunes
Hot Nectarine Sauce (see recipe below)
1 small (3-ounce) package cream cheese, cut into 6 pieces

1  Position the rack in the center of the oven and preheat to 400 degrees F. Lightly grease or line with paper baking cups six 3-inch muffin cups.

2  In a large bowl, blend together the two flours, baking powder, baking soda, and salt. In a medi-

um bowl, beat the egg until foamy. Beat in the butter, milk, and honey. Stir in the prunes. Combine the two mixtures, blending until the dry ingredients are just moistened.

3  Spoon 2 tablespoons of the batter into each of the prepared muffin cups. Press one piece of the cheese into the center of each. Top each with an additional 1 tablespoon of the remaining batter. Bake for 15 to 20 minutes, or until the tops just begin to turn golden and a cake tester or wooden toothpick inserted near the edge of a muffin (not into the cream cheese) comes out clean. Cool in the pan on a wire rack for 5 to 7 minutes. Serve warm, or invert onto the rack to cool completely. Top with Hot Nectarine Sauce.

## HOT NECTARINE SAUCE

MAKES: *2½ cups*

2 cups peeled and thinly sliced fresh nectarines
½ cup granulated sugar
½ cup orange juice
2 tablespoons Triple Sec liqueur

In a medium saucepan, combine the nectarines, sugar, and orange juice. Place the pan over medium heat and cook, stirring constantly, until the sugar dissolves and the mixture thickens, about 5 to 7 minutes. Remove from the heat and stir in the liqueur.

1½ cups all-purpose flour
1½ cups rolled oats
1 tablespoon baking powder
½ teaspoon salt
1 large egg
1 cup milk
3 tablespoons butter or margarine, melted
1 cup honey
2 medium bananas, sliced
Cherry Sauce (see recipe page 52)

**1** Position the rack in the center of the oven and preheat to 400 degrees F. Lightly grease or line with paper baking cups sixteen 2¾-inch muffin cups.

**2** In a large bowl, blend together the flour, oats, baking powder, and salt. In a medium bowl, beat the egg, milk, butter, and honey until smooth. Combine the two mixtures, blending until the dry ingredients are just moistened.

**3** Spoon the batter into the prepared muffin cups, filling each about three-quarters full. Press a slice of banana into the center of each cup. Bake for 15 to 20 minutes, or until a cake tester or wooden toothpick inserted into the edge of a muffin (not into the center) comes out clean. Cool in the pan on a wire rack for 5 to 7 minutes. Serve warm, or invert onto the rack to cool completely. Top with Cherry Sauce.

# HONEY–BANANA– OATMEAL SURPRISE MUFFINS

MAKES: *14 to 16 muffins*

---

1 cup whole-wheat flour
1 teaspoon baking soda
1 cup All-Bran® cereal
Pinch salt
1 large egg
1 cup sour milk or buttermilk
1 banana, mashed
¼ cup canola oil
¼ cup plus 2 tablespoons warmed honey
Black Treacle Sauce (see recipe page 60)
2 tablespoons butter or margarine, at room temperature

**1** Position the rack in the center of the oven and preheat to 375 degrees F. Lightly grease or line with paper baking cups twelve 2¾-inch muffin cups.

**2** In a large bowl, blend together the flour, baking soda, cereal, and salt. In a medium bowl, beat the egg until thick and light-colored. Beat in the milk, banana, oil, ¼ cup of the honey, and the butter. Combine the two mixtures, blending until the dry ingredients are just moistened.

**3** Spoon the batter into the prepared muffin cups, filling each about three-quarters full. Bake for 15 to 20 minutes, or until a cake tester or wooden toothpick inserted into the center of a muffin comes out clean. Remove from the oven and brush the tops of the muffins with the warmed honey. Cool in the pan on a wire rack for 5 to 7 minutes. Serve warm, or transfer to the rack to cool completely. Top with Black Treacle Sauce.

# HONEYED-BANANA– BRAN MUFFINS

MAKES: *11 to 12 muffins*

# HONEYED CHEESE MUFFINS

MAKES: *12 to 14 muffins*

2 cups all-purpose flour
1 tablespoon baking powder
2 to 3 tablespoons grated sharp
    Cheddar cheese
2 tablespoons granulated sugar
½ teaspoon salt
1 large egg
1 cup skim milk
¼ cup canola oil
¼ cup warmed honey
2 tablespoons toasted sesame seeds
Cucumber Juice (see recipe below)

1  Position the rack in the center of the oven and preheat to 425 degrees F. Lightly grease and line with paper baking cups fourteen 2¾-inch muffin cups.

2  In a large bowl, blend together the flour, baking powder, Cheddar cheese, sugar, and salt. In a medium bowl, beat the egg until foamy. Beat in the milk and oil. Combine the two mixtures, blending until the dry ingredients are just moistened.

3  Spoon the mixture into the prepared muffin cups, filling each about three-quarters full. Bake for 15 to 20 minutes, or until a cake tester or wooden toothpick inserted into the center of a muffin comes out clean. Remove from the oven and immediately brush with honey and sprinkle with sesame seeds. Cool in the pan on a wire rack for 5 to 7 minutes. Serve warm, or transfer to the rack to cool completely. Serve with Cucumber Juice.

## CUCUMBER JUICE

MAKES: *About 2 cups*

2 cups V-8® vegetable juice
2 tablespoons finely chopped
    cucumbers
¼ teaspoon crushed dill
Sour cream for garnish

In a small saucepan, combine the juice, cucumbers, and dill and cook over medium heat until bubbles start to form around the edges of the pan. Remove from the heat, pour into a cup, and garnish with a dab of sour cream.

1 cup graham flour
1 cup corn flour
2 teaspoons baking powder
2 tablespoons granulated sugar
1 teaspoon salt
2 large eggs
1 cup milk
¼ cup honey
1 tablespoon butter or margarine
Hot Curry Spread (see recipe below)

**1** Position the rack in the center of the oven and preheat to 425 degrees F. Lightly grease or line with paper baking cups seventeen 2¾-inch muffin cups.

**2** In a large bowl, blend together the two flours, baking powder, sugar, and salt. In a medium bowl, beat the eggs until foamy. Beat in the milk, honey, and butter. Combine the two mixtures, blending until the dry ingredients are just moistened.

**3** Drop 1 heaping tablespoon of the mixture into each of the prepared muffin cups. Bake for 15 to 20 minutes, or until a cake tester or wooden toothpick inserted into the center of a muffin comes out clean. Cool in the pan on a wire rack for 5 to 7 minutes. Serve warm, or invert onto the rack to cool completely. Serve with Hot Curry Spread.

# HONEY–GRAHAM MUFFINS

MAKES: *15 to 17 muffins*

## HOT CURRY SPREAD

MAKES: *About 1¼ cups*

1 cup butter or margarine, at room temperature
2 tablespoons fresh snipped parsley
1 tablespoon curry powder
¼ cup white port wine
Salt to taste

In a small bowl, using an electric mixer on medium speed, beat all of the ingredients together until smooth. Cover and refrigerate until ready to serve.

---

2 cups all-purpose flour
3 tablespoons granulated sugar
1 tablespoon baking powder
½ teaspoon baking soda
1 teaspoon salt
2 large eggs
¾ cup milk
1 tablespoon butter or margarine, melted
1 cup huckleberries
New Spread (see recipe below)

**1** Position the rack in the center of the oven and preheat to 400 degrees F. Lightly grease or line with paper baking cups twelve 2¾-inch muffin cups.

**2** In a large bowl, blend together the flour, sugar, baking powder, baking soda, and salt. In a medium bowl, beat the eggs until thick and light-colored. Beat in the milk and butter. Combine the two mixtures, blending until the dry ingredients are just moistened. Stir in the berries.

**3** Spoon the batter into the prepared muffin cups, filling each about three-quarters full. Bake for 15 to 20 minutes, or until a cake tester or wooden toothpick inserted into the center of a muffin comes out clean. Cool in the pan on a wire rack for 5 to 7 minutes. Serve warm, or invert onto the rack to cool completely. Serve with New Spread.

# HUCKLEBERRY MUFFINS

MAKES: *11 to 12 muffins*

## NEW SPREAD

MAKES: *About 2 cups*

One 8-ounce package cream cheese
One 7-ounce jar marshmallow cream

In a small bowl, beat the cream cheese and marshmallow cream together until smooth. Chill until ready to serve.

# INDIAN MUFFINS

MAKES: *11 to 12 muffins*

1½ cups all-purpose flour
2 heaping tablespoons yellow
  cornmeal
2 teaspoons baking powder
¼ teaspoon salt
1 large egg
1 teaspoon butter or margarine,
  melted
1 cup milk
Tomato Relish (see recipe below)

**1** Position the rack in the center of the oven and preheat to 450 degrees F. Lightly grease or line with paper baking cups twelve 2-inch muffin cups.

**2** In a medium bowl, blend together the flour, cornmeal, baking powder, and salt. In another medium bowl, beat the egg, butter, and milk until smooth. Combine the two mixtures, blending until the dry ingredients are just moistened.

**3** Spoon 1 tablespoon of the batter into each of the prepared muffin cups. Bake for 18 to 20 minutes, or until a cake tester or wooden toothpick inserted into the center of a muffin comes out clean. Cool in the pan on a wire rack for 5 to 7 minutes. Serve warm, or invert onto the rack to cool completely. Serve with Tomato Relish.

## TOMATO RELISH

MAKES: *1 to 1½ cups*

⅓ cup canola oil
¼ teaspoon ground cumin
2 large cloves garlic, mashed
6 small green chili peppers,
  stemmed, seeded, and diced
1 teaspoon cayenne pepper
1 tablespoon vinegar
1 tablespoon molasses
4 medium tomatoes, peeled and
  finely diced

In a medium saucepan set over medium-low heat, combine the oil, cumin, garlic, peppers, cayenne, and vinegar, stirring frequently until the garlic is translucent. Remove from the heat and stir in the molasses and tomatoes. Serve at once.

# IRISH COFFEE MUFFINS

MAKES: *11 to 12 muffins*

2 cups all-purpose flour
1 tablespoon baking powder
½ teaspoon salt
1 large egg
½ cup granulated sugar
⅓ cup butter or margarine, melted
½ cup heavy cream
¼ cup Irish whiskey
½ cup coffee-flavored liqueur
Sugarless Cranberry Sauce (see
  recipe page 86)

**1** Position the rack in the center of the oven and preheat to 400 degrees F. Lightly grease or line with paper baking cups twelve 2¾-inch muffin cups.

**2** In a large bowl, blend together the flour, baking powder, and salt. In a medium bowl, beat the egg, sugar, butter, cream, whiskey, and liqueur until smooth. Combine the two mixtures, blending until the dry ingredients are just moistened.

**3** Spoon the batter into the prepared muffin cups, filling each about three-quarters full. Bake for 15 to 20 minutes, or until a cake tester or wooden toothpick inserted into the center of a muffin comes out clean. Cool in the pan on a wire rack for 5 to 7 minutes. Serve warm, or invert onto the rack to cool completely. Serve with Sugarless Cranberry Sauce.

1 cup quick-cooking oats
1 cup sour milk or buttermilk
1 cup all-purpose flour
1 teaspoon baking powder
½ teaspoon baking soda
½ cup seedless raisins (optional)
½ teaspoon salt
1 large egg
¼ cup packed light-brown sugar
⅓ cup butter or margarine, melted
Make It Quick Spread (see recipe
   below)

**1** The day before baking, combine the oats and sour milk in a small bowl. Cover and refrigerate overnight.

**2** When ready to bake, position the rack in the center of the oven and preheat to 400 degrees F. Lightly grease or line with paper baking cups twelve 2¾-inch muffin cups.

**3** In a large bowl, blend together the flour, baking powder, baking soda, raisins, and salt. In a medium bowl, beat the egg until foamy. Beat in the brown sugar and butter. Stir in the oat and milk mixture until well blended. Combine the two mixtures, blending until the dry ingredients are just moistened.

**4** Spoon one tablespoon of batter into the prepared muffin cups. Bake for 15 to 20 minutes, or until a cake tester or wooden toothpick inserted into the center of a muffin comes out clean. Cool in the pan on a wire rack for 5 to 7 minutes. Serve warm, or invert onto the rack to cool completely. Serve with Make It Quick Spread.

# IRISH SODA BREAD MUFFINS

MAKES: *10 to 12 muffins*

## MAKE IT QUICK SPREAD

MAKES: *About 1½ cups*

One 8-ounce package cream cheese
½ cup mayonnaise
½ cup shredded Cheddar cheese
½ cup peeled, cored, and finely
   chopped apple
¼ cup finely chopped pecans

In a small bowl, blend together the cream cheese and mayonnaise until smooth. Stir in the Cheddar cheese, apples, and pecans. Chill until ready to use.

# ISRAELI MUFFINS

MAKES: *20 muffins*

2½ cups unbleached all-purpose
    flour
⅓ cup matzo meal
¼ cup granulated sugar
2½ teaspoons baking powder
1½ teaspoons baking soda
1 tablespoon grated fresh orange
    zest
1½ teaspoons salt
3 large eggs
¾ cup clarified butter
½ cup honey
¼ cup orange-juice concentrate
Cheese-and-Horseradish Spread
    (see recipe below)

1  Position the rack in the center of the oven and preheat to 375 degrees F. Lightly grease or line with paper baking cups twenty 2¾-inch muffin cups.

2  In a large bowl, blend together the flour, matzo meal, sugar, baking powder, baking soda, orange zest, and salt. In a medium bowl, beat the eggs until foamy. Beat in the butter, honey, and orange juice. Combine the two mixtures, blending until the dry ingredients are just moistened.

3  Spoon one tablespoon of the batter into the prepared muffin cups. Bake for 15 to 20 minutes, or until the tops are golden brown and a cake tester or wooden toothpick inserted into the center of a muffin comes out clean. Cool in the pan on a wire rack for 5 to 7 minutes. Serve warm, or invert onto the rack to cool completely. Serve with Cheese-and-Horseradish Spread.

## CHEESE-AND-HORSERADISH SPREAD

MAKES: *About 1 cup*

One 8-ounce package cream
    cheese, at room temperature
½ cup prepared horseradish,
    drained through a fine sieve
Ground white pepper to taste

In a small bowl, using a spatula, combine the cheese and horseradish until smooth. Adjust the seasoning, cover with plastic wrap, and refrigerate until ready to serve.

2 cups all-purpose flour
2 teaspoons baking powder
1 cup granulated sugar
½ teaspoon ground nutmeg
½ teaspoon salt
2 large eggs
5 tablespoons butter or margarine, melted
¾ cup milk
1 teaspoon ground cinnamon
Blender Apricot Sauce (see recipe page 25)

1 Position the rack in the center of the oven and preheat to 400 degrees F. Lightly grease or line with paper baking cups twelve 2¾-inch muffin cups.

2 In a large bowl, blend together the flour, baking powder, ½ cup of the sugar, the nutmeg, and salt. In a medium bowl, beat the eggs, butter, and milk until smooth. Combine the two mixtures, blending until the dry ingredients are just moistened.

3 Spoon the batter into the prepared muffin cups, filling each about three-quarters full. In a cup or small bowl, combine the remaining ½ cup sugar and the cinnamon and stir until mixed. Sprinkle the sugar liberally over the tops of the muffins. Bake for 15 to 20 minutes, or until a cake tester or wooden toothpick inserted into the center of a muffin comes out clean. Cool in the pan on a wire rack for 5 to 7 minutes. Serve warm, or transfer to the rack to cool completely. Top with Blender Apricot Sauce.

# KING'S LYNN BREAKFAST BUN

MAKES: *11 to 12 muffins*

---

2 cups all-purpose flour
1 tablespoon baking powder
1 teaspoon baking soda
1 cup powdered sugar
¼ teaspoon salt
3 large kiwi fruits, peeled and finely chopped
2 large eggs
¾ cup canola oil
¾ cup skim milk
Lemon Glaze (see recipe below)

1 Position the rack in the center of the oven and preheat to 375 degrees F. Lightly grease or line with paper baking cups eighteen 2¾-inch muffin cups.

2 In a large bowl, blend together the flour, baking powder, baking soda, sugar, salt, and fruit. In a medium bowl, beat the eggs until thick and light-colored. Beat in the oil and milk. Combine the two mixtures, blending until the dry ingredients are just moistened.

3 Spoon the batter into the prepared muffin cups, filling each about three-quarters full. Bake for 15 to 20 minutes, or until the tops are golden brown and a cake tester or wooden toothpick inserted into a muffin is removed clean. Cool in the pan on a wire rack for 5 to 7 minutes. Brush with Lemon Glaze. Serve warm, or invert onto the rack to cool completely.

# KIWI MUFFINS

MAKES: *16 to 18 muffins*

# LEMON GLAZE

MAKES: *½ cup*

1 cup powdered sugar
2 tablespoons milk
1 tablespoon fresh lemon juice

In a small bowl, blend together the sugar, milk, and lemon juice until smooth. Brush on muffins hot from the oven.

# LARGE-BATCH PLAIN MUFFINS

MAKES: *88 dozen muffins*

9 pounds light-brown sugar
9 pounds granulated sugar
10 pounds vegetable shortening
8 ounces salt
11 pounds whole eggs
20 ounces baking powder
25 pounds all-purpose flour
19 pounds milk

**1** Position the rack in the center of the oven and preheat to 400 degrees F. Lightly grease or line with paper baking cups seven or eight 2½-inch size muffin cups.

**2** In a large bowl of a mixer, on medium speed, cream the sugars, shortening, and salt together until light and fluffy. Beat in the eggs, scraping down the sides of the bowl, and continue mixing until the eggs are blended. In a large bowl, blend together the baking powder and flour. Gradually blend the flour into the egg mixture, alternating with the milk. Scrape down the sides of the bowl and blend until just smooth. (Do not overmix.)

**3** Spoon 1½ to 2 ounces of batter into each of the prepared muffin cups, filling each at least two-thirds full. Bake for 14 to 18 minutes, or until a cake tester or wooden toothpick inserted into the center of a muffin comes out clean. Cool in the pan on a wire rack for 5 to 7 minutes. Serve warm, or invert onto the rack to cool completely.

**SERVING SUGGESTION: Serve with any topping, spread, or sauce of choice.**

# LEMON, CHIVE AND PEPPER MUFFINS

MAKES: *18 to 20 muffins*

2 cups all-purpose flour
1 tablespoon baking powder
1 tablespoon fresh grated lemon zest
¼ cup fresh snipped chives
1 teaspoon salt
½ teaspoon cracked black pepper
1 large egg
½ cup granulated sugar
¾ cup milk
⅓ cup canola oil
Cheese Sauce (see recipe page 57)

**1** Position the rack in the center of the oven and preheat to 375 degrees F. Lightly grease or line with paper baking cups twenty 2¾-inch muffin cups.

**2** In a large bowl, blend together the flour, baking powder, lemon zest, chives, salt, and pepper. In a medium bowl, beat together the egg, sugar, milk, and oil until smooth. Combine the two mixtures, blending until the dry ingredients are just moistened.

**3** Spoon the batter into the prepared muffin cups, filling each about three-quarters full. Bake for 15 to 20 minutes, or until a cake tester or wooden toothpick inserted into the center of a muffin comes out clean. Cool in the pan on a wire rack for 5 to 7 minutes. Serve warm, or invert onto the rack to cool completely. Top with Cheese Sauce.

1 pound finely ground lamb
¼ cup plain yogurt
⅓ cup chopped fresh cilantro
(coriander) leaves
1 clove garlic, minced
1 cup all-purpose flour
2 teaspoons baking powder
2 teaspoons ground coriander
¼ teaspoon salt
2 large eggs
1 cup milk
¼ cup canola oil
Cheese-and-Olive Spread (see recipe
below)

**1** Position the rack in the center of the oven and preheat to 400 degrees F. Lightly grease or line with paper baking cups fourteen 2¾-inch muffin cups.

**2** In a nonstick medium skillet set over high heat, cook the lamb, stirring and breaking up any large chunks of meat, until light-ly browned. Stir in the yogurt, fresh cilantro, and garlic. Remove from the heat and set aside.

**3** In a large bowl, blend together the flour, baking powder, ground coriander, and salt. In a medium bowl, beat the eggs until foamy. Beat in the milk and oil. Stir in the cooked lamb. Combine the two mixtures, blending until the dry ingredients are just moistened.

**4** Spoon the batter into the pre-pared muffin cups, filling each about three-quarters full. Bake for 15 to 20 minutes, or until a wooden toothpick inserted into the center of a muffin comes out clean. Cool in the pan on a wire rack for 5 to 7 minutes. Serve warm, or invert onto the rack to cool completely. Serve with Cheese-and-Olive Spread.

# LEBANESE LAMB MUFFINS

MAKES: *12 to 14 muffins*

## CHEESE-AND-OLIVE SPREAD

MAKES: *About 2½ cups*

Two 8-ounce packages cream
cheese, at room temperature
1 cup pitted black olives
¼ cup pimento, chopped
¼ cup sour cream or yogurt
1 tablespoon freshly squeezed
lime juice
Ground black pepper to taste

In the container of a blender or food processor, combine all of the ingredients and process on medium speed until smooth. Transfer the spread to a bowl, cover with plastic wrap, and refrigerate until ready to serve.

## LEMON, DATE AND PECAN MUFFINS

MAKES: *24 to 28 muffins*

½ cup packed brown sugar
6 tablespoons butter or margarine
¼ cup honey
1 tablespoon grated lemon zest
1¾ cups all-purpose flour
1½ teaspoons baking powder
½ teaspoon baking soda
1 cup chopped, pitted dates
⅔ cup chopped pecans
½ teaspoon salt
1 large egg
½ cup sour cream
¼ cup hot water
Lemon Syrup (see recipe below)

1  Position the rack in the center of the oven and preheat to 400 degrees F. Lightly grease or line with paper baking cups twenty-eight 2¾-inch muffin cups.

2  In a small saucepan, combine the brown sugar, butter, honey, and lemon zest and set over medium-low heat. Bring to a boil, remove from the heat, and set aside.

3  In a large bowl, blend together the flour, baking powder, baking soda, dates, pecans, and salt. In a medium bowl, beat the egg and sour cream until smooth. Beat in the brown sugar mixture and the hot water. Combine the two mixtures, blending until the dry ingredients are just moistened.

4  Drop 1 heaping tablespoon of the mixture into each of the prepared muffin cups and bake for 15 to 20 minutes, or until a cake tester or wooden toothpick inserted into the center of a muffin comes out clean. Remove from the oven and brush the tops of the muffins with the lemon glaze. Cool in the pan on a wire rack for 5 to 7 minutes. Serve warm, or transfer to the rack to cool completely. Top with Lemon Syrup.

## LEMON SYRUP

MAKES: *½ cup*

½ cup granulated sugar
¼ cup lemon juice
¼ cup water
2 teaspoons fresh grated lemon zest

In a small saucepan set over low heat, combine the sugar, lemon juice, water, and lemon zest. Cook, stirring, until the sugar is completely dissolved and the mixture comes to a boil. Remove from the heat and pour into a serving bowl.

2 cups all-purpose flour
1 teaspoon baking soda
1 tablespoon grated lemon zest
¼ teaspoon salt
¾ cup (4.5 ounces) semisweet
   chocolate chips
2 large eggs
½ cup butter or margarine, melted
1¼ cups granulated sugar
1 cup chocolate-flavored yogurt
¼ cup fresh lemon juice
Chocolate Sauce (see recipe page 26)

**1** Position a rack in the center of the oven and preheat to 375 degrees F. Lightly grease or line with paper baking cups eighteen 2¾-inch muffin cups.

**2** In a large bowl, blend together the flour, baking soda, lemon zest, salt, and chocolate chips. In a medium bowl, beat the eggs, butter, sugar, yogurt, and lemon juice until smooth. Combine the two mixtures, blending until the dry ingredients are just moistened.

**3** Spoon the batter into the prepared muffin cups, filling each about three-quarters full. Bake for 15 to 20 minutes, or until a cake tester or wooden toothpick inserted into the center of a muffin comes out clean. Cool in the pan on a wire rack for 5 to 7 minutes. Serve warm, or invert onto the rack to cool completely. Top with Chocolate Sauce.

# LEMON-FLAVORED CHOCOLATE MUFFINS
MAKES: *16 to 18 muffins*

---

1 cup all-purpose flour
2 teaspoons baking powder
1½ tablespoons grated lemon zest
⅛ teaspoon salt
2 large eggs, separated
½ cup granulated sugar
½ cup butter or margarine, melted
¼ cup undiluted lemon juice
   concentrate

**1** Position the rack in the center of the oven and preheat to 400 degrees F. Lightly grease or line with paper baking cups five 3-inch muffin cups.

**2** In a large bowl, blend together the flour, baking powder, lemon zest, and salt. In a medium bowl, beat the egg whites until stiff but not dry. Beat in the egg yolks, sugar, butter, and lemon juice. Combine the two mixtures, blending until the dry ingredients are just moistened.

**3** Drop 3 heaping tablespoons of the batter into the prepared muffin cups, filling each about three-quarters full. Bake for 18 to 22 minutes, or until a cake tester or wooden toothpick inserted into the center of a muffin comes out clean. Cool in the pan on a wire rack for 5 to 7 minutes. Serve warm, or invert onto the rack to cool completely.

**SERVING SUGGESTION: Serve with cheese of choice and a sweet red wine.**

# LEMON-FLAVORED MUFFINS
MAKES: *4 to 5 muffins*

## LEMON MUFFINS

MAKES: *5 to 6 muffins*

2 cups all-purpose flour
1 cup granulated sugar
2 teaspoons baking powder
2 teaspoons grated lemon zest
1 teaspoon salt
4 large eggs, separated
1 cup butter or margarine, melted
½ cup lemon juice

**1** Position the rack in the center of the oven and preheat to 375 degrees F. Lightly grease or line with paper baking cups six 3-inch muffin cups.

**2** In a large bowl, blend together the flour, sugar, baking powder, lemon zest, and salt. In a medium bowl, beat the egg whites until stiff but not dry. Beat in the egg yolks, butter, and lemon juice. Combine the two mixtures, blending until the dry ingredients are just moistened.

**3** Spoon 3 heaping tablespoons of the batter into the prepared muffin cups, filling each about three-quarters full. Bake for 18 to 22 minutes, or until a cake tester or wooden toothpick inserted into the center of a muffin comes out clean. Cool in the pan on a wire rack for 5 to 7 minutes. Serve warm, or invert onto the rack to cool completely.

**SERVING SUGGESTION: Roll in butter and sugar.**

## LEMON–PECAN MUFFINS

MAKES: *5 to 6 muffins*

2 cups all-purpose flour
1 cup granulated sugar
2 teaspoons baking powder
2 tablespoons grated lemon zest
¼ teaspoon salt
1 cup finely chopped pecans
4 large eggs, separated
1 cup butter or margarine, melted
6 tablespoons lemon juice
Whipped Cream-Cheese Topping
　(see recipe below)

**1** Position the rack in the center of the oven and preheat to 375 degrees F. Lightly grease or line with paper baking cups six 3-inch muffin cups.

**2** In a large bowl, blend together the flour, sugar, baking powder, lemon zest, salt, and pecans. In a small bowl, beat the egg whites until stiff but not dry. In a medium bowl, beat the egg yolks, but-ter, and lemon juice until smooth. Fold in the egg whites. Fold in the dry ingredients until just blended.

**3** Spoon 3 heaping tablespoons of the batter into each of the pre-pared muffin cups, filling each about three-quarters full. Bake for about 18 to 22 minutes, or until the tops of the muffins are golden and until a cake tester or wooden toothpick inserted into the center of a muffin comes out clean. Remove from the oven and immediately brush the tops of the muffins with the glaze. Cool in the pan on a wire rack for 5 to 7 minutes. Serve warm, or trans-fer to the rack to cool completely. Serve with Whipped Cream-Cheese Topping.

## WHIPPED CREAM-CHEESE TOPPING

MAKES: *1¼ cups*

1 small (3-ounce) package cream
　cheese, at room temperature
1 cup powdered sugar
½ teaspoon vanilla extract
½ teaspoon evaporated milk

In a medium bowl, combine the cream cheese and sugar and beat until smooth. Add the vanilla extract and milk and continue beating until smooth.

1¾ cups all-purpose flour
⅓ cup plus 2 tablespoons
   granulated sugar
2 teaspoons baking powder
2 tablespoons grated lemon zest
¼ teaspoon salt
1 large egg
3 tablespoons canola oil
1 tablespoon plus 2 teaspoons
   poppy seeds
1 cup milk
1 tablespoon lemon juice

**1** Position the rack in the center of the oven and preheat to 400 degrees F. Lightly grease or line with paper baking cups twelve 2¾-inch muffin cups.

**2** In a large bowl, blend together the flour, ⅓ cup of the sugar, the baking powder, lemon zest, and salt. In a medium bowl, beat together the remaining 2 table-spoons of sugar, the egg, oil, 1 tablespoon of the poppy seeds, the milk, and lemon juice. Combine the two mixtures, blending until the dry ingredients are just moistened.

**3** Spoon the batter into the prepared muffin cups, filling each about three-quarters full. Sprinkle the remaining 2 teaspoons of poppy seeds over the tops of the muffins. Bake for 15 to 20 minutes, or until a cake tester or wooden toothpick inserted into the center of a muffin comes out clean. Cool in the pan on a wire rack for 5 to 7 minutes. Serve warm, or invert onto the rack to cool completely.

**SERVING SUGGESTION: Serve with a vanilla custard or tapioca pudding.**

# LEMON-AND-POPPY-SEED MUFFINS

MAKES: *11 to 12 muffins*

2 cups all-purpose flour
1 cup granulated sugar
1 tablespoon baking powder
½ teaspoon salt
2 large eggs
1 cup milk
1 cup canola oil
1 teaspoon lemon extract
1 cup raspberries, fresh or frozen
Wine Spread with Blue Cheese (see
   recipe below)

**1** Position the rack in the center of the oven and preheat to 425 degrees F. Lightly grease or line with paper baking cups twelve 2¾-inch muffin cups.

**2** In a large bowl, blend together the flour, sugar, baking powder, and salt. In a medium bowl, beat the eggs, milk, oil, and lemon extract until smooth. Combine the two mixtures, blending until the dry ingredients are just moistened. Stir in the raspberries.

**3** Spoon the batter into the prepared muffin cups, filling each about three-quarters full. Bake for 15 to 20 minutes, or until a cake tester or wooden toothpick inserted into the center of a muffin comes out clean. Cool in the pan on a wire rack for 5 to 7 minutes. Serve warm, or invert onto the rack to cool completely. Serve with Wine Spread with Blue Cheese.

# LEMON–RASPBERRY MUFFINS

MAKES: *11 to 12 muffins*

## WINE SPREAD WITH BLUE CHEESE

MAKES: *About 1½ cups*

¼ cup white port wine
6 tablespoons butter, at room
   temperature
8 ounces blue cheese
¼ teaspoon ground white pepper
Pinch cayenne pepper
¾ cup finely ground pecans

In a medium-size bowl using an electric mixer on medium-high speed, combine all of the ingredients and beat until smooth. Cover with plastic wrap and refrigerate for at least 1 hour before serving.

# LETTUCE MUFFINS

MAKES: *11 to 12 muffins*

2½ cups all-purpose flour
1 teaspoon baking powder
1 cup grated Cheddar cheese
1 small white onion, finely chopped
½ cup fresh chopped parsley
1½ cups shredded lettuce
½ teaspoon salt
2 large eggs
¼ cup canola oil
½ teaspoon chili sauce
1 cup milk
2 tablespoons sesame seeds
Chicken Spread (see recipe below)

**1** Position the rack in the center of the oven and preheat to 400 degrees F. Lightly grease or line with paper baking cups twelve 2¾-inch muffin cups.

**2** In a large bowl, blend together the flour, baking powder, ½ cup of the cheese, the onions, parsley, lettuce, and salt. In a medium bowl, beat the eggs until foamy. Beat in the oil, chili sauce, and milk. Combine the two mixtures, blending until the dry ingredients are just moistened.

**3** Spoon the batter into the prepared muffin cups, filling each about three-quarters full. In a small cup, combine the remaining ½ cup of cheese and sesame seeds and sprinkle this lightly over the tops of the muffins. Bake for about 20 to 25 minutes, or until a cake tester or wooden toothpick inserted into the center of a muffin comes out clean. Cool in the pan on a wire rack for 5 to 7 minutes. Serve warm, or invert onto the rack to cool completely. Serve with Chicken Spread.

## CHICKEN SPREAD

MAKES: *About 1½ cups*

One 8-ounce package cream cheese, at room temperature
One 5-ounce can prepared chicken spread
2 tablespoons mayonnaise
½ teaspoon prepared horseradish
¼ teaspoon Worcestershire sauce
¼ teaspoon prepared mustard

In a medium bowl, combine all of the ingredients, blending until smooth. Refrigerate until ready to use.

1½ cups all-purpose flour
¼ cup granulated sugar
4 teaspoons baking powder
2 teaspoons anise seeds
¼ teaspoon salt
1 large egg white
¾ cup skim milk
¼ cup lite (reduced calorie)
    margarine, melted
5 apple slices
Fig Sauce (see recipe below)

**1** Position the rack in the center of the oven and preheat to 400 degrees F. Lightly grease or line with paper baking cups five 3-inch muffin cups.

**2** In a large bowl, blend together the flour, sugar, baking powder, anise seed, and salt. In a large bowl, beat the egg white until stiff but not dry. Beat in the yolk, milk, and margarine. Combine the two mixtures, blending until the dry ingredients are just moistened.

**3** Drop 3 heaping tablespoons of the mixture into each of the prepared muffin cups, filling each about three-quarters full. Press a slice of apple into the top of each muffin. Bake for 15 to 20 minutes, or until a cake tester or wooden toothpick inserted into the center of a muffin comes out clean. Cool in the pan on a wire rack for 5 to 7 minutes. Serve warm, or invert onto the rack to cool completely. Serve with Fig Sauce.

# LIGHT MUFFINS

MAKES: *4 to 5 muffins*

# FIG SAUCE

MAKES: *1¼ cups*

½ cup finely chopped fresh figs
⅓ cup water
½ cup ricotta cheese
¼ cup finely ground hazelnuts
1 tablespoon granulated sugar
¼ teaspoon ground cinnamon

In the container of a blender, combine the figs and water. Blend on high until smooth. Add the cheese, nuts, sugar, and cinnamon to the blender and blend on high until the mixture is very smooth. Pour into a serving bowl.

# LIME-FLAVORED MUFFINS

MAKES: *11 to 12 muffins*

2 cups all-purpose flour
2 teaspoons baking powder
½ teaspoon salt
1 large egg
¾ cup evaporated milk
½ cup canola oil
⅓ cup packed light-brown sugar
¼ cup lime-juice concentrate
2 tablespoons freshly grated lime zest
⅔ cup miniature chocolate chips (optional)
Lime Glaze (see recipe below)

**1** Position the rack in the center of the oven and preheat to 400 degrees F. Lightly grease or line with paper baking cups twelve 2¾ muffin cups.

**2** In a large bowl, blend together the flour, baking powder, and salt. In a medium bowl, beat the egg until foamy. Beat in the milk, oil, sugar, lime juice, and lime zest. Combine the two mixtures, blending until the dry ingredients are just moistened. Stir in the optional chocolate chips.

**3** Spoon the batter into the prepared muffin cups, filling each about three-quarters full. Bake for 15 to 20 minutes, or until a cake tester or wooden toothpick inserted into the center of a muffin comes out clean. Cool in the pan on a wire rack for 5 to 7 minutes. Serve warm, or invert onto the rack to cool completely. Brush with Lime Glaze.

## LIME GLAZE

MAKES: *¾ to 1 cup*

3 tablespoons Piña Colada concentrate
2 teaspoons lime juice
1½ cups sifted powdered sugar

In a small bowl, combine the concentrate, lime juice, and sugar, blending until smooth. Brush on hot muffins.

1 cup all-purpose flour
1 cup yellow cornmeal
2 tablespoons granulated sugar
2½ teaspoons baking powder
One 8-ounce can whole-kernel corn, drained
½ teaspoon salt
2 large eggs
½ cup canola oil
1 cup milk
½ teaspoon pepper sauce
Paprika for sprinkling
Savory Sauce (see recipe below)

**1** Position the rack in the center of the oven and preheat to 400 degrees F. Lightly grease or line with paper baking cups fourteen 2¾-inch muffin cups.

**2** In a large bowl, blend together the flour, cornmeal, sugar, baking powder, corn, and salt. In a medi-um bowl, beat the eggs, oil, milk, and pepper sauce until smooth. Combine the two mixtures, blending until the dry ingredients are just moistened.

**3** Spoon the batter into the prepared muffin cups, filling each cup two-thirds full. Sprinkle the top of each muffin lightly with paprika. Bake for 15 to 20 minutes, or until a cake tester or wooden toothpick inserted into the center of a muffin comes out clean. Cool in the pan on a wire rack for 5 to 7 minutes. Serve warm, or invert onto the rack to cool completely. Top with Savory Sauce.

# LOUISIANA CORN MUFFINS
MAKES: *12 to 14 muffins*

## SAVORY SAUCE
MAKES: *About ⅓ cup*

¼ cup canola oil
1 tablespoon onion juice
1 tablespoon grated celery
1 teaspoon celery seeds
Pinch ground nutmeg
1 tablespoon brewers yeast
Pinch sea salt

In the container of a blender, combine all of the ingredients and process on medium speed until smooth. Serve cold.

---

1½ cups corn flour
½ cup all-purpose flour
4 teaspoons baking powder
1 teaspoon salt
2 large eggs
2 cups milk
1 tablespoon butter or margarine, melted
2 tablespoons finely chopped jalapeño peppers
Peppery Lemon Butter (see recipe page 74)

**1** Position the rack in the center of the oven and preheat to 425 degrees F. Lightly grease or line with paper baking cups twelve 2¾-inch muffin cups.

**2** In a large bowl, blend together the corn flour, flour, baking powder, and salt. In a medium bowl, beat the eggs until foamy. Beat in the milk and butter. Stir in the jalapeño. Combine the two mixtures, blending until the dry ingredients are just moistened.

**3** Spoon the batter into the prepared muffin cups, filling each about three-quarters full. Bake for 15 to 20 minutes, or until a cake tester or wooden toothpick inserted into the center of a muffin comes out clean. Cool in the pan on a wire rack for 5 to 7 minutes. Serve warm, or invert onto the rack to cool completely. Serve with Peppery Lemon Butter.

# LOUISIANA HOT CORN MUFFINS
MAKES: *11 to 12 muffins*

## MAISMEEL KADETJES-CORNMEAL MUFFINS

MAKES: *11 to 12 muffins*

1 cup all-purpose flour
1 cup cornmeal
1 tablespoon granulated sugar
2 teaspoons baking powder
½ teaspoon salt
1 cup milk
2 large eggs
¼ cup butter or margarine, melted
¼ cup toasted sesame seeds

**1** Position the rack in the center of the oven and preheat to 400 degrees F. Lightly grease or line with paper baking cups twelve 2¾-inch muffin cups.

**2** In a large bowl, blend together the flour, cornmeal, sugar, baking powder, and salt. In a medium bowl, beat the milk, eggs, and butter until smooth. Combine the two mixtures, blending until the dry ingredients are just moistened.

**3** Spoon the batter into the prepared muffin cups, filling each about three-quarters full. Sprinkle the tops of the muffins with the sesame seeds. Bake for 15 to 20 minutes, or until a cake tester or wooden toothpick inserted into the center of a muffin comes out clean. Cool in the pan on a wire rack for 5 to 7 minutes. Serve warm, or invert onto the rack to cool completely.

**SERVING SUGGESTION: Serve with a seafood salad.**

## MANGO MUFFINS

MAKES: *11 to 12 muffins*

1 cup rice flour
½ cup millet flour
½ cup oat flour
1 teaspoon baking powder
¼ teaspoon salt
1 large mango, peeled, seeded and chopped fine
¼ cup finely chopped almonds
1 large egg
½ cup honey
3 tablespoons butter or margarine, melted
2 tablespoons coconut flavoring
Sweet-and-Sour Mango Relish (see recipe below)

**1** Position the rack in the center of the oven and preheat to 375 degrees F. Lightly grease or line with paper baking cups twelve 2¾-inch muffin cups.

**2** In a large bowl, combine the three flours, baking powder, salt, mango, and almonds. In a medium bowl, beat the egg, honey, butter, and coconut flavoring until smooth. Combine the two mixtures, blending until the dry ingredients are just moistened.

**3** Spoon the batter into the prepared muffin cups, filling each about three-quarters full. Bake for 15 to 20 minutes, or until a cake tester or wooden toothpick inserted into the center of a muffin comes out clean. Remove from the oven and brush with Citrus Glaze. Cool in the pan on a wire rack for 5 to 7 minutes. Serve warm, or transfer the muffins to the rack to cool completely. Serve with Sweet-and-Sour Mango Relish.

## SWEET-AND-SOUR MANGO RELISH

MAKES: *About 1½ cups*

Flesh from 2 medium unripe (but not green) mangoes, diced
¼ cup molasses
1 tablespoon cider vinegar
1 tablespoon ground coriander
1 teaspoon ground cumin
1 teaspoon ground ginger
¼ teaspoon ground nutmeg
½ teaspoon cayenne
½ cup very finely chopped onion
Salt to taste

In the container of a blender, combine all of the ingredients except the onion and salt and process on medium speed until smooth. Pour into a bowl and stir in the onion. Season to taste with salt and refrigerate until ready to use.

1½ cups whole-wheat flour
¾ cup wheat bran
1 tablespoon baking powder
⅓ cup chopped walnuts
½ teaspoon salt
1 large egg
½ cup milk
¼ cup canola oil
½ cup maple syrup
Sweet Vanilla Sauce (see recipe
    below)

**1** Position the rack in the center of the oven and preheat to 400 degrees F. Lightly grease or line with paper baking cups six 3-inch muffin cups.

**2** In a large bowl, blend together the flour, bran, baking powder, walnuts, and salt. In a medium bowl, beat the egg, milk, oil, and maple syrup until smooth. Combine the two mixtures, blending until the dry ingredients are just moistened.

**3** Drop 3 heaping tablespoons of the batter into each of the prepared muffin cups, filling each about three-quarters full. Bake for 15 to 20 minutes, or until a cake tester or wooden toothpick inserted into the center of a muffin comes out clean. Remove from the oven and brush the tops of the muffins with Maple Glaze. Cool in the pan on a wire rack for 5 to 7 minutes. Serve warm, or transfer to the rack to cool completely. Top with Sweet Vanilla Sauce.

# MAPLE–BRAN MUFFINS

MAKES: *5 to 6 muffins*

# SWEET VANILLA SAUCE

MAKES: *About 1 cup*

1 tablespoon cornstarch
1 cup milk
1 tablespoon butter
1 tablespoon granulated sugar
1 teaspoon vanilla extract

In a cup, combine the cornstarch and 1 tablespoon of the milk and stir until it forms a smooth paste. In a small saucepan set over medium-low heat, warm the remaining milk slightly before stirring in the cornstarch. Cook, stirring, until the mixture boils and thickens. Reduce the heat to low and simmer for 2 minutes, stirring constantly. Remove from the heat and stir in the butter, sugar, and vanilla extract. Serve warm or cold.

## MAPLE, OAT BRAN, AND FIG MUFFINS

MAKES: *3 to 4 muffins*

2 cups oat bran
2 teaspoons baking powder
1 teaspoon ground cinnamon
¾ cup diced dried figs
2 tablespoons grated orange zest
½ teaspoon salt
1 large egg
¼ cup canola oil
½ cup plain yogurt
½ cup maple syrup
**Fig Sauce (see recipe page 189)**

**1** Position the rack in the center of the oven and preheat to 400 degrees F. Lightly grease or line with paper baking cups four 3-inch muffin cups.

**2** In a large bowl, blend together the oat bran, baking powder, cinnamon, figs, orange zest, and salt. In a medium bowl, beat the egg, oil, yogurt, and maple syrup until smooth. Combine the two mixtures, blending until the dry ingredients are just moistened.

**3** Drop 3 heaping tablespoons of the batter into each of the prepared muffin cups, filling each about three-quarters full. Bake for 15 to 20 minutes, or until a cake tester or wooden toothpick inserted into the center of a muffin comes out clean. Cool in the pan on a wire rack for 5 to 7 minutes. Serve warm, or invert onto the rack to cool completely. Top with Fig Sauce.

## MAPLE–PECAN MUFFINS

MAKES: *3 to 4 muffins*

1½ cups whole-wheat flour
1½ teaspoons baking powder
½ cup finely chopped pecans
¼ teaspoon salt
¼ cup maple syrup
2 tablespoons butter or margarine, melted
1 large egg
⅔ cup water
1 teaspoon vanilla extract
**Maple Butter (see recipe page 35)**

**1** Position the rack in the center of the oven and preheat to 375 degrees F. Lightly grease or line with paper baking cups four 3-inch muffin cups.

**2** In a large bowl, blend together the flour, baking powder, pecans, and salt. In a medium bowl, beat the syrup, butter, egg, water, and vanilla extract until smooth. Combine the two mixtures, blending until the dry ingredients are just moistened.

**3** Drop 3 heaping tablespoons of the batter into each of the prepared muffin cups, filling each about three-quarters full. Bake for 15 to 20 minutes, or until a cake tester or wooden toothpick inserted into the center of a muffin comes out clean. Cool in the pan on a wire rack for 5 to 7 minutes. Serve warm, or invert onto the rack to cool completely. Serve with Maple Butter.

2 cups all-purpose flour
2 teaspoons baking powder
½ teaspoon salt
1 large egg
½ cup milk
¼ cup canola oil
½ cup maple syrup
4 chunks pineapple, drained
Blender Apricot Sauce (see recipe
  page 25)

**1** Position the rack in the center of the oven and preheat to 375 degrees F. Light grease or line with paper baking cups four 3-inch muffin cups.

**2** In a large bowl, blend together the flour, baking powder, and salt. In a medium bowl, beat the egg, milk, oil, and maple syrup until smooth. Combine the two mixtures, blending until the dry ingredients are just moistened.

**3** Drop 3 heaping tablespoons of the batter into each of the prepared muffin cups, filling each about three-quarters full. Push a chunk of pineapple deep into the batter. Bake for 15 to 20 minutes, or until a cake tester or wooden toothpick inserted into the edge of a muffin comes out clean. Cool in the pan on a wire rack for 5 to 7 minutes. Serve warm, or invert onto the rack to cool completely. Serve with Blender Apricot Sauce.

# Maple–Pineapple Muffins

MAKES: *3 to 4 muffins*

---

1⅓ cups all-purpose flour
1 cup yellow cornmeal
1 tablespoon granulated sugar
1 tablespoon baking powder
½ teaspoon baking soda
½ teaspoon salt
2 large eggs
¼ cup butter or margarine, melted
1⅓ cups buttermilk or sour milk
Cottage Cheese Dip (see recipe
  below)

**1** Position the rack in the center of the oven and preheat to 375 degrees F. Lightly grease or line with paper baking cups twenty 2¾-inch muffin cups.

**2** In a large bowl, blend together the flour, cornmeal, sugar, baking powder, baking soda, and salt. In a medium bowl, beat the eggs, butter, and buttermilk until smooth. Combine the two mixtures, blending until the dry ingredients are just moistened.

**3** Spoon the batter into the prepared muffin cups, filling each about three-quarters full. Bake for 15 to 20 minutes, or until a cake tester or wooden toothpick inserted into the center of a muffin comes out clean. Cool in the pan on a wire rack for 5 to 7 minutes. Serve warm, or invert onto the rack to cool completely. Serve with Cottage Cheese Dip.

# Maple, Walnut, and Corn Muffins

MAKES: *18 to 20 muffins*

## Cottage Cheese Dip

MAKES: *About 1½ cups*

1 cup large-curd cottage cheese
1 medium ripe avocado, peeled
  and seeded
1 tablespoon minced onion
1 tablespoon finely minced
  pimento

In the container of a blender, combine all of the ingredients and process on low speed until smooth. Pour into a bowl and refrigerate until ready to serve.

## MARMALADE–ALMOND MUFFINS

MAKES: *11 to 12 muffins*

2 cups all-purpose flour
3 tablespoons baking powder
⅔ cup granulated sugar
2 tablespoons grated orange zest
1 cup ground almonds
2 large eggs
¼ cup butter or margarine, melted
½ cup milk
⅔ cup orange marmalade
¼ cup slivered almonds

**1** Position the rack in the center of the oven and preheat to 375 degrees F. Lightly grease or line with paper baking cups twelve 2¾-inch muffin cups.

**2** In a large bowl, blend together the flour, baking powder, sugar, orange zest, and ground almonds. In a medium bowl, beat the eggs until foamy. Beat in the butter and milk. Stir in the marmalade. Combine the two mixtures, blending until the dry ingredients are just moistened.

**3** Spoon the batter into the prepared muffin cups, filling each about three-quarters full. Sprinkle the slivered almonds over the tops of the muffins. Bake for 15 to 20 minutes, or until a cake tester or wooden toothpick inserted into the center of a muffin comes out clean. Cool in the pan on a wire rack for 5 to 7 minutes. Serve warm, or invert onto the rack to cool completely.

**SERVING SUGGESTION: Serve with fresh fruit salad.**

## MAYONNAISE MUFFINS

MAKES: *8 to 10 muffins*

2 cups all-purpose flour
1 tablespoon baking powder
1 tablespoon granulated sugar
¼ teaspoon salt
1 cup milk
2 tablespoons mayonnaise
Cheese Sauce (see recipe page 57)

**1** Position the rack in the center of the oven and preheat to 400 degrees F. Lightly grease or line with paper baking cups ten 2¾-inch muffin cups.

**2** In a large bowl, blend together the flour, baking powder, sugar, and salt. In a small bowl, beat the milk and mayonnaise until smooth. Combine the two mixtures, blending until the dry ingredients are just moistened.

**3** Spoon the batter into the prepared muffin cups, filling each about three-quarters full. Bake for 15 to 20 minutes, or until a cake tester or wooden toothpick inserted into the center of a muffin comes out clean. Cool in the pan on a wire rack for 5 to 7 minutes. Serve warm, or invert onto the rack to cool completely. Serve with Cheese Sauce.

2 cups all-purpose flour
5 teaspoons baking powder
1 tablespoon granulated sugar
2 tablespoons fresh snipped chives
2 teaspoons fresh chopped tarragon
1 teaspoon fresh chopped basil
¼ teaspoon salt
1 cup milk
2 tablespoons mayonnaise
Savory Sauce (see recipe page 191)

**1** Position the rack in the center of the oven and preheat to 400 degrees F. Lightly grease or line with paper baking cups twelve 2¾-inch muffin cups.

**2** In a large bowl, blend together the flour, baking powder, sugar, chives, tarragon, basil, and salt.

In a small bowl, beat the milk and mayonnaise until smooth. Combine the two mixtures, blending until the dry ingredients are just moistened.

**3** Drop a scant 2 tablespoons of the batter into each of the prepared muffin cups. Bake for 15 to 20 minutes, or until a cake tester or wooden toothpick inserted into the center of a muffin comes out clean. Cool in the pan on a wire rack for 5 to 7 minutes. Serve warm, or invert onto the rack to cool completely. Top with Savory Sauce.

## MAYONNAISE MUFFINS WITH CHIVES AND HERBS
MAKES: *11 to 12 muffins*

2 cups all-purpose flour
1 tablespoon baking powder
1 tablespoon granulated sugar
2 tablespoons fresh snipped chives
¼ teaspoon salt
1 cup milk
2 tablespoons mayonnaise
Sliced olives for topping
Herb Salsa (see recipe below)

**1** Position the rack in the center of the oven and preheat to 400 degrees F. Lightly grease or line with paper baking cups ten 2¾-inch muffin cups.

**2** In a large bowl, blend together the flour, baking powder, sugar, chives, and salt. In a small bowl,

beat the milk and mayonnaise until smooth. Combine the two mixtures, blending until the dry ingredients are just moistened.

**3** Spoon the batter into the prepared muffin cups, filling each about three-quarters full, and press several slices of olives into the top of each muffin. Bake for 15 to 20 minutes, or until a cake tester or wooden toothpick inserted into the center of a muffin comes out clean. Cool in the pan on a wire rack for 5 to 7 minutes. Serve warm, or invert onto the rack to cool completely. Serve with Herb Salsa.

## MAYONNAISE MUFFINS WITH CHIVES
MAKES: *8 to 10 muffins*

## HERB SALSA
MAKES: *About 2 cups*

½ cup fresh snipped parsley
½ cup fresh snipped chives
2 tablespoons crushed basil
⅔ cup finely chopped ripe tomatoes
2 medium cloves garlic, peeled and finely chopped
1 jalapeño pepper, stemmed, seeded, and finely chopped

2 tablespoons lemon juice
Salt and ground black pepper to taste

In the container of a blender or food processor, combine all the ingredients and process on low for 3 to 5 seconds. Pour into a small bowl and serve.

# MINCEMEAT MUFFINS

MAKES: *11 to 12 muffins*

2 cups all-purpose flour
2 teaspoons baking powder
⅓ cup granulated sugar
¼ teaspoon freshly grated nutmeg
1 teaspoon grated orange zest
1 cup chopped pecans
2 large eggs
⅓ cup milk
1¼ cups prepared mincemeat
6 thin slices orange, halved
Mincemeat Sauce (see recipe page 142)

**1** Position the rack in the center of the oven and preheat to 400 degrees F. Lightly grease or line with paper baking cups twelve 2¾-inch muffin cups.

**2** In a large bowl, blend together the flour, baking powder, sugar, nutmeg, orange zest, and pecans.

In a medium bowl, beat the eggs until foamy. Beat in the milk. Stir in the mincemeat. Combine the two mixtures, blending until the dry ingredients are just moistened.

**3** Spoon the batter into the prepared muffin cups, filling each about three-quarters full. Press a half slice of orange into each of the muffins. Bake for 15 to 20 minutes, or until a cake tester or wooden toothpick inserted into the center of a muffin comes out clean. Cool in the pan on a wire rack for 5 to 7 minutes. Serve warm, or invert onto the rack to cool completely. Serve with Mincemeat Sauce.

# MINESTRONE MUFFINS

MAKES: *12 to 14 muffins*

1½ cups all-purpose flour
½ cup yellow cornmeal
1 tablespoon baking powder
2 large eggs
¼ cup packed light-brown sugar
3 tablespoons molasses
2 cups thick minestrone soup
¼ cup beef broth

**1** Position the rack in the center of the oven and preheat to 425 degrees F. Lightly grease or line with paper baking cups fourteen 2¾-inch muffin cups.

**2** In a large bowl, blend together the flour, cornmeal, and baking powder. In a medium bowl, beat the eggs until foamy. Beat in the

sugar, molasses, soup, and broth. Combine the two mixtures, blending until the dry ingredients are just moistened.

**3** Spoon the batter into the prepared muffin cups, filling each about three-quarters full. Baking for 15 to 20 minutes, or until a cake tester or wooden toothpick inserted into the center of a muffin comes out clean. Cool in the pan on a wire rack for 5 to 7 minutes. Serve warm, or invert onto the rack to cool completely.

SERVING SUGGESTION: **Serve with a thin-bodied soup.**

1 cup all-purpose flour
1¼ cups wheat germ
1¼ cups quick-cooking oats
½ cup packed light-brown sugar
1 tablespoon baking powder
1 teaspoon baking soda
¼ teaspoon salt
¾ cup unsweetened applesauce
½ cup canola oil
1 large egg
1 teaspoon almond extract
Peanut Dip (see recipe below)

**1** Position the rack in the center of the oven and preheat to 400 degrees F. Lightly grease or line with paper baking cups thirty-six 1¾-inch muffin cups.

**2** In a large bowl, blend together the flour, wheat germ, oats, sugar, baking powder, baking soda, and salt. In a medium bowl, beat the applesauce, oil, egg, and almonds extract until smooth. Combine the two mixtures, blending until the dry ingredients are just moistened.

**3** Drop 1 heaping tablespoon of the mixture into each of the prepared muffin cups, filling each about three-quarters full. Bake for about 12 to 15 minutes, or until a cake tester or wooden toothpick inserted into the center of a muffin comes out clean. Cool in the pan on a wire rack for 5 to 7 minutes. Serve warm, or invert onto the rack to cool completely. Serve with Peanut Dip.

# MINI MUFFINS

MAKES: *35 to 36 muffins*

# PEANUT DIP

MAKES: *1½ to 1⅔ cups*

1½ cups roasted unsalted peanuts
3 tablespoons peeled, sliced fresh
    ginger root
1 small clove garlic, peeled and
    mashed
2 teaspoons brown sugar
½ teaspoon cayenne pepper
1 tablespoon soy sauce

1 tablespoon red wine vinegar
¾ cup water
¼ cup orange juice

In the container of a blender or food processor, combine all the ingredients and process on low for 3 to 5 seconds. Pour into a small bowl and serve.

---

1 cup all-purpose flour
1 cup graham flour
2 teaspoons baking powder
1 cup chopped pitted prunes
1 teaspoon salt
1 large egg
1½ cups milk
¼ cup canola oil
½ cup molasses
1 tablespoon coffee liqueur or
    strong brewed fresh coffee
Tropical Sauce (see recipe page 81)

**1** Position the rack in the center of the oven and preheat to 400 degrees F. Lightly grease or line with paper baking cups fourteen 2¾-inch muffin cups.

**2** In a large bowl, blend together the two flours, baking powder, prunes, and salt. In a medium bowl, beat the egg, milk, oil, molasses, and liqueur until smooth. Combine the two mixtures, blending until the dry ingredients are just moistened.

**3** Spoon the batter into the prepared muffin cups, filling each about three-quarters full. Bake for 15 to 20 minutes, or until a cake tester or wooden toothpick inserted into the center of a muffin comes out clean. Cool in the pan on a wire rack for 5 to 7 minutes. Serve warm, or invert onto the rack to cool completely. Top with Tropical Sauce.

# MISTER'S MUFFINS

MAKES: *12 to 14 muffins*

## MOCHA MUFFINS WITH PECANS

MAKES: *11 to 12 muffins*

1 tablespoon instant espresso coffee powder
¼ cup hot water
1¾ cups all-purpose flour
½ cup granulated sugar
½ cup packed light-brown sugar
2 teaspoons baking powder
1 teaspoon baking soda
1 tablespoon Dutch-processed cocoa powder
1 cup chopped pecans
1 teaspoon salt
2 large eggs
½ cup sour milk or buttermilk
½ cup canola oil
1 teaspoon chocolate extract
Chocolate Sauce (see recipe page 26)

**1** Position the rack in the center of the oven and preheat to 375 degrees F. Lightly grease or line with paper baking cups twelve 2¾-inch muffin cups.

**2** In a cup, dissolve the coffee in the hot water. In a large bowl, blend together the flour, two sugars, baking powder, baking soda, cocoa, pecans, and salt. In a medium bowl, beat the eggs until foamy. Beat in the espresso, sour milk, oil, and chocolate extract. Combine the two mixtures, blending until the dry ingredients are just moistened.

**3** Spoon the batter into the prepared muffin cups, filling each about three-quarters full. Bake for 15 to 20 minutes, or until a cake tester or wooden toothpick inserted into the center of a muffin comes out clean. Cool in the pan on a wire rack for 5 to 7 minutes. Serve warm, or invert onto the rack to cool completely. Serve with Chocolate Sauce.

## MOLASSES–BRAN MUFFINS

MAKES: *6 to 8 muffins*

1 large egg
¼ cup molasses
¾ cup milk
2 tablespoons butter or margarine, melted
1 cup All-Bran® cereal
1 cup all-purpose flour
1 tablespoon baking powder
½ teaspoon salt

**1** Position the rack in the center of the oven and preheat to 400 degrees F. Lightly grease or line with paper baking cups eight 2¾-inch muffin cups.

**2** In a medium bowl, beat the egg, molasses, milk, and butter until smooth. Add the cereal and set aside for 10 minutes.

**3** Meanwhile, in a large bowl, blend together the flour, baking powder, and salt. When the cereal mixture is ready, combine the two mixtures, blending until the dry ingredients are just moistened.

**4** Spoon the batter into the prepared muffin cups, filling each about three-quarters full. Bake for 15 to 20 minutes, or until a cake tester or wooden toothpick inserted into the center of a muffin comes out clean. Remove from the oven. Cool in the pan on a wire rack for 5 to 7 minutes. Serve warm, or transfer to the rack to cool completely.

1¾ cups all-purpose flour
¼ cup rye flour
2 tablespoons granulated sugar
1 teaspoon baking powder
½ teaspoon baking soda
½ teaspoon salt
½ cup sour milk or buttermilk
1 large egg
2 tablespoons butter or margarine, melted
½ cup molasses
Blender Apricot Sauce (see recipe page 25)

**1** Position the rack in the center of the oven and preheat to 400 degrees F. Lightly grease or line with paper baking cups twelve 2¾-inch muffin cups.

**2** In a large bowl, blend together the two flours, sugar, baking powder, baking soda, and salt. In a medium bowl, beat the milk, egg, butter, and molasses until smooth. Combine the two mixtures, blending until the dry ingredients are just moistened.

**3** Spoon the batter into the prepared muffin cups, filling each about three-quarters full. Bake for 15 to 20 minutes, or until a cake tester or wooden toothpick inserted into the center of a muffin comes out clean. Cool in the pan on a wire rack for 5 to 7 minutes. Serve warm, or invert onto the rack to cool completely. Top with Blender Apricot Sauce.

## MOLASSES MUFFINS

MAKES: *11 to 12 muffins*

---

½ cup seedless raisins
¼ cup boiling water
1½ cups bran cereal
1 cup all-purpose flour
1½ teaspoons baking soda
¼ teaspoon salt
1 large egg
½ cup unsweetened apple juice
¼ cup dark molasses
¼ cup apple-flavored yogurt
¼ cup canola oil
Peanut Sauce (see recipe below)

**1** Place the raisins in a cup or small bowl and add the boiling water. Set aside for 20 minutes. Meanwhile, position the rack in the center of the oven and preheat to 400 degrees F. Lightly grease or line with paper baking cups twelve 2¾-inch muffin cups.

**2** In a large bowl, blend together the cereal, flour, baking soda, and salt. In a medium bowl, beat the egg, apple juice, molasses, yogurt, and oil until smooth. Combine the two mixtures, blending until the dry ingredients are just moistened. Drain the raisins, discarding the liquid, and fold the raisins into the batter.

**3** Spoon the batter into the prepared muffin cups, filling each about three-quarters full. Bake for 15 to 20 minutes, or until a cake tester or wooden toothpick inserted into the center of a muffin comes out clean. Cool in the pan on a wire rack for 5 to 7 minutes. Serve warm, or invert onto the rack to cool completely. Top with Peanut Sauce.

## MOLASSES, RAISIN, AND BRAN MUFFINS

MAKES: *11 to 12 muffins*

## PEANUT SAUCE

MAKES: *About 1 cup*

½ cup creamy-style peanut butter
½ cup warmed heavy cream
3 tablespoons honey

In a small bowl, beat the ingredients together until smooth. Serve at once.

## MUSHROOM MUFFINS

MAKES: *11 to 12 muffins*

2 cups all-purpose flour
1 tablespoon baking powder
One 4-ounce can chopped
    mushrooms, drained and liquid
    reserved
1 teaspoon salt
1 large egg
¾ cup milk
¼ cup granulated sugar
¼ cup butter or margarine, melted
½ cup grated cheese
Parsley Sauce (see recipe below)

1  Position the rack in the center of the oven and preheat to 400 degrees F. Lightly grease or line with paper baking cups twelve 2¾-inch muffin cups.

2  In a large bowl, blend together the flour, baking powder, mushrooms, and salt. In a medium bowl, beat the egg until thick and light-colored. Beat in the reserved liquid from the mushrooms, the milk, sugar, and butter. Stir in the cheese. Combine the two mixtures, blending until the dry ingredients are just moistened.

3  Spoon the batter into the prepared muffin cups, filling each about three-quarters full. Bake for 15 to 20 minutes, or until a cake tester or wooden toothpick inserted into the center of a muffin comes out clean. Cool in the pan on a wire rack for 5 to 7 minutes. Serve warm, or invert onto the rack to cool completely. Top with Parsley Sauce.

### PARSLEY SAUCE

MAKES: *About 1 cup*

4 large egg whites
Pinch sea salt
1 teaspoon onion juice
6 tablespoons hot soy milk
½ cup fresh snipped parsley

In a medium bowl, beat the egg whites and salt together until stiff but not dry. Fold in the onion juice. Gradually stir in the soy milk, stirring constantly until the mixture thickens. Fold in the parsley and serve warm.

## NEW ENGLAND CLAM CHOWDER MUFFINS

MAKES: *12 to 14 muffins*

1 cup corn flour
½ cup all-purpose flour
1 cup cornmeal
1 tablespoon baking powder
¼ teaspoon ground nutmeg
2 large eggs
¾ cup milk
One 18.5-ounce can (2½ cups)
    Progresso® New England Clam
    Chowder soup

1  Position the rack in the center of the oven and preheat to 375 degrees F. Lightly grease or line with paper baking cups fourteen 2¾-inch muffin cups.

2  In a large bowl, blend together the two flours, cornmeal, baking powder, and nutmeg. In a medium bowl, beat the eggs until foamy. Beat in the milk and soup. Combine the two mixtures, blending until the dry ingredients are just moistened.

3  Spoon the batter into the prepared muffin cups, filling each about three-quarters full. Bake for 15 to 20 minutes, or until a cake tester or wooden toothpick inserted into the center of a muffin comes out clean. Cool in the pan on a wire rack for 5 to 7 minutes. Serve warm, or invert onto the rack to cool completely.

**SERVING SUGGESTION: Serve with a thick chowderlike soup.**

1 teaspoon ground cinnamon
¼ cup plus 1 teaspoon granulated
   sugar
1 cup all-purpose flour
1 cup bran flakes
1 tablespoon baking powder
½ cup finely chopped walnuts or
   pecans
¼ cup chopped pitted dates
½ teaspoon salt
1 large egg
¼ cup milk
⅓ cup melted butter
Raspberry Melba Sauce (see recipe
   below)

**1** Position the rack in the center of the oven and preheat to 400 degrees F. Lightly grease or line with paper baking cups six 3-inch muffin cups. In a cup, combine the cinnamon and 1 teaspoon of the sugar and set aside.

**2** In a large bowl, blend together the flour, bran flakes, baking powder, the remaining quarter cup of sugar, the walnuts, dates, and salt. In a medium bowl, beat the egg until foamy. Beat in the milk and butter. Combine the two mixtures, blending until the dry ingredients are just moistened.

**3** Spoon the batter into the prepared muffin cups, filling each about three-quarters full. Sprinkle the tops of the muffins with the cinnamon-and-sugar mixture. Bake for 15 to 20 minutes, or until a cake tester or wooden toothpick inserted into the center of a muffin comes out clean. Cool in the pan on a wire rack for 5 to 7 minutes. Serve warm, or invert onto the rack to cool completely. Top with Raspberry Melba Sauce.

# Nut–Bran Muffins

MAKES: *5 to 6 muffins*

## Raspberry Melba Sauce

MAKES: *About 1½ cups*

1 package frozen red raspberries
3 tablespoons powdered sugar
1 teaspoon arrowroot
1 tablespoon cold water
1 tablespoon fresh lemon juice
1 tablespoon Kirsch liqueur

In the container of a blender, combine the raspberries, sugar, arrowroot, and water and process on low speed just until smooth (do not overprocess). Pour into a small saucepan and cook over low heat until the mixture thickens. Remove from the heat and stir in the lemon juice and liqueur. Serve hot or cold.

# NUTMEG MUFFINS

MAKES: *16 to 18 muffins*

3 cups all-purpose flour
1½ cups packed brown sugar
¾ cup chilled butter or margarine, cut into chunks
2 teaspoons baking powder
½ teaspoon baking soda
2 teaspoons ground nutmeg
½ teaspoon salt
2 large eggs
1½ cups buttermilk
Foamy Orange Sauce (see recipe below)

1  Position the rack in the center of the oven and preheat to 375 degrees F. Lightly grease or line with paper baking cups eighteen 2¾-inch muffin cups.

2  In a large bowl, blend together 2 cups of the flour and the brown sugar. Using a pastry cutter or two knives scissor-fashion, cut the butter into the mixture until it resembles coarse meal. Measure out three-quarter cup of this mixture and set it aside for topping the muffins.

3  To the mixture remaining in the bowl, stir in the remaining 1 cup of flour, the baking powder, baking soda, nutmeg, and salt. In a medium bowl, beat the eggs and buttermilk until smooth. Combine the two mixtures, blending until the dry ingredients are just moistened.

4  Spoon the batter into the prepared muffin cups, filling each about three-quarters full. Sprinkle the reserved flour-and-brown sugar mixture over the tops of the muffins. Bake for 15 to 20 minutes, or until a cake tester or wooden toothpick inserted into the center of a muffin comes out clean. Cool in the pan on a wire rack for 5 to 7 minutes. Serve warm, or transfer to the rack to cool completely. Serve with Foamy Orange Sauce.

## FOAMY ORANGE SAUCE

MAKES: *1 cup*

1 large egg
¼ cup butter or margarine
1 cup sifted powdered sugar
1 tablespoon orange juice
Pinch salt
1¼ teaspoons vanilla extract
1 tablespoon grated orange zest

In a small cup, beat the egg until foamy. In the top of a double boiler set over simmering water, combine the butter and sugar. Cook, stirring, until the butter is melted and the mixture is smooth. Stir in the orange juice and salt. Cook, stirring frequently, until the mixture is glossy and smooth. Remove from the heat, stir in the egg, vanilla and orange zest, and pour into a serving bowl.

WARNING: **Serve immediately as this recipe contains raw egg and the sauce will not keep.**

1 cup rolled oats
1 cup sour milk or buttermilk
½ cup packed dark-brown sugar
1 cup all-purpose flour
2 teaspoons baking powder
1 teaspoon baking soda
1 teaspoon nutmeg or mace
½ teaspoon salt
1 large egg
½ cup butter or margarine, melted
2 tablespoons jam or preserves, warmed
Sweet or Sour Lemon Sauce (see recipe below)

1  Position the rack in the center of the oven and preheat to 375 degrees F. Lightly grease or line with paper baking cups twelve 2¾-inch muffin cups.

2  In a small bowl, blend together the oats, buttermilk, and brown sugar. Set aside for 5 to 7 minutes. Meanwhile, in a large bowl,

blend together the flour, baking powder, baking soda, nutmeg, and salt. In a medium bowl, beat the egg until foamy. Beat in the butter. Fold in the oat mixture. Combine the two mixtures, blending until the dry ingredients are just moistened.

3  Spoon the batter into the prepared muffin cups, filling each about three-quarters full. Bake for 15 to 20 minutes, or until a cake tester or wooden toothpick inserted into the center of a muffin comes out clean. Remove from the oven and brush the warm jam over the tops of the muffins. Cool in the pan on a wire rack for 5 to 7 minutes. Serve warm, or invert onto the rack to cool completely. Top with Sweet or Sour Lemon Sauce.

## OAT-AND-JAM MUFFINS

MAKES: *11 to 12 muffins*

## SWEET OR SOUR LEMON SAUCE

MAKES: *About ¾ to 1 cup*

½ cup water
2 tablespoons lemon juice
½ cup potato flour
2 tablespoons honey (for a sweet sauce) or 1 tablespoon cider vinegar (for a sour sauce)

1  In the container of a blender, combine the water, lemon juice, and potato flour and process on medium speed until smooth.

2  Pour into a small saucepan and heat over medium-low heat, stirring frequently until the mixture thickens. For a sweet sauce, stir in the honey; for a sour sauce, stir in the vinegar.

1 cup all-purpose flour
2 cups oat-bran cereal
2 tablespoons baking powder
¼ teaspoon salt
4 large eggs
2 cups skim milk
½ cup packed light-brown sugar
¼ cup light corn syrup
½ cup molasses
Papaya Salsa (see recipe page 123)

1  Position the rack in the center of the oven and preheat to 425 degrees F. Lightly grease or line with paper baking cups twelve 3-inch muffin cups.

2  In a large bowl, blend together the flour, cereal, baking powder, and salt. In a medium bowl, beat

the eggs, milk, sugar, corn syrup, and molasses until smooth. Combine the two mixtures, blending until the dry ingredients are just moistened.

3  Drop 3 heaping tablespoons of the batter into each of the prepared muffin cups, filling each about three-quarters full. Bake for 15 to 20 minutes, or until a cake tester or wooden toothpick inserted into the center of a muffin comes out clean. Cool in the pan on a wire rack for 5 to 7 minutes. Serve warm, or invert onto the rack to cool completely. Serve with Papaya Salsa.

## OAT-BRAN-CEREAL MUFFINS

MAKES: *12 muffins*

# Oat-Bran–Molasses Muffins with Raisins

MAKES: *12 to 14 muffins*

¾ cup seedless raisins
2 tablespoons brandy, warmed
1 cup oat bran
1 cup quick-cooking oats
1 tablespoon baking powder
½ teaspoon baking soda
¾ teaspoon ground cinnamon
¼ teaspoon ground nutmeg
1 cup buttermilk or sour milk
1 large egg
2 tablespoons canola oil
½ cup molasses
Berry Sauce (see recipe page 38)

1  In a cup or small bowl, combine the raisins and warm brandy and set aside for 20 minutes. Meanwhile, position the rack in the center of the oven and preheat to 425 degrees F. Lightly grease or line with paper baking cups fourteen 2¾-inch muffin cups.

2  In a large bowl, blend together the bran, oats, baking powder, baking soda, cinnamon, and nutmeg. In a medium bowl, beat the milk, egg, oil, and molasses until smooth. Stir in the raisins and brandy. Combine the two mixtures, blending until the dry ingredients are just moistened.

3  Spoon the batter into the prepared muffin cups, filling each about three quartets full. Bake for 15 to 20 minutes, or until a cake tester or wooden toothpick inserted into the center of a muffin comes out clean. Cool in the pan on a wire rack for 5 to 7 minutes. Serve warm, or invert onto the rack to cool completely. Top with Berry Sauce.

# Oat-Bran Muffins with Almonds

MAKES: *12 to 14 muffins*

2¼ cups oat-bran cereal
¼ cup ground almonds
¼ cup golden raisins
2 teaspoons baking powder
¼ teaspoon salt
4 large egg whites
⅓ cup honey
2 tablespoons canola oil
¾ cup milk
Blender Apricot Sauce (see recipe page 25)

1  Position the rack in the center of the oven and preheat to 425 degrees F. Lightly grease or line with paper baking cups fourteen 2¾-inch muffin cups.

2  In a large bowl, blend together the cereal, almonds, raisins, baking powder, and salt. In a medium bowl, beat the egg whites, honey, oil, and milk until smooth. Combine the two mixtures, blending until the dry ingredients are just moistened.

3  Spoon the batter into the prepared muffin cups, filling each about three-quarters full. Bake for 15 to 20 minutes, or until a cake tester or wooden toothpick inserted into the center of a muffin comes out clean. Cool in the pan on a wire rack for 5 to 7 minutes. Serve warm, or invert onto the rack to cool completely. Serve with Blender Apricot Sauce.

1 cup quick-cooking oats
1 cup all-purpose flour
½ cup granulated sugar
2 teaspoons baking powder
1½ teaspoons ground cinnamon
½ teaspoon ground nutmeg
¼ teaspoon salt
2 large egg whites
¾ cup milk
½ cup canola oil
1 cup black currants
1 medium apple, peeled, cored, and
    diced
Molasses Sauce (see recipe page 125)

1  Position the rack in the center of the oven and preheat to 400 degrees F. Lightly grease or line with paper baking cups eighteen 2¾-inch muffin cups.

2  In a large bowl, blend together the oats, flour, sugar, baking powder, cinnamon, nutmeg, and salt. In a medium bowl, beat the egg whites until foamy. Beat in the milk and oil. Combine the two mixtures, blending until the dry ingredients are just moistened. Stir in the currants and apples.

3  Spoon the batter into the prepared muffin cups, filling each about three-quarters full. Bake for 15 to 20 minutes, or until a cake tester or wooden toothpick inserted into the center of a muffin comes out clean. Cool in the pan on a wire rack for 5 to 7 minutes. Serve warm, or invert onto the rack to cool completely. Top with Molasses Sauce.

# OATMEAL–APPLE MUFFINS

MAKES: *16 to 18 muffins*

---

¾ cup all-purpose flour
¾ cup quick-cooking oats
2 teaspoons baking powder
2 teaspoons ground cinnamon
1 teaspoon ground ginger
¼ teaspoon salt
2 large eggs
½ cup milk
2 tablespoons canola oil
¼ cup packed light-brown sugar
2 teaspoons vanilla extract
½ cup unsweetened applesauce
Apple–Cinnamon Syrup (see recipe
    page 168)

1  Position the rack in the center of the oven and preheat to 375 degrees F. Lightly grease or line with paper baking cups ten 2¾-inch muffin cups.

2  In a large bowl, blend together the flour, oats, baking powder, cinnamon, ginger, and salt. In a medium bowl, beat the eggs until thick and light-colored. Beat in the milk, oil, sugar, and vanilla extract. Stir in the applesauce. Combine the two mixtures, blending until the dry ingredients are just moistened.

3  Spoon the batter into the prepared muffin cups, filling each about three-quarters full. Bake for 15 to 20 minutes, or until a cake tester or wooden toothpick inserted into the center of a muffin comes out clean. Cool in the pan on a wire rack for 5 to 7 minutes. Serve warm, or invert onto the rack to cool completely. Serve with Apple–Cinnamon Syrup.

# OATMEAL– APPLESAUCE MUFFINS

MAKES: *10 muffins*

# OATMEAL-AND-MANGO MUFFINS WITH RAISINS

MAKES: *11 to 12 muffins*

1 cup finely chopped dried mango or papaya
1 cup graham flour
1 cup quick oats
⅓ cup granulated sugar
1 tablespoon baking powder
1 teaspoon ground cinnamon
½ teaspoon ground nutmeg or mace
1 cup golden raisins
1 large egg
¾ cup milk
½ cup canola oil
Whipped Cream Topping (see recipe below)

1 In a cup or small bowl, place the chopped mango and warm water to cover and set aside for 30 minutes.

2 When ready to bake, position the rack in the center of the oven and preheat to 400 degrees F. Lightly grease or line with paper baking cups twelve 2¾-inch muffin cups.

3 In a large bowl, blend together the flour, oats, sugar, baking powder, cinnamon, nutmeg, apples, and raisins. Drain the mango, discarding the liquid, and stir it into the flour mixture, coating thoroughly. In a medium bowl, beat the egg, milk, and oil until smooth. Combine the two mixtures, blending until the dry ingredients are just moistened.

4 Spoon the batter into the prepared muffin cups, filling each about three-quarters full. Bake for 15 to 20 minutes, or until a cake tester or wooden toothpick inserted into a muffin is removed clean. Cool in the pan on a wire rack for 5 to 7 minutes. Serve warm, or invert onto the rack to cool completely. Top with Whipped Cream Topping.

## WHIPPED CREAM TOPPING

MAKES: *2 cups*

1 cup heavy cream
¼ cup powdered sugar
1 teaspoon vanilla extract

In a medium bowl, using a whisk or an electric mixer on high speed, beat the cream until foamy. Add the sugar and vanilla and continue beating until soft peaks form. Refrigerate until ready to use.

# OATMEAL, MAPLE, AND PECAN MUFFINS

MAKES: *12 to 14 muffins*

2 cups finely ground oatmeal (see Note)
¼ cup whole-wheat flour
2 teaspoons baking powder
½ cup finely chopped pecans
½ cup finely chopped, pitted dates
2 large eggs
½ cup maple syrup
¾ cup water
2 teaspoons maple flavoring
2 tablespoons safflower or canola oil

1 Position the rack in the center of the oven and preheat to 375 degrees F. Lightly grease or line with paper baking cups fourteen 2¾-inch muffin cups.

2 In a large bowl, blend together the oatmeal, flour, baking powder, pecans, and dates. In a medium bowl, beat the eggs, syrup, water, maple flavoring, and oil until smooth. Combine the two mixtures, blending until the dry ingredients are just moistened.

3 Spoon the batter into the prepared muffin cups, filling each about three-quarters full. Bake for 15 to 20 minutes, or until a cake tester or wooden toothpick inserted into the center of a muffin comes out clean. Cool in the pan on a wire rack for 5 to 7 minutes. Serve warm, or invert onto the rack to cool completely.

NOTE: **If you purchase coarse oatmeal, it can be ground finely in a blender or food processor.**

1 cup all-purpose flour
1 cup rolled oats
1 teaspoon baking powder
½ teaspoon baking soda
¾ cup golden raisins
⅛ teaspoon salt
1 large egg
1 tablespoon canola oil
2 tablespoons granulated sugar
¼ cup molasses
½ cup buttermilk or sour milk
¼ cup unsweetened applesauce
Rhubarb Sauce (see recipe page 245)

1 Position the rack in the center of the oven and preheat to 375 degrees F. Lightly grease or line with paper baking cups six 3-inch muffin cups.

2 In a large bowl, blend together the flour, oats, baking powder, baking soda, raisins, and salt. In a medium bowl, beat the egg until thick and light-colored. Beat in the oil, sugar, molasses, and buttermilk until smooth. Stir in the applesauce. Combine the two mixtures, blending until the dry ingredients are just moistened.

3 Spoon 3 heaping tablespoons of the batter into the prepared muffin cups, filling each about three-quarters full. Bake for 15 to 20 minutes, or until a cake tester or wooden toothpick inserted into the center of a muffin comes out clean. Cool in the pan on a wire rack for 5 to 7 minutes. Serve warm, or invert onto the rack to cool completely. Serve with Rhubarb Sauce.

## Oatmeal Muffins with Raisins

Makes: *5 to 6 muffins*

---

1 cup quick-cooking oats
1 cup sour milk or buttermilk
1 cup all-purpose flour
1 teaspoon baking powder
½ teaspoon baking soda
½ cup packed light-brown sugar
½ teaspoon salt
1 large egg
½ cup canola oil
Raspberry Melba Sauce (see recipe page 203)

1 In a small bowl, combine the oats and milk. Set aside for 1 hour.

2 When ready to bake, position the rack in the center of the oven and preheat to 375 degrees F. Lightly grease or line with paper baking cups six 3-inch muffin cups.

3 In a large bowl, blend together the flour, baking powder, baking soda, sugar, and salt. In a medium bowl, beat the egg and oil until smooth. Stir in the oats and milk. Combine the two mixtures, blending until the dry ingredients are just moistened.

4 Spoon the batter into the prepared muffin cups, filling each about three-quarters full. Bake for 15 to 20 minutes, or until a cake tester or wooden toothpick inserted into the center of a muffin comes out clean. Cool in the pan on a wire rack for 5 to 7 minutes. Serve warm, or invert onto the rack to cool completely. Top with Raspberry Melba Sauce.

## Oatmeal Muffins

Makes: *5 to 6 muffins*

# OATMEAL–RAISIN MUFFINS

MAKES: *12 to 14 muffins*

1¼ cups all-purpose flour
1 cup rolled oats
¼ cup packed brown sugar
1 tablespoon baking powder
¾ teaspoon ground cinnamon
½ teaspoon salt
1 large egg
¼ cup canola oil
1 cup milk
½ cup seedless raisins
raspberry preserves for brushing
Whipped Butter (see recipe page 23)

1  Position the rack in the center of the oven and preheat to 400 degrees F. Lightly grease or line with paper baking cups twelve 2¾-inch muffin cups.

2  In a large bowl, blend together the flour, oats, sugar, baking powder, cinnamon, and salt. In a medium bowl, beat the egg until thick and light-colored. Beat in the oil and milk. Stir in the raisins. Combine the two mixtures, until the dry ingredients are just blended.

3  Spoon the batter into the prepared muffin cups, filling each about three-quarters full. Bake for 15 to 20 minutes, or until a cake tester or wooden toothpick inserted into the center of a muffin comes out clean. Remove from the oven and brush the tops of the muffins with raspberry preserves before cooling in the pan on a wire rack for 5 to 7 minutes. Serve warm, or transfer to the rack to cool completely. Serve with Whipped Butter.

# OLD-FASHIONED GERMAN MUFFINS

MAKES: *9 to 11 muffins*

2¼ cups all-purpose flour
2 teaspoons baking powder
¼ cup ground hazelnuts or almonds
1 tablespoon grated orange zest
½ teaspoon ground mace or nutmeg
¼ teaspoon salt
¾ cup butter or margarine, at room temperature
½ cup granulated sugar
2 large eggs
3 tablespoons milk
1 tablespoon rum or brandy
1 teaspoon almond extract
2 tablespoons raspberry preserves
Orange Marshmallow Sauce (see recipe page 22)

1  Position the rack in the center of the oven and preheat to 375 degrees F. Lightly grease or line with paper baking cups twelve 2¾-inch muffin cups.

2  In a large bowl, blend together the flour, baking powder, hazelnuts, orange zest, and mace. In a medium bowl, beat the butter and sugar until light and fluffy. Beat in the eggs, milk, rum, and almond extract until smooth. Combine the two mixtures, blending until the dry ingredients are just moistened.

3  Spoon the batter into the prepared muffin cups, filling each about three-quarters full. Press ½ teaspoon of the raspberry preserves into the center of each muffin. Bake for 15 to 20 minutes, or until a cake tester or wooden toothpick inserted at the edge of a muffin (not into the preserves) comes out clean. Cool in the pan on a wire rack for 5 to 7 minutes. Serve warm, or invert onto the rack to cool completely. Top with Orange Marshmallow Sauce.

2 cups all-purpose flour
1 tablespoon baking powder
1 cup chopped black olives
1 teaspoon salt
1 large egg
1 cup milk
¼ cup granulated sugar
¼ cup butter or margarine, melted
½ cup grated cheese
Cheese-and-Olive Spread (see recipe page 183)

1  Position the rack in the center of the oven and preheat to 400 degrees F. Lightly grease or line with paper baking cups twelve 2¾-inch muffin cups.

2  In a large bowl, blend together the flour, baking powder, olives, and salt. In a medium bowl, beat the egg until thick and light-colored. Beat in the milk, sugar, and butter. Stir in the cheese. Combine the two mixtures, blending until the dry ingredients are just moistened.

3  Spoon the batter into the prepared muffin cups, filling each about three-quarters full. Bake for 15 to 20 minutes, or until a cake tester or wooden toothpick inserted into the center of a muffin comes out clean. Cool in the pan on a wire rack for 5 to 7 minutes. Serve warm, or invert onto the rack to cool completely. Serve with Cheese & Olive Spread.

## OLIVE-AND-CHEESE MUFFINS

MAKES: *11 to 12 muffins*

---

1¾ cups all-purpose flour
2 tablespoons baking powder
1 teaspoon baking soda
¾ cup grated Cheddar cheese, plus more for topping the muffins
½ cup grated onion
1 tablespoon fresh snipped chives
1 large egg
2 tablespoons butter or margarine, melted
1¼ cups buttermilk or sour milk
½ cup canola oil
Shrimp Spread (see recipe page 145)

1  Position the rack in the center of the oven and preheat to 375 degrees F. Lightly grease or line with paper baking cups twelve 2¾-inch muffin cups.

2  In a large bowl, blend together the flour, baking powder, baking soda, ¾ cup cheese, onion, and chives. In a medium bowl, beat the egg until foamy. Beat in the butter, milk, and oil. Combine the two mixtures, blending until the dry ingredients are just moistened.

3  Spoon the batter into the prepared muffin cups, filling each about three-quarters full. Sprinkle the tops of the muffins lightly with grated cheese. Bake for 15 to 20 minutes, or until a cake tester or wooden toothpick inserted into the center of a muffin comes out clean. Cool in the pan on a wire rack for 5 to 7 minutes. Serve warm, or invert onto the rack to cool completely. Serve with Shrimp Spread.

## ONION-AND-CHEESE MUFFINS

MAKES: *12 to 14 muffins*

# ORANGE–CORN MUFFINS

MAKES: *11 to 12 muffins*

1 cup all-purpose flour
1 cup yellow cornmeal
⅓ cup granulated sugar
4 teaspoons baking powder
½ teaspoon baking soda
1 tablespoon grated orange zest
½ teaspoon salt
1 large egg
¼ cup canola oil
2 tablespoons fresh squeezed orange juice
¾ cup sour milk or buttermilk
Foamy Orange Sauce (see recipe page 204)

1  Position the rack in the center of the oven and preheat to 425 degrees F. Lightly grease or line with paper baking cups twelve 2¾-inch muffin cups.

2  In a large bowl, blend together the flour, cornmeal, sugar, baking powder, baking soda, orange zest, and salt. In a medium bowl, beat the egg until thick and light-colored. Beat in the oil, orange juice, and milk. Combine the two mixtures, blending until the dry ingredients are just moistened.

3  Spoon the batter into the prepared muffin cups, filling each about three-quarters full. Bake for 15 to 20 minutes, or until a cake tester or wooden toothpick inserted into the center of a muffin comes out clean. Remove from the oven and immediately brush the tops of the muffins with the glaze. Cool in the pan on a wire rack for 5 to 7 minutes. Serve warm, or transfer to the rack to cool completely. Top with Foamy Orange Sauce.

# ORANGE–CRANBERRY MUFFINS

MAKES: *12 to 14 muffins*

TOPPING
¼ cup packed brown sugar
½ teaspoon ground cinnamon
⅓ cup chopped walnuts

MUFFIN
2 cups all-purpose flour
¼ cup granulated sugar
1 tablespoon baking powder
½ teaspoon baking soda
½ teaspoon salt
1 large egg
1 cup orange juice
1 teaspoon grated orange zest
¼ cup canola oil
1 cup chopped cranberries
Cranberry Sauce (see recipe page 108)

1  To make the topping, in a small-size bowl, blend together the brown sugar, cinnamon, and walnuts. Set aside. Position the rack in the center of the oven and preheat to 375 degrees F. Lightly grease or line with paper baking cups twelve 2¾-inch muffin cups.

2  In a large bowl, blend together the flour, granulated sugar, baking powder, baking soda, and salt. In a medium bowl, beat the egg, orange juice, orange zest, and oil until smooth. Stir in the cranberries. Combine the two mixtures, blending until the dry ingredients are just moistened.

3  Spoon the batter into the prepared muffin cups, filling each about three-quarters full. Sprinkle the topping over each cup full of batter. Bake for 15 to 20 minutes, or until a cake tester or wooden toothpick inserted into the center of a muffin comes out clean. Cool in the pan on a wire rack for 5 to 7 minutes. Serve warm, or invert onto the rack to cool completely. Serve with Cranberry Sauce.

1¾ cups all-purpose flour
2 teaspoons baking powder
½ teaspoon salt
⅓ cup granulated sugar
2 large eggs
⅓ cup butter or margarine, melted
⅓ cup milk
1 tablespoon Triple Sec or 1
   teaspoon orange extract
½ cup Marmalade Filling (see recipe
   below)
Orange Sauce (see recipe page 33)

**1** Position the rack in the center of the oven and preheat to 375 degrees F. Lightly grease or line with paper baking cups twelve 2¾-inch muffin cups.

**2** In a large bowl, blend together the flour, baking powder, and salt. In a medium bowl, beat the sugar, eggs, butter, milk, and Triple Sec until smooth. Combine the two mixtures, blending until the dry ingredients are just moistened.

**3** Spoon the batter into the prepared muffin cups, filling each about three-quarters full.

**4** Dividing evenly between the muffin cups, press the filling into the center of each muffin. Bake for 15 to 20 minutes, or until a cake tester or wooden toothpick inserted near the edge of a muffin (not into the filling) comes out clean. Cool in the pan on a wire rack for 5 to 7 minutes. Serve warm, or invert onto the rack to cool completely. Serve with Orange Sauce.

## MARMALADE FILLING

MAKES: ⅔ cup

¼ cup all-purpose flour
¼ cup packed brown sugar
1 teaspoon light cream
1 tablespoon butter or margarine,
   at room temperature
2 tablespoons orange marmalade

In a small bowl, combine the flour, sugar, cream, butter, and marmalade. Beat until smooth.

# ORANGE MARMALADE MUFFINS

MAKES: *10 to 12 muffins*

---

1½ cups cake flour
⅓ cup granulated sugar
2 teaspoons baking powder
1 large egg
¼ cup butter or margarine, melted
¼ cup condensed milk
¼ cup orange juice
Freshly grated zest from orange
Whipped Cream Topping (see recipe
   page 208)

**1** Position the rack in the center of the oven and preheat to 375 degrees F. Lightly grease or line with paper baking cups eight 2¾-inch muffin cups.

**2** In a large bowl, blend together the flour, sugar, and baking powder. In a medium bowl, beat the egg, butter, milk, orange juice, and orange zest until smooth. Combine the two mixtures, blending until the dry ingredients are just moistened.

**3** Spoon the batter into the prepared muffin cups, filling each about three-quarters full. Bake for 15 to 20 minutes, or until a cake tester or wooden toothpick inserted into the center of a muffin comes out clean. Cool in the pan on a wire rack for 5 to 7 minutes. Serve warm, or invert onto the rack to cool completely. Serve with Whipped Cream Topping.

# ORANGE MUFFINS

MAKES: *7 to 8 muffins*

## PAPAYA MUFFINS

MAKES: *11 to 12 muffins*

1 cup dried papaya, finely diced
¼ cup peach-flavored brandy
1¼ cups all-purpose flour
1 cup whole-wheat flour
½ cup granulated sugar
1 tablespoon baking powder
1 teaspoon baking soda
4 large egg whites
1 cup plain yogurt
2 tablespoons butter or margarine, melted
Tropical Sauce (see recipe page 81)

**1** In a cup or small bowl, combine the papaya and brandy. Set aside for 1 hour.

**2** When ready to bake, position the rack in the center of the oven and preheat to 375 degrees F. Lightly grease or line with paper baking cups twelve 2¾-inch muffin cups.

**3** In a large bowl, blend together the two flours, sugar, baking powder, and baking soda. In a medium bowl, beat the egg whites until stiff but not dry. Beat in the yogurt and butter. Stir in the papaya and brandy. Combine the two mixtures, until the dry ingredients are just blended.

**4** Spoon the batter into the prepared muffin cups, filling each about three-quarters full. Bake for 15 to 20 minutes, or until a cake tester or wooden toothpick inserted into the center of a muffin comes out clean. Cool in the pan on a wire rack for 5 to 7 minutes. Serve warm, or invert onto the rack to cool completely. Top with Tropical Sauce.

## PARMESAN MUFFINS

MAKES: *11 to 12 muffins*

2 cups all-purpose flour
1½ teaspoons baking powder
½ teaspoon baking soda
½ cup grated Parmesan cheese
½ cup chopped fresh parsley
½ teaspoon dried crushed marjoram
¼ cup butter or margarine, melted
1 tablespoon granulated sugar
1¼ cups buttermilk or sour milk
1 large egg
Mexican Sauce (see recipe page 77)

**1** Position the rack in the center of the oven and preheat to 400 degrees F. Lightly grease or line with paper baking cups twelve 2¾-inch muffin cups.

**2** In large bowl, blend together the flour, baking powder, baking soda, parsley, cheese, and marjoram. In a medium bowl, beat the butter, sugar, buttermilk, and egg until smooth. Combine the two mixtures, blending until the dry ingredients are just moistened.

**3** Spoon the batter into the prepared muffin cups, filling each about three-quarters full. Bake for 15 to 20 minutes, or until a cake tester or wooden toothpick inserted into the center of a muffin comes out clean. Cool in the pan on a wire rack for 5 to 7 minutes. Serve warm, or invert onto the rack to cool completely. Top with Mexican Sauce.

1 to 2 tablespoons schmaltz
1½ cups matzoh farfel
1 to 1½ cups boiling water
4 large eggs
¼ teaspoon ground white pepper
¼ teaspoon salt
Whipped Butter (see recipe page 23)

**1** Position the rack in the center of the oven and preheat to 400 degrees F. Place a small piece of schmaltz in the bottom of each of eight 2¾-inch muffin cups. Place the muffin cups in the oven while preparing the batter.

**2** Place the farfel into a fine-mesh strainer and place the strainer in a large bowl in which the strainer touches the bottom. Gently pour the boiling water over the farfel and let set for 5 minutes or until soggy. Remove the strainer from the bowl, and drain completely. Transfer the farfel to a medium bowl. Using a fork, whip in the eggs, one at a time, beating thoroughly after each addition. Stir in salt and pepper.

**3** Remove the muffin cups from the oven and pour out the schmaltz. Spoon the batter into the muffin cups, filling each about three-quarters full. Bake for about 25 to 30 minutes, or until the tops are a golden brown and a cake tester or wooden toothpick inserted into the center of a muffin comes out clean. Cool in the pan on a wire rack for 5 to 7 minutes. Serve warm, or invert onto the rack to cool completely. Serve with Whipped Butter.

**BAKING NOTE: The muffins will rise during baking, but will fall as they start to cool.**

# PASSOVER MUFFINS
MAKES: *7 to 8 muffins*

---

1 cup all-purpose flour
1 teaspoon baking powder
1 teaspoon baking soda
¾ cup granulated sugar
½ teaspoon ground cinnamon
½ teaspoon ground nutmeg
1 cup finely chopped pecans
1 cup fresh persimmon pulp
2 tablespoons butter or margarine, melted
1 to 2 tablespoons milk
Whipped Cream Topping (see recipe page 208)

**1** Position the rack in the center of the oven and preheat to 400 degrees F. Lightly grease or line with paper baking cups twelve 2¾-inch muffin cups.

**2** In a large bowl, blend together the flour, baking powder, baking soda, sugar, cinnamon, nutmeg, and pecans. In a small bowl, beat the persimmon and butter until smooth. Combine the two mixtures, blending until the dry ingredients are just moistened. If mixture seems dry, gently stir in the milk 1 tablespoon at a time.

**3** Spoon the batter into the prepared muffin cups, filling each about three-quarters full. Bake for 15 to 20 minutes, or until a cake tester or wooden toothpick inserted into the center of a muffin comes out clean. Cool in the pan on a wire rack for 5 to 7 minutes. Serve warm, or invert onto the rack to cool completely. Serve with Whipped Cream Topping.

# PERSIMMON MUFFINS
MAKES: *12 muffins*

# PESTO MUFFINS

MAKES: *12 to 14 muffins*

1½ cups all-purpose flour
1 cup whole-wheat flour
2 teaspoons baking powder
½ teaspoon baking soda
1 tablespoon chopped fresh basil
½ cup grated Cheddar cheese
2 large eggs
¼ cup canola oil
1 cup milk
⅓ cup prepared Pesto sauce
½ cup finely chopped shallots
Paprika
Pesto Cream (see recipe page 169)

**1** Position the rack in the center of the oven and preheat to 400 degrees F. Lightly grease or line with paper baking cups fourteen 2¾-inch muffin cups.

**2** In a large bowl, blend together the two flours, baking powder, baking soda, basil, and cheese. In a medium bowl, beat the eggs until thick and light-colored. Beat in the oil, milk, Pesto, and shallots. Combine the two mixtures, blending until the dry ingredients are just moistened.

**3** Spoon the batter into the prepared muffin cups, filling each about three-quarters full. Sprinkle the tops of the muffins lightly with paprika. Bake for 15 to 20 minutes, or until a cake tester or wooden toothpick inserted into the center of a muffin comes out clean. Cool in the pan on a wire rack for 5 to 7 minutes. Serve warm, or invert onto the rack to cool completely. Top with Pesto Cream.

# PICK-NIC B & B MUFFINS

MAKES: *16 to 18 muffins*

2 cups all-purpose flour
1½ cups bran flakes
2 tablespoons packed light-brown sugar
1 teaspoon baking powder
1¼ teaspoons baking soda
2 tablespoons grated orange zest
1 cup chopped walnuts
¼ teaspoon salt
1 large egg
2 cups buttermilk
¼ cup butter or margarine, melted
½ cup molasses
2 large bananas, mashed

**1** Position the rack in the center of the oven and preheat to 375 degrees F. Lightly grease or line with paper baking cups eighteen 2¾-inch muffin cups.

**2** In a large bowl, blend together the flour, bran flakes, sugar, baking powder, baking soda, orange zest, walnuts, and salt. In a medium bowl, beat the egg until foamy. Beat in the buttermilk, butter, molasses, and bananas. Combine the two mixtures, blending until the dry ingredients are just moistened.

**3** Spoon the batter into the prepared muffin cups, filling each about three-quarters full. Bake for 15 to 20 minutes, or until a cake tester or wooden toothpick inserted into the center of a muffin comes out clean. Cool in the pan on a wire rack for 5 to 7 minutes. Serve warm, or invert onto the rack to cool completely.

SERVING SUGGESTION: **Serve with grilled apples.**

1½ cups all-purpose flour
½ cup granulated sugar
2 tablespoons baking powder
¼ cup toasted pine nuts
¼ cup chopped pecans
¼ cup shelled sunflower seeds
1 large egg
½ cup milk
¼ cup butter or margarine, melted
Energy Drink (see recipe page 165)

**1** Position the rack in the center of the oven and preheat to 400 degrees F. Lightly grease or line with paper baking cups twelve 2¾-inch muffin cups.

**2** In a large bowl, blend together the flour, sugar, baking powder, pine nuts, pecans, and sunflower seeds. In a medium bowl, beat the eggs until foamy. Beat in the milk and butter. Combine the two mixtures, blending until the dry ingredients are just moistened.

**3** Spoon the batter into the prepared muffin cups, filling each about three-quarters full. Bake for 15 to 20 minutes, or until a cake tester or wooden toothpick inserted into the center of a muffin comes out clean. Cool in the pan on a wire rack for 5 to 7 minutes. Serve warm, or invert onto the rack to cool completely. Serve with Energy Drink.

# PINE NUT, PECAN, AND SUNFLOWER SEED MUFFINS

MAKES: *10 to 12 muffins*

---

2 cups all-purpose flour
¼ cup packed dark-brown sugar
2 tablespoons granulated sugar
1 tablespoon baking powder
½ teaspoon ground nutmeg
½ teaspoon salt
1 large egg
2 tablespoons butter or margarine, melted
1 cup milk
¼ cup canola oil
½ cup crushed pineapple, drained
Coconut Chutney (see recipe page 65)
Flaked coconut for sprinkling

**1** Position the rack in the center of the oven and preheat to 400 degrees F. Lightly grease or line with paper baking cups fourteen 2¾-inch muffin cups.

**2** In a large bowl, blend together the flour, two sugars, baking powder, nutmeg, and salt. In a medium bowl, beat the egg foamy before beating in the butter, milk, oil, and pineapple. Combine the two mixtures, blending until the dry ingredients are just moistened.

**3** Spoon the batter into the prepared muffin cups, filling each about three-quarters full. Bake for 15 to 20 minutes, or until a cake tester or wooden toothpick inserted into the center of a muffin comes out clean. Remove from the oven and sprinkle the tops of the muffins with flaked coconut. Cool in the pan on a wire rack for 5 to 7 minutes. Serve warm, or transfer to the rack to cool completely. Serve with Coconut Chutney.

# PINEAPPLE MUFFINS

MAKES: *12 to 14 muffins*

# PINEAPPLE–OATMEAL MUFFINS

MAKES: *11 to 12 muffins*

1 cup rolled oats
One 8-ounce can crushed pineapple (do not drain)
½ cup sour cream or buttermilk
1¼ cups all-purpose flour
1 teaspoon baking powder
½ teaspoon baking soda
1 teaspoon salt
1 large egg
⅓ cup butter or margarine, melted
⅓ cup packed brown sugar
1 teaspoon grated orange zest
Whipped Cream Topping (see recipe page 208)

1  In a medium bowl, combine the oats, pineapple, and sour cream. Set aside for 10 minutes.

2  Meanwhile, position the rack in the center of the oven and preheat to 400 degrees F. Lightly grease or line with paper baking cups twelve 2 ¾-inch muffin cups.

3  In a large bowl, blend together the flour, baking powder, baking soda, and salt. In a medium bowl, beat the egg until foamy. Beat in the butter, sugar, and orange zest. Stir in the oat-and-pineapple mixture. Combine the two mixtures, blending until the dry ingredients are just moistened.

4  Spoon the batter into the prepared muffin cups, filling each about three-quarters full. Bake for 15 to 20 minutes, or until a cake tester or wooden toothpick inserted into the center of a muffin comes out clean. Cool in the pan on a wire rack for 5 to 7 minutes. Serve warm, or invert onto the rack to cool completely. Serve with Whipped Cream Topping.

# PINEAPPLE–BACON MUFFINS

MAKES: *11 to 12 muffins*

1 cup all-purpose flour
1 cup cornmeal
1 teaspoon baking powder
¾ teaspoon baking soda
2 large eggs
2 tablespoons brown sugar
1½ cups sour milk or buttermilk
¼ cup bacon drippings
4 strips crisply cooked bacon, crumbled
¾ cup crushed pineapple, drained and mashed
Horseradish Sauce with Bacon (see recipe below)

1  Position the rack in the center of the oven and preheat to 425 degrees F. Lightly grease or line with paper baking cups twelve 2¾-inch muffin cups.

2  In a large bowl, blend together the flour, cornmeal, baking powder, and baking soda. In a medium bowl, beat the eggs until thick and light-colored. Beat in the sugar, milk, and bacon drippings. Stir in the bacon and pineapple. Combine the two mixtures, blending until the dry ingredients are just moistened.

3  Spoon the batter into the prepared muffin cups, filling each about three-quarters full. Bake for 15 to 20 minutes, or until a cake tester or wooden toothpick inserted into the center of a muffin comes out clean. Cool in the pan on a wire rack for 5 to 7 minutes. Serve warm, or invert onto the rack to cool completely. Serve with Horseradish Sauce with Bacon.

## HORSERADISH SAUCE WITH BACON

MAKES: *About 2 cups*

1 cup mayonnaise
1 cup sour cream or yogurt
¼ cup crumbled bacon or bacon bits
¼ cup prepared horseradish

In a medium bowl, combine all of the ingredients and blend until smooth. Cover with plastic wrap and refrigerate until ready to serve.

2 cups all-purpose flour
2 teaspoons baking powder
2 teaspoons chopped fresh basil
½ teaspoon paprika
1 medium tomato, finely chopped
12 black olives, chopped
½ cup grated Provolone cheese, plus
   more for topping
¼ teaspoon salt
2 large eggs
1 tablespoon olive oil
¾ cup milk
12 slices dry salami
Tomato Sauce (see recipe below)

**1** Position the rack in the center of the oven and preheat to 400 degrees F. Lightly grease or line with paper baking cups twelve 2¾-inch muffin cups.

**2** In a large bowl, blend together the flour, baking powder, basil, paprika, tomato, olives, ½ cup of the cheese, and salt. In a medium bowl, beat the eggs until thick and light-colored. Beat in the oil and milk. Combine the two mixtures, blending until the dry ingredients are just moistened.

**3** Spoon the batter into the prepared muffin cups, filling each about three-quarters full. Lay a slice of salami on the top of each muffin and sprinkle the tops lightly with cheese. Bake for 15 to 20 minutes, or until a cake tester or wooden toothpick inserted into the center of a muffin comes out clean. Cool in the pan on a wire rack for 5 to 7 minutes. Serve warm, or transfer to the rack to cool completely. Serve with Tomato Sauce.

## TOMATO SAUCE

MAKES: *About 1 cup*

4 medium tomatoes, quartered
1 medium shallot, peeled and
   quartered
2 teaspoons honey
Pinch dry mustard
Salt to taste

In the container of a blender, combine all of the ingredients except the salt and process on medium speed until smooth. Pour into a small saucepan and set over medium heat. Cook, stirring constantly, until the mixture just starts to bubble. Remove from the heat and season to taste with salt. Serve hot or cold.

---

3 cups all-purpose flour
1 tablespoon granulated sugar
4 teaspoons baking powder
½ teaspoon salt
2 large eggs
⅔ cup milk
2 tablespoons butter or margarine,
   melted
Whipped Butter (see recipe page 23)

**1** Position the rack in the center of the oven and preheat to 425 degrees F. Lightly grease or line with paper baking cups twelve 2¾-inch muffin cups.

**2** In a large bowl, blend together the flour, sugar, baking powder, and salt. In a medium bowl, beat the eggs until foamy. Beat in the milk and butter. Combine the two mixtures, blending until the dry ingredients are just moistened.

**3** Spoon the batter into the prepared muffin cups, filling each about three-quarters full. Bake for 15 to 20 minutes, or until cake tester or wooden toothpick inserted into the center of a muffin comes out clean. Cool in the pan on a wire rack for 5 to 7 minutes. Serve warm, or invert onto the rack to cool completely. Serve with Whipped Butter.

# PLAIN MUFFINS
MAKES: *12 to 14 muffins*

## PLAIN MUFFINS WITH APRICOTS

MAKES: *11 to 12 muffins*

¾ cup finely chopped dried apricots
⅓ cup warmed brandy
2 cups all-purpose flour
1 tablespoon baking powder
½ teaspoon baking soda
1 teaspoon salt
¼ cup butter-flavored vegetable shortening
½ cup packed light-brown sugar
1 large egg
¾ cup sour cream or plain yogurt

**1** In a cup or small bowl, combine the apricots and warm brandy and set aside for 30 minutes.

**2** When ready to bake, position the rack in the center of the oven and preheat 400 degrees F. Lightly grease or line with paper baking cups twelve 2¾-inch muffin cups.

**3** In a large bowl, blend together the flour, baking powder, baking soda, and salt. In a medium bowl, beat the shortening and sugar light and fluffy. Beating in the egg and sour cream. Drain the apricots, discarding the brandy or saving it for another use, and stir in the apricots. Combine the two mixtures, blending until the dry ingredients are just moistened.

**4** Spoon the batter into the prepared muffin cups, filling each about three-quarters full. Bake for 20 to 25 minutes, or until a cake tester or wooden toothpick inserted into the center of a muffin comes out clean. Remove from the oven and brush with the glaze. Cool in the pan on a wire rack for 5 to 7 minutes. Serve warm, or transfer to the rack to cool completely.

## POPPY SEED MUFFINS

MAKES: *14 to 16 muffins*

2 cups all-purpose flour
¾ cup granulated sugar
1 tablespoon baking powder
½ teaspoon grated orange zest
¼ teaspoon ground nutmeg
¼ cup chopped pecans
2 tablespoons poppy seeds
½ cup seedless raisins (optional)
½ teaspoon salt
2 large eggs
1 cup butter or margarine, melted
1 cup milk
Whipped Cream (see recipe page 208)

**1** Position the rack in the center of the oven and preheat to 400 degrees F. Lightly grease or line with paper baking cups sixteen 2¾-inch muffin cups.

**2** In a large bowl, blend together the flour, sugar, baking powder, orange zest, nutmeg, nuts, poppy seeds, raisins, and salt. In a medium bowl, beat the eggs until foamy. Beat in the butter and milk. Combine the two mixtures, blending until the dry ingredients are just moistened.

**3** Spoon the batter into the prepared muffin cups, filling each about three-quarters full. Bake for 15 to 20 minutes, or until a cake tester or wooden toothpick inserted into the center of a muffin comes out clean. Cool in the pan on a wire rack for 5 to 7 minutes. Serve warm, or invert onto the rack to cool completely. Serve with Whipped Cream.

**SERVING SUGGESTION: Serve with black currant jam.**

3 cups all-purpose flour
5 teaspoons baking powder
1 tablespoon granulated sugar
½ cup grated Swiss cheese
½ teaspoon salt
2 cups white port wine

**1** Position the rack in the center of the oven and preheat to 375 degrees F. Lightly grease or line with paper baking cups eighteen 2¾-inch muffin cups.

**2** In a large bowl, blend together the flour, baking powder, sugar, cheese, and salt. Add the port wine and stir until the dry ingredients are just moistened.

**3** Spoon the batter into the prepared muffin cups, filling each about three-quarters full. Bake for 15 to 20 minutes, or until a cake tester or wooden toothpick inserted into the center of a muffin comes out clean. Cool in the pan on a wire rack for 5 to 7 minutes. Serve warm, or invert onto the rack to cool completely.

**SERVING SUGGESTION: Serve with thinly sliced Swiss cheese and a sweet white wine.**

# PORTS-O-CALL MUFFINS

MAKES: *16 to 18 muffins*

---

2 cups all-purpose flour
3 tablespoons granulated sugar
1 tablespoon baking powder
1 teaspoon ground sage
½ teaspoon onion powder
½ teaspoon salt
1 large egg
¼ cup butter or margarine, melted
1 cup milk
1 cup mashed potatoes
Shredded Swiss cheese for topping
Savory Sauce (see recipe page 191)

**1** Position the rack in the center of the oven and preheat to 375 degrees F. Lightly grease or line with paper baking cups twelve 2¾-inch muffin cups.

**2** In a large bowl, blend together the flour, sugar, baking powder, sage, onion powder, and salt. In a medium bowl, beat the egg until foamy. Beat in the butter, milk, and mashed potatoes. Combine the two mixtures, blending until the dry ingredients are just moistened.

**3** Spoon the batter into the prepared muffin cups, filling each about three-quarters full. Sprinkle the tops of the muffins lightly with the shredded cheese. Bake for 15 to 20 minutes, or until the tops of the muffins are golden brown and a cake tester or wooden toothpick inserted into a muffin is removed clean. Cool in the pan on a wire rack for 5 to 7 minutes. Serve warm, or invert onto the rack to cool completely. Serve with Savory Sauce.

# POTATO MUFFINS

MAKES: *11 to 12 muffins*

# PRUNE MUFFINS

MAKES: *8 to 10 muffins*

1 cup all-purpose flour
½ cup graham flour
2 teaspoons baking powder
½ teaspoon baking soda
½ cup chopped dried prunes
½ teaspoon salt
1 large egg
½ cup sour milk or buttermilk
½ cup warm honey
¼ cup butter or margarine, melted
Prune Spread (see recipe page 117)

1  Position the rack in the center of the oven and preheat to 375 degrees F. Lightly grease or line with paper baking cups ten 2¾-inch muffin cups.

2  In a large bowl, blend together the two flours, baking powder, baking soda, prunes, and salt. In a medium bowl, beat the egg until thick and light-colored. Beat in the milk, honey, and butter. Combine the two mixtures, blending until the dry ingredients are just moistened.

3  Spoon the batter into the prepared muffin cups, filling each about three-quarters full. Bake for 15 to 20 minutes, or until a cake tester or wooden toothpick inserted into the center of a muffin comes out clean. Cool in the pan on a wire rack for 5 to 7 minutes. Serve warm, or invert onto the rack to cool completely. Top with Prune Spread.

# PRUNE-AND-BRAN MUFFINS

MAKES: *11 to 12 muffins*

½ cup oat bran
½ cup unsweetened prune juice
½ cup milk
½ cup packed light-brown sugar
1½ cups all-purpose flour
2 teaspoons baking powder
1 teaspoon ground nutmeg
½ teaspoon salt
2 large eggs
½ cup butter or margarine, melted
1 cup chopped, pitted dried prunes

1  Position the rack in the center of the oven and preheat to 375 degrees F. Lightly grease or line with paper baking cups twelve 2¾-inch muffin cups.

2  In a medium bowl, combine the oat bran, prune juice, milk, and brown sugar and set aside for 5 minutes.

3  In a large bowl, blend together the flour, baking powder, nutmeg, and salt. To the soaked oat bran, add the eggs, butter, and prunes and stir until well incorporated. Combine the two mixtures, blending until the dry ingredients are just moistened.

4  Spoon the batter into the prepared muffin cups, filling each about three-quarters full. Bake for 15 to 20 minutes, or until a cake tester or wooden toothpick inserted into the center of a muffin comes out clean. Cool in the pan on a wire rack for 5 to 7 minutes. Serve warm, or invert onto the rack to cool completely.

1¾ cups all-purpose flour
1½ teaspoons baking powder
1 teaspoon baking soda
¼ teaspoon salt
1 large egg
¼ cup packed light-brown sugar
½ cup butter or margarine, melted
¼ cup molasses
1 cup cooked fresh or canned
  pumpkin pulp
Pumpkin Butter (see recipe page
  122)

**1** Position the rack in the center of the oven and preheat to 375 degrees F. Lightly grease or line with paper baking cups twelve 2¾-inch muffin cups.

**2** In a large bowl, blend together the flour, baking powder, baking soda, and salt. In a medium bowl, beat the egg until foamy. Beat in the brown sugar, butter, and molasses until smooth. Stir in the pumpkin. Combine the two mixtures, blending until the dry ingredients are just moistened.

**3** Spoon the batter into the prepared baking cups, filling each about three-quarters full. Bake for 15 to 20 minutes, or until a cake tester or wooden toothpick inserted into the center of a muffin comes out clean. Cool in the pan on a wire rack for 5 to 7 minutes. Serve warm, or invert onto the rack to cool completely. Serve with Pumpkin Butter.

# Pumpkin Muffins

MAKES: *11 to 12 muffins*

---

2 cups All-Bran® cereal
4 large shredded-wheat squares,
  crushed
½ cup boiling water
5 cups all-purpose flour
5 teaspoons baking soda
1 teaspoon baking powder
2 teaspoons salt
1 cup vegetable shortening
3 cups granulated sugar
4 large eggs
1 quart buttermilk or sour milk

**1** In a large bowl, combine the cereal, shredded wheat, and boiling water. Set aside for 10 minutes. Preheat the oven to 400 degrees F. Lightly grease or line with paper baking cups sixty 2¾-inch muffin cups.

**2** In a large bowl, blend together the flour, baking soda, baking powder, and salt. In another large bowl, cream the shortening and sugar together until light and fluffy. Beat in the eggs, one at a time, beating vigorously after each addition. Beat in the buttermilk. Stir in the soaked cereals. Combine the two mixtures, blending until the dry ingredients are just moistened.

**3** Spoon the batter into the prepared muffin cups, filling each about three-quarters full. Bake for 15 to 20 minutes, or until a cake tester or wooden toothpick inserted into the center of a muffin comes out clean. Cool in the pan on a wire rack for 5 to 7 minutes. Serve warm, or invert onto the rack to cool completely. (Large quantities of muffins should not be made unless you have room in the oven to bake the entire batch in two insertions into the oven. If you do not have enough room, you can refrigerate the batter up to 1½ hours and bake in batches. )

**Serving suggestion: Serve with any topping, sauce, or item listed.**

# Quantity Muffin Recipe

MAKES: *50 to 60 muffins*

## RASPBERRY-FILLED BRAN MUFFINS

MAKES: *14 to 16 muffins*

1¼ cups bran cereal, crushed
1 cup milk
1¼ cups all-purpose flour
½ cup granulated sugar
1 tablespoon baking powder
½ cup golden raisins
½ cup chopped walnuts or pecans
½ teaspoon salt
1 large egg
¼ cup canola oil
⅔ cup raspberry preserves
Raspberry Sauce (see recipe page 48)
Whipped Cream (see recipe page 208)

1 Position the rack in the center of the oven and preheat to 375 degrees F. Lightly grease or line with paper baking cups sixteen 2¾-inch muffin cups.

2 In a small bowl, blend together the bran cereal and milk. Set aside for 2 to 3 minutes. Meanwhile, in a large bowl, blend together the flour, sugar, baking powder, raisins, walnuts, and salt. In a medium bowl, beat the egg until foamy. Beat in the oil. Stir in the cereal. Combine the two mixtures, blending until the dry ingredients are just moistened.

3 Spoon the batter into the prepared muffin cups, filling each about three-quarters full, and press a spoonful of the raspberry preserves into the center of each cup. Bake for 15 to 20 minutes, or until a cake tester or wooden toothpick inserted at the edge of a muffin (not into the jam) comes out clean. Cool in the pan on a wire rack for 5 to 7 minutes. Serve warm, or invert onto the rack to cool completely. Serve with Raspberry Sauce and Whipped Cream.

## RENO MUFFINS

MAKES: *15 to 16 muffins*

¼ pound American cheese, very finely chopped
2 cups all-purpose flour
1 tablespoon baking powder
½ teaspoon baking soda
1 tablespoon granulated sugar
½ teaspoon salt
⅓ cup butter or margarine, melted
⅔ cup sour milk or buttermilk
Paprika

1 Position the rack in the center of the oven and preheat to 400 degrees F. Lightly grease or line with paper baking cups sixteen 2¾-inch size muffin cups.

2 In a large bowl, using a fork or wire whisk, blend together the cheese, flour, baking powder, baking soda, sugar and salt. In a medium bowl, beat the butter and milk together until smooth. Combine the two mixtures, blending until the dry ingredients are just moistened.

3 Spoon the batter into the prepared muffin cups, filling each about three-quarters full. Sprinkle a little paprika on top of each muffin. Bake for 15 to 20 minutes, or until a cake tester or wooden toothpick inserted into the center of a muffin comes out clean. Cool in the pan on a wire rack for 5 to 7 minutes. Serve warm, or invert onto the rack to cool completely.

**SERVING SUGGESTION: Serve with a chilled seafood salad.**

1½ cups chopped fresh rhubarb
¼ cup granulated sugar
¼ teaspoon grated lemon zest
1 tablespoon fresh lemon juice
1 tablespoon water
2½ cups all-purpose flour
2 tablespoons baking powder
1 large egg
3 tablespoons butter or margarine, melted
1 cup milk
StrawberrySauce (see recipe page 144)
Whipped Cream (see recipe page 208)

**1** Position the rack in the center of the oven and preheat to 400 degrees F. Lightly grease or line with paper baking cups fourteen 2¾-inch muffin cups.

**2** In a small bowl, combine the rhubarb, sugar, lemon zest, lemon juice, and water and thoroughly blend. Set aside. In a medium bowl, blend the flour and baking powder together. In another medium bowl, beat the egg until thick and light-colored. Beat in the butter and milk. Combine the flour and egg mixtures, blending until the dry ingredients are just moistened.

**3** Spoon the batter into the prepared muffin cups, filling each about three-quarters full. Press a tablespoonful into the center of each muffin. Bake for 15 to 20 minutes, or until the tops are golden brown and a cake tester or wooden toothpick inserted into the edge of a muffin (not into the filling) comes out clean. Remove from the oven and immediately brush with the glaze. Cool in the pan on a wire rack for 5 to 7 minutes. Serve warm, or transfer to the rack to cool completely. Serve with Strawberry Sauce and Whipped Cream.

# RHUBARB-FILLED MUFFINS

MAKES: *12 to 14 muffins*

---

2½ cups all-purpose flour
¾ cup granulated sugar
1½ teaspoons baking powder
1 teaspoon baking soda
¼ teaspoon salt
3 large eggs
3 tablespoons butter or margarine, melted
1 cup sour milk or buttermilk
1 teaspoon grated lemon zest
2 cups chopped rhubarb
1 cup chopped water chestnuts
Peanut Butter–Fudge Sauce (see recipe below)

**1** Position the rack in the center of the oven and preheat to 375 degrees F. Lightly grease or line with paper baking cups fourteen 2¾-inch muffin cups.

**2** In a large bowl, blend together the flour, sugar, baking powder, baking soda, and salt. In a medium bowl, beat the eggs until foamy. Beat in the butter, milk, and lemon zest. Stir in the rhubarb and chestnuts. Combine the two mixtures, blending until the dry ingredients are just moistened.

**3** Spoon the batter into the prepared muffin cups, filling each about three-quarters full. Bake for 15 to 20 minutes, or until a cake tester or wooden toothpick inserted into the center of a muffin comes out clean. Cool in the pan on a wire rack for 5 to 7 minutes. Serve warm, or invert onto the rack to cool completely. Top with Peanut Butter–Fudge Sauce.

# RHUBARB MUFFINS WITH WATER CHESTNUTS

MAKES: *12 to 14 muffins*

---

# PEANUT BUTTER– FUDGE SAUCE

MAKES: *1¼ cups*

½ cup store-bought chocolate-fudge sauce
½ cup chocolate syrup
¼ cup creamy-style peanut butter

In a small saucepan set over low heat, combine the fudge sauce, syrup, and peanut butter. Cook, stirring frequently, for 3 to 5 minutes, or until the mixture thickens slightly. Pour into a serving bowl.

## RHUBARB–PECAN MUFFINS

MAKES: *11 to 12 muffins*

2 cups all-purpose flour
¾ cup granulated sugar
1½ teaspoons baking powder
½ teaspoon baking soda
¾ cup chopped pecans
2 teaspoons grated orange zest
½ teaspoon salt
1 large egg
½ cup canola oil
¾ cup fresh orange juice
1¼ cups finely chopped fresh
   rhubarb
Hot Crab Sauce (see recipe below)

**1** Position the rack in the center of the oven and preheat to 375 degrees F. Lightly grease or line with paper baking cups twelve 2¾-inch muffin cups.

**2** In a large bowl, blend together the flour, sugar, baking powder, baking soda, pecans, orange zest, and salt. In a medium bowl, beat the egg until foamy. Beat in the oil and orange juice. Stir in the rhubarb. Combine the two mixtures, blending until the dry ingredients are just moistened.

**3** Spoon the batter into the prepared muffin cups, filling each about three-quarters full. Bake for 15 to 20 minutes, or until a cake tester or wooden toothpick inserted into the center of a muffin comes out clean. Cool in the pan on a wire rack for 5 to 7 minutes. Serve warm, or invert onto the rack to cool completely. Serve with Hot Crab Sauce.

## HOT CRAB SAUCE

MAKES: *About 1 cup*

One 3-ounce package cream
   cheese, at room temperature
½ cup mayonnaise
One 6-ounce can crabmeat,
   drained
¼ cup finely chopped scallions
   (green onions)
1 tablespoon fresh lemon juice
¼ teaspoon Tabasco® sauce

In a small bowl, beat the cream cheese smooth before stirring in the remaining ingredients. Transfer the mixture to a small saucepan and set over low heat. Cook, stirring frequently, until the mixture bubbles. Remove from the heat and serve warm.

## RICE MUFFINS

MAKES: *11 to 12 muffins*

1½ cups all-purpose flour
¼ cup granulated sugar
2 teaspoons baking powder
½ teaspoon salt
1 large egg
3 tablespoons butter or margarine,
   melted
1 cup milk
1½ teaspoons almond extract
1 cup cold cooked flavored rice (such
   as Jasmine or Basmati)
Hot Nectarine Sauce (see recipe
   page 174)

**1** Position the rack in the center of the oven and preheat to 425 degrees F. Lightly grease or line with paper baking cups twelve 2¾-inch muffin cups.

**2** In a large bowl, blend together the flour, sugar, baking powder, and salt. In a medium bowl, beat the egg, butter, milk, and almond extract until smooth. Stir in the rice. Combine the two mixtures, blending until the dry ingredients are just moistened.

**3** Spoon the mixture into the prepared muffin cups, filling each about three-quarters full. Bake for 15 to 20 minutes, or until a cake tester or wooden toothpick inserted into the center of a muffin comes out clean. Cool in the pan on a wire rack for 5 to 7 minutes. Serve warm, or invert onto the rack to cool completely. Top with Hot Nectarine Sauce.

1¼ cups cooked Jasmine rice (or Basmati)
1 cup white cornmeal
2 tablespoons granulated sugar
2 large eggs, separated
½ teaspoon plus ⅛ teaspoon salt
2 tablespoons butter or margarine, at room temperature
2 teaspoons baking powder
¾ cup plus 1 tablespoon milk

**1** Position the rack in the center of the oven and preheat to 400 degrees F. Lightly grease or line with paper baking cups fourteen 2¾-inch muffin cups.

**2** In a large bowl, using a fork or wire whisk, blend together the rice, cornmeal, and sugar. In a small bowl, beat the egg whites and ⅛ teaspoon salt until the whites are stiff but not dry. In a medium bowl, beat the remaining ½ teaspoon salt, butter, baking powder, and milk until smooth. Stir the milk mixture into the rice and cornmeal mixture, blending until the ingredients are just combined. Fold in the egg whites.

**3** Spoon the batter into the prepared muffin cups, filling each about three-quarters full. Bake for 15 to 20 minutes, or until a cake tester or wooden toothpick inserted into the center of a muffin comes out clean. Cool in the pan on a wire rack for 5 to 7 minutes. Serve warm, or invert onto the rack to cool completely.

# RICE-AND-CORNMEAL MUFFINS

MAKES: *12 to 14 muffins*

---

1½ cups all-purpose flour
½ cup finely grated Swiss cheese, plus more for topping the muffins
1 tablespoon granulated sugar
1 tablespoon baking powder
½ teaspoon salt
2 large eggs, separated
1 cup cooked flavored rice (such as Jasmine or Basmati)
1¼ cups milk
2 tablespoons butter or margarine, melted

**1** Position the rack in the center of the oven and preheat to 425 degrees F. Lightly grease or line with paper baking cups fourteen 2¾-inch muffin cups.

**2** In a large bowl, blend together the flour, cheese, sugar, baking powder, and salt. In a small bowl, beat the egg whites until stiff but not dry. In a medium bowl, beat the egg yolks thick before beating in the rice, milk, and butter. Stir the flour and cheese mixture into yolk-and-rice mixture, blending until the dry ingredients are just moistened. Fold in the egg whites.

**3** Spoon the batter into the prepared muffin cups, filling each about three-quarters full. Bake for 15 to 20 minutes, or until a cake tester or wooden toothpick inserted into the center of a muffin comes out clean. Cool in the pan on a wire rack for 5 to 7 minutes. Serve warm, or invert onto the rack to cool completely.

**SERVING SUGGESTION: Serve with cubed Swiss cheese and a dry red wine.**

# RICE-AND-CHEESE MUFFINS

MAKES: *12 to 14 muffins*

## RICE MUFFINS WITH BLACK CURRANTS

MAKES: *11 to 12 muffins*

1 cup all-purpose flour
1 tablespoon granulated sugar
1½ teaspoons baking powder
¼ cup black or red currants
½ teaspoon salt
1 large egg
⅔ cup milk
1 cup cooked rice
2 tablespoons vegetable shortening, melted
Whipped Cream Topping (see recipe page 208)

1  Position the rack in the center of the oven and preheat to 425 degrees F. Lightly grease or line with paper baking cups twelve 2¾-inch muffin cups.

2  In a large bowl, blend together the flour, sugar, baking powder, currants, and salt. In a medium bowl, beat the egg, milk, rice, and shortening until smooth. Combine the two mixtures, blending until the dry ingredients are just moistened.

3  Spoon the batter into the prepared muffin cups, filling each about three-quarters full. Bake for 15 to 20 minutes, or until a cake tester or wooden toothpick inserted into the center of a muffin comes out clean. Cool in the pan on a wire rack for 5 to 7 minutes. Serve warm, or invert onto the rack to cool completely. Serve with Whipped Cream Topping.

## RICOTTA CHEESE MUFFINS

MAKES: *12 to 14 muffins*

1 cup all-purpose flour
½ cup whole-wheat flour
2 teaspoons baking powder
½ teaspoon baking soda
¼ cup Dutch-processed cocoa powder
¼ teaspoon salt
3 large eggs
½ cup butter or margarine, melted
¼ cup honey
½ cup milk
1 cup ricotta or cream cheese
¼ cup coarsely ground walnuts
Ham Spread (see recipe page 57)

1  Position the rack in the center of the oven and preheat to 375 degrees F. Lightly grease or line with paper baking cups fourteen 2¾-inch muffin cups. In a large bowl, blend together the two flours, baking powder, baking soda, cocoa powder, and salt.

2  In a medium bowl, beat the eggs, butter, honey, milk, and ricotta cheese until smooth. Combine the two mixtures, blending until the dry ingredients are just moistened.

3  Spoon the batter into the prepared muffin cups, filling each about three-quarters full. Sprinkle the ground nuts over the top of the muffins. Bake for 15 to 20 minutes, or until a cake tester or wooden toothpick inserted into the center of a muffin comes out clean. Cool in the pan on a wire rack for 5 to 7 minutes. Serve warm, or invert onto the rack to cool completely. Serve with Ham Spread.

2 cups all-purpose flour
2 teaspoons baking powder
½ teaspoon baking soda
½ teaspoon dried crushed tarragon
¾ cup grated Romano cheese, plus more for topping the muffins
½ cup chopped fresh parsley
1 can or package (14 ounces) chopped mixed vegetables, drained
1 large egg
¼ cup butter or margarine, melted
1 tablespoon granulated sugar
1¼ cups buttermilk or sour milk

**1** Position the rack in the center of the oven and preheat to 325 degrees F. Lightly grease or line with paper baking cups sixteen 2¾-inch muffin cups.

**2** In a large bowl, blend together the flour, baking powder, baking soda, tarragon, ¾ cup of the cheese, parsley, and vegetables. In a medium bowl, beat the egg, butter, sugar, and buttermilk until smooth. Combine the two mixtures, blending until the dry ingredients are just moistened.

**3** Drop 1 heaping tablespoon of the battter into the prepared muffin cups. Sprinkle a little cheese over the tops of the muffins. Bake for 15 to 20 minutes, or until a cake tester or wooden toothpick inserted into the center of a muffin comes out clean. Cool in the pan on a wire rack for 5 to 7 minutes. Serve warm, or invert onto the rack to cool completely.

**SERVING SUGGESTION: Serve with a creamy-style French dressing.**

# ROMANO MUFFINS WITH VEGETABLES

MAKES: *15 to 16 muffins*

2 cups Bisquick® baking mix
2 teaspoons ground cinnamon
½ cup chopped pecans
1 large egg
2 teaspoons brown sugar
¼ cup honey
½ cup milk
¼ cup rum
Hot Buttered Rum Sauce (see recipe page 37)

**1** Position the rack in the center of the oven and preheat to 400 degrees F. Lightly grease or line with paper baking cups twelve 2¾-inch muffin cups.

**2** In a large bowl, blend together the baking mix, cinnamon, and nuts. In a medium bowl, beat the egg, brown sugar, honey, milk, and rum until smooth. Combine the two mixtures, blending until the dry ingredients are just moistened.

**3** Spoon the batter into the prepared muffin cups, filling each about three-quarters full. Bake for 15 to 20 minutes, or until a cake tester or wooden toothpick inserted into the center of a muffin comes out clean. Cool in the pan on a wire rack for 5 to 7 minutes. Serve warm, or invert onto the rack to cool completely. Serve with Hot Buttered Rum Sauce.

# RUM-AND-PECAN MUFFINS

MAKES: *11 to 12 muffins*

# RYE MUFFINS

MAKES: *8 to 10 muffins*

1 cup rye flour
1 cup all-purpose flour
2 tablespoons packed brown sugar
1¼ teaspoons baking powder
¾ teaspoon baking soda
2 teaspoons caraway seeds
½ teaspoon salt
1 large egg
1½ cups sour milk or buttermilk
2 tablespoons butter or margarine, melted
Mustard Butter (see recipe page 42)

**1** Position the rack in the center of the oven and preheat to 400 degrees F. Lightly grease or line with paper baking cups ten 2¾-inch muffin cups.

**2** In a large bowl, blend together the two flours, sugar, baking powder, baking soda, caraway seeds, and salt. In a medium bowl, beat the egg until foamy. Beat in the milk and butter. Combine the two mixtures, blending until the dry ingredients are just moistened.

**3** Spoon the batter into the prepared muffin cups, filling each about three-quarters full. Bake for 15 to 20 minutes, or until a cake tester or wooden toothpick inserted into the center of a muffin comes out clean. Cool in the pan on a wire rack for 5 to 7 minutes. Serve warm, or invert onto the rack to cool completely. Serve with Mustard Sauce.

# RYE MUFFINS WITH SAUSAGE

MAKES: *12 to 14 muffins*

1¼ cups rye flour
¾ cup all-purpose flour
2 teaspoons baking powder
¾ teaspoon baking soda
1 tablespoon caraway seeds
½ teaspoon salt
1 large egg
1½ cups sour milk or buttermilk
3 tablespoons molasses
12 to 14 small cocktail sausages
Mustard Butter (see recipe page 42)

**1** Position the rack in the center of the oven and preheat to 400 degrees F. Lightly grease or line with paper baking cups fourteen 2¾-inch muffin cups.

**2** In a large-size bowl, blend together the two flours, baking powder, caraway seeds, and salt. In a medium bowl, beat the egg until foamy. Beat in the milk and molasses. Combine the two mixtures, blending until the dry ingredients are just moistened.

**3** Spoon the batter into the prepared muffin cups, filling each about three-quarters full. Press a sausage into the center of each muffin. Bake for 15 to 20 minutes, or until the tops of the muffins are golden brown, and a cake tester or wooden toothpick inserted near the edge of a muffin (not into the sausage) comes out clean. Cool in the pan on a wire rack for 5 to 7 minutes. Serve warm, or invert onto the rack to cool completely. Serve with Mustard Sauce.

2½ cups all-purpose flour
1 tablespoon baking powder
¾ pound boiled or canned asparagus spears, chopped fine
½ pound smoked salmon, finely chopped
2 large eggs
1 cup buttermilk
¼ cup butter or margarine, melted
2 tablespoons prepared mustard
Flavored Mayonnaise (see recipe page 324)

**1** Position the rack in the center of the oven and preheat to 400 degrees F. Lightly grease or line with paper baking cups twenty-eight 2¾-inch muffin cups.

**2** In a large bowl, blend together the flour, baking powder, aspara-gus, and salmon. In a medium bowl, beat the eggs until foamy. Beat in the buttermilk, butter, and mustard. Combine the two mixtures, blending until the dry ingredients are just moistened.

**3** Drop 1 heaping tablespoon of the mixture into each of the pre-pared muffin cups. Bake for 15 to 20 minutes, or until a cake tester or wooden toothpick inserted into the center of a muffin comes out clean. Cool in the pan on a wire rack for 5 to 7 minutes. Serve warm, or invert onto the rack to cool completely. Serve with Flavored Mayonnaise.

# SALMON-AND-MUSTARD MUFFINS WITH ASPARAGUS

MAKES: *24 to 28 muffins*

---

3 cups all-purpose flour
1 tablespoon baking powder
½ teaspoon granulated sugar
1 tablespoon fresh chopped tarragon
1 tablespoon fresh snipped chives
1 tablespoon fresh chopped parsley
1 tablespoon fresh chopped cilantro (coriander) leaves
¼ teaspoon salt
3 large eggs
2 tablespoons butter or margarine, melted
1½ cups milk
2 ounces finely chopped canned salmon
Hot Curry Spread (see recipe page 177)

**1** Position the rack in the center of the oven and preheat to 400 degrees F. Lightly grease or line with paper baking cups fourteen 2¾-inch muffin cups.

**2** In a large bowl, blend together the flour, baking powder, sugar, tarragon, chives, parsley, cilantro, and salt. In a medium bowl, beat the eggs until foamy. Beat in the butter and milk. Stir in the salmon. Combine the two mix-tures, blending until the dry ingredients are just moistened.

**3** Spoon the batter into the pre-pared muffin cups, filling each about three-quarters full. Bake for 15 to 20 minutes, or until a cake tester or wooden toothpick inserted into a muffin comes out clean. Cool in the pan on a wire rack for 5 to 7 minutes. Serve warm, or invert onto the rack to cool completely. Serve with Hot Curry Spread.

# SALMON MUFFINS

MAKES: *12 to 14 muffins*

## SALSA-BEAN MUFFINS

MAKES: *18 to 20 muffins*

1²⁄₃ cups all-purpose flour
½ cup corn flour
½ cup cornmeal
1 tablespoon baking powder
1 large egg
3 tablespoons granulated sugar
1½ cups milk
One 19-ounce can (2½ cups)
   Campbell's® Salsa Bean soup
Bean Salad (see recipe page 92)

**1** Position the rack in the center of the oven and preheat to 425 degrees F. Lightly grease or line with paper baking cups twenty 2¾-inch muffin cups.

**2** In a large bowl, blend together the two flours, cornmeal, and baking powder. In a medium bowl, beat the egg until foamy. Beat in the sugar, milk, and soup. Combine the two mixtures, blending until the dry ingredients are just moistened.

**3** Spoon the batter into the prepared muffin cups, filling each about three-quarters full. Bake for 15 to 20 minutes, or until a cake tester or wooden toothpick inserted into the center of a muffin comes out clean. Cool in the pan on a wire rack for 5 to 7 minutes. Serve warm, or invert onto the rack to cool completely. Serve with Bean Salad.

## SAUERKRAUT-AND-PICKLE MUFFINS

MAKES: *11 to 12 muffins*

2 cups all-purpose flour
1 tablespoon baking powder
½ teaspoon baking soda
1 teaspoon salt
1 large egg
½ cup packed light-brown sugar
¼ cup butter or margarine, at room
   temperature
¾ cup plain yogurt or sour cream
One 14.5-ounce can sauerkraut,
   drained and finely chopped
½ cup finely chopped kosher dill
   pickles
½ cup crumbled, crisply cooked
   bacon
Mustard Butter (see recipe page 42)

**1** Position the rack in the center of the oven and preheat to 400 degrees F. Lightly grease or line with paper baking cups twelve 2¾-inch muffin cups.

**2** In a large bowl, blend together the flour, baking powder, baking soda, and salt. In a medium bowl, beat the egg until foamy. Beat in the sugar. Beat in the butter, yogurt, and sauerkraut. Stir in the pickles. Combine the two mixtures, blending until the dry ingredients are just moistened.

**3** Spoon the batter into the prepared muffin cups, filling each about three-quarters full. Sprinkle the tops of the muffins with the crumbled bacon. Bake for 20 to 25 minutes, or until a cake tester or wooden toothpick inserted into a muffin is removed clean and the tops are golden brown. Cool in the pan on a wire rack for 5 to 7 minutes. Serve warm, or invert onto the rack to cool completely. Serve with Mustard Sauce.

2 cups all-purpose flour
½ cup granulated sugar
¼ cup Dutch-processed cocoa powder
2 teaspoons baking powder
½ teaspoon baking soda
2 large eggs
¼ cup butter-flavored vegetable shortening
1 cup canned sauerkraut, drained and finely chopped
¼ cup water
Chocolate Sauce (see recipe page 26)

**1** Position the rack in the center of the oven and preheat to 400 degrees F. Lightly grease or line with paper baking cups twelve 2¾-inch muffin cups.

**2** In a large bowl, blend together the flour, sugar, cocoa powder, baking powder, and baking soda.

In a medium bowl, beat the eggs until foamy. Beat in the shortening, sauerkraut, and water. Combine the two mixtures, blending until the dry ingredients are just moistened.

**3** Spoon the batter into the prepared muffin cups, filling each about three-quarters full. Bake for 20 to 25 minutes, or until a cake tester or wooden toothpick inserted into the center of a muffin comes out clean. Cool in the pan on a wire rack for 5 to 7 minutes. Remove the muffins from the pan and drizzle the tops with the glaze. Serve warm, or transfer to the rack to cool completely. Top with Chocolate Sauce.

## SAUERKRAUT–FUDGE MUFFINS
MAKES: *11 to 12 muffins*

2 cups all-purpose flour
1 tablespoon baking powder
½ teaspoon baking soda
1 teaspoon salt
¼ cup butter-flavored vegetable shortening
½ cup packed light-brown sugar
1 large egg
½ cup canned sauerkraut, drained and finely chopped
¾ cup sour cream or plain yogurt
½ cup dried apple slices, finely chopped
Bacon bits
Applesauce (see recipe page 138)

**1** Position the rack in the center of the oven and preheat to 400 degrees F. Lightly grease or line with paper baking cups twelve 2¾-inch muffin cups.

**2** In a large bowl, blend together the flour, baking powder, baking soda, and salt. In a medium

bowl, beat the shortening and sugar until light and fluffy. Beat in the egg, sauerkraut, sour cream, and apples. Combine the two mixtures, blending until the dry ingredients are just moistened.

**3** Spoon the batter into the prepared muffin cups, filling each about three-quarters full. Sprinkle bacon bits lightly over the top of each muffin. Bake for about 20 to 25 minutes, or until a cake tester or wooden toothpick inserted into the center of a muffin comes out clean. Cool in the pan on a wire rack for 5 to 7 minutes. Serve warm, or invert onto the rack to cool completely. Serve with Applesauce.

## SAUERKRAUT-AND-APPLE MUFFINS
MAKES: *11 to 12 muffins*

# SAUSAGE MUFFINS

MAKES: *11 to 12 muffins*

¼ pound fresh ground pork sausage
1 small (3-ounce) package cream
   cheese, diced
½ cup shredded Cheddar cheese
¼ cup finely chopped scallions
   (green onions), green tops only
1 cup Bisquick® baking mix
2 large eggs
⅔ cup milk
Chili Butter (see recipe page 119)

1  Position the rack in the center of the oven and preheat to 375 degrees F. Lightly grease or line with paper baking cups twelve 2¾-inch muffin cups.

2  In a large bowl, blend together the pork, cream cheese, Cheddar cheese, scallion, and baking mix.

In a small bowl, beat together the eggs and milk. Combine the two mixtures, blending until the dry ingredients are just moistened.

3  Spoon the batter into the prepared muffin cups, filling each about three-quarters full. Bake for 15 to 20 minutes, or until a cake tester or wooden toothpick inserted into the center of a muffin comes out clean. Cool in the pan on a wire rack for 5 to 7 minutes. Serve warm, or invert onto the rack to cool completely. Serve with Chili Butter.

# SAUSAGE MUFFINS WITH CHEESE

MAKES: *11 to 12 muffins*

¾ cup bulk pork-sausage meat
Butter or margarine, melted
2 cups all-purpose flour
2 tablespoons granulated sugar
1 tablespoon baking powder
½ cup shredded Cheddar cheese,
   plus more for topping the muffins
¼ teaspoon salt
1 large egg
1 cup milk
1 teaspoon prepared mustard
Cheese-and-Olive Spread (see recipe
   page 183)

1  Position the rack in the center of the oven and preheat to 375 degrees F. Lightly grease or line with paper baking cups twelve 2¾-inch muffin cups.

2  In a skillet set over medium heat, cook the sausage until browned, stirring to break up any large chunks. Remove from the heat and drain well, reserving the drippings. Add enough but-

ter to the drippings to measure ¼ cup. Set the cooked sausage and drippings aside.

3  In a large bowl, blend together the flour, sugar, baking powder, cheese, and salt. In a medium bowl, beat the egg until foamy. Beat in the milk, mustard, and the reserved ¼ cup drippings. Stir in the sausage. Combine the two mixtures, blending until the dry ingredients are just moistened.

4  Spoon the batter into the prepared muffin cups, filling each about three-quarters full. Bake for 15 to 20 minutes, or until a cake tester or wooden toothpick inserted into the center of a muffin comes out clean. Cool in the pan on a wire rack for 5 to 7 minutes. Serve warm, or invert onto the rack to cool completely. Serve with Cheese & Olive Spread.

2 cups all-purpose flour
4 teaspoons baking powder
½ teaspoon dried rosemary, crushed
½ teaspoon dried fennel seeds, crushed
½ teaspoon dried tarragon
½ teaspoon dried chopped chives
⅓ teaspoon salt
1 large egg
1 cup milk
2 tablespoons butter or margarine, melted
1 cup minced cooked ham or chicken
Tomato Sauce (see recipe page 219)

# SAVORY MUFFINS

MAKES: *11 to 12 muffins*

**1** Position the rack in the center of the oven and preheat to 400 degrees F. Lightly grease or line with paper baking cups twelve 2¾-inch muffin cups.

**2** In a large bowl, blend together the flour, baking powder, rosemary, fennel seeds, tarragon, chives, and salt. In a medium bowl, beat the egg until thick and light-colored. Beat in the milk and butter. Stir in the chopped ham. Combine the two mixtures, blending until the dry ingredients are just moistened.

**3** Spoon the batter into the prepared muffin cups, filling each about three-quarters full. Bake for 15 to 20 minutes, or until a cake tester or wooden toothpick inserted into the center of a muffin comes out clean. Cool in the pan on a wire rack for 5 to 7 minutes. Serve warm, or invert onto the rack to cool completely. Serve with Tomato Sauce.

---

1 cup all-purpose flour
¼ cup granulated sugar
2 teaspoons baking powder
½ teaspoon salt
1 large egg
2 tablespoons butter or margarine, melted
¾ cup milk
1 cup shredded whole bran
Honey Butter (see recipe page 146)

# SHREDDED BRAN MUFFINS

MAKES: *5 to 6 muffins*

**1** Position the rack in the center of the oven and preheat to 400 degrees F. Lightly grease or line with paper baking cups six 2¾-inch muffin cups.

**2** In a large bowl, blend together the flour, sugar, baking powder, and salt. In a medium bowl, beat the egg, butter, and milk until smooth. Stir in the bran and let stand for 2 to 3 minutes. Combine the two mixtures, blending until the dry ingredients are just moistened.

**3** Spoon the batter into the prepared muffin cups, filling each about three-quarters full. Bake for 15 to 20 minutes, or until a cake tester or wooden toothpick inserted into the center of a muffin comes out clean. Cool for 5 to 7 minutes. Serve with Honey Butter.

# SHRIMP MUFFINS

MAKES: *16 to 18 muffins*

3 cups all-purpose flour
5 teaspoons baking powder
¼ tablespoon granulated sugar
¼ teaspoon salt
½ cup grated Swiss cheese
1 tablespoon finely chopped fresh
    ginger root
One 4½-ounce can tiny deveined
    shrimp, drained, rinsed, and
    finely chopped
2 cups dry sherry
Chili–Tomato Sauce (see recipe page
    116)

**1** Position the rack in the center of the oven and preheat to 375 degrees F. Lightly grease or line with paper baking cups eighteen 2¾-inch muffin cups.

**2** In a large bowl, blend together the flour, baking powder, sugar, cheese, ginger, and salt. Stir in the shrimp. Then stir the sherry into the dry ingredients until they are just moistened.

**3** Spoon the mixture into the prepared muffin cups, filling each about three-quarters full. Bake for 15 to 20 minutes, or until a cake tester or wooden toothpick inserted into the center of a muffin comes out clean. Cool in the pan on a wire rack for 5 to 7 minutes. Serve warm, or invert onto the rack to cool completely. Serve with Chili Tomato Sauce.

# SHRIMP SAMBAL MUFFINS

MAKES: *12 to 14 muffins*

3 cups all-purpose flour
1 tablespoon granulated sugar
4 teaspoons baking powder
2 tablespoons finely chopped onion
¼ teaspoon dried crushed red
    pepper
2 cans (4½ ounces each) tiny
    deveined shrimp, drained and
    rinsed
2 large eggs
⅔ cup milk
5 teaspoons peanut oil
3 tablespoons peanut butter
Lemon Butter (see recipe below)

**1** Position the rack in the center of the oven and preheat to 425 degrees F. Lightly grease or line with paper baking cups fourteen 2¾-inch muffin cups.

**2** In a large bowl, blend together the flour, sugar, baking powder, onions, pepper, and salt. Stir in the shrimp. In a medium bowl, beat the eggs until foamy. Beat in the milk, oil, and peanut butter. Combine the two mixtures, blending until the dry ingredients are just moistened.

**3** Spoon the batter into the prepared muffin cups, filling each about three-quarters full. Bake for 15 to 20 minutes, or until a cake tester or wooden toothpick inserted into the center of a muffin comes out clean. Cool in the pan on a wire rack for 5 to 7 minutes. Serve warm, or invert onto the rack to cool completely. Serve with Lemon Butter.

# LEMON BUTTER

MAKES: *About ¼ cup*

2 tablespoons butter, at room
    temperature
1 tablespoon fresh lemon juice
1 teaspoon finely chopped mint
    leaves

In a small bowl, combine all of the ingredients and blend until smooth. Chill in the refrigerator before serving.

2 cups all-purpose flour
¼ cup powdered sugar
1 tablespoon baking powder
½ teaspoon baking soda
1½ cups shredded Tilsit or other soft cheese, plus more for topping the muffins
2 large eggs
¼ cup butter or margarine, melted
1 cup sour cream or plain yogurt

**1** Position the rack in the center of the oven and preheat to 375 degrees F. Lightly grease or line with paper baking cups twelve 2¾-inch muffin cups.

**2** In a large bowl, blend together the flour, sugar, baking powder, baking soda, and cheese. In a medium bowl, beat the eggs until foamy. Beat in the butter and sour cream. Combine the two mixtures, blending until the dry ingredients are just moistened.

**3** Spoon the batter into the prepared muffin cups, filling each cup about three-quarters full. Sprinkle the tops of the muffins lightly with cheese. Bake for 15 to 20 minutes, or until the tops of the muffins are golden and a cake tester or wooden toothpick inserted into the center of a muffin comes out clean. Cool in the pan on a wire rack for 5 to 7 minutes. Serve warm, or invert onto the rack to cool completely.

**SERVING SUGGESTION: Serve with a glass of dry white wine.**

# SOFT-CHEESE MUFFINS

MAKES: *11 to 12 muffins*

---

1¾ cups all-purpose flour
2 tablespoons granulated sugar
1 teaspoon baking powder
½ teaspoon baking soda
½ teaspoon ground nutmeg
½ teaspoon salt
1 large egg
1 cup sour cream
Chocolate Sauce (see recipe page 26)

**1** Position the rack in the center of the oven and preheat to 400 degrees F. Lightly grease or line with paper baking cups twenty-four 2¾-inch muffin cups.

**2** In a large bowl, blend together the flour, sugar, baking powder, baking soda, nutmeg, and salt. In a medium bowl, beat the egg until foamy. Beat in the sour cream. Combine the two mixtures, blending until the dry ingredients are just moistened.

**3** Drop 1 heaping tablespoon of the batter into each of the prepared muffin cups. Press ½ teaspoon of the custard into the center of each muffin. Bake for 12 to 18 minutes, or until a cake tester or wooden toothpick inserted into the edge of a muffin (not into the filling) comes out clean. Cool in the pan on a wire rack for 5 to 7 minutes. Serve warm, or invert onto the rack to cool completely. Top with Chocolate Sauce.

# SOUR CREAM MUFFINS

MAKES: *23 to 24 muffins*

## SOUR CREAM MUFFINS WITH CHOCOLATE CHIPS

MAKES: *27 to 28 muffins*

2 cups all-purpose flour
1 teaspoon baking powder
1 teaspoon baking soda
2 tablespoons fresh grated orange zest
1 cup Hershey's® milk-chocolate-bar sprinkles or miniature chocolate chips
2 large eggs
1¼ cups granulated sugar
½ cup butter or margarine, melted
1 cup chocolate-flavored yogurt or sour cream
¼ cup fresh orange juice or crème de cacao
Custard Sauce (see recipe page 29)

1  Position the rack in the center of the oven and preheat to 375 degrees F. Lightly grease or line with paper baking cups twenty-eight 2¾-inch muffin cups.

2  In a large bowl, blend together the flour, baking powder, baking soda, orange zest, and sprinkles. In a medium bowl, beat the eggs until foamy. Beat in the sugar, yogurt, and orange juice. Combine the two mixtures, blending until the dry ingredients are just moistened.

3  Drop 1 heaping tablespoon of the mixture into the prepared muffin cups. Bake for 15 to 20 minutes, or until a cake tester or wooden toothpick inserted into the center of a muffin comes out clean. Cool in the pan on a wire rack for 5 to 7 minutes. Serve warm, or invert onto the rack to cool completely. Top with Custard Sauce.

## SOUTHEAST ASIA MUFFINS

MAKES: *16 to 18 muffins*

1½ cups rice flour
¾ cup soy flour
2 cups flaked unsweetened coconut, plus more for sprinkling on the muffins
1 tablespoon baking powder
¼ teaspoon five-star spice powder
¼ teaspoon salt
2 large eggs
¼ teaspoon honey
1 cup milk
½ cup canola oil
Coconut Chutney (see recipe page 65)

1  Position the rack in the center of the oven and preheat to 375 degrees F. Lightly grease or line with paper baking cups eighteen 2¾-inch muffin cups.

2  In a large bowl, blend together the two flours, coconut, baking powder, spice powder, and salt. In a medium bowl, beat the egg until foamy. Beat in the honey, milk, and oil. Combine the two mixtures, blending until the dry ingredients are just moistened.

3  Spoon the batter into the prepared muffin cups, filling each about three-quarters full. Sprinkle a little flaked coconut over the top of each muffin. Bake for 15 to 20 minutes, or until a cake tester or wooden toothpick inserted into the center of a muffin comes out clean. Cool in the pan on a wire rack for 5 to 7 minutes. Serve warm, or invert onto the rack to cool completely. Serve with Coconut Chutney.

2¼ cups all-purpose flour
½ cup granulated sugar
1 tablespoon baking powder
1½ cups drained, canned crushed
   pineapple
¼ teaspoon salt
6 tablespoons butter or margarine,
   melted
½ cup pineapple juice
¼ cup rum
½ teaspoon coconut flavoring
Tropical Sauce (see recipe page 81)

**1** Position the rack in the center of the oven and preheat to 375 degrees F. Lightly grease or line with paper baking cups twelve 2¾-inch muffin cups.

**2** In a large bowl, blend together the flour, sugar, baking powder, and salt. Stir in drained pineapple. In a medium bowl, beat together the butter, pineapple juice, rum, and coconut flavoring. Combine the two mixtures, blending until the dry ingredients are just moistened.

**3** Spoon the batter into the prepared muffin cups, filling each about three-quarters full. Bake for 15 to 20 minutes, or until a cake tester or wooden toothpick inserted into the center of a muffin comes out clean. Remove from the oven and cool in the pan on a wire rack for 5 to 7 minutes. Serve warm, or invert onto the rack to cool completely. Serve with Tropical Sauce.

## SOUTH SEA ISLAND MUFFINS

MAKES: *11 to 12 muffins*

---

1 cup milk
¼ cup canola oil
1 large egg
1¾ cups all-purpose flour
¼ cup white cornmeal
1 tablespoon baking powder
1 teaspoon granulated sugar
⅛ teaspoon chili powder
½ cup whole-kernel corn
¼ cup grated Cheddar cheese
2 tablespoons chopped fresh green
   chili peppers
⅛ teaspoon salt
Honey Glaze (see recipe page 53)

**1** Position the rack in the center of the oven and preheat to 400 degrees F. Lightly grease or line with paper baking cups twelve 2¾-inch muffin cups.

**2** In a medium bowl, beat the milk, oil, and egg until smooth. In a large bowl, blend together the flour, cornmeal, baking powder, sugar, chili powder, corn, cheese, peppers, and salt. Combine the two mixtures, blending until the dry ingredients are just moistened.

**3** Spoon the batter into the prepared muffin cups, filling each about three-quarters full. Bake for 15 to 20 minutes, or until a cake tester or wooden toothpick inserted into the center of a muffin comes out clean. Cool in the pan on a wire rack for 5 to 7 minutes. Serve warm, or invert onto the rack to cool completely. Brush with Honey Glaze.

## SOUTHWESTERN CHEESE MUFFINS

MAKES: *11 to 12 muffins*

## SOUTHWESTERN SALSA MUFFINS

MAKES: *11 to 12 muffins*

1 cup all-purpose flour
1 cup cornmeal
4 teaspoons baking powder
2 tablespoons crumbled crisply
  cooked bacon
½ teaspoon finely chopped hot fresh
  chili peppers
½ teaspoon salt
1 large egg
1 tablespoon granulated sugar
1 cup milk
¼ cup mild salsa
Chili Butter (see recipe page 119)

1  Position the rack in the center of the oven and preheat to 400 degrees F. Lightly grease or line with paper baking cups twelve 2¾-inch muffin cups.

2  In a large bowl, blend together the flour, cornmeal, baking powder, bacon, chilies, and salt. In a medium bowl, beat the egg until foamy. Beat in the sugar, milk, and salsa. Combine the two mixtures, blending until the dry ingredients are just moistened.

3  Spoon the batter into the prepared muffin cups, filling each about three-quarters full. Bake for 15 to 20 minutes, or until a cake tester or wooden toothpick inserted into the center of a muffin comes out clean. Cool in the pan on a wire rack for 5 to 7 minutes. Serve warm, or invert onto the rack to cool completely. Serve with Chili Butter.

## SOY MUFFINS

MAKES: *11 to 12 muffins*

1⅔ cups all-purpose flour
½ cup soy flour
3 tablespoons granulated sugar
1 tablespoon baking powder
1½ teaspoons salt
1 large egg
1¼ cups milk
2 tablespoons butter or margarine,
  melted
Strawberry Sauce (see recipe page
  144)

1  Position the rack in the center of the oven and preheat to 425 degrees F. Lightly grease or line with paper baking cups twelve 2¾-inch muffin cups.

2  In a large bowl, blend together the two flours, sugar, baking powder, and salt. In a medium bowl, beat the egg until foamy. Beat in the milk and butter. Combine the two mixtures, blending until the dry ingredients are just moistened.

3  Drop 2 tablespoons of the mixture into the prepared muffin cups, filling each cup half full. Bake for 15 to 20 minutes, or until a cake tester or wooden toothpick inserted into the center of a muffin comes out clean. Cool in the pan on a wire rack for 5 to 7 minutes. Serve warm, or invert onto the rack to cool completely. Top with Strawberry Sauce.

1⅔ cups all-purpose flour
1 tablespoon baking powder
1 teaspoon ground cinnamon
¼ teaspoon ground nutmeg or mace
½ teaspoon ground cloves
3 tablespoons granulated sugar
1 medium apple, peeled, cored and diced
½ teaspoon salt
1 large egg
⅔ cup milk
¼ cup butter or margarine, melted
10 apple wedges from a peeled and cored apple
Alcohol-Free Hard Sauce (see recipe page 111)

**1** Position the rack in the center of the oven and preheat to 400 degrees F. Lightly grease or line with paper baking cups ten 2¾-inch muffin cups.

**2** In a large bowl, blend together the flour, baking powder, cinnamon, nutmeg, cloves, sugar, apple, and salt. In a medium bowl, beat together the egg, milk, and butter until smooth. Combine the two mixtures, blending until the dry ingredients are just moistened.

**3** Spoon the batter into the prepared muffin cups, filling each about three-quarters full. Press an apple wedge into the top of each muffin. Bake for 15 to 20 minutes, or until a cake tester or wooden toothpick inserted into the center of a muffin comes out clean. Cool in the pan on a wire rack for 5 to 7 minutes. Serve warm, or invert onto the rack to cool completely. Serve with Alcohol-Free Hard Sauce.

# SPICED APPLE MUFFINS

MAKES: *8 to 10 muffins*

¾ cup white corn flour
⅔ cup all-purpose flour
½ cup granulated sugar
2 tablespoons baking powder
1 teaspoon baking soda
1½ teaspoons pumpkin-pie spice
½ cup seedless raisins
½ cup chopped pecans
½ teaspoon salt
2 large eggs
2 tablespoons butter or margarine, at room temperature
⅔ cup sour milk or buttermilk
1 tablespoon coffee-flavored liqueur or strong brewed coffee
1 teaspoon almond extract
2 cups mashed, peeled sweet potatoes
Marshmallow Sauce (see recipe page 131)

**1** Position the rack in the center of the oven and preheat to 400 degrees F. Lightly grease or line with paper baking cups twelve 2¾-inch muffin cups.

**2** In a large bowl, blend together the two flours, sugar, baking powder, baking soda, pumpkin-pie spice, raisins, pecans, and salt. In a medium bowl, beat the eggs until thick and light-colored. Beat in the butter, milk, liqueur, almond extract, and potatoes. Combine the two mixtures, blending until the dry ingredients are just moistened.

**3** Spoon the batter into the prepared muffin cups, filling each about three-quarters full. Bake for 15 to 20 minutes, or until a cake tester or wooden toothpick inserted into the center of a muffin comes out clean. Remove from the oven and immediately brush the tops of the muffins with the glaze. Cool in the pan on a wire rack for 5 to 7 minutes. Serve warm, or transfer to the rack to cool completely. Top with Marshmallow Sauce.

# SPICED SWEET-POTATO MUFFINS

MAKES: *11 to 12 muffins*

## SPICED ZUCCHINI MUFFINS

MAKES: *11 to 12 muffins*

1½ cups bran
1¼ cups all-purpose flour
2 teaspoons baking powder
¼ teaspoon ground cinnamon
¼ teaspoon ground nutmeg
¼ teaspoon ground cloves
¼ teaspoon salt
¼ cup cholesterol-free egg
    substitute
¼ cup packed light-brown sugar
1¼ cups skim milk
⅓ cup butter or margarine, melted
½ cup golden raisins
½ cup grated zucchini
Papaya Salsa (see recipe page 123)

1  Position the rack in the center of the oven and preheat to 400 degrees F. Lightly grease or line with paper baking cups twelve cup 2¾-inch muffin cups.

2  In a large bowl, blend together the bran, flour, baking powder, cinnamon, nutmeg, cloves, and salt. In a medium bowl, stir the egg substitute and sugar until smooth. Beat in the milk and butter. Fold in the raisins and zucchini. Combine the two mixtures, blending until the dry ingredients are just moistened.

3  Spoon the batter into the prepared muffin cups, filling each about three-quarters full. Bake for 15 to 20 minutes, or until a cake tester or wooden toothpick inserted into the center of a muffin comes out clean. Cool in the pan on a wire rack for 5 to 7 minutes. Serve warm, or invert onto the rack to cool completely. Serve with Papaya Salsa.

## SPICY MUFFINS WITH CREAM CHEESE

MAKES: *11 to 12 muffins*

2 cups all-purpose flour
½ cup granulated sugar
1 teaspoon baking powder
1 teaspoon ground nutmeg
1 teaspoon ground cinnamon
1 teaspoon ground ginger
1 teaspoon salt
1 large egg
1 cup milk
¼ cup canola oil
Honey Glaze (see recipe page 53)
Whipped Cream-Cheese Topping
    (see recipe page 186)

1  Position the rack in the center of the oven and preheat to 425 degrees F. Lightly grease or line with paper baking cups twelve 2¾-inch muffin cups.

2  In a large bowl, blend together the flour, sugar, baking powder, nutmeg, cinnamon, ginger, and salt. In a medium bowl, beat the egg until foamy. Beat in the milk and oil. Combine the two mixtures, blending until the dry ingredients are just moistened.

3  Spoon the batter into the prepared muffin cups, filling each about three-quarters full. Bake for 15 to 20 minutes, or until a cake tester or wooden toothpick inserted into the center of a muffin comes out clean. Remove from the oven and immediately brush the tops with Honey Glaze. Cool in the pan on a wire rack for 5 to 7 minutes. Serve warm, or invert onto the rack to cool completely. Serve with Whipped Cream-Cheese Topping.

1 cup rolled oats
1 cup all-purpose flour
½ cup chopped pecans
1 tablespoon baking powder
1½ teaspoons ground cinnamon
¼ teaspoon ground nutmeg
¼ teaspoon ground cloves
½ teaspoon salt
2 large egg whites
1 cup milk
¼ cup packed light-brown sugar
½ cup light corn syrup
2 tablespoons canola oil
Molasses Sauce (see recipe page 125)

**1** Position the rack in the center of the oven and preheat to 400 degrees F. Line with paper baking cups twelve 2¾-inch muffin cups. (Do not grease the baking pan for these muffins.)

**2** In a large bowl, blend together the oats, flour, pecans, baking powder, cinnamon, nutmeg, cloves, and salt. In a small bowl, beat the egg whites until stiff but not dry. In a medium bowl, beat the milk, brown sugar, corn syrup, and oil until smooth. Fold in the egg whites. Combine the two mixtures, blending until the dry ingredients are just moistened. (This is a very moist mixture, and should not be overmixed.)

**3** Drop ⅓ cup of the batter into each of the prepared muffin cups. Bake for about 18 to 22 minutes, or until the tops are golden brown and a cake tester or wooden toothpick inserted into a muffin is removed clean. Cool in the pan on a wire rack for 5 to 7 minutes. Serve warm, or invert onto the rack to cool completely. Top with Molasses Sauce.

## SPICY OATMEAL MUFFINS

MAKES: *11 to 12 muffins*

---

1 cup all-purpose flour
½ cup rolled oats
1 teaspoon baking powder
¼ teaspoon baking soda
2 tablespoons granulated sugar
1 teaspoon ground ginger
⅔ cup chopped dried figs
¼ teaspoon salt
1 large egg
1 cup milk
3 tablespoons butter or margarine, melted
Flaked coconut for topping
Fig Sauce (see recipe page 189)
Tropical Sauce (see recipe page 81)

**1** Position the rack in the center of the oven and preheat to 400 degrees F. Lightly grease or line with paper baking cups ten 2¾-inch muffin cups.

**2** In a large bowl, blend together the flour, oats, baking powder, baking soda, sugar, ginger, figs, and salt. In a medium bowl, beat the egg until foamy. Beat in the milk and butter. Combine the two mixtures, blending until the dry ingredients are just moistened.

**3** Spoon the batter into the prepared muffin cups, filling each three-quarters full. Sprinkle the tops of the muffins with coconut. Bake for 15 to 20 minutes, or until a cake tester or wooden toothpick inserted into the center of a muffin comes out clean. Cool in the pan on a wire rack for 5 to 7 minutes. Serve warm, or invert onto the rack to cool completely. Serve with Fig Sauce and Tropical Sauce.

## SPICY OATMEAL MUFFINS WITH FIGS AND COCONUT

MAKES: *8 to 10 muffins*

# SPINACH-AND-RICE MUFFINS WITH OLIVES

MAKES: *11 to 12 muffins*

1 cup all-purpose flour
½ cup whole-wheat flour
¼ cup cornmeal
2 teaspoons baking powder
1½ teaspoons ground cumin
½ teaspoon salt
1 large egg
3 tablespoons butter or margarine, melted
1 cup milk
1 cup cold cooked basmati rice
Savory Sauce (see recipe page 191)

1  Position the rack in the center of the oven and preheat to 425 degrees F. Lightly grease or line with paper baking cups twelve 2¾-inch muffin cups.

2  In a large bowl, blend together the two flours, cornmeal, baking powder, cumin, and salt. In a medium bowl, beat the egg until foamy. Beat in the butter and milk. Stir in the rice. Combine the two mixtures, blending until the dry ingredients are just moistened.

3  Spoon the mixture into the prepared muffin cups, filling each about three-quarters full. Bake for 15 to 20 minutes, or until a cake tester or wooden toothpick inserted into the center of a muffin comes out clean. Cool in the pan on a wire rack for 5 to 7 minutes. Serve warm, or invert onto the rack to cool completely. Top with Savory Sauce.

# SPINACH MUFFINS WITH CHICK PEAS

MAKES: *11 to 12 muffins*

2 tablespoons butter or margarine
4 scallions (green onions), chopped fine
1 cup finely chopped fresh spinach leaves
1 tablespoon garlic powder
2 cups all-purpose flour
1 cup cornmeal
2 teaspoons baking powder
¼ teaspoon dried tarragon, crushed
One 15-ounce can chick peas, drained and rinsed
2 tablespoons grated Romano cheese
3 large eggs
1¼ cups milk
3 tablespoons butter or margarine, melted
Flavored Mayonnaise (see recipe page 324)

1  Position the rack in the center of the oven and preheat to 375 degrees F. Lightly grease or line with paper baking cups twelve 2¾-inch muffin cups.

2  In a small skillet set over a medium heat, melt the butter. Add onion, spinach, and garlic powder. Cook, stirring, until the onion just starts to turn translucent and the spinach is wilted. Remove from the heat and set aside.

3  In a large bowl, blend together the flour, cornmeal, baking powder, tarragon, chick peas, and cheese. In a medium bowl, beat the eggs until foamy. Beat in the milk and butter. Stir in the spinach mixture. Combine the two mixtures, blending until the dry ingredients are just moistened.

4  Spoon the batter into the prepared muffin cups, filling each about three-quarters full. Bake for 15 to 20 minutes, or until a cake tester or wooden toothpick inserted into the center of a muffin comes out clean. Cool in the pan on a wire rack for 5 to 7 minutes. Serve warm, or invert onto the rack to cool completely. Serve with Flavored Mayonnaise.

1½ cups all-purpose flour
½ cup whole-wheat flour
1 tablespoon baking powder
½ teaspoon Cunningham® English
    Mixture Spice or ground
    cinnamon
¼ teaspoon ground cloves
½ teaspoon salt
2 large eggs
¼ cup packed light-brown sugar
¼ cup canola oil
¾ cup milk
½ cup mashed cooked summer
    squash
Cinnamon–Rhubarb Sauce (see
    recipe page 68)

**1** Position the rack in the center of the oven and preheat to 400 degrees F. Lightly grease or line with paper baking cups twelve 2¾-inch muffin cups.

**2** In a large bowl, blend together the two flours, baking powder, spice, cloves, and salt. In a medium bowl, beat the egg and sugar smooth. Beat in the oil, milk, and squash. Combine the two mixtures, blending until the dry ingredients are just moistened.

**3** Spoon the batter into the prepared muffin cups, filling each about three-quarters full. Bake for 15 to 20 minutes, or until a cake tester or wooden toothpick inserted into the center of a muffin comes out clean. Cool in the pan on a wire rack for 5 to 7 minutes. Serve warm, or invert onto the rack to cool completely. Top with Cinnamon–Rhubarb Sauce.

# SQUASH DINNER MUFFINS

MAKES: *11 to 12 muffins*

---

2¼ cups all-purpose flour
⅓ cup granulated sugar
1 tablespoon baking powder
½ teaspoon salt
2 large eggs
½ cup milk
1 teaspoon vanilla
1 cup sliced strawberries
Rhubarb Sauce (see recipe below)

**1** Position the rack in the center of the oven and preheat to 400 degrees F. Lightly grease or line with paper baking cups fourteen 2¾-inch muffin cups.

**2** In a large bowl, blend together the flour, sugar, baking powder, and salt. In a medium bowl, beat the eggs until thick and light-colored. Beat in the milk and vanilla extract. Stir in the strawberries. Combine the two mixtures, blending until the dry ingredients are just moistened.

**3** Spoon the batter into the prepared muffin cups, filling each about three-quarters full. Bake for about 15 to 20 minutes, or until a cake tester or wooden toothpick inserted into the center of a muffin comes out clean. Remove from the oven and immediately brush the tops of the muffins with Strawberry Glaze. Cool in the pan on a wire rack for 5 to 7 minutes. Serve warm, or transfer to the rack to cool completely. Top with Rhubarb Sauce.

# STRAWBERRY MUFFINS

MAKES: *12 to 14 muffins*

# RHUBARB SAUCE

MAKES: *About 1 cup*

1 cup fresh rhubarb, finely
    chopped
2 tablespoons water
2 tablespoons cornstarch
3 tablespoons honey

In the container of a blender, combine all of the ingredients and process until smooth. Pour into a small saucepan, set over medium heat and cook until bubbles just start to form around the edges of the pan. Remove from the heat, pour into a sieve, and serve hot.

## SUGARED PUMPKIN MUFFINS

MAKES: *11 to 12 muffins*

1½ cups all-purpose flour
½ cup granulated sugar
2 teaspoons baking powder
½ teaspoon ground cinnamon
½ teaspoon grated nutmeg
½ cup miniature marshmallows
½ teaspoon salt
1 large egg
¼ cup butter or margarine, melted
½ cup milk
½ cup cooked mashed pumpkin
¼ cup granulated sugar for topping
Marshmallow Sauce (see recipe
  page 131)

1  Position the rack in the center of the oven and preheat to 400 degrees F. Lightly grease or line with paper baking cups twelve 2¾-inch muffin cups.

2  In a large bowl, blend together the flour, brown sugar, baking powder, cinnamon, nutmeg, marshmallows, and salt. In a medium bowl, beat the egg until foamy. Beat in the butter and milk. Stir in the pumpkin. Combine the two mixtures, blending until the dry ingredients are just moistened.

3  Spoon the batter into the prepared muffin cups, filling each about three-quarters full. Sprinkle a generous coating of sugar over the top of each muffin. Bake for 15 to 20 minutes, or until a cake tester or wooden toothpick inserted into the center of a muffin comes out clean. Cool in the pan on a wire rack for 5 to 7 minutes. Serve warm, or invert onto the rack to cool completely. Serve with Marshmallow Sauce.

## SWEET POTATO-AND-MARSHMALLOW SURPRISE MUFFINS

MAKES: *24 to 26 muffins*

3 cups all-purpose flour
2 teaspoons baking powder
1½ teaspoons baking soda
1 cup granulated sugar
2 teaspoons ground black pepper
½ teaspoon salt
3 large eggs
½ cup milk
1 cup plus 2 tablespoons canola oil
2 cups (about 2) mashed sweet
  potatoes
78 miniature marshmallows
Apple–Cinnamon Glaze (see recipe
  page 171)

1  Position the rack in the center of the oven and preheat to 375 degrees F. Lightly grease or line with paper baking cups twenty-six 2¾-inch muffin cups.

2  In a large bowl, blend together the flour, baking powder, baking soda, sugar, pepper, and salt. In a medium bowl, beat the eggs until foamy. Beat in the milk, oil, and sweet potatoes. Combine the two mixtures, blending until the dry ingredients are just moistened.

3  Drop 1 heaping tablespoon of the batter into each of the prepared muffin cups. Press two miniature marshmallows into the batter in each cup and top each with 1 heaping tablespoon of the remaining batter. (The muffin cups should be about two-thirds full). Press one or more miniature marshmallows onto the top of each muffin.

4  Bake for 15 to 20 minutes, or until a cake tester or wooden toothpick inserted into the edge of a muffin (not into the marshmallows) comes out clean. Cool in the pan on a wire rack for 5 to 7 minutes. Serve warm, or transfer to the rack to cool completely. Top with Apple–Cinnamon Glaze.

1½ cups all-purpose flour
½ cup crushed shredded wheat
¼ cup packed light-brown sugar
2 teaspoons baking powder
1 teaspoon baking soda
1 teaspoon ground nutmeg
1 cup golden raisins
½ teaspoon salt
2 large eggs
¾ cup sour milk or buttermilk
¼ cup butter or margarine, melted
½ cup mashed sweet potato
Marshmallow Sauce (see recipe
    page 131)

**1** Position the rack in the center of the oven and preheat to 400 degrees F. Lightly grease or line with paper baking cups six 3-inch muffin cups.

**2** In a large bowl, blend together the flour, shredded wheat, brown sugar, baking powder, baking soda, nutmeg, and salt. In a medium bowl, beat the eggs until thick and light-colored. Beat in the milk, butter, and potatoes. Combine the two mixtures, blending until the dry ingredients are just moistened.

**3** Spoon the batter into the prepared muffin cups, filling each about three-quarters full. Bake for 20 to 25 minutes, or until a cake tester or wooden toothpick inserted into the center of a muffin comes out clean. Cool in the pan on a wire rack for 5 to 7 minutes. Serve warm, or invert onto the rack to cool completely. Top with Marshmallow Sauce.

## SWEET-POTATO MUFFINS

MAKES: *5 to 6 muffins*

---

1½ cups all-purpose flour
¼ cup cornmeal
4 tablespoons powdered sugar
1½ teaspoons baking powder
1¼ teaspoons baking soda
¼ teaspoon paprika
½ cup finely diced cooked ham
2 large eggs
3 tablespoons butter or margarine, melted
2 teaspoons prepared mustard
1 cup buttermilk
Grated Swiss cheese for topping
Sweet Mustard Sauce (see recipe
    page 85)

**1** Position the rack in the center of oven and preheat to 400 degrees F. Lightly grease or line with paper baking cups six 3-inch muffin cups.

**2** In a large bowl, blend together the flour, cornmeal, sugar, baking powder, baking soda, paprika, and diced ham. In a medium bowl, beat the eggs until foamy. Beat in the butter, mustard, and buttermilk. Combine the two mixtures, blending until the dry ingredients are just moistened.

**3** Spoon the batter into the prepared muffin cups, filling each about three-quarters full. Bake for 20 to 25 minutes, or until a cake tester or wooden toothpick inserted into the center of a muffin comes out clean. Remove from the oven and sprinkle grated Swiss cheese on top of each muffin. Cool in the pan on a wire rack for 5 to 7 minutes. Serve warm, or invert onto the rack to cool completely. Serve with Sweet Mustard Sauce.

## THE MUFFINS OF ST. PATRICK

MAKES: *5 to 6 muffins*

## THE SCOTSMAN MUFFINS

MAKES: *14 to 16 muffins*

½ cup all-purpose flour
½ cup cornmeal
½ teaspoon baking powder
½ teaspoon baking soda
½ cup cooked ground sausage meat
½ teaspoon ground cumin
½ teaspoon ground coriander
½ teaspoon garlic powder
½ teaspoon onion powder
½ teaspoon salt
2 large eggs
3 tablespoons butter or margarine, melted
1 cup buttermilk or sour milk
1 can (15 ounces) cream-style corn
3 drops Tabasco®

1  Position the rack in the center of the oven and preheat to 375 degrees F. Lightly grease or line with paper baking cups sixteen 2¾-inch muffin cups.

2  In a large bowl, blend together the flour, cornmeal, baking powder, baking soda, sausage, cumin, coriander, garlic powder, onion powder, and salt. In a medium bowl, beat the eggs until foamy. Beat in the butter and buttermilk. Stir in the corn and Tabasco. Combine the two mixtures, blending until the dry ingredients are just moistened.

3  Spoon the batter into the prepared muffin cups, filling each about three-quarters full. Bake for 15 to 20 minutes, or until a cake tester or wooden toothpick inserted into the center of a muffin comes out clean. Cool in the pan on a wire rack for 5 to 7 minutes. Serve warm, or invert onto the rack to cool completely.

SERVING SUGGESTION: **Serve with a thick bean soup.**

## TUNA MUFFINS

MAKES: *16 to 18 muffins*

3 cups all-purpose flour
5 teaspoons baking powder
1 tablespoon granulated sugar
1 tablespoon finely chopped onion
1 can (6 ounces) chunk light tuna in water, drained and finely chopped
2 cups dry sherry or white port wine
Shredded Cheddar cheese for topping the muffins
Lemon Butter (see recipe page 236)

1  Position the rack in the center of the oven and preheat to 375 degrees F. Lightly grease or line with paper baking cups eighteen 2¾-inch muffin cups.

2  In a large bowl, blend together the flour, baking powder, sugar, and onion. Stir in the tuna. Add the sherry and stir until the dry ingredients are just moistened.

3  Spoon the batter into the prepared muffin cups, filling each about three-quarters full. Sprinkle the tops of the muffins with cheese. Bake for 15 to 20 minutes, or until a cake tester or wooden toothpick inserted into the center of a muffin comes out clean. Cool in the pan on a wire rack for 5 to 7 minutes. Serve warm, or invert onto the rack to cool completely. Serve with Lemon Butter.

2 cups all-purpose flour
½ cup granulated sugar
1 tablespoon baking powder
¼ cup Dutch-processed cocoa
  powder
2 large eggs
6 tablespoons butter or margarine,
  melted
1 cup sour cream
1 cup evaporated milk
1 tablespoon instant coffee
freshly grated zest from two oranges

**1** Position the rack in the center of the oven and preheat to 400 degrees F. Lightly grease or line with paper baking cups twelve 2¾-inch muffin cups.

**2** In a large bowl, blend together the flour, sugar, baking powder, and cocoa powder. In a medium bowl, beat the eggs until thick and light-colored. Beat in the butter, sour cream, milk, coffee, and orange zest. Combine the two mixtures, blending until the dry ingredients are just moistened.

**3** Spoon the batter into the prepared muffin cups, filling each about three-quarters full. Press half an orange slice into each muffin. Bake for 15 to 20 minutes, or until a cake tester or wooden toothpick inserted into a muffin is removed clean. Cool in the pan on a wire rack for 5 to 7 minutes. Serve warm, or invert onto the rack to cool completely.

# VARIETY COFFEE MUFFINS

MAKES: *11 to 12 muffins*

# VEGETABLE-SALAD MUFFINS

MAKES: *5 to 6 muffins*

**BATTER**
1 cup all-purpose flour
½ cup whole-wheat flour
½ cup corn flour
1 tablespoon baking powder
1 teaspoon salt
2 large eggs
½ cup canola oil
1 cup milk
½ teaspoon Tabasco®

**1ST LAYER**
½ cup finely chopped broccoli
1 tablespoon grated Romano cheese

**2ND LAYER**
½ cup whole-kernel corn
¼ teaspoon garlic powder

**3RD LAYER**
One 4-ounce can chopped
  mushrooms, drained

**TOPPING**
½ teaspoon onion powder
¼ teaspoon garlic powder
¼ cup crumbled, crisply cooked
  bacon

**1** Position the rack in the center of the oven and preheat to 375 degrees F. Lightly grease or line with paper baking cups six 3-inch muffin cups.

**2** To make the batter, in a large bowl, blend together the three flours, baking powder, and salt. In a medium bowl, beat the eggs until foamy. Beat in the oil, milk, and Tabasco®. Combine the two mixtures, blending until the dry ingredients are just moistened.

**3** To make the layers, divide the batter evenly between 3 small bowls. To the first bowl, stir in the chopped broccoli and Romano cheese. To the second, stir in the corn and garlic powder. To the third, stir in the chopped mushrooms. In another small bowl, combine the topping ingredients.

**4** Drop 1 heaping tablespoon of the broccoli batter into each of the prepared muffin cups. Drop 1 heaping tablespoon of the corn batter on top of the first in the pan, and top with 1 heaping tablespoon of the mushroom mixture. Sprinkle the tops of the muffins with the bacon mixture. Bake for about 20 to 25 minutes, or until a cake tester or wooden toothpick inserted into the center of a muffin comes out clean. Cool in the pan on a wire rack for 5 to 7 minutes. Serve warm, or invert onto the rack to cool completely.

**SERVING SUGGESTION: Serve with a fresh seafood salad.**

# VEGGIE MUFFINS

MAKES: *11 to 12 muffins*

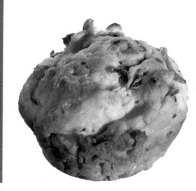

2 cups all-purpose flour
2 tablespoons granulated sugar
1 tablespoon baking powder
½ cup finely chopped pitted olives
½ cup grated carrots
2 tablespoons fresh snipped chives
¼ teaspoon dried red pepper flakes
¼ teaspoon salt
1 large egg
¾ cup milk
¼ cup canola oil
1 small package (3 ounces) cream
   cheese, cut into 12 chunks

**1** Position the rack in the center of the oven and preheat to 400 degrees F. Lightly grease or line with paper baking cups twelve 2¾-inch muffin cups.

**2** In a large bowl, blend together the flour, sugar, baking powder, olives, carrots, chives, red pepper flakes, and salt. In a medium bowl, beat the egg, milk, and oil until smooth. Combine the two mixtures, blending until the dry ingredients are just moistened.

**3** Spoon the batter into the prepared muffin cups, filling each about three-quarters full. Press one chunk of cream cheese into the center of the batter in each muffin cup. Bake for 15 to 20 minutes, or until a cake tester or wooden toothpick inserted into the center of a muffin comes out clean. Cool in the pan on a wire rack for 5 to 7 minutes. Serve warm, or invert onto the rack to cool completely.

**SERVING SUGGESTION: Serve with a thick soup.**

# WHOLE-GRAIN ENGLISH-STYLE MUFFINS

MAKES: *11 to 12 muffins*

1½ cups wheat flour
½ cup cornmeal
3 tablespoons granulated sugar
1 tablespoon baking powder
1 teaspoon Cunningham® English
   Mixture Spice or ground
   cinnamon
1¾ cups heavy cream
2 tablespoons butter or margarine,
   melted
Whipped Cream-Cheese Topping
   (see recipe page 186)

**1** Position the rack in the center of the oven and preheat to 375 degrees F. Lightly grease or line with paper baking cups twelve 2¾-inch muffin cups.

**2** In a large bowl, blend together the flour, cornmeal, sugar, baking powder, and spice. In a medium bowl, beat the cream until foamy. Beat in the butter. Combine the two mixtures, blending until the dry ingredients are just moistened.

**3** Spoon the batter into the prepared muffin cups, filling each about three-quarters full. Bake for 15 to 20 minutes, or until a cake tester or wooden toothpick inserted into the center of a muffin comes out clean. Remove from the oven and immediately brush the top of each muffin with the glaze. Cool in the pan on a wire rack for 5 to 7 minutes. Serve warm, or invert onto the rack to cool completely. Serve with Whipped Cream-Cheese Topping.

**SERVING SUGGESTION: Serve with strawberry jam.**

1½ cups all-purpose flour
½ cup soy flour
¼ cup turbinado sugar
1 tablespoon baking powder
½ teaspoon baking soda
½ teaspoon salt
1 large egg
¼ cup canola oil
1 cup sour milk or buttermilk
1 cup cooked wild rice
1 tablespoon chopped scallion
   (green onion)
1 tablespoon chopped fresh parsley
Tomato–Basil Dip (see recipe page
   130)

**1** Position the rack in the center of the oven and preheat to 400 degrees F. Lightly grease or line with paper baking cups fourteen 2¾-inch muffin cups.

**2** In a large bowl, blend together the two flours, sugar, baking powder, baking soda, and salt. In a medium bowl, beat the egg until foamy. Beat in the oil and milk. Stir in the rice, scallion, and parsley. Combine the two mixtures, blending until the dry ingredients are just moistened.

**3** Spoon the batter into the prepared muffin cups, filling each about three-quarters full. Bake for 15 to 20 minutes, or until a cake tester or wooden toothpick inserted into the center of a muffin comes out clean. Cool in the pan on a wire rack for 5 to 7 minutes. Serve warm, or invert onto the rack to cool completely. Serve with Tomato–Basil Dip.

# WILD RICE MUFFINS

MAKES: *12 to 14 muffins*

---

1½ cups all-purpose flour
½ cup yellow cornmeal
1 tablespoon baking powder
1 large egg
1½ cups condensed canned turkey
   soup
¼ cup butter or margarine, melted
3 tablespoons jellied cranberry
   sauce
Sweet Onion Relish (see recipe page
   89)

**1** Position the rack in the center of the oven and preheat to 375 degrees F. Lightly grease or line with paper baking cups twelve 2¾-inch muffin cups.

**2** In a large bowl, blend together the flour, cornmeal, and baking powder. In a medium bowl, beat the egg until foamy. Beat in the soup and butter. Stir in the cranberry sauce. Combine the two mixtures, blending until the dry ingredients are just moistened.

**3** Spoon the batter into the prepared muffin cups, filling each about three-quarters full. Bake for 15 to 20 minutes, or until a cake tester or wooden toothpick inserted into the center of a muffin comes out clean. Cool in the pan on a wire rack for 5 to 7 minutes. Serve warm, or invert onto the rack to cool completely. Serve with Sweet Onion Relish.

# WILD-WEST TURKEY-SOUP MUFFINS

MAKES: *11 to 12 muffins*

# YANKEE MAPLE MUFFINS

MAKES: *12 to 14 muffins*

2 cups all-purpose flour
1 cup yellow cornmeal
1 tablespoon baking powder
2 large eggs
¼ cup packed light-brown sugar
1 cup milk
⅓ cup maple syrup
¼ cup butter or margarine, melted
½ cup crushed, canned pineapple, drained
Bean Salad (see recipe page 42)

1  Position the rack in the center of the oven and preheat to 375 degrees F. Lightly grease or line with paper baking cups fourteen 2¾-inch muffin cups.

2  In a large bowl, blend together the flour, cornmeal, and baking powder. In a medium bowl, beat the eggs until foamy. Beat in the sugar. Beat in the milk, syrup, butter, and pineapple. Combine the two mixtures, blending until the dry ingredients are just moistened.

3  Spoon the batter into the prepared muffin cups, filling each about three-quarters full. Bake for 25 to 30 minutes, or until a cake tester or wooden toothpick inserted into the center of a muffin comes out clean. Remove from the oven and brush the top of each muffin with the butter. Cool in the pan on a wire rack for 5 to 7 minutes. Serve warm, or transfer to the rack to cool completely. Serve with Bean Salad.

# ZUCCHINI-AND-BASIL MUFFINS

MAKES: *11 to 12 muffins*

2 cups all-purpose flour
¼ cup granulated sugar
1 tablespoon baking powder
3 tablespoons minced fresh basil
1 tablespoon minced fresh oregano
¼ teaspoon salt
2 large eggs
¾ cup milk
⅔ cup canola oil
2 cups shredded zucchini
¼ cup grated Parmesan cheese
Cottage Cheese Dip (see recipe page 195)

1  Position the rack in the center of the oven and preheat to 425 degrees F. Lightly grease or line with paper baking cups twelve 2¾-inch muffin cups.

2  In a large bowl, blend together the flour, sugar, baking powder, basil, oregano, and salt. In a medium bowl, beat the eggs until foamy. Beat in the milk and oil. Stir in the zucchini. Combine the two mixtures, blending until the dry ingredients are just moistened.

3  Spoon the batter into the prepared muffin cups, filling each about three-quarters full. Sprinkle Parmesan cheese over the tops of the muffins. Bake for 15 to 20 minutes, or until a cake tester or wooden toothpick inserted into the center of a muffin comes out clean. Cool in the pan on a wire rack for 5 to 7 minutes. Serve warm, or invert onto the rack to cool completely. Serve with Cottage Cheese Dip.

1¼ cups rye flour
¾ cup all-purpose flour
2 teaspoons baking powder
½ teaspoon baking soda
1 tablespoon caraway seeds
½ teaspoon salt
1 large egg
1½ cups sour milk or buttermilk
3 tablespoons molasses
1 cup finely chopped zucchini
¼ cup finely chopped pitted olives
Thin slices of your favorite grated
    cheese for topping
Cheese-and-Olive Spread (see recipe
    page 183)

**1** Position the rack in the center of the oven and preheat to 375 degrees F. Lightly grease a 6 cup, 4-inch-size, muffin top baking pan.

**2** In a large bowl, blend together the two flours, baking powder, baking soda, caraway seeds, and salt. In a medium bowl, beat the egg, milk, molasses, zucchini, and olives until smooth. Combine the two mixtures, blending until the dry ingredients are just moistened.

**3** Drop 3 heaping tablespoons of the batter into each of the prepared muffin cups. Top each with a slice of cheese. Bake for 20 to 25 minutes, or until a cake tester or wooden toothpick inserted into the center of a muffin comes out clean. Cool in the pan on a wire rack for 5 to 7 minutes. Serve warm, or transfer to the rack to cool completely. Serve with Cheese-and-Olive Spread.

## ZUCCHINI-AND-SWEET-RYE MUFFINS WITH OLIVES

MAKES: *6 to 8 muffins*

2 cups all-purpose flour
1 cup granulated sugar
1 teaspoon baking soda
¼ teaspoon baking powder
1½ teaspoons ground cinnamon
1 cup golden raisins
½ cup chopped walnuts
½ teaspoon salt
2 large eggs
½ cup canola oil
1 tablespoon vanilla extract
2 cups shredded zucchini
Blueberry Spread (see recipe page
    62)

**1** Position the rack in the center of the oven and preheat to 375 degrees F. Lightly grease or line with paper baking cups twenty-four 2¾-inch muffin cups.

**2** In a large bowl, blend together the flour, sugar, baking soda, baking powder, cinnamon, raisins, walnuts, and salt. In a medium bowl, beat the eggs until foamy. Beat in the oil and vanilla extract. Stir in zucchini. Combine the two mixtures, blending until the dry ingredients are just moistened.

**3** Spoon the batter into the prepared muffin cups, filling each about three-quarters full. Bake for 15 to 20 minutes, or until a cake tester or wooden toothpick inserted into the center of a muffin is removed clean. Cool in the pan on a wire rack for 5 to 7 minutes. Serve warm, or invert onto the rack to cool completely. Serve with Blueberry Spread.

## ZUCCHINI MUFFINS

MAKES: *23 to 24 muffins*

# Chapter 3

# BISCUITS

Biscuits are one of those traditionally American creations that are appropriate when served many different times of the day. They can be made fresh, in the morning, and served hot with breakfast. Biscuits can be made in the morning and rewarmed to go with a lunchtime meal. You'll find them wrapped in waxed paper, plastic wrap, or even a napkin, to be taken along on a business trip or in a lunch box. These snacks-on-the-run travel well and can be something eaten by itself or as an accompaniment or side dish to many meals.

# APPLESAUCE BISCUITS

*MAKES: 6 to 8 biscuits*

2 cups all-purpose flour
1 tablespoon baking powder
¼ teaspoon baking soda
1 teaspoon salt
3 tablespoons vegetable shortening, chilled
1 large egg
¼ cup sour cream
½ cup applesauce
½ cup grated cheese
Apple–Cinnamon Syrup (see recipe page 168)

**1** Position the rack in the center of the oven and preheat to 425 degrees F.

**2** In a large bowl, blend together the flour, baking powder, baking soda, and salt. Using a pastry blender or two knives scissor-fashion, cut in the shortening until the mixture resembles fine meal. In a small bowl, combine the egg, sour cream, and apple-sauce. (Do not beat.) Pour into the dry mixture all at one time and stir briefly until the dough holds together.

**3** Turn the dough out onto a lightly floured surface and knead 7 to 8 times. Using a rolling pin, roll the dough out to a thickness of ½ inch. Using a 2-inch round cutter, cut out as many biscuits as possible. Place the biscuits 1 inch apart on an ungreased baking sheet. Rework the scraps until all the biscuits are cut.

**4** Sprinkle the cheese over the tops of the biscuits and bake for 10 to 12 minutes, or the tops are golden brown. Serve warm and with Apple–Cinnamon Syrup.

# AUSTRALIAN CHEESE– CURRY BISCUITS

*MAKES: 4 to 6 biscuits*

¾ cup all-purpose flour
½ teaspoon baking powder
2 teaspoons curry powder
¼ cup butter or margarine, at room temperature
⅔ cup grated cheese
1 large egg yolk
2 tablespoons milk
⅛ teaspoon dry mustard powder
¼ teaspoon salt
Dash of cayenne pepper
Hot Curry Spread (see recipe page 177)

**1** Position the rack in the center of the oven and preheat to 425 degrees F.

**2** In a large bowl, blend together the flour, baking powder, and curry powder. Using a pastry blender or two knives scissor-fashion, cut in the butter until the mixture resembles fine meal. Fold in the cheese. In a small bowl, combine the egg yolk, milk, dry mustard, salt, and cayenne. (Do not beat.) Pour into the dry ingredients all at one time and stir briefly until the dough holds together.

**3** Turn the dough out onto a lightly floured surface and knead 7 to 8 times. Using a rolling pin, roll the dough out to a thickness of ¼ inch. Using a 2-inch round cutter, cut out as many biscuits as possible. Place the biscuits 1 inch apart on an ungreased baking sheet. Rework the scraps until all the dough is used. Bake for 7 to 10 minutes, or until the tops of the biscuits are golden brown. Serve warm and with Hot Curry Spread.

1 can (12 ounces) beer
4 cups Bisquick® baking mix
3 tablespoons granulated sugar
Blueberry Spread (see recipe page
   62)

**1** Thirty minutes before baking, pour the beer into a glass and set aside. Position the rack in the center of the oven and preheat to 375 degrees F.

**2** In a large bowl, blend together the biscuit mix and sugar. Stir in the flat beer, stirring until the dough holds together.

**3** Turn the dough out onto a lightly floured surface. Using a rolling pin, roll the dough out to a thickness of ½-inch. Using a 2-inch round cutter, cut out as many biscuits as possible. Place the biscuits 1 inch apart on ungreased baking sheets. Rework the scraps until all the dough is used. Bake for 12 to 15 minutes, or until the tops of the biscuits are golden brown. Serve warm and with Blueberry Spread.

# BEER BISCUITS

MAKES: *12 to 14 biscuits*

---

2¼ cups Bisquick® baking mix
⅔ cup white port wine
1½ cups shredded sharp Cheddar
   cheese
Cheese Spread (see recipe below)

**1** Position the rack in the center of the oven and preheat to 425 degrees F.

**2** In a large bowl, combine the baking mix and wine and stir just until the dough holds together. (Do not overmix.) Stir in the cheese.

**3** Turn the dough out onto a lightly floured surface and knead 7 to 8 times. Using a rolling pin, roll the dough out to a thickness of ½ inch. Using a 2-inch round cutter, cut out as many biscuits as possible. Place the biscuits 1 inch apart on an ungreased baking sheet. Rework the scraps until all the dough is used and brush with the remaining butter. Bake for 10 to 12 minutes, or until the tops of the biscuits are golden brown. Serve warm and with Cheese Spread.

# BISQUICK® CHEESE BISCUITS

MAKES: *4 to 6 biscuits.*

---

# CHEESE SPREAD

MAKES: *About 1¼ cups*

One 3-ounce package Neufchatel
   cream cheese
1 teaspoon finely chopped pimento
One 5-ounce jar Old English®
   sharp pasteurized processed
   cheese spread
3 tablespoons heavy cream
1 teaspoon fresh snipped chives

In a small bowl, combine all of the ingredients and stir until mixed. Refrigerate until ready to serve.

## BLACKBERRY BISCUITS

MAKES: *6 to 8 biscuits*

1 cup all-purpose flour
¼ cup graham flour
1½ teaspoons baking powder
¼ cup granulated sugar
½ teaspoon salt
¼ cup heavy cream
½ cup berry-flavored yogurt
½ cup blackberries
**Whipped Cream-Cheese Topping**
  **(see recipe page 186)**

**1** Position the rack in the center of the oven and preheat to 425 degrees F.

**2** In a large bowl, blend together the two flours, baking powder, sugar, salt, cream, and yogurt, stirring just until the dough holds together. (Do not overmix.) Stir in the blackberries.

**3** Turn the dough out onto a lightly floured surface and knead 7 to 8 times. Using a rolling pin, roll the dough out to a thickness of ½ inch. Using a 2-inch round cutter, cut out as many biscuits as possible. Place the biscuits 1 inch apart on an ungreased baking sheet. Rework the scraps until all the dough is used. Bake for 10 to 12 minutes, or until the tops of the biscuits are golden brown. Serve warm and with Whipped Cream-Cheese Topping.

## BREAKFAST BISCUITS

MAKES: *12 to 14 biscuits.*

2 cups all-purpose flour, sifted
1 cup sugar
1 tablespoon baking powder
1 teaspoon salt
2½ tablespoons butter or margarine
¼ cup melted butter or margarine
  (for brushing)
¾ cup milk
**Whipped Butter (see recipe page 23)**

**1** Position the rack in the center of the oven and preheat to 425 degrees F.

**2** In a large bowl, blend together the flour, baking powder, sugar, and salt. Using a pastry blender or two knives scissor-fashion, cut in the shortening until the mixture resembles fine meal. Pour in the milk all at one time and stir just until the dough holds together. (Do not overmix.)

**3** Turn the dough out onto a lightly floured surface and knead 7 to 8 times. Using a rolling pin, roll the dough out to a thickness of ¾-inch. Using a 2- to 2½-inch round cutter, cut out as may biscuits as possible. Place the biscuits 1 inch apart on ungreased baking sheets. Rework the scraps until all the dough is used. Brush with the remaining butter. Bake for 10 to 12 minutes, or until the tops of the biscuits are golden brown. Serve warm and with Whipped Butter.

2 cups all-purpose flour
2½ teaspoons baking powder
¼ teaspoon baking soda
1 tablespoon granulated sugar
¼ teaspoon salt
6 tablespoons butter or margarine,
   chilled
¼ cup melted butter or margarine,
   melted (for brushing)
¾ cup buttermilk or sour milk
Prune Spread (see recipe page 117)

**1** Position the rack in the center of the oven and preheat to 425 degrees F.

**2** In a large bowl, blend together the flour, baking powder, baking soda, sugar, and salt. Using a pastry blender or two knives scissor-fashion, cut in the butter until the mixture resembles fine

meal. Add the buttermilk all at one time and stir just until the dough holds together. (Do not overmix.)

**3** Turn the dough out onto a lightly floured surface and knead 7 to 8 times. Using a rolling pin, roll the dough out to a thickness of ½ inch. Using a 2-inch round cutter, cut out as many biscuits as possible. Place the biscuits 1 inch apart on an ungreased baking sheet. Rework the scraps until all the dough is used. Brush with the melted butter. Bake for 10 to 12 minutes, or until the tops of the biscuits are golden brown. Serve warm and with Prune Spread.

# BUTTERMILK BISCUITS
MAKES: *10 to 12 biscuits*

---

2 cups all-purpose flour
3¾ teaspoons baking powder
1 teaspoon salt
6 tablespoons butter or margarine, at
   room temperature
¾ cup milk
Zucchini Spread (see recipe page
   170)

**1** Lightly grease a skillet and preheat it over a low flame.

**2** In a large bowl, blend together the flour, baking powder, and salt. Using a pastry blender or two knives scissor-fashion, cut in the butter until the mixture resembles fine meal. Add the

milk all at one time and stir just until the dough holds together. (Do not overmix.)

**3** Turn the dough out onto a lightly floured surface and knead 7 to 8 times. Using a rolling pin, roll the dough out to a thickness of ½ inch. Using a 2-inch round cutter or the top of a cup or glass, cut out as many biscuits as possible. Place the biscuits 1 inch apart on the prepared skillet (you may have to work in batches). Cook until the biscuits are light brown on the underside. Turn and brown on the other side. Serve at once and with Zucchini Spread.

# CAMP BISCUITS
MAKES: *16 to 18 biscuits*

# CHEDDAR CHEESE BISCUITS

MAKES: *6 to 8 biscuits*

2 cups all-purpose flour
4 teaspoons baking powder
2 teaspoons granulated sugar
½ teaspoon salt
2 tablespoons butter or margarine, at room temperature
1 large egg
¾ cup milk
½ cup grated Cheddar cheese
Chicken Spread (see recipe page 188)

1 Position the rack in the center of the oven and preheat to 425 degrees F.

2 In a large bowl, blend together the flour, baking powder, sugar, and salt. In a medium bowl, beat the egg, butter, and milk together before stirring in the Cheddar cheese. Then combine the two mixes, blending just until the dough holds together. (Do not overmix.)

3 Turn the dough out onto a lightly floured surface and knead 7 to 8 times. Using a rolling pin, roll the dough out to a thickness of ½ inch. Cut with a 1-inch round cutter. Place the biscuits 1 inch apart on an ungreased baking sheet. Rework the scraps until all the dough is used. Bake for 10 to 12 minutes, or until the tops of the biscuits are golden brown. Serve warm and with Chicken Spread.

# CHEESE BISCUITS

MAKES: *16 to 18 biscuits*

2 cups all-purpose flour
2 teaspoons baking powder
½ teaspoon salt
4 tablespoons vegetable shortening, chilled
1 cup grated American cheese
1 cup milk
Ham Spread (see recipe page 57)

1 Position the rack in the center of the oven and preheat to 425 degrees F.

2 In a large bowl, blend together the flour, baking powder, and salt. Using a pastry blender or two knives scissor-fashion, cut in the shortening until the mixture resembles fine meal. Add the cheese and milk all at one time and stir just until the dough holds together. (Do not overmix.)

3 Turn the dough out onto a lightly floured surface and knead 7 to 8 times. Using a rolling pin, roll the dough out to a thickness of ½ inch. Using a 2-inch round cutter, cut out as many biscuits as possible. Place the biscuits 1 inch apart on ungreased baking sheets. Rework the scraps until all the dough is used. Bake for 10 to 12 minutes, or until the tops of the biscuits are golden brown. Serve warm and with Ham Spread.

1 cup all-purpose flour
1 cup graham flour
1 tablespoon baking powder
¼ cup snipped fresh chives
1 teaspoon salt
⅔ cup milk
⅓ cup canola oil
Shrimp Spread (see recipe page 145)

**1** Position the rack in the center of the oven and preheat to 425 degrees F.

**2** In a large bowl, blend together the two flours, baking powder, chives, and salt. Add the milk and oil all at one time and stir just until the dough holds together. (Do not overmix.)

**3** Turn the dough out onto a lightly floured surface and knead 7 to 8 times. Using a rolling pin, roll the dough out to a thickness of ¾ inch. Using a 2-inch round cutter, cut out as many biscuits as possible. Place the biscuits 1 inch apart on an ungreased baking sheet. Rework the scraps until all the dough is used. Bake for 10 to 12 minutes, or until the tops of the biscuits are golden brown. Serve warm and with Shrimp Spread.

## CHIVE BISCUITS

---

1½ cups all-purpose flour
1 tablespoon baking powder
1½ teaspoons granulated sugar
½ teaspoon cream of tartar
¼ cup finely chopped dried cherries
½ teaspoon salt
¼ cup vegetable shortening, chilled
½ cup milk
¾ cup butter or margarine, melted
Apricot Spread (see recipe below)

**1** Position the rack in the center of the oven and preheat to 425 degrees F.

**2** In a large bowl, blend together the flour, baking powder, chopped dried cherries, sugar, salt, and cream of tartar. Using a pastry blender or two knives scissor-fashion, cut in the shortening until the mixture resembles fine meal. Pour the milk and ½ cup of the butter in all at one time and stir just until the dough holds together. (Do not overmix.)

**3** Turn the dough out onto a lightly floured surface and knead 7 to 8 times. Using a rolling pin, roll the dough out to a thickness of ½ inch. Using a 2-inch round cutter, cut out as many biscuits as possible. Place the biscuits 1 inch apart on an ungreased baking sheet. Rework the scraps until all the dough is used and brush with the remaining butter. Bake for 12 to 15 minutes, or until the tops of the biscuits are golden brown. Serve warm and with Apricot Spread.

## CHOPPED CHERRY BISCUITS

MAKES: *8 to 10 biscuits*

---

## APRICOT SPREAD

MAKES: *About ½ cup*

½ cup finely chopped dried apricots, plumped in brandy and drained
2 tablespoons evaporated milk
1 teaspoon almond extract
1 tablespoon granulated sugar
1 tablespoon packed light-brown sugar

In the container of a blender, combine all of the ingredients and process on medium speed until smooth. Pour into a bowl and refrigerate until ready to serve.

## CURRANT BISCUITS

MAKES: *10 to 12 biscuits*

1½ cups all-purpose flour
½ cup soy flour
2 teaspoons baking powder
½ teaspoon salt
¼ cup butter or margarine, at room temperature
½ cup black currants or finely chopped raisins
½ cup milk
Cheese Spread (see recipe page 257)

**1** Position the rack in the center of the oven and preheat to 425 degrees F.

**2** In a large bowl, blend together the two flours, baking powder, and salt. Work in the butter until the mixture resembles fine meal. Stir in the currants. Add the milk all at one time, stirring briefly until the dough holds together. (Do not overmix.)

**3** Turn the dough out onto a lightly floured surface and knead 7 to 8 times. Using a rolling pin, roll the dough out to a thickness of ½ inch. Using a 2-inch round cutter, cut out as many biscuits as possible. Place the biscuits 1 inch apart on an ungreased baking sheet. Rework the scraps until all the dough is used. Bake for 10 to 12 minutes, or until the tops of the biscuits are golden brown. Serve warm and with Cheese Spread.

## GRAHAM BISCUITS

MAKES: *8 to 10 biscuits*

2 cups graham flour
1 cup all-purpose flour
2 tablespoons baking powder
¾ teaspoon salt
½ cup vegetable shortening, chilled
1 cup milk
Herb Butter (see recipe page 149)

**1** Position the rack in the center of the oven and preheat to 425 degrees F.

**2** In a large bowl, blend together the two flours, baking powder, and salt. Using a pastry cutter or two knives scissor-fashion, cut in the shortening until the mixture resembles fine meal. Add the milk all at one time and stir just until the dough holds together. (Do not overmix.)

**3** Turn the dough out onto a lightly floured surface and knead 7 to 8 times. Using a rolling pin, roll the dough out to a thickness of ½ inch. Using a 2-inch round cutter, cut out as many biscuits as possible. Place the biscuits 1 inch apart on an ungreased baking sheet. Rework the scraps until all the dough is used. Bake for 10 to 12 minutes, or until the tops of the biscuits are golden brown. Serve warm and with Herb Butter.

1 cup all-purpose flour
1 cup whole-wheat flour
1 tablespoon baking powder
¼ cup grated Romano cheese
¾ teaspoon salt
2 large eggs
½ cup chopped green tomatoes
1 teaspoon wine vinegar
6 tablespoons butter or margarine,
   melted
Peppery Lemon Butter (see recipe
   page 74)

**1** Position the rack in the center of the oven and preheat to 425 degrees F.

**2** In a large bowl, blend together the two flours, baking powder, cheese, and salt. In a medium bowl, blend together the egg, green tomatoes, vinegar, and butter. Then combine the two mixtures, blending until the dry ingredients are just moistened. (Do not overmix.)

**3** Turn the dough out onto a lightly floured surface and knead 7 to 8 times. Using a rolling pin, roll the dough out to a thickness of ½ inch. Using a 2-inch round cutter, cut out as many biscuits as possible. Place the biscuits 1 inch apart on an ungreased baking sheet. Rework the scraps until all the dough is used. Bake for 10 to 12 minutes, or until the tops of the biscuits are golden brown. Serve warm and with Peppery Lemon Butter.

# GREEN TOMATO BISCUITS

MAKES: *14 to 16 biscuits*

---

1¾ cups all-purpose flour
2½ teaspoons baking powder
1 cup heavy cream
½ teaspoon salt
Pumpkin Butter (see recipe page
   122)

**1** Position the rack in the center of the oven and preheat to 450 degrees F.

**2** In a large bowl, combine the flour, baking powder, cream, and salt and stir just until the dough holds together. (Do not overmix.)

**3** Turn the dough out onto a lightly floured surface and knead 7 or 8 times. Using a rolling pin, roll the dough out to a thickness of ½ inch. Using a 2-inch round cutter, cut out as many biscuits as possible. Place the biscuits 1-inch apart on an ungreased baking sheet. Rework the scraps until all the dough is used. Bake for 10 to 12 minutes, or until the tops of the biscuits are golden brown. Serve warm and with Pumpkin Butter.

# HEAVY CREAM BISCUITS

MAKES: *4 to 6 biscuits*

# HONEY BISCUITS

MAKES: *10 to 12 biscuits*

**FILLING**

⅓ cup butter or margarine, at room temperature
¼ cup honey

**DOUGH**

2 cups all-purpose flour
4 teaspoons baking powder
½ tablespoon salt
¼ cup butter, at room temperature
⅔ cup milk
¼ cup sesame seeds
Blueberry Spread (see recipe page 62)

**1** Position the rack in the center of the oven and preheat to 325 degrees F.

**2** To make the filling, in a small bowl, beat together the butter and honey until smooth. Set aside.

**3** To make the dough, in a large bowl, blend together the flour, baking powder, and salt. Work in the butter until the mixture resembles fine meal. Add the milk all at one time and stir just until the dough holds together. (Do not overmix.)

**4** Turn the dough out onto a lightly floured surface and knead 7 to 8 times. Roll out to a rectangle ½ inch thick. Brush the rectangle with the honey butter. Roll the rectangle up jelly-roll fashion and cut into 1-inch slices. Place the slices on an ungreased baking sheet, and brush with any remaining honey butter. Sprinkle the tops of the biscuits with sesame seeds. Bake for 10 to 12 minutes, or until the tops of the biscuits are golden brown. Serve warm and with Blueberry Spread.

# INDIAN FRIED BISCUITS

MAKES: *12 to 16 biscuits*

Oil for deep frying
2 cups all-purpose flour
3 tablespoons baking powder
2 tablespoons granulated sugar
½ teaspoon salt
¾ cup milk
Pumpkin Butter (see recipe page 122)

**1** Pour ½-inch of oil into a large skillet and preheat over a medium heat.

**2** In a large bowl, blend together the flour, baking powder, sugar, and salt. Stir in the milk, stirring just until the dough holds together. (Do not overmix.)

**3** Turn the dough out onto a lightly floured surface and knead 7 to 8 times. Using a rolling pin, roll the dough out to a thickness of ½ inch. Using a 2-inch round cutter, cut out as many biscuits as possible. Rework the scraps until all the dough is used.

**4** Carefully slip as many of the rounds as possible into the hot oil without overcrowding the skillet. Cook until the biscuits are browned on both sides. Remove the biscuits from the oil and drain them on paper towels or on a wire rack. Continue until all the biscuits are fried. Serve warm and with Pumpkin Butter.

1 cup all-purpose flour
2 tablespoons cornmeal
1½ teaspoons baking powder
½ cup finely grated sharp cheese
2 tablespoons peeled and chopped tomato
1 teaspoon seeded, minced jalapeño pepper
½ teaspoon salt
½ cup milk
Cheese Spread (see recipe page 257)

1 Position the rack in the center of the oven and preheat to 425 degrees F.

2 In a large bowl, blend together the flour, cornmeal, baking pow-der, cheese, tomatoes, peppers, and salt. Add the milk all at one time and stir just until the dough holds together. (Do not overmix.)

3 Turn the dough out onto a lightly floured surface and knead 7 to 8 times. Divide the dough into 6 equal balls and place the balls on an ungreased baking sheet. Pat the balls into 3-inch rounds. Bake for 10 to 12 min-utes, or until the tops of the bis-cuits are golden brown. Serve warm and with Cheese Spread.

## JALAPEÑO PEPPER– CHEESE BISCUITS

MAKES: *6 biscuits*

---

1½ cups all-purpose flour
1 tablespoon baking powder
1 tablespoon granulated sugar
1 teaspoon salt
⅓ cup vegetable shortening, chilled
¼ cup whiskey
¼ cup milk
Honey Butter (see recipe page 146)

1 Position the rack in the center of the oven and preheat to 425 degrees F.

2 In a large bowl, blend together the flour, baking powder, sugar, and salt. Using a pastry blender or two knives scissor-fashion, cut in the shortening until the mix-ture resembles fine meal. Add the whiskey and milk all at one time and stir just until the dough just holds together. (Do not overmix.)

3 Turn the dough out onto a lightly floured surface and knead 7 to 8 times. Using a rolling pin, roll the dough out to a thickness of ½ inch. Using a 2-inch round cutter, cut out as many biscuits as possible. Place the biscuits 1 inch apart on an ungreased baking sheet. Rework the scraps until all the dough is used. Bake for 10 to 12 minutes, or until the tops of the biscuits are golden brown. Serve warm and with Honey Butter.

## KENTUCKY BLEND BISCUITS

MAKES: *4 to 6 biscuits*

# LEMON BISCUITS

MAKES: *14 to 16 biscuits*

2 cups all-purpose flour
¾ teaspoon baking soda
¼ cup granulated sugar
½ teaspoon salt
⅓ cup vegetable shortening, chilled
2 teaspoons grated lemon zest
½ cup milk
3 tablespoons lemon juice
Lemon Butter (see recipe page 236)

**1** Position the rack in the center of the oven and preheat to 425 degrees F.

**2** In a large bowl, blend together the flour, baking soda, sugar, and salt. Using a pastry blender or two knives scissor-fashion, cut in the shortening until the mixture resembles fine meal. Stir in the lemon zest. Add the milk and lemon juice all at one time and stir just until the dough holds together. (Do not overmix.)

**3** Turn the dough out onto a lightly floured surface and knead 7 to 8 times. Using a rolling pin, roll the dough out to a thickness of ½ inch. Using a 2-inch round cutter, cut out as many biscuits as possible. Place the biscuits 1 inch apart on an ungreased baking sheet. Rework the scraps until all the dough is used. Bake for 10 to 12 minutes, or until the tops of the biscuits are golden brown. Serve warm and with Lemon Butter.

# MASHED POTATO BISCUITS

MAKES: *10 to 12 biscuits*

1¾ cups all-purpose flour
1 teaspoon salt
½ cup chilled butter
4 large egg yolks
2 tablespoons sour cream
1 cup cold mashed potatoes
Peach Butter (see recipe page 124)

**1** Position the rack in the center of the oven and preheat to 425 degrees F.

**2** In a large bowl, blend together the flour and salt. Using a pastry blender or two knives scissor-fashion, cut in the butter until the mixture resembles fine meal. In a medium bowl, beat 3 of the egg yolks until foamy before beating in the sour cream and potatoes. Combine the two mixtures, blending until the dry ingredients are just moistened and the dough holds together. (Do not overmix.)

**3** Turn the dough out onto a lightly floured surface and knead 7 to 8 times. Using a rolling pin, roll the dough out to a thickness of ½ inch. Using a 2-inch round cutter, cut out as many biscuits as possible. Place the biscuits 1 inch apart on an ungreased baking sheet. Rework the scraps until all the dough is used. Brush the tops of the biscuits with the remaining egg yolk. Bake for 10 to 12 minutes, or until the tops of the biscuits are golden brown. Serve warm and with Peach Butter.

2 cups all-purpose flour
1 teaspoon granulated sugar
4 strips crisply cooked bacon, crumbled
½ teaspoon salt
1 cup milk
3 tablespoons mayonnaise
1 tablespoon bacon drippings
Hot Curry Spread (see recipe page 177)

**1** Position the rack in the center of the oven and preheat to 425 degrees F.

**2** In a large bowl, blend together the flour, sugar, bacon, and salt. Add the milk, mayonnaise, and bacon drippings. Stir briefly until the dough just holds together.

**3** Turn the dough out onto a lightly floured surface and knead 7 to 8 times. Using a rolling pin, roll the dough out to a thickness of 1 inch. Using a 2-inch round cutter, cut out as many biscuits as possible. Place the biscuits 1 inch apart on an ungreased baking sheet. Rework the scraps until all the dough is used. Bake for 10 to 12 minutes, or until the tops of the biscuits are golden brown. Serve warm and with Hot Curry Spread.

# MAYONNAISE-AND-BACON BISCUITS

MAKES: *6 to 8 biscuits*

---

1 cup all-purpose flour
1 cup rice flour
1 tablespoon baking powder
½ teaspoon dry mustard powder
¼ cup butter or margarine, at room temperature
1 cup shredded Cheddar cheese
1 large egg, lightly beaten
⅓ cup milk
Mustard Sauce (see recipe page 42)

**1** Position the rack in the center of the oven and preheat to 425 degrees F.

**2** In a large bowl, blend together the two flours, baking powder, and mustard. Work in the butter until the mixture resembles fine meal. Stir in the cheese. Add the egg and milk all at one time and stir just until the dough holds together. (Do not overmix.)

**3** Turn the dough out onto a lightly floured surface and knead 7 to 8 times. Using a rolling pin, roll the dough out to a thickness of ½ inch. Using a 2-inch round cutter, cut out as many biscuits as possible. Place the biscuits 1 inch apart on an ungreased baking sheet. Rework the scraps until all the dough is used. Bake for 10 to 12 minutes, or until the tops of the biscuits are golden brown. Serve warm and with Mustard Sauce.

# MUSTARD-AND-CHEESE BISCUITS

MAKES: *8 to 10 biscuits*

# ONION BISCUITS

MAKES: *10 to 12 biscuits*

3 cups all-purpose flour
1 teaspoon baking powder
½ teaspoon baking soda
1 teaspoon granulated sugar
2 tablespoons poppy seeds
2 medium onions, grated
1 teaspoon salt
2 large eggs
¼ cup vegetable oil
3 cups water
2 teaspoons cider vinegar
Mustard–Anchovy Spread (see
    recipe page 157)

**1** Position the rack in the center of the oven and preheat to 425 degrees F.

**2** In a large bowl, blend together the flour, baking powder, baking soda, poppy seeds, onion, and salt. In a small bowl, beat the eggs, oil, water, and vinegar together. Combine the two mixtures, blending until the dry ingredients are just moistened.

**3** Turn the dough out onto a lightly floured surface and knead 7 to 8 times. Using a rolling pin, roll the dough out to a thickness of ¼ inch. Using a 2-inch round cutter, cut out as many biscuits as possible. Place the biscuits 1 inch apart on ungreased baking sheets. Rework the scraps until all the dough is used. Bake for 10 to 12 minutes, or until the tops of the biscuits are golden brown. Serve warm and with Mustard–Anchovy Spread.

# PATRIOTIC BISCUITS

MAKES: *10 to 12 biscuits*

2 cups all-purpose flour
1 tablespoon baking powder
2 tablespoons granulated sugar
½ teaspoon salt
½ cup butter or margarine, at room
    temperature
¼ cup finely chopped cranberries
¼ cup finely chopped blueberries
1 large egg, lightly beaten
½ cup milk
Onion-and-Pepper Relish (see
    recipe page 76)

**1** Position the rack in the center of the oven and preheat to 425 degrees F.

**2** In a large bowl, blend together the flour, baking powder, sugar, and salt. Work in the butter until the mixture resembles fine meal. Stir in the cranberries and blue-berries. Add the egg and milk all at one time, and stir just until the dough holds together.

**3** Turn the dough out onto a lightly floured surface and knead 7 to 8 times. Using a rolling pin, roll the dough out to a thickness of ½ inch. Using a 2-inch round cutter, cut out as many biscuits as possible. Place the biscuits 1 inch apart on an ungreased baking sheet. Rework the scraps until all the dough is used. Bake for 10 to 12 minutes, or until the tops of the biscuits are golden brown. Serve warm and with Onion-and-Pepper Relish.

3 cups all-purpose flour
4½ teaspoons baking powder
1 tablespoon granulated sugar
¾ teaspoon salt
½ cup chilled butter or margarine
1 large bell pepper, seeded and
 finely diced
1 large egg
¾ cup milk
Tomato–Onion Fried Relish (see
 recipe page 120)

**1** Position the rack in the center of the oven and preheat to 425 degrees F.

**2** In a large bowl, blend together the flour, baking powder, sugar, and salt. Using a pastry blender or two knives scissor-fashion, cut in the butter until the mixture resembles fine meal. Stir in the pepper. In a small bowl, whisk together the egg and milk and add it to the dry ingredients, stirring just until the dough holds together. (Do not overmix.)

**3** Turn the dough out onto a lightly floured surface and knead 7 to 8 times. Using a rolling pin, roll the dough out to a thickness of ½ inch. Using a 2-inch round cutter, cut out as many biscuits as possible. Place the biscuits 1 inch apart on an ungreased baking sheet. Rework the scraps until all the dough is used. Bake for 10 to 12 minutes, or until the tops of the biscuits are golden brown. Serve warm and with Tomato–Onion Fried Relish.

# PEPPER EGG BISCUITS
MAKES: *10 to 12 biscuits*

# PIONEER BISCUITS
MAKES: *10 to 12 biscuits*

2 cups all-purpose flour
1 tablespoon baking powder
2 tablespoons granulated sugar
½ teaspoon salt
½ cup butter or margarine, at room
 temperature
1 large egg, lightly beaten
½ cup milk
Chili Butter (see recipe page 119)

**1** Position the rack in the center of the oven and preheat to 425 degrees F.

**2** In a large bowl, blend together the flour, baking powder, sugar, and salt. Work in the butter until the mixture resembles fine meal. Add the egg and milk all at one time and stir just until the dough holds together. (Do not overmix.)

**3** Turn the dough out onto a lightly floured surface and knead 7 to 8 times. Using a rolling pin, roll the dough out to a thickness of ½ inch. Using a 2-inch round cutter, cut out as many biscuits as possible. Place the biscuits 1 inch apart on an ungreased baking sheet. Rework the scraps until all the dough is used. Bake for 10 to 12 minutes, or until the tops of the biscuits are golden brown. Serve warm and with Chili Butter.

## POPPY SEED-AND-BUTTERMILK BISCUITS

MAKES: *14 to 16 biscuits*

2 cups all-purpose flour
1½ teaspoons baking powder
½ teaspoon baking soda
1½ teaspoons granulated sugar
1 teaspoon salt
6 tablespoons butter or margarine, at room temperature
⅔ cup buttermilk
Melted butter for brushing
Poppy seeds for sprinkling
Poppy Seed Butter (see recipe page 96)

**1** Position the rack in the center of the oven and preheat to 425 degrees F.

**2** In a large bowl, blend together the flour, baking powder, baking soda, sugar, and salt. Work in the butter until the mixture resembles fine meal. Add the butter-milk all at one time, and stir just until the dough holds together. (Do not overmix.)

**3** Turn the dough out onto a lightly floured surface and knead 7 to 8 times. Using a rolling pin, roll the dough out to a thickness of ½ inch. Using a 2-inch round cutter, cut out as many biscuits as possible. Place the biscuits 1 inch apart on ungreased baking sheets. Rework the scraps until all the dough is used. Brush the tops of the biscuits with butter and sprinkle them with poppy seeds. Bake for 10 to 12 minutes, or until the tops of the biscuits are golden brown. Serve warm and with Poppy Seed Butter.

## RUM BISCUITS

MAKES: *10 to 12 biscuits*

2 cups all-purpose flour
2 teaspoons baking powder
½ teaspoon salt
3 tablespoons butter or margarine, chilled
¾ cup milk
12 sugar cubes
¼ cup rum
Plum Butter (see recipe page 47)

**1** Position the rack in the center of the oven and preheat to 425 degrees F.

**2** In a large bowl, blend together the flour, baking powder, and salt. Using a pastry blender or two knives scissor-fashion, cut in the butter until the mixture resembles fine meal. Add the milk all at one time and stir just until the dough holds together.

**3** Turn the dough out onto a lightly floured surface and knead 7 to 8 times. Using a rolling pin, roll the dough out to a thickness of ½ inch. Using a 2-inch round cutter, cut out as many biscuits as possible. Place the biscuits 1 inch apart on an ungreased baking sheet. Rework the scraps until all the dough is used. Push a sugar cube into the center of each biscuit. Spoon the rum evenly over the sugar cubes. Bake for 10 to 12 minutes, or until the tops of the biscuits are golden brown. Serve warm and with Plum Butter.

1½ cups all-purpose flour
½ cup whole-wheat flour
1 tablespoon baking powder
½ teaspoon salt
⅓ cup vegetable shortening, chilled
¾ cup milk
Sesame seeds for sprinkling
Sweet-and-Sour Mango Relish (see
recipe page 192)

**1** Position the rack in the center of the oven and preheat to 425 degrees F.

**2** In a large bowl, blend together the two flours, baking powder, and salt. Using a pastry blender or two knives scissor-fashion, cut in the shortening until the mixture resembles fine meal. Add the milk all at one time and stir just until the dough holds together. (Do not overmix.)

**3** Turn the dough out onto a lightly floured surface and knead 7 to 8 times. Using a rolling pin, roll the dough out to a thickness of ½ inch. Using a 2-inch round cutter, cut out as many biscuits as possible. Place the biscuits 1 inch apart on an ungreased baking sheet. Rework the scraps until all the dough is used. Sprinkle the tops of the biscuits with sesame seeds. Bake for 10 to 12 minutes, or until the tops of the biscuits are golden brown. Serve warm and with Sweet-and-Sour Mango Relish.

## SUGARLESS WHOLE-WHEAT BISCUITS

MAKES: *8 to 10 biscuits*

2 cups all-purpose flour
1 tablespoon granulated sugar
1 tablespoon baking powder
½ teaspoon salt
½ cup cooked, mashed sweet potato
½ cup butter or margarine, at room
temperature
½ cup milk
Shrimp Spread (see recipe page 145)

**1** Position the rack in the center of the oven and preheat to 450 degrees F.

**2** In a large bowl, blend together the flour, sugar, baking powder, and salt. Work in the potatoes and butter. Add the milk all at one time and stir just until the dough holds together.

**3** Transfer the dough to a lightly floured board and knead 7 or 8 times. Using a rolling pin, roll the dough out to a thickness of ½-inch. Using a 2-inch round cutter, cut out as many biscuits as possible. Place the biscuits 1 inch apart on ungreased baking sheets. Rework the scraps until all the biscuits are cut. Bake for 10 to 12 minutes, or until the tops of the biscuits are golden brown. Serve warm and with Shrimp Spread.

## SWEET-POTATO BISCUITS

MAKES: *12 to 14 biscuits*

# TOMATO-FLAVORED BISCUITS

MAKES: *14 to 16 biscuits*

1 cup all-purpose flour
1 cup whole-wheat flour
1 tablespoon baking powder
½ teaspoon dried oregano
¼ cup grated Parmesan cheese
¾ teaspoon salt
⅔ cup tomato juice
6 tablespoons melted butter or
  margarine
Peppery Lemon Butter (see recipe
  page 74)

1 Position the rack in the center of the oven and preheat to 425 degrees F.

2 In a large bowl, blend together the two flours, baking powder, oregano, cheese, salt, tomato juice, and butter, stirring just until the dough holds together.

3 Turn the dough out onto a lightly floured surface and knead 7 to 8 times. Using a rolling pin, roll the dough out to a thickness of ½ inch. Using a 2-inch round cutter, cut out as many biscuits as possible. Place the biscuits 1 inch apart on an ungreased baking sheet. Rework the scraps until all the dough is used. Bake for 10 to 12 minutes, or until the tops of the biscuits are golden brown. Serve warm and with Peppery Lemon Butter.

# WHEAT-GERM DROP BISCUITS

MAKES: *8 to 10 biscuits*

2 cups all-purpose flour
¼ cup wheat germ
1 tablespoon baking powder
1 teaspoon salt
¼ cup melted butter or margarine
1 cup milk
Cheese-and-Horseradish Spread
  (see recipe page 180)

1 Position the rack in the center of the oven and preheat to 425 degrees F.

2 In a large bowl, blend together the flour, wheat germ, baking powder, salt, butter, and milk, stirring just until the dough holds together. (Do not overmix.)

3 Drop the dough by heaping tablespoons onto an ungreased baking sheet, leaving 2 inches between the biscuits. Bake for 10 to 12 minutes, or until the tops of the biscuits are golden brown. Serve warm and with Cheese-and-Horseradish Spread.

# Chapter 4

# COBBLERS

Cobblers are not made as often as they used to be—and that is a pity. The cobbler, however, is the perfect comfort food, and may be coming back into the baking mainstream, as homey recipes appear more and more in the baker's kitchen. They are similar to a fruit pie, without the difficulty of making the pie crust. They can be made with fresh, frozen, or canned fruit—and can be as large or as small as you desire. Cobblers are usually made using a square or round individual-size pan. Cobblers are like a tart without a crust. Straight from the oven, these warm, bubbly desserts may have cheese or other toppings of your choice sprinkled on them. The problem with the cobbler is that it is always so hard to determine who will get the last piece!

# APPLE COBBLER WITH CHEDDAR CHEESE

MAKES: *4 to 6 servings*

**FILLING**
1 cup granulated sugar
¼ cup all-purpose flour
¼ teaspoon ground cinnamon
6 cups sliced apples, peeled and cored

**TOPPING**
1 cup all-purpose flour
¼ cup granulated sugar
1½ teaspoons baking powder
½ teaspoon salt
1½ cups shredded cheddar cheese
⅓ cup melted butter or margarine
¼ cup milk

**1** Position the rack in the center of the oven and preheat to 400 degrees F. Lightly grease and flour the bottom of a 9-inch square baking pan or chaffing dish.

**2** To make the filling, in a plastic or paper bag, combine the sugar, flour cinnamon, and apple and shake to coat before spreading evenly into the prepared baking pan. To make the topping, in a large bowl, combine the flour, sugar, baking powder, salt, and cheese. Stir in the butter and milk, combining until the dry ingredients are just moistened and spread over the top of the apple mixture in the pan.

**3** Bake for 28 to 30 minutes, until the topping is a golden brown color. Cool in the pan on a wire rack for 5 to 7 minutes. Serve warm.

# BISQUICK COBBLER

MAKES: *6 to 8 servings*

1 cup Bisquick® baking mix
1 cup milk
1 cup granulated sugar
½ cup melted butter or margarine
One 16-ounce can sliced peaches in heavy syrup

**1** Position the rack in the center of the oven and preheat to 350 degrees F. In a large bowl, beat the baking mix, milk, sugar, and butter until smooth. Spoon the mixture into a 13-by-9-inch baking dish.

**2** Drain the peaches, reserving the liquid. Arrange the sliced peaches over the top of the batter in the pan. Drizzle half of the reserved syrup over the top.

**3** Bake for 40 to 45 minutes, or until a cake tester or wooden toothpick inserted into the cobbler is removed clean. Cool in the pan on a wire rack for 5 to 7 minutes. Serve warm.

## FILLING

3 cups sliced apple, cored
1 cup fresh cranberries
1 cup sliced pear, cored
¼ cup chopped pitted fresh dates
¼ cup maple syrup
1 tablespoon cornstarch
2 teaspoons ground allspice
¼ teaspoon fresh lemon juice

## TOPPING

1½ cups rolled oats
¾ cup unsweetened apple juice
1 teaspoon ground nutmeg
¼ teaspoon vanilla extract

**1** Position the rack in the center of the oven and preheat to 375 degrees F. Lightly grease a 13-by-9-inch baking pan or chafing dish.

**2** To make the filling, spread the apples, cranberries, and pears evenly over the bottom of the prepared pan. In the container of a blender, combine the dates, maple syrup, cornstarch, allspice, and lemon juice and process on high for 5 to 6 seconds, or until smooth. Pour over the fruit in the baking pan.

**3** To make the topping, in a medium bowl, combine the oats, apple juice, nutmeg, and vanilla extract, stirring until the dry ingredients are just moistened. Spoon the topping evenly over the fruit in the pan.

**4** Bake for 35 to 40 minutes, or until the topping starts to brown and the filling begins to bubble up around the edges of the pan. Cool in the pan on a wire rack for 5 to 7 minutes. Serve warm.

# CRAN-APPLE COBBLER

MAKES: *6 to 8 servings*

---

## FILLING

2 cans (13 ounces each) tart cherries in syrup, pitted and drained (reserve the syrup)
¼ cup packed light-brown sugar
2 tablespoons tapioca, quick-cooking
2 tablespoons Kirsch liqueur
1½ tablespoons melted butter or margarine

## TOPPING

1½ cups all-purpose flour
2 teaspoons baking powder
3½ tablespoons granulated sugar, plus more for sprinkling over the top of the cobbler
1 small (3-ounce) package cream cheese
¼ cup melted butter or margarine
¾ cup milk

**1** Position the rack in the center of the oven and preheat to 425 degrees F. Lightly grease and flour the bottom of an 8-inch square baking pan or chafing dish.

**2** To make the filling, in a large bowl, combine the cherries, ⅓ cup of the reserved syrup, the brown sugar, tapioca, and Kirsch. Spread evenly over the bottom of the prepared pan. Drizzle the butter over the top.

**3** To make the topping, in a large bowl, combine the flour, baking powder, and sugar. Using a pastry cutter or two knives scissor-fashion, cut in the cream cheese until the mixture resembles coarse meal. In a small bowl, combine the butter and milk. Combine the two mixtures, blending until the dry ingredients are just moistened. Drop spoonfuls of the topping mixture over the cherries in the pan. Sprinkle lightly with granulated sugar.

**4** Bake for 20 to 25 minutes, or until the topping is golden brown. Cool in the pan on a wire rack for 5 to 7 minutes. Serve warm.

# CREAM CHEESE COBBLER WITH CHERRIES

MAKES: *8 to 10 servings*

## QUICK PEACH COBBLER

MAKES: *6 to 8 servings*

¼ cup butter or margarine, at room temperature
1 cup granulated sugar
1 large egg
3 large fresh peaches, peeled, pitted, and finely chopped
1 cup all-purpose flour
1 teaspoon baking soda
½ teaspoon ground nutmeg
½ teaspoon ground cinnamon
½ cup chopped walnuts

**1** Position the rack in the center of the oven and preheat to 325 degrees F. Lightly grease and flour the bottom of a 9-inch square baking pan or chafing dish.

**2** In a large bowl, beat the butter and sugar until light and fluffy. Beat in the egg. Stir in the peaches. In a medium bowl, combine the flour, baking soda, nutmeg, and cinnamon. Combine the two mixtures, blending until the dry ingredients are just moistened. Pour the mixture into the prepared pan. Sprinkle the top with chopped walnuts.

**3** Bake for about 35 to 40 minutes, or until the cobbler is golden and the center of the topping is set. Cool in the pan on a wire rack for 5 to 7 minutes. Serve warm.

## RHUBARB– STRAWBERRY COBBLER

MAKES: *6 to 8 servings*

FILLING

1¼ cups granulated sugar
3 tablespoons all-purpose flour
1½ teaspoons ground cinnamon
1½ teaspoons fresh frated orange zest
6 cups chopped fresh rhubarb
3 cups sliced fresh strawberries

CRUST

1½ cups all-purpose flour
3 tablespoons granulated sugar
1½ teaspoons baking powder
½ teaspoon baking soda
¼ teaspoon salt
3 tablespoons chilled butter or margarine
1 cup buttermilk or sour milk

**1** Position the rack in the center of the oven and preheat to 400 degrees F. Lightly grease a 13-by-9-inch baking pan or chafing dish.

**2** To make the filling, in a large bowl combine the sugar, flour, cinnamon, orange zest, rhubarb, and strawberries and spread the mixture evenly over the bottom of the prepared baking pan. Bake for 10 minutes, or until the mixture begins to bubble. To make the crust, in a large bowl, combine the flour, sugar, baking powder, and baking soda. Cut in the butter until the mix resembles a coarse meal. Add the milk and blend to a soft dough.

**3** Remove the pan from the oven and spoon the mixture onto the hot fruit, and continue baking for 20 to 25 minutes, or until the crust is a golden brown color. Remove the pan from the oven and cool on a wire rack for 5 to 7 minutes and serve warm.

## CRUST

3 cups all-purpose flour

2 teaspoons baking powder

½ teaspoon baking soda

¼ teaspoon salt

¾ cup butter or margarine, at room temperature

1¼ cups buttermilk or sour milk

## FILLING

3 cups fresh blueberries washed and rinsed

¾ cup granulated sugar

2 teaspoons grated lemon zest

½ teaspoon grated nutmeg

½ teapoon ground cinnamon

3 tablespoons butter or margarine, chilled and diced finely

**1** Position the rack in the center of the oven and preheat to 450 degrees F. Lightly grease a 13-by-9-inch baking pan or chafing dish.

**2** To make the crust, in a large bowl, combine the flour, baking powder, baking soda, and salt. Cut the butter into the dry mixture until the mixture resembles coarse meal. Stir in 1 cup of the buttmilk to form a dry stiff dough adding the remaining ¼ cup, a tablespoon at a time, to soften the dough as needed. Pat the dough out on a floured surface to let it set.

**3** To make the filling, in a plastic or paper bag, place the blueberries, sugar, lemon zest, nutmeg, and cinnamon, and shake gently to evenly coat the berries. Dot the top of the cobbler with the butter.

# ROYAL BLUEBERRY LEMON COBBLER

MAKES: *6 to 8 servings*

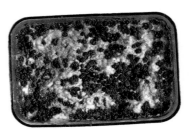

# Chapter 5

# COFFEE CAKE

Too many people think coffee cakes are too difficult to prepare, and therefore will tend to skip this chapter. Quick bread coffee cakes are not hard to make, nor do they have complex ingredients. Most of the quick bread coffee cakes in this chapter can be assembled with ordinary ingredients found in the average kitchen. They are easy, and have all been thoroughly tested so that even a novice baker will have no problems producing a fine, finished product.

## ALASKAN BLUEBERRY COFFEE CAKE

MAKES: *6 to 8 servings*

**TOPPING**
⅓ cup all-purpose flour
½ cup firmly packed brown sugar
½ teaspoon ground cinnamon
¼ cup chilled butter or margarine

**BATTER**
1½ cups all-purpose flour
¾ cup granulated sugar
2½ teaspoons baking powder
1 teaspoon salt
1 large egg
¼ cup canola oil
¾ cup milk
1½ cups fresh blueberries
Blueberry Spread (see recipe page 62)

**1** Position the rack in the center of the oven and preheat to 375 degrees F. Grease and flour the bottom of a 9-inch square or round baking pan.

**2** To make the topping, in a small bowl, combine the flour, brown sugar, and cinnamon. Using a pastry blender or two knives scissor-fashion, cut in the butter until the mixture resembles coarse crumbs. Set aside.

**3** To make the batter, in a large bowl, blend together the flour, sugar, baking powder, and salt. In a medium bowl, beat the egg until foamy before beating in the oil and milk. Fold in 1 cup of the blueberries. Combine the two mixtures, blending until the dry ingredients are just moistened.

**4** Spread the batter into the prepared baking pan. Sprinkle on the topping mixture and top with the remaining ½ cup blueberries. Bake for 25 to 30 minutes, or until a cake tester or wooden toothpick inserted into the cake comes out clean and the berries on top appear dried out. Remove the pan from the oven and cool on a wire rack for 5 to 8 minutes. Serve warm or cooled, and with Blueberry Spread.

## ALMOND STREUSEL COFFEE CAKE

MAKES: *6 to 8 servings*

**STREUSEL**
½ cup granulated sugar
½ cup firmly packed brown sugar
¼ cup all-purpose flour
4 teaspoons ground cinnamon
¼ cup butter or margarine, at room temperature
1 cup quick-cooking rolled oats
½ cup toasted chopped almonds

**BATTER**
¾ cup margarine, at room temperature
1½ cups granulated sugar
3 large eggs
1 cup plain yogurt or sour cream
1½ teaspoons vanilla extract
½ teaspoon almond extract
2½ cups all-purpose flour
2 teaspoons baking powder
1 teaspoon baking soda
1 teaspoon salt

**1** Position the rack in the center of the oven and preheat to 350 degrees F. Lightly grease and flour the bottom of a 13-by-9-inch baking pan.

**2** To make the streusel, in a medium bowl, blend together the two sugars, flour, and cinnamon. Using a pastry blender or two knives scissor-fashion, cut in the butter until the mixture resembles coarse crumbs. Stir in the oats and almonds. Set aside.

**3** To make the batter, in a medium bowl, beat the margarine and sugar until light and fluffy. Beat in the eggs, one at a time, beating vigorously after each addition. Beat in the sour cream, vanilla and almond extract. In a large bowl, blend together the flour, baking powder, baking soda, and salt. Combine the two mixtures, blending until the dry ingredients are moistened.

**4** Spoon half of the batter into the prepared pan. Sprinkle on half of the streusel mixture over the top of the batter in the pan. Top with the remaining batter and sprinkle with the remaining streusel.

**5** Bake for 45 to 50 minutes, or until a cake tester or wooden pick inserted into the cake comes out clean. Remove the pan from the oven and cool on a wire rack for 5 to 7 minutes. Serve warm.

**SERVING SUGGESTION: Serve with a bowl of fruit.**

## TOPPING

½ cup firmly packed light-brown
  sugar
2 tablespoons butter or margarine, at
  room temperature
2 tablespoons all-purpose flour
1 teaspoon ground cinnamon

## BATTER

½ cup granulated sugar
¼ cup vegetable shortening
1 large egg
½ cup milk
1½ cups all-purpose flour
2 teaspoons baking powder
½ teaspoon salt
2 cups peeled, cored, and thinly
  sliced apples

**1** Position the rack in the center
of the oven and preheat to 375
degrees F. Lightly grease and
flour the bottom of an 8-inch
square or round baking pan.

**2** To make the topping, in a small
bowl, beat the brown sugar and

butter until light and fluffy. Beat
in the flour and cinnamon. Set
aside.

**3** To make the batter, in a medium bowl, beat the sugar and
shortening together until light
and fluffy. Beat in the egg and
milk. In a large bowl, combine
the flour, baking powder, and
salt. Combine the two mixtures,
blending until smooth. Spoon
half of the batter into the prepared baking pan. Top with the
apples and spoon the remaining
batter on top.

**4** Bake for 45 to 50 minutes, or
until a cake tester or wooden
toothpick inserted into the cake
comes out clean. Remove the pan
from the oven and cool on a wire
rack for 5 to 7 minutes. Serve
warm.

**SERVING SUGGESTION: Serve
with warm applesauce.**

# APPLE COFFEE CAKE

MAKES: *4 to 6 servings*

---

## FILLING

2 tablespoons packed light-brown
  sugar
2 tablespoons cornstarch or
  arrowroot
One 16-ounce can pitted red cherries
1 teaspoon almond extract
6 to 8 drops red food color (optional)
1 cup finely ground almonds
  (optional)

## BATTER

½ cup all-purpose flour
2 tablespoons Dutch-processed
  cocoa powder
1 tablespoon packed light-brown
  sugar
¾ teaspoon baking powder
Pinch of salt
2 tablespoons butter or margarine, at
  room temperature
⅓ cup evaporated milk or heavy
  cream
1 teaspoon chocolate or vanilla
  extract
Cherry Sauce (see recipe page 52)

**1** Position the rack in the center
of the oven and preheat to 375
degrees F. Lightly grease and
flour the bottom of a 13-by-9-inch
baking pan.

**2** To make the filling, combine
the brown sugar, cornstarch, and
cherries in a saucepan. Place the
pan over medium heat and cook,
stirring occasionally, until the
mixture boils and thickens slightly. Remove from the heat and stir
in the almond extract, food color,
and almonds. Spoon into the prepared baking pan.

**3** To make the batter, in a large
bowl, combine the flour, cocoa
powder, brown sugar, baking
powder, and salt. Using a pastry
blender or two knives scissor-
fashion, cut in the butter until the
mixture resembles fine meal.
Add the milk and chocolate
extract and blend until smooth.
Spoon the batter over the cherries
in the pan.

**4** Bake for 20 to 25 minutes, or
until a cake tester or wooden
toothpick inserted into the cake
batter comes out clean. Remove
the pan from the oven and cool
on a wire rack for 5 to 7 minutes.
Serve warm or cooled, and with
Cherry Sauce.

# BLACK FOREST
# CHERRY COFFEE CAKE

MAKES: *6 to 8 servings*

# BLACKBERRY–LEMON COFFEE CAKE

MAKES: *6 to 8 servings*

¾ cup crushed Rice Krispies™ cereal
1½ cups all-purpose flour
¾ cup granulated sugar
½ cup butter or margarine, at room temperature
½ teaspoon baking powder
½ teaspoon baking soda
¼ teaspoon salt
1 large egg
¾ cup buttermilk
1 teaspoon grated lemon zest
½ cup blackberry preserves
Lemon Sauce (see recipe page 61)

**1** Position the rack in the center of the oven and preheat to 350 degrees F. Lightly grease a 9-inch square or round baking pan.

**2** In a large bowl, blend together the cereal, flour, and sugar. Using a pastry cutter or two knives scissor-fashion, cut in the margarine until the mixture resembles coarse meal. Reserve ½ cup of this mixture for topping. To the remainder, blend in the baking powder, baking soda, and salt. In a medium bowl, beat the egg until foamy before beating in the buttermilk and lemon zest. Combine the two mixtures, blending until the dry ingredients are moistened.

**3** Spoon two-thirds of the batter into the prepared pan. Gently spread the blackberry preserves over the top. Dot the remaining batter over the top of the preserves. Sprinkle the reserved crumble mix over the top.

**4** Bake for 35 to 40 minutes, or until a cake tester or wooden toothpick inserted near the edge of the cake (not into the preserves) comes out clean. Remove the pan from the oven and cool on a wire rack for 5 to 7 minutes. Serve warm and with Lemon Sauce.

# BLUEBERRY COFFEE CAKE

MAKES: *6 to 8 servings*

⅔ cup butter or margarine
1 cup granulated sugar
3 large eggs, separated
3 cups all-purpose flour
2 teaspoons baking powder
¼ teaspoon salt
1 cup milk
One 10-ounce package frozen blueberries, thawed and drained
4 tablespoons brown sugar
Fresh Blueberry Sauce (see recipe page 78)

**1** Position the rack in the center of the oven and preheat to 375 degrees F. Grease a 9-inch square or round baking pan.

**2** In a large bowl, combine the flour, baking powder, and salt. In a medium bowl, beat the butter and granulated sugar together until light and fluffy. Beat in the egg yolks. Combine the two mixtures, blending until smooth. Fold in the blueberries. In a small bowl, beat the egg whites until stiff but not dry and fold them into the batter. Scrape the batter into the prepared baking pan.

**3** Bake for 35 to 40 minutes or until a cake tester or wooden toothpick inserted into the cake comes out clean. Remove the pan from the oven and cool on a wire rack for 5 to 7 minutes. Serve warm or cooled, and with Fresh Blueberry Sauce.

## TOPPING

⅓ cup firmly packed brown sugar
¼ cup cream of wheat cereal
½ teaspoon ground cinnamon
3 tablespoons butter or margarine, at room temperature

## BATTER

1 cup cream of wheat cereal
1 cup all-purpose flour
¾ cup granulated sugar
1 tablespoon baking powder
1 teaspoon salt
1 large egg
1 cup milk
¼ cup canola oil

**1** Position the rack in the center of the oven and preheat to 375 degrees F. Lightly grease and flour the bottom of an 8-inch square or round baking pan.

**2** To make the topping, in a medium bowl, blend the brown sugar, cereal, and cinnamon together. Using a pastry blender or two knives scissor-fashion, cut in the butter until the mixture resembles coarse crumbs. Set aside.

**3** To make the batter, in a large bowl, blend together the cereal, flour, sugar, baking powder, and salt. In a medium bowl, beat the egg until foamy before beating in the milk and oil. Combine the two mixtures, blending until the dry ingredients are just moistened. Scrape the batter into the prepared pan and sprinkle on the topping.

**4** Bake for 30 minutes, or until a cake tester or wooden toothpick inserted into the cake comes out clean. Remove the pan from the oven and cool on a wire rack for 5 to 7 minutes. Serve warm or cooled.

**SERVING SUGGESTION: Serve with maple syrup.**

# BREAKFAST COFFEE CAKE

MAKES: *6 to 9 servings*

## BASE

½ cup all-purpose flour
½ cup packed light-brown sugar
1½ teaspoons Dutch-processed cocoa powder
¼ cup butter or margarine, at room temperature
½ cup finely chopped walnuts or pecans

## BATTER

2 cups all-purpose flour
1 teaspoon baking powder
1 teaspoon baking soda
½ teaspoon salt
1 cup sour cream or plain yogurt
1 cup granulated sugar
2 large eggs
1 teaspoon Amaretto liqueur
½ cup (8 ounces) semisweet chocolate chips

**1** Position a rack in the center of the oven and preheat to 350 degrees F. Lightly grease and flour the bottom of a 14-by-9-inch Bundt bakeware mini-loaf baking pan.

**2** To make the base, in a medium bowl, combine the flour, sugar, and cocoa. Using a pastry blender or two knives scissor-fashion, cut in the butter until mixture is crumbly. Stir in the walnuts and sprinkle into the bottom of three or four cups of the prepared baking pan.

**3** To make the batter, in a large bowl blend together the flour, baking powder, baking soda, and salt. In a medium bowl, beat the sour cream, sugar, eggs, and Amaretto smooth. Combine the two mixtures, blending until the dry ingredients are just moistened. Fold in the chocolate chips and spoon the batter into the cups of the prepared baking pan, filling each cup ½ full.

**4** Bake for 60 to 65 minutes, or until a cake tester or wooden toothpick inserted into the cake comes out clean. Remove the pan from the oven and cool on a wire rack for 5 to 7 minutes. Serve warm or cooled.

# BRUNCH COFFEE RING

MAKES: *6 to 9 servings*

# BUTTER CREAM-AND-CHEESE COFFEE CAKE

MAKES: *6 to 8 servings*

**TOPPING**
½ cup all-purpose flour
½ cup firmly packed brown sugar
¼ cup butter or margarine, at room temperature

**BATTER**
2 cups all-purpose flour
1¼ cups granulated sugar
2 teaspoons baking powder
½ teaspoon baking soda
½ teaspoon salt
½ cup butter or margarine, at room temperature
One 8-ounce package cream cheese
2 large eggs
½ cup milk

1 Position the rack in the center of the oven and preheat to 350 degrees F. Lightly grease and flour the bottom of a 13-by-9-inch baking pan.

2 To make the topping, in a small bowl, combine the flour, brown sugar, and butter until crumbly. Set aside.

3 To make the batter, in a large bowl, blend together the flour, sugar, baking powder, baking soda, and salt. In a medium bowl, beat the butter and cream cheese until smooth. Beat in the eggs and milk. Then combine the two mixtures, blending until the dry ingredients are moistened.

4 Scrape the batter into the prepared baking pan and sprinkle the topping over the batter. Bake for 30 to 35 minutes, or until a cake tester or wooden toothpick inserted into the cake comes out clean. Remove the pan from the oven and cool on a wire rack for 5 to 7 minutes. Serve warm or cooled.

**SERVING SUGGESTION: Serve wih hot chocolate.**

# CEREAL COFFEE CAKE

MAKES: *10 to 12 servings*

**TOPPING**
¼ cup firmly packed dark-brown sugar
2 tablespoons all-purpose flour
1 teaspoon ground allspice
2 tablespoons chilled butter or margarine, diced

**BATTER**
1¾ cups all-purpose flour
1 cup granulated sugar
1 tablespoon baking powder
1 teaspoon salt
⅓ cup butter or margarine, at room temperature
1 large egg
1 cup milk
1½ cups cornflake cereal

1 Position the rack in the center of the oven and preheat to 350 degrees F. Lightly grease and flour the bottom of a 9-inch square or round baking pan.

2 To make the topping, in a small bowl, combine the sugar, flour, and allspice. Using a pastry blender or two knives scissor-fashion, cut in the butter until the mixture is crumbly. Set aside.

3 To make the batter, in a large bowl, blend together the flour, sugar, baking powder, salt, butter, egg, and milk until smooth. Fold in the cereal. Spoon the batter into the prepared baking pan and sprinkle the topping over the batter.

4 Bake for 35 to 40 minutes, or until a cake tester or wooden toothpick inserted into the cake comes out clean and the top is a golden color. Serve warm or cooled.

**SERVING SUGGESTION: Serve with hot chocolate.**

TOPPING

½ cup raisins
¼ cup firmly packed brown sugar
¼ teaspoon ground cinnamon

BATTER

1½ cups all-purpose flour
¼ cup granulated sugar
2½ teaspoons baking powder
¾ teaspoon salt
¾ cup milk
¼ cup vegetable shortening
1 large egg
⅔ cup cherry-pie filling
Cherry Sauce (see recipe page 52)

1  Position the rack in the center of the oven and preheat to 375 degrees F. Lightly grease and flour the bottom of an 8-inch square or round baking pan.

2  To make the topping, in a small bowl, combine the raisins, brown sugar, and cinnamon. Set aside.

3  To make the batter, in a large bowl, combine the flour, sugar, baking powder, salt, milk, shortening, and egg, beating vigorously until smooth. Scrape the mixture into the prepared pan. Drop the cherry-pie filling from the tip of a spoon onto the batter in the baking pan. Sprinkle the topping over the top.

4  Bake for 25 to 30 minutes, or until a cake tester or wooden toothpick inserted near the edge of the cake (not into the cherry filling) comes out clean. Remove the pan from the oven and cool on a wire rack for 5 to 7 minutes. Serve warm or cooled, and with Cherry Sauce.

# CHERRY–RAISIN COFFEE CAKE

MAKES: *10 to 12 servings*

---

½ cup finely ground almonds
2½ cups all-purpose flour
2 teaspoons baking powder
1 teaspoon baking soda
¼ teaspoon salt
½ cup Dutch-processed cocoa powder
1½ cups dried apricots, finely diced
1 cup vegetable shortening
One 8-ounce package cream cheese, at room temperature
2¼ cups granulated sugar
5 large eggs
1½ teaspoons Amaretto liqueur
Chocolate Sauce (see recipe page 26)

1  Position the rack in the center of the oven and preheat to 350 degrees F. Grease and flour a 10-inch Bundt pan. Press ¼ cup of the almonds up the outer sides of the pan.

2  In a large bowl, blend together the remaining almonds, flour, baking powder, baking soda, salt, cocoa powder, and diced apricots. In a medium bowl, beat shortening, cream cheese, and sugar until smooth. Beat in the eggs one at a time, beating vigorously after each addition. Beat in the Amaretto. Combine the two mixtures, blending until the dry ingredients are just moistened.

3  Carefully spoon the batter into the prepared baking pan. Bake for 45 to 50 minutes, or until a cake tester or wooden toothpick inserted into the cake comes out clean. Remove the pan from the oven and cool on a wire rack for 5 to 7 minutes before inverting onto a wire rack to cool completely. Serve warm and with Chocolate Sauce.

# CHOCOLATE COFFEE CAKE

MAKES: *10 to 12 servings*

# CHOCOLATE TEA CAKE

MAKES: *8 to 16 servings*

8 ounces unsweetened chocolate, grated
¾ cup butter or margarine
¾ cup granulated sugar
4 large eggs
½ cup all-purpose flour
2 tablespoons powdered sugar
Strawberry Sauce (see recipe page 144)

**1** Position the rack in the center of the oven and preheat to 350 degrees F. Lightly grease and flour the bottom of a 9-inch square or round baking pan.

**2** In the top of a double boiler set over simmering water, stirring occasionally, melt the chocolate. Set aside to cool slightly.

**3** In a small bowl, beat the butter and sugar until light and fluffy. Beat in the chocolate. Add the eggs, one at a time, beating vigorously after each addition. Stir in the flour until just combined.

**4** Scrape the batter into the prepared baking pan. Bake for 25 to 30 minutes, or until a cake tester or wooden toothpick inserted into the cake comes out clean. Remove the pan from the oven, sprinkle the top of the cake with powdered sugar, and cool on a wire rack for 5 to 7 minutes. Serve warm or cooled and with Strawberry Sauce.

---

# CINNAMON COFFEE CAKE

MAKES: *8 to 10 servings*

**TOPPING**
½ cup firmly packed brown sugar
½ cup finely chopped walnuts
2 tablespoons all-purpose flour
2 teaspoons ground cinnamon
2 tablespoons canola oil

**BATTER**
1½ cups all-purpose flour
½ cup granulated sugar
2½ teaspoons baking powder
½ teaspoon salt
1 large egg white
¼ cup canola oil
¾ cup milk
Whipped Cream-Cheese Topping (see recipe page 186)

**1** Position the rack in the center of the oven and preheat to 375 degrees F. Lightly grease and flour the bottom of an 8-inch square or round baking pan.

**2** To make the topping, in a small bowl, combine the brown sugar, walnuts, flour, cinnamon, and oil and mix until crumbly. Set aside.

**3** To make the batter, in a large bowl, blend together the flour, sugar, baking powder, and salt. In a medium bowl, beat the egg white until foamy before beating in the oil and milk. Combine the two mixtures, blending until the dry ingredients are moistened.

**4** Spoon half of the batter into the prepared baking pan and top the batter with half of the topping. Spoon the remaining batter into the pan and top with the remaining topping. Bake for 30 to 35 minutes, or until a cake tester or wooden toothpick inserted into the cake comes out clean. Remove the pan from the oven and cool on a wire rack for 5 to 7 minutes. Serve warm or cooled and with Whipped Cream-Cheese Topping.

## TOPPING

½ cup crushed cornflake cereal
3 tablespoons melted butter or margarine
3 tablespoons firmly packed brown sugar
½ teaspoon ground cinnamon

## BATTER

1¼ cups all-purpose flour
1½ teaspoons baking powder
2 teaspoons ground cinnamon
½ teaspoon salt
½ cup vegetable shortening
⅓ cup firmly packed brown sugar
1 large egg
¾ cup milk
1 teaspoon grated orange zest
½ cup crushed cornflake cereal

**1** Position the rack in the center of the oven and preheat to 375 degrees F. Lightly grease and flour the bottom of an 8-inch square or round baking pan.

**2** To make the topping, in a small bowl, combine the cornflakes, butter, sugar, and cinnamon and stir until crumbly. Set aside.

**3** To make the batter, in a large bowl, blend together the flour, baking powder, cinnamon, and salt. In a medium bowl, beat the shortening and brown sugar until light and fluffy. Beat in the egg, milk, and orange zest. Stir in the crushed cornflakes. Combine the two mixtures, blending until the dry ingredients are moistened. Spoon the batter into the prepared pan. Sprinkle the topping over the batter and press it gently into the batter.

**4** Bake for 20 to 25 minutes, or until a cake tester or wooden toothpick inserted into the cake comes out clean. Remove the pan from the oven and cool on a wire rack for 5 to 7 minutes. Serve warm.

# CINNAMON–CORNFLAKE COFFEE CAKE

MAKES: *6 to 8 servings*

---

2 cups all-purpose flour
1 cup granulated sugar
1 tablespoon baking powder
¼ teaspoon salt
½ cup vegetable shortening, chilled
2 large eggs
1 cup milk
1½ cups frozen blueberries, thawed
1⅓ cups shredded coconut

**1** Position the rack in the center of the oven and preheat to 350 degrees F. Lightly grease and flour the bottom of two 9-inch square or round baking pans.

**2** In a large bowl, blend together the flour, sugar, baking powder, and salt. Using a pastry blender or two knives scissor-fashion, cut the shortening into the dry ingre-dients until the mixture is crumbly. In a small bowl, beat the eggs until foamy before beating in the milk. Combine the two mixtures, blending until the dry ingredients are moistened. Fold in the blueberries.

**3** Divide the batter evenly between the two prepared pans and sprinkle each with coconut. Bake for 20 to 25 minutes, or until a cake tester or wooden toothpick inserted into the cake comes out clean. Remove the pan from the oven and cool on a wire rack for 5 to 7 minutes. Serve warm.

**SERVING SUGGESTION: Serve with a bowl of fresh fruit.**

# COCONUT-AND-BLUEBERRY COFFEE CAKE

MAKES: *14 to 16 servings*

# CRANBERRY COFFEE CAKE

MAKES: *14 to 16 servings*

CAKE

2 cups all-purpose flour
1 teaspoon baking powder
1 teaspoon baking soda
1 teaspoon salt
½ cup butter or margarine, at room temperature
2 large eggs
1½ cups granulated sugar
1 cup sour cream or plain yogurt
1½ teaspoons almond extract
1 teaspoon vanilla extract
1 cup cranberry sauce

GLAZE

1 cup sifted powdered sugar
3 tablespoons milk
½ teaspoon almond extract
Cranberry Sauce (see recipe page 108)

**1** Position the rack in the center of the oven and preheat to 350 degrees F. Lightly grease and flour the bottom of a 9- or 10-inch tube pan.

**2** To make the cake, in a large bowl, blend together the flour, baking powder, baking soda, and salt. In a medium bowl, beat the eggs until foamy before beating in the sugar, sour cream, almond extract, and vanilla extract. Combine the two mixtures, blending until the dry ingredients are moistened.

**3** Spoon ½ of the batter into the prepared baking pan. Spoon the cranberry sauce over the top of the batter and top it with the remaining batter. Bake for 45 to 50 minutes, or until a cake tester or wooden toothpick inserted into the top half of the cake comes out clean.

**4** Meanwhile, to make the glaze, in a small bowl, blend together the sugar, milk, and almond extract. When the cake is baked, remove the pan from the oven and drizzle the top of the cake with the glaze. Cool in the pan on a wire rack for 5 to 7 minutes. Serve at room temperature and with Cranberry Sauce.

# CREAM CHEESE COFFEE CAKE

MAKES: *6 to 8 servings*

2 packages refrigerated, ready-to-bake crescent rolls
Two 8-ounce packages cream cheese, at room temperature
1 large egg, separated
1 cup plus 2 tablespoons granulated sugar
½ cup chopped walnuts or pecans
Whipped Cream-Cheese Topping (see recipe page 186)

**1** Position the rack in the center of the oven and preheat to 325 degrees F. Lightly grease and flour the bottom of a 13-by-9-inch baking pan.

**2** Open the package of rolls, separate them, and arrange the rolls to completely cover the bottom of the prepared pan. Set aside.

**3** In a large bowl, beat the cream cheese, egg yolk, and 1 cup of the sugar until smooth. Spoon this mixture over the rolls in the pan. In a small bowl, beat the egg white until stiff but not dry and spread evenly over the top of the cream cheese mixture in the pan. Sprinkle the nuts and remaining 2 tablespoons of sugar over the top.

**4** Bake for 25 to 30 minutes, or until the top is golden brown. Remove the pan from the oven and cool on a wire rack for 8 to 10 minutes. Serve at room temperature and with Whipped Cream-Cheese Topping.

1½ cups all-purpose flour
1 cup firmly packed brown sugar
½ cup butter or margarine, at room temperature
1½ teaspoons baking powder
½ teaspoon ground cinnamon
½ teaspoon salt
1 large egg
⅔ cup milk

**1** Position the rack in the center of the oven and preheat to 375 degrees F. Lightly grease and flour the bottom of an 8-inch square or round baking pan.

**2** In a large bowl, blend together the flour and sugar. Using a pastry cutter or two knives scissor-fashion, cut in the butter until the mixture resembles fine meal. Measure out 1 cup of this mixture and set it aside to use as the topping.

**3** Add the baking powder, cinnamon, and salt to the mixture remaining in the bowl. In a small bowl, beat the egg until foamy before beating in the milk. Combine the two mixtures, blending until the dry ingredients are just moistened. Spoon the batter into the prepared baking pan and sprinkle the top with the reserved one-cup topping mixture.

**4** Bake for 35 to 40 minutes, or until a cake tester or wooden toothpick inserted into the cake comes out clean. Remove the pan from the oven and cool on a wire rack for 5 to 7 minutes. Serve warm.

# CRUMB-TOP COFFEE CAKE

MAKES: *6 to 8 servings*

---

**TOPPING**
¼ cup sliced almonds
2 tablespoons granulated sugar

**BATTER**
¾ cup butter or margarine, at room temperature
1 cup granulated sugar
3 large eggs
½ cup milk
1½ cups all-purpose flour
2 teaspoons baking powder
2 large tart apples, peeled, cored, and diced
1¼ cups flaked coconut
¼ teaspoon salt
Whipped Butter (see recipe page 23)

**1** Position the rack in the center of the oven and preheat to 350 degrees F. Grease and flour the bottom of a 13-by-9-inch baking dish.

**2** To make the topping, in a cup, combine the almonds and sugar and stir until mixed. Set aside.

**3** To make the batter, in a medium bowl, beat the butter and sugar until light and fluffy. Add the eggs, one at a time, beating vigorously after each addition. In a large bowl, blend together the flour, baking powder, apples, coconut, and salt. Combine the two mixtures, blending until the dry ingredients are moistened.

**4** Spoon the batter into the prepared baking pan and sprinkle the topping mixture over the top. Bake for 30 to 35 minutes, or until a cake tester or wooden toothpick inserted into the cake comes out clean. Remove the pan from the oven and cool on a wire rack for 5 to 7 minutes. Serve warm or cooled and with Whipped Butter.

# DANISH APPLE-AND-COCONUT COFFEE CAKE

MAKES: *10 to 12 servings*

# DATE-AND-WALNUT COFFEE CAKE

MAKES: *6 to 8 servings*

**TOPPING**
1 tablespoon melted butter
¼ cup firmly packed brown sugar
¼ cup chopped walnuts

**BATTER**
1½ cups all-purpose flour
4 teaspoons baking powder
½ cup granulated sugar
½ teaspoon salt
¼ cup butter or margarine, at room
    temperature
2 large eggs, lightly beaten
½ cup milk
¾ cup rolled oats
½ cup chopped dates
Fig Sauce (see recipe page 189)

1  Position the rack in the center of the oven and preheat to 400 degrees F. Lightly grease and flour the bottom of an 8-inch ring-style baking pan.

2  To make the topping, in a small bowl, blend together the butter, brown sugar, and walnuts until the mixture is crumbly. Set aside.

3  To make the batter, in a large bowl, blend together the flour, baking powder, sugar, and salt. Using a pastry blender or two knives scissor-fashion, cut in the butter until the mixture resembles coarse meal. Add the eggs and milk, blending until the dry ingredients are just moistened. Fold in the oats. Spoon half the batter into the prepared pan and sprinkle the dates over the batter. Top with the remaining batter and sprinkle the topping mixture over the batter.

4  Bake for 20 to 25 minutes, or until a cake tester or wooden toothpick inserted into the cake comes out clean. Remove the pan from the oven and cool on a wire rack for 8 to 10 minutes. Serve at room temperature and with Fig Sauce.

# FAT-FREE APPLE COFFEE CAKE

MAKES: *8 to 10 servings*

1 cup all-purpose flour
1½ teaspoons baking powder
¾ cup granulated sugar
½ teaspoon salt
2 large egg whites
⅓ cup skim milk
⅓ cup Karo® light or dark corn
    syrup
2 apples, peeled, cored, and halved
2 tablespoons cinnamon sugar for
    sprinkling
Sugarless Apricot Sauce (see recipe
    page 40)

1  Position the rack in the center of the oven and preheat to 350 degrees F. Lightly grease and flour the bottom of a 9-inch square or round baking pan.

2  In a large bowl, blend together the flour, baking powder, sugar, and salt. In a medium bowl, beat the egg whites stiff but not dry before beating in the milk and corn syrup. Combine the two mixtures, blending until the dry ingredients are moistened. Spoon the batter into the prepared pan, arrange the apples over the top, and sprinkle with cinnamon sugar.

3  Bake for 45 to 50 minutes, or until a cake tester or wooden toothpick inserted into the cake comes out clean. Remove the pan from the oven and cool on a wire rack for 5 to 7 minutes. Serve warm and with Sugarless Apricot Sauce.

# FRUIT-AND-YOGURT COFFEE CAKE

MAKES: *7 to 9 servings*

**TOPPING**

¼ cup Bisquick® buttermilk baking mix

¼ cup granulated sugar

2 tablespoons chilled butter or margarine

1 tablespoon grated orange or lemon zest

**BATTER**

2 cups Bisquick® buttermilk baking mix

¼ cup granulated sugar

2 tablespoons butter or margarine, at room temperature

1 large egg, lightly beaten

¾ cup fruit-flavored yogurt

1 teaspoon vanilla extract

Yogurt Cream (see recipe page 55)

**1** Position the rack in the center of the oven and preheat to 375 degrees F. Lightly grease and flour the bottom of an 8-inch square or round baking pan.

**2** To make the topping, in a small bowl, combine the baking mix, sugar, and butter until crumbly. Stir in the lemon zest. Set aside.

**3** To make the batter, in a large bowl, blend together the baking mix and sugar. Using a pastry blender or two knives scissor-fashion, cut in the butter until the mixture is crumbly. Add the egg, yogurt, and vanilla extract, blending until the dry ingredients are moistened.

**4** Scrape the batter into the prepared pan and sprinkle the topping over the batter. Bake for 30 to 35 minutes, or until a cake tester or wooden toothpick inserted into the cake comes out clean. Remove the pan from the oven and cool on a wire rack for 5 to 7 minutes. Serve warm and with Yogurt Cream.

# GOLDEN-SEEDLESS-RAISIN COFFEE CAKE

MAKES: *6 to 8 servings*

**TOPPING**

⅓ cup Bisquick® baking mix

3 tablespoons granulated sugar

2 tablespoons butter or margarine, melted

**BATTER**

2⅓ cups Bisquick® baking mix

⅓ cup granulated sugar

1 cup seedless golden raisins

1 large egg

⅔ cup milk

2 tablespoons melted butter or margarine

**1** Position the rack in the center of the oven and preheat to 375 degrees F. Lightly grease and flour the bottom of a 9-inch square or round baking pan.

**2** To make the topping, in a small bowl, combine the baking mix, sugar, and butter and stir until the mixture is crumbly. Set aside.

**3** To make the batter, in a large bowl, combine the baking mix, sugar, and raisins. In a small bowl, beat the egg until foamy before beating in the milk and butter. Combine the two mixtures, blending until the dry ingredients are moistened.

**4** Scrape the batter into the prepared baking pan and sprinkle the topping mixture over the batter. Bake for 30 to 35 minutes, or until a cake tester or wooden toothpick inserted into the cake comes out clean. Remove the pan from the oven and cool on a wire rack for 5 to 7 minutes. Serve at room temperature.

**SERVING SUGGESTION: Serve with jam or jelly of your choice.**

# GRANOLA COFFEE CAKE

MAKES: *6 to 8 servings*

**TOPPING**

1 cup granola
¼ cup firmly packed brown sugar
¼ teaspoon ground nutmeg
⅔ cup cranberry sauce

**BATTER**

1½ cups Bisquick® buttermilk
 baking mix
½ cup granulated sugar
1 large egg
½ cup milk
2 tablespoons vegetable shortening
1 teaspoon vanilla extract

**GLAZE**

1 cup powdered sugar
1 tablespoon light corn syrup
1 to 2 tablespoons milk

**1** Position the rack in the center of the oven and preheat to 375 degrees F. Lightly grease and flour the bottom of a 9-inch square or round baking pan.

**2** To make the topping, in a small bowl, combine the granola, brown sugar, and nutmeg and stir until well mixed. Set aside.

**3** To make the batter, in a large bowl, combine the baking mix, granulated sugar, egg, milk, shortening, and vanilla and beat until smooth. Scrape the batter into the prepared baking pan. Sprinkle the topping over the batter and spoon on the cranberry sauce. Bake for 35 to 40 minutes, or until a cake tester or wooden toothpick inserted into the cake comes out clean.

**4** Meanwhile, make the glaze: In a small bowl, combine the sugar, corn syrup, and enough milk to make a pourable glaze. When the cake is done, remove the pan from the oven and drizzle the glaze over the top of the cake. Cool on a wire rack for 5 to 7 minutes. Serve warm.

**SERVING SUGGESTION: Serve with jam or jelly of your choice.**

# IMPERIAL COFFEE CAKE

MAKES: *6 to 8 servings*

**TOPPING**

½ cup chopped almonds or pecans
1 cup granulated sugar
1 teaspoon ground cinnamon
1 tablespoon butter or margarine, at
 room temperature

**BATTER**

2 cups all-purpose flour
1 teaspoon baking powder
1 teaspoon baking soda
½ teaspoon ground nutmeg
1 tablespoon grated orange zest
1 cup raisins
1 large egg
1 cup buttermilk or sour milk
⅓ cup melted butter or margarine

**1** Position the rack in the center of the oven and preheat to 350 degrees F. Lightly grease and flour the bottom of a 13-by-9-by-1½-inch baking pan.

**2** To make the topping, in a small bowl, combine the almonds, sugar, cinnamon, and butter and stir until the mixture is crumbly. Set aside.

**3** To make the batter, in a large bowl, combine the flour, baking powder, baking soda, nutmeg, orange zest, and raisins. In a small bowl, beat together the egg, buttermilk, and butter. Combine the two mixtures, blending until the dry ingredients are moistened.

**4** Spoon the batter into the prepared baking pan and sprinkle the topping over the batter. Bake for 30 to 35 minutes, or until a cake tester or wooden toothpick inserted into the cake comes out clean. Remove the pan from the oven and cool on a wire rack for 5 to 7 minutes. Serve warm.

## TOPPING

1¼ cups firmly packed brown sugar
1 cup chopped walnuts
2 teaspoons ground cinnamon
3 tablespoons butter or margarine, melted

## BATTER

¾ cup granulated sugar
½ cup butter or margarine, at room temperature
3 large eggs
1 cup sour cream
1 teaspoon vanilla extract
2 cups all-purpose flour
1 teaspoon baking powder
1 teaspoon baking soda
¼ teaspoon salt
Whipped Cream-Cheese Topping (see recipe page 186)

**1** Position the rack in the center of the oven and preheat to 350 degrees F. Lightly grease and flour the bottom of a 10-inch tube or Bundt pan.

**2** To make the topping, in a small bowl, combine the brown sugar, walnuts, cinnamon, and butter and stir until the mixture is crumbly. Set aside.

**3** To make the batter, in a large bowl, beat the sugar and butter until light and fluffy. Beat in the eggs, one at a time, beating vigorously after each addition. Beat in the sour cream and vanilla extract. In a large bowl, blend together the flour, baking powder, baking soda, and salt. Combine the two mixtures, blending until the dry ingredients are moistened.

**4** Spoon half the batter into the prepared baking pan. Sprinkle half of the topping mix over the batter, spoon in the remaining batter and top with the remaining topping. Bake for 35 to 40 minutes, or until a cake tester or wooden toothpick inserted into the cake comes out clean. Remove the pan from the oven and cool in the upright position for 10 to 12 minutes before inverting onto a serving plate to cool completely. Serve cooled and with Whipped Cream-Cheese Topping.

# JEWISH SOUR-CREAM COFFEE CAKE

MAKES: *8 to 10 servings*

## TOPPING

½ cup chopped walnuts
1 cup crushed cornflake cereal
¼ cup granulated sugar
½ teaspoon ground cinnamon
2 tablespoons melted butter or margarine

## BATTER

2 cups Bisquick® baking mix
½ cup chopped walnuts
1 large egg
½ cup milk
½ cup firmly packed brown sugar
3 tablespoons melted butter or margarine
1 tablespoon lemon juice
2 teaspoons grated lemon zest
Lemon Sauce (see recipe page 61)

**1** Position the rack in the center of the oven and preheat to 400 degrees F. Lightly grease and flour the bottom of an 8-inch square or round baking pan.

**2** To make the topping, in a small bowl, combine the walnuts, cornflakes, sugar, cinnamon, and melted butter and stir until well mixed. Set aside.

**3** To make the batter, in a large bowl, blend together the baking mix and walnuts. In a medium bowl, beat the egg until foamy before beating in the milk, sugar, butter, lemon juice, and lemon zest. Combine the two mixtures, blending until the dry ingredients are moistened.

**4** Spoon the batter into the prepared pan. Sprinkle the topping mixture over the batter. Bake for 28 to 30 minutes, or until a cake tester or wooden toothpick inserted into the cake comes out clean. Remove the pan from the oven and cool on a wire rack for 5 to 7 minutes. Serve warm and with Lemon Sauce.

# LEMON–WALNUT COFFEE CAKE

MAKES: *6 to 8 servings*

## MOLASSES–WALNUT GINGERBREAD

MAKES: *6 to 8 servings*

3½ cups all-purpose flour
2 teaspoons baking soda
½ teaspoon ground ginger
½ teaspoon ground cinnamon
¼ teaspoon ground cloves
¼ teaspoon salt
1 cup chopped walnuts
½ cup vegetable shortening
1 cup packed dark-brown sugar
½ cup dark molasses
1 cup boiling water
2 large eggs
Whipped Cream Topping (see recipe page 208)

**1** Position the rack in the center of the oven and preheat to 350 degrees F. Lightly grease and flour the bottom of a 9¼-by-5¼-by-2¾-inch loaf baking pan.

**2** In a large bowl, blend together the flour, baking soda, salt, ginger, cinnamon, cloves, and walnuts. In a medium bowl, beat the shortening and sugar until light and fluffy before beating in the molasses and boiling water. Add the eggs, one at a time, beating vigorously after each addition. Combine the two mixtures, blending until the dry ingredients are moistened.

**3** Spoon the batter into the prepared pan. Bake for 30 to 35 minutes, or until a cake tester or wooden toothpick inserted into the cake comes out clean. Remove the pan from the oven and cool on a wire rack for 5 to 7 minutes. Serve warm or cooled.

## NUTMEG COFFEE CAKE

MAKES: *6 to 8 servings*

2 cups all-purpose flour
2 cups firmly packed brown sugar
½ cup butter or margarine, at room temperature
1 large egg
1 cup sour cream
1 teaspoon baking soda
1 teaspoon nutmeg
½ cup finely chopped pecans
Whipped Cream Topping (see recipe page 208)

**1** Position the rack in the center of the oven and preheat to 325 degrees F. Lightly grease and flour the bottom of an 8-inch square or round baking pan.

**2** In a large bowl, blend together the flour, brown sugar, and butter until the mixture is crumbly.

Press 2 cups of this mix into the bottom of the prepared pan. To the mixture remaining in the bowl, add the egg, sour cream, baking soda, and nutmeg and beat until smooth.

**3** Scrape the batter into the pan and sprinkle the chopped nuts over the top. Bake for 55 to 60 minutes, or until a cake tester or wooden toothpick inserted into the cake comes out clean. Remove the pan from the oven and cool on a wire rack for 5 to 7 minutes. Serve at room temperature and with Whipped Cream Topping.

## TOPPING

¼ cup granulated sugar
2 teaspoons grated orange zest

## BATTER

½ cup butter or margarine, at room
   temperature
1¼ cups granulated sugar
2 large eggs
1 cup milk
2¼ cups all-purpose flour
1 tablespoon baking powder
1 teaspoon salt
One 8-ounce package cream cheese,
   finely diced
½ cup chopped almonds
1 tablespoon grated orange zest
Whipped Cream Topping (see recipe
   page XXX)

**1** Position the rack in the center of the oven and preheat to 375 degrees F. Lightly grease and flour the bottom of a 13-by-9-by-1½-inch baking pan.

**2** To make the topping, in a cup, combine the sugar and orange zest. Set aside.

**3** To make the batter, in a medium bowl, beat the margarine and sugar until light and fluffy. Beat in the eggs and milk. In a large bowl, blend together the flour, baking powder, and salt. Combine the two mixtures, blending until the dry ingredients are moistened. Fold in the diced cream cheese, almonds, and orange zest.

**4** Scrape the batter into the prepared baking pan, and sprinkle the topping mixture over the batter. Bake for 35 to 40 minutes, or until a cake tester or wooden toothpick inserted into the cake comes out clean. Remove the pan from the oven and cool on a wire rack for 5 to 7 minutes. Serve warm or cooled, and with Whipped Cream Topping.

# ORANGE CREAM-CHEESE COFFEE CAKE

MAKES: *6 to 8 servings*

---

## TOPPING

¾ cup firmly packed brown sugar
1 tablespoon all-purpose flour
1 teaspoon ground cinnamon
2 tablespoons butter or margarine, at
   room temperature
1 cup chopped pecans

## BATTER

½ cup butter or margarine
1 cup granulated sugar
3 large eggs
1 cup sour cream
2 cups all-purpose flour
1 teaspoon baking powder
1 teaspoon baking soda
½ cup raisins
¼ teaspoon salt
Peach Sauce (see recipe page 41)

**1** Position the rack in the center of the oven and preheat to 350 degrees F. Lightly grease and flour the bottom of a 13-by-9-inch baking pan.

**2** To make the topping, in a small bowl, combine the brown sugar, flour, and cinnamon. Cut in the butter until mixture is crumbly. Set aside.

**3** To make the batter, in a medium bowl, beat the butter and sugar until light and fluffy. Add the eggs, one at a time, beating vigorously after each addition. Add the sour cream. In a large bowl, blend together the flour, the baking powder, baking soda, raisins, and salt. Combine the two mixtures, blending until the dry ingredients are moistened.

**4** Scrape the batter into the prepared pan and sprinkle the topping over the batter. Bake for 28 to 30 minutes, or until a cake tester or wooden toothpick inserted into the cake comes out clean. Remove the pan from the oven and cool on a wire rack for 5 to 7 minutes. Serve warm and with Peach Sauce.

# PECAN–SOUR CREAM COFFEE CAKE

MAKES: *10 to 12 servings*

## SHOO-FLY COFFEE CAKE

MAKES: *6 to 8 servings*

**FILLING**
½ cup firmly packed brown sugar
½ cup chopped walnuts or pecans
1½ teaspoons ground cinnamon

**BATTER**
¾ cup butter or margarine, at room temperature
1 cup granulated sugar
3 large eggs
1½ teaspoons vanilla extract
½ cup light molasses
1½ cups sour cream
3 cups all-purpose flour
1½ teaspoons baking powder
2 teaspoons baking soda
¼ teaspoon salt
Molasses Sauce (see recipe page 125)

1  Position the rack in the center of the oven and preheat to 350 degrees F. Lightly grease and flour the bottom of a 10-inch tube pan.

2  To make the filling, in a small bowl, combine the sugar, walnuts, and cinnamon until well mixed. Set aside.

3  To make the batter, in a medium bowl, beat together the butter and sugar until light and fluffy. Beat in the eggs, one at a time, beating vigorously after each addition. Beat in the vanilla extract and molasses. Stir in the sour cream. In a large bowl, blend together the flour, baking powder, baking soda, and salt. Combine the two mixtures, blending until the dry ingredients are moistened.

4  Spoon about 2 cups of the batter into the prepared pan, sprinkle ⅓ of the filling over the top, and repeat until the batter and filling are all used. Bake for 55 to 60 minutes, or until a cake tester or wooden toothpick inserted into the cake comes out clean. Remove from the oven and cool on a wire rack for 5 to 7 minutes. Serve warm and with Molasses Sauce.

## SOUR CREAM-AND-PECAN COFFEE CAKE

MAKES: *6 to 8 servings*

**TOPPING**
¾ cup firmly packed brown sugar
½ cup chopped pecans
1 teaspoon ground cinnamon

**BATTER**
¾ cup butter or margarine, at room temperature
1 cup granulated sugar
2 large eggs
1 cup sour cream
2 cups all-purpose flour
1 teaspoon baking powder
1 teaspoon baking soda
1 teaspoon ground nutmeg
½ teaspoon salt
Fresh Blueberry Sauce (see recipe page 78)

1  Position the rack in the center of the oven and preheat to 350 degrees F. Lightly grease and flour the bottom of a 13-by-9-inch baking pan.

2  To make the topping, in a small bowl, combine the brown sugar, pecans, and cinnamon until well mixed. Set aside.

3  To make the batter, in a medium bowl, beat the butter and sugar until light and fluffy. Beat in the eggs, one at a time, beating vigorously after each addition. Beat in the sour cream. In a large bowl, blend together the flour, baking powder, baking soda, nutmeg, and salt. Combine the two mixtures, blending until the dry ingredients are moistened.

4  Scrape the batter into the prepared pan. Spoon half of the topping mix in a straight line down the center of the mixture in the pan. Gently swirl a spoon several times, back and forth, through the batter. Sprinkle the remaining topping mix over the top. Bake for 35 to 45 minutes or until a cake tester or wooden toothpick inserted into the cake comes out clean. Remove the pan from the oven and cool on a wire rack for 5 to 7 minutes. Serve warm or cooled and with Fresh Blueberry Sauce.

# Chapter 6

# DOUGHNUTS AND FRITTERS

One of the secrets to good doughnuts is not to handle the dough more than necessary. Temperature control on the frying oil is also a very important element in the outcome of the end product. When making the doughnuts, do not forget that the centers cut out of the doughnut rings also make great snack foods.

Fritters appear in this chapter because they are similar in style to doughnuts. They are nothing more than batter that is dropped from the end of a spoon into hot oil. The secret to successful fritters is the amount of batter used and the heat of the frying oil. Do not get impatient and make them too large—the bigger they get, the doughier they are. After frying, fritters can be rolled in almost any substance such as granulated sugar, powdered sugar, sugar and cinnamon mixture, white frosting, jams, and jellies. These treats are perfect for the baker who likes to experiment with shapes and flavors.

# APPLESAUCE FRITTERS

MAKES: *40 to 45 fritters*

4 large eggs
½ cup milk
2 cups canned applesauce
1 cup granulated sugar, plus more
    for rolling the doughnuts in
1 cup packed brown sugar
3 tablespoons vegetable oil
1 teaspoon vanilla extract
1 tablespoon baking powder
1 teaspoon baking soda
1 teaspoon ground cinnamon
1 teaspoon ground nutmeg
½ teaspoon ground cloves
½ teaspoon salt
4½ cups all-purpose flour
Oil for deep frying

**1** In a medium bowl, beat the eggs foamy before beating in the milk, applesauce, two sugars, oil, and vanilla extract. Stir in the baking powder, baking soda, cinnamon, nutmeg, cloves, and salt. Gently stir in the flour, ½ cup at a time, until smooth.

**2** In a deep-fryer, heavy skillet, or Dutch oven, preheat 3 to 4 inches of oil to 370 to 375 degrees F. When the oil is hot, drop the dough by tablespoonfuls into the oil and for fry 1 to 2 minutes, turning occasionally, until the fritters are golden brown. Using a slotted spoon, lift the doughnut from the oil and drain on a double thickness of paper towels or on a wire rack for 1 to 2 minutes. Continue until all the doughnuts are cooked. Roll each in granulated sugar and serve warm or cooled.

# BUTTERMILK–MASHED POTATO DOUGHNUTS

MAKES: *24 to 30 doughnuts*

3 large eggs
2 cups granulated sugar
1½ cups cooked mashed potatoes
⅓ cup melted butter or margarine
1 cup buttermilk or sour milk
1 teaspoon vanilla extract
4 teaspoons baking powder
1½ teaspoons baking soda
½ teaspoon ground nutmeg
1 teaspoon salt
5 cups all-purpose flour
Oil for deep frying

**1** In a medium bowl, beat the eggs until foamy before beating in the sugar, potatoes, butter, buttermilk, and vanilla extract. Stir in the baking powder, baking soda, nutmeg, and salt. Gently stir in the flour, ½ cup at a time, until the dough holds together. Cover with plastic wrap and refrigerate for at least 1 hour.

**2** When ready to cook, in a deep-fryer, heavy skillet, or Dutch oven, preheat 3 to 4 inches of oil to 370 to 375 degrees F.

**3** Turn the dough out onto a floured surface, and with floured hands pat the dough out to a thickness of ½ inch. Using a doughnut cutter, cut out as many doughnuts as possible, reworking the scraps as you go.

**4** Slip the doughnuts into the preheated oil, three or four at a time (depending on the size of your deep fryer). Cook until lightly browned on one side (2 to 3 minutes). Gently turn the doughnuts and brown the other side. Using a slotted spoon, lift the doughnuts from the oil and drain them on a double thickness of paper towels or on a wire rack for 1 to 2 minutes. Continue until all the doughnuts are cooked. Repeat until all the doughnuts are cooked. Serve warm or cooled.

1 large egg
2 large egg yolks
¼ cup granulated sugar
2 tablespoons melted butter or
   margarine
¼ cup vegetable oil
¼ cup milk
1½ teaspoons vanilla
1½ teaspoons baking powder
¼ teaspoon salt
1½ cups all-purpose flour
Oil for deep frying
Cinnamon sugar for rolling the
   doughnuts

1  In a medium bowl, beat together the egg, egg yolks, sugar, butter, oil, milk, and vanilla extract until smooth. Stir in the baking powder and salt. Gently stir in the flour, ½ cup at a time, until the dough holds together.

2  In a deep-fryer, heavy skillet, or Dutch oven, preheat 3 to 4 inches of oil to 370 to 375 degrees F. When the oil is hot, drop the dough by tablespoonfuls into the hot oil, 3 to 4 at a time (depending on the size of your deep fryer). Cook, turning occasionally, until the fritters are golden brown. Using a slotted spoon, lift the doughnuts from the oil and drain on a double thickness of paper towels or on a wire rack for 1 to 2 minutes. Continue until all the fritters are cooked. Roll the fritters in the cinnamon sugar. Serve warm or cooled.

# CHANUKAH FRITTERS
MAKES: *25 to 30 fritters*

3 tablespoons butter or margarine, at
   room temperature
⅔ cup granulated sugar
1 large egg
⅔ cup milk
½ cup cocoa powder
1 tablespoon baking powder
½ teaspoon ground nutmeg
½ teaspoon salt
2½ cups all-purpose flour
Oil for deep frying
Powdered sugar for dusting

1  In a medium bowl, beat the butter and sugar until fluffy. Beat in the egg and milk. Stir in the cocoa powder, baking powder, nutmeg, and salt. Gently stir in the flour, ½ cup at a time, until the dough holds together.

2  In a deep-fryer, heavy skillet, or Dutch oven, preheat 3 to 4 inches of oil to 370 to 375 degrees F. Turn the dough out onto a floured surface, and with floured hands pat it out to a thickness of ½ inch. Using a doughnut cutter, cut out as many doughnuts as possible, reworking the scraps as you go.

3  Slip the doughnuts into the preheated oil, three or four at a time (depending on the size of your deep-fryer). Cook until lightly browned on one side (2 to 3 minutes). Gently turn and brown the other side. Using a slotted spoon, lift the doughnuts from the hot oil and drain on a double thickness of paper towels or on a wire rack for 1 to 2 minutes. Continue until all the doughnuts are cooked. Sprinkle the doughnuts with powdered sugar. Serve warm or cooled.

# CHOCOLATE DOUGHNUTS
MAKES: *12 to 14 doughnuts*

## COFFEE–WALNUT FRITTERS

MAKES: *20 to 24 fritters*

3 large eggs
1 tablespoon melted vegetable
   shortening
1 cup strong brewed coffee
1 tablespoon baking powder
½ teaspoon baking soda
1 cup granulated sugar
½ cup chopped walnuts
½ teaspoon salt
3 cups all-purpose flour
Oil for deep frying
Cinnamon sugar for rolling the
   fritters

**1** In a medium bowl, beat the eggs until foamy. Beat in the shortening and coffee. Stir in the baking powder, baking soda, sugar, walnuts, and salt. Gently stir in the flour, ½ cup at a time, until the dough holds together.

**2** In a deep-fryer, heavy skillet, or Dutch oven, preheat 3 to 4 inches of oil to 370 to 375 degrees F. Drop the dough by tablespoonfuls into the hot oil 3 to 4 at a time (depending on the size of your deep-fryer). Cook, turning occasionally, until the fritters are golden brown. Using a slotted spoon, lift the fritters from the oil and drain on a double thickness of paper towels or on a wire rack for 1 to 2 minutes. Roll the fritters in the cinnamon sugar. Serve warm or cooled.

## DUTCH FRITTERS

MAKES: *20 to 24 fritters*

2 large eggs
¾ cup milk
¼ cup vegetable oil
1 tablespoon baking powder
½ cup granulated sugar
½ teaspoon ground mace
½ cup raisins or currants (optional)
½ teaspoon salt
2½ cups all-purpose flour
Oil for deep frying
Cinnamon sugar for rolling the
   fritters

**1** In a medium bowl, beat the eggs until foamy. Beat in the milk and oil. Stir in the baking powder, sugar, mace, raisins, and salt. Gently stir in the flour, ½ cup at a time, until the dough holds together.

**2** In a deep-fryer, heavy skillet, or Dutch oven, preheat 3 to 4 inches of oil to 370 to 375 degrees F. Drop the dough by tablespoonfuls into the hot oil, 3 to 4 at a time (depending on the size of your deep-fryer). Cook, turning occasionally, until the fritters are golden brown. Using a slotted spoon, lift the doughnuts from the hot oil and drain on a double thickness of paper towels or on a wire rack for 1 to 2 minutes. Continue until all the fritters are cooked. Roll the fritters in cinnamon sugar. Serve warm or cooled.

1 cup hot mashed potatoes
2 tablespoons butter or margarine, at
	room temperature
1½ cups sweet milk
4 teaspoons baking powder
1½ cups granulated sugar, plus more
	for sprinkling on the doughnuts
4 cups all-purpose flour
Oil for deep frying

**1** In a medium bowl, beat the potatoes, butter, and milk until smooth. Stir in the baking powder and sugar. Gently stir in the flour, ½ cup at a time, until the dough holds together.

**2** In a deep-fryer, heavy skillet, or Dutch oven, preheat 3 to 4 inches of oil to 370 to 375 degrees F. Turn the dough out onto a floured surface, and with floured hands pat it out to a thickness of ½ inch. Using a doughnut cutter, cut out as many doughnuts as possible, reworking the scraps as you go.

**3** Slip the doughnuts into the preheated oil, three or four at a time (depending on the size of your deep-fryer). Cook until lightly browned on one side (2 to 3 minutes). Gently turn and brown the other side. Using a slotted spoon, lift the doughnuts from the hot oil and drain on a double thickness of paper towels or on a wire rack for 1 to 2 minutes. Continue until all the doughnuts are cooked. Sprinkle with granulated sugar. Serve warm or cooled.

# EGGLESS DOUGHNUTS

MAKES: *16 to 18 doughnuts*

⅓ cup vegetable shortening
½ cup granulated sugar
1 large egg
½ cup milk
1½ teaspoons baking powder
¼ teaspoon ground nutmeg
½ teaspoon salt
1½ cups all-purpose flour
Powdered sugar for dusting

**1** Position the rack in the center of the oven and preheat to 350 degrees F. Lightly grease a 12-cup muffin baking pan.

**2** In a medium bowl, beat the shortening and sugar until light and fluffy. Beat in the egg and milk until smooth. Stir in the baking powder, nutmeg and salt. Add the flour, ½ cup at a time, stirring until smooth.

**3** Spoon the mixture evenly into the prepared baking pan, and bake for 20 to 25 minutes, or until the top is a light golden brown. Remove from the oven and cool in the pan on a wire rack for 5 to 7 minutes before removing the doughnuts. Dust with powdered sugar.

# FRENCH MUFFIN DOUGHNUTS

MAKES: *10 to 12 doughnuts*

## GERMAN FRITTERS (TROPFRAPKEN)

MAKES: *30 to 36 fritters*

2 large egg yolks
1 large egg
¼ cup butter or margarine, at room temperature
1 cup granulated sugar
¾ cup buttermilk or sour milk
2 teaspoons baking powder
½ teaspoon baking soda
¼ teaspoon ground nutmeg
4 cups all-purpose flour
Oil for deep frying
Powdered sugar for dusting

**1** In a medium bowl, beat the egg yolks and egg until foamy before beating in the butter, sugar, and buttermilk. Stir in the baking powder, baking soda, and nutmeg. Gently stir in the flour, ½ cup at a time, until the dough holds together.

**2** In a deep-fryer, heavy skillet, or Dutch oven, preheat 3 to 4 inches of oil to 370 to 375 degrees F. Drop the dough by tablespoonfuls into the hot oil, 3 to 4 at a time and cook (depending on the size of your deep-fryer). Cook, turning occasionally, until the fritters are golden brown. Using a slotted spoon, lift the doughnuts from the hot oil and drain on a double thickness of paper towels or on a wire rack for 1 to 2 minutes. Repeat until all the batter is used. Dust the fritters with powdered sugar and serve warm or cooled.

## GERMAN POTATO DOUGHNUTS

MAKES: *14 to 18 doughnuts*

2 large eggs
1 tablespoon butter
1 cup mashed potatoes
½ cup milk
1 tablespoon baking powder
1 cup granulated sugar
½ teaspoon salt
3 cups all-purpose flour
Oil for deep frying
Powdered sugar for dusting

**1** In a medium bowl, beat the eggs until foamy. Beat in the butter, potatoes, and milk. Stir in the baking powder, sugar, and salt. Gently stir in the flour, ½ cup at a time, until the dough holds together.

**2** In a deep-fryer, heavy skillet, or Dutch oven, preheat 3 to 4 inches of oil to 375 degrees F. Turn the dough out onto a floured surface, and with floured hands pat it out to a thickness of ½ inch. Using a doughnut cutter, cut out as many doughnuts as possible, reworking the scraps as you go.

**3** Slip the doughnuts into the preheated oil, three or four at a time (depending on the size of your deep-fryer). Cook until lightly browned on one side (2 to 3 minutes). Gently turn and brown the other side. Using a slotted spoon, lift the doughnuts from the hot oil and drain on a double thickness of paper towels or on a wire rack for 1 to 2 minutes. Continue until all the doughnuts are cooked. Dust the doughnuts with powdered sugar. Serve warm or cooled.

3 large eggs
1 cup granulated sugar
½ cup molasses
1 cup sour cream
2 teaspoons baking powder
1 teaspoon baking soda
1½ teaspoons ground ginger
¼ teaspoon ground cinnamon
¼ teaspoon ground nutmeg
1 tablespoon grated lemon zest
½ teaspoon salt
4 cups all-purpose flour
Oil for deep frying

**1** In a medium bowl, beat the eggs until foamy. Beat in the sugar, molasses, and sour cream. Stir in the baking powder, baking soda, ginger, cinnamon, nutmeg, lemon zest, and salt. Gently stir in the flour a half cup at a time.

**2** In a deep-fryer, heavy skillet, or Dutch oven, preheat 3 to 4 inches of oil to 370 to 375 degrees F. Turn the dough out onto a floured surface, and with floured hands, pat it out to a thickness of ½ inch. Using a doughnut cutter, cut out as many doughnuts as possible, reworking the scraps as you go.

**3** Slip the doughnuts into the preheated oil, three or four at a time (depending on the size of your deep-fryer). Cook until lightly browned on one side (2 to 3 minutes). Gently turn and brown the other side. Using a slotted spoon, lift the doughnuts from the hot oil and drain on a double thickness of paper towels or on a wire rack for 1 to 2 minutes. Continue until all the doughnuts are cooked. Serve warm or cooled.

## GINGER–MOLASSES DOUGHNUTS

MAKES: *20 to 24 doughnuts*

2 eggs
¾ cup milk
1 cup granulated sugar
½ cup creamy peanut butter
1 tablespoon baking powder
½ teaspoon salt
½ cup chopped peanuts
3⅓ cups all-purpose flour
Oil for deep frying

**1** In a medium bowl, beat the eggs until foamy. Beat in the milk, sugar, and peanut butter. Stir in the baking powder, salt, and peanuts. Gently stir in the flour, ½ cup at a time, until the dough holds together.

**2** In a deep-fryer, heavy skillet, or Dutch oven, preheat 3 to 4 inches of oil to 370 to 375 degrees F. Turn the dough out onto a floured surface, and with floured hands, pat it out to a thickness of ½ inch. Using a doughnut cutter, cut out as many doughnuts as possible, reworking the scraps as you go.

**3** Slip the doughnuts into the preheated oil, three or four at a time (depending on the size of your deep-fryer). Cook until lightly browned on one side (2 to 3 minutes). Gently turn and brown the other side. Using a slotted spoon, lift the doughnuts from the hot oil and drain on a double thickness of paper towels or on a wire rack for 1 to 2 minutes. Continue until all the doughnuts are cooked. Serve warm or cooled.

## PEANUT BUTTER DOUGHNUTS

MAKES: *14 to 16 doughnuts*

# PUMPKIN DOUGHNUTS

MAKES: *20 to 24 doughnuts*

1 large egg
1¼ cups milk
1 cup granulated sugar
2 tablespoons melted butter
½ teaspoon vanilla
¾ cup canned pumpkin
4 teaspoons baking powder
1 teaspoon ground nutmeg
¾ teaspoon salt
4½ cups all-purpose flour
Oil for deep frying

**1** In a medium bowl, beat the egg until foamy before beating in the milk, sugar, butter, vanilla, and pumpkin. Stir in the baking powder, nutmeg, and salt. Gently stir in the flour, ½ cup at a time, until the dough holds together.

**2** In a deep-fryer, heavy skillet, or Dutch oven, preheat 3 to 4 inches of oil to 370 to 375 degrees

F. Turn the dough out onto a floured surface, and with floured hands, pat it out to a thickness of ½ inch. Using a doughnut cutter, cut out as many doughnuts as possible, reworking the scraps as you go.

**3** Slip the doughnuts into the preheated oil, three or four at a time (depending on the size of your deep-fryer). Cook until lightly browned on one side (2 to 3 minutes). Gently turn and brown the other side. Using a slotted spoon, lift the doughnuts from the hot oil and drain on a double thickness of paper towels or on a wire rack for 1 to 2 minutes. Continue until all the doughnuts are cooked. Serve warm or cooled.

# RICOTTA CHEESE FRITTERS

MAKES: *14 to 16 fritters*

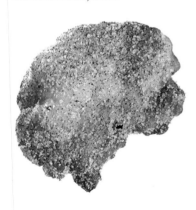

2 large eggs
1 cup Ricotta cheese
1½ teaspoons granulated sugar
1½ teaspoons baking soda
¼ teaspoon salt
1 cup all-purpose flour
Cinnamon sugar for rolling fritters in

**1** In a medium bowl, beat the eggs until foamy. Beat in the cheese and sugar. Stir in the baking soda and salt. Gently stir in the flour, ½ cup at a time, until the dough holds together.

**2** In a deep-fryer, heavy skillet, or Dutch oven, preheat 3 to 4 inches of oil to 370 to 375 degrees

F. Drop the dough by tablespoonfuls in the hot oil, 3 to 4 at a time (depending on the size of your deep-fryer). Cook, turning occasiionally, until the fritters are golden brown. Using a slotted spoon, lift the doughnuts from the hot oil and drain on a double thickness of paper towels or on a wore rack for 1 to 2 minutes. Continue until all the fritters are cooked. Roll the fritters in cinnamon sugar. Serve warm or cooled.

1 large egg
1½ cups sour cream or plain yogurt
¼ cup granulated sugar
1 teaspoon baking soda
¼ teaspoon salt
4 cups all-purpose flour

**1** In a medium bowl, beat the egg foamy before beating in the sour cream and sugar. Stir in the baking soda and salt. Gently stir in the flour a half a cup at a time until the dough holds together.

**2** In a deep-fryer, heavy skillet, or Dutch oven, preheat 3 to 4 inches of oil to 370 to 375 degrees F. Turn the dough out onto a floured surface, and with floured hands pat it out to a thickness of ½ inch. Using a doughnut cutter, cut out as many doughnuts as possible, reworking the scraps as you go.

**3** Slip the doughnuts into the preheated oil, three or four at a time (depending on the size of your deep-fryer). Cook until lightly browned on one side (2 to 3 minutes). Gently turn and brown the other side. Using a slotted spoon, lift the doughnuts from the hot oil and drain on a double thickness of paper towels or on a wire rack for 1 to 2 minutes. Continue until all the doughnuts are cooked. Serve warm or cooled.

# SOUR CREAM DOUGHNUTS

MAKES: *22 to 24 doughnuts*

---

2 tablespoons butter or margarine, at room temperature
1 cup granulated sugar
3 large eggs
1 cup milk
2 tablespoons baking powder
½ teaspoon ground nutmeg
2½ cups all-purpose flour
Powdered sugar for dusting

**1** In a medium bowl, beat the butter and sugar until fluffy. Add the eggs one at a time, beating vigorously after each addition. Beat in the milk. Stir in the baking powder and nutmeg. Gently stir in the flour, ½ cup at a time, until the dough holds together.

**2** In a deep-fryer, heavy skillet, or Dutch oven, preheat 3 to 4 inches of oil to 370 to 375 degrees F. Turn the dough out onto a floured surface, and with floured hands, pat it out to a thickness of ½ inch. Using a doughnut cutter, cut out as many fritters as possible, reworking the scraps as you go.

**3** Slip the fritters into the pre-heated oil, three or four at a time (depending on the size of your deep-fryer). Cook until lightly browned on one side (2 to 3 minutes). Gently turn and brown on the other side. Using a slotted spoon, lift the fritters from the hot oil and drain on a double thickness of paper towels or on a wire rack for 1 to 2 minutes. Continue until all the fritters are cooked. Dust with the powdered sugar. Serve warm or cold.

# SOUTHERN-STYLE FRITTERS

MAKES: *14 to 16 fritters*

# SPICY MOLASSES DOUGHNUTS

MAKES: *20 to 24 doughnuts*

2 large eggs
1 cup molasses
2 tablespoons melted butter or margarine
1 cup sour milk or buttermilk
½ cup granulated sugar
1 teaspoon baking powder
2 teaspoons baking soda
1 teaspoon ground nutmeg
½ teaspoon ground cinnamon
¼ teaspoon ground ginger
4 cups all-purpose flour
Oil for deep frying

**1** In a medium bowl, beat the eggs until foamy. Beat in the molasses, butter, sour milk, and sugar. Stir in the baking powder, baking soda, nutmeg, cinnamon, and ginger. Gently stir in the flour, ½ cup at a time, until the dough holds together.

**2** In a deep-fryer, heavy skillet, or Dutch oven, preheat 3 to 4 inches of oil to 370 to 375 degrees F. Turn the dough out onto a floured surface, and with floured hands pat it out to a thickness of ½ inch. Using a doughnut cutter, cut out as many doughnuts as possible, reworking the scraps as you go.

3 Slip the doughnuts into the preheated oil, three or four at a time (depending on the size of your deep-fryer). Cook until lightly browned on one side (2 to 3 minutes). Gently turn and brown the other side. Using a slotted spoon, lift the doughnuts from the hot oil and drain on a double thickness of paper towels or on a wire rack for 1 to 2 minutes. Continue until all the doughnuts are cooked. Serve warm or cooled.

# SWEET-POTATO DOUGHNUTS

MAKES: *20 to 24 doughnuts*

3 large eggs
¾ cup granulated sugar
3 tablespoons melted butter or margarine
¾ cup mashed sweet potatoes
1½ teaspoons baking powder
1 teaspoon ground cloves
2 teaspoons allspice
¼ teaspoon salt
3 cups all-purpose flour
Oil for deep frying

**1** In a medium bowl, beat the eggs until foamy. Beat in the sugar, butter, and potatoes. Stir in the baking powder, cloves, allspice, and salt. Gently stir in the flour, ½ cup at a time, until the dough holds together.

**2** In a deep-fryer, heavy skillet, or Dutch oven, preheat 3 to 4 inches of oil to 370 to 375 degrees F. Turn the dough out onto a floured surface, and with floured hands pat it out to a thickness of ½ inch. Using a doughnut cutter, cut out as many doughnuts as possible, reworking the scraps as you go.

3 Slip the doughnuts into the preheated oil, three or four at a time (depending on the size of your deep-fryer). Cook until lightly browned on one side (2 to 3 minutes). Gently turn and brown the other side. Using a slotted spoon, lift the doughnuts from the hot oil and drain on a double thickness of paper towels or on a wire rack for 1 to 2 minutes. Continue until all the doughnuts are cooked. Serve warm or cooled.

# Chapter 7

# QUICK BREADS

Years ago, it was the custom for the home maker to make a little loaf, or quick bread for a holiday celebration. Usually these baked treats were nut breads, or cranberry-nut breads. Seldom if ever did any of those home makers consider making the little loaves for a lunchtime snack or evening meal.

In our diverse and curious world, food is valued for the variety of flavors and tastes available. Muffins, as well as quick breads, are the perfect medium for a melange of flavors. Imagine replacing potatoes or a starch, at meal time, with a few slices of freshly-baked quick bread. Try using the broccoli bread, the bean bread, or any other savory recipe offered in this collection.

The pan sizes listed here are for recommendation only. If the suggested size for a loaf pan is not available then two loaf pans in a smaller size may be used. If only one loaf pan is available, and the recipe calls for two, then divide the batter in half and bake the quick breads one at a time. (Remember to refrigerate the reserved batter while the first loaf is baking.) Some adjustments may be necessary if pan size or oven accuracy varies—but the test for doneness will always be a good way to measure how much baking time is needed.

# ALMOND BREAD

MAKES: *1 loaf*

1¼ cups sifted all-purpose flour
1½ teaspoons baking powder
¼ cup almond halves
⅛ teaspoon salt
⅓ cup granulated sugar
4 large eggs
2 tablespoons lemon juice
2 tablespoons melted butter or
   margarine
Apple–Cinnamon Syrup (see recipe
   page 168)

1  Position the rack in the center of the oven and preheat to 375 degrees F. Lightly grease and flour an 8-inch square baking pan.

2  In a large bowl, blend together the flour, baking powder, almonds, and salt. In a medium bowl, beat the sugar and eggs until smooth before beating in the lemon juice and butter. Combine the two mixtures, blending until the dry ingredients are moistened.

3  Scrape the batter into the prepared baking pan and bake for 35 to 40 minutes, or until a cake tester or wooden toothpick inserted into the center of the bread comes out clean and the top is golden brown. Remove from the oven and cool in the pan on a wire rack for 5 to 10 minutes before cutting into squares and serving. Serve with Apple–Cinnamon Syrup.

# ALMOND-FLAVORED RAISIN BREAD

MAKES: *1 loaf*

3¼ cups all-purpose flour
1 tablespoon baking powder
1 cup granulated sugar
1 cup finely chopped seedless raisin
1 cup golden raisins
½ teaspoon salt
1 large egg
1½ cups milk
1 teaspoon almond extract

1  Position the rack in the center of the oven and preheat to 325 degrees F. Lightly grease and flour a 9¼-by-5¼-by-2¾-inch loaf pan.

2  In a large bowl, blend together the flour, baking powder, sugar, raisins, and salt. In a medium bowl, beat the egg until foamy before beating in the milk and the almond extract. Combine the two mixtures, blending until the dry ingredients are well moistened.

3  Scrape the batter into the prepared pan and bake for 55 to 60 minutes, or until a cake tester or wooden toothpick inserted into the center of the bread comes out clean and the top is golden. Remove from the oven and cool in the pan on a wire rack for 5 to 10 minutes before removing the loaf from the pan.

1½ cups whole-wheat flour
1 cup all-purpose flour
1 cup rolled oats
1 tablespoon baking powder
1½ teaspoons ground cinnamon
2 medium apples, peeled, cored, and finely chopped
1 cup candied cherry halves
½ cup golden raisins
1 teaspoon grated lemon or orange zest
4 large eggs
¾ cup milk
½ cup apple-flavored yogurt
¼ cup unsweetened frozen apple-juice concentrate, thawed
Cherry Sauce (see recipe page 52)

1 Position the rack in the center of the oven and preheat to 350 degrees F. Lightly grease and flour a 9¼-by-5½-by-2¾-inch loaf pan.

2 In a large bowl, blend together the two flours, oats, baking powder, cinnamon, apples, cherries, raisins, and lemon zest. In a medium bowl, beat the eggs until foamy before beating in the milk, yogurt, and apple juice. Combine the two mixtures, blending until the dry ingredients are thoroughly moistened.

3 Scrape the batter into the prepared pan and bake for 55 to 60 minutes, or until a cake tester or wooden toothpick inserted into the center of the bread comes out clean and the top is golden. Remove the pan from the oven and cool on a wire rack for 5 to 10 minutes before removing the loaf from the pan. Serve with Cherry Sauce.

# APPLE-AND-CHERRY BREAD

MAKES: *1 loaf*

2 cups all-purpose flour
1 cup granulated sugar
1 teaspoon baking soda
2 cups finely chopped apples, peeled and cored
¼ teaspoon salt
2 large eggs
½ cup melted butter or margarine
2 tablespoons sour milk or buttermilk
1 teaspoon vanilla extract

1 Position the rack in the center of the oven and preheat to 350 degrees F. Lightly grease and flour a 9¼-by-5¼-by-2¾-inch loaf pan.

2 In a large bowl, blend together the flour, sugar, baking soda, salt, and apples. In a medium bowl, beat the eggs until foamy before beating in the butter, milk, and vanilla extract. Combine the two mixtures, blending until the dry ingredients are moistened.

3 Scrape the batter into the prepared pan and bake for 55 to 60 minutes, or until a cake tester or wooden toothpick inserted into the center of the bread comes out clean and the top is golden brown. Remove the pan from the oven and invert onto a wire rack to cool for 5 to 10 minutes before removing the loaf from the pan.

**SERVING SUGGESTION: Serve with apple butter.**

# APPLE BREAD

MAKES: *1 loaf*

## APPLE–CHEESE BREAD

MAKES: *1 loaf*

2 cups all-purpose flour
1 teaspoon baking powder
½ teaspoon baking soda
⅓ cup chopped walnuts or pecans
½ cup grated Monterey Jack cheese
½ teaspoon salt
½ cup butter or margarine, at room temperature
⅔ cup granulated sugar
3 large eggs
2 medium apples, peeled, cored, and grated
Cheese Sauce (see recipe page 57)

1  Position the rack in the center of the oven and preheat to 350 degrees F. Lightly grease and flour a 9¼-by-5¼-by-2¾-inch loaf pan.

2  In a large bowl, blend together the flour, baking powder, baking soda, nuts, cheese, and salt. In a medium bowl, beat the butter and sugar together until light and fluffy. Beat in the eggs, one at a time, beating vigorously after each addition. Stir in the apples. Combine the two mixtures, blending until the dry ingredients are well moistened.

3  Scrape the batter into the prepared pan and bake for 55 to 60 minutes, or until a cake tester or wooden toothpick inserted into the center of the bread comes out clean and the top is golden. Remove the pan from the oven and cool on a wire rack for 5 to 10 minutes before removing the loaf from the pan. Serve with Cheese Sauce.

## APPLE-FLAVORED CHOCOLATE TEA BREAD

MAKES: *1 loaf*

1¾ cups all-purpose flour
1 cup granulated sugar
1 teaspoon baking soda
⅓ cup Dutch-processed cocoa
⅓ cup semisweet chocolate chips
½ cup chopped walnuts
¾ teaspoon salt
2 large eggs
½ cup unsweetened applesauce
⅓ cup butter or margarine, at room temperature
⅓ cup water, at room temperature
½ teaspoon vanilla extract
Chocolate Sauce (see recipe page 26)

1  Position the rack in the center of the oven and preheat to 350 degrees F. Lightly grease and flour a 9¼-by-5¼-by-2¾-inch loaf pan.

2  In a large bowl, blend together the flour, sugar, baking soda, cocoa, chocolate chips, walnuts, and salt. In a medium bowl, beat the eggs until foamy before beating in the applesauce, butter, water, and vanilla extract. Combine the two mixtures, blending until the dry ingredients are moistened.

3  Scrape the batter into the prepared pan and bake for 55 to 60 minutes, or until a cake tester or wooden toothpick inserted into the center of the bread comes out clean and the top is golden. Remove the pan from the oven and cool on a wire rack for 5 minutes before removing the loaf from the pan. Serve with Chocolate Sauce.

2 cups all-purpose flour
1 teaspoon baking powder
½ teaspoon ground cinnamon
½ teaspoon ground nutmeg
1 cup raisins, plumped and drained
½ cup chopped pecans
½ teaspoon salt
1 cup granulated sugar
½ cup butter or margarine, at room temperature
3 large eggs
¼ cup molasses
1 cup unsweetened applesauce
Molasses Sauce (see recipe page 125)

1  Position the rack in the center of the oven and preheat to 350 degrees F. Lightly grease and flour a 9¼-by-5¼-by-2¾-inch loaf pan.

2  In a large bowl, blend together the flour, baking powder, cinnamon, nutmeg, raisins, pecans, and salt. In a medium bowl, beat the sugar and butter until fluffy. Beat in the eggs, one at a time, beating vigorously after each addition. Beat in the molasses and applesauce. Combine the two mixtures, blending until the dry ingredients are moistened.

3  Scrape the batter into the prepared pan and bake for 55 to 60 minutes, or until a cake tester or wooden toothpick inserted into the center of the bread comes out clean and the top is golden. Remove the pan from the oven and cool on a wire rack for 5 to 10 minutes before removing the loaf from the pan. Serve with Chocolate Sauce.

# APPLE–MOLASSES BREAD

MAKES: *1 loaf*

---

2 cups all-purpose flour
1 teaspoon baking soda
½ cup packed light-brown sugar
½ cup granulated sugar
2 teaspoons ground cinnamon
1 cup chopped peanuts
2 large apples, peeled, cored, and grated
2 large eggs
½ cup peanut oil
2 tablespoons orange juice
¼ cup creamy peanut butter
Peanut Sauce (see recipe page 201) or Peanut Butter Sauce (see recipe page 156)

1  Position the rack in the center of the oven and preheat to 350 degrees F. Lightly grease and flour a 9¼-by-5¼-by-2¾-inch loaf pan.

2  In a large bowl, blend together the flour, baking soda, two sugars, cinnamon, peanuts, and apples. In a medium bowl, beat the eggs until foamy before beating in the peanut oil, orange juice, and peanut butter. Combine the two mixtures, blending until the dry ingredients are moistened.

3  Scrape the batter into the prepared pan and bake for 55 to 60 minutes, or until a cake tester or wooden toothpick inserted into the center of the bread comes out clean and the top is golden brown. Remove from the oven and cool the pan on a wire rack for 5 to 10 minutes before removing the loaf from the pan. Serve with Peanut Sauce or Peanut Butter Sauce.

# APPLE–PEANUT BREAD

MAKES: *1 loaf*

# APPLE–RAISIN–NUT BREAD

MAKES: *1 loaf*

1½ cups all-purpose flour
¾ cup granulated sugar
1 teaspoon baking powder
½ teaspoon baking soda
1½ teaspoons ground cinnamon
2 medium apples, unpared, cored and shredded
1 cup chopped walnuts
1 cup seedless raisins
½ teaspoon salt
2 large eggs
½ cup canola oil
1 teaspoon vanilla extract

1  Position the rack in the center of the oven and preheat to 375 degrees F. Lightly grease and flour an 8½-by-4½-by-2½-inch loaf pan.

2  In a large bowl, blend together the flour, sugar, baking powder, baking soda, cinnamon, apples, walnuts, raisins, and salt. In a small bowl, beat the eggs until foamy before beating in the oil and vanilla extract. Combine the two mixtures, blending until the dry ingredients are just moistened.

3  Scrape the batter into the prepared pan and bake for 45 to 50 minutes, or until a cake tester or wooden toothpick inserted into the center of the bread comes out clean and the top is golden brown. Remove the pan from the oven and cool on a wire rack for 5 to 10 minutes before removing the loaf from the pan.

**SERVING SUGGESTION: Serve with apple butter.**

---

# APRICOT BREAD

MAKES: *1 loaf*

1 cup diced dried apricots
¼ cup apricot-flavored brandy or liqueur
1 cup all-purpose flour
1 cup whole-wheat flour
1 cup oat bran
1 teaspoon baking powder
1 teaspoon baking soda
1 cup chopped almonds
½ teaspoon salt
¼ cup butter or margarine
½ cup granulated sugar
1 large egg
1 cup buttermilk or sour milk
Blender Apricot Sauce (see recipe page 25)

1  Thirty minutes before baking, in a small bowl, combine the apricots and brandy and set aside.

2  Position the rack in the center of the oven and preheat to 350 degrees F. Lightly grease and flour a 9¼-by-5¼-by-2¾-inch loaf pan.

3  In a large bowl, blend together the two flours, oat bran, baking powder, baking soda, almonds, and salt. In a medium bowl, beat the butter and sugar until light and fluffy. Beat in the egg and buttermilk. Stir in the apricots and brandy. Combine the two mixtures, blending until the dry ingredients are just moistened.

4  Scrape the batter into the prepared pan and bake for 55 to 60 minutes, or until a cake tester or wooden toothpick inserted into the center of the bread comes out clean and the top is golden. Remove the pan from the oven and cool on a wire rack for 5 to 10 minutes before removing the loaf from the pan. Serve with Blender Apricot Sauce.

1 cup dried apricot halves
2 cups all-purpose flour
1½ cups bran flakes
½ cup granulated sugar
2 teaspoons baking powder
½ teaspoon baking soda
1 teaspoon ground cinnamon
½ teaspoon ground nutmeg
¾ cup chopped walnuts
½ teaspoon salt
1 large egg
3 tablespoons melted butter or
  margarine
1½ cups buttermilk or sour milk, at
  room temperature
Blender Apricot Sauce (see recipe
  page 25)

1 Thirty minutes before baking, place the apricots in a small bowl and add enough boiling water to just cover them. Set aside.

2 Position the rack in the center of the oven and preheat to 350 degrees F. Lightly grease and flour a 9¼-by-5¼-by-2¾-inch loaf pan.

3 In a large bowl, blend together the flour, bran flakes, sugar, baking powder, baking soda, cinnamon, nutmeg, walnuts, and salt. In a small bowl, beat the egg, butter, and buttermilk until smooth. Drain and finely chop the apricots before stirring them into the egg mixture. Combine the wet and dry ingredients, blending until the dry ingredients are just moistened.

3 Scrape the batter into the prepared pan and bake for 55 to 60 minutes, or until a cake tester or wooden toothpick inserted into the center of the bread comes out clean and the top is golden. Remove from the oven and cool the pan on a wire rack for 5 to 10 minutes before removing the loaf from the pan. Serve with Blender Apricot Sauce.

# Apricot–Buttermilk Bread

Makes: *1 loaf*

---

1 cup all-purpose flour
½ cup whole-wheat flour
½ cup granulated sugar
2 teaspoons baking powder
¼ teaspoon baking soda
1 tablespoon grated orange zest
½ cup finely chopped dried apricots
½ cup finely chopped pitted dates
½ teaspoon salt
¾ cup milk or light cream, at room
  temperature
1 large egg
1 tablespoon melted butter or
  margarine
Apricot Spread (see recipe page 261)

1 Position the rack in the center of oven and preheat to 375 degrees F. Lightly grease and flour an 8½-by-4½-by-2½-inch loaf pan.

2 In a large bowl, blend together the two flours, sugar, baking powder, baking soda, orange zest, apricots, dates, and salt. In a small bowl, beat the milk, egg, and butter until smooth. Combine the two mixtures, blending until the dry ingredients are just moistened.

3 Scrape the batter into the prepared pan and bake for 40 to 45 minutes, or until a cake tester or wooden toothpick inserted into the center of the bread comes out clean and the top is golden. Remove from the oven and cool the pan on a wire rack for 5 to 10 minutes before removing the loaf from the pan. Serve with Apricot Spread.

# Apricot–Date Bread

Makes: *1 loaf*

# APRICOT–GINGER BREAD

MAKES: *1 loaf*

2 cups all-purpose flour
1½ teaspoons baking powder
½ teaspoon baking soda
3 tablespoons granulated sugar
¾ cup finely chopped dried apricots
1½ teaspoons coarsely grated lemon zest
2 teaspoons ground ginger
2 large eggs
¾ cup milk
⅓ cup melted butter or margarine
Ginger Cream (see recipe page 21)

1  Position the rack in the center of the oven and preheat to 350 degrees F. Lightly grease and flour an 8½-by-4½-by-2½-inch loaf pan.

2  In a large bowl, blend together the flour, baking powder, baking soda, sugar, apricots, zest, and ginger. In a medium bowl, beat the eggs until foamy before beating in the milk and butter. Combine the two mixtures, blending until the dry ingredients are just moistened.

3  Scrape the batter into the prepared pan and bake for 35 to 40 minutes, or until a cake tester or wooden toothpick inserted into the center of the bread comes out clean and the top is golden brown. Remove from the oven and cool the pan on a wire rack for 5 to 10 minutes before removing the loaf from the pan. Serve with Ginger Cream.

# ASIAN RICE FLOUR BREAD

MAKES: *1 loaf*

1 cup millet flour
¾ cup rice flour
1 teaspoon baking soda
2 teaspoons cream of tartar
½ teaspoon salt
1 large egg
1 cup milk or goat's milk
Tropical Sauce (see recipe page 81)

1  Position the rack in the center of the oven and preheat to 350 degrees F. Lightly grease and flour a 9-inch square baking pan.

2  In a large bowl, blend together the 2 flours, baking soda, cream of tartar, and salt. In a medium bowl, beat the egg until foamy before beating in the milk. Combine the two mixtures, blending until the dry ingredients are moistened.

3  Scrape the batter into the prepared pan and bake for 25 to 30 minutes, or until a cake tester or wooden toothpick inserted into the center of the bread comes out clean and the top is golden brown. Remove from the oven and cool the pan on a wire rack for 5 to 10 minutes before removing the loaf from the pan. Cut into squares and serve with Tropical Sauce.

2 cups all-purpose flour
1½ teaspoons baking powder
¼ cup granulated sugar
1 large egg
¼ cup melted butter or margarine
1 cup milk, at room temperature
1 medium avocado, pureed
1 cup toasted slivered almonds for
    topping
Guacamole (see recipe below)

**1** Position the rack in the center of the oven and preheat to 350 degrees F. Lightly grease and flour an 8½-by-4½-by-2½-inch loaf pan.

**2** In a large bowl, blend together the flour, baking powder, and sugar. In a medium bowl, beat the egg until foamy before beating in the butter, milk, and avocado. Combine the two mixtures, blending until the dry ingredients are moistened.

**3** Scrape the batter into the prepared pan and bake for 45 to 50 minutes, or until a cake tester or wooden toothpick inserted into the center of the bread comes out clean and the top is golden brown. Remove from the oven and cool the pan on a wire rack for 5 to 10 minutes before removing the loaf from the pan. Sprinkle top with almonds and serve with Guacamole.

## AVOCADO BREAD

MAKES: *1 loaf*

## GUACAMOLE

MAKES: *About 2 cups*

2 medium avocados, peeled, cut in
    half and pitted
2 tablespoons fresh lemon juice
2 tablespoons mayonnaise
1¼ teaspoons salt
½ small onion, minced
1 small clove garlic, minced
1 can (4 ounces) chopped green
    chilies, drained

In a medium bowl, using potato masher or back of a fork, mash the avocado with the lemon juice and mayonnaise until smooth. Stir in the salt, onion, garlic, and chilies. Spoon into a bowl and serve.

---

8 ounces sliced bacon
2 cups all-purpose flour
1½ cups cornmeal
¼ cup granulated sugar
2 tablespoons baking powder
2 teaspoons salt
2 large eggs
1¼ cups milk
¼ cup vegetable oil
Whipped Cream-Cheese Topping
    (see recipe page 186)

**1** In a large skillet, cook the bacon until crisp. Drain, reserving ½ cup of the drippings, and cool the bacon on paper towels. When cooled, crumble and set aside.

**2** Position the rack in the center of the oven and preheat to 400 degrees F. Lightly grease and flour a 9-inch square baking pan.

**3** In a large bowl, blend together the flour, cornmeal, sugar, baking powder, and salt. In a medium bowl, beat the eggs until foamy before beating in the milk, oil, and ½ cup reserved drippings. Combine the two mixtures, blending until the dry ingredients are just moistened.

**4** Scrape the batter into the prepared pan and sprinkle the crumbled bacon over the top. Bake for 20 to 25 minutes, or until a cake tester or wooden toothpick inserted into the center of the bread comes out clean and the top is golden. Remove from the oven and cool the pan on a wire rack for 5 to 10 minutes before cutting into squares and serving. Serve with Whipped Cream-Cheese Topping.

## BACON–CORN BREAD

MAKES: *1 loaf*

## BANANA–GREEN-GINGER BREAD

MAKES: *1 loaf*

**2½ cups all-purpose flour**
**1½ teaspoons baking soda**
**¼ teaspoon salt**
**¼ cup granulated sugar**
**¼ cup diced fresh green ginger**
**2 large eggs**
**½ cup melted butter or margarine**
**2 medium bananas, mashed**

**1** Position the rack in the center of the oven and preheat to 350 degrees F. Lightly grease and flour an 8½-by-4½-by-2½-inch loaf pan.

**2** In a large bowl, blend together the flour, baking powder, baking soda, salt, sugar, and ginger. In a medium bowl, beat the eggs until foamy before beating in the butter and bananas. Combine the two mixtures, blending until the dry ingredients are moistened.

**3** Scrape the batter into the prepared pan and bake for 45 to 50 minutes, or until a cake tester or wooden toothpick inserted into the center of the bread comes out clean and the top is golden. Remove from the oven and cool the pan on a wire rack for 5 to 10 minutes before removing the loaf from the pan.

## BANANA–APPLESAUCE BREAD

MAKES: *1 loaf*

**1½ cups whole-wheat flour**
**¾ cup all-purpose flour**
**1 teaspoon baking soda**
**¼ cup seedless raisins**
**¼ cup chopped walnuts or pecans**
**2 large egg whites**
**¼ cup canola oil**
**¾ cup frozen unsweetened apple-juice concentrate, thawed**
**2 medium bananas, mashed**
**½ cup unsweetened applesauce**

**1** Position the rack in the center of the oven and preheat to 325 degrees F. Lightly grease and flour an 8½-by-4½-by-2½-inch loaf pan.

**2** In a large bowl, blend together the two flours, baking soda, raisins, and walnuts. In a medium bowl, beat the egg whites until stiff but not dry. Stir in the oil, apple juice, bananas, and applesauce until smooth. Combine the two mixtures, blending until the dry ingredients are moistened.

**3** Scrape the batter into the prepared pan and bake for 50 to 55 minutes, or until a cake tester or wooden toothpick inserted into the center of the bread comes out clean and the top is golden. Remove from the oven and cool the pan on a wire rack for 5 to 10 minutes before removing the loaf from the pan.

**SERVING SUGGESTION: Serve with warm unsweetened applesauce.**

1¾ cups all-purpose flour
¾ cup granulated sugar
1¼ teaspoons baking powder
½ teaspoon baking soda
½ cup chopped walnuts
¾ teaspoon salt
2 large eggs
2 medium bananas, mashed
⅓ cup melted butter or margarine
¼ cup beer

**1** Position the rack in the center of the oven and preheat to 350 degrees F. Lightly grease and flour a 9¼-by-5¼-by-2¾-inch loaf pan.

**2** In a large bowl, blend together the flour, sugar, baking powder, baking soda, walnuts, and salt. In a medium bowl, beat the eggs until foamy before beating in the bananas, butter, and beer. Combine the two mixtures, blending until the dry ingredients are moistened.

**3** Scrape the batter into the prepared pan and bake for 55 to 60 minutes, or until a cake tester or wooden toothpick inserted into the center of the bread comes out clean and the top is golden. Remove from the oven and cool the pan on a wire rack for 5 to 10 minutes before removing the loaf from the pan.

**SERVING SUGGESTION: Serve with cold beer and sliced cheese of choice.**

# BANANA BEER BREAD

MAKES: *1 loaf*

---

1½ cups whole-wheat flour
½ cup all-purpose flour
½ cup rolled oats
2 teaspoons baking powder
½ teaspoon baking soda
½ cup fresh or frozen blueberries
2 large egg whites
¼ cup melted butter or margarine
1 cup mashed bananas
¾ cup frozen apple-juice
  concentrate, thawed
Blueberry Syrup (see recipe page 43)

**1** Position the rack in the center of the oven and preheat to 325 degrees F. Lightly grease and flour an 8½-by-4½-by-2½-inch loaf pan.

**2** In a large bowl, blend together the two flours, oats, baking powder, and baking soda. Stir in the blueberries. In a medium bowl, beat the egg whites until stiff but not dry. Stir in the butter, bananas, and apple juice. Combine the two mixtures, blending until the dry ingredients are moistened.

**3** Scrape the batter into the prepared pan and bake for 50 to 55 minutes, or until a cake tester or wooden toothpick inserted into the center of the bread comes out clean and the top is golden. Remove from the oven and cool the pan on a wire rack for 5 to 10 minutes before removing the loaf from the pan. Serve with Blueberry Syrup.

# BANANA–BLUEBERRY BREAD

MAKES: *1 loaf*

# BANANA BREAD

MAKES: *1 loaf*

1½ cups all-purpose flour
1 cup oat flour
½ cup granulated sugar
1 teaspoon baking powder
1 teaspoon baking soda
1 teaspoon ground cinnamon
½ cup flaked coconut
½ teaspoon salt
2 large eggs
3 medium bananas, mashed
¼ cup canola oil
One 8-ounce can crushed pineapple (do not drain)
¼ cup shredded coconut for topping

1  Position the rack in the center of the oven and preheat to 350 degrees F. Lightly grease and flour an 8½-by-4½-by-2½-inch loaf pan.

2  In a large bowl, blend together the flour, oat flour, sugar, baking powder, baking soda, cinnamon, coconut, and salt. In a medium bowl, beat the eggs until foamy before beating in the bananas, oil, and pineapple with its juice. Combine the two mixtures, blending until the dry ingredients are moistened.

3  Scrape the batter into the prepared pan and sprinkle the shredded coconut over the top. Bake for 45 to 50 minutes, or until a cake tester or wooden toothpick inserted into the center of the bread comes out clean and the top is golden. Remove from the oven and cool the pan on a wire rack for 5 to 10 minutes before removing the loaf from the pan.

# BANANA–CHOCOLATE CHIP BREAD

MAKES: *1 loaf*

2 cups all-purpose flour
1 cup granulated sugar
1½ teaspoons baking powder
½ teaspoon baking soda
¼ cup finely chopped walnuts
½ cup chopped maraschino cherries
¼ cup semisweet chocolate chips
⅛ teaspoon salt
2 large eggs
½ cup melted butter or margarine
3 medium bananas, mashed
Chocolate Sauce (see recipe page 26)

1  Position the rack in the center of the oven and preheat to 350 degrees F. Lightly grease and flour a 9¼-by-5¼-by-2¾-inch loaf pan.

2  In a large bowl, blend together the flour, sugar, baking powder, baking soda, walnuts, cherries, chocolate chips, and salt. In a small bowl, beat the eggs, butter, and bananas until smooth. Combine the two mixtures, blending until the dry ingredients are just moistened.

3  Scrape the batter into the prepared pan and bake for 40 to 45 minutes, or until a cake tester or wooden toothpick inserted into the center of the bread comes out clean and the top is golden brown. Remove from the oven and cool the pan on a wire rack for 5 to 10 minutes before removing the loaf from the pan. Serve with Chocolate Sauce.

3 cups all-purpose flour
2 cups granulated sugar
¼ cup Dutch-processed cocoa powder
2 teaspoons baking soda
1 teaspoon ground cinnamon
1 cup finely chopped pecans
1 cup semisweet chocolate chips
4 large eggs
1 cup melted butter or margarine
6 medium bananas, mashed
1 cup banana-flavored yogurt or plain sour cream
2 teaspoons vanilla extract
Chocolate–Honey Sauce (see recipe page 30)

**1** Position the rack in the center of the oven and preheat to 350 degrees F. Lightly grease and flour the bottom of two 8½-by-4½-by-2½-inch loaf pans.

**2** In a large bowl, blend together the flour, sugar, cocoa, baking soda, cinnamon, pecans, and chocolate chips. In a large bowl, beat the eggs until foamy before beating in the butter, bananas, yogurt, and vanilla extract. Combine the two mixtures, blending until the dry ingredients are moistened.

**3** Scrape the batter into the prepared pans and bake for 45 to 50 minutes, or until a cake tester or wooden toothpick inserted into the center of the bread comes out clean and the tops are golden. Remove from the oven and cool the pans on a wire rack for 5 to 10 minutes before removing the loaves from the pans. Serve with Chocolate–Honey Sauce.

# Banana–Chocolate Tea Bread

Makes: *2 loaves*

2¼ cups whole-wheat flour
¼ cup all-purpose flour
1 teaspoon baking powder
½ teaspoon baking soda
¼ cup poppy seeds
1 large egg white
¾ cup frozen unsweetened apple-juice concentrate, thawed
¼ cup melted butter or margarine
3 medium bananas, mashed
Whipped Cream Topping (see recipe page 208)

**1** Position the rack in the center of the oven and preheat to 325 degrees F. Lightly grease and flour an 8½-by-4½-by-2½-inch loaf pan.

**2** In a large bowl, blend together the two flours, baking powder, baking soda, and poppy seeds. In a small bowl, beat the egg white until stiff but not dry. Stir in the apple juice, butter, and banana until smooth. Combine the two mixtures, blending until the dry ingredients are just moistened.

**3** Scrape the batter into the prepared pan and bake for 40 to 45 minutes, or until a cake tester or wooden toothpick inserted into the center of the bread comes out clean and the top is golden brown. Remove from the oven and cool the pan on a wire rack for 5 to 10 minutes before removing the loaf from the pan. Serve with Whipped Cream Topping.

**Serving suggestion: Serve with black currant jam.**

# Banana–Poppy Seed Bread

Makes: *1 loaf*

# BANANA TEA BREAD

MAKES: *1 loaf*

2 cups all-purpose flour
1 teaspoon baking powder
1 teaspoon baking soda
1⅓ cups granulated sugar
1½ cups finely chopped pecans
1½ teaspoons salt
2 large eggs
½ cup plain yogurt or sour cream
2 tablespoons rum or rum flavoring
1 teaspoon almond extract
½ cup melted butter or margarine,
    at room temperature
3 medium bananas, mashed
Pineapple Syrup (see recipe page 46)

**1** Position the rack in the center of the oven and preheat to 350 degrees F. Lightly grease and flour a 9¼-by-5¼-by-2¾-inch loaf pan.

**2** In a large bowl, blend together the flour, baking powder, baking soda, sugar, pecans, and salt. In a medium bowl, beat the eggs until foamy before beating in the yogurt, rum, almond extract, butter, and bananas. Combine the two mixtures, blending until the dry ingredients are moistened.

**3** Scrape the batter into the prepared pan and bake for 55 to 60 minutes, or until a cake tester or wooden toothpick inserted into the center of the bread comes out clean and the top is golden brown. Remove from the oven and cool the pan on a wire rack for 5 to 10 minutes before removing the loaf from the pan. Serve with Pineapple Syrup.

# BEAN BREAD

MAKES: *1 loaf*

1 large egg
1½ cups milk
½ cup molasses
1½ cups cooked and drained
    Anasazi beans or red kidney
    beans
1 cup whole-wheat flour
½ cup all-purpose flour
2 teaspoons baking powder
⅓ cup Dutch-processed cocoa
    powder
1 teaspoon ground cardamom
¼ teaspoon salt
1 tablespoon finely ground almonds

**1** Position the rack in the center of the oven and preheat to 350 degrees F. Lightly grease and flour an 8½-by-4½-by-2½-inch loaf pan.

**2** In the container of a blender, combine the egg, milk, molasses, and cooked beans. Process on high for 5 to 10 seconds or until the mixture is smooth. Set aside. In a large bowl, blend together the two flours, baking powder, cocoa, cardamom, salt, and almonds. Combine the dry ingredients and the bean mixture, blending until the dry ingredients are moistened.

**3** Scrape the batter into the prepared pan and bake for 45 to 50 minutes, or until a cake tester or wooden toothpick inserted into the center of the bread comes out clean and the top is a deep golden brown. Remove from the oven and cool the pan on a wire rack for 5 to 10 minutes before removing the loaf from the pan.

**SERVING SUGGESTION: Serve with a thick soup.**

2 cups all-purpose flour
1 cup granulated sugar
2 teaspoons baking powder
¼ teaspoon ground cardamom
¼ cup poppy seeds
1 teaspoon grated lemon zest
2 large eggs
½ cup butter or margarine, melted
2 medium ripe bananas, mashed

**1** Position the rack in the center of the oven and preheat to 350 degrees F. Lightly grease and flour an 8½-by-4½-by-2½-inch loaf pan.

**2** In a large bowl, blend together the flour, sugar, baking powder, cardamom, poppy seeds, and lemon zest. In a medium bowl, beat the eggs until foamy before beating in the butter and bananas. Combine the two mixtures, blending until the dry ingredients are thoroughly moistened.

**3** Scrape the batter into the prepared pan and bake for 45 to 50 minutes, or until a cake tester or wooden toothpick inserted into the center of the bread comes out clean and the top is golden brown. Remove from the oven and cool the pan on a wire rack for 5 to 10 minutes before removing the loaf from the pan.

## BIRDSEED BREAD

MAKES: *1 loaf*

---

1 cup all-purpose flour
2 teaspoons baking powder
1 cup raisins
1 cup chopped almonds
¼ teaspoon salt
4 large eggs, separated
1 cup granulated sugar
1 teaspoon almond extract
Powdered sugar for topping
Sliced almonds for topping
Amaretto–Peach Sauce (see recipe
    page 152)

**1** Position the rack in the center of the oven and preheat to 350 degrees F. Lightly grease and flour a 9¼-by-5¼-by-2¾-inch loaf pan.

**2** In a large bowl, blend together the flour, baking powder, raisins, almonds, and salt. In a small bowl, beat the egg yolks until foamy before beating in the sugar and extract. In a medium bowl, beat the egg whites until stiff but not dry. Then combine the egg yolks and dry ingredients, blending until the dry ingredients are just moistened. Fold in the egg whites until incorporated.

**3** Scrape the batter into the prepared pan and bake for 20 to 25 minutes, or until a cake tester or wooden toothpick inserted into the center of the bread comes out clean. Remove from the oven and cool the pan on a wire rack for 5 to 10 minutes before removing the loaf from the pan. Sprinkle the loaf with powdered sugar and sliced almonds. Serve with Amaretto–Peach Sauce.

## BISHOP'S ALMOND BREAD

MAKES: *1 loaf*

## BISHOP'S BREAD

MAKES: *1 loaf*

2 cups all-purpose flour
1 tablespoon baking powder
½ cup wheat germ
1 cup (6 ounces) semisweet
    chocolate chips, chopped
¼ cup golden raisins
¼ cup candied cherry halves
¼ cup finely chopped walnuts
1 teaspoon salt
⅓ cup butter or margarine, at room
    temperature
1 cup granulated sugar
1 large egg
1 tablespoon grated orange zest,
    plus more for topping the loaf
1½ cups orange juice
3 tablespoons canola oil
Blender Apricot Sauce (see recipe
    page 25)

1  Position the rack in the center of the oven and preheat to 350 degrees F. Lightly grease and flour a 9¼-by-5¼-by-2¾-inch loaf pan.

2  In a large bowl, blend together the flour, baking powder, wheat germ, chocolate chips, raisins, cherries, walnuts, and salt. In a medium bowl, beat the butter and sugar until light and fluffy. Beat in the egg, 1 tablespoon of orange zest, orange juice, and oil. Combine the two mixtures, blending until the dry ingredients are moistened.

3  Scrape the batter into the prepared pan and bake for 55 to 60 minutes, or until a cake tester or wooden toothpick inserted into the center of the bread comes out clean and the top is golden. Remove from the oven and cool the pan on a wire rack for 5 to 10 minutes before removing the loaf from the pan. Sprinkle freshly grated orange zest over the top. Serve with Blender Apricot Butter.

## BISHOP'S HEALTH BREAD

MAKES: *1 loaf*

½ cup tofu, at room temperature
¾ cup honey, at room temperature
½ cup canola oil
1 teaspoon almond extract
Egg substitute to equal 1 egg
3 medium bananas
2½ cups whole-wheat flour
½ cup graham flour
½ teaspoon baking powder
½ teaspoon baking soda
1 tablespoon poppy seeds
Berry Sauce (see recipe page 38)

1  Position the rack in the center of the oven and preheat to 350 degrees F. Lightly grease and flour a 9¼-by-5¼-by-2¾-inch baking pan.

2  In the container of a food processor, blend together the tofu, honey, oil, almond extract, egg substitute, and bananas. In a large bowl, blend together the two flours, baking powder, baking soda, and poppy seeds. Then slowly pulse the dry ingredients into the food processor until smooth.

3  Scrape the batter into the prepared baking pan and bake for 30 to 35 minutes, or until a cake tester or wooden toothpick inserted into the center of the bread comes out clean. Remove from the oven and cool the pan on a wire rack for 5 to 10 minutes before removing the loaf from the pan.

1 cup all-purpose flour
1 cup rye flour
1½ teaspoons baking powder
½ teaspoon baking soda
2 large eggs
½ cup milk
2 tablespoons melted butter or
  margarine
2 teaspoons prepared horseradish
1 cup finely chopped yellow onion
3½ ounces crumbled blue cheese
Salt and pepper to taste

**1** Position the rack in the center of the oven and preheat to 350 degrees F. Lightly grease and flour an 8-inch square baking pan.

**2** In a large bowl, blend together the two flours, baking powder, and baking soda. In a medium bowl, beat the eggs until foamy before beating in the milk, butter, and horseradish. Stir in the onion and cheese before adjusting the seasoning to taste. Combine the two mixtures, blending until the dry ingredients are well moistened.

**3** Scrape the batter into the prepared pan and bake for 35 to 40 minutes, or until a cake tester or wooden toothpick inserted into the center of the bread comes out clean and the top is starting to turn golden brown. Remove from the oven and cool the pan on a wire rack for 5 to 10 minutes before cutting the bread into squares.

**SERVING SUGGESTION: Serve with white wine of choice.**

# BLUE CHEESE BREAD

MAKES: *1 loaf*

---

1 cup blue cornmeal
¾ cup all-purpose flour
2 teaspoons baking powder
½ teaspoon garlic powder
1 small red bell pepper, cored,
  seeded, and diced
1 small jalapeño pepper, cored,
  seeded, and very finely diced
½ teaspoon salt
2 large eggs
2 tablespoons canola oil
3 tablespoons butter or margarine, at
  room temperature
¾ cup buttermilk or sour milk
Flavored Mayonnaise of Choice (see
  recipe page 324)

**1** Position the rack in the center of the oven and preheat to 350 degrees F. Lightly grease and flour an 8-inch square baking pan.

**2** In a large bowl, blend together the cornmeal, flour, baking powder, garlic powder, two peppers, and salt. In a medium bowl, beat the eggs, oil, butter, and buttermilk until smooth. Combine the two mixtures, blending until the dry ingredients are well moistened.

**3** Scrape the batter into the prepared pan and bake for 45 to 50 minutes, or until a cake tester or wooden toothpick inserted into the center of the bread comes out clean and the top is starting to turn a lemon yellow color. Remove from the oven and cool the pan on a wire rack for 5 to 10 minutes before cutting the bread into squares. Serve with Flavored Mayonnaise of Choice.

# BLUE CORN–PEPPER BREAD

MAKES: *1 loaf*

## BASIC MAYONNAISE

MAKES: *About 2 cups*

**1 large egg**
**1 teaspoon salt**
**1 teaspoon dry mustard**
**2 tablespoons cider vinegar**
**1 tablespoon fresh lemon juice**
**1½ cups olive or salad oil**

In the container of a blender, combine the egg, salt, mustard, vinegar, and lemon juice. Cover and process on high for 1 to 2 seconds. With the motor running on slow speed, uncover and gradually add, in a narrow stream, the oil. Continue blending until the mix is very thick. Pour from the blender container to a bowl, cover and chill until ready to use.

## FLAVORED MAYONNAISE

MAKES: *About 2 cups*

To make a Flavored Mayonnaise, add one of the following to this Basic Mayonnaise:

**Anchovy Mayonnaise:** add 2 tablespoons anchovy paste.

Blueberry Mayonnaise: add 1 cup finely chopped, fresh, firm blueberries.

**Cheese-Flavored Mayonnaise:** add 3 ounces cream cheese and 2½ tablespoons Camembert cheese.

**Relish Mayonnaise:** add 2 tablespoons finely chopped red and green peppers, 1 tablespoon finely chopped olives and sweet pickles, and 1 tablespoon horseradish.

**Cranberry Mayonnaise:** add 1 cup finely minced fresh cranberries.

**Cranberry Mayonnaise Cream:** add 1 cup cranberry jelly and ¾ cup whipped cream.

**Garlic Mayonnaise:** add 1 cup garlic-flavored French-style dressing.

**Herb Mayonnaise:** add 1 tablespoon fresh snipped parsley, taragon, watercress, chives, and basil. Blend well.

**Lemon Cream Mayonnaise:** add ½ cup powdered sugar, ¼ cup fresh lemon juice, 1 cup whipped heavy cream.

**Pimiento Cheese Mayonnaise:** add 1 ounce pimiento cream cheese, 2 tablespoons bottled chili sauce, and ½ teaspoon Worcestershire Sauce.

**Seafood-Flavored Mayonnaise:** add 1 cup bottled chili sauce, 2 finely chopped hard cooked eggs, 2 minced sweet pickles, ½ cup finely chopped ripe olives, ¼ pound shredded crab, shrimp or lobster.

**Thousand Island Mayonnaise:** add ¼ cup bottled chili sauce, 2 tablespoons chopped pimiento-stuffed olives, 1 teaspoon finely chopped capers, 1 teaspon finely chopped chives.

2 cups all-purpose flour
1½ teaspoons baking powder
½ teaspoon baking soda
¼ cup finely chopped hazelnuts
¼ teaspoon salt
1 large egg
1 cup powdered sugar
2 tablespoons butter or margarine, at
    room temperature
¼ cup orange-juice concentrate,
    undiluted
¾ cup boiling water
2 tablespoons grated orange zest
1 cup blueberries
Fresh Blueberry Sauce (see recipe
    page 78)

**1** Position the rack in the center of the oven and preheat to 350 degrees F. Lightly grease and flour an 8½-by-4½-by-2½-inch loaf pan.

**2** In a large bowl, blend together the flour, baking powder, baking soda, hazelnuts, and salt. In a medium bowl, beat the egg until foamy before beating in the sugar, butter, orange juice, water, and orange zest. Stir in the blueberries. Combine the two mixtures, blending until the dry ingredients are just moistened.

**3** Scrape the batter into the prepared pan and bake for 55 to 60 minutes, or until a cake tester or wooden toothpick inserted into the center of the bread comes out clean and the top is golden. Remove from the oven and cool the pan on a wire rack for 5 to 10 minutes before removing the loaf from the pan. Serve with Fresh Blueberry Sauce.

# BLUEBERRY BREAD
MAKES: *1 loaf*

---

3 cups all-purpose flour
1 tablespoon baking powder
¾ cup granulated sugar
1 teaspoon grated lemon zest
½ cup finely chopped pecans or
    walnuts
1½ teaspoons salt
1 large egg
¼ cup melted butter or margarine
1 cup blueberries

**1** Position the rack in the center of the oven and preheat to 325 degrees F. Lightly grease and flour a 9¼-by-5¼-by-2¾-inch loaf pan.

**2** In a large bowl, blend together the flour, baking powder, sugar, lemon zest, walnuts, and salt. In

a medium bowl, beat the egg until foamy before beating in the butter. Stir in the blueberries. Combine the two mixtures, blending until the dry ingredients are just moistened.

**3** Scrape the batter into the prepared pan and bake for 60 to 65 minutes, or until a cake tester or wooden toothpick inserted into the center of the bread comes out clean and the top is golden. Remove from the oven and cool the pan on a wire rack for 5 to 10 minutes before removing the loaf from the pan.

# BLUEBERRY–
# WALNUT BREAD
MAKES: *1 loaf*

# BOSTON BRAN BREAD

*MAKES: 2 loaves*

1½ cups All-Bran™ cereal
1 cup sour milk or buttermilk
½ cup molasses
1½ cups all-purpose flour
¼ cup granulated sugar
1 teaspoon baking soda
½ cup plumped seedless raisins
⅓ cup chopped hazelnuts
½ teaspoon salt
Whipped Cream-Cheese Topping
  (see recipe page 186)

1 Position the rack in the center of the oven and preheat to 350 degrees F. Lightly grease and flour two 16-ounce food cans, opened at one end and well washed. (Alternatively, use an 8½-by-4½-by-2½-inch loaf pan.)

2 In a small bowl, combine the cereal, milk, and molasses and set aside for at least 5 minutes. In a large bowl, blend together the flour, sugar, baking soda, raisins, hazelnuts, and salt. Combine the two mixtures, blending until the dry ingredients are just moistened.

3 Scrape the batter into the prepared cans, set the cans on a tray, and bake for 40 to 45 minutes, or until a cake tester or wooden toothpick inserted deep into the loaf is removed clean. Remove the cans from the oven and cool on a wire rack to room temperature before handling. Allow to set in the refrigerator for at least 24 hours.

4 To remove the bread from the cans, use a can opener to remove the bottom of the can and carefully push the loaf out the other end. Slice and serve with Whipped Cream-Cheese Topping.

# BOSTON BROWN BREAD

*MAKES: 3 to 4 small loaves*

1 cup all-purpose flour
1 cup graham flour
1 cup cornmeal
1½ teaspoons baking soda
1 teaspoon salt
¾ cup molasses
2 cups sour milk or buttermilk, warmed
Whipped Cream-Cheese Topping
  (see recipe page 186)
Molasses Sauce (see recipe page 125)

1 Position the rack in the center of the oven and preheat to 350 degrees F. Lightly grease and flour four 5¾-by-3-by-2⅛-inch loaf pans.

2 In a large bowl, blend together the two flours, cornmeal, baking soda, and salt. In a medium bowl, blend the molasses and warmed sour milk until smooth. Combine the two mixtures, blending until the dry ingredients are just moistened.

3 Scrape the batter into the prepared baking pans and bake for 40 to 45 minutes, or until a cake tester or wooden toothpick inserted into the center of the bread comes out clean and the tops are golden. Remove from the oven and cool the pans on a wire rack for 5 to 10 minutes before removing the loaves from the pans. Drizzle with Molasses Sauce and serve with Whipped Cream-Cheese Topping.

1 cup oat bran cereal
1 cup pitted dates, chopped
⅔ cup hot water
1½ cups all-purpose flour
1 tablespoon baking soda
⅔ cup granulated sugar
1 teaspoon ground cinnamon
½ cup finely chopped walnuts or pecans
1 teaspoon salt
2 large eggs
2 tablespoons melted butter or margarine
Fig Sauce (see recipe page 189)

**1** Position the rack in the center of the oven and preheat to 350 degrees F. Lightly grease and flour an 8½-by-4½-by-2½-inch loaf pan.

**2** In a small bowl, combine the bran, dates, and hot water. In a large bowl, blend together the flour, baking soda, sugar, cinnamon, walnuts, and salt. In a medium bowl, beat the eggs and butter until smooth before stirring in the bran mixture. Pour this mixture into the dry ingredients and blend until the dry ingredients are well moistened.

**3** Scrape the batter into the prepared pan and bake for 45 to 50 minutes, or a cake tester or wooden toothpick inserted into the center of the bread comes out clean and the top is golden. Remove from the oven and cool the pan on a wire rack for 5 to 10 minutes before removing the loaf from the pan. Serve with Fig Sauce.

## BRAN-AND-DATE BREAD

MAKES: *1 loaf*

---

2 cups all-purpose flour
1 cup rolled oats
1 teaspoon bran
1 tablespoon baking powder
2 teaspoons ground cinnamon
⅛ teaspoon ground nutmeg
2 medium apples, peeled, cored, and finely chopped
⅓ cup seedless raisins
¼ teaspoon salt
2 large egg whites
⅓ cup honey, at room temperature
½ cup melted butter or margarine
½ cup plus 1 teaspoon skim milk

**1** Position the rack in the center of the oven and preheat to 350 degrees F. Lightly grease and flour a 9¼-by-5¼-by-2¾-inch loaf pan.

**2** In a large bowl, blend together the flour, oats, bran, baking powder, cinnamon, nutmeg, apples, raisins, and salt. In a medium bowl, beat the egg whites until stiff but not dry. Stir in the honey, butter, and milk until smooth. Combine the two mixtures, blending until the dry ingredients are just moistened.

**3** Scrape the batter into the prepared pan and bake for 55 to 60 minutes, or until a cake tester or wooden toothpick inserted into the center of the bread comes out clean and the top is golden brown. Remove the pan from the oven and cool on a wire rack for 5 to 10 minutes before removing the loaf from the pan.

## BRAN–APPLE NUT BREAD

MAKES: *1 loaf*

## BRAN–BANANA–NUT BREAD

MAKES: *1 loaf*

1 cup All-Bran™ cereal
½ cup buttermilk or sour milk
1½ cups all-purpose flour
2 teaspoons baking powder
½ teaspoon baking soda
½ cup chopped walnuts
½ teaspoon salt
¼ cup butter or margarine, at room temperature
½ cup granulated sugar
1 large egg
1 teaspoon vanilla extract
5 medium bananas, mashed
Powdered sugar for sprinkling
Banana Cream (see recipe page 56)

1 Position the rack in the center of the oven and preheat to 350 degrees F. Lightly grease and flour an 8½-by-4½-by-2½-inch loaf pan.

2 In a small bowl, combine the cereal and buttermilk. In a large bowl, blend together the flour, baking powder, baking soda, walnuts, and salt. In a medium bowl, beat the butter and sugar until light and fluffy. Beat in the egg, vanilla extract, and bananas. Stir in the cereal and buttermilk. Combine the wet and dry mixtures, blending until the dry ingredients are just moistened.

3 Scrape the batter into the prepared pan and bake for 45 to 50 minutes, or until a cake tester or wooden toothpick inserted into the middle of the bread is removed clean and the top is golden. Remove from the oven and cool the pan on a wire rack for 5 to 10 minutes before removing the loaf from the pan. Sprinkle the top of the loaf with powdered sugar. Serve with Banana Cream.

## BRAZIL NUT–APRICOT BREAD

MAKES: *1 loaf*

2 cups all-purpose flour
1 cup granulated sugar
1 tablespoon baking powder
¼ teaspoon baking soda
1 cup finely chopped Brazil nuts
½ cup chopped dried apricots
¾ teaspoon salt
1 large egg
2 tablespoons melted butter or margarine
¾ cup fresh-squeezed orange juice
Orange Glaze (see recipe page 67)

1 Position the rack in the center of the oven and preheat to 350 degrees F. Lightly grease and flour an 8¼-by-4½-by-2½-inch loaf pan.

2 In a large bowl, blend together the flour, sugar, baking powder, baking soda, nuts, apricots, and salt. In a small bowl, beat the egg, butter, and orange juice until smooth. Combine the two mixtures, blending until the dry ingredients are just moistened.

3 Scrape the batter into prepared pan and bake for 45 to 50 minutes, or until a cake tester or wooden toothpick inserted into the center of the bread comes out clean and the top is golden. Remove from the oven and cool the pan on a wire rack for 5 to 10 minutes before removing the loaf from the pan. Brush the top of the loaf with the Orange Glaze.

1 box corn muffin mix
1 cup grated cheese
½ cup chopped onion
1 box frozen chopped broccoli,
 cooked according to package
 directions and drained
4 large eggs
½ cup melted butter or margarine
Flavored Mayonnaise of Choice (see
 recipe page 324)

**1** Position the rack in the center of the oven and preheat to 425 degrees F. Lightly grease and flour a 9-inch square baking pan.
**2** In a large bowl, blend together the muffin mix, cheese, onion, and broccoli. In a medium bowl, beat the eggs until foamy before beating in the butter. Combine the two mixtures, blending until the dry ingredients are just moistened.

**3** Scrape the batter into the prepared pan and bake for 18 to 20 minutes, or until the top is a lemon-yellow color and a cake tester or wooden toothpick inserted into the bread is removed clean. Remove from the oven and cool the pan on a wire rack for 3 to 5 minutes before cutting into squares and serving warm. Serve with Flavored Mayonnaise of Choice.

# BROCCOLI BREAD
MAKES: *1 loaf*

1½ cups all-purpose flour
1½ cups rye flour
1 cup yellow cornmeal
1 teaspoon baking soda
½ cup chopped pecans
½ cup seedless raisins
1 teaspoon salt
2 cups buttermilk or sour milk
½ cup molasses
Berrry Sauce (see recipe page 38)

**1** Position the rack in the center of the oven and preheat to 375 degrees F. Lightly grease and flour a 9¼-by-5¼-by-2¾-inch loaf pan.
**2** In a large bowl, blend together the two flours, cornmeal, baking soda, pecans, raisins, and salt. In a medium bowl, beat the buttermilk and molasses until smooth. Combine the two mixtures, blending until the dry ingredients are just moistened.

**3** Scrape the batter into the prepared pan and bake for 50 to 55 minutes, or until a cake tester or wooden toothpick inserted into the center of the bread comes out clean and the top is golden. Remove from the oven and cool the pan on a wire rack for 5 to 10 minutes before removing the loaf from the pan. When at room temperature, wrap in plastic wrap and hold for one day before serving. Serve with Berry Sauce.

# BROWN BREAD
MAKES: *1 loaf*

## BUTTERMILK CORN BREAD

MAKES: *1 loaf*

1 cup all-purpose flour
¾ cup blue cornmeal
1 teaspoon baking soda
3 tablespoons granulated sugar
½ teaspoon salt
1 large egg
1 cup buttermilk or sour milk
2 tablespoons melted butter or
  margarine
Cheese Spread (see recipe page 257)

1 Position the rack in the center of the oven and preheat to 400 degrees F. Lightly grease and flour the bottom of a 9-inch square baking pan.

2 In a large bowl, blend together the flour, cornmeal, baking soda, sugar, and salt. In a medium bowl, blend the milk, egg, and butter until smooth. Combine the two mixtures, blending until the dry ingredients are just moistened.

3 Scrape the batter into the prepared pan and bake for 20 to 25 minutes, or until a cake tester or wooden toothpick inserted into the center of the bread comes out clean and the top is golden. Remove from the oven and cool in the pan on a wire rack for 5 to 10 minutes before cutting into squares. Serve with Cheese Spread.

## BUTTERNUT SQUASH- AND-RAISIN BREAD

MAKES: *2 loaves*

3 cups all-purpose flour
½ cup graham flour
1 cup granulated sugar
1 cup packed light-brown sugar
2 teaspoons baking soda
1 cup raisins
1 teaspoon ground nutmeg
1 teaspoon ground cinnamon
1 teaspoon salt
4 large eggs
1 cup canola oil
½ cup honey
1 cup white port wine
1½ cups cooked butternut squash,
  mashed
Dieter's Butter (see recipe page 63)

1 Position the rack in the center of the oven and preheat to 350 degrees F. Lightly grease and flour two 8½-by-3½-by-2½-inch loaf pans.

2 In a large bowl, blend together the two flours, two sugars, baking soda, raisins, nutmeg, cinnamon, and salt. In a medium bowl, beat the eggs until foamy before beating in the oil, honey, wine, and squash. Combine the two mixtures, blending until the dry ingredients are moistened.

3 Scrape the batter into the prepared pans and bake for 45 to 50 minutes, or until a cake tester or wooden toothpick inserted into the center of the bread comes out clean and the tops are golden. Remove from the oven and cool the pans on a wire rack for 5 to 10 minutes before removing the loaves from the pans. Serve with Dieter's Butter.

2 cups all-purpose flour
1 cup packed light-brown sugar
1 teaspoon baking powder
½ teaspoon baking soda
½ cup chopped hazelnuts
¼ teaspoon salt
1½ tablespoons melted butter or
   margarine
1 cup buttermilk or sour milk
1 large egg
Dutch-Style Hard Sauce (see recipe
   page 154)

**1** Position the rack in the center of the oven and preheat to 350 degrees F. Lightly grease and flour a 9¼-by-5¼-by-2¾-inch loaf pan.

**2** In a large bowl, blend together the flour, brown sugar, baking powder, baking soda, hazelnuts, and salt. In a medium bowl, beat the butter, buttermilk, and egg until smooth. Combine the two mixtures, blending until the dry ingredients are moistened.

**3** Scrape the batter into the prepared pan and bake for 55 to 60 minutes, or until a cake tester or wooden toothpick inserted into the center of the bread comes out clean and the top is golden. Remove from the oven and cool the pan on a wire rack for 5 to 10 minutes before removing the loaf from the pan. Serve wih Dutch-Style Hard Sauce.

# BUTTERSCOTCH–HAZELNUT BREAD

MAKES: *1 loaf*

---

1⅓ cups all-purpose flour
2 cups whole-wheat flour
1 cup granulated sugar
1 tablespoon baking powder
1 teaspoon baking soda
¼ cup crushed hard candy
1 teaspoon salt
2 large eggs
½ cup packed light-brown sugar
1¼ cups milk, at room temperature
½ cup light corn syrup, slightly
   warmed
Chocolate Sauce (see recipe page 26)

**1** Position the rack in the center of the oven and preheat to 350 degrees F. Lightly grease and flour a 9¼-by-5¼-by-2¾-inch loaf pan.

**2** In a large bowl, blend together the two flours, granulated sugar, baking powder, baking soda, candy, and salt. In a medium bowl, beat the eggs, brown sugar, milk, and corn syrup together until smooth. Combine the two mixtures, blending until the dry ingredients are moistened.

**3** Scrape the batter into the prepared pan and bake for 55 to 60 minutes, or until a cake tester or wooden toothpick inserted into the center of the cake comes out clean and the top is golden. Remove from the oven and place the pan on a wire rack to cool for 5 to 10 minutes before removing the loaf from the pan. Serve with Chocolate Sauce.

# CANDY BREAD

MAKES: *1 loaf*

# CAPPUCCINO BREAD

MAKES: *1 loaf*

½ teaspoon ground cinnamon
¾ cup plus 1 tablespoon granulated sugar
2 cups all-purpose flour
2½ teaspoons baking powder
¾ cup grated semisweet chocolate
2 teaspoons instant espresso coffee powder
1 large egg
½ cup melted butter or margarine
1 cup scalded milk
1 teaspoon chocolate extract

**1** Position the rack in the center of the oven and preheat to 350 degrees F. Lightly grease and flour a 9¼-by-5¼-by-2¾-inch loaf pan.

**2** In a cup, blend together the cinnamon and 1 tablespoon of the sugar. Set aside.

**3** In a large bowl, blend together the remaining ½ cup sugar, the flour, baking powder, chocolate, and coffee powder. In a medium bowl, beat the egg until foamy before beating in the milk and chocolate extract. Combine the two mixtures, blending until the dry ingredients are moistened.

**4** Scrape the batter into the prepared pan and sprinkle the cinnamon-sugar mixture over the top of the batter. Bake for 45 to 50 minutes, or until a cake tester or wooden toothpick inserted into the center of the bread comes out clean and the top is golden. Remove from the oven and cool the pan on a wire rack for 5 to 10 minutes before removing the loaf from the pan.

# CARAWAY–BEER BREAD

MAKES: *1 loaf*

2 cups whole-wheat flour
1 cup all-purpose flour
1 cup granulated sugar
4 teaspoons baking powder
1 teaspoon baking soda
3 tablespoons caraway seeds
1 teaspoon salt
2 large eggs
½ cup packed light-brown sugar
1¼ cups beer, at room temperature
½ cup maple syrup, slightly warmed

**1** Position the rack in the center of the oven and preheat to 350 degrees F. Lightly grease and flour a 9¼-by-5¼-by-2¾-inch loaf pan.

**2** In a large bowl, blend together the two flours, granulated sugar, baking powder, baking soda, seeds, and salt. In a small bowl, beat the eggs, brown sugar, beer, and maple syrup until smooth. Combine the two mixtures, blending until the dry ingredients are moistened.

**3** Scrape the batter into the prepared pan and bake for 55 to 60 minutes, or until a cake tester or wooden toothpick inserted into the center of the bread comes out clean and the top is golden. Remove from the oven and cool the pan on a wire rack for 5 to 10 minutes before removing the loaf from the pan.

**SERVING SUGGESTION: Serve with a cold beer and thinly sliced cheese of choice.**

## CARDAMOM–HONEY BREAD

MAKES: *1 loaf*

1 cup all-purpose flour
1 cup whole-wheat flour
2½ cups oat or wheat bran
2 teaspoons baking powder
1 teaspoon baking soda
1 teaspoon ground cardamom
¼ teaspoon salt
4 large eggs
½ cup warmed honey
½ cup canola oil
¼ teaspoon vanilla extract
2 cups unsweetened applesauce
Honey Glaze (see recipe page 53)

**1** Position the rack in the center of the oven and preheat to 350 degrees F. Lightly grease and flour a 9¼-by-5¼-by-2¾-inch loaf pan.

**2** In a large bowl, blend together the two flours, bran, baking powder, baking soda, salt, and cardamom. In a medium bowl, beat the eggs until foamy before beating in the honey, oil, and vanilla extract. Stir in the applesauce. Combine the two mixtures, blending until the dry ingredients are moistened.

**3** Scrape the batter into the prepared pan and bake for 55 to 60 minutes, or until a cake tester or wooden toothpick inserted into the center of the bread comes out clean and the top is golden. Remove the pan from the oven and cool on a wire rack for 5 to 10 minutes before removing the loaf from the pan. Serve with Honey Glaze.

## CARROT, ALMOND, AND RAISIN BREAD

MAKES: *1 loaf*

2 cups all-purpose flour
¼ cup graham flour
1¼ teaspoons baking soda
1 cup granulated sugar
½ cup packed light-brown sugar
1½ teaspoons ground cinnamon
1½ teaspoons ground nutmeg
1¼ cups finely chopped almonds
1¼ cups golden raisins
2¼ cups grated carrots
½ teaspoon salt
3 large eggs
1 cup canola oil
1 teaspoon almond extract
Carrot Butter (see recipe page 64)

**1** Position the rack in the center of the oven and preheat to 350 degrees F. Lightly grease and flour a 9¼-by-5¼-by-2¾-inch loaf pan.

**2** In a large bowl, blend together the two flours, baking soda, two sugars, cinnamon, nutmeg, almonds, raisins, carrots, and salt. In a medium bowl, beat the eggs until foamy before beating in the oil and extract. Combine the two mixtures, blending until the dry ingredients are moistened.

**3** Scrape the batter into the prepared pan and bake for 55 to 60 minutes, or until a cake tester or wooden toothpick inserted into the bread comes out clean and the top is golden. Remove from the oven and cool the pan on a wire rack for 5 to 10 minutes before removing the loaf from the pan. Serve with Carrot Butter.

## CARROT BREAD

MAKES: *1 loaf*

1½ cups all-purpose flour
1 teaspoon baking powder
1 teaspoon baking soda
1 teaspoon ground cinnamon
½ cup raisins
½ cup chopped almonds
1 cup grated carrots
½ teaspoon salt
2 large eggs
1 cup packed light-brown sugar
¾ cup canola oil
Molasses Sauce (see recipe page 125)

1  Position the rack in the center of the oven and preheat to 375 degrees F. Lightly grease and flour an 8½-by-4½-by-2½-inch loaf pan.

2  In a large bowl, blend together the flour, baking powder, baking soda, cinnamon, raisins, almonds, carrots, and salt. In a medium bowl, beat the eggs until foamy before beating in the sugar and oil. Combine the two mixtures, blending until the dry ingredients are moistened.

3  Scrape the batter into the prepared pan and bake for 45 to 50 minutes, or until a cake tester or wooden toothpick inserted into the center of the bread comes out clean and the top is golden. Remove from the oven and cool the pan on a wire rack for 5 to 10 minutes before removing the loaf from the pan. Serve with Molasses Sauce.

## CHEDDAR SPOON BREAD

MAKES: *1 loaf*

4 large eggs, separated
2 cups milk
1 cup cornmeal
2 cups (8 ounces) Kraft® sharp
    Cheddar cheese, grated
½ cup margarine
1 teaspoon salt
Pinch ground cayenne
Cheese Sauce (see recipe page 57)

1  Position the rack in the center of the oven and preheat to 375 degrees F. Lightly grease and flour a 2-quart casserole dish.

2  In a medium bowl, beat the egg whites until stiff but not dry. Set aside. In a medium saucepan set over medium heat, heat the milk until bubbles start to form around the edges. Add the cornmeal and cook, stirring constantly, until the mixture is very thick and smooth. Remove from the heat and quickly stir in the cheese, margarine, salt, and cayenne, stirring until smooth. Stir in egg yolks. Fold in the egg whites.

3  Pour the mixture into the prepared baking dish and bake for 35 to 40 minutes, or until the top is golden brown. Remove the casserole from the oven and serve immediately. Serve with Cheese Sauce.

2 cups sifted all-purpose flour
1 tablespoon granulated sugar
2 teaspoons baking powder
1 cup grated sharp Cheddar cheese
1½ teaspoons dried dill weed
½ teaspoon salt
1 large egg
¼ cup melted butter or margarine
1 grated onion
¾ cup milk or light cream
Whipped Cream Topping (see recipe
     page 208)

1  Position the rack in the center
of the oven and preheat to 350
degrees F. Lightly grease and
flour an 8½-by-4½-by-2½-inch
loaf pan.

2  In a large bowl, blend together
the flour, sugar, baking powder,
cheese, dill, and salt. In a medium bowl, beat the egg until
foamy before beating in the butter, onion, and milk. Combine the
two mixtures, blending until the
dry ingredients are moistened.

3  Scrape the batter into the prepared pan and bake for 45 to 50
minutes, or until a cake tester or
wooden toothpick inserted into
the center of the bread comes out
clean and the top is golden.
Remove from the oven and cool
the pan on a wire rack for 5 to 10
minutes before removing the loaf
from the pan. Serve with
Whipped Cream Topping.

## CHEESE BREAD

MAKES: *1 loaf*

2 cups Bisquick® baking mix
1 teaspoon baking powder
½ teaspoon baking soda
½ cup crumbled crisply cooked
     bacon
1 large egg
¾ cup sour milk
6 ounces Swiss cheese, cut into ½-
     inch cubes
Chicken Spread (see recipe page
     188)

1  Position the rack in the center
of the oven and preheat to 375
degrees F. Lightly grease and
flour an 8½-by-4½-by-2½-inch
loaf pan.

2  In a large bowl, blend together
the baking mix, baking powder,
baking soda, and bacon. In a

medium bowl, beat the egg until
foamy before beating in the milk.
Combine the two mixtures,
blending until the dry ingredients are moistened.

3  Spread ½ of the batter into the
prepared baking pan and dot
with the Swiss cheese. Spread the
remaining batter evenly over the
top of the cheese. Bake for 40 to
45 minutes, or until a cake tester
or wooden toothpick inserted
along the edge of the pan (not
into the cheese) comes out clean
and the top is golden. Remove
from the oven and cool on a wire
rack for 5 to 10 minutes before
removing the loaf from the pan.
Serve with Chicken Spread.

## CHEESE-AND-BACON-FILLED BREAD

MAKES: *1 loaf*

# CHERRY–BRAN BREAD

MAKES: *1 loaf*

2 cups all-purpose flour
1 tablespoon bran
2 teaspoons baking powder
½ teaspoon salt
2 large eggs
3 tablespoons granulated sugar
½ cup milk
½ cup melted vegetable shortening
1 cup stemmed, pitted, and chopped cherries

1 Position the rack in the center of the oven and preheat to 350 degrees F. Lightly grease and flour a 9-inch square baking pan.

2 In a large bowl, blend together the flour, bran, baking powder, and salt. In a medium bowl, beat the eggs and sugar until foamy before beating in the milk, shortening, and cherries. Combine the two mixtures, blending until the dry ingredients are thoroughly moistened.

3 Scrape the batter into the prepared baking pan and bake for 45 to 50 minutes, or until a cake tester or wooden toothpick inserted into the center of the bread comes out clean and the top is golden brown. Remove from the oven and cool the pan on a wire rack for 5 to 10 minutes before cutting the bread into squares and serving.

# CHERRY BREAD

MAKES: *2 small loaves*

1½ cups all-purpose flour
2 teaspoons baking powder
½ cup granulated sugar
½ cup finely chopped candied red cherries
¼ teaspoon salt
2 large eggs
3 tablespoons melted butter or margarine
1 cup Peter Herring liqueur or cherry-flavored brandy
Whipped Cream Topping (see recipe page 208)

1 Position the rack in the center of the oven and preheat to 350 degrees F. Lightly grease and flour two 5¾-by-3-by-2⅛-inch loaf pans.

2 In a large bowl, blend together the flour, baking powder, sugar, cherries, and salt. In a medium bowl, beat the eggs until foamy before beating in the butter and liqueur. Combine the two mixtures, blending until the dry ingredients are moistened.

3 Scrape the batter into the prepared pans and bake for 20 to 25 minutes, or until a cake tester or wooden toothpick inserted into the center of the bread comes out clean and the tops are golden. Remove from the oven and cool the pans on a wire rack for 5 to 10 minutes before removing the loaves from the pans.

2 cups all-purpose flour
½ cup graham flour
½ cup granulated sugar
1 tablespoon baking powder
1½ cups shredded mild cheese
1 teaspoon salt
1 large egg
½ cup packed light-brown sugar
1¼ cups milk
1¼ cups frozen pitted sweet
    cherries, thawed, drained, and
    halved
3 tablespoons melted butter or
    margarine
Cherry Sauce (see recipe page 52)

**1** Position the rack in the center of the oven and preheat to 350 degrees F. Lightly grease and flour a 9¼-by-5¼-by-2¾-inch loaf pan.

**2** In a large bowl, blend together the two flours, granulated sugar, baking powder, cheese, and salt. In a medium bowl, beat the egg until foamy before beating in the brown sugar and milk. Stir in the cherries. Combine the two mixtures, blending until the dry ingredients are moistened.

**3** Scrape the batter into the prepared pan, brush top with melted butter or margarine, and bake for 55 to 60 minutes, or until a cake tester or wooden toothpick inserted into the center of the bread comes out clean and the top is golden. Remove from the oven and cool the pan on a wire rack for 5 to 10 minutes before removing the loaf from the pan. Brush the bread with Cherry Sauce.

# CHERRY–CHEESE BREAD

MAKES: *1 loaf*

---

¼ cup cherry-flavored brandy or
    liqueur
1 cup diced dried cherries
1 cup all-purpose flour
½ cup whole-wheat flour
1 cup oat bran
½ cup wheat germ
1 teaspoon baking soda
1 cup chopped almonds
½ teaspoon salt
¼ cup butter or margarine, at room
    temperature
½ cup granulated sugar
1 large egg
1 cup buttermilk
Brazil Nut Cream Sauce (see recipe
    page 70)

**1** Thirty minutes before baking, in a small bowl, combine the brandy and diced cherries. Cover with plastic wrap and set in a warm place.

**2** Position the rack in the center of the oven and preheat to 350 degrees F. Lightly grease and flour three 5¾-by-3-by-2½-inch loaf pans.

**3** In a large bowl, blend together the two flours, oat bran, wheat germ, baking soda, almonds, and salt. In a medium bowl, beat the butter and sugar together until light and fluffy. Beat in the egg and buttermilk. Stir in the cherries and brandy. Combine the two mixtures, blending until the dry ingredients are just moistened.

**4** Scrape the batter into the prepared pans and bake for 40 to 45 minutes, or until a cake tester or wooden toothpick inserted into the center of the bread comes out clean and the tops are golden. Remove from the oven and cool the pans on a wire rack for 5 to 10 minutes before removing the loaves from the pans. Serve with Brazil Nut Cream Sauce.

# CHERRY–NUT BREAD

MAKES: *3 small loaves*

## CHILI–CHEESE BREAD

MAKES: *1 loaf*

2 cups Bisquick® baking mix
½ teaspoon baking powder
1 cup grated sharp Cheddar cheese
1 teaspoon Spice Island® Chili Con Carne Seasoning
½ teaspoon crushed dried oregano
2 teaspoons crushed dried chervil
1 large egg
¾ cup milk
Chili–Tomato Sauce (see recipe page 116)

**1** Position the rack in the center of the oven and preheat to 350 degrees F. Lightly grease and flour an 8½-by-4½-by-2½-inch loaf pan.

**2** In a large bowl, blend together the baking mix, baking powder, cheese, seasoning, oregano, and chervil. In a small bowl, beat the egg until foamy before beating in the milk. Combine the two mixtures, blending until the dry ingredients are just moistened.

**3** Scrape the batter into the prepared pan and bake for 40 to 45 minutes, or until a cake tester or wooden toothpick inserted into the center of the bread comes out clean and the top is golden. Remove from the oven and cool the pan on a wire rack for 5 to 10 minutes before removing the loaf from the pan. Serve with Chili–Tomato Sauce.

## CHOCOLATE BANANA BREAD

MAKES: *1 loaf*

½ cup all-purpose flour
¾ cup whole-wheat flour
½ cup rolled oats, processed to a powder in a food processor
1¼ teaspoons baking powder
½ teaspoon baking soda
½ cup Dutch-processed cocoa powder
½ teaspoon salt
⅔ cup granulated sugar
⅓ cup butter or margarine, at room temperature
2 large eggs
2 tablespoons heavy cream or milk
1 teaspoon chocolate or vanilla extract
1 cup mashed ripe bananas
Banana Cream (see recipe page 56)

**1** Position the rack in the center of the oven and preheat to 350 degrees F. Lightly grease and flour an 8½-by-4½-by-2½-inch loaf pan.

**2** In a large bowl, blend the two flours, oats, baking powder, baking soda, cocoa powder, and salt. In a medium bowl, beat the sugar and butter together until light and fluffy. Beat in the eggs, one at a time, beating vigorously after each addition. Beat in the cream, chocolate extract, and bananas. Combine the two mixtures, blending until the dry ingredients are moistened.

**3** Scrape the batter into the prepared pan and bake for 40 to 45 minutes, or until a cake tester or wooden toothpick inserted into the center of the bread comes out clean and the top is golden. Remove from the oven and cool the pan on a wire rack for 5 to 10 minutes before removing the loaf from the pan. Serve with Banana Cream.

½ cup chopped hazelnuts
1¾ cups all-purpose flour
1¼ teaspoons cream of tartar
¾ teaspoon baking soda
¾ cup granulated sugar
½ teaspoon ground allspice
½ cup semisweet chocolate chips
2 large eggs
½ cup canola oil
½ teaspoon vanilla extract
2 medium bananas, mashed
Chocolate–Honey Sauce (see recipe
    page 30)

**1** Position the rack in the center of the oven and preheat to 350 degrees F. Lightly brush oil into the bottom of an 8½-by-4½-by-2½-inch loaf pan and sprinkle the hazelnuts across the bottom. Set aside.

**2** In a large bowl, blend together the flour, cream of tartar, baking soda, sugar, allspice, and chocolate chips. In a medium bowl, beat the eggs, oil, vanilla extract, and bananas until smooth. Combine the two mixtures, blending until the dry ingredients are moistened.

**3** Scrape the batter into the prepared pan and bake for 30 to 35 minutes, or until a cake tester or wooden toothpick inserted into the center of the bread comes out clean and the top is golden. Remove from the oven and cool the pan on a wire rack for 5 to 10 minutes before removing the loaf from the pan. Serve with Chocolate–Honey Sauce.

# CHOCOLATE CHIP–BANANA BREAD

MAKES: *1 loaf*

---

3 cups Bisquick® baking mix
½ cup granulated sugar
5 ounces (5 squares) semisweet
    chocolate, grated
½ cup finely chopped hazelnuts
1 large egg
¾ cup evaporated milk
½ cup crème de cacao
¼ cup honey, slightly warmed
Chocolate Sauce (see recipe page 26)

**1** Position the rack in the center of the oven and preheat to 350 degrees F. Lightly grease and flour a 9¼-by-5¼-by-2¾-inch loaf pan.

**2** In a large bowl, blend together the baking mix, sugar, chocolate, and nuts. In a medium bowl, beat the egg until foamy before beating in the milk, crème de cacao, and honey. Combine the two mixtures, blending until the dry ingredients are well moistened.

**3** Scrape the batter into the prepared pan and bake for 45 to 50 minutes, or until a cake tester or wooden toothpick inserted into the center of the bread comes out clean and the top is golden. Remove from the oven and cool the pan on a wire rack for 5 to 10 minutes before removing the loaf from the pan. Cool the bread completely on the rack before spreading the whipped cream over the top. Serve with Chocolate Sauce.

# CHOCOLATE NUT BREAD

MAKES: *1 loaf*

# CHOCOLATE–NUT TEA BREAD

MAKES: *1 loaf*

2 cups all-purpose flour
1 teaspoon baking soda
½ cup chopped hazelnuts
¼ cup chopped pecans
2 ounces (2 squares) unsweetened chocolate, grated
½ teaspoon salt
¼ cup butter-flavored vegetable shortening
1 cup granulated sugar
1 large egg
1 cup double-strength brewed coffee
1½ teaspoons coffee- or hazelnut-flavored brandy
Crushed chocolate wafer cookies for sprinkling
Chocolate Sauce (see recipe page 26)

1  Position the rack in the center of the oven and preheat to 350 degrees F. Lightly grease and flour a 9¼-by-5¼-by-2¾-inch loaf pan.

2  In a large bowl, blend together the flour, baking soda, hazelnuts, pecans, chocolate, and salt. In a medium bowl, beat the shortening and sugar until fluffy before beating in the egg, coffee, and brandy. Combine the two mixtures, blending until the dry ingredients are well moistened.

3  Scrape the batter into the prepared pan and bake for 55 to 60 minutes, or until a cake tester or wooden toothpick inserted into the center of the bread comes out clean and the top is golden. Remove from the oven and cool the pan on a wire rack for 5 to 10 minutes before removing the loaf from the pan. Immediately brush the top of the warm bread with the Chocolate Sauce and sprinkle with crushed chocolate wafers.

# CHOCOLATE, PECAN, AND DATE LOAF

MAKES: *2 small loaves*

1½ cups all-purpose flour
1 teaspoon baking powder
1 teaspoon baking soda
¼ cup Dutch-processed cocoa powder
2 teaspoons ground cinnamon
1 teaspoon ground nutmeg
¼ teaspoon ground cloves
1 cup (6 ounces) mint-flavored semisweet chocolate chips
½ cup pitted dates, finely chopped
½ cup finely ground pecans
¼ cup butter or margarine, at room temperature
1 cup granulated sugar
2 large eggs
1 cup sour milk or buttermilk
Fresh mint leaves for garnish
Date Sauce (see recipe page 136)

1  Position the rack in the center of the oven and preheat to 350 degrees F. Lightly grease and flour the bottom of two 5¾-by-3-by-2-inch loaf pans.

2  In a large bowl, blend together the flour, baking powder, baking soda, cocoa powder, cinnamon, nutmeg, cloves, chocolate chips, dates, and pecans. In a medium bowl, beat the butter and sugar together until light and fluffy; beating in the eggs, one at a time, beating vigorously after each addition. Beat in the sour milk. Combine the two mixtures, blending until the dry ingredients are well moistened.

3  Scrape the batter into the prepared pans and bake for 45 to 50 minutes, or until a cake tester or wooden toothpick inserted into the center of the bread comes out clean and the tops are golden. Remove from the oven and cool the pans on a wire rack for 5 to 10 minutes before removing the loaves from the pans. Serve with Date Sauce.

1½ cups all-purpose flour
1½ teaspoons baking powder
½ teaspoon baking soda
½ cup Dutch-processed cocoa
  powder
2 teaspoons ground cinnamon
1 teaspoon ground nutmeg
½ teaspoon ground allspice
1 cup (6 ounces) chocolate candy bar
  sprinkles
½ cup pitted dates, finely chopped
½ cup coarsely chopped pecans
½ cup butter or margarine, at room
  temperature
1 cup granulated sugar
2 large eggs
1 cup sour milk or buttermilk
Cherry Sauce (see recipe page 52)

**1** Position the rack in the center of the oven and preheat to 350 degrees F. Lightly grease and flour an 8½-by-4½-by-2½-inch loaf pan.

**2** In a large bowl, blend together the flour, baking powder, baking soda, cocoa powder, cinnamon, nutmeg, allspice, sprinkles, dates, and pecans. In a medium bowl, beat the butter and sugar together until light and fluffy before beating in the eggs, one at a time, beating vigorously after each addition. Beat in the sour milk. Combine the two mixtures, blending until the dry ingredients are just moistened.

**3** Scrape the batter into the prepared pan and bake for 45 to 50 minutes, or until a cake tester or wooden toothpick inserted into the center of the bread comes out clean and the top is dry-looking and a deep chocolate color. Remove from the oven and cool the pan on a wire rack for 5 to 10 minutes before removing the loaf from the pan. Brush the loaf with Cherry Sauce.

# CHOCOLATE PUMPKIN BREAD

MAKES: *1 loaf*

---

2 cups all-purpose flour
2 teaspoons baking powder
¼ teaspoon baking soda
¼ teaspoon salt
2 teaspoons ground cinnamon
1 teaspoon ground ginger
1½ ounces unsweetened chocolate,
  grated
⅓ cup vegetable shortening
2 large eggs
¼ cup granulated sugar
¼ cup packed light-brown sugar
¼ cup dark molasses
½ cup milk

**1** Position the rack in the center of the oven and preheat to 350 degrees F. Lightly grease a 13-by-9-inch baking pan.

**2** In a large bowl, blend together the flour, baking powder, baking soda, salt, and spices. In the top of a double boiler set over simmering water, melt the chocolate and shortening, stirring until smooth. Remove from the heat and beat in the eggs, one at a time, beating vigorously after each addition. Beat in the sugars, molasses, and milk. Combine the two mixtures, blending until the dry ingredients are moistened.

**3** Spoon the batter into the prepared baking pan. Bake for 20 to 25 minutes, or until a cake tester or wooden toothpick inserted into the cake comes out clean. Remove the pan from the oven and cool on a wire rack for 5 to 7 minutes. Sprinkle with powdered sugar and serve warm or cooled.

# CHOCOLATE TEA BREAD

MAKES: *6 to 8 servings*

# CHOCOLATE ZUCCHINI BREAD

MAKES: *1 loaf*

3 cups all-purpose flour
1 teaspoon baking soda
¼ teaspoon baking powder
½ teaspoon salt
2 cups granulated sugar
1 teaspoon ground cinnamon
2 cups grated zucchini
1 cup finely chopped almonds
3 large eggs
1 cup vegetable oil
2 squares baking chocolate, melted
1 teaspoon vanilla extract
Fresh Cucumber Sauce (see recipe below)

1  Position the rack in the center of the oven and preheat to 350 degrees F. Lightly grease and flour one 9¼-by-5¼-by-2¾-inch loaf pan.

2  In a large bowl, blend together the flour, baking soda, baking powder, sugar, cinnamon, zucchini, almonds, and salt. In a medium bowl, beat the eggs, oil, chocolate, and vanilla extract until smooth. Combine the two mixtures, blending until the dry ingredients are well moistened.

3  Scrape the batter into the prepared pan and bake for 55 to 60 minutes, or until a cake tester or wooden toothpick inserted into the center of the bread comes out clean and the top is a deep golden color. Remove from the oven and cool the pan on a wire rack for 5 to 10 minutes before removing the loaf from the pans. Serve with Fresh Cucumber Sauce.

# FRESH CUCUMBER SAUCE

MAKES: *About 2 cups*

2 large fresh cucumbers, peeled and finely chopped
1 large white onion, peeled and finely chopped
2 stalks celery, finely chopped
½ cup chicken stock
1 tablespoon fresh lemon juice
2 tablespoons butter or margarine
1 tablespoon finely chopped parsley

In a medium saucepan set over medium-low heat, combine the cucumbers, onion, celery, stock, and lemon juice and simmer until the vegetables are tender. Remove from the heat, cool slightly, and pour into the container of a blender. Process on medium speed until smooth. Pour into a bowl and stir in the butter and parsley.

2 cups all-purpose flour
2 teaspoons baking powder
½ teaspoon baking soda
1 tablespoon grated orange zest
1 cup chopped fresh cranberries
½ cup green candied cherries
1 teaspoon salt
2 large eggs
¾ cup granulated sugar
¼ cup melted butter or margarine
¾ cup fresh-squeezed orange juice
Holiday Sauce (see recipe page 172)

**1** Position the rack in the center of the oven and preheat to 350 degrees F. Lightly grease a 1½-quart casserole dish.

**2** In a large bowl, blend together the flour, baking powder, baking soda, orange zest, cranberries, cherries, and salt. In a medium bowl, beat the eggs until foamy before beating in the sugar, butter, and orange juice. Combine the two mixtures, blending until the dry ingredients are well moistened.

**3** Scrape the batter into the prepared pan and bake for 45 to 50 minutes, or until a cake tester or wooden toothpick inserted into the center of the bread comes out clean and the top is golden. Remove from the oven and cool the pan on a wire rack for 5 to 10 minutes before removing the loaf from the pan. Serve with Holiday Sauce.

# CHRISTMAS CRANBERRY BREAD

MAKES: *1 loaf*

---

2½ cups sifted all-purpose flour
4 teaspoons baking powder
1½ cups mixed candied fruit
¼ cup chopped seedless raisins
¾ cup chopped walnuts
¼ teaspoon salt
½ cup butter-flavored vegetable shortening
¾ cup granulated sugar
3 large eggs
3 medium bananas, mashed
½ cup orange juice
Holiday Sauce (see recipe page 172)

**1** Position the rack in the center of the oven and preheat to 350 degrees F. Lightly grease an 8½-by-4½-by-2½-inch loaf pan.

**2** In a large bowl, blend together the flour, baking powder, fruit, raisins, walnuts, and salt. In a medium bowl, beat the shortening and sugar together until light and fluffy before beating in the eggs, one at a time, beating vigorously after each addition. Beat in the bananas and orange juice. Combine the two mixtures, blending until the dry ingredients are well moistened.

**3** Scrape the batter into the prepared pan and bake for 45 to 50 minutes, or until a cake tester or wooden toothpick inserted into the center of the bread comes out clean and the top is golden. Remove from the oven and cool the pan on a wire rack for 5 to 10 minutes before removing the loaf from the pan. Serve with Holiday Sauce.

# CHRISTMAS FRUIT BREAD

MAKES: *1 loaf*

# COCOA BREAD

MAKES: *1 loaf*

1¾ cups all-purpose flour
¼ cup Dutch-processed cocoa
  powder
¼ teaspoon baking powder
⅛ teaspoon baking soda
¾ teaspoon ground allspice
½ teaspoon salt
2 large eggs
¼ cup butter or margarine
¾ cup packed light-brown sugar
¾ cup sour cream or chocolate-
  flavored yogurt
Chocolate Sauce (see recipe page 26)

**1** Position the rack in the center of the oven and preheat to 375 degrees F. Lightly grease and flour an 8½-by-4½-by-2½-inch loaf pan.

**2** In a large bowl, blend together the flour, cocoa, baking powder, baking soda, allspice, and salt. In a medium bowl, beat the eggs until foamy before beating in the butter, brown sugar, and sour cream. Combine the two mixtures, blending until the dry ingredients are moistened.

**3** Scrape the batter into the prepared pan and bake for 45 to 50 minutes, or until a cake tester or wooden toothpick inserted into the center of the bread comes out clean and the top is golden. Remove from the oven and cool the pan on a wire rack for 5 to 10 minutes before removing the loaf from the pan. Serve with Chocolate Sauce.

# COCONUT BREAD

MAKES: *1 loaf*

2 cups Bisquick® mix
¼ cup granulated sugar
1 teaspoon ground cinnamon
1 cup flaked coconut
¾ cup chopped pecans
2 large eggs, lightly beaten
3 tablespoons melted margarine
1½ cups milk
Coconut Chutney (see recipe page
  65)

**1** Position the rack in the center of the oven and preheat to 350 degrees F. Lightly grease and flour an 8½-by-4½-by-2½-inch loaf pan.

**2** In a large bowl, blend together the Bisquick, sugar, cinnamon, coconut, and pecans. Form a well in the center of the mixture and add the eggs, butter, and milk all at one time. Using a large spoon or spatula, stir the mixture until smooth.

**3** Scrape the batter into the prepared pan and bake for 45 to 50 minutes, or until a cake tester or wooden toothpick inserted into the center of the bread comes out clean and the top is golden. Remove from the oven and cool the pan on a wire rack for 5 to 10 minutes before removing the loaf from the pan. Serve with Coconut Chutney.

2 cups all-purpose flour
1½ teaspoons baking powder
¾ cup granulated sugar
¼ teaspoon salt
1 cup flaked coconut, unsweetened
¼ cup candied lemon peel
1 large egg
¼ cup melted butter or margarine
1½ cups coconut milk
2 tablespoons shredded coconut for topping

**1** Position the rack in the center of the oven and preheat to 400 degrees F. Lightly grease and flour the bottom of an 8½-by-4½-by-2½-inch loaf baking pan.

**2** In a large bowl, blend together the flour, baking powder, sugar, salt, flaked coconut, and lemon peel. In a medium bowl, beat the egg, butter, and coconut milk until smooth. Combine the two mixtures, blending until the dry ingredients are just moistened.

**3** Spoon the batter into the prepared baking pan and sprinkle the shredded coconut on top of the batter. Bake for about 45 to 50 minutes, or until the top starts to turn a light golden and a cake tester or wooden toothpick inserted into the center of the bread comes out clean. Remove from the oven and cool on a wire rack for 5 to 10 minutes before inverting the loaf pan.

# Coconut–Lemon Bread

Makes: *1 loaf*

---

2½ cups all-purpose flour
2 teaspoons baking powder
½ teaspoon baking soda
1 cup granulated sugar
2 large eggs
¼ cup melted butter or margarine
1 cup triple-strength brewed coffee
Coffee Cream Sauce (see recipe page 79)

**1** Position the rack in the center of the oven and preheat to 350 degrees F. Lightly grease and flour an 8½-by-4½-by-2½-inch loaf pan.

**2** In a large bowl, blend together the flour, baking powder, baking soda, and sugar. In a medium bowl, beat the eggs until foamy before beating in the butter and coffee. Combine the two mixtures, blending until the dry ingredients are moistened.

**3** Scrape the batter into the prepared pan and bake for 40 to 45 minutes, or until a cake tester or wooden toothpick inserted into the center of the bread comes out clean and the top is golden. Remove from the oven and cool the pan on a wire rack for 5 to 10 minutes before removing the loaf from the pan. Serve with Coffee Cream Sauce.

# Coffee-Flavored Bread

Makes: *1 loaf*

# CORN BREAD

MAKES: *4 to 6 servings*

1 cup cornmeal
2 cups boiling water
1 tablespoon vegetable shortening
2 teaspoons salt
1 cup milk
2 large eggs

**1** Position the rack in the center of the oven and preheat to 350 degrees F. Lightly grease and flour a 9-inch square baking dish.

**2** In the top of a double boiler set over simmering water, blend together the cornmeal and boiling water and cook, stirring frequently, for about 5 to 8 minutes, or until the mixture pulls away from the side of the pan. Stir in the shortening and salt before removing from the heat. Beat in the milk and eggs.

**3** Immediately pour the batter into the prepared baking dish and score the top with a knife. Bake for 20 to 25 minutes, or until a cake tester or wooden toothpick inserted into the center of the bread comes out clean. Remove the dish from the oven and cool on a wire rack for about 5 minutes before serving hot.

# CORN BREAD SURPRISE

MAKES: *1 loaf*

1 cup all-purpose flour
1 cup cornmeal
1 tablespoon baking powder
3 lean hot dogs, diced
1 teaspoon salt
¼ cup vegetable shortening
1 tablespoon granulated sugar
1 large egg
1 cup milk
Chili Butter (see recipe page 119)

**1** Position the rack in the center of the oven and preheat to 425 degrees F. Lightly grease and flour a 9-inch square baking pan.

**2** In a large bowl, blend together the flour, cornmeal, baking powder, diced hot dogs, and salt. In a medium bowl, beat the shortening and sugar until light and fluffy before beating in the egg and milk. Combine the two mixtures, blending until the dry ingredients are just moistened.

**3** Scrape the batter into the prepared pan and bake for 25 to 30 minutes, or until a cake tester or wooden toothpick inserted into the center of the bread comes out clean and the top is starting to turn a golden-yellow color. Remove from the oven and cool in the pan on a wire rack for 5 to 10 minutes before cutting into squares and serving. Serve with Chili Butter.

2¾ cups all-purpose flour
1 cup granulated sugar
2½ teaspoons baking powder
½ cup raisins
½ cup chopped hazelnuts
2 large eggs
1 cup milk
1 cup cottage or ricotta cheese
2 tablespoons hazelnut extract or
   liqueur

**1** Position the rack in the center of the oven and preheat to 350 degrees F. Lightly grease and flour a 9¼-by-5¼-by-2¾-inch loaf pan.

**2** In a large bowl, blend together the flour, sugar, baking powder, raisins, and nuts. In a medium bowl, beat the eggs until foamy before beating in the milk, cottage cheese, and hazelnut extract. Combine the two mixtures, blending until the dry ingredients are well moistened.

**3** Scrape the batter into the prepared pan and bake for 65 to 70 minutes, or until a cake tester or wooden toothpick inserted into the center of the bread comes out clean and the top is golden. Remove from the oven and cool the pan on a wire rack for 5 to 10 minutes before removing the loaf from the pan.

## COTTAGE CHEESE BREAD

MAKES: *1 loaf*

¼ cup Amaretto liqueur
1 cup diced dried cranberries
1 cup all-purpose flour
1½ cups whole-wheat flour
½ cup oat bran
1 teaspoon baking powder
1 teaspoon baking soda
1 cup chopped almonds
¼ cup butter or margarine, at room
   temperature
½ cup granulated sugar
1 large egg
1 cup sour milk or buttermilk
Cranberry Sauce (see recipe page
   108)

**1** Thirty minutes before baking, in a small bowl, combine the liqueur and cranberries, cover, and set aside in a warm place until ready.

**2** Position the rack in the center of the oven and preheat to 350 degrees F. Lightly grease and flour an 8½-by-4½-by-2½-inch loaf pan.

**3** In a large bowl, blend together the two flours, oat bran, baking powder, baking soda, and almonds. In a medium bowl, beat the butter and sugar together until light and fluffy. Beat in the egg and sour milk. Combine the two mixtures, blending until the dry ingredients are well moistened.

**4** Scrape the batter into the prepared pan and bake for 45 to 50 minutes, or until a cake tester or wooden toothpick inserted into the center of the bread comes out clean and the top is golden. Remove from the oven and cool the pan on a wire rack for 5 to 10 minutes before removing the loaf from the pan. Serve with Cranberry Sauce.

## CRANBERRY BREAD

MAKES: *1 loaf*

## CRANBERRY–PECAN BREAD WITH APPLES

MAKES: *1 loaf*

2 cups all-purpose flour
¾ cup granulated sugar
2 teaspoons baking powder
½ teaspoon baking soda
1 cup chopped fresh cranberries
½ cup coarsely chopped pecans
1 medium apple, peeled, cored, and finely diced
1 large egg
½ cup unsweetened apple cider
⅓ cup Kraft® real mayonnaise
Strawberry Sauce (see recipe page 144)

1 Position the rack in the center of the oven and preheat to 350 degrees F. Lightly grease and flour an 8½-by-4½-by-2½-inch loaf pan.

2 In a large bowl, blend together the flour, sugar, baking powder, baking soda, cranberries, pecans, and apples. In a medium bowl, beat the egg until foamy before beating in the apple cider and mayonnaise. Combine the two mixtures, blending until the dry ingredients are well moistened.

3 Scrape the batter into the prepared pan and bake for 45 to 50 minutes, or until a cake tester or wooden toothpick inserted into the center of the bread comes out clean and the top is golden. Remove from the oven and cool the pan on a wire rack for 5 to 10 minutes before removing the loaf from the pan. Serve with Strawberry Sauce.

## CRANBERRY– PUMPKIN BREAD

MAKES: *2 small loaves*

3½ cups all-purpose flour
1⅔ cups granulated sugar
1½ teaspoons baking powder
1 teaspoon baking soda
¾ cup finely chopped pecans
½ cup finely chopped seedless raisins
2 teaspoons pumpkin-pie spice
½ teaspoon salt
4 large eggs
One 16-ounce can pumpkin puree
One 16-ounce can cranberry sauce (not jellied)
⅔ cup canola oil
Rhubarb Sauce (see recipe page 245)

1 Position the rack in the center of the oven and preheat to 350 degrees F. Lightly grease and flour two 5¾-by-3-by-2-inch loaf pans.

2 In a large bowl, blend together the flour, sugar, baking powder, baking soda, pecans, raisins, pumpkin-pie spice, and salt. In a medium bowl, beat the eggs until foamy before beating in the pumpkin, cranberry sauce, and oil. Combine the two mixtures, blending until the dry ingredients are well moistened.

3 Scrape the batter into the prepared pans and bake for 40 to 45 minutes, or until a cake tester or wooden toothpick inserted into the center of the bread comes out clean and the top is golden. Remove from the oven and cool the pans on a wire rack for 5 to 10 minutes before removing the loaves from the pans. Serve with Rhubarb Sauce.

1½ cups finely chopped dried
  cranberries
½ cup Triple Sec liqueur
2 cups all-purpose flour
1 cup whole-wheat flour
1 cup granulated sugar
1 tablespoon baking powder
½ teaspoon baking soda
2 teaspoons grated orange zest
2 large eggs
½ cup melted butter or margarine
1 cup orange juice
Honey Glaze (see recipe page 53)

**1** In a small bowl, combine the
cranberries and liqueur and set
aside for 10 minutes.

**2** Position the rack in the center
of the oven and preheat to 350
degrees F. Lightly grease and
flour a 9¼-by-5¼-by-2¾-inch loaf
pan.

**3** In a large bowl, blend together
the two flours, sugar, baking
powder, baking soda, and orange
zest. In a medium bowl, beat the
eggs until foamy before beating
in the butter and orange juice.
Stir in the cranberries and
liqueur. Combine the wet and
dry ingredients, blending until
the dry ingredients are well
moistened.

**4** Scrape the batter into the prepared pan and bake for 55 to 60
minutes, or until a cake tester or
wooden toothpick inserted into
the center of the bread comes out
clean and the top is golden.
Remove from the oven and cool
the pan on a wire rack for 5 to 10
minutes before removing the loaf
from the pan. Serve with Honey
Glaze.

# CRANBERRY WHOLE-WHEAT BREAD
MAKES: *1 loaf*

2 cups all-purpose flour
1¼ teaspoons baking powder
1 teaspoon salt
One 8-ounce package cream cheese,
  at room temperature
1 cup butter or margarine, at room
  temperature
1 cup granulated sugar
3 large eggs
Flavored Mayonnaise (see recipe
  page 324)

**1** Position the rack in the center
of the oven and preheat to 350
degrees F. Lightly grease and
flour two 8½-by-4½-by-2½-inch
loaf pans.

**2** In a large bowl, blend together
the flour, baking powder, and
salt. In a medium bowl, beat the

cheese, butter, and sugar together
until smooth. Beat in the eggs,
one at a time, beating vigorously
after each addition. Combine the
two mixtures, blending until the
dry ingredients are well
moistened.

**3** Scrape the batter into the prepared pans and bake for 45 to 50
minutes, or until a cake tester or
wooden toothpick inserted into
the center of the bread comes out
clean and the tops are golden.
Remove from the oven and cool
the pans on a wire rack for 5 to
10 minutes before removing the
loaves from the pans. Serve with
Flavored Mayonnaise.

# CREAM CHEESE BREAD
MAKES: *2 loaves*

## CREAM CHEESE–PUMPKIN BREAD

MAKES: *1 loaf*

One 8-ounce package cream cheese, at room temperature
1 large egg
1¼ cups granulated sugar
1 cup all-purpose flour
¾ cup graham flour
1½ cups granulated sugar
1 teaspoon baking soda
1 teaspoon ground cinnamon
¼ teaspoon ground nutmeg
½ teaspoon salt
1 large egg
½ cup packed light-brown sugar
1 cup canned pumpkin puree
½ cup butter or margarine, melted
⅓ cup brandy

1  Position the rack in the center of the oven and preheat to 350 degrees F. Lightly grease and flour an 8½-by-4½-by-2½-inch loaf pan.

2  In a small bowl, blend together the cream cheese, egg, and ¼ cup of the granulated sugar, beating until the sugar is dissolved. Set aside.

3  In a large bowl, blend together the two flours, the remaining 1 ¼ cups sugar, the baking soda, cinnamon, nutmeg, and salt. In a medium bowl, beat the egg and brown sugar smooth before beating in the pumpkin, butter, and brandy. Combine the two mixtures, blending until the dry ingredients are well moistened.

4  Scrape the batter into the prepared pan. Spoon the cream cheese mixture over the top and, using a knife or spatula, swirl it back and forth several times to make swirls throughout the batter. Bake for 50 to 55 minutes, or until a cake tester or wooden toothpick inserted into the center of the bread comes out clean and the top is golden. Remove from the oven and cool the pan on a wire rack for 5 to 10 minutes before removing the loaf from the pan.

## CREAM-OF-WHEAT BREAD WITH BANANAS

MAKES: *1 loaf*

2 cups Quaker® Cream of Wheat cereal
1 cup all-purpose flour
4 teaspoons baking powder
1 teaspoon ground nutmeg
½ teaspoon salt
2 large eggs
2 tablespoons packed light-brown sugar
1½ cups cream or evaporated milk
1 cup canola oil
3 medium bananas, mashed
Shredded coconut for topping
Finely chopped seedless raisins for topping
Raspberry Sauce (see recipe page 48)

1  Position the rack in the center of the oven and preheat to 350 degrees F. Lightly grease and flour a 13-by-9-inch baking pan.

2  In a large bowl, blend together the cream of wheat, flour, baking powder, nutmeg, and salt. In a medium bowl, beat the eggs until foamy before beating in the sugar, cream, oil, and bananas. Combine the two mixtures, blending until the dry ingredients are moistened.

3  Scrape the batter into the prepared pan and sprinkle the shredded coconut and raisins over the top. Bake for 40 to 45 minutes, or until a cake tester or wooden toothpick inserted into the center of the bread comes out clean and the top is golden. Remove from the oven and cool the pan on a wire rack for 5 to 10 minutes before removing the loaf from the pan and cutting into squares. Serve wih Raspberry Sauce.

2 cups all-purpose flour
1½ teaspoons baking powder
1 teaspoon curry powder
½ cup finely grated Cheddar cheese
1 small white onion, diced
One 3-ounce package Kraft®
  Philadelphia® cream cheese
½ cup fruit chutney
½ teaspoon bottled chili sauce
2 large eggs
¾ cup water
Freshly grated Romano cheese
  for topping
Hot Curry Spread (see recipe
  page 177)

1  Position the rack in the center of the oven and preheat to 350 degrees F. Lightly grease and flour an 8½-by-4½-by-2½-inch loaf pan.

2  In a large bowl, blend together the flour, baking powder, curry powder, cheese, and onion. In a medium bowl, beat the cream cheese, chutney, and chili sauce until smooth. Beat in the eggs, one at a time, beating vigorously after each addition. Beat in the water. Combine the two mixtures, blending until the dry ingredients are well moistened.

3  Scrape the batter into the prepared pan and sprinkle Romano cheese over the top. Bake for 45 to 50 minutes, or until a cake tester or wooden toothpick inserted into the center of the bread comes out clean and the top is golden brown. Remove from the oven and cool the pan on a wire rack for 5 to 10 minutes before removing the loaf from the pan. Serve with Hot Curry Spread.

# CURRY-FLAVORED CHEESE BREAD
MAKES: *1 loaf*

---

2⅔ cups all-purpose flour
2 teaspoons baking powder
¼ teaspoon baking soda
¾ cup packed light-brown sugar
2 tablespoons Bird's® Dessert Mix
½ teaspoon ground allspice
¼ teaspoon ground cloves
2 large eggs
1 cup milk
2 tablespoons melted butter or
  margarine
Custard Sauce (see recipe page 29)
  or Lemon Sauce (see recipe page
  61)

1  Position the rack in the center of the oven and preheat to 350 degrees F. Lightly grease and flour an 8½-by-4½-by-2½-inch loaf pan.

2  In a large bowl, blend together the flour, baking powder, baking soda, brown sugar, dessert mix, allspice, and cloves. In a small bowl, beat the eggs, milk, and butter until smooth. Combine the two mixtures, blending until the dry ingredients are well moistened.

3  Scrape the batter into the prepared pan and bake for 55 to 60 minutes, or until a cake tester or wooden toothpick inserted into the center of the bread comes out clean and the top is golden brown. Remove from the oven and cool the pan on a wire rack for 5 to 10 minutes before removing the loaf from the pan. Serve with Custard Sauce or Lemon Sauce.

# CUSTARD BREAD
MAKES: *1 loaf*

## DARK-BROWN BREAD

MAKES: *1 loaf*

1 cup All-Bran™ cereal
1 cup sour milk
1 cup all-purpose flour
¼ cup granulated sugar
1 teaspoon baking soda
¼ cup plumped and drained raisins
½ teaspoon salt
1 large egg
2 tablespoons melted butter or
    margarine
¼ cup molasses
Whipped Cream-Cheese Topping
    (see recipe page 186)

1 Position the rack in the center of the oven and preheat to 350 degrees F. Lightly grease and flour an 8½-by-4½-by-2½-inch loaf pan.

2 In a small bowl, pour the milk over the cereal and set aside. In a large bowl, blend together the flour, sugar, baking soda, raisins, and salt. In a medium bowl, beat the egg until foamy before beating in the butter and molasses. Stir in the cereal and milk. Combine the two mixtures, blending until the dry ingredients are moistened.

3 Scrape the batter into the prepared pan and bake for 45 to 50 minutes, or until a cake tester or wooden toothpick inserted into the center of the bread comes out clean and the top is golden. Remove from the oven and cool the pan on a wire rack for 5 to 10 minutes before removing the loaf from the pan. Serve with Whipped Cream-Cheese Topping.

## DATE–NUT BREAD

MAKES: *2 small loaves*

1 cup finely chopped pitted dates
3 tablespoons butter or margarine
1 cup boiling water
1 cup all-purpose flour
1½ cups whole-wheat flour
½ cup granulated sugar
1½ teaspoons baking powder
½ teaspoon baking soda
¾ cup finely chopped walnuts
1 teaspoon salt
3 large eggs
½ cup granulated sugar
1 teaspoon vanilla extract
Date Sauce (see recipe page 136)

1 Position the rack in the center of the oven and preheat to 350 degrees F. Lightly grease and flour two 5¼-by-3-by-2-inch loaf pans.

2 In a small bowl, combine the dates, butter, and boiling water. Set aside to cool slightly. In a large bowl, blend together the two flours, baking powder, baking soda, walnuts, and salt. In a medium bowl, beat the eggs and sugar until smooth before stirring in the cooled date mixture and vanilla extract. Combine the two mixtures, blending until the dry ingredients are moistened.

3 Scrape the batter into the prepared pans and bake for 45 to 50 minutes, or until a cake tester or wooden toothpick inserted into the center of the bread comes out clean and the tops are golden. Remove from the oven and cool the pans on a wire rack for 5 to 10 minutes before removing the loaves from the pans. Serve with Date Sauce.

1 cup finely chopped pitted dates
1¼ cups hot scalded milk
2 cups all-purpose flour
1 cup rolled oats
4 teaspoons baking powder
½ teaspoon ground nutmeg
1 teaspoon salt
1 large egg
¾ cup light corn syrup
Fig Sauce (see recipe page 189)

**1** Position the rack in the center of the oven and preheat to 350 degrees F. Lightly grease and flour a 9¼-by-5¼-by-2¾-inch loaf pan.

**2** In a small bowl, combine the dates and hot milk. Set aside to cool slightly. In a large bowl, blend together the flour, oats, baking powder, nutmeg, and salt. In a medium bowl, beat the egg until foamy before beating in the corn syrup. Beat in the date mixture. Combine the two mixtures, blending until the dry ingredients are moistened.

**3** Scrape the batter into the prepared pan and bake for 55 to 60 minutes, or until a cake tester or wooden toothpick inserted into the center of the bread comes out clean and the top is golden. Remove from the oven and cool the pan on a wire rack for 5 to 10 minutes before removing the loaf from the pan. Serve with Fig Sauce.

# DATE–OATMEAL BREAD

MAKES: *1 loaf*

2 cups all-purpose flour
2 teaspoons baking powder
½ teaspoon ground nutmeg
1 cup grated Gruyére cheese
1 medium clove garlic, minced
1 large egg
1 cup milk
3 tablespoons melted butter or
    margarine
3 tablespoons Kirsch
Cheese Sauce (see recipe page 57)
    or Chocolate Sauce (see recipe
    page 26)

**1** Position the rack in the center of the oven and preheat to 350 degrees F. Lightly grease and flour a 9-inch square baking pan.

**2** In a large bowl, blend together the flour, baking powder, nutmeg, cheese, and garlic. In a medium bowl, beat the egg until foamy before beating in the milk, butter, and Kirsch. Combine the two mixtures, blending until the dry ingredients are moistened.

**3** Scrape the batter into the prepared pan and bake for 30 to 35 minutes, or until a cake tester or wooden toothpick inserted into the center of the bread comes out clean and the top is a light golden color. Remove from the oven and cool the pan on a wire rack for 5 to 10 minutes before cutting into squares and serving. Serve with Cheese Sauce or Chocolate Sauce.

# DIPPIN BREAD

MAKES: *1 loaf*

## DOUBLE CHOCOLATE ZUCCHINI BREAD

MAKES: *2 loaves*

2½ cups all-purpose flour
1 teaspoon baking powder
1 teaspoon ground cinnamon
¼ teaspoon ground cloves
1 cup finely chopped hazelnuts
½ cup (3 ounces) semisweet chocolate chips
¼ teaspoon salt
3 large eggs
2 cups granulated sugar
1 cup canola oil
1 tablespoon crème de cacao
2 ounces (2 squares) unsweetened chocolate, melted
2 cups grated zucchini
Cheese Sauce (see recipe page 57)

1  Position the rack in the center of the oven and preheat to 350 degrees F. Lightly grease and flour the bottoms of two 8½-by-4½-by-2½-inch loaf pans.

2  In a large bowl, blend together the flour, baking powder, cinnamon, cloves, nuts, chocolate chips, and salt. In a medium bowl, beat the eggs until foamy before beating in the sugar, oil, crème de cacao, and melted chocolate. Stir in the zucchini. Combine the two mixtures, blending until the dry ingredients are moistened.

3  Scrape the batter into the prepared pans and bake for 55 to 60 minutes, or until a cake tester or wooden toothpick inserted into the center of the bread comes out clean and the tops are golden. Remove from the oven and cool the pans on a wire rack for 5 to 10 minutes before removing the loaves from the pans. Serve with Cheese Sauce.

## EGGNOG BREAD

MAKES: *1 loaf*

BATTER
3 cups all-purpose flour
½ cup powdered sugar
4 teaspoons baking powder
¾ teaspoon ground nutmeg
½ cup finely chopped pecans or hazelnuts
1 large egg
½ cup canola oil
1¾ cups prepared eggnog

TOPPING
½ cup powdered sugar
1 tablespoon prepared eggnog
½ cup finely chopped raisins
Honey Glaze (see recipe page 53)

1  Position the rack in the center of the oven and preheat to 350 degrees F. Lightly grease and flour a 9¼-by-5¼-by-2¾-inch loaf pan.

2  To make the batter, in a large bowl, blend together the flour, sugar, baking powder, nutmeg, and nuts. In a medium bowl, beat the egg until foamy before beating in the oil and eggnog. Combine the two mixtures, blending until the dry ingredients are moistened.

3  Scrape the batter into the prepared pan and bake for 55 to 60 minutes, or until a cake tester or wooden toothpick inserted into the center of the bread comes out clean and the top is golden. Remove from the oven and cool the pan on a wire rack for 5 to 10 minutes before removing the loaf from the pan.

4  Meanwhile, to prepare the topping, in a small bowl or cup, using a fork or wire whisk, blend together the powdered sugar and eggnog. Stir in the raisins. Drizzling over the top of the cooled bread. Serve with Honey Glaze.

1 package (12 ounces) pitted prunes, coarsely chopped
1 cup freshly squeezed orange juice
⅔ cup granulated sugar
¼ cup butter or margarine, at room temperature
⅓ cup Triple Sec liqueur
1 teaspoon lemon or orange extract
1½ cups all-purpose flour
½ cup whole-wheat flour
1 teaspoon baking powder
1 teaspoon baking soda
¾ teaspoon ground cinnamon
¼ teaspoon ground cloves
Coarsely grated orange zest for topping
Plum Topping (see recipe page 101)

**1** Position the rack in the center of the oven and preheat to 350 degrees F. Lightly grease and flour an 8½-by-4½-by-2½-inch loaf pan.

**2** In a medium saucepan, combine the prunes, orange juice, sugar, and butter and set over medium heat. Cook until bubbles form around the edges of the pan. Remove from the heat and stir in the Triple Sec and lemon extract. Set aside to cool.

**3** In a large bowl, blend together the two flours, baking powder, baking soda, cinnamon, and cloves. Combine the dry ingredients with the prune mixture, blending until the dry ingredients are moistened.

**4** Scrape the batter into the prepared pan and sprinkle the orange zest over the top. Bake for 45 to 50 minutes, or until a cake tester or wooden toothpick inserted into the center of the bread comes out clean and the top is golden. Remove from the oven and cool the pan on a wire rack for 5 to 10 minutes before removing the loaf from the pan. Serve with Plum Topping.

# Enriched Prune Bread

MAKES: *1 loaf*

---

2 cups all-purpose flour
½ cup graham flour
1 teaspoon baking powder
½ teaspoon baking soda
1 cup finely chopped pistachio nuts
½ cup finely chopped raisins
½ cup finely chopped fresh figs
½ teaspoon salt
1 large egg
1 cup warmed honey
2 tablespoons butter or margarine
1 cup sour milk or buttermilk
Fig Sauce (see recipe page 189)

**1** Position the rack in the center of the oven and preheat to 325 degrees F. Lightly grease and flour a 9¼-by-5¼-by-2¾-inch loaf pan.

**2** In a large bowl, blend together the two flours, baking powder, baking soda, nuts, raisins, figs, and salt. In a medium bowl, beat the egg, honey, butter, and buttermilk together until smooth. Combine the two mixtures, blending until the dry ingredients are moistened.

**3** Scrape the batter into the prepared pan and bake for 60 to 65 minutes, or until a cake tester or wooden toothpick inserted into the center of the bread comes out clean and the top is golden. Remove from the oven and cool the pan on a wire rack for 5 to 10 minutes before removing the loaf from the pan. Serve with Fig Sauce.

# Fig Bread

MAKES: *1 loaf*

## FRESH STRAWBERRY BREAD

MAKES: *1 loaf*

1½ cups fresh sliced strawberries
1 cup granulated sugar
1½ cups all-purpose flour
1 teaspoon baking powder
½ teaspoon baking soda
½ teaspoon ground cinnamon
½ teaspoon ground nutmeg
¼ teaspoon salt
2 large eggs
½ cup melted butter or margarine
Fresh mint leaves for garnish
Rhubarb Sauce (see recipe page 245)

**1** Position the rack in the center of the oven and preheat to 350 degrees F. Lightly grease and flour an 8½-by-5½-by-2½-inch loaf pan.

**2** Place the strawberries in a small bowl and sprinkle with ½ cup of the sugar. Set aside.

**3** In a large bowl, blend together the remaining sugar, the flour, baking powder, baking soda, salt, cinnamon, and nutmeg. In a medium bowl, beat the eggs until foamy before beating in the butter. Stir in the strawberries. Combine the two mixtures, blending until the dry ingredients are moistened.

**4** Scrape the batter into the prepared pan and bake for 45 to 50 minutes, or until a cake tester or wooden toothpick inserted into the center of the bread comes out clean and the top is golden. Remove from the oven and cool the pan on a wire rack for 5 to 10 minutes before removing the loaf from the pan. Serve with Rhubarb Sauce.

## FRIED ONION-AND-CHEESE BREAD

MAKES: *1 loaf*

1 tablespoon light olive oil
2¼ cups all-purpose flour
1 tablespoon melted butter or margarine
1 to 2 tablespoons water
1 medium white onion, sliced thin and separated into rings
1½ teaspoons baking powder
½ teaspoon baking soda
¼ teaspoon salt
¾ cup grated brick cheese
1 tablespoon snipped fresh chives
1 large egg
1¼ cups buttermilk or sour milk
2 tablespoons canola oil
Cheese-and-Horseradish Spread (see recipe page 180)

**1** Position the rack in the center of the oven and preheat to 350 degrees F. Lightly grease and flour an 8½-by-4½-by-2½-inch loaf pan.

**2** Place the oil in a medium skillet and set it over medium heat. In a small bowl using a fork, blend together ½ cup of the flour, the butter, and enough water to make a paste about the thickness of a thin mayonnaise. Dip each ring of onion into the paste and immediately place in the hot skillet. Cooking, turning as required, until the onions are browned and crisp on both sides. Remove and thoroughly drain on a double thickness of paper towels. Set aside.

**3** In a large bowl, blend together the remaining 2 cups of flour, the baking powder, baking soda, salt, cheese, and chives. In a medium bowl, beat the egg until foamy before beating in the buttermilk and oil. Combine the two mixtures, blending until the dry ingredients are thoroughly moistened. Adjust the seasoning.

**4** Spread ⅓ of the batter into the prepared baking pan, layer ½ of the onions on top. Cover the onions with half the remaining batter, top with the remaining onions, and finish with the remaining batter. Bake for 55 to 60 minutes, or until a cake tester or wooden toothpick inserted into the center of the bread comes out clean and the top is golden. Remove from the oven and cool the pan on a wire rack for 5 to 10 minutes before removing the loaf from the pan. Serve with Cheese-and-Horseradish Spread.

1½ cups all-purpose flour
1 teaspoon baking powder
1 cup oat bran
2 ounces (2 squares) unsweetened chocolate, grated
½ cup chopped golden raisins
½ cup chopped dried cherries
1 cup chopped almonds or hazelnuts
½ teaspoon salt
½ cup butter or margarine, at room temperature
1⅓ cups granulated sugar
3 large eggs
1 teaspoon chocolate extract
1 cup heavy cream or evaporated milk
Powdered sugar for dusting
Raspberry Melba Sauce (see recipe page 203)

**1** Position the rack in the oven and preheat to 350 degrees F. Lightly grease and flour a kuglehof baking pan.

**2** In a large bowl, blend together the flour, baking powder, oat bran, chocolate, raisins, cherries, almonds, and salt. In a medium bowl, beat the butter and sugar until light and fluffy. Beat in the eggs, chocolate extract, and milk. Combine the two mixtures, blending until the dry ingredients are thoroughly moistened.

**3** Scrape the batter into the prepared pan and bake for 55 to 60 minutes, or until a cake tester or wooden toothpick inserted into the center of the bread comes out clean and the top is golden. Remove from the oven and cool the pan on a wire rack for 5 to 10 minutes before removing the loaf from the pan. Dust with powdered sugar and serve with Raspberry Melba Sauce.

# GERMAN-STYLE SWEET BREAD

MAKES: *1 loaf*

---

2 cups all-purpose flour
1½ teaspoons baking powder
½ teaspoon baking soda
½ cup granulated sugar
¼ cup finely chopped fresh ginger root
Pinch curry powder
1 large egg
½ cup light corn syrup
¼ cup canola oil
½ cup plain yogurt or sour cream
Ginger Cream (see recipe page 21)

**1** Position the rack in the center of the oven and preheat to 350 degrees F. Lightly grease and flour an 8½-by-4½-by-2½-inch loaf pan.

**2** In a large bowl, blend together the flour, baking powder, baking soda, sugar, ginger, and curry powder. In a medium bowl, beat the egg until foamy before beating in the syrup, oil, and yogurt. Combine the two mixtures, blending until the dry ingredients are moistened.

**3** Scrape the batter into the prepared pan and bake for 40 to 45 minutes, or until a cake tester or wooden toothpick inserted into the center of the bread comes out clean and the top is golden. Remove from the oven and cool the pan on a wire rack for 5 to 10 minutes before removing the loaf from the pan. Serve with Ginger Cream.

# GINGER-FLAVORED BREAD

MAKES: *1 loaf*

## GRAPE NUT– APRICOT BREAD

MAKES: *1 loaf*

2 cups hot scalded milk
1 cup grape nuts
1 cup finely chopped dried apricots
3 cups all-purpose flour
½ cup granulated sugar
4 teaspoons baking powder
1½ teaspoons salt
1 large egg
3 tablespoons melted butter or
   margarine
Grand Marnier Sauce (see recipe
   page 98)

1 Position the rack in the center of the oven and preheat to 350 degrees F. Lightly grease and flour a 9¼-by-5¼-by-2¾-inch loaf pan.

2 In a small bowl, combine the milk, grape nuts, and apricots. Set aside to cool.

3 In a large bowl, blend together the flour, sugar, baking powder, and salt. In a medium bowl, beat the egg until foamy before beating in the butter. Stir in the cooled grape nut mixture. Combine the wet and dry mixtures, blending until the dry ingredients are thoroughly moistened.

4 Scrape the batter into the prepared pan and bake for 55 to 60 minutes, or until a cake tester or wooden toothpick inserted into the center of the bread comes out clean and the top is golden. Remove from the oven and cool the pan on a wire rack for 5 to 10 minutes before removing the loaf from the pan. Serve with Grand Marnier Sauce.

## GREEN TOMATO BREAD

MAKES: *1 loaf*

3 cups all-purpose flour
1 teaspoon baking powder
1 teaspoon baking soda
2 teaspoons ground cinnamon
1 teaspoon ground cloves
½ teaspoon salt
3 large eggs
2 cups granulated sugar
1 cup canola oil
1 tablespoon vanilla extract
2 cups grated unpeeled green
   tomatoes
Savory Sauce (see recipe page 191)

1 Position the rack in the center of the oven and preheat to 325 degrees F. Lightly grease and flour a 9¼-by-5¼-by-2¾-inch loaf pans.

2 In a large bowl, blend together the flour, baking powder, baking soda, cinnamon, cloves, and salt. In a medium bowl, beat the eggs until foamy before beating in the sugar, oil, vanilla, and tomatoes. Combine the two mixtures, blending until the dry ingredients are thoroughly moistened.

3 Scrape the batter into the prepared pan and bake for 55 to 60 minutes, or until a cake tester or wooden toothpick inserted into the center of the bread comes out clean and the top is golden. Remove from the oven and cool the pan on a wire rack for 5 to 10 minutes before removing the loaf from the pan. Serve with Savory Sauce.

2 cups all-purpose flour
1½ teaspoons baking powder
½ teaspoon Herb Ox® chicken broth powder
½ teaspoon paprika
6 slices honey-baked ham, finely chopped
1½ cups grated Tillamook or Colby cheese
1 large egg
2 tablespoons melted butter or margarine
1½ cups milk
1 teaspoon prepared mustard
Sliced, pitted black olives for topping
Ham Spread (see recipe page 57)

**1** Position the rack in the center of the oven and preheat to 350 degrees F. Lightly grease and flour an 8½-by-4½-by-2½-inch loaf pan.

**2** In a large bowl, blend together the flour, baking powder, chicken broth powder, paprika, ham, and cheese. In a medium bowl, beat the egg, butter, milk, and mustard until smooth. Combine the two mixtures, blending until the dry ingredients are moistened.

**3** Scrape the batter into the prepared pan and sprinkle the top with sliced olives. Bake for 45 to 50 minutes, or until a cake tester or wooden toothpick inserted into the center of the bread comes out clean and the top is golden. Remove from the oven and cool the pan on a wire rack for 5 to 10 minutes before removing the loaf from the pan. Serve with Ham Spread.

# HAM-AND-CHEESE BREAD
MAKES: *1 loaf*

---

4 cups all-purpose flour
2 teaspoons baking soda
One 10-ounce package flaked coconut
2 teaspoons salt
4 large eggs
½ cup packed light-brown sugar
1 can (2½ ounce) undrained crushed pineapple
8 whole candied cherries for garnish
Coconut Chutney (see recipe page 65)
Tropical Sauce (see recipe page 81)

**1** Position the rack in the center of the oven and preheat to 350 degrees F. Lightly grease and flour the bottom of two 8½-by-4½-by-2½-inch loaf pans.

**2** In a large bowl, blend together the flour, baking soda, coconut, and salt. In a second large bowl, beat the eggs until foamy before beating in the brown sugar. Stir in the pineapple. Combine the two mixtures, blending until the dry ingredients are thoroughly moistened.

**3** Scrape the batter into the prepared pans and press four cherries down the center of each loaf. Bake for 55 to 60 minutes, or until a cake tester or wooden toothpick inserted into the center of the bread comes out clean and the tops are golden brown. Remove from the oven and cool the pans on a wire rack for 5 to 10 minutes before removing the loaves from the pans. Serve with Coconut Chutney and Tropical Sauce.

# HAWAIIAN BREAD
MAKES: *2 loaves*

# HAZELNUT BREAD

MAKES: *2 small loaves*

1½ cups all-purpose flour
2½ teaspoons baking powder
½ cup granulated sugar
½ cup finely chopped hazelnuts
2 large eggs
½ cup melted butter or margarine
¾ cup plain yogurt or sour cream
½ cup Cafe de Torani or Frangelico liqueur
Nut Spread (see recipe page 121)

**1** Position the rack in the center of the oven and preheat to 350 degrees F. Lightly grease and flour two 5¾-by-3-by-2⅛-inch loaf pans.

**2** In a large bowl, blend together the flour, baking powder, sugar, and nuts. In a medium bowl, beat the eggs until foamy before beating in the butter, yogurt, and liqueur. Combine the two mixtures, blending until the dry ingredients are moistened.

**3** Scrape the batter into the prepared pans and bake for 30 to 35 minutes, or until a cake tester or wooden toothpick inserted into the center of the bread comes out clean and the tops are golden. Remove from the oven and cool the pans on a wire rack for 5 to 10 minutes before removing the loaves from the pans. Serve with Nut Spread.

# HERBED CHERRY BREAD

MAKES: *1 loaf*

1 cup all-purpose flour
1 cup whole-wheat flour
¾ cup crushed Rice Krispies™ cereal
⅓ cup granulated sugar
1 tablespoon baking powder
1 teaspoon baking soda
3 tablespoons dried chives
1 tablespoon snipped fresh mint
1½ cups finely chopped dried cherries
2 large eggs
¼ cup melted butter or margarine
1⅓ cups buttermilk or sour milk
Cherry Sauce (see recipe page 52)

**1** Position the rack in the center of the oven and preheat to 350 degrees F. Lightly grease and flour a 9¼-by-5¼-by-2¾-inch loaf pan.

**2** In a large bowl, blend together the two flours, cereal, sugar, baking powder, baking soda, chives, mint, and cherries. In a large bowl, beat the eggs until foamy before beating in the butter and buttermilk. Combine the two mixtures, blending until the dry ingredients are thoroughly moistened.

**3** Scrape the batter into the prepared pan and bake for 55 to 60 minutes, or until a cake tester or wooden toothpick inserted into the center of the bread comes out clean and the top is golden. Remove from the oven and cool the pan on a wire rack for 5 to 10 minutes before removing the loaf from the pan. Serve with Cherry Sauce.

3 cups all-purpose flour
2½ teaspoons baking powder
½ teaspoon baking soda
2 tablespoons snipped fresh tarragon
1 tablespoon snipped fresh parsley
1 tablespoon granulated sugar
1 cup finely grated Cheddar cheese
½ teaspoon salt
2 large eggs
1 cup milk
¼ cup canola oil
2 tablespoons tomato paste
1 small yellow onion, finely chopped
1 teaspoon ketchup
½ cup grated provolone cheese for topping
Tomato–Basil Dip (see recipe page 130)

1 Position the rack in the center of the oven and preheat to 350 degrees F. Lightly grease and flour a 9¼-by-5¼-by-2¾-inch loaf pan.

2 In a large bowl, blend together the flour, baking powder, baking soda, tarragon, parsley, sugar, cheese, and salt. In a medium bowl, beat the eggs until foamy before beating in the milk, oil, tomato paste, onion, and ketchup. Combine the two mixtures, blending until the dry ingredients are moistened.

3 Scrape the batter into the prepared pan and sprinkle the provolone over the top. Bake for 55 to 60 minutes, or until a cake tester or wooden toothpick inserted into the center of the bread comes out clean and the top is golden. Remove from the oven and cool the pan on a wire rack for 5 to 10 minutes before removing the loaf from the pan. Serve with Tomato–Basil Dip.

# HERBED TOMATO BREAD

MAKES: *1 loaf*

2¾ cups all-purpose flour
2 teaspoons baking soda
1 tablespoon grated orange zest
⅓ cup finely chopped dried apricots
1 cup finely chopped seedless raisins
½ cup finely chopped golden raisins
½ cup finely chopped walnuts
1 teaspoon salt
1 large egg
1 cup granulated sugar
⅓ cup heavy cream
1 tablespoon melted butter or margarine
1½ cups apricot nectar
Apricot Spread (see recipe page 261)

1 Position the rack in the center of the oven and preheat to 350 degrees F. Lightly grease and flour an 8½-by-4½-by-2½-inch loaf pan.

2 In a large bowl, blend together the flour, baking soda, orange zest, apricots, raisins, walnuts, and salt. In a medium bowl, beat the egg until foamy before beating in the sugar, cream, butter, and apricot nectar. Combine the two mixtures, blending until the dry ingredients are thoroughly moistened.

3 Scrape the batter into the prepared pan and bake for 55 to 60 minutes, or until a cake tester or wooden toothpick inserted into the center of the bread comes out clean and the top is golden. Remove from the oven and cool the pan on a wire rack for 5 to 10 minutes before removing the loaf from the pan. Serve with Apricot Spread.

# HOLIDAY APRICOT BREAD

MAKES: *1 loaf*

# HOLIDAY PUMPKIN LOAF

MAKES: *2 small loaves*

1¾ cups all-purpose flour
1 teaspoon baking soda
2 teaspoons ground allspice
1 cup (6 ounces) semisweet
  chocolate chips
¼ teaspoon salt
¼ cup butter-flavored vegetable
  shortening
1 cup granulated sugar
2 large eggs
¾ cup canned pumpkin puree
1 teaspoon vanilla or almond extract
Marshmallow Sauce (see recipe
  page 131)
Peach or apricot wedges for garnish

1  Position the rack in the center of the oven and preheat to 350 degrees F. Lightly grease and flour two 5¾-by-3-by-2½-inch loaf pans.

2  In a large bowl, blend together the flour, baking soda, allspice, chocolate chips, and salt. In a medium bowl, beat the shortening and sugar together until light and fluffy. Beat in the eggs, one at a time, beating vigorously after each addition. Beat in the pumpkin and vanilla extract. Combine the two mixtures, blending until the dry ingredients are thoroughly moistened.

3  Scrape the batter into the prepared pans and bake for 55 to 60 minutes, or until a cake tester or wooden toothpick inserted into the center of the bread comes out clean and the tops are golden. Remove from the oven and cool the pans on a wire rack for 5 to 10 minutes before removing the loaves from the pans. Garnish with peach or apricot wedges and serve with Marshmallow Sauce.

# HOMINY BREAD

MAKES: *1 loaf*

2 cups cold cooked hominy
1½ tablespoons melted vegetable
  shortening
¼ teaspoon salt
2 large eggs, separated
1½ cups milk
Chili–Tomato Sauce (see recipe page
  116)

1  Position the rack in the center of the oven and preheat to 400 degrees F. Lightly grease and flour an 8-inch square baking pan.

2  In a large bowl, combine the hominy, shortening, and salt. In a medium bowl, beat the egg yolks and milk until smooth before stirring in the hominy mixture. In a small bowl, beat the egg whites until stiff but not dry and fold into the hominy mixture.

3  Scrape the batter into the prepared pan and bake for 55 to 60 minutes, or until a cake tester or wooden toothpick inserted into the center of the bread comes out clean and the top is golden brown. Remove from the oven and cool the pan on a wire rack for 5 to 10 minutes before cutting the bread into squares. Serve with Chili–Tomato Sauce.

2 cups all-purpose flour
1½ teaspoons baking soda
1 cup finely chopped pecans
½ teaspoon salt
½ cup butter-flavored vegetable
    shortening, at room temperature
1 cup honey
2 large eggs
1 cup unsweetened applesauce
12 red candied cherries for topping
Fresh mint leaves for garnish
Apple–Cinnamon Syrup (see recipe
    page 168)

**1** Position the rack in the center of the oven and preheat to 325 degrees F. Lightly grease and flour an 8½-by-4½-by-2½-inch loaf pan.

**2** In a large bowl, blend together the flour, baking soda, pecans, and salt. In a medium bowl, beat the shortening and honey until smooth before beating in the eggs, one at a time, beating vigorously after each addition. Beat in the applesauce. Combine the two mixtures, blending until the dry ingredients are thoroughly moistened.

**3** Scrape the batter into the prepared pan and press the cherries into the top of the batter. Bake for 55 to 60 minutes, or until a cake tester or wooden toothpick inserted into the center of the bread comes out clean and the top is golden brown. Remove from the oven and cool the pan on a wire rack for 5 to 10 minutes before removing the loaf from the pan. Garnish with fresh mint leaves. Serve with Apple–Cinnamon Syrup.

# HONEY–APPLE BREAD

MAKES: *1 loaf*

2 cups all-purpose flour
1 teaspoon baking soda
½ teaspoon ground cinnamon
¼ teaspoon ground nutmeg
½ cup finely chopped dried apricots
¼ cup finely chopped almonds
1 teaspoon grated lemon zest
½ teaspoon salt
¾ cup honey
½ cup mayonnaise
1 cup apricot brandy
Sugarless Apricot Sauce (see recipe
    page 40)

**1** Position the rack in the center of the oven and preheat to 325 degrees F. Lightly grease and paper line the bottom of an 8½-by-4½-by-2½-inch loaf pan.

**2** In a large bowl, blend together the flour, baking soda, cinnamon, nutmeg, apricots, almonds, lemon zest, and salt. In a medium bowl, beat the honey and mayonnaise together until smooth before beating in the brandy. Combine the two mixtures, blending until the dry ingredients are thoroughly moistened.

**3** Scrape the batter into the prepared pan and bake for 55 to 60 minutes, or until a cake tester or wooden toothpick inserted into the center of the bread comes out clean and the top is golden brown. Remove from the oven and cool the pan on a wire rack for 5 to 10 minutes before removing the loaf from the pan. Serve with Sugarless Apricot Sauce.

# HONEY–APRICOT BREAD

MAKES: *1 loaf*

## HONEY BREAD

MAKES: *1 loaf*

2 cups all-purpose flour
1 tablespoon baking powder
2 teaspoons ground cinnamon
¼ teaspoon ground nutmeg
¼ teaspoon ground cloves
1 teaspoon salt
1 large egg
¾ cup packed light-brown sugar
1 cup sour cream or plain yogurt
¼ cup honey
Whipped Cream-Cheese Topping
   (see recipe page 186)

**1** Position the rack in the center of the oven and preheat to 325 degrees F. Lightly grease and flour an 8½-by-4½-by-2½-inch loaf pan.

**2** In a large bowl, blend together the flour, baking powder, cinnamon, nutmeg, cloves, and salt. In a medium bowl, beat the egg until foamy before beating in the brown sugar, sour cream, and honey. Combine the two mixtures, blending until the dry ingredients are thoroughly moistened.

**3** Scrape the batter into the prepared pan and bake for 55 to 60 minutes, or until a cake tester or wooden toothpick inserted into the center of the bread comes out clean and the top is golden brown. Remove from the oven and cool the pan on a wire rack for 5 to 10 minutes before removing the loaf from the pan. Serve with Whipped Cream-Cheese Topping.

## HONEY–DATE–NUT BREAD

MAKES: *2 small loaves*

1 cup water
1 cup finely chopped dates
¾ cup honey, plus more for
   brushing the loaf
2 tablespoons butter or margarine
1½ cups Bisquick® baking mix
½ teaspoon baking powder
1 cup finely chopped walnuts
1 large egg
Date Sauce (see recipe page 136)

**1** Position the rack in the center of the oven and preheat to 325 degrees F. Lightly grease and flour two 5¾-by-3-by-2-inch loaf pans.

**2** In a small saucepan, combine the dates and water and cook, stirring constantly, until the mixture thickens. Remove from the heat and stir in the ½ cup of honey and the butter. Set aside until cooled.

**3** In a large bowl, blend together the baking mix, baking powder, and nuts. In a medium bowl, beat the egg until foamy. Beat in the date mixture. Combine with the dry ingredients, blending until the dry ingredients are thoroughly moistened.

**4** Scrape the batter into the prepared pans and bake for 55 to 60 minutes, or until a cake tester or wooden toothpick inserted into the center of the bread comes out clean and the tops are golden brown. Remove from the oven and cool the pans on a wire rack for 5 to 10 minutes before removing the loaves from the pans. Brush each loaf with honey. Serve with Date Sauce.

One 28-ounce can pear halves in
   heavy syrup
2 cups all-purpose flour
2 cups graham flour
1 tablespoon baking powder
1 teaspoon baking soda
1 teaspoon ground nutmeg
½ teaspoon ground cloves
2 teaspoons fresh grated lemon zest
2 teaspoons fresh grated orange zest
¾ cup finely chopped pecans
1½ teaspoons salt
2 large eggs
⅔ cup packed light-brown sugar
½ cup canola oil
¾ cup honey, plus more for
   brushing the bread
Mint Jelly (see recipe page 28)

**1** Position the rack in the center
of the oven and preheat to 350
degrees F. Lightly grease and
flour two 8½-by-4½-by-2½-inch
loaf pans.

**2** Drain the pears, reserving the
juice, and dice them. In a large
bowl, blend together the two
flours, baking powder, baking
soda, nutmeg, cloves, lemon zest,
orange zest, pecans, and salt. In a
medium bowl, beat the eggs and
sugar until smooth before beating in the oil, ½ cup honey, and
reserved pear juice. Stir in the
diced pears. Combine the two
mixtures, blending until the dry
ingredients are thoroughly
moistened.

**3** Scrape the batter into the prepared pans and bake for 55 to 60
minutes, or until a cake tester or
wooden toothpick inserted into
the center of the bread comes out
clean and the tops are golden
brown. Remove from the oven
and cool the pans on a wire rack
for 5 to 10 minutes before removing the loaves from the pans and
brushing with honey. Serve with
Mint Jelly.

# HONEY–PEAR BREAD
MAKES: *2 loaves*

¾ cup sour milk
1 cup honey, plus more for brushing
   the bread
2 tablespoons vegetable shortening
2 tablespoons finely chopped
   candied orange peel
2½ cups all-purpose flour
½ cup rye flour
1 teaspoon baking powder
1 teaspoon baking soda
½ cup finely chopped seedless
   raisins
½ cup finely chopped hazelnuts
1 teaspoon salt
1 large egg
2 tablespoons Triple Sec liqueur
Foamy Orange Sauce (see recipe
   page 204)

**1** Position the rack in the center
of the oven and preheat to 325
degrees F. Lightly grease and
flour a 9¼-by-5¼-by-2¾-inch loaf
pan.

**2** In a small saucepan, combine
the milk, 1 cup of honey, shortening, and orange peel and place
over low heat. Cook, stirring
occasionally, until bubbles start
to form around the edges of the
pan. Remove from the heat and
set aside until cooled.

**3** In a large bowl, blend together
the two flours, baking powder,
baking soda, raisins, hazelnuts,
and salt. In a small bowl, beat the
egg until foamy before beating it
into the cooled honey mixture.
Stir in the liqueur. Combine dry
and wet ingredients, blending
until the dry ingredients are thoroughly moistened.

**4** Scrape the batter into the prepared pan and bake for 55 to 60
minutes, or until a cake tester or
wooden toothpick inserted into
the center of the bread comes out
clean and the top is golden
brown. Remove from the oven
and cool the pan on a wire rack
for 5 to 10 minutes before removing the loaf from the pan. Brush
the loaf with honey and serve
with Foamy Orange Sauce.

# HONEY, ORANGE,
# AND NUT BREAD
MAKES: *1 loaf*

## HONEYED PEANUT BUTTER BREAD

MAKES: *1 loaf*

2 cups all-purpose flour
½ cup whole-wheat flour
1 teaspoon baking powder
1 teaspoon baking soda
1 teaspoon salt
1 large egg
½ cup honey
½ cup creamy-style peanut butter
1½ cups buttermilk or sour milk
½ cup finely chopped peanuts for topping
Peanut Butter Sauce (see recipe page 156)

1  Position the rack in the center of the oven and preheat to 350 degrees F. Lightly grease and flour a 9¼-by-5¼-by-2¾-inch loaf pan.

2  In a large bowl, blend together the two flours, baking powder, baking soda, and salt. In a medi-um bowl, beat the egg, honey, peanut butter, and buttermilk together until smooth. Combine the two mixtures, blending until the dry ingredients are thorough-ly moistened.

3  Scrape the batter into the pre-pared pan and sprinkle the peanuts over the top, pressing them lightly into the batter. Bake for 55 to 60 minutes, or until a cake tester or wooden toothpick inserted into the center of the bread comes out clean. Remove from the oven and cool the pan on a wire rack for 5 to 10 minutes before removing the loaf from the pan. Serve with Peanut Butter Sauce.

## ICE CREAM BREAD

MAKES: *1 loaf*

1½ cups all-purpose flour
1 teaspoon baking powder
2 cups soft but not melted vanilla ice cream
Cherry Sauce (see recipe page 52) or Caramel Sauce (see recipe page 32)

1  Position the rack in the center of the oven and preheat to 350 degrees F. Lightly grease and flour an 8½-by-4½-by-2½-inch loaf pan.

2  In a medium bowl, blend the flour and baking powder togeth-er. Working quickly, blend in the ice cream, blending until the dry ingredients are just moistened.

3  Immediately spoon the mix-ture into the prepared baking pan and bake for 20 to 25 min-utes, or until the top is golden brown. Remove from the oven and cool the pan on a wire rack for 5 to 10 minutes before remov-ing the loaf from the pan. Serve with Cherry Sauce or Caramel Sauce.

2 cups all-purpose flour
1 teaspoon baking soda
2 cups brown sugar
½ cup butter or margarine, at room temperature
2 large eggs, separated
½ cup chocolate-flavored yogurt or plain sour cream
1 teaspoon vanilla or chocolate extract
3 ounces (3 squares) semisweet chocolate, melted
½ cup ice-cold water
Marshmallow Sauce (see recipe page 131)

1  Position the rack in the center of the oven and preheat to 375 degrees F. Lightly grease and flour a 9¼-by-5¼-by-2¾-inch loaf pan.

2  In a large bowl, blend together the flour and baking soda. In a medium bowl, beat the sugar and butter together until light and fluffy. Beat in the egg yolks, yogurt, vanilla extract, melted chocolate, and ice water. Combine the two mixtures, blending until the dry ingredients are thoroughly moistened. In a small bowl, beat the egg whites until stiff but not dry and fold them into the batter.

3  Scrape the batter into the prepared pan and bake for 45 to 50 minutes, or until a cake tester or wooden toothpick inserted into the center of the bread comes out clean and the top is golden brown. Remove from the oven and cool the pan on a wire rack for 5 to 10 minutes before removing the loaf from the pan. Serve with Marshmallow Sauce.

## ICE WATER CHOCOLATE LOAF

MAKES: *1 loaf*

1½ cups whole-wheat bread
½ cup all-purpose flour
1 teaspoon baking powder
½ teaspoon baking soda
¼ cup black currants or finely chopped seedless raisins
1 teaspoon caraway seeds
1 heaping tablespoon sugar
¼ teaspoon salt
1 large egg
⅔ cup buttermilk or sour milk
3 tablespoons melted butter or margarine
Berry Sauce (see recipe page 38)

1  Position the rack in the center of the oven and preheat to 350 degrees. Lightly grease and flour a 9-inch square baking pan.

2  In a large bowl, blend together the two flours, baking powder, baking soda, black currants, caraway seeds, sugar, and salt. In a small bowl, beat the egg until foamy before beating in the buttermilk and butter. Combine the two mixtures, blending until the dry ingredients are moistened.

3  Scrape the batter into the prepared pan and bake for 30 to 35 minutes, or until a cake tester or wooden toothpick inserted into the center of the bread comes out clean and the top is a light golden color. Remove from the oven and cool the pan on a wire rack for 5 to 10 minutes before cutting into squares and serving. Serve with Berry Sauce.

## IRISH BREAD

MAKES: *1 loaf*

## ITALIAN-STYLE HERB BREAD WITH SPINACH

MAKES: *1 loaf*

2 cups all-purpose flour
1¼ cups cornmeal
1 teaspoon baking powder
1 teaspoon garlic powder
¼ teaspoon salt
4 medium scallions (green onions), chopped
One 8-ounce package frozen chopped spinach, thawed and drained
1 can (15⅓ ounces) chick peas, drained, rinsed, and drained again
2 tablespoons grated Parmesan or Romano cheese
1 large egg
1¼ cups milk
⅓ cup melted butter or margarine
Tomato Relish (see recipe page 178) or Chili Butter (see recipe page 119)

1  Position the rack in the center of the oven and preheat to 350 degrees F. Lightly grease and flour a 9¼-by-5¼-by-2¾-inch loaf pan.

2  In a large bowl, blend together the flour, cornmeal, baking powder, garlic powder, salt, scallions, spinach, chick peas, and cheese. In a medium bowl, beat the egg, milk, and butter together until smooth. Combine the two mixtures, blending until the dry ingredients are moistened.

3  Scrape the batter into the prepared pan and bake for 55 to 60 minutes, or until a cake tester or wooden toothpick inserted into the center of the bread comes out clean and the top is golden. Remove from the oven and cool the pan on a wire rack for 5 to 10 minutes before removing the loaf from the pan. Serve with Tomato Relish or Chili Butter.

## ITALIAN-STYLE OLIVE BREAD

MAKES: *2 loaves*

3 cups all-purpose flour
2 teaspoons baking powder
½ teaspoon baking soda
1½ teaspoons garlic powder
⅓ cup grated Parmesan or Romano cheese
¾ cup pitted black olives, sliced
2 tablespoons snipped fresh basil
1 tablespoon snipped fresh oregano
2 large eggs
2 tablespoons tomato paste
½ teaspoon hot sauce
¾ cup canola oil
1½ cups buttermilk or sour milk
Cheese-and-Olive Spread (see recipe page 183)

1  Position the rack in the center of the oven and preheat to 350 degrees F. Lightly grease and flour a 9¼-by-5¼-by-2¾-inch loaf pan.

2  In a large bowl, blend together the flour, baking powder, baking soda, garlic powder, cheese, olives, basil, and oregano. In a medium bowl, beat the eggs until foamy before beating in the tomato paste, hot sauce, oil, and buttermilk. Combine the two mixtures, blending until the dry ingredients are moistened.

3  Scrape the batter into the prepared pans and bake for 55 to 60 minutes, or until a cake tester or wooden toothpick inserted into the center of the bread comes out clean and the top is golden. Remove from the oven and cool the pan on a wire rack for 5 to 10 minutes before removing the loaf from the pan. Serve with Cheese-and-Olive Spread.

2½ cups all-purpose flour
1¾ teaspoons baking powder
½ teaspoon baking soda
5 slices Parma ham (Prosciutto), chopped
⅓ cup chopped sun-dried tomatoes
2 tablespoons snipped fresh basil
1½ teaspoons garlic powder
1 large egg
½ cup light olive oil
1¼ cups buttermilk or sour milk
Freshly ground black pepper to taste
Shredded Provolone cheese for topping
Herb Butter (see recipe page 149)

**1** Position the rack in the center of the oven and preheat to 350 degrees F. Lightly grease and flour a 9-inch square baking pan.

**2** In a large bowl, blend together the flour, baking powder, baking soda, ham, tomatoes, basil, and garlic powder. In a medium bowl, beat the egg, oil, and buttermilk until smooth. Combine the two mixtures, blending until the dry ingredients are moistened.

**3** Scrape the batter into the prepared pan and sprinkle with Provolone cheese. Bake for 40 to 45 minutes, or until a cake tester or wooden toothpick inserted into the center of the bread comes out clean and the top is golden. Remove from the oven and cool in the pan on a wire rack for 5 to 10 minutes before removing the loaf from the pan. Serve with Herb Butter.

# ITALIAN-STYLE PROSCIUTTO BREAD
MAKES: *1 loaf*

One 8-ounce package finely chopped pitted dates
2 teaspoons baking soda
1 cup boiling water
3 cups all-purpose flour
1 cup finely chopped pecans
Pinch salt
2 large eggs, separated
1 cup packed dark-brown sugar
2 tablespoons melted butter or margarine
¾ cup Jamaican rum
Flaked coconut for topping
Coconut Chutney (see recipe page 65)

**1** Position the rack in the center of the oven and preheat to 375 degrees F. Lightly grease and flour a 9¼-by-5¼-by-2¾-inch loaf pan.

**2** In a medium bowl, combine the dates, baking soda, and water (the water will fizz, so pour the water over the dates slowly). Set aside to cool.

**3** In a large bowl, blend together the flour, pecans, and salt. In a medium bowl, beat the egg yolks until foamy before beating in the sugar, butter, and rum. Stir in the date mixture. Combine the dry and wet ingredients, blending until the dry ingredients are thoroughly moistened. In a small bowl, beat the egg whites until stiff but not dry and fold them into the batter.

**4** Scrape the batter into the prepared pan and bake for 55 to 60 minutes, or until a cake tester or wooden toothpick inserted into the center of the bread comes out clean and the top is golden brown. Remove from the oven and cool the pan on a wire rack for 5 to 10 minutes before removing the loaf from the pan. Sprinkle with coconut and serve with Coconut Chutney.

# JAMAICAN-STYLE DATE-AND-WALNUT BREAD
MAKES: *1 loaf*

# KIWI FRUIT BREAD

MAKES: *2 loaves*

**3 cups all-purpose flour**
**2 teaspoons baking powder**
**¼ teaspoon salt**
**¼ cup granulated sugar**
**2 large eggs**
**¼ cup packed light-brown sugar**
**¼ cup oil**
**¾ cup milk**
**4 large kiwi fruit, peeled and
    mashed**
**1 tablespoon fresh lemon juice**
**¼ teaspoon almond extract**
**Powdered sugar for sprinkling**
**Tropical Sauce (see recipe page 81)**

**1** Position the rack in the center of the oven and preheat to 350 degrees F. Lightly grease and flour the bottom of two 8½-by-4½-by-2½-inch loaf pans.

**2** In a large bowl, blend together the flour, baking powder, salt, and sugar. In a medium bowl, beat the eggs and sugar until smooth before beating in the oil, milk, kiwi fruit, lemon juice, and almond extract. Combine the two mixtures, blending until the dry ingredients are moistened.

**3** Scrape the batter into the prepared pans, sprinkle a light coating of powdered sugar over the top, and bake for 40 to 45 minutes, or until a cake tester or wooden toothpick inserted into the center of the bread comes out clean and the tops are golden. Remove from the oven and cool the pans on a wire rack for 5 to 10 minutes before removing the loaves from the pans and sprinkling them a second time with powdered sugar. Serve with Tropical Sauce.

# KUMQUAT BREAD

MAKES: *1 loaf*

**3 cups finely crushed vanilla wafers**
**½ teaspoon baking powder**
**3 large eggs**
**½ cup melted butter or margarine**
**½ cup beer**
**8 medium kumquats, thinly sliced
    and seeded (do not peel)**
**2 tablespoons finely ground pecans
    for topping**
**Date Sauce (see recipe page 136)**

**1** Position the rack in the center of the oven and preheat to 350 degrees F. Lightly grease and flour an 8½-by-4½-by-2½-inch loaf pan.

**2** In a large bowl, combine the wafer crumbs and baking powder. In a medium bowl, beat the eggs until foamy before beating in the butter and beer. Fold in the kumquats. Combine the two mixtures, blending until the dry ingredients are well moistened.

**3** Scrape the batter into the prepared pan, sprinkle with the pecans, and bake for 45 to 50 minutes, or until a cake tester or wooden toothpick inserted into the center of the bread comes out clean and the top is golden. Remove from the oven and cool the pan on a wire rack for 5 to 10 minutes before removing the loaf from the pan. Serve with Date Sauce.

3 cups all-purpose flour
½ teaspoon baking soda
1 cup chopped walnuts
3 tablespoons freshly grated lemon
  zest
2 cups granulated sugar
½ cup butter or margarine, at room
  temperature
4 large eggs
1 cup buttermilk or sour milk
Lemon Butter (see recipe page 236)

**1** Position the rack in the center of the oven and preheat to 350 degrees. Lightly grease and flour a 9¼-by-5¼-by-2¾-inch loaf pan.

**2** In a large bowl, blend together the flour, baking soda, walnuts and zest. In a medium bowl, beat the sugar and butter together until light and fluffy. Beat in the eggs, one at a time, beating vigorously after each addition. Beat in the buttermilk. Combine the two mixtures, blending until the dry ingredients are thoroughly moistened.

**3** Scrape the batter into the prepared pan and bake for 35 to 40 minutes, or until a cake tester or wooden toothpick inserted into the center of the bread comes out clean and the top is golden. Remove from the oven and cool the pan on a wire rack for 5 to 10 minutes before removing the loaf from the pan. Serve with Lemon Butter.

## LEMON BREAD

MAKES: *1 loaf*

---

1 cup all-purpose flour
½ cup oat flour
1 cup granulated sugar
1 teaspoon baking powder
5 teaspoons grated lemon zest
½ cup coarsely chopped pecans
1 teaspoon salt
2 large eggs
⅓ cup melted butter or margarine
½ cup milk
3 tablespoons lemon extract
½ cup shredded coconut
Lemon Sauce (see recipe page 61)

**1** Position the rack in the center of the oven and preheat to 350 degrees F. Lightly grease and flour an 8½-by-4½-by-2½-inch loaf pan.

**2** In a large bowl, blend together the two flours, sugar, baking powder, lemon zest, pecans, and salt. In a medium bowl, beat the eggs until foamy before beating in the butter, milk, and extract. Combine the two mixtures, blending until the dry ingredients are moistened.

**3** Scrape the batter into the prepared pan and sprinkle the shredded coconut over the top. Bake for 45 to 50 minutes, or until a cake tester or wooden toothpick inserted into the center of the bread comes out clean and the top is golden. Remove from the oven and cool the pan on a wire rack for 5 to 10 minutes before removing the loaf from the pan. Serve with Lemon Sauce.

**SERVING SUGGESTION: Serve with ice cream.**

## LEMON–PECAN BREAD

MAKES: *1 loaf*

## LEMON–POTATO BREAD

MAKES: *1 loaf*

1 cup all-purpose flour
1½ teaspoons baking powder
½ teaspoon baking soda
1 cup granulated sugar
1 teaspoon grated lemon zest
½ teaspoon salt
2 large eggs
1 cup cooked mashed potatoes
6 tablespoons melted butter or margarine
Poppy Seed Butter (see recipe page 96)

1 Position the rack in the center of the oven and preheat to 350 degrees F. Lightly grease and flour an 8½-by-4½-by-2½-inch loaf pan.

2 In a large bowl, beat the butter and sugar together until light and fluffy. Beat in the eggs, potatoes, butter, and lemon juice. Combine the two mixtures, blending until the dry ingredients are moistened.

3 Scrape the batter into the prepared pan. Bake for 45 to 50 minutes, or until a cake tester or wooden toothpick inserted into the center of the bread comes out clean and the top is golden. Remove from the oven and cool the pan on a wire rack for 5 to 10 minutes before removing the loaf from the pan. Serve with Poppy Seed Butter.

## LEMONADE QUICK BREAD

MAKES: *2 loaves*

1 cup granulated sugar
2 teaspoons baking powder
1 tablespoon grated lemon zest
¼ teaspoon salt
2 large eggs
½ cup melted butter or margarine
1 tablespoon fresh lemon juice
⅓ cup frozen lemonade concentrate, thawed

1 Position the rack in the center of the oven and preheat to 350 degrees F. Lightly grease and flour the bottoms of two 5¾-by-3-by-2⅛-inch loaf baking pans.

2 In a large bowl, blend together the sugar, baking powder, lemon zest, and salt. In a medium bowl, beat the eggs until foamy before beating in the butter and lemon juice. Combine the two mixtures, blending until the dry ingredients are just moistened.

3 Spoon the batter into the prepared baking pans. Bake for 45 to 50 minutes, or or until the top starts to turn a light golden and a cake tester or wooden toothpick inserted into the center of the bread comes out clean. Remove from the oven and cool inverted in the pan on a wire rack for 5 to 10 minutes. Remove pans and pour the lemonade concentrate over the top of the loaves.

1½ cups all-purpose flour
2 teaspoons baking powder
½ teaspoon baking soda
¼ teaspoon salt
1 cup granulated sugar
Pinch ground nutmeg
Pinch ground ginger
2 tablespoons finely chopped
   sun-dried tomatoes
1½ teaspoons grated lemon zest
1 cup finely chopped iceberg lettuce
¼ cup finely chopped walnuts or
   pecans
2 large eggs
½ cup canola oil
Ham Spread (see recipe page 57)

**1** Position the rack in the center of the oven and preheat to 350 degrees F. Lightly grease and flour an 8½-by-4½-by-2½-inch loaf pan.

**2** In a large bowl, blend together the flour, baking powder, baking soda, salt, sugar, nutmeg, ginger, tomatoes, lemon zest, lettuce, and nuts. In a medium bowl, beat the eggs until foamy before beating in the oil. Combine the two mixtures, blending until the dry ingredients are moistened.

**3** Scrape the batter into the prepared pan. Bake for 45 to 50 minutes, or until a cake tester or wooden toothpick inserted into the center of the bread comes out clean and the top is golden. Remove from the oven and cool the pan on a wire rack for 5 to 10 minutes before removing the loaf from the pan. Serve with Ham Spread.

# LETTUCE BREAD
MAKES: *1 loaf*

---

3 cups all-purpose flour
¾ cup plus 2 tablespoons granulated
   sugar
1 tablespoon baking powder
¼ teaspoon baking soda
2 tablespoons finely chopped lime
   peel
½ teaspoon salt
1 large egg
¼ cup canola oil
1½ cups milk
5 tablespoons lime juice
Mandarin Orange Gelatin Salad (see
   recipe page 104)

**1** Position the rack in the center of the oven and preheat to 350 degrees F. Lightly grease and flour a 9¼-by-5¼-by-2¾-inch loaf pan.

**2** In a large bowl, blend together the flour, ¾ cup of the sugar, the baking powder, baking soda, peel, and salt. In a medium bowl, beat the egg until foamy before beating in the oil, milk, and 4 tablespoons of lime juice. Combine the two mixtures, blending until the dry ingredients are moistened.

**3** Scrape the batter into the prepared pan and bake for 55 to 60 minutes, or until a cake tester or wooden toothpick inserted into the center of the bread is removed clean and the top is golden brown. Remove from the oven and cool the pan on a wire rack for 5 to 10 minutes before removing the loaf from the pan.

**4** Meanwhile, in a cup, combine the remaining 2 tablespoons of sugar and the remaining tablespoon of lime juice. Brush over the bread as soon as it is removed from the pan. Serve with Mandarin Orange Gelatin Salad.

# LIME BREAD
MAKES: *1 loaf*

## MARBLEIZED CHOCOLATE LOAF

MAKES: *1 loaf*

1¾ cups all-purpose flour
¾ teaspoon baking powder
¾ teaspoon baking soda
1 tablespoon grated orange zest
1 cup butter-flavored vegetable
  shortening
1 cup granulated sugar
3 large eggs
1 cup chocolate-flavored yogurt or
  plain sour cream
2 teaspoons chocolate or orange
  extract
2 ounces (2 squares) unsweetened
  chocolate, melted
⅓ cup crème de cacao
Chocolate Sauce (see recipe page 26)

**1** Position the rack in the center of the oven and preheat to 350 degrees F. Lightly grease and flour an 8½-by-4½-by-2½-inch loaf pan.

**2** In a large bowl, blend together the flour, baking powder, baking soda, and orange zest. In a medium bowl, beat the shortening and sugar until light and fluffy.

Beat in the eggs, one at a time, beating vigorously after each addition. Beat in ¾ cup of the yogurt and the chocolate extract. Scrape the batter into the prepared pan.

**3** In a small bowl, combine the remaining ¼ cup of yogurt, the melted chocolate, and crème de cacao and beat until smooth. Spoon over the top of the mixture in the pan, and using a knife or spatula, swirl it back and forth several times to make swirls throughout the batter.

**4** Bake for 45 to 50 minutes, or until a cake tester or wooden toothpick inserted into the center of the bread comes out clean. Remove from the oven and cool the pan on a wire rack for 10 minutes before removing the loaf from the pan. Transfer the loaf to the rack to cool completely. Spread with the Chocolate Sauce, slice and serve.

## MARMALADE BREAD

MAKES: *1 loaf*

2 cups all-purpose flour
⅔ cup granulated sugar
1½ teaspoons baking powder
2 tablespoons orange peel, pith
  removed, cut into matchsticks
1 cup coarsely ground almonds
2 large eggs
¼ cup melted butter or margarine
½ cup milk
½ cup orange marmalade
¼ cup slivered almonds
2 tablespoons powdered sugar
1 teaspoon freshly squeezed orange
  juice
Orange Marshmallow Sauce (see
  recipe page 22)

**1** Position the rack in the center of the oven and preheat to 350 degrees F. Lightly grease and flour an 8½-by-4½-by-2½-inch loaf pan.

**2** In a large bowl, blend together the flour, sugar, baking powder, orange peel, and ground almonds. In a medium bowl, beat

the eggs until foamy before beating in the butter and milk. Stir in the marmalade. Combine the two mixtures, blending until the dry ingredients are moistened.

**3** Scrape the batter into the prepared pan and sprinkle the slivered almonds over the top. Bake for 45 to 50 minutes, or until a cake tester or wooden toothpick inserted into the center of the bread is removed clean and the top is golden brown. Remove from the oven and cool the pan on a wire rack for 5 to 10 minutes before removing the loaf from the pan.

**4** Meanwhile, in a cup, blend together the powdered sugar and orange juice. As soon as the loaf is removed from the pan, brush with the sugar mixture. Serve with Orange Marshmallow Sauce.

1 cup finely chopped pitted dates
½ cup boiling water
2 cups all-purpose flour
1 teaspoon baking powder
1 teaspoon baking soda
1 cup finely chopped hazelnuts
1 cup granulated sugar
1 cup Kraft's® real mayonnaise
½ cup heavy cream or evaporated
  milk
Flavored Mayonnaise of Choice (see
  recipe page 324)

1  Position the rack in the center of the oven and preheat to 350 degrees F. Lightly grease and flour an 8½-by-4½-by-2½-inch loaf pan.

2  In a small bowl, combine the dates and boiling water. Set aside to cool. In a large bowl, blend together the flour, baking powder, baking soda, and nuts. In a small bowl, beat the sugar and mayonnaise smooth before beating in the cream and cooled date mixture. Combine the wet and dry ingredients, blending until the dry ingredients are moistened.

3  Scrape the batter into the prepared pan and bake for 45 to 50 minutes, or until a cake tester or wooden toothpick inserted into the center of the bread comes out clean and the top is golden. Remove from the oven and cool the pan on a wire rack for 5 to 10 minutes before removing the loaf from the pan. Serve with Flavored Mayonnaise of Choice.

## MAYONNAISE DATE BREAD

MAKES: *1 loaf*

---

2 cups all-purpose flour
2 teaspoons baking powder
¼ cup granulated sugar
½ teaspoon salt
2 large eggs
½ cup melted butter or margarine
1 cup prepared mincemeat
½ cup unsweetened apple juice
3 tablespoons powdered sugar
1 tablespoon rum or fruit-flavored
  liqueur
Mincemeat Sauce (see recipe page
  142)

1  Position the rack in the center of the oven and preheat to 350 degrees F. Lightly grease and flour an 8½-by-4½-by-2½-inch loaf pan.

2  In a large bowl, blend together the flour, baking powder, granulated sugar, and salt. In a medium bowl, beat the eggs until foamy before stirring in the butter, mincemeat, and apple juice. Combine the two mixtures, blending until the dry ingredients are moistened.

3  Scrape the batter into the prepared pan and bake for 40 to 45 minutes, or until a cake tester or wooden toothpick inserted into the center of the bread comes out clean and the top is a light golden color.

4  Meanwhile, in a cup, combine the powdered sugar and rum. Remove the baked bread from the oven and cool the pan on a wire rack for 5 to 10 minutes before removing the loaf from the pan. Brush the loaf with the sugar-and-rum mixture. Serve with Mincemeat Sauce.

## MINCEMEAT BREAD

MAKES: *1 loaf*

# MÜESLI BREAD WITH NUTS

MAKES: *1 loaf*

2 cups all-purpose flour
1 cup crushed vanilla wafer cookies
1½ teaspoons baking powder
½ cup Müesli cereal, plus more for sprinkling
2 large eggs
¾ cup melted butter or margarine
¾ cup milk
⅔ cup sweetened condensed milk
Orange Sauce (see recipe page 33)

**1** Position the rack in the center of the oven and preheat to 350 degrees F. Lightly grease and flour an 8-inch square baking pan.

**2** In a large bowl, blend together the flour, vanilla wafers, baking powder, and ½ cup cereal. In a medium bowl, beat the eggs, butter, milk, and condensed milk until smooth. Combine the two mixtures, blending until the dry ingredients are moistened.

**3** Scrape the batter into the prepared pan and sprinkle the top with additional cereal. Bake for 35 to 40 minutes, or until a cake tester or wooden toothpick inserted into the center of the bread comes out clean and the top is golden. Remove from the oven and cool the pan on a wire rack for 5 to 10 minutes before cutting into squares and serving. Serve with Orange Sauce.

# NATURAL SPELT BREAD

MAKES: *1 loaf*

3½ cups spelt flour
2 tablespoons baking soda
½ teaspoon vitamin C crystals
½ cup natural unsweetened applesauce
1¼ cups water
Berry Sauce (see recipe page 38)

**1** Position the rack in the center of the oven and preheat to 350 degrees F. Lightly grease and flour a 9¼-by-5¼-by-2¾-inch loaf pan.

**2** In a large bowl, blend together the flour, baking soda, vitamin C, applesauce, and water, blending until the dry ingredients are moistened.

**3** Scrape the batter into the prepared pan and bake for 35 to 40 minutes, or until a cake tester or wooden toothpick inserted into the center of the bread comes out clean and the top is golden brown. Remove from the oven and cool in the pan on a wire rack before removing the loaf from the pan and transferring it to the rack to cool completely. Refrigerate until slicing and serving. Serve with Berry Sauce.

2 cups all-purpose flour
¾ cup sifted powdered sugar
½ teaspoon baking powder
½ teaspoon baking soda
½ teaspoon ground nutmeg
1 cup chopped pecans
½ teaspoon salt
¼ cup butter or margarine, at room temperature
2 large bananas, mashed
3 tablespoons sour milk or buttermilk
Nut Spread (see recipe page 121)

1 Position the rack in the center of the oven and preheat to 350 degrees F. Lightly grease and flour a 9¼-by-5¼-by-2¾-inch loaf pan.

2 In a large bowl, blend together the flour, sugar, baking powder, baking soda, nutmeg, pecans, and salt. Using a pastry blender or two knives scissor-fashion, cut the butter into the dry ingredients until the mixture resembles coarse meal. In a small bowl, blend together the bananas and sour milk. Using your hands, combine the two mixes until the dry ingredients are just moistened. If the dough is too dry, add additional sour milk, a tablespoonful at a time.

3 Press the dough evenly into the prepared baking pan and bake for 55 to 60 minutes, or until a cake tester or wooden toothpick inserted into the center of the bread comes out clean and the top is golden. Remove the loaf from the oven and cool the pan on a wire rack for 5 to 10 minutes before removing the loaf from the pan. Serve with Nut Spread.

## NUTTY BANANA BREAD

MAKES: *1 loaf*

2 cups all-purpose flour
½ cup whole-wheat flour
1½ cups quick-cooking rolled oats
2 teaspoons baking soda
3 ¼ cups flaked coconut
2 teaspoons salt
4 large eggs
1½ cups packed light-brown sugar
One 20-ounce can crushed pineapple (do not drain)
Creamy Pecan–Rum Sauce (see recipe page 147)

1 Position the rack in the center of the oven and preheat to 325 degrees F. Lightly grease and flour two 9¼-by-5¼-by-2¾-inch loaf pans.

2 In a large bowl, blend together the two flours, oats, baking soda, 3 cups of the coconut, and salt. In a medium bowl, beat the eggs until foamy before beating in the brown sugar. Stir in the undrained pineapple. Combine the two mixtures, blending until the dry ingredients are moistened.

3 Scrape the batter into the prepared pans and sprinkle the remaining ¼ cup of coconut over the tops. Bake for 55 to 60 minutes, or until a cake tester or wooden toothpick inserted into the center of the bread comes out clean and the tops are golden. Remove from the oven and cool the pans on a wire rack for 5 to 10 minutes before removing the loaves from the pans. Serve with Creamy Pecan–Rum Sauce.

## OATMEAL– COCONUT BREAD

MAKES: *2 loaves*

## OATMEAL DATE-AND-NUT BREAD

MAKES: *2 loaves*

3 cups all-purpose flour
1 cup granulated sugar
1 teaspoon baking powder
2 teaspoons baking soda
1½ cups rolled oats
1½ cups chopped almonds
1½ cups finely chopped dates
1 teaspoon salt
2 large eggs
⅔ cup molasses
2 cups buttermilk or sour milk
Custard Sauce (see recipe page 29)

1  Position the rack in the center of the oven and preheat to 350 degrees F. Lightly grease and flour two 8½-by-4½-by-2½-inch loaf pans.

2  In a large bowl, blend together the flour, sugar, baking powder, baking soda, oats, dates, almonds, and salt. In a medium bowl, beat the eggs, molasses, and buttermilk smooth. Combine the two mixtures, blending until the dry ingredients are moistened.

3  Scrape the batter into the prepared pans and bake for 45 to 50 minutes, or until a cake tester or wooden toothpick inserted into the center of the bread comes out clean and the tops are golden. Remove from the oven and cool the pans on a wire rack for 5 to 10 minutes before removing the loaves from the pans. Serve with Custard Sauce.

## OATMEAL–PRUNE BREAD

MAKES: *1 loaf*

2 cups all-purpose flour
1 cup rolled oats
2 teaspoons baking powder
¾ teaspoon baking soda
½ teaspoon salt
¼ cup butter or margarine, at room temperature
6 tablespoons firmly packed dark-brown sugar
1 large egg
1 cup buttermilk or sour milk
¼ cup plum-flavored yogurt (or any berry-flavored yogurt)
¾ cup finely chopped pitted dried prunes
Cranberry Sauce (see recipe page 108)

1  Position the rack in the center of the oven and preheat to 350 degrees F. Lightly grease and flour an 8¼-by-4½-by-2½-inch loaf pan.

2  In a large bowl, blend together the flour, oats, baking powder, baking soda, and salt. In a medium bowl, beat the butter and sugar together until light and fluffy before beating in the egg, buttermilk, yogurt. Stir in a ½ cup of the prunes. Combine the two mixtures, blending until the dry ingredients are just moistened.

3  Scrape the batter into the prepared pan and sprinkle the remaining ¼ cup of prunes over the top. Bake for 45 to 50 minutes, or until a cake tester or wooden toothpick inserted into the center of the bread comes out clean and the top is golden. Remove from the oven and cool the pan on a wire rack for 5 to 10 minutes before removing the loaf from the pan. Serve with Cranberry Sauce.

²⁄₃ cup all-purpose flour
1 cup whole-wheat flour
¹⁄₃ cup granulated sugar
1 teaspoon baking soda
½ teaspoon salt
1 large egg
1 cup milk
²⁄₃ cup molasses
2 teaspoons vinegar
**Strawberry Sauce (see recipe page 144)**

**1** Position the rack in the center of the oven and preheat to 350 degrees F. Lightly grease and flour an 8½-by-4½-by-2½-inch loaf pan.

**2** In a large bowl, blend together the two flours, sugar, baking soda, and salt. In a medium bowl, beat the egg, milk, molasses, and vinegar until smooth. Combine the two mixtures, blending until the dry ingredients are moistened.

**3** Scrape the batter into the prepared pan and bake for 45 to 50 minutes, or until a cake tester or wooden toothpick inserted into the center of the bread comes out clean and the top is golden. Remove from the oven and cool the pan on a wire rack for 5 to 10 minutes before removing the loaf from the pan. Serve with Strawberry Sauce.

# OLD-FASHIONED BROWN BREAD

MAKES: *1 loaf*

---

2 cups all-purpose flour
1 tablespoon baking powder
¼ cup granulated sugar
1 tablespoon grated orange zest
1 cup sliced almonds
1 large egg
2 tablespoons melted vegetable shortening
1 cup orange juice
**Raspberry-Rhubarb Blend (see recipe page 87)**

**1** Position the rack in the center of the oven and preheat to 350 degrees F. Lightly grease and flour an 8½-by-4½-by-2½-inch loaf pan.

**2** In a large bowl, blend together the flour, baking powder, sugar, orange zest, and almonds. In a medium bowl, beat the egg, shortening, and orange juice until smooth. Combine the two mixtures, blending until the dry ingredients are moistened.

**3** Scrape the batter into the prepared pan and bake for 45 to 50 minutes, or until a cake tester or wooden toothpick inserted into the center of the bread comes out clean and the top is golden. Remove from the oven and cool the pan on a wire rack for 5 to 10 minutes before removing the loaf from the pan. Serve with Raspberry-Rhubarb Blend.

# ORANGE-ALMOND BREAD

MAKES: *1 loaf*

## ORANGE BREAD

MAKES: *1 loaf*

2 cups all-purpose flour
4 teaspoons baking powder
½ cup granulated sugar
1 cup chopped candied orange peel
½ teaspoon salt
2 large eggs
3 tablespoons melted butter or
  margarine
½ cup freshly squeezed orange juice
Plum Topping (see recipe page 101)

**1** Position the rack in the center of the oven and preheat to 350 degrees F. Lightly grease and flour an 8½-by-4½-by-2½-inch loaf pan.

**2** In a large bowl, blend together the flour, baking powder, sugar, peel, and salt. In a medium bowl, beat the eggs, butter, and orange juice until smooth. Combine the two mixtures, blending until the dry ingredients are thoroughly moistened.

**3** Scrape the batter into the prepared pan and bake for 45 to 50 minutes, or until a cake tester or wooden toothpick inserted into the center of the bread comes out clean and the top is golden. Remove from the oven and cool the pan on a wire rack for 5 to 10 minutes before removing the loaf from the pan. Serve with Plum Topping.

## ORANGE–DATE BREAD

MAKES: *1 loaf*

⅔ cup coarsely chopped dates
½ cup hot water
2 cups sifted all-purpose flour
1½ teaspoons baking powder
½ teaspoon baking soda
¾ cup granulated sugar
½ teaspoon salt
1 large egg
1 medium orange, peeled, seeded,
  and diced
2 tablespoons melted butter or
  margarine
Fig Sauce (see recipe page 189)

**1** Position the rack in the center of the oven and preheat to 350 degrees F. Lightly grease and flour an 8½-by-4½-by-2½-inch loaf pan.

**2** In the container of a blender or food processor, combine the dates and water and process on high speed until the dates are finely chopped. In a large bowl, blend together the flour, baking powder, baking soda, sugar, and salt. In a medium bowl, beat the egg until foamy before beating in the orange and butter. Stir in the date mixture. Combine the dry and wet ingredients, blending until the dry ingredients are moistened.

**3** Scrape the batter into the prepared pan and bake for 45 to 50 minutes, or until a cake tester or wooden toothpick inserted into the center of the bread comes out clean and the top is golden. Remove from the oven and cool the pan on a wire rack for 5 to 10 minutes before removing the loaf from the pan. Serve with Fig Sauce.

2 cups all-purpose flour
²⁄₃ cup whole wheat flour
2 teaspoons baking powder
½ teaspoon baking soda
½ cup granulated sugar
1 cup coarsely chopped pecans
3 ounces semisweet chocolate, grated
½ teaspoon salt
²⁄₃ cup buttermilk or sour milk
½ cup Triple Sec
2 tablespoons canola oil
½ cup molasses

**1** Position the rack in the center of the oven and preheat to 325 degrees F. Lightly grease and flour the bottom of a 9¼-by-5-by-2¾-inch loaf baking pan.

**2** In a large bowl, blend together the flour, baking powder, baking soda, sugar, pecans, chocolate, and salt. In a medium bowl, beat the milk, Triple Sec, canola oil, and molasses until smooth. Combine the mixtures, blending until the dry ingredients are just moistened.

**3** Spoon the batter into the prepared baking pan. Bake for 60 to 65 minutes, or until a cake tester or a wooden totohpick inserted into the center comes out of the bread clean. Remove from the oven and cool in the pan on a wire rack for 5 to 10 minutes before removing the loaf from the pan.

# ORANGE–FLAVORED CHOCOLATE NUT BREAD

MAKES: *1 loaf*

2¾ cups (approximately 38 crackers) finely crushed graham cracker crumbs
½ teaspoon baking powder
½ teaspoon baking soda
½ cup granulated sugar
½ teaspoon salt
3 large eggs
½ cup melted butter-flavored vegetable shortening
½ cup orange juice
1 tablespoon grated orange zest
Herbed Orange Sauce (see recipe page 163)
Thinly sliced almonds for topping

**1** Position the rack in the center of the oven and preheat to 350 degrees F. Lightly grease and flour an 8½-by-4½-by-2½-inch loaf pan.

**2** In a large bowl, blend together the cracker crumbs, baking powder, baking soda, sugar, and salt. In a medium bowl, beat the eggs until foamy before beating in the butter and orange juice. Stir in the orange zest. Combine the two mixtures, blending until the dry ingredients are moistened.

**3** Scrape the batter into the prepared pan and bake for 45 to 50 minutes, or until a cake tester or wooden toothpick inserted into the center of the bread comes out clean and the top is golden. Remove from the oven and cool the pan on a wire rack for 5 to 10 minutes before removing the loaf from the pan. Brush the loaf with the Herbed Orange Sauce and sprinkle with the sliced almonds.

# ORANGE–GRAHAM CRACKER BREAD

MAKES: *1 loaf*

## ORANGE GUMDROP BREAD

MAKES: *2 loaves*

1½ cups finely chopped dates
½ cup hot water
½ cup Triple Sec liqueur
4 cups all-purpose flour
¾ cup granulated sugar
2 teaspoons baking powder
2 teaspoons baking soda
1 teaspoon grated orange zest
2 cups orange gumdrop candies
½ teaspoon salt
2 large eggs
¾ cup packed brown sugar
½ cup butter or margarine, at room
    temperature
1 cup orange juice
Flaked coconut for topping

**1** Position the rack in the center of the oven and preheat to 350 degrees F. Lightly grease and flour the bottom of two 8½-by-4½-by-2½-inch loaf pans.

**2** In a small bowl, using a fork, combine the dates, water, and liqueur. Set aside to cool. In a large bowl, blend together the flour, granulated sugar, baking powder, baking soda, orange zest, candies, and salt. In a medium bowl, beat the eggs until foamy before beating in the brown sugar, butter, and orange juice. Stir in the date mixture. Combine the two mixtures, blending until the dry ingredients are moistened.

**3** Scrape the batter into the prepared pans and bake for 45 to 50 minutes, or until a cake tester or wooden toothpick inserted into the center of the bread comes out clean and the tops are golden. Remove from the oven and cool the pans on a wire rack for 5 to 10 minutes before removing the loaves from the pans. Sprinkle top of loaves with the coconut.

## ORANGE-HONEY BREAD

MAKES: *1 loaf*

2⅔ cups all-purpose flour
2½ teaspoons baking powder
½ teaspoon baking soda
2 tablespoons finely grated orange
    zest
¾ cup finely chopped hazelnuts
½ teaspoon salt
1 large egg
1 cup honey
2 tablespoons melted vegetable
    shortening
½ cup orange juice
Caramel Sauce (see recipe page 32)

**1** Position the rack in the center of the oven and preheat to 325 degrees F. Lightly grease and flour an 8½-by-4½-by-2½-inch loaf pan.

**2** In a large bowl, blend together the flour, baking powder, baking soda, orange zest, hazelnuts, and salt. In a medium bowl, beat the egg until foamy before beating in the honey, shortening, and juice. Combine the two mixtures, blending until the dry ingredients are moistened.

**3** Scrape the batter into the prepared pan and bake for 45 to 50 minutes, or until a cake tester or wooden toothpick inserted into the center of the bread comes out clean and the top is golden. Remove from the oven and cool the pan on a wire rack for 5 to 10 minutes before removing the loaf from the pan. Serve with hot Caramel Sauce.

2 cups all-purpose flour
¾ cup graham flour
2 teaspoons baking powder
½ teaspoon baking soda
½ cup chopped walnuts
½ teaspoon salt
½ cup butter or margarine, at room
temperature
½ cup packed light-brown sugar
2 large eggs
One 10-ounce jar orange marmalade
½ cup freshly squeezed orange juice
Golden Sauce (see recipe page 151)

1  Position the rack in the center of the oven and preheat to 350 degrees F. Lightly grease and flour an 8½-by-4½-by-2½-inch loaf pan.

2  In a large bowl, blend together the two flours, baking powder, baking soda, walnuts, and salt. In a medium bowl, beat the butter and brown sugar until smooth before beating in the eggs, one at a time, beating vigorously after each addition. Beat in the marmalade and juice. Combine the two mixtures, blending until the dry ingredients are moistened.

3  Scrape the batter into the prepared pan and bake for 55 to 60 minutes, or until a cake tester or wooden toothpick inserted into the center of the bread comes out clean and the top is golden. Remove from the oven and cool the pan on a wire rack for 5 to 10 minutes before removing the loaf from the pan. Serve with Golden Sauce.

# ORANGE MARMALADE NUT BREAD

MAKES: *1 loaf*

2¾ cups all-purpose flour
1 cup granulated sugar
1 tablespoon baking powder
1 teaspoon baking soda
½ cup coarsely chopped hazelnuts
1 tablespoon coarsely grated orange
zest
¾ cup finely diced cooked potatoes
½ cup coarsely chopped seedless
raisins
1 teaspoon salt
1 large egg
1 tablespoon canola oil
1¼ cups orange juice
½ teaspoon almond extract
Herb Salsa (see recipe page 197)

1  Position the rack in the center of the oven and preheat to 350 degrees F. Lightly grease and flour a 9¼-by-5¼-by-2¾-inch loaf pan.

2  In a large bowl, blend together the flour, sugar, baking powder, baking soda, nuts, zest, potatoes, raisins, and salt. In a medium bowl, beat the egg until foamy before beating in the oil, orange juice, and almond extract. Combine the two mixtures, blending until the dry ingredients are moistened.

3  Scrape the batter into the prepared pan and bake for 55 to 60 minutes, or until a cake tester or wooden toothpick inserted into the center of the bread comes out clean and the top is golden. Remove from the oven and cool the pan on a wire rack for 5 to 10 minutes before removing the loaf from the pan. Serve with Herb Salsa

# ORANGE–POTATO BREAD

MAKES: *1 loaf*

## PEACH–PECAN BREAD

MAKES: *1 loaf*

2 cups all-purpose flour
¾ cup granulated sugar
1 tablespoon baking powder
1 cup coarsely chopped pecans
1 teaspoon salt
2 large eggs
6 tablespoons melted butter or
    margarine
1 tablespoon lemon juice
¼ cup peach-flavored brandy
One 16-ounce can finely diced
    peaches, drained
Peach Butter (see recipe page 124)
Pecan halves for topping

1  Position the rack in the center of the oven and preheat to 350 degrees F. Lightly grease and flour an 8½-by-4½-by-2½-inch loaf pan.

2  In a large bowl, blend together the flour, sugar, baking powder, pecans, and salt. In a medium bowl, beat the eggs until foamy before beating in the butter, lemon juice, and brandy. Stir in the peaches. Combine the two mixtures, blending until the dry ingredients are moistened.

3  Scrape the batter into the prepared pan and bake for 45 to 50 minutes, or until a cake tester or wooden toothpick inserted into the center of the bread comes out clean and the top is golden. Remove from the oven and cool the pan on a wire rack for 5 to 10 minutes before removing the loaf from the pan. Sprinkle top of loaf with pecan halves and serve with Peach Butter.

## PEANUT BUTTER BREAD

MAKES: *1 loaf*

1 cup all-purpose flour
1 cup whole-wheat flour
4 teaspoons baking powder
¾ cup dry nonfat milk powder
¾ cup chopped peanuts
¼ teaspoon salt
1 large egg
½ cup granulated sugar
1½ cups warm water
¾ cup creamy peanut butter

1  Position the rack in the center of the oven and preheat to 325 degrees F. Lightly grease and flour an 8½-by-4½-by-2½-inch loaf pan.

2  In a large bowl, blend together the two flours, baking powder, dry milk, peanuts, and salt. In a medium bowl, beat the egg until foamy before beating in the sugar, warm water, and peanut butter. Combine the two mixtures, blending until the dry ingredients are moistened.

3  Scrape the batter into the prepared pan and bake for 55 to 60 minutes, or until a cake tester or wooden toothpick inserted into the center of the bread comes out clean and the top is golden brown. Remove from the oven and cool the pan on a wire rack for 5 to 10 minutes before removing the loaf from the pan.

2 cups all-purpose flour
1 cup granulated sugar
1 tablespoon baking powder
1 cup crumbled crisply cooked
  bacon, plus more for topping the
  bread
1 cup coarsely chopped unsalted
  peanuts
½ teaspoon salt
1 large egg
1 tablespoon melted butter or
  margarine
1 cup milk
1 cup peanut butter
Honey for brushing
Peppery Lemon Butter (see recipe
  page 74)

**1** Position the rack in the center of the oven and preheat to 350 degrees F. Lightly grease and flour an 8½-by-4½-by-2½-inch loaf pan.

**2** In a large bowl, blend together the flour, sugar, baking powder,1 cup crumbled bacon, peanuts, and salt. In a medium bowl, beat the egg until foamy before beating in the butter, milk, and peanut butter. Combine the two mixtures, blending until the dry ingredients are moistened.

**3** Scrape the batter into the prepared pan and bake for 45 to 50 minutes, or until a cake tester or wooden toothpick inserted into the center of the bread comes out clean and the top is golden. Remove from the oven and cool the pan on a wire rack for 5 to 10 minutes before removing the loaf from the pan. Brush the loaf with honey and sprinkle with additional crumbled bacon. Serve with Peppery Lemon Butter.

# PEANUT BUTTER–
# BACON BREAD

MAKES: *1 loaf*

---

1¾ cups all-purpose flour
⅔ cup granulated sugar
2 teaspoons baking powder
½ teaspoon baking soda
¼ teaspoon salt
2 large eggs
⅓ cup melted butter or margarine
¾ chunky-style peanut butter
1 cup mashed bananas
Banana Cream (see recipe page 56)

**1** Position the rack in the center of the oven and preheat to 350 degrees F. Lightly grease and flour an 8½-by-4½-by-2½-inch loaf pan.

**2** In a large bowl, blend together the flour, sugar, baking powder, baking soda, and salt. In a medium bowl, beat the eggs until foamy before beating in the butter, peanut butter, and bananas. Combine the two mixtures, blending until the dry ingredients are moistened.

**3** Scrape the batter into the prepared pan and bake for 45 to 50 minutes, or until a cake tester or wooden toothpick inserted into the center of the bread comes out clean and the top is golden. Remove from the oven and cool the pan on a wire rack for 5 to 10 minutes before removing the loaf from the pan. Serve with Banana Cream.

# PEANUT BUTTER–
# BANANA BREAD

MAKES: *1 loaf*

## PEANUT BUTTER BREAD

MAKES: *1 loaf*

2 cups Bisquick® baking mix
2 teaspoons baking powder
⅓ cup granulated sugar
1 large egg
1 cup milk
¾ cup peanut butter
Peanut Sauce (see recipe page 201)

**1** Position the rack in the center of the oven and preheat to 350 degrees F. Lightly grease and flour an 8½-by-4½-by-2½-inch loaf pan. In a large bowl, blend together the baking mix, baking powder, and sugar.

**2** In a small bowl, beat the egg until foamy before beating in the milk and peanut butter. Combine the two mixtures, blending until the dry ingredients are thoroughly moistened.

**3** Scrape the batter into the prepared pan and bake for 55 to 60 minutes, or until a cake tester or wooden toothpick inserted into the center of the bread comes out clean and the top is golden. Remove from the oven and cool the pan on a wire rack for 5 to 10 minutes before removing the loaf from the pan. Serve with Peanut Sauce.

## PEAR-AND-WALNUT BREAD

MAKES: *1 loaf*

2½ cups all-purpose flour
1¼ cups granulated sugar
2 teaspoons baking powder
1 teaspoon baking soda
½ teaspoon ground cinnamon
¼ teaspoon ground ginger
1 tablespoon grated lemon zest
2 large eggs
½ cup canola oil
¼ teaspoon lemon extract
1 cup coarsely chopped fresh pears
2 cups finely diced canned pears
Maple-Flavored Whipped Cream
(see recipe page 94)

**1** Position the rack in the center of the oven and preheat to 350 degrees F. Lightly grease and flour a 9¼-by-5¼-by-2¾-inch loaf pan.

**2** In a large bowl, blend together the flour, sugar, baking powder, baking soda, cinnamon, ginger, and lemon zest. In a medium bowl, beat the eggs until foamy before beating in the oil and extract. Stir in both types of pears. Combine the two mixtures, blending until the dry ingredients are moistened.

**3** Scrape the batter into the prepared pan and bake for 45 to 50 minutes, or until a cake tester or wooden toothpick inserted into the center of the bread comes out clean and the top is golden. Remove from the oven and cool the pan on a wire rack for 5 to 10 minutes before removing the loaf from the pan. Serve with Maple-Flavored Whipped Cream.

2 cups all-purpose flour
4 teaspoons baking powder
1 cup finely chopped pecans
¼ teaspoon ground nutmeg
1 large egg
1 large egg yolk
3 tablespoons packed light-brown
    sugar
1 cup milk
5 tablespoons melted butter or
    margarine
Hard Sauce (see recipe page 97)
Flaked coconut for sprinkling

**1** Position the rack in the center of the oven and preheat to 350 degrees F. Lightly grease and flour an 8½-by-4½-by-2½-inch loaf pan.

**2** In a large bowl, blend together the flour, baking powder, pecans, and nutmeg. In a medium bowl,

beat the egg and egg yolk until foamy before beating in the sugar, milk, and butter. Combine the two mixtures, blending until the dry ingredients are moistened.

**3** Scrape the batter into the prepared pan and bake for 45 to 50 minutes, or until a cake tester or wooden toothpick inserted into the center of the bread comes out clean and the top is golden. Remove from the oven and cool the pan on a wire rack for 5 to 10 minutes before removing the loaf from the pan. Sprinkle with coconut and serve with Hard Sauce.

## PECAN BREAD
MAKES: *1 loaf*

---

1 cup all-purpose flour
1½ cups yellow cornmeal
½ cup granulated sugar
1 tablespoon baking powder
1 cup finely chopped pecans
1 teaspoon salt
2 large eggs
¾ cup melted butter
1½ cups half-and-half
Flaked coconut for sprinkling
Coarsely ground pecans for
    sprinkling
Cottage Cheese Dip (see recipe
    page 195)

**1** Position the rack in the center of the oven and preheat to 375 degrees F. Lightly grease and flour an 8½-by-4½-by-2½-inch loaf pan.

**2** In a large bowl, blend together the flour, cornmeal, sugar, baking powder, and salt. In a medium bowl, beat together the eggs, butter, and half-and-half. Combine the two mixtures, blending until the dry ingredients are moistened.

**3** Scrape the batter into the prepared pan and bake for 45 to 50 minutes, or until a cake tester or wooden toothpick inserted into the center of the bread comes out clean and the top is golden. Remove from the oven and cool the pan on a wire rack for 5 to 10 minutes before removing the loaf from the pan. Sprinkle with coconut and ground pecans. Serve with Cottage Cheese Dip.

## PECAN CORN BREAD
MAKES: *1 loaf*

## PEPPARKAKOR BREAD

MAKES: *1 loaf*

1½ cups all-purpose flour
1 teaspoon baking soda
1 cup granulated sugar
1 teaspoon cloves
1 teaspoon ground cinnamon
¼ teaspoon ground cardamom
2 large eggs
1 cup sour cream or plain yogurt
½ cup melted butter or margarine
Flaked coconut from sprinkling
Whipped Cream-Cheese Topping
  (see recipe page 186)

1  Position the rack in the center of the oven and preheat to 350 degrees F. Lightly grease and flour a 5¾-by-3-by-2-inch loaf pan.

2  In a large bowl, blend together the flour, baking soda, sugar, cloves, cinnamon, and cardamom. In a medium bowl, beat the eggs until foamy before beating in the sour cream and butter. Combine the two mixtures, blending until the dry ingredients are moistened.

3  Scrape the batter into the prepared pan and bake for 35 to 40 minutes, or until a cake tester or wooden toothpick inserted into the center of the bread comes out clean and the top is golden. Remove from the oven and cool the pan on a wire rack for 5 to 10 minutes before removing the loaf from the pan. Sprinkle with the coconut and serve with Whipped Cream-Cheese Topping.

## PEPPER-AND-FETA BREAD

MAKES: *1 loaf*

1 medium red bell pepper, seeded and finely chopped
1 medium yellow bell pepper, seeded washed, and finely chopped
1 tablespoon olive oil
2½ cups all-purpose flour
1¼ teaspoons baking powder
¼ teaspoon baking soda
¼ teaspoon salt
½ cup crumbled Feta cheese
1 tablespoon snipped fresh rosemary
3 tablespoons melted butter or margarine
1 large egg
1¼ cup milk
Freshly ground black pepper to taste
Shrimp Spread (see recipe page 145)

1  Position the rack in the center of the oven and preheat to 350 degrees F. Lightly grease and flour a 9¼-by-5¼-by-2¾-inch loaf pan.

2  In a medium skillet set over a medium heat, sauté the peppers in the olive oil until tender. Set aside.

3  In a large bowl, blend together the flour, baking powder, baking soda, salt, rosemary, and cheese. In a small bowl, beat the butter and egg until smooth before beating in the milk. Stir in the cooked peppers. Combine the two mixtures, blending until the dry ingredients are thoroughly moistened. Adjust the seasoning.

4  Scrape the batter into the prepared baking pan and bake for 55 to 60 minutes, or until a cake tester or wooden toothpick inserted into the center of the bread comes out clean and the top is golden. Remove from the oven and cool the pan on a wire rack for 5 to 10 minutes before removing the loaf from the pan. Serve with Shrimp Spread.

3 tablespoons extra-virgin olive oil
1 teaspoon garlic powder
1 medium leek, trimmed, washed, and sliced
2 cups all-purpose flour
1½ teaspoons baking powder
2 teaspoons curry powder
1 teaspoon freshly ground coriander seeds
1 teaspoon ground cumin
½ cup grated Cheddar cheese
2 large eggs
1 cup milk
⅓ cup melted butter or margarine
1 cup finely grated zucchini
Flavored Mayonnaise of Choice (see recipe page 324)

**1** Position the rack in the center of the oven and preheat to 350 degrees F. Lightly grease and flour an 8½-by-4½-by-2½-inch loaf pan.

**2** In a small skillet set over medium heat, warm the olive oil and garlic powder, blending until smooth. Add the leeks and sauté until translucent. Remove from the heat and set aside.

**3** In a large bowl, blend together the flour, baking powder, curry powder, coriander, cumin, and cheese. In a medium bowl, beat the eggs until foamy before beating in the milk and butter. Stir in the leeks and zucchini. Combine the two mixtures, blending until the dry ingredients are moistened.

**4** Scrape the batter into the prepared pan and bake for 55 to 60 minutes, or until a cake tester or wooden toothpick inserted into the center of the bread comes out clean and the top is golden. Remove from the oven and invert on a wire rack to cool for 5 to 10 minutes before removing the loaf from the pan. Serve with Flavored Mayonnaise of Choice.

# PEPPERED ZUCCHINI BREAD

MAKES: *1 loaf*

---

2 cups all-purpose flour
1½ teaspoons baking powder
⅔ cup granulated sugar
2 tablespoons snipped fresh mint
½ cup glacé pineapple, finely chopped
2 large eggs
½ cup evaporated milk
1 cup persimmon pulp
½ cup melted butter or margarine
Tropical Sauce (see recipe page 81)

**1** Position the rack in the center of the oven and preheat to 350 degrees F. Lightly grease and flour the bottom of two 8½-by-4½-by-2½-inch loaf pans.

**2** In a large bowl, blend together the flour, baking powder, sugar, mint, and pineapple. In a medium bowl, beat the eggs until foamy before beating in the milk, persimmon pulp, and butter. Combine the two mixtures, blending until the dry ingredients are well moistened.

**3** Scrape the batter into the prepared pans and bake for 45 to 50 minutes, or until a cake tester or wooden toothpick inserted into the center of the bread comes out clean and the tops are golden brown. Remove from the oven and cool the pans on a wire rack for 3 to 5 minutes before removing the loaves from the pans. Serve with Tropical Sauce.

# PERSIMMON– PINEAPPLE BREAD

MAKES: *2 loaves*

## PESTO BREAD WITH SALAMI

MAKES: *1 loaf*

2 cups all-purpose flour
1½ teaspoons baking powder
½ teaspoon baking soda
⅔ cup grated Gruyére or Swiss cheese
1½ cups chopped dry salami
3 large eggs
⅓ cup canola oil
½ cup buttermilk or sour milk
⅓ cup prepared pesto
Pesto Cream (see recipe page 169)

1 Position the rack in the center of the oven and preheat to 350 degrees F. Lightly grease and flour an 8-inch square baking pan.

2 In a large bowl, blend together the flour, baking powder, baking soda, cheese, and salami. In a medium bowl, beat the eggs until foamy before beating in the oil, buttermilk, and pesto. Combine the two mixtures, blending until the dry ingredients are thoroughly moistened. Adjust the seasoning.

3 Scrape the mixture into the prepared baking pan and bake for 35 to 40 minutes, or until a cake tester or wooden toothpick inserted into the center of the bread comes out clean and the tops are golden brown. Remove from the oven and cool the pans on a wire rack for 5 to 10 minutes before cutting into squares and serving. Serve with Pesto Cream.

## PIÑA COLADA BREAD

MAKES: *1 loaf*

1½ cups all-purpose flour
1 teaspoon baking powder
½ teaspoon baking soda
½ cup granulated sugar
½ cup flaked coconut
1 large egg
¼ cup melted butter or margarine
1 cup coconut milk
½ teaspoon rum or rum extract
One 15.5-ounce can crushed pineapple, drained
Whipped Cream-Cheese Topping (see recipe page 186)

1 Position the rack in the center of the oven and preheat to 350 degrees F. Lightly grease and flour an 8½-by-4½-by-2½-inch loaf pan.

2 In a large bowl, blend together the flour baking powder, baking soda, sugar, and coconut. In a medium bowl, beat the egg until foamy before beating in the butter, coconut milk, and rum. Stir in the pineapple. Combine the two mixtures, blending until the dry ingredients are moistened.

3 Scrape the batter into the prepared pan and bake for 40 to 45 minutes, or until a cake tester or wooden toothpick inserted into the center of the bread comes out clean and the top is golden. Remove from the oven and cool the pan on a wire rack for 5 to 10 minutes before removing the loaf from the pan. Serve with Whipped Cream-Cheese Topping.

1¼ cups all-purpose flour
1 cup whole-wheat flour
1 cup granulated sugar
1 teaspoon baking soda
1 cup finely chopped almonds
1 teaspoon salt
1 large egg
2 tablespoons melted butter or
    margarine
1 cup water
¼ cup pineapple juice
2 cups crushed pineapple, drained
½ cup slivered almonds for topping
Tropical Sauce (see recipe page 81)

1 Position the rack in the center of the oven and preheat to 350 degrees F. Lightly grease and flour a 9¼-by-5¼-by-2¾-inch loaf pan.

2 In a large bowl, blend together the two flours, sugar, baking soda, almonds, and salt. In a medium bowl, beat the eggs until foamy before beating in the butter, water, and pineapple. Combine the two mixtures, blending until the dry ingredients are thoroughly moistened.

3 Scrape the batter into the prepared pan, sprinkle the slivered almond on top, and bake for 55 to 60 minutes, or until a cake tester or wooden toothpick inserted into the center of the bread comes out clean and the top is golden brown. Remove from the oven and cool on a wire rack for 5 to 10 minutes before removing the loaf from the pan. Serve with Tropical Sauce.

# PINEAPPLE– ALMOND BREAD

MAKES: *1 loaf*

---

¼ cup cherry-flavored brandy or
    liqueur
1 cup diced dried cherries
1 cup all-purpose flour
1 cup whole-wheat flour
1 cup oat bran
1 teaspoon baking soda
1 cup chopped almonds
¼ cup vegetable shortening
½ cup granulated sugar
1 large egg
½ cup crushed pineapple, drained
1 cup buttermilk or sour milk
Cherry Sauce (see recipe page 52)

1 Thirty minutes before baking, in a small bowl, combine the liqueur and diced cherries. Cover and set in a warm place until ready.

2 Position the rack in the center of the oven and preheat to 350 degrees F. Lightly grease and flour a 9¼-by-5¼-by-2¾-inch loaf pan.

3 In a large bowl, blend together the two flours, oat bran, baking soda, and almonds. In a medium bowl, beat the shortening and sugar until light and fluffy before beating in the egg, pineapple, and buttermilk. Stir in the cherries and brandy. Combine the two mixtures, blending until the dry ingredients are thoroughly moistened.

4 Scrape the batter into the prepared pan and bake for 55 to 60 minutes, or until a cake tester or wooden toothpick inserted into the center of the bread comes out clean and the top is golden brown. Remove from the oven and cool on a wire rack for 5 to 10 minutes before removing the loaf from the pan. Serve with Cherry Sauce.

# PINEAPPLE– CHERRY BREAD

MAKES: *1 loaf*

# PINEAPPLE–NUT BREAD

MAKES: *1 loaf*

2 cups all-purpose flour
2 teaspoons baking powder
¼ teaspoon baking soda
2 tablespoons granulated sugar
½ teaspoon ground cardamom
¾ cup chopped chestnuts or black walnuts
½ cup finely chopped seedless raisins
2 large eggs
¾ cup packed dark-brown sugar
3 tablespoons melted butter or margarine
One 8-ounce can crushed pineapple, undrained
Custard Sauce (see recipe page 29)

**1** Position the rack in the center of the oven and preheat to 350 degrees F. Lightly grease and flour an 8½-by-4½-by-2½-inch loaf pan.

**2** In a large bowl, blend together the flour, baking powder, baking soda, granulated sugar, cardamom, chestnuts, and raisins. In a medium bowl, beat the eggs until foamy before beating in the brown sugar and butter. Stir in the pineapple. Combine the two mixtures, blending until the dry ingredients are thoroughly moistened.

**3** Scrape the batter into the prepared pan and bake for 55 to 60 minutes, or until a cake tester or wooden toothpick inserted into the center of the bread comes out clean and the top is golden brown. Remove from the oven and cool the pan on a wire rack for 5 to 10 minutes before removing the loaf from the pan. Serve with Custard Sauce.

# PINEAPPLE–PECAN BREAD

MAKES: *1 loaf*

1¼ cups all-purpose flour
1 tablespoon baking powder
½ teaspoon baking soda
1 cup coarsely chopped pecans
½ cup crushed Rice Krispies® cereal
2 large eggs
3 tablespoons canola oil
½ cup firmly packed light-brown sugar
1 cup buttermilk or sour milk
One 8-ounce can crushed pineapple, drained
Jelly Sauce (see recipe page 23)

**1** Position the rack in the center of the oven and preheat to 350 degrees F. Lightly grease and flour a 9¼-by-4¼-by-2¾-inch loaf pan.

**2** In a large bowl, blend together the flour, baking powder, baking soda, pecans, and cereal. In a medium bowl, beat the eggs until foamy before beating in the oil, sugar, and buttermilk. Stir in the pineapple. Combine the two mixtures, blending until the dry ingredients are thoroughly moistened.

**3** Scrape the batter into the prepared pan and bake for 55 to 60 minutes, or until a cake tester or wooden toothpick inserted into the center of the bread comes out clean and the top is golden brown. Remove from the oven and cool the pan on a wire rack for 5 to 10 minutes before removing the loaf from the pan. Serve wih Jelly Sauce.

3 cups all-purpose flour
1½ teaspoons baking powder
½ teaspoon baking soda
1½ teaspoons allspice
1 cup chopped almonds
1 cup chopped seedless raisins
½ teaspoon salt
3 large eggs
1 cup granulated sugar
1 cup packed light-brown sugar
1 cup canola oil
1 teaspoon almond extract
2 cups shredded zucchini
One 8-ounce can crushed pineapple, drained
Whipped Cream Topping (see recipe page 208)

1  Position the rack in the center of the oven and preheat to 350 degrees F. Lightly grease and flour a 9¼-by-5¼-by-2¾-inch loaf pan.

2  In a large bowl, blend together the flour, baking powder, baking soda, allspice, almonds, raisins, and salt. In a medium bowl, beat the eggs until foamy before beating in the two sugars, oil, and almond extract. Stir in the zucchini and pineapple.

3  Scrape the batter into the prepared pan and bake for 55 to 60 minutes, or until a cake tester or wooden toothpick inserted into the center of the bread comes out clean and the top is golden. Remove from the oven and cool the pan on a wire rack for 5 to 10 minutes before removing the loaf from the pan. Serve with Whipped Cream Topping.

## PINEAPPLE–ZUCCHINI BREAD

MAKES: *1 loaf*

---

1 small red bell pepper, seeded and diced
⅓ cup light olive oil
2½ cups all-purpose flour
1½ teaspoons baking powder
½ teaspoon baking soda
½ cup grated Cheddar cheese, plus ¼ cup for topping
¼ cup grated Parmesan or Romano cheese
½ cup pitted black olives, halved
¼ cup sun-dried tomatoes, washed drained and finely chopped
2 tablespoons snipped fresh basil
2 teaspoons snipped fresh rosemary
½ teaspoon garlic powder
1 large egg
1¼ cups buttermilk or sour milk
Tomato Sauce (see recipe page 219)

1  Position the rack in the center of the oven and preheat to 350 degrees F. Lightly grease and flour an 8½-by-4½-by-2¾-inch loaf pan.

2  In a small skillet over a medium heat, sauté the pepper in 2 tablespoons of the oil until tender. Remove from the heat and set aside.

3  In a large bowl, blend together the flour, baking powder, baking soda, the half cup of Cheddar cheese, the Parmesan cheese, olives, tomatoes, basil, rosemary, and garlic powder. In a medium bowl, beat the egg until foamy before beating in the buttermilk and remaining oil. Combine the two mixtures, blending until the dry ingredients are well moistened.

4  Scrape the batter into the prepared pan and sprinkle with the remaining ¼ cup Cheddar cheese. Bake for 45 to 50 minutes, or until a cake tester or wooden toothpick inserted into the center of the bread comes out clean and the top is golden brown. Remove from the oven and cool the pan on a wire rack for 3 to 5 minutes before removing the loaf from the pan. Serve with Tomato Sauce.

## PIZZA CHEESE BREAD

MAKES: *1 loaf*

## PLANTATION HERB BREAD

MAKES: *1 loaf*

2 cups all-purpose flour
1 tablespoon baking powder
1 cup cooked brown or wild rice
¼ teaspoon dried crushed thyme
½ teaspoon dried crushed basil
¼ teaspoon dried crushed parsley
¼ cup grated Parmesan or Romano cheese
2 large eggs
1 cup milk
3 tablespoons melted butter or margarine
Cheese Sauce (see recipe page 57)

**1** Position the rack in the center of the oven and preheat to 350 degrees F. Lightly grease and flour a 9¼-by-5¼-by-2¾-inch loaf pan.

**2** In a large bowl, blend together the flour, baking powder, rice, herbs, and cheese. In a medium bowl, beat the eggs until foamy before beating in the milk and butter. Combine the two mixtures, blending until the dry ingredients are well moistened.

**3** Scrape the batter into the prepared pan and bake for 55 to 60 minutes, or until a cake tester or wooden toothpick inserted into the center of the bread comes out clean and the top is golden brown. Remove from the oven and cool the pan on a wire rack for 5 to 10 minutes before removing the loaf from the pan. Serve with Cheese Sauce.

## PLUM BREAD WITH WHEAT GERM

MAKES: *1 loaf*

1½ cups all-purpose flour
1½ teaspoons baking powder
½ teaspoon baking soda
½ cup wheat germ
½ cup Turbinado sugar
1 large egg
¾ cup buttermilk or sour milk
3 tablespoons melted butter or margarine
5 large ripe plums, peeled, pitted, and diced
Plum Butter (see recipe page 47)

**1** Position the rack in the center of the oven and preheat to 350 degrees F. Lightly grease and flour an 8½-by-4½-by-2½-inch loaf pan.

**2** In a large bowl, blend together the flour, baking powder, baking soda, wheat germ, and sugar. In a medium bowl, beat the egg until foamy before beating in the buttermilk, butter, and plums. Combine the two mixtures, blending until the dry ingredients are moistened.

**3** Scrape the batter into the prepared pan and bake for 35 to 40 minutes, or until a cake tester or wooden toothpick inserted into the center of the bread comes out clean and the top is a light golden color. Remove from the oven and cool the pan on a wire rack for 5 to 10 minutes before removing the loaf from the pan. Serve with Plum Butter.

3 cups all-purpose flour
2¼ cups granulated sugar
1½ teaspoons baking powder
1½ tablespoons poppy seeds
3 large eggs
1½ cups heavy cream or evaporated milk
1⅛ cups canola oil
1½ teaspoons Molly McButter® powdered butter flavoring
1½ teaspoons vanilla extract
Poppy Seed Butter (see recipe page 96)

**1** Position the rack in the center of the oven and preheat to 350 degrees F. Lightly grease and flour a 9¼-by-5¼-by-2¾-inch loaf pan.

**2** In a large bowl, blend together the flour, sugar, baking powder, and poppy seeds. In a medium bowl, beat the eggs until foamy before beating in the cream, oil, butter flavoring, and vanilla extract. Combine the two mixtures, blending until the dry ingredients are thoroughly moistened.

**3** Scrape the batter into the prepared pan and bake for 55 to 60 minutes, or until a cake tester or wooden toothpick inserted into the center of the bread comes out clean and the top is golden brown. Remove from the oven and cool on a wire rack for 5 to 10 minutes before removing the loaf from the pan. Serve with Poppy Seed Butter

# POPPY SEED BREAD

MAKES: *1 loaf*

---

1 cup all-purpose flour
1 cup whole-wheat flour
1 cup oat flour
5 teaspoons baking powder
1 teaspoon baking soda
2 cups finely chopped pitted prunes
1 cup chopped chestnuts
½ teaspoon salt
1 cup granulated sugar
1 large egg
1 tablespoon melted vegetable shortening
½ cup prune juice
1¼ cups sour milk or buttermilk
Whipped Cream-Cheese Topping (see recipe page 186)

**1** Position the rack in the center of the oven and preheat to 350 degrees F. Lightly grease and flour two 8½-by-4½-by-2½-inch loaf pans.

**2** In a large bowl, blend together the three flours, baking powder, baking soda, prunes, chestnuts, and salt. In a medium bowl, beat the sugar and egg until smooth before beating in the shortening, prune juice, and sour milk. Combine the two mixtures, blending until the dry ingredients are thoroughly moistened.

**3** Scrape the batter into the prepared pans and bake for 45 to 50 minutes, or until a cake tester or wooden toothpick inserted into the center of the bread comes out clean and the top is golden brown. Remove from the oven and cool the pans on a wire rack for 5 to 10 minutes before removing the loaves from the pans. Serve with Whipped Cream-Cheese Topping.

# PRUNE–NUT BREAD

MAKES: *2 loaves*

# PUMPKIN BREAD

MAKES: *1 loaf*

2 cups all-purpose flour
1 teaspoon baking powder
1 teaspoon baking soda
1 teaspoon salt
1 cup packed dark-brown sugar
3 large eggs
½ cup butter or margarine, at room
   temperature
1½ teaspoons ground cinnamon
½ teaspoon ground cloves
½ teaspoon ground ginger
1 cup canned pumpkin puree
Whipped Cream-Cheese Topping
   (see recipe page 186)

1  Position the rack in the center of the oven and preheat to 350 degrees F. Lightly grease and flour an 8½-by-4½-by-2½-inch loaf pan.

2  In a large bowl, blend together the flour, baking powder, baking soda, and salt. In a medium bowl, beat the brown sugar and eggs until smooth before beating in the butter, cinnamon, cloves, ginger, and pumpkin. Combine the two mixtures, blending until the dry ingredients are thoroughly moistened.

3  Scrape the batter into the prepared pan and bake for 50 to 55 minutes, or until a cake tester or wooden toothpick inserted into the center of the bread comes out clean and the top is golden brown. Remove from the oven and cool the pan on a wire rack for 5 to 10 minutes before removing the loaf from the pan. Serve with Whipped Cream-Cheese Topping.

# PUMPKIN BREAD WITH ORANGE

MAKES: *2 loaves*

1 whole Valencia orange, peeled and
   diced into small pieces
⅔ cup Triple Sec liqueur
3½ cups all-purpose flour
2⅔ cups granulated sugar
2 teaspoons baking soda
½ teaspoon baking powder
1 teaspoon ground cinnamon
1 teaspoon ground cloves
1½ teaspoons salt
4 large eggs, at room temperature
⅔ cup vegetable shortening, at room
   temperature
One 16-ounce can pumpkin puree
¼ cup slivered almonds for topping
Miniature marshmallows for
   topping
Foamy Orange Sauce (see recipe
   page 204)

1  Position the rack in the center of the oven and preheat to 350 degrees F. Lightly grease and flour two 8½-by-4½-by-2½-inch loaf pans.

2  In a small bowl, combine the orange and liqueur and set aside. In a large bowl, blend together the flour, sugar, baking soda, baking powder, cinnamon, cloves, and salt. In a medium bowl, beat the eggs until foamy before beating in the shortening and pumpkin. Combine the two mixtures, blending until the dry ingredients are thoroughly moistened.

3  Scrape the batter into the prepared pans and bake for 45 to 50 minutes, or until a cake tester or wooden toothpick inserted into the center of the bread comes out clean and the tops are golden brown. Remove from the oven and cool the pans on a wire rack for 5 to 10 minutes before removing the loaves from the pans. Sprinkle almonds and miniature marshmallows on loaves. Serve wih Foamy Orange Sauce.

3 cups all-purpose flour
½ cup graham flour
1 teaspoon baking powder
1 teaspoon baking soda
1 teaspoon ground cinnamon
1 teaspoon ground cloves
½ teaspoon salt
⅔ cup chopped dried cranberries
⅔ cup finely chopped pecans or chestnuts
⅔ cup butter or margarine, at room temperature
2⅔ cups granulated sugar
4 large eggs
⅔ cup canned pumpkin puree
⅓ cup water
⅓ cup white port wine
Cranberry Sauce (see recipe page 108)

**1** Position the rack in the center of the oven and preheat to 350 degrees F. Lightly grease and flour two 8½-by-4½-by-2½-inch loaf pans.

**2** In a large bowl, blend together the two flours, baking powder, baking soda, dried cranberries, pecans or chestnuts, cinnamon, cloves, and salt. In a medium bowl, beat the butter and sugar until fluffy before beating in the eggs, one at a time, beating vigorously after each addition. Beat in the pumpkin, water, and port wine. Combine the two mixtures, blending until the dry ingredients are well moistened.

**3** Scrape the batter into the prepared pans and bake for 50 to 55 minutes, or until a cake tester or wooden toothpick inserted into the center of the bread comes out clean and the tops are golden. Remove from the oven and cool the pans on a wire rack for 5 to 10 minutes before removing the loaves from the pans. Serve with Cranberry Sauce.

## PUMPKIN– CRANBERRY BREAD

MAKES: *2 loaves*

---

3 cups all-purpose flour
¼ cup whole-wheat flour
1½ cups granulated sugar
¾ cups rolled oats
½ teaspoon baking powder
2 teaspoons baking soda
1 cup chopped black walnuts
½ teaspoon salt
1½ cups packed brown sugar
3 large eggs
½ cup canola oil
½ cup heavy cream or evaporated milk
½ cup white port wine or brandy
1½ teaspoons pumpkin-pie spice
1¾ cups canned pumpkin
Pumpkin Butter (see recipe page 122)

**1** Position the rack in the center of the oven and preheat to 350 degrees F. Lightly grease and flour two 9¼-by-5¼-by-2¾-inch loaf pans.

**2** In a large bowl, blend together the two flours, granulated sugar, oats, nuts, baking powder, baking soda, and salt. In a medium bowl, beat the brown sugar and eggs until smooth before beating in the oil, cream, wine, pumpkin-pie spice, and pumpkin. Combine the two mixtures, blending until the dry ingredients are well moistened.

**3** Scrape the batter into the prepared pans and bake for 50 to 55 minutes, or until a cake tester or wooden toothpick inserted into the center of the bread comes out clean and the tops are golden. Remove from the oven and cool the pans on a wire rack for 5 to 10 minutes before removing the loaves from the pans. Serve with Pumpkin Butter.

## PUMPKIN–NUT BREAD

MAKES: *2 loaves*

# QUICK FRUIT BREAD

MAKES: *1 loaf*

1 cup all-purpose flour
1 cup whole-wheat flour
½ cup soy flour
½ cup oat bran
1 teaspoon baking soda
1 cup chopped nuts (optional)
½ teaspoon salt
¼ cup butter or margarine, at room temperature
½ cup granulated sugar
1 large egg
¼ cup fresh juice or berry-flavored liqueur
1 cup fruit pulp
1 cup sour milk or buttermilk
Whipped Cream-Cheese Topping (see recipe page 186)

1 Position the rack in the center of the oven and preheat to 350 degrees F. Lightly grease and flour a 9¼-by-5¼-by-2¾-inch loaf pan.

2 In a large bowl, blend together the three flours, oat bran, baking soda, nuts, and salt. In a medium bowl, beat the butter and sugar until light and fluffy. Beat in the egg, juice, pulp, and sour milk. Combine the two mixtures, blending until the dry ingredients are well moistened.

3 Scrape the batter into the prepared pan and bake for 55 to 60 minutes, or until a cake tester or wooden toothpick inserted into the center of the bread comes out clean and the top is golden. Remove from the oven and cool the pan on a wire rack for 5 to 10 minutes before removing the loaf from the pan. Serve with Whipped Cream-Cheese Topping.

# QUICKIE COCOA BREAD

MAKES: *1 loaf*

2½ cups all-purpose flour
⅓ cup granulated sugar
1 tablespoon baking powder
½ teaspoon baking soda
¼ cup Dutch-processed cocoa powder
½ teaspoon salt
1 large egg
1⅓ cups milk
¼ cup melted vegetable shortening
Chocolate Sauce (see recipe page 26)

1 Position the rack in the center of the oven and preheat to 350 degrees F. Lightly grease and flour an 8½-by-4½-by-2½-inch loaf pan.

2 In a large bowl, blend together the flour, sugar, baking powder, baking soda, cocoa, and salt. In a medium bowl, beat the egg until foamy before beating in the milk and shortening. Combine the two mixtures, blending until the dry ingredients are well moistened.

3 Scrape the batter into the prepared pan and bake for 40 to 45 minutes, or until a cake tester or wooden toothpick inserted into the center of the bread comes out clean and the top is golden. Remove from the oven and cool the pan on a wire rack for 5 to 10 minutes before removing the loaf from the pan. Serve with Chocolate Sauce.

2 cups all-purpose flour
1 cup granulated sugar
1 tablespoon baking powder
½ teaspoon ground cinnamon
½ teaspoon ground nutmeg
1½ cups seedless raisins
1 cup chopped pecans
½ teaspoon salt
1 large egg
1¼ cups milk
2 tablespoons canola oil
1 tablespoon melted butter or
  margarine
1½ cups oat bran
Honey-Orange Marmalade Sauce
  (see recipe page 148)

**1** Position the rack in the center of the oven and preheat to 350 degrees F. Lightly grease and flour an 8½-by-4½-by-2½-inch loaf pan.

**2** In a large bowl, blend together the flour, ¾ cup of the sugar, the baking powder, cinnamon, nutmeg, raisins, pecans, and salt. In a medium bowl, beat the egg until foamy before beating in the milk, oil, and butter. Stir in the bran. Combine the two mixtures, blending until the dry ingredients are well moistened.

**3** Scrape the batter into the prepared pan and bake for 45 to 50 minutes, or until a cake tester or wooden toothpick inserted into the center of the bread comes out clean and the top is golden. Remove from the oven and cool the pan on a wire rack for 5 to 10 minutes before removing the loaf from the pan. Serve with Honey-Orange Marmalade Sauce.

# RAISIN, BRAN, AND NUT BREAD

MAKES: *1 loaf*

---

2 cups all-purpose flour
1 cup whole-wheat flour
1½ teaspoons baking powder
½ teaspoon baking soda
1 teaspoon ground cinnamon
½ teaspoon ground nutmeg
¼ teaspoon salt
⅛ teaspoon ground cloves
1 cup finely chopped raisins
One 16-ounce can beer

**1** Position the rack in the center of the oven and preheat to 350 degrees F. Lightly grease and flour a 9¼-by-5¼-by-2¾-inch loaf pan.

**2** In a large bowl, blend together the two flours, baking powder, baking soda, cinnamon, nutmeg, salt, cloves, and raisins. Make an indentation in the center of the ingredients and pour in the beer all at one time. Blend until the dry ingredients are moistened.

**3** Scrape the batter into the prepared pan and bake for 50 to 55 minutes, or until a cake tester or wooden toothpick inserted into the center of the bread comes out clean and the top is golden brown. Remove from the oven and cool the pan on a wire rack for 3 to 5 minutes before removing the loaf from the pan.

**SERVING SUGGESTION: Serve with a cold beer and cheese.**

# RAISIN, CINNAMON, AND BEER BREAD

MAKES: *1 loaf*

## REAL COCONUT BREAD

MAKES: *1 loaf*

2¾ cups all-purpose flour
1 cup powdered sugar
4 teaspoons baking powder
1¼ cups flaked coconut
1 teaspoon salt
1 large egg
1½ cups coconut milk
2 tablespoons peanut oil
1 teaspoon coconut extract
Coconut Chutney (see recipe
  page 65)

**1** Position the rack in the center of the oven and preheat to 375 degrees F. Lightly grease and flour a 9¼-by-5¼-by-2¾-inch loaf pan.

**2** In a large bowl, blend together the flour, sugar, baking powder, coconut, and salt. In a medium bowl, beat the egg, coconut milk, oil, and coconut extract until smooth. Combine the two mixtures, blending until the dry ingredients are thoroughly moistened.

**3** Scrape the batter into the prepared pan and bake for 55 to 60 minutes, or until a cake tester or wooden toothpick inserted into the center of the bread comes out clean and the top is golden. Remove from the oven and cool the pan on a wire rack for 5 to 10 minutes before removing the loaf from the pan. Serve with Coconut Chutney.

## RHUBARB BREAD

MAKES: *1 loaf*

2½ cups all-purpose flour
1 teaspoon baking soda
1½ cups diced fresh rhubarb
1½ cups chopped walnuts or pecans
1 teaspoon salt
1 large egg
1½ cups packed brown sugar
⅔ cup canola oil
1 cup buttermilk or sour milk
1 teaspoon vanilla extract
Strawberry Sauce (see recipe
  page 144)

**1** Position the rack in the center of the oven and preheat to 350 degrees F. Lightly grease and flour an 8½-by-4½-by-2½-inch loaf pan.

**2** In a large bowl, blend together the flour, baking soda, rhubarb, walnuts, and salt. In a medium bowl, beat the egg and brown sugar until smooth before beating in the oil, sour milk, and vanilla extract. Combine the two mixtures, blending until the dry ingredients are thoroughly moistened.

**3** Scrape the batter into the prepared pan and bake for 45 to 50 minutes, or until a cake tester or wooden toothpick inserted into the center of the bread comes out clean and the top is golden. Remove from the oven and cool the pan on a wire rack for 5 to 10 minutes before removing the loaf from the pan. Serve with Strawberry Sauce.

2 cups all-purpose flour
¼ cup granulated sugar
1 tablespoon baking powder
¼ cup chopped raisins
½ teaspoon salt
2 large eggs
1 cup milk
2 tablespoons melted butter or
　margarine
1 cup cold cooked rice
Cheese Spread (see recipe page 257)

**1** Position the rack in the center of the oven and preheat to 350 degrees F. Lightly grease and flour a 9¼-by-5¼-by-2¾-inch loaf pan.

**2** In a large bowl, blend together the flour, sugar, baking powder, raisins, and salt. In a medium bowl, beat the eggs until foamy before beating in the milk and butter. Stir in the rice. Combine the two mixtures, blending until the dry ingredients are just moistened.

**3** Scrape the batter into the prepared pan and bake for 45 to 50 minutes, or until a cake tester or wooden toothpick inserted into the center of the bread comes out clean. Remove from the oven and cool the pan on a wire rack for 5 to 10 minutes before removing the loaf from the pan. Serve with Cheese Spread.

# RICE BREAD WITH RAISINS

MAKES: *1 loaf*

---

1¾ cups all-purpose flour
2 teaspoons baking powder
¼ teaspoon baking soda
½ teaspoon salt
2 large eggs
⅔ cup granulated sugar
⅓ cup butter or margarine, at room
　temperature
1 teaspoon rum or brandy
2 large bananas, mashed
Banana Cream (see recipe page 56)

**1** Position the rack in the center of the oven and preheat to 350 degrees F. Lightly grease and flour an 8½-by-4½-by-2½-inch loaf pan.

**2** In a large bowl, blend together the flour, baking powder, baking soda, and salt. In a medium bowl, beat the eggs and sugar until smooth before beating in the butter, rum, and bananas. Combine the two mixtures, blending until the dry ingredients are thoroughly moistened.

**3** Scrape the batter into the prepared pan and bake for 55 to 60 minutes, or until a cake tester or wooden toothpick inserted into the center of the bread comes out clean and the top is golden. Remove from the oven and cool the pan on a wire rack for 5 to 10 minutes before removing the loaf from the pan. Serve with Banana Cream.

# RICH BANANA TEA BREAD

MAKES: *1 loaf*

## SALAMI CHEESE BREAD

MAKES: *1 loaf*

3 cups all-purpose flour
2 teaspoons baking powder
½ teaspoon baking soda
12 slices dry salami, sliced into matchsticks
½ cup grated Edam or Jarlsberg cheese
1 tablespoon snipped fresh parsley
2 teaspoons snipped fresh thyme
5 tablespoons melted butter or margarine
1 large egg
1½ cups buttermilk or sour milk
Salt and pepper to taste
Cheese-and-Olive Spread (see recipe page 183)

1  Position the rack in the center of the oven and preheat to 350 degrees F. Lightly grease and flour a 9¼-by-5¼-by-2¾-inch loaf pan.

2  In a large bowl, blend together the flour, baking powder, baking soda, salami, cheese, parsley, and thyme. In a medium bowl, beat the butter and egg until smooth before beating in the milk. Combine the two mixtures, blending until the dry ingredients are thoroughly moistened. Adjust the seasoning.

3  Scrape the batter into the prepared pan and bake for 55 to 60 minutes, or until a cake tester or wooden toothpick inserted into the center of the bread comes out clean and the top is golden brown. Remove from the oven and cool the pan on a wire rack for 5 to 10 minutes before removing the loaf from the pan. Serve with Cheese-and-Olive Spread.

## SALMON BREAD WITH ASPARAGUS

MAKES: *1 loaf*

2½ cups all-purpose flour
1½ teaspoons baking powder
½ teaspoon baking soda
One 7.5-ounce can sockeye salmon, drained
8 ounces fresh asparagus, chopped
2 large eggs
1 cup buttermilk or sour milk
¼ cup melted butter or margarine
1 tablespoon prepared mustard
Pepper to taste
Grated Parmesan or Romano cheese for topping
Chili Butter (see recipe page 119)

1  Position the rack in the center of the oven and preheat to 350 degrees F. Lightly grease and flour a 9¼-by-5¼-by-2¾-inch loaf pan.

2  In a large bowl, blend together the flour, baking powder, baking soda, salmon, and asparagus. In a medium bowl, beat the eggs until foamy before beating in the buttermilk, butter, and mustard. Combine the two mixtures, blending until the dry ingredients are thoroughly moistened. Adjust the seasoning.

3  Scrape the batter into the prepared baking pan and sprinkle the top with cheese. Bake for 55 to 60 minutes, or until a cake tester or wooden toothpick inserted into the center of the bread comes out clean and the top is golden brown. Remove from the oven and cool the pan on a wire rack for 5 to 10 minutes before removing the loaf from the pan. Serve with Chili Butter.

3 cups all-purpose flour
1 teaspoon baking powder
1 teaspoon baking soda
½ teaspoon onion powder
½ teaspoon garlic powder
1 cup chopped dried cranberries
(optional)
1 teaspoon salt
2 large eggs
¼ cup granulated sugar
1 pound pork sausage meat, cooked,
finely minced, and drained
1¼ cups beef or chicken broth
Flavored Mayonnaise of Choice (see
recipe page 324)

**1** Position the rack in the center of the oven and preheat to 350 degrees F. Lightly grease and flour a ring-mold baking pan.

**2** In a large bowl, blend together the flour, baking powder, baking soda, onion powder, garlic powder, cranberries, and salt. In a medium bowl, beat the eggs until foamy before beating in the sugar. Stir in the pork and broth. Combine the two mixtures, blending until the dry ingredients are well moistened.

**3** Scrape the batter into the prepared pan and bake for 55 to 60 minutes, or until a cake tester or wooden toothpick inserted into the center of the bread comes out clean and the top is golden brown. Remove from the oven, and cool on a wire rack for 3 to 5 minutes before removing the loaf from the pan. Serve with Flavored Mayonnaise of Choice.

## SAUSAGE BREAD

MAKES: *1 loaf*

---

1 cup all-purpose flour
2 cups cornmeal
1¼ teaspoons baking soda
½ cup sesame seeds
1 teaspoon salt
3 large eggs
⅓ packed light-brown sugar
2 cups buttermilk or sour milk
⅔ cup vegetable oil
Sesame Sauce (see recipe page 75)

**1** Position the rack in the center of the oven and preheat to 375 degrees F. Lightly grease and flour a 9-inch square baking pan. In a large bowl, blend together the flour, cornmeal, baking soda, sesame seeds, and salt. In a medi-

um bowl, beat the eggs and brown sugar until smooth before beating in the buttermilk and oil. Combine the two mixtures, blending until the dry ingredients are thoroughly moistened.

**3** Scrape the batter into the prepared pan and bake for 35 to 40 minutes, or until a cake tester or wooden toothpick inserted into the center of the bread comes out clean and the top is golden brown. Remove from the oven and cool the pan on a wire rack for 5 to 10 minutes before cutting the bread into squares and serving. Serve with Sesame Sauce.

## SESAME CORN BREAD

MAKES: *1 loaf*

## SHORT NEN BREAD

MAKES: *1 loaf*

1½ cups cornmeal
¾ cup wheat flour
½ teaspoon baking soda
1 cup finely chopped crisply cooked
 bacon
½ teaspoon salt
1 cup sour milk or buttermilk
Molasses Sauce (see recipe page 125)

1  Position the rack in the center of the oven and preheat to 425 degrees F. Lightly grease and flour a 9-inch square baking pan.

2  In a large bowl, blend together the cornmeal, flour, baking soda, bacon, and salt. Add the milk, blending until the dry ingredients are just moistened.

3  Scrape the batter into the prepared pan and bake for 25 to 30 minutes, or until a cake tester or wooden toothpick inserted into the center of the bread is removed clean and the top is a light golden brown. Remove from the oven and cool the pan on a wire rack for 5 to 10 minutes before cutting the bread into squares and serving. Serve with Molasses Sauce.

## SHREDDED WHEAT BREAD

MAKES: *1 loaf*

1½ cups all-purpose flour
½ cup whole-wheat flour
1 teaspoon baking powder
¼ teaspoon baking soda
2 cups finely crushed Nabisco®
 Shredded Wheat
1 cup granulated sugar
¾ cup golden raisins
2 tablespoons orange zest
2 large eggs
1½ cups milk
2 tablespoons melted butter or
 margarine
Berry Sauce (see recipe page 38)

1  Position the rack in the center of the oven and preheat to 350 degrees F. Lightly grease and flour an 8½-by-4½-by-2½-inch loaf pan.

2  In a large bowl, blend together the two flours, baking powder, baking soda, crushed wheat, sugar, raisins, and orange zest. In a medium bowl, beat the eggs until foamy before beating in the milk and butter. Combine the two mixtures, blending until the dry ingredients are just moistened.

3  Scrape the batter into the prepared pan and bake for 40 to 45 minutes, or until a cake tester or wooden toothpick inserted into the center of the bread comes out clean and the top is golden brown. Remove from the oven and cool the pan on a wire rack for 5 to 10 minutes before removing the loaf from the pan. Serve with Berry Sauce.

1½ cups all-purpose flour
½ cup whole-wheat flour
2 teaspoons baking powder
¼ cup grated Parmesan or Romano cheese
¼ teaspoon crushed thyme
¼ cup dried parsley
¼ cup finely chopped parsley
⅓ cup sour cream
⅓ cup canola oil
¾ cup milk
1 can deveined chopped shrimp, drained
½ cup finely crushed potato chips
Tomato–Basil Dip (see recipe page 130)

**1** Position the rack in the center of the oven and preheat to 350 degrees F. Lightly grease and flour a 9-inch square baking pan.

# SHRIMP BOAT BREAD

MAKES: *1 loaf*

**2** In a large bowl, blend together the two flours, baking powder, cheese, thyme, and parsley. In a medium bowl, beat the sour cream, oil, and milk until smooth. Stir in the shrimp. Combine the two mixtures, blending until the dry ingredients are moistened.

**3** Scrape the batter into the prepared pan and sprinkle the potato chips over the top. Bake for 30 to 55 minutes, or until a cake tester or wooden toothpick inserted into the center of the bread comes out clean and the top is golden. Remove from the oven and cool the pan on a wire rack for 5 to 10 minutes before cutting into squares and serving. Serve with Tomato–Basil Dip.

---

1 cup all-purpose flour
¾ cup yellow cornmeal
¼ cup granulated sugar
2 teaspoons baking powder
½ teaspoon salt
1 large egg
2 tablespoons canola oil
1 cup sour cream or plain yogurt
¼ cup milk
Parsley Sauce (see recipe page 202)

**1** Position the rack in the center of the oven and preheat to 425 degrees F. Lightly grease and flour an 8-inch square baking pan.

**2** In a large bowl, blend together the flour, cornmeal, sugar, baking powder, and salt. In a medium

# SOUR CREAM CORN BREAD

MAKES: *1 loaf*

bowl, beat the egg until foamy before beating in the oil, sour cream, and milk. Combine the two mixtures, blending until the dry ingredients are thoroughly moistened.

**3** Scrape the batter into the prepared pan and bake for 35 to 50 minutes, or until a cake tester or wooden toothpick inserted into the center of the bread comes out clean and the top is golden brown. Remove from the oven and cool the pan on a wire rack for 5 to 10 minutes before cutting into squares and serving. Serve with Parsley Sauce.

## SOUTHERN-STYLE SWEET POTATO BREAD

MAKES: *1 loaf*

2 cups all-purpose flour
1½ teaspoons baking powder
¼ teaspoon ground allspice
¼ teaspoon ground nutmeg
¼ cup finely chopped pecans
1 teaspoon freshly grated orange zest
¼ cup butter or margarine, at room temperature
½ cup packed dark-brown sugar
2 large eggs
1 cup cooked mashed sweet potatoes or yams
3 tablespoons milk or cream
Marshmallow Sauce (see recipe page 131)

1 Position the rack in the center of the oven and preheat to 350 degrees F. Lightly grease and flour a 9¼-by-5¼-by-2¾-inch loaf pan.

2 In a large bowl, blend together the flour, baking powder, spices, pecans, and orange zest. In a medium bowl, beat the butter and brown sugar until light and fluffy before beating in the eggs, one at a time, beating vigorously after each addition. Beat in the potatoes and milk. Combine the two mixtures, blending until the dry ingredients are well moistened.

3 Scrape the batter into the prepared pan and bake for 45 to 50 minutes, or until a cake tester or wooden toothpick inserted into the center of the bread comes out clean and the top is golden. Remove from the oven and cool the pan on a wire rack for 5 to 10 minutes before removing the loaf from the pan. Serve with Marshmallow Sauce.

## SOUTHWEST CORN BREAD

MAKES: *1 loaf*

1 cup all-purpose flour
1 cup yellow cornmeal
1½ teaspoons baking soda
4 tablespoons granulated sugar
2 teaspoons cream of tartar
½ cup canned whole-kernel corn, drained
⅔ teaspoon salt
2 large eggs, lightly beaten
1 cup sour cream
½ cup melted butter or margarine
¼ cup sour milk or buttermilk
Mexican Sauce (see recipe page 77)

1 Position the rack in the center of the oven and preheat to 425 degrees F. Lightly grease a 9-inch square baking pan.

2 In a large bowl, blend together the flour, cornmeal, baking soda, sugar, cream of tartar, corn, and salt. Make an indentation in the center of the dry ingredients and add the eggs, sour cream, butter, and sour milk all at one time. Blend until smooth.

3 Scrape the batter into the prepared pan and bake for 20 to 25 minutes, or until a cake tester or wooden toothpick inserted into the center of the bread comes out clean and the top is a golden yellow color. Remove from the oven and cool the pan on a wire rack for 5 to 10 minutes before cutting into squares and serving. Serve with Mexican Sauce.

1½ cups all-purpose flour
1 cup soy flour
1 tablespoon baking powder
2 tablespoons granulated sugar
½ teaspoon ground nutmeg
1 cup coarsely chopped brazil nuts
1 teaspoon salt
3 large eggs
1 cup milk
½ cup vegetable shortening, at room temperature
Papaya Salsa (see recipe page 123)

**1** Position the rack in the center of the oven and preheat to 350 degrees F. Lightly grease and flour an 8½-by-4½-by-2½-inch loaf pan.

**2** In a large bowl, blend together the flour, soy flour, baking powder, sugar, nutmeg, nuts, and salt. In a medium bowl, beat the eggs until foamy before beating in the milk and shortening. Combine the two mixtures, blending until the dry ingredients are thoroughly moistened.

**3** Scrape the batter into the prepared pan and bake for 45 to 50 minutes, or until a cake tester or wooden toothpick inserted into the center of the bread comes out clean and the top is golden brown. Remove from the oven and cool the pan on a wire rack for 5 to 10 minutes before removing the loaf from the pan. Serve with Papaya Salsa.

# Soy–Nut Bread

MAKES: *1 loaf*

---

2 cups yellow cornmeal
½ teaspoon baking soda
1 tablespoon granulated sugar
One 6-ounce can green chilies, drained and finely chopped
2 cups grated Cheddar cheese
½ teaspoon salt
4 large eggs
¾ cup buttermilk or sour milk
⅓ cup melted butter or margarine
One 15-ounce can cream-style corn
Tomato Sauce (see recipe page 219)

**1** Position the rack in the center of the oven and preheat to 400 degrees F. Lightly grease and flour a 13-by-9-inch baking pan.

**2** In a large bowl, blend together the cornmeal, baking soda, sugar, chilies, cheese, and salt. In a medium bowl, beat the eggs until foamy before beating in the buttermilk, butter, and corn. Combine the two mixtures, blending until the dry ingredients are thoroughly moistened.

**3** Scrape the batter into the prepared pan and bake for 35 to 40 minutes, or until a cake tester or wooden toothpick inserted into the center of the bread comes out clean and the top is golden brown. Remove from the oven and cool the pan on a wire rack for 5 to 10 minutes before cutting into squares and serving. Serve with Tomato Sauce.

# Spanish Corn Bread

MAKES: *1 loaf*

## SPECKLED ZUCCHINI BREAD

MAKES: *2 loaves*

3 cups all-purpose flour
2 cups granulated sugar
1 teaspoon baking powder
1 teaspoon baking soda
1 teaspoon ground cinnamon
1 cup semisweet chocolate chips
3 large eggs
1 cup vegetable oil
1 teaspoon vanilla extract
½ cup sour cream or plain yogurt
2 cups shredded zucchini
Nut Spread (see recipe page 121)

1  Position the rack in the center of the oven and preheat to 350 degrees F. Lightly grease and flour the two 8½-by-4½-by-2½-inch loaf pans.

2  In a large bowl, blend together the flour, sugar, baking powder, baking soda, cinnamon, and chocolate chips. In a medium bowl, beat the eggs until foamy before beating in the oil, vanilla extract, and sour cream. Using a spoon, stir in the zucchini. Combine the two mixtures, blending until the dry ingredients are well moistened.

3  Scrape the batter into the prepared pans and bake for 45 to 50 minutes, or until a cake tester or wooden toothpick inserted into the center of the bread comes out clean and the tops are golden. Remove from the oven and cool the pans on a wire rack for 5 to

## SPICE-AND-PEACH BREAD

MAKES: *1 loaf*

1 cup all-purpose flour
½ cup soy flour
½ cup granulated sugar
1 tablespoon baking powder
1 teaspoon ground allspice
½ teaspoon ground ginger
¼ cup finely chopped hazelnuts
¼ teaspoon salt
3 large egg whites
1 cup powdered sugar
4 cups Rice Krispies® cereal, crushed
One 16-ounce can diced peaches, drained and liquid reserved
Peach Sauce (see recipe page 41)

1  Position the rack in the center of the oven and preheat to 350 degrees F. Lightly grease and flour a 9¼-by-5¼-by-2¾-inch loaf pan.

2  In a large bowl, blend together the two flours, granulated sugar, baking powder, allspice, ginger, nuts, and salt. In a medium bowl, beat the egg whites until foamy before beating in the powdered sugar. Stir in the cereal, peaches, and ¾ cup of the reserved peach liquid. Combine the two mixtures, blending until the dry ingredients are just moistened.

3  Scrape the batter into the prepared pan and bake for 45 to 50 minutes, or until the top is a golden brown color, and a cake tester or wooden toothpick inserted into the center of the bread comes out clean and the top is golden. Remove from the oven and cool on a wire rack for 5 to 10 minutes before removing the loaf from the pan. Serve with Peach Sauce.

2½ cups all-purpose flour
1 tablespoon baking powder
½ teaspoon baking soda
¼ teaspoon salt
1 cup finely crushed hard
    peppermint candies
2 large eggs
½ cup sugar
¼ cup melted butter or margarine
1¼ cups buttermilk or sour milk
1 teaspoon vanilla extract
Whipped Cream Topping (see recipe
    page 208)
Caramel Sauce (see recipe page 32)

1  Position the rack in the center of the oven and preheat to 350 degrees F. Lightly grease and flour an 8½-by-4½-by-2½-inch loaf pan.

2  In a large bowl, blend together the flour, baking powder, baking soda, candy, and salt. In a medium bowl, beat the eggs until foamy before beating in the sugar, butter, buttermilk, and vanilla extract. Combine the two mixtures, blending until the dry ingredients are moistened.

3  Scrape the batter into the prepared pan and bake for 45 to 50 minutes, or until a cake tester or wooden toothpick inserted into the center of the bread comes out clean and the top is golden. Remove from the oven and cool the pan on a wire rack for 5 to 10 minutes before removing the loaf from the pan. Drizzle with Caramel Sauce and serve with

# SPICED CANDY DROP BREAD

MAKES: *1 loaf*

---

1 cup all-purpose flour
1 cup whole-wheat flour
1¼ cups rolled oats
1 tablespoon baking powder
½ teaspoon baking soda
½ teaspoon ground nutmeg
¼ teaspoon ground cloves
½ cup finely chopped seedless
    raisins
1 cup finely shredded carrots
4 large egg whites
¼ cup light corn syrup
¾ cup plus 2 tablespoons bottled
    carrot juice
Carrot Butter (see recipe page 64)

1  Position the rack in the center of the oven and preheat to 350 degrees F. Lightly grease and flour a 9¼-by-5¼-by-2¾-inch loaf pan.

2  In a large bowl, blend together the two flours, the oats, baking powder, baking soda, nutmeg, cloves, raisins, and carrots. In a medium bowl, beat the egg whites until foamy before beating in the corn syrup and carrot juice. Combine the two mixtures, blending until the dry ingredients are just moistened.

3  Scrape the batter into the prepared pan and bake for 55 to 60 minutes, or until a cake tester or wooden toothpick inserted into the center of the bread comes out clean and the top is golden. Remove from the oven and cool the pan on a wire rack for 5 to 10 minutes before removing the loaf from the pan. Serve with Carrot Butter.

# SPICED CARROT BREAD

MAKES: *1 loaf*

## SPICY BANANA BREAD

MAKES: *1 loaf*

1 cup rice flour
½ cup whole-wheat flour
⅓ cup soy flour
2 teaspoons baking powder
½ teaspoon ground allspice
¼ teaspoon ground nutmeg
½ cup golden raisins
½ cup finely chopped dried apricots
1 cup plain yogurt
½ cup honey
½ cup molasses
2 medium bananas, mashed
¼ cup canola oil
Fresh Blueberry Sauce (see recipe page 78)

1 Position the rack in the center of the oven and preheat to 350 degrees F. Lightly grease and flour a 9-inch square baking pan.

2 In a large bowl, blend together the three flours, baking powder, allspice, nutmeg, raisins, and apricots. In a medium bowl, beat the yogurt, honey, molasses, bananas, and oil until smooth. Combine the two mixtures, blending until the dry ingredients are just moistened.

3 Scrape the batter into the prepared pan and bake for 30 to 35 minutes, or until a cake tester or wooden toothpick inserted into the center of the bread comes out clean and the top is golden. Remove from the oven and cool the pan on a wire rack for 5 to 10 minutes before cutting into squares and serving with Fresh Blueberry Sauce.

## SPICY BANANA–WALNUT BREAD

MAKES: *1 loaf*

1¾ cups all-purpose flour
2 teaspoons baking powder
⅔ cup granulated sugar
1 teaspoon ground cinnamon
⅛ teaspoon ground mace or nutmeg
⅛ teaspoon ground cardamom
½ cup finely chopped hazelnuts
2 large eggs
⅓ cup vegetable shortening, at room temperature
1 teaspoon vanilla extract
1 cup mashed bananas
Strawberry Sauce (see recipe page 144)

1 Position the rack in the center of the oven and preheat to 350 degrees F. Lightly grease and flour an 8½-by-4½-by-2½-inch loaf pan.

2 In a large bowl, blend together the flour, baking powder, sugar, cinnamon, cardamom, and nuts. In a medium bowl, beat the eggs until foamy before beating in the shortening, vanilla extract, and bananas. Combine the two mixtures, blending until the dry ingredients are thoroughly moistened.

3 Scrape the batter into the prepared pan and bake for 45 to 50 minutes, or until a cake tester or wooden toothpick inserted into the center of the bread comes out clean and the top is golden brown. Remove from the oven and cool the pan on a wire rack for 5 to 10 minutes before removing the loaf from the pan. Serve with Strawberry Sauce.

2 cups all-purpose flour
1 cup granulated sugar
½ cup packed brown sugar
1 teaspoon baking soda
½ teaspoon ground cinnamon
½ teaspoon ground ginger
½ teaspoon ground nutmeg
1 cup raisins
½ cup chopped pecans
½ teaspoon salt
2 large eggs
¼ cup water
½ cup canola oil
1 cup cooked mashed squash
Nut Spread (see recipe page 121)

1  Position the rack in the center of the oven and preheat to 350 degrees F. Lightly grease and flour an 8½-by-4½-by-2½-inch loaf pan.

2  In a large bowl, blend together the flour, sugar, baking soda, cinnamon, ginger, nutmeg, raisins, nuts, and salt. In a medium bowl, beat the eggs until foamy before beating in the water, oil, and squash, beating until smooth. Combine the two mixtures, blending until the dry ingredients are thoroughly moistened.

3  Scrape the batter into the prepared pan and bake for 45 to 50 minutes, or until a cake tester or wooden toothpick inserted into the center of the bread comes out clean and the top is golden brown. Remove from the oven and cool the pan on a wire rack for 5 to 10 minutes before removing the loaf from the pan. Serve with Nut Spread.

## SQUASH BREAD

MAKES: *1 loaf*

---

3 cups all-purpose flour
2 cups granulated sugar
1 tablespoon cinnamon
1 teaspoon baking soda
½ teaspoon salt
3 large eggs
1 cup canola oil
Two 10-ounce packages frozen strawberries, thawed and drained
Rhubarb Sauce (see recipe page 245)

1  Position the rack in the center of the oven and preheat to 350 degrees F. Lightly grease and flour a 9¼-by-5½-by-2¾-inch loaf pan.

2  In a large bowl, blend together the flour, sugar, cinnamon, baking soda, and salt. In a medium bowl, beat the eggs until foamy before beating in the oil. Add the strawberries. Combine the two mixtures, blending until the dry ingredients are well moistened.

3  Scrape the mixture into the two baking pans and bake for 45 to 50 minutes, or until a cake tester or wooden toothpick inserted into the center of the bread comes out clean and the top is golden. Remove from the oven and cool the pan on a wire rack for 5 to 10 minutes before removing the loaf from the pan. Serve with Rhubarb Sauce.

## STRAWBERRY BREAD

MAKES: *2 loaves*

# STRAWBERRY–NUT BREAD

MAKES: *1 loaf*

1½ cups all-purpose flour
1 cup granulated sugar
½ teaspoon baking soda
1½ cups finely chopped almond
½ teaspoon salt
2 large eggs
⅔ cup melted butter or margarine
1 teaspoon orange extract
One 10-ounce package frozen
  strawberries, thawed and drained
Pumpkin Butter (see recipe page
  122)

1  Position the rack in the center of the oven and preheat to 350 degrees F. Lightly grease and flour a 9¼-by-5¼-by-2¾-inch loaf pan.

2  In a large bowl, blend together the flour, sugar, baking soda, almonds, and salt. In a small bowl, beat the eggs until foamy before beating in the butter and orange extract. Stir in the strawberries. Combine the two mixtures, blending until the dry ingredients are well moistened and a pink color.

3  Scrape the batter into the prepared pan and bake for 55 to 60 minutes, or until a cake tester or wooden toothpick inserted into the center of the bread comes out clean and the top is golden. Remove from the oven and cool the pan on a wire rack for 5 to 10 minutes before removing the loaf from the pan. Serve with Pumpkin Butter.

# SUGAR-FREE BREAD

MAKES: *1 loaf*

1 cup whole-wheat flour
1 cup rye flour
1 tablespoon baking powder
1½ cups unsweetened flaked
  coconut
2 tablespoons sesame seeds
1 teaspoon ground allspice
1 cup finely grated carrots
1 cup seedless raisins
2 large eggs
1 cup soy milk
3 tablespoons canola oil
Alcohol-Free Hard Sauce (see recipe
  page 111)

1  Position the rack in the center of the oven and preheat to 350 degrees F. Lightly grease and flour an 8½-by-4½-by-2½-inch loaf pan.

2  In a large bowl, blend together the two flours, baking powder, coconut, sesame seeds, allspice, carrots, and raisins. In a medium bowl, beat the eggs until foamy before beating in the soy milk and oil. Combine the two mixtures, blending until the dry ingredients are well moistened.

3  Scrape the batter into the prepared pan and bake for 45 to 50 minutes, or until a cake tester or wooden toothpick inserted into the center of the bread comes out clean and the top is golden. Remove from the oven and cool the pan on a wire rack for 5 to 10 minutes before removing the loaf from the pan. Transfer the loaf to a serving plate or platter and serve with whipped, unsalted butter on the side. Serve with Alcohol-Free Hard Sauce.

2 cups all-purpose flour
1 cup granulated sugar
¼ teaspoon baking powder
1 teaspoon baking soda
1 cup finely chopped pecans
2 teaspoons pumpkin-pie spice
½ teaspoon salt
2 large eggs
½ cup packed light-brown sugar
⅓ cup vegetable shortening, melted
½ cup buttermilk or sour milk
1 cup cooked, mashed sweet
   potatoes
One 8-ounce can crushed pineapple,
   drained
Marshmallow Sauce (see recipe
   page 131)

**1** Position the rack in the center of the oven and preheat to 350 degrees F. Lightly grease and flour an 8½-by-4½-by-2½-inch loaf pan.

**2** In a large bowl, blend together the flour, granulated sugar, baking powder, baking soda, pecans, pumpkin-pie spice, and salt. In a large bowl, beat the eggs until foamy before beating in the brown sugar, shortening, buttermilk, potatoes, and pineapple. Combine the two mixtures, blending until the dry ingredients are well moistened.

**3** Scrape the batter into the prepared pan and bake for 60 to 65 minutes, or until a cake tester or wooden toothpick inserted into the center of the bread comes out clean and the top is golden. Remove from the oven and cool the pan on a wire rack for 5 to 10 minutes before removing the loaf from the pan. Serve with Marshmallow Sauce.

# SWEET-POTATO BREAD
MAKES: *1 loaf*

---

2 cups all-purpose flour
1 teaspoon baking powder
½ teaspoon baking soda
1 teaspoon ground allspice
½ teaspoon ground nutmeg
1 cup finely chopped pecans
½ cup butter or margarine, at room
   temperature
½ cup vanilla-flavored yogurt or
   unflavored sour cream
1¼ cups granulated sugar
3 large eggs
½ cup cooked mashed sweet potato
Raspberry–Rhubarb Blend (see
   recipe page 87)

**1** Position the rack in the center of the oven and preheat to 350 degrees F. Lightly grease and flour a 9¼-by-5½-by-2¾-inch loaf pan.

**2** In a large bowl, blend together the flour, baking powder, baking soda, allspice, and nutmeg. In a medium bowl, beat the butter, yogurt, and sugar together until smooth before beating in the eggs, one at a time, beating vigorously after each addition. Beat in the sweet potato. Combine the two mixtures, blending until the dry ingredients are thoroughly moistened.

**3** Scrape the batter into the prepared pan and bake for 45 to 50 minutes, or until a cake tester or wooden toothpick inserted into the center of the bread comes out clean and the top is golden. Remove from the oven and cool the pan on a wire rack for 5 to 10 minutes before removing the loaf from the pan. Serve with Raspberry–Rhubarb Blend.

# SWEET-POTATO BREAD WITH PECANS
MAKES: *1 loaf*

## SWEET TATA BREAD

MAKES: *1 loaf*

1½ cups all-purpose flour
2 teaspoons baking powder
1 teaspoon ground mace or nutmeg
½ teaspoon ground cinnamon
1 cup finely chopped pecans
½ cup golden raisins
¼ teaspoon salt
2 large eggs
1 cup granulated sugar
½ cup unsweetened applesauce
2 tablespoons milk or cream
1 cup cooked, mashed sweet potatoes (not yams)
Blender Apricot Sauce (see recipe page 25)

**1** Position the rack in the center of the oven and preheat to 350 degrees F. Lightly grease and flour an 8½-by-4½-by-2½-inch loaf pan.

**2** In a large bowl, blend together the flour, baking powder, mace, cinnamon, pecans, raisins, and salt. In a medium bowl, beat the eggs until foamy before beating in the sugar, applesauce, milk, and sweet potatoes. Combine the two mixtures, blending until the dry ingredients are thoroughly moistened.

**3** Scrape the batter into the prepared pan and bake for 45 to 50 minutes, or until a cake tester or wooden toothpick inserted into the center of the bread comes out clean and the top is golden. Remove from the oven and cool the pan on a wire rack for 5 to 10 minutes before removing the loaf from the pan. Serve with Blender Apricot Sauce.

## TAFFY APPLE BREAD

MAKES: *1 loaf*

**BREAD**
2 cups all-purpose flour
1 tablespoon baking powder
½ teaspoon baking soda
½ cup granulated sugar
¼ teaspoon ground nutmeg
¼ teaspoon salt
1 medium apple, peeled, cored, and finely chopped
2 large eggs
½ cup milk
¼ cup melted butter or margarine

**TOPPING**
½ cup honey, at room temperature
½ cup packed light-brown sugar
½ teaspoon peppermint extract
¼ cup finely chopped walnuts
Mint Jelly (see recipe page 28)

**1** Position the rack in the center of the oven and preheat to 350 degrees F. Lightly grease and flour an 8½-by-4½-by-2½-inch loaf pan.

**2** To make the bread, in a large bowl, blend together the flour, baking powder, baking soda, salt, sugar, nutmeg, and apples. In a medium bowl, beat the eggs until foamy before beating in the milk and butter. Combine the two mixtures, blending until the dry ingredients are thoroughly moistened.

**3** Scrape the batter into the prepared pan and bake for 45 to 50 minutes, or until a cake tester or wooden toothpick inserted into the center of the bread comes out clean and the top is golden.

**4** Meanwhile, in a small saucepan set over medium heat, combine the honey and brown sugar, stirring until the sugar is completely dissolved and the mixture starts to boil. Remove from the heat and stir in the peppermint extract.

**5** When the bread is done, remove the pan from the oven and cool the pan on a wire rack for 5 to 10 minutes before removing the loaf from the pan. Using a pastry brush, brush the honey mixture over the top and sides of the loaf. Sprinkle the walnuts over the top. Serve with Mint Jelly.

1½ cups all-purpose flour
½ cup graham flour
2½ teaspoons baking powder
¼ teaspoon baking soda
3 tablespoons finely minced
  tangerine peel
½ cup chopped pecans or
  macadamia nuts
1 teaspoon salt
1 large egg
½ cup freshly squeezed tangerine
  juice
½ cup milk or light cream
¼ cup melted butter or margarine
Fluffy Cream Dressing (see recipe
  page 34)

**1** Position the rack in the center of the oven and preheat to 350 degrees F. Lightly grease and flour or paper line an 8½-by-4½-by-2½-inch loaf pan.

**2** In a large bowl, blend together the two flours, baking powder, baking soda, peel, pecans, and salt. In a small bowl, beat the egg until foamy before beating in the juice, milk, and butter. Combine the two mixtures, blending until the dry ingredients are moistened.

**3** Scrape the batter into the prepared pan and bake for 55 to 60 minutes, or until a cake tester or wooden toothpick inserted into the center of the bread comes out clean and the top is golden. Remove from the oven and cool the pan on a wire rack for 5 to 10 minutes before removing the loaf from the pan. Serve with Fluffy Cream Dressing.

## TANGERINE TEA BREAD

MAKES: *1 loaf*

---

3 cups all-purpose flour
1¼ cups granulated sugar
1 tablespoon baking powder
1 teaspoon baking soda
2 tablespoons grated orange zest
2 cups finely chopped cranberries
1½ cups finely chopped walnuts and
  pecans
3 large eggs
⅓ cup canola oil
1½ cups milk or evaporated milk
½ cup fresh orange juice or Triple
  Sec liqueur
Fig Sauce (see recipe page 189)

**1** Position the rack in the center of the oven and preheat to 350 degrees F. Lightly grease and flour a 9¼-by-5¼-by-2¾-inch loaf pan.

**2** In a large bowl, blend together the flour, sugar, baking powder, baking soda, orange zest, cranberries, and nuts. In a medium bowl, beat the eggs until foamy before beating in the oil, milk, and orange juice. Combine the two mixtures, blending until the dry ingredients are well moistened.

**3** Scrape the batter into the prepared pan and bake for 55 to 60 minutes, or until a cake tester or wooden toothpick inserted into the center of the bread comes out clean and the top is golden. Remove from the oven and cool the pan on a wire rack for 5 to 10 minutes before removing the loaf from the pan. Serve with Fig Sauce.

## THANKSGIVING CRANBERRY– NUT BREAD

MAKES: *1 loaf*

## THREE-GRAIN BREAD

MAKES: *1 loaf*

1 cup graham flour
1 cup rye flour
1 cup yellow cornmeal
2 teaspoons baking soda
½ teaspoon ground allspice
¼ teaspoon ground ginger
1 teaspoon salt
1¾ cups sour milk or buttermilk
¾ cup molasses
¼ cup light cream or evaporated milk
Cheese Sauce (see recipe page 57)

1 Position the rack in the center of the oven and preheat to 350 degrees F. Lightly grease and flour a 9¼-by-5¼-by-2¾-inch loaf pan.

2 In a large bowl, blend together the two flours, cornmeal, baking soda, allspice, ginger, and salt. In a medium bowl, beat the sour milk, molasses, and cream until smooth. Combine the two mixtures, blending until the dry ingredients are well moistened.

3 Scrape the batter into the prepared pan and bake for 55 to 60 minutes, or until a cake tester or wooden toothpick inserted into the center of the bread comes out clean and the top is golden. Remove from the oven and cool the pan on a wire rack for 5 to 10 minutes before removing the loaf from the pan. Serve with Cheese Sauce.

## TOFU–COCONUT BREAD

MAKES: *1 loaf*

2 cups all-purpose flour
½ cup graham flour
1 tablespoon baking powder
1 cup unsweetened coconut flakes
¼ teaspoon salt
One 14-ounce can coconut milk
1 cup Turbinado sugar
¼ cup Amaretto liqueur
One 4-ounce package tofu, diced
Cucumber Dill Sauce (see recipe page 91)

1 Position the rack in the center of the oven and preheat to 350 degrees F. Lightly grease and flour a 9¼-by-5½-by-2¾-inch loaf pan.

2 In a large bowl, blend together the two flours, baking powder, coconut, and salt. In the container of a blender, combine the milk, sugar, Amaretto, and tofu. Process on high for 5 to 10 seconds or until smooth. Combine the two mixtures, blending until the dry ingredients are moistened.

3 Scrape the batter into the prepared pan and bake for 55 to 60 minutes, or until a cake tester or wooden toothpick inserted into the center of the bread comes out clean and the top is golden brown. Remove from the oven and cool the pan on a wire rack for 5 to 10 minutes before removing the loaf from the pan. Serve with Cucumber Dill Sauce.

**BREAD**
**2 cups all-purpose flour**
**⅓ cup soy flour**
**1½ teaspoons baking powder**
**1 teaspoon ground ginger**
**1 cup flaked coconut**
**½ cup chopped glacé ginger**
**½ cup chopped glacé (candied)
    pineapple**
**2 large eggs, at room temperature**
**⅔ cup milk, at room temperature**
**¼ cup light corn syrup**
**⅔ cup Turbinado sugar, or light-
    brown sugar**
**Tropical Sauce (see recipe page 81)**

**1** Position the rack in the center of the oven and preheat to 350 degrees F. Lightly grease and flour an 8½-by-4½-by-2½-inch loaf pan.

**2** To make the bread, in a large bowl, blend together the two flours, baking powder, ground ginger, and coconut. Fold in the candied fruit. In a medium bowl, beat the eggs until foamy before beating in the milk. In a small bowl, blend the Turbinado sugar and corn syrup together before beating them into the egg mixture. Combine the wet and dry ingredients, blending until the dry ingredients are moistened.

**3** Scrape the batter into the prepared pan and bake for 45 to 50 minutes, or until a cake tester or wooden toothpick inserted into the center of the bread comes out clean and the top is golden brown. Remove from the oven and cool the pan on a wire rack for 5 to 10 minutes before removing the loaf from the pan. Sprinkle with coconut and serve with Tropical Sauce.

# TROPICAL BREAD
MAKES: *2 loaves*

---

**1¼ cups all-purpose flour**
**1 cup whole bran**
**¾ cup finely chopped dried apricots**
**½ cup finely chopped Brazil nuts**
**¼ cup finely chopped peanuts**
**⅔ cup granulated sugar**
**1 teaspoon baking powder**
**½ teaspoon baking soda**
**½ cup flaked coconut**
**½ teaspoon salt**
**3 large eggs**
**⅓ cup melted vegetable shortening**
**¼ cup buttermilk or sour milk**
**1 cup mashed bananas**
**Coconut Chutney (see recipe
    page 65)**

**1** Position the rack in the center of the oven and preheat to 350 degrees F. Lightly grease and flour a 9¼-by-5¼-by-2¾-inch loaf pan.

**2** In a large bowl, blend together the flour, bran, apricots, Brazil nuts, peanuts, sugar, baking powder, baking soda, coconut, and salt. In a medium bowl, beat the eggs until foamy before beating in the shortening, buttermilk, and bananas. Combine the two mixtures, blending until the dry ingredients are well moistened.

**3** Scrape the batter into the prepared pan and bake for 55 to 60 minutes, or until a cake tester or wooden toothpick inserted into the center of the bread comes out clean and the top is golden. Remove from the oven and cool the pan on a wire rack for 5 to 10 minutes before removing the loaf from the pan. Serve with Coconut Chutney.

# TROPICAL FRUIT BREAD
MAKES: *1 loaf*

# TROPICAL MANGO BREAD

MAKES: *2 loaves*

3 cups all-purpose flour
1½ teaspoons baking powder
½ teaspoon baking soda
½ teaspoon ground cinnamon
¼ teaspoon ground nutmeg or mace
¼ teaspoon salt
1 cup golden raisins
½ cup shredded coconut
1 cup butter or margarine, at room temperature
1¼ cups packed dark-brown sugar
3 large eggs
5 medium bananas
1 medium mango, peeled, pitted, and pureed
Sweet-and-Sour Mango Relish (see recipe page 192)

**1** Position the rack in the center of the oven and preheat to 350 degrees F. Lightly grease and flour two 8½-by-4½-by-2½-inch loaf pans.

**2** In a large bowl, blend together the flour, baking powder, baking soda, salt, cinnamon, nutmeg, raisins, and coconut. In a medium bowl, beat the butter and sugar until smooth. Beat in the eggs, one at a time, beating vigorously after each addition. Beat in the banana and pureed mango. Combine the two mixtures, blending until the dry ingredients are well moistened.

**3** Scrape the batter into the prepared pans and bake for 45 to 50 minutes, or until a cake tester or wooden toothpick inserted into the center of the bread comes out clean and the top is golden. Remove from the oven and cool the pans on a wire rack for 5 to 10 minutes before removing the loaves from the pans. Serve with Sweet-and-Sour Mango Relish.

# TURKEY BREAD

MAKES: *1 loaf*

2 cups whole-wheat flour
1 cup all-purpose flour
1 teaspoon baking powder
1 teaspoon baking soda
½ teaspoon onion powder
½ teaspoon garlic powder
1 cup chopped dried cranberries (optional)
1 teaspoon salt
2 large eggs
¼ cup granulated sugar
1 pound cooked, finely minced turkey
1¼ cups beef or chicken broth
Flavored Mayonnaise of Choice (see recipe page 324)

**1** Position the rack in the center of the oven and preheat to 350 degrees F. Lightly grease and flour a ring-mold baking pan.

**2** In a large bowl, blend together the two flours, baking powder, baking soda, onion powder, garlic powder, cranberries, and salt. In a medium bowl, beat the eggs until foamy before beating in the sugar. Stir in the turkey and broth. Combine the two mixtures, blending until the dry ingredients are well moistened.

**3** Scrape the batter into the prepared pan and bake for 65 to 70 minutes, or until a cake tester or wooden toothpick inserted into the center of the bread comes out clean and the top is golden brown. Remove from the oven, cool on a wire rack for 3 to 5 minutes before removing the loaf from the pan. Serve with Flavored Mayonnaise of Choice.

1½ cups frozen mixed vegetables, thawed
1 small white onion, finely chopped
2½ cups all-purpose flour
1½ teaspoons baking powder
½ teaspoon baking soda
¼ teaspoon salt
1 tablespoon grated Romano or Parmesan cheese
2 tablespoons snipped fresh thyme
1 tablespoon snipped fresh parsley
2 large eggs
1½ cups buttermilk or sour milk
5 tablespoons melted butter or margarine
Flavored Mayonnaise of Choice (see recipe page 324)

**1** Position the rack in the center of the oven and preheat to 350 degrees F. Lightly grease and flour an 8½-by-4½-by-2¾-inch loaf pan.

**2** In the container of a food processor, or using a sharp knife, chop the vegetables into fine pieces about the size used for relish or chutney. In a large bowl, blend together the vegetables, onion, flour, baking powder, baking soda, salt, cheese, thyme, and parsley. In a medium bowl, beat the eggs until foamy before beating in the buttermilk and butter. Combine the two mixtures, blending until the dry ingredients are well moistened.

**3** Scrape the batter into the prepared pan and bake for 55 to 60 minutes, or until a cake tester or wooden toothpick inserted into the center of the bread comes out clean and the top is golden brown. Remove from the oven and cool the pan on a wire rack for 3 to 5 minutes before removing the loaf from the pan. Serve with Flavored Mayonnaise of Choice.

## VEGETABLE BREAD

MAKES: *1 loaf*

1 cup all-purpose flour
2 cups graham flour
1½ teaspoons baking soda
1 teaspoon salt
½ cup maple syrup or brown sugar
2 cups buttermilk or sour milk
Blueberry Syrup (see recipe page 43)

**1** Position the rack in the center of the oven and preheat to 350 degrees F. Lightly grease and flour a 9¼-by-5¼-by-2¾-inch loaf pan.

**2** In a large bowl, blend together the two flours, baking soda, and salt. In a medium bowl, beat the maple sugar and buttermilk until smooth. Combine the two mixtures, blending until the dry ingredients are moistened.

**3** Scrape the batter into the prepared pan and bake for 55 to 60 minutes, or until a cake tester or wooden toothpick inserted into the center of the bread comes out clean and the top is golden. Remove from the oven and cool the pan on a wire rack for 5 to 10 minutes before removing the loaf from the pan. Serve with Blueberry Syrup.

## VERMONT GRAHAM BREAD

MAKES: *1 loaf*

## VERMONT JOHNNYCAKE

MAKES: *1 loaf*

2 cups all-purpose flour
1 cup corn flour
4½ teaspoons baking powder
¾ teaspoon salt
3 large eggs
1 cup milk
¾ cup melted vegetable shortening
½ cup maple syrup
Maple-Flavored Whipped Cream
  (see recipe page 94)

**1** Position the rack in the center of the oven and preheat to 400 degrees F. Lightly grease and flour a 9-inch square baking pan.

**2** In a large bowl, blend together the flour, corn flour, baking powder, and salt. In a medium bowl, beat the eggs until foamy before beating in the milk, shortening, and syrup. Combine the two mixtures, blending until the dry ingredients are well moistened.

**3** Scrape the batter into the prepared pan and bake for 35 to 40 minutes, or until a cake tester or wooden toothpick inserted into the center of the bread comes out clean and the top is golden. Remove from the oven and cool the pan on a wire rack for 5 to 10 minutes before removing the loaf from the pan. Serve with Maple-Flavored Whipped Cream.

## WHISKEY BREAD

MAKES: *1 loaf*

2½ cups all-purpose flour
2 teaspoons baking powder
1 teaspoon ground nutmeg or mace
½ cup finely ground pecans
½ cup golden raisins
½ cup candied red cherry halves
¼ cup chopped candied pineapple
3 large eggs, separated
1 cup granulated sugar
½ cup packed light-brown sugar
⅓ cup butter or margarine, at room
  temperature
1 cup whiskey

**1** Position the rack in the center of the oven and preheat to 350 degrees F. Lightly grease and flour a 9¼-by-5¼-by-2¾-inch loaf pan.

**2** In a large bowl, blend together the flour, baking powder, nutmeg, pecans, raisins, cherries, and pineapple. In a small bowl, beat the egg whites until stiff but not dry. In a medium bowl, beat the egg yolks foamy before beating in the two sugars, butter, and whiskey. Combine the wet and dry ingredients, blending until the dry ingredients are moistened. Fold in the egg whites.

**3** Scrape the batter into the prepared pan and bake for 55 to 60 minutes, or until a cake tester or wooden toothpick inserted into the center of the bread comes out clean and the top is golden. Remove from the oven and cool the pan on a wire rack for 5 to 10 minutes before removing the loaf from the pan.

**SERVING SUGGESTION: Serve with a glass of dry white wine and thinly sliced cheese.**

4 cups sifted all-purpose flour
1 teaspoon baking soda
2 cups granulated sugar
1½ teaspoons ground ginger
½ teaspoon ground cinnamon
½ teaspoon ground nutmeg
¼ teaspoon salt
2 large eggs
1 cup sour milk or buttermilk
1 cup melted butter or margarine
2 tablespoons finely grated
    crystallized ginger for topping
Ginger Cream (see recipe page 21)

1  Position the rack in the center of the oven and preheat to 350 degrees F. Lightly grease and flour a 13-by-9-by-1½-inch baking pan.

2  In a large bowl, blend together the flour, baking soda, salt, sugar, ginger, nutmeg, and cinnamon.

In a medium bowl, beat the eggs until foamy before beating in the sour milk and butter. Combine the two mixtures, blending until the dry ingredients are well moistened.

3  Scrape the batter into the prepared pan and bake for 35 to 40 minutes, or until a cake tester or wooden toothpick inserted into the center of the bread comes out clean and the top is golden. Remove from the oven and cool the pan on a wire rack for 5 to 10 minutes before cutting into squares. Garnish with grated crystallized ginger and serve with Ginger Cream.

## WHITE GINGER BREAD

MAKES: *1 loaf*

---

1 cup all-purpose flour
½ cup whole-wheat flour
2 teaspoons baking powder
½ teaspoon ground cinnamon
¼ teaspoon ground allspice
¼ teaspoon ground nutmeg
¾ cup granulated sugar
½ cup chopped walnuts
¼ teaspoon salt
2 large eggs
⅔ cup milk or evaporated milk
½ teaspoon vanilla extract
¼ cup melted margarine or butter
Golden Sauce (see recipe page 151)

1  Position the rack in the center of the oven and preheat to 350 degrees F. Lightly grease and flour an 8½-by-4½-by-2½-inch loaf pan.

2  In a large bowl, blend together the two flours, baking powder, cinnamon, allspice, nutmeg, sugar, walnuts, and salt. In a medium bowl, beat the eggs until foamy before beating in the milk, vanilla extract, and margarine. Combine the two mixtures, blending until the dry ingredients are well moistened.

3  Scrape the batter into the prepared pan and bake for 45 to 50 minutes, or until a cake tester or wooden toothpick inserted into the center of the bread comes out clean and the top is golden. Remove from the oven and cool the pan on a wire rack for 5 to 10 minutes before cutting into squares and serving. Serve with Golden Sauce.

## WHOLE-WHEAT WALNUT BREAD

MAKES: *1 loaf*

## YOUR CHOICE FRUIT-AND-NUT BREAD

MAKES: *1 loaf*

1½ cups whole-wheat flour
1½ cups all-purpose flour
1 teaspoon baking powder
1 teaspoon baking soda
1 cup chopped nuts of choice
¼ cup melted butter or margarine
½ cup granulated sugar
1 large egg
¼ cup fruit juice of choice
1 cup finely diced fruit pulp of choice
1 cup sour milk or buttermilk
Fresh mint leaves for garnish
Blender Apricot Sauce (see recipe page 25)

1  Position the rack in the center of the oven and preheat to 350 degrees F. Lightly grease and flour a 9¼-by-5¼-by-2¾-inch loaf pan.

2  In a large bowl, blend together the two flours, baking powder, baking soda, and nuts. In a medium bowl, beat the butter, sugar, egg, juice, fruit, and sour milk until combined. Combine the two mixtures, blending until the dry ingredients are moistened.

3  Scrape the batter into the prepared pan and bake for 55 to 60 minutes, or until a cake tester or wooden toothpick inserted into the center of the bread comes out clean and the top is golden. Remove from the oven and cool the pan on a wire rack for 5 to 10 minutes before removing the loaf from the pan. Garnish with fresh mint leaves and serve with Blender Apricot Sauce.

## ZUCCHINI BREAD

MAKES: *1 loaf*

2½ cups all-purpose flour
1 teaspoon baking powder
1 teaspoon baking soda
2 teaspoons ground cinnamon
1 cup finely chopped seedless raisins
½ teaspoon salt
2 large eggs
¾ cup melted margarine or butter
1 teaspoon almond extract
1½ cups warm honey
2 cups grated zucchini
Cranberry Sauce (see recipe page 108)

1  Position the rack in the center of the oven and preheat to 350 degrees F. Lightly grease and flour a 9¼-by-5¼-by-2¾-inch loaf pan.

2  In a large bowl, blend together the flour, baking powder, baking soda, cinnamon, raisins, and salt. In a medium bowl, beat the eggs until foamy before beating in the margarine, almond extract, and honey. Stir in the zucchini. Combine the two mixtures, blending until the dry ingredients are well moistened.

3  Scrape the batter into the prepared pan and bake for 55 to 60 minutes, or until a cake tester or wooden toothpick inserted into the center of the bread comes out clean and the top is golden. Remove from the oven and cool the pan on a wire rack for 5 to 10 minutes before removing the loaf from the pan. Serve with Cranberry Sauce.

2½ cups whole-wheat flour
½ cup All-Bran™ cereal
1 teaspoon baking soda
2 teaspoons ground cinnamon
1 teaspoon ground nutmeg
1 cup finely chopped unsalted
 peanuts
1 cup finely grated carrots
1 teaspoon salt
3 large eggs
1½ cups packed light-brown sugar
1 cup canola oil
1 cup grated zucchini
2 teaspoons vanilla or almond
 extract
Carrot Butter (see recipe page 64)

**1** Position the rack in the center of the oven and preheat to 350 degrees F. Lightly grease and flour a 9¼-by-5¼-by-2¾-inch loaf pan.

**2** In a large bowl, blend together the flour, cereal, baking soda, cinnamon, nutmeg, nuts, carrots, and salt. In a medium bowl, beat the eggs until foamy before beating in the brown sugar and oil. Stir in the zucchini and extract. Combine the two mixtures, blending until the dry ingredients are well moistened.

**3** Scrape the batter into the prepared pan and bake for 55 to 60 minutes, or until a cake tester or wooden toothpick inserted into the center of the bread comes out clean and the top is golden. Remove from the oven and cool the pan on a wire rack for 5 to 10 minutes before removing the loaf from the pan. Serve with Carrot Butter.

# ZUCCHINI–CARROT BREAD
MAKES: *1 loaf*

¼ cup butter or margarine
1 cup finely chopped onions
2½ cups Bisquick® baking mix
1 tablespoon fresh snipped parsley
½ teaspoon fresh snipped basil
½ teaspoon fresh snipped lemon
 thyme
¼ cup walnuts or pecans
3 large eggs
½ cup milk or cream
1½ cups grated zucchini
1 cup grated sharp cheese

**1** Position the rack in the center of the oven and preheat to 350 degrees F. Lightly grease and flour a 9-inch square baking pan.

**2** In a medium skillet set over medium heat, melt the butter and sauté the onions until translucent. Remove from the heat and set aside.

**3** In a large bowl, blend together the Bisquick, parsley, basil, thyme, and pecans. In a medium bowl, beat the eggs until light-colored before beating in the milk. Stir in the onion mixture, zucchini, and cheese. Combine the wet and dry ingredients, blending until the dry ingredients are well moistened.

**4** Scrape the batter into the prepared pan and bake for 40 to 45 minutes, or until a cake tester or wooden toothpick inserted into the center of the bread comes out clean. Remove from the oven and cool the pan on a wire rack for 5 to 10 minutes before removing the bread from the pan.

**SERVING SUGGESTION: Serve with a glass of beer and sliced cheese.**

# ZUCCHINI–CHEESE BREAD
MAKES: *1 loaf*

# Chapter 8

# PANCAKES

There are many ways to vary pancake batter. Generally, when making pancakes for breakfast, cooks tend to use sweet fillings. Brunch, however, is fast becoming a popular meal. This breakfast/lunch combination thankfully opens the door to a world of other meal items—especially savory pancakes. Don't be afraid to add shrimp or cooked chopped turkey to your basic pancake batter for an interesting twist on brunch, lunch, or dinner.

## APPLE FLAPJACKS

MAKES: *14 to 16 pancakes*

1 cup all-purpose flour
½ cup graham flour
1 tablespoon granulated sugar
1 teaspoon baking powder
½ teaspoon ground cinnamon
1 medium apple, peeled, cored and
   finely chopped
2 large eggs
1 tablespoon canola oil
1 cup milk

**1** Preheat a large skillet or griddle over medium heat.

**2** In a large bowl, blend together the two flours, sugar, baking powder, cinnamon, and apple. Make an indentation in the center of the ingredients and add the eggs, oil, and milk. Stir until the ingredients are combined but the batter is still slightly lumpy.

**3** Brush the skillet with oil. Drop a heaping serving spoonful of the batter onto the prepared skillet and cook for 3 to 5 minutes, or until the bottom is golden brown and the top is speckled with holes. Turn and brown the other side. Transfer the pancake to a plate and continue until all the batter is used. Serve warm.

**SERVING SUGGESTION: Serve with apple butter and sweet whipped cream on the side.**

## AUSTRIAN BREAD PANCAKES

MAKES: *4 to 6 servings*

2 large eggs
1 cup milk
¼ cup butter or margarine, melted
½ teaspoon vanilla extract
⅛ teaspoon salt
6 slices stale white bread, crusts
   removed, diced

**1** In a medium bowl, beat the eggs until foamy. Beat in the milk, butter, vanilla extract, and salt. Stir in the bread. Set aside at room temperature for about 30 minutes.

**2** When ready to cook, preheat a large skillet over medium heat and brush it with oil.

**3** Pour all of the batter into the skillet at one time and cook until the bottom of the pancake is light brown. Using a large spatula, turn the pancake and cook on the other side until browned. Remove the pan from the heat and use a knife to cut the pancake into wedges. Serve warm.

**SERVING SUGGESTION: Serve with whipped, unsalted butter and honey on the side.**

1½ cups all-purpose flour
1½ teaspoons granulated sugar
1½ teaspoons baking powder
½ teaspoon baking soda
½ teaspoon salt
1 large egg
2 tablespoons butter or margarine,
   melted
¾ cup milk
½ cup beer

**1** Preheat a large skillet or griddle over medium heat.

**2** In a large bowl, blend together the flour, sugar, baking powder, baking soda, and salt. Make an indentation in the center of the ingredients and add the egg, butter, milk, and beer. Stir until the ingredients are combined and the batter is smooth.

**3** Brush the skillet with oil. Drop a heaping serving spoonful of the batter onto the prepared skillet and cook for 3 to 5 minutes, or until the bottom is golden brown and the top is speckled with holes. Turn and brown the other side. Transfer the pancake to plate and continue until all the batter is used. Serve warm.

# BEER PANCAKES

MAKES: *4 to 6 pancakes*

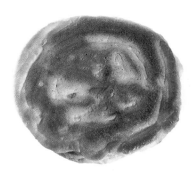

¼ cup all-purpose flour
¾ cup buckwheat flour
3 tablespoons granulated sugar
1 teaspoon baking powder
½ teaspoon salt
½ cup seedless raisins, plumped in
   boiling water
3 large eggs
1¾ cups milk
6 tablespoons butter or margarine,
   melted

**1** Preheat a large skillet or griddle over medium heat.

**2** In a large bowl, blend together the two flours, sugar, baking powder, and salt. Drain the water from the raisins, pat them dry between paper towels and fold them into the dry ingredients.

Make an indentation in the center of the mixture and add the eggs, milk, and butter all at one time. Stir until the ingredients are combined but the batter is still slightly lumpy.

**3** Brush the skillet with oil. Drop a heaping serving spoonful of the batter onto the prepared skillet and cook for 3 to 5 minutes, or until the bottom is golden brown and the top is speckled with holes. Turn and brown the other side. Transfer the pancake to a plate and continue until all the batter is used. Serve warm.

**SERVING SUGGESTION: Serve with honey and fresh fruit on the side.**

# BELGIAN BUCKWHEAT PANCAKES

MAKES: *16 to 18 pancakes*

## BLUEBERRY PANCAKES

MAKES: *8 to 10 pancakes*

1 cup all-purpose flour
1 tablespoon granulated sugar
1½ teaspoons baking powder
¼ teaspoon ground cinnamon
¾ cup fresh blueberries
½ teaspoon salt
1 large egg, separated
¾ cup milk
2 tablespoons butter or margarine,
  melted

**1** Preheat a large skillet or griddle over medium heat.

**2** In a large bowl, blend together the flour, sugar, baking powder, cinnamon, blueberries, and salt. In a medium bowl, beat the egg until foamy. Beat in the milk and butter. Combine the two mixtures, stirring until the ingredients are combined but the batter is still slightly lumpy.

**3** Brush the skillet with oil. Drop a heaping serving spoonful of the batter onto the prepared skillet and cook for 3 to 5 minutes, or until the bottom is golden brown and the top is speckled with holes. Turn and brown the other side. Transfer the pancake to a plate and continue until all the batter is used. Serve warm.

**SERVING SUGGESTION: Serve with syrup and sweet whipped cream on the side.**

## BUTTERMILK PANCAKES

MAKES: *24 pancakes*

2 cups all-purpose flour
2 tablespoons granulated sugar
2 teaspoons baking powder
½ teaspoon baking soda
½ teaspoon ground nutmeg
½ teaspoon salt
2 large eggs
2 cups buttermilk or sour milk
2 tablespoons canola oil

**1** Preheat a large skillet or griddle over medium heat.

**2** In a large bowl, blend together the flour, sugar, baking powder, baking soda, nutmeg, and salt. Make an indentation in the center of the dry ingredients and add the eggs, buttermilk, and oil. Beat until smooth.

**3** Brush the skillet with oil. Drop a heaping serving spoon of the batter onto the prepared skillet and cook for 3 to 5 minutes, or until the bottom is golden brown and the top is speckled with holes. Turn the pancake and brown the other side. Transfer the pancake to a plate and continue until all the batter is used.

**SERVING SUGGESTION: Serve with a fruit butter on the side.**

## CARROT PANCAKES

MAKES: *4 to 6 pancakes*

2 large eggs
½ cup milk
¼ cup butter or margarine, melted
2 teaspoons granulated sugar
¼ teaspoon salt
2¼ cups all-purpose flour
¾ cup very finely chopped carrots

**1** Preheat a large skillet or griddle over medium heat.

**2** In the container of a blender or food processor, combine the eggs, milk, butter, salt, and sugar and process on high for 2 to 3 seconds. Add the flour and carrots and process for 6 to 7 seconds more, or until the batter is fairly smooth.

**3** Brush the skillet with oil. Drop a heaping serving spoonful of the batter onto the prepared skillet and cook for 3 to 5 minutes, or until the bottom is golden brown and the top is speckled with holes. Turn the pancake and brown the other side. Transfer the pancake to a plate and continue until all the batter is used. Serve warm.

1 cup all-purpose flour
½ cup Dutch-processed cocoa
   powder
2 teaspoons grated orange zest
1 cup finely ground hazelnuts
1 cup heavy cream
½ cup granulated sugar
2 large egg yolks
1 large egg, separated
¼ cup butter or margarine, melted
Powdered sugar for sprinkling

**1** Preheat a large skillet or griddle over medium heat.

**2** In a large bowl, blend together the flour, cocoa powder, orange zest, and nuts. In a medium bowl, beat the cream and sugar until soft peaks form. Add the 3 egg yolks, one at a time, beating vigorously after each addition. Beat in the butter. In a small bowl, beat the egg white until stiff but not dry. Combine the flour and the cream mixtures, beating until smooth. Fold in the egg white.

**3** Drop a heaping serving spoonful of the batter onto the prepared skillet and cook for 3 to 5 minutes, or until the bottom is golden brown and the top is speckled with holes. Turn the pancake and brown the other side. Transfer the pancake to a plate and roll it into a cylinder. Continue until all the batter is used. Just before serving, sprinkle the pancakes with powdered sugar.

# CHOCOLATE–NUT PANCAKES

MAKES: *14 to 16 pancakes*

½ cup all-purpose flour
3 tablespoons Dutch-processed
   cocoa powder
3 tablespoons granulated sugar
1 large egg
½ cup minus 1 tablespoon
   evaporated milk
1 tablespoon butter or margarine,
   melted
1 tablespoon chocolate extract

**1** Preheat a large skillet or griddle over medium heat.

**2** In a large bowl, blend together the flour, cocoa powder, and sugar. In a medium bowl, beat the egg, milk, butter, and chocolate extract until smooth. Combine the two mixtures, beating until smooth.

**3** Brush the skillet with oil. Drop a heaping serving spoonful of the batter onto the prepared skillet and cook for 3 to 5 minutes, or until the bottom is golden brown and the top is speckled with holes. Turn the pancake and brown the other side. Transfer the pancake to a plate and continue until all the batter is used. Serve warm.

**SERVING SUGGESTION: Serve with fresh fruit and hot chocolate syrup on the side.**

# CHOCOLATE PANCAKES

MAKES: *4 to 6 servings*

## CORN MEAL GRIDDLECAKES

MAKES: *30 to 35 pancakes*

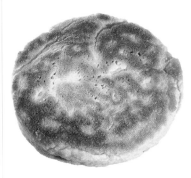

2 cups boiling water
1 cup cornmeal
1 tablespoon granulated sugar
1 teaspoon salt
1½ cups milk
2 cups all-purpose flour
1 tablespoon baking powder
2 large eggs

**1** In a large bowl, blend together the boiling water, cornmeal, sugar, and salt. Set aside for 5 minutes. Stir in the milk and set aside for an additional 5 minutes. In a medium bowl, combine the flour and baking powder. Beat the eggs into the cornmeal mix, and beat in the flour until smooth.

**2** Heat a large skillet or griddle over medium heat and brush it with oil. Drop a heaping serving spoonful of the batter onto the prepared skillet and cook for 3 to 5 minutes, or until the bottom is golden brown and the top is speckled with holes. Turn the pancake and brown the other side. Transfer the pancake to a plate and continue until all the batter is used. Serve warm.

## COTTAGE CHEESE PANCAKES

MAKES: *8 to 10 pancakes*

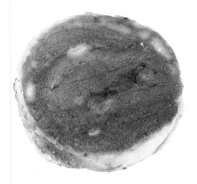

2 large eggs
⅓ cup cottage cheese
¾ cup sour cream or plain yogurt
½ cup all-purpose flour
½ teaspoon baking soda
½ teaspoon salt

**1** Preheat a large skillet or griddle over medium heat.

**2** In the container of a blender or food processor, combine the eggs, cottage cheese, sour cream, flour, baking soda, and salt. Process on high for 20 to 25 seconds, or until the mixture is smooth.

**3** Brush the skillet with oil. Drop a heaping serving spoonful of the batter onto the prepared skillet and cook for 3 to 5 minutes, or until the bottom is golden brown and the top is speckled with holes. Turn the pancake and brown the other side. Transfer the pancake to a plate and continue until all the batter is used.

## CREAM CHEESE PANCAKES

MAKES: *8 to 10 servings*

1 cup all-purpose flour
½ teaspoon salt
3 large egg yolks, beaten
1 large (8-ounce) package cream cheese
2 tablespoons butter or margarine, melted
1½ cups light cream or evaporated milk

**1** Preheat a large skillet or griddle over medium heat.

**2** In a large bowl, beat the flour, salt, egg yolks, cream cheese, butter, and cream until smooth.

**3** Brush the skillet with oil. Drop a heaping serving spoonful of the batter onto the prepared skillet and cook for 3 to 5 minutes, or until the bottom is golden brown and the top is speckled with holes. Turn the pancake and brown the other side. Transfer the pancake to a plate and continue until all the batter is used. Serve warm.

¾ cup all-purpose flour
1½ teaspoons baking soda
¼ teaspoon salt
1 large egg
½ cup cooked cream of wheat cereal
¼ cup butter or margarine, melted
1 cup buttermilk or sour milk

**1** Preheat a large skillet or griddle over medium heat.

**2** In a small bowl, blend together the flour, baking soda, and salt. In a large bowl, beat the egg until foamy. Beat in the cream of wheat, butter, and buttermilk. Combine the two mixtures, beating until smooth.

**3** Bush the skillet with oil. Drop a heaping serving spoonful of the batter onto the prepared skillet and cook for 3 to 5 minutes, or until the bottom is golden brown and the top is speckled with holes. Turn the pancake and brown the other side. Transfer the pancake to a plate and continue until all the batter is used. Serve warm.

**SERVING SUGGESTION: Serve with grape jelly and whipped butter on the side.**

## CREAM OF WHEAT PANCAKES

MAKES: *4 to 6 pancakes*

2 cups all-purpose flour
3 tablespoons granulated sugar
1 teaspoon baking soda
1 teaspoon ground cinnamon
½ teaspoon ground nutmeg
¾ teaspoon salt
2 large eggs
¼ cup lemon juice
1¾ cups milk
¼ cup butter or margarine, melted
1 medium-size apple, peeled, cored, and grated
Ginger Cream (see recipe page 21)

**1** Preheat a large skillet or griddle over medium heat.

**2** In a large bowl, blend together the flour, sugar, baking soda, cinnamon, nutmeg, and salt. Make an indentation in the dry ingredients and add the eggs, lemon juice, milk, and butter all at once. Beat until smooth. Fold in the apples.

**3** Brush the skillet with oil. Drop a heaping serving spoonful of the batter onto the prepared skillet and cook for 3 to 5 minutes, or until the bottom is golden brown and the top is speckled with holes. Turn the pancake and brown the other side. Transfer the pancake to a plate and continue until all the batter is used. Serve warm with Ginger Cream.

## MAINE PAN-APPLE-CAKES

MAKES: *14 to 16 pancakes*

# OAT BRAN GRIDDLECAKES

MAKES: *14 to 16 pancakes*

½ cup all-purpose flour
¾ cup oat bran
2 teaspoons granulated sugar
2 teaspoons baking powder
¼ teaspoon ground nutmeg
¼ teaspoon salt
1 large egg
¾ cup milk
1 tablespoon butter or margarine, melted

**1** Preheat a large skillet or griddle over medium heat.

**2** In a large bowl, blend together the flour, oat bran, sugar, baking powder, nutmeg, and salt. In a medium bowl, beat the egg until foamy. Beat in the milk and butter. Combine the two mixtures, beating until smooth.

**3** Brush the skillet with oil. Drop a heaping serving spoonful of the batter onto the prepared skillet and cook for 3 to 5 minutes, or until the bottom of the pancake is golden brown and the top is speckled with holes. Turn the pancake and brown the other side. Transfer the pancake to a plate and continue until all the batter is used. Serve warm.

**SERVING SUGGESTION: Serve with hot maple syrup and sweet whipped cream on the side.**

# OATMEAL PANCAKES

MAKES: *4 to 6 pancakes*

⅓ cup all-purpose flour
2 cups rolled oats
2½ teaspoons baking powder
2 teaspoons granulated sugar
1 teaspoon salt
2 large eggs, separated
2 cups milk
⅓ cup butter or margarine, melted

**1** Preheat a large skillet or griddle over medium heat.

**2** In a large bowl, blend together the flour, oats, baking powder, sugar, and salt. In a small bowl, beat the egg whites until stiff but not dry. In a medium bowl, beat the egg yolks, milk, and butter together. Combine the oat and the milk mixtures, beating until smooth. Fold in the egg whites.

**3** Brush the skillet with oil. Drop a heaping serving spoonful of the batter onto the prepared skillet and cook for 3 to 5 minutes, or until the bottom is golden brown and the top is speckled with holes. Turn the pancake and brown the other side. Transfer the pancake to a plate and continue until all the batter is used. Serve warm.

**SERVING SUGGESTION: Serve with cherry preserves and sweet whipped cream on the side.**

# ORANGE PANCAKES

MAKES: *4 to 6 pancakes*

1 large egg
2 tablespoons butter or margarine, melted
1 cup orange juice
1 cup all-purpose flour
1 tablespoon granulated sugar
2 teaspoons baking powder
½ teaspoon salt

**1** Preheat a large skillet or griddle over medium heat.

**2** In the container of a blender or food processor, combine the egg, butter, and orange juice. Process on high for about 20 seconds or until smooth. Add the flour, sugar, baking powder, and salt and process for an additional 20 seconds or until smooth.

**3** Brush the skillet with oil. Drop a heaping serving spoonful of the batter onto the prepared skillet and cook for 3 to 5 minutes, or until the bottom is golden brown and the top is speckled with holes. Turn the pancake and brown the other side. Transfer the pancake to a plate and continue until all the batter is used. Serve warm.

**SERVING SUGGESTION: Serve with orange marmalade and whipped cream-cheese on the side.**

¾ cup all-purpose flour
¾ cup cooked Jasmine (or other flavored) rice
2½ teaspoons baking powder
1 large egg
1 cup milk
3 tablespoons canola oil
¼ teaspoon salt

1  Preheat a large skillet or griddle over medium heat.

2  In the container of a blender or food processor, combine the flour, rice, baking powder, egg, milk, oil, and salt. Process on high for 10 to 20 seconds or until smooth.

3  Brush the skillet with oil. Drop a heaping serving spoonful of the batter onto the prepared skillet and cook for 3 to 5 minutes, or until the bottom is golden brown and the top is speckled with holes. Turn the pancake and brown the other side. Transfer the pancake to a plate and continue until all the batter is used. Serve hot.

**SERVING SUGGESTION: Serve with syrup or honey and whipped butter on the side, or with fresh fruit and sweet whipped cream.**

## RICE PANCAKES

MAKES: *14 to 16 pancakes*

---

⅓ cup heavy cream
3 large eggs
¼ cup butter or margarine, melted
⅓ cup sherry
½ cup all-purpose flour
¼ cup graham flour
1 tablespoon granulated sugar
¼ teaspoon salt

1  Preheat a large skillet or griddle over medium heat.

2  In a large bowl, beat the heavy cream until slightly thickened. Beat in the eggs, butter, and sherry. In a small bowl, blend together the two flours, sugar, and salt. Combine the two mixtures, beating until smooth.

3  Brush the skillet with oil. Drop a heaping serving spoonful of the batter onto the prepared skillet and cook for 3 to 5 minutes, or until the bottom is golden brown and the top is speckled with holes. Turn the pancake and brown the other side. Transfer the pancake to a plate and continue until all the batter is used. Serve warm.

**SERVING SUGGESTION: Serve with fruit-flavored yogurt on the side.**

## SHERRY PANCAKES

MAKES: *4 to 6 pancakes*

---

3 tablespoons all-purpose flour
2 tablespoons granulated sugar
¼ teaspoon salt
9 ounces (3 small packages) cream cheese
3 tablespoons sour cream or plain yogurt
¼ cup butter or margarine, melted
3 large eggs

1  Preheat a large skillet or griddle over medium heat.

2  In a small bowl, combine the flour, sugar, and salt. In a large bowl, beat the cream cheese until soft before beating in the sour cream and butter. Add the eggs, one at a time, beating vigorously after each addition. Combine the two mixtures, beating until smooth.

3  Brush the skillet with oil. Drop a heaping serving spoonful of the batter onto the prepared skillet and cook for 3 to 5 minutes, or until the bottom is golden brown and the top is speckled with holes. Turn the pancake and brown the other side. Transfer the pancake to a plate and continue until all the batter is used. Serve warm.

## SOUR CREAM-AND-CHEESE PANCAKES

MAKES: *4 to 6 servings*

## SOY PANCAKES

MAKES: *14 to 16 pancakes*

1 large egg
1 cup milk
3 tablespoons canola oil
1 cup soy flour
½ cup rice flour
2½ teaspoons baking powder
¾ teaspoon salt

1  Preheat a large skillet or griddle over medium heat.

2  In the container of a blender or food processor, combine the egg, milk, oil, two flours, baking powder, and salt. Process on high speed for 10 to 20 seconds or until smooth.

3  Brush the skillet with oil. Drop a heaping serving spoonful of the batter onto the prepared skillet and cook for 3 to 5 minutes, or until the bottom is golden brown and the top is speckled with holes. Turn the pancake and brown the other side. Transfer the pancake to a plate and continue until all the batter is used. Serve warm.

**SERVING SUGGESTION: Serve with syrup, honey, and whipped butter on the side, or with fresh fruit and sweet whipped cream.**

## YOGURT PANCAKES

MAKES: *4 to 6 pancakes*

¾ cup all-purpose flour
1 teaspoon baking soda
¼ teaspoon ground allspice
¼ teaspoon salt
1 large egg
½ cup cooked oatmeal
¼ cup butter or margarine, melted
1 cup plain yogurt or sour cream

1  Preheat a large skillet or griddle over medium heat.

2  In a small bowl, blend together the flour, baking soda, allspice, and salt. In a large bowl, beat the egg until foamy. Beat in the oatmeal, butter, and yogurt. Combine the two mixtures, beating until combined.

3  Brush the skillet with oil. Drop a heaping serving spoonful of the batter onto the prepared skillet and cook for 3 to 5 minutes, or until the bottom is golden brown and the top is speckled with holes. Turn the pancake and brown the other side. Transfer the pancake to a plate and continue until all the batter is used. Serve warm.

**SERVING SUGGESTION: Serve with grape jelly and whipped butter on the side.**

## ZUCCHINI–CHEESE PANCAKES

MAKES: *6 to 8 pancakes*

⅔ cup Bisquick® baking mix
¼ cup wheat germ
1 medium zucchini, grated
1 cup grated Cheddar cheese
¼ cup grated Parmesan cheese
¼ teaspoon ground white pepper
2 large eggs
¾ cup milk
Herb Butter (see recipe page 149)

1  Preheat a large skillet or griddle over medium heat.

2  In a large bowl, blend together the baking mix, wheat germ, zucchini, cheeses, and pepper. In a small bowl, beat the eggs and milk smooth. Combine the two mixtures, beating until smooth.

3  Brush the skillet with oil. Drop a heaping serving spoonful of the batter onto the prepared skillet and cook for 3 to 5 minutes, or until the bottom is golden brown and the top is speckled with holes. Turn the pancake and brown the other side. Transfer the pancake to a plate and continue until all the batter is used. Serve warm with Herb Butter.

# Chapter 9

# POPOVERS

This chapter contains recipes for the lightest, crispy, flakey, and flavorful baked good known as a popover. Unfortunately the popover is seldom seen anymore. Many people who have eaten English Yorkshire Pudding do not realize that it is just an oversized popover. One of the most important secrets in popover-baking is the intense heat of the oven.

## BASIC POPOVERS

MAKES: *10 to 12 popovers*

1 cup all-purpose flour
½ teaspoon salt
2 large eggs
1 cup milk
1 tablespoon butter or margarine, melted

**1** Position the rack in the center of the oven and preheat to 425 degrees F. Liberally grease a 12-cup muffin baking pan or 12 oven-proof custard cups. Place in the oven until needed.

**2** In a small bowl, blend together the flour and salt. In a medium bowl, beat the eggs until foamy. Beat in the milk and butter. Add the dry ingredients all at one time and beat until smooth.

**3** Spoon the batter into the hot cups, filling each about three-quarters full. Bake for 15 minutes (do not open the oven door). Reduce the heat to 375 degrees F and bake for an additional 20 to 25 minutes, or until the tops are firm to the touch and a deep golden brown.

**4** Turn off the oven, remove the popovers from the oven and prick the side of each popover with a fork. Return the popovers to the oven for an additional 5 minutes. Remove the popovers from the baking cups (run a knife around the edges of cups if necessary) and serve hot.

## CHEDDAR CHEESE POPOVERS

MAKES: *10 to 12 popovers*

1 cup all-purpose flour
½ cup grated cheddar cheese
¼ teaspoon salt
2 large eggs
1 cup milk

**1** Position the rack in the center of the oven and preheat to 425 degrees F. Liberally grease a popover pan or custard cups. Place in the oven until needed.

**2** In a small bowl, blend together the flour, cheese, and salt. In a medium bowl beat the eggs until foamy. Beat in the milk. Add the dry ingredients all at one time and beat until smooth.

**3** Spoon the batter into the hot cups, filling each about three-quarters full. Bake for 15 minutes (do not open the oven door). Reduce the heat to 375 degrees F and bake for an additional 20 to 25 minutes, or until the tops are firm to the touch and a deep golden brown.

**4** Turn off the oven, remove the popovers from the oven and prick the side of each popover with a fork. Return the popovers for an additional 5 minutes. Remove the popovers from the baking cups (run a knife around the edges of cups if necessary) and serve hot.

1⅓ cups all-purpose flour
½ cup shredded Swiss cheese
½ teaspoon salt
4 large eggs
⅔ cup milk
⅔ cup water

**1** Position the rack in the center of the oven and preheat to 425 degrees F. Liberally grease a 12-cup muffin baking pan or 12 oven-proof custard cups. Place in the oven until needed.

**2** In a small bowl, blend together the flour, cheese, and salt. In a medium bowl, beat the eggs until foamy. Beat in the milk and water. Add the dry ingredients all at one time and beat until smooth.

**3** Spoon the batter into the hot cups, filling each about three-quarters full. Bake for 15 minutes (do not open the oven door). Reduce the heat to 375 degrees F and bake for an additional 20 to 25 minutes, or until the tops are firm to the touch and a deep golden brown.

**4** Turn off the oven, remove the popovers from the oven and prick the side of each popover with a fork. Return the popovers to the oven for an additional 5 minutes. Remove the popovers from the baking cups (run a knife around the edges of cups if necessary) and serve hot.

## CHEESY MORNING POPOVERS

MAKES: *6 to 8 popovers*

---

1 tablespoon butter or margarine
2 pounds tart apples, peeled, cored and diced
3 tablespoons granulated sugar
1 teaspoon vanilla extract
¼ teaspoon ground allspice
1 cup milk
2 large eggs, separated
1 cup all-purpose flour
¼ teaspoon salt

**1** In a large oven-proof skillet set over medium heat, melt the butter. Add the apples and 2 tablespoons of the sugar. Cook, stirring frequently, for 15 to 20 minutes or until the apples are tender and most of the liquid has evaporated. Remove from the heat and stir in the vanilla extract and allspice. Set aside.

**2** Position the rack in the center of the oven and preheat to 425 degrees F. In a medium bowl, beat the remaining tablespoon of sugar, the milk, egg yolks, flour, and salt until smooth. In a small bowl, beat the egg whites until stiff but not dry. Fold the egg whites into the yolk mixture.

**3** Spoon the batter over the top of the apples in the pan. Bake for 20 minutes (do not open the oven door). Reduce the heat to 350 degrees F. and bake for an additional 10 to 15 minutes, or until the top of the popover is firm to the touch and golden brown. Remove the pan from the oven and cool it on a wire rack for 3 to 5 minutes before cutting into wedges and serving.

## NEW ENGLAND FAMILY POPOVERS

MAKES: *6 to 8 servings*

## PARMESAN CHEESE POPOVERS

MAKES: *6 to 8 popovers*

4 large eggs
1 cup milk
⅔ cup all-purpose flour
½ teaspoon salt
½ cup grated Parmesan cheese

**1** Position the rack in the center of the oven and preheat to 425 degrees F. Liberally grease 8 muffin baking cups or 8 oven-proof custard cups. Place the cups in the oven until needed.

**2** In the container of a blender, combine the eggs, milk, flour, salt, and cheese and process on high for 3 to 4 seconds or until smooth.

**3** Pour the batter into the hot cups, filling each about three-quarters full. Bake for 15 minutes (do not open the oven door) and reduce the heat to 375 degrees F and bake for an additional 20 to 25 minutes, or until the tops are firm to the touch and a deep golden brown.

**4** Turn off the oven, remove the popovers from the oven and prick the side of each with a fork. Return them to the oven for an additional 5 minutes. Remove the popovers from the baking cups (run a knife around the edges of cups if necessary) and serve hot.

## PASSOVER POPOVERS

MAKES: *10 to 12 popovers*

4 large eggs
½ cup unsalted butter or margarine, melted
1 cup water
½ cup cake meal
½ cup matzo meal
¼ teaspoon salt

**1** Position the rack in the center of the oven and preheat to 425 degrees F. Liberally grease a 12-cup muffin baking pan or 12 oven-proof custard cups. Place in the oven until needed.

**2** In the container of a blender, combine the eggs, butter, water, cake meal, matzo meal, and salt and process on high for 3 to 4 seconds or until smooth.

**3** Pour the batter into the hot cups, filling each about three-quarters full. Bake for 15 minutes (do not open the oven door). Reduce the heat to 375 degrees F and bake for an additional 20 to 25 minutes, or until the tops are firm to the touch and a deep golden brown.

**4** Turn off the oven, remove the popovers from the oven and prick the side of each popover with a fork. Return the popovers to the oven for an additional 5 minutes. Remove the popovers from the baking cups (run a knife around the edges of cups if necessary) and serve hot.

½ cup cooked rice, cold
1 cup all-purpose flour
1 teaspoon grated orange rind
½ teaspoon salt
3 teaspoons granulated sugar
1 large egg, separated
2 teaspoons butter, melted

**1** Position the rack in the center of the oven and preheat to 425 degrees F. Liberally grease a popover pan or custard cups. Place in the oven until needed.

**2** In a medium bowl, blend together the rice, flour, baking powder, orange zest, and salt stirring until the grains of rice are separated. In a small bowl, beat the sugar, egg yolk, and butter until smooth. In another small bowl, beat the egg white until stiff but not dry. Combine the rice mixture and the sugar mixture until smooth. Fold in the egg white.

**3** Spoon the batter into the hot cups, filling each about three-quarters full. Bake for 15 minutes (do not open the oven door). Reduce the heat to 375 degrees F and bake for an additional 20 to 25 minutes, or until the tops are firm to the touch and a deep golden brown.

**4** Turn off the oven, remove the popovers from the oven and prick the side of each popover with a fork. Return the popovers for an additional 5 minutes. Remove the popovers from the baking cups (run a knife around the edges of cups if necessary) and serve hot.

# RICE POPOVERS

MAKES: *8 to 10 popovers*

# Chapter 10

# SCONES

No one knows exactly when the first scone was made, who made it, nor from which culture it derives. As far as we can tell, the original scone was formed in the shape of a triangle and cooked on a griddle. Today, they are baked in a variety of shapes, but are mostly found in various sized rounds, and cut or scored into wedge shapes to follow tradition. They can be baked to adapt and please almost any type of taste. Scones are more popular in the United Kingdom than in the United States, but Americans have their own version of the scone—the biscuit. In the United Kingdom, scones are considered appropriate for afternoon tea served with a hot beverage, more as a snack, than as part of a meal.

# All-Grain Scones

Makes: *8 scones*

½ cup buttermilk
1 large egg
1 tablespoon honey
1 tablespoon molasses
¼ cup unprocessed bran
½ cup all-purpose flour
½ cup whole-wheat flour
¼ cup rye flour
⅓ cup rolled oats
¼ cup cornmeal
2 teaspoons baking powder
½ teaspoon baking soda
½ teaspoon salt
6 tablespoons chilled butter or
  margarine, diced

**1** Position the rack in the center of the oven and preheat to 400 degrees F. Lightly grease and flour a baking sheet.

**2** In a medium bowl, beat the buttermilk, egg, honey, and molasses until smooth. Stir in the bran. In a large bowl, blend together the three flours, rolled oats, cornmeal, baking powder, baking soda, and salt. Using a pastry blender or two knives scissor-fashion, cut the butter into the mixture until it resembles coarse meal. Gently stir in the wet ingredients until the dough just holds together.

**3** Transfer the dough to the prepared baking sheet and pat it into an 8-inch circle. Using a serrated knife, score into 8 wedges (do not cut all the way through the dough). Bake for 18 to 20 minutes, or until the top is golden. Remove from the oven, cut into wedges, and serve hot.

# Aloha Scones

Makes: *8 scones*

2 cups all-purpose flour
2 teaspoons baking powder
¼ cup granulated sugar
¼ teaspoon salt
5 tablespoons chilled butter, diced
½ cup chopped dried papaya
½ cup chopped dried pineapple
½ cup chopped macadamia nuts
½ cup shredded coconut
3 ounces white chocolate, cut into
  very small pieces
1 large egg, beaten
½ cup milk
1½ teaspoons rum

**1** Position the rack in the center of the oven and preheat to 400 degrees F. Lightly grease and flour a baking sheet.

**2** In a large bowl, blend together the flour, baking powder, sugar, and salt. Using a pastry blender or two knives scissor-fashion, cut the butter into the mixture until it resembles coarse meal. Stir in the papaya, pineapple, nuts, coconut, and white chocolate. Add the egg, milk, and rum, stirring gently until the dough holds together.

**3** Transfer the dough to the prepared baking sheet and pat it into an 8-inch circle. Using a serrated knife, score into 8 wedges (do not cut all the way through the dough). Bake for 18 to 20 minutes, or until the top is golden brown. Remove from the oven and cool on a wire rack for 5 to 7 minutes before serving warm or cold.

1½ cups all-purpose flour
1 cup rolled oats
2½ teaspoons baking powder
⅓ cup packed brown sugar
½ teaspoon salt
½ cup chilled butter or margarine, diced
¾ cup chopped apples, unpeeled and cored
⅔ cup chopped pitted dates
1 large egg, beaten
¼ cup milk, plus more for brushing the scones
2 tablespoons molasses
1 teaspoon vanilla extract

1 Position the rack in the center of the oven and preheat to 400 degrees F. Lightly grease and flour a baking sheet.

2 In a large bowl, blend together the oats, baking powder, brown sugar, and salt. Using a pastry blender or two knives scissor-fashion, cut the butter into the mixture until it resembles coarse meal. Stir in the apples and dates. Add the egg, milk, molasses, and vanilla extract, stirring gently until the dough just holds together.

3 Transfer the dough to the prepared baking sheet and pat it into an 8-inch circle. Using a serrated knife, score the dough into 8 wedges (do not cut all the way through the dough). Brush the top of the scone with milk and bake for 18 to 20 minutes, or until the top is golden brown. Remove from the oven and serve hot.

# APPLE–OATMEAL SCONES

MAKES: *8 scones*

---

1¾ cups all-purpose flour
½ teaspoon baking powder
¼ teaspoon baking soda
3 tablespoons granulated sugar
¼ cup chilled butter or margarine, diced
1 teaspoon grated lemon zest
¾ cup peeled, cored, and chopped apples
¼ cup chopped pecans
½ cup lemon-flavored yogurt
Cinnamon sugar for sprinkling

1 Position the rack in the center of the oven and preheat to 400 degrees F. Lightly grease and flour a baking sheet.

2 In a large bowl, blend together the flour, baking powder, baking soda, and sugar. Using a pastry blender or two knives scissor-fashion, cut in the butter until the mixture resembles fine meal. Stir in the lemon zest, apples, and pecans. Add the yogurt, stirring gently until the dough holds together.

3 Turn the dough out onto the prepared baking sheet and pat it into an 8-inch circle. Using a serrated knife, score the dough into 8 wedges (do not cut all the way through the dough). Sprinkle the top with cinnamon sugar and bake for 15 to 20 minutes, or until the top is golden brown. Remove from the oven and serve hot.

# APPLE–PECAN SCONES

MAKES: *8 scones*

## AUNT ETHEL'S ABERDEEN SCONES

MAKES: *4 large scones*

3 cups all-purpose flour
6 teaspoons baking powder
6 tablespoons granulated sugar
1 teaspoon salt
2 tablespoons chilled vegetable
    shortening
1 cup buttermilk
1 large egg, beaten

**1** In a large bowl, blend together the flour, baking powder, sugar, and salt. Using a pastry blender or two knives scissor-fashion, cut in the shortening until the mixture forms fine crumbs. Add the buttermilk and egg, stirring gently until the dough holds together.

**2** Turn the dough out onto a floured surface and pat it out to a thickness of ¾-inch. Cut the dough into four wedges.

**3** Preheat a large skillet over medium heat. Place the pieces, one at a time, in the heated skillet and fry until browned on both sides. Remove from the pan and serve hot.

## BACON, CHEDDAR, AND CHIVE SCONES

MAKES: *16 scones*

3 large eggs
1 tablespoon warm water
2 cups all-purpose flour
2 teaspoons baking powder
¼ cup chilled butter or margarine
1½ cups shredded Cheddar cheese
8 slices crisply cooked bacon,
    crumbled
1 tablespoon fresh chopped chives
½ cup light cream

**1** Position the rack in the center of the oven and preheat to 450 degrees F. Lightly grease and flour a baking sheet. In a cup, combine one of the eggs and the water and whisk until smooth. Set aside.

**2** In a large bowl, blend together the flour and baking powder. Using a pastry blender or two knives scissor-fashion, cut in the butter until the mixture forms fine crumbs. Stir in the cheese, bacon, and chives. In a medium bowl, beat the remaining two eggs and cream until smooth. Add to the dry ingredients, stirring gently until the dough holds together.

**3** Turn the dough out onto a lightly floured surface and roll it into a 12-by-6-inch rectangle. Cut the dough into 3-inch squares, and then cut each square into halves from corner to corner to form rectangles

**4** Place the rectangles on the prepared baking sheet and brush with the reserved egg and water mixture. Bake for 14 to 16 minutes, or until the tops are golden brown. Remove from the oven and serve hot.

2 cups rolled oats
2 cups all-purpose flour
¼ cup granulated sugar
1¼ teaspoons baking powder
¼ teaspoon salt
2 ripe bananas
1 cup milk

**1** Position the rack in the center of the oven and preheat to 425 degrees F. Lightly grease and flour a baking sheet.

**2** Place 1 cup of the oats in the container of a food processor and process until fine. Add the flour, sugar, baking powder, salt, and bananas and process again until smooth. Pour mixture into a large bowl and add the remaining oats and milk, stirring gently until the dough holds together.

**3** Divide the dough into three equal pieces, and form each into a ball. Place the balls on the prepared baking sheet and pat each down to a thickness of ½-inch. Using a serrated knife, score the top of each into 4 wedges (do not cut all the way through the dough). Bake for 18 to 20 minutes, or until the tops are golden brown. Remove from the oven and serve hot.

# BANANA–OATMEAL SCONES

MAKES: *12 scones*

---

1 cup all-purpose flour
2 teaspoons baking powder
Dash of white pepper
¼ cup chilled butter or margarine
¼ cup crumbled blue cheese
¼ cup golden raisins
½ cup milk

**1** Position the rack in the center of the oven and preheat to 425 degrees F. Lightly grease and flour a baking sheet.

**2** In a large bowl, blend together the flour, baking powder, and pepper. Using a pastry blender or two knives scissor-fashion, cut in the butter until the mixture resembles coarse meal. Stir in the cheese and raisins. Add the milk, stirring gently until the dough holds together.

**3** Turn the dough out onto a lightly floured surface and knead a few times. Shape into a ball, place the ball on the prepared baking sheet, and pat into a ½-inch-thick circle. Using a serrated knife, score into 8 wedges (do not cut all the way through the dough). Bake for 10 to 15 minutes, or until golden brown. Remove from the oven and serve hot.

# BLUE CHEESE-AND-GOLDEN RAISIN SCONES

MAKES: *8 scones*

## BLUEBERRY, BANANA, AND WALNUT SCONES

MAKES: *8 scones*

1¼ cups all-purpose flour
½ cup whole-wheat flour
1 teaspoon baking powder
½ teaspoon baking soda
¼ cup granulated sugar
¼ teaspoon salt
¼ cup chilled butter or margarine, diced
¼ cup chopped walnuts
½ cup blueberries
½ cup blueberry-flavored yogurt
½ cup mashed bananas
1 tablespoon brown sugar

**1** Position the rack in the center of the oven and preheat to 350 degrees F. Lightly grease and flour a baking sheet.

**2** In a large bowl, blend together the two flours, baking powder, baking soda, granulated sugar, and salt. Using a pastry blender or two knives scissor-fashion, cut in the butter until the mixture resembles coarse crumbs. Stir in the walnuts and blueberries. In a small bowl, beat the yogurt and banana until smooth before gently stirring it into the dry ingredients, stirring until the dough holds together.

**3** Turn the dough out onto the prepared baking sheet and pat it into a ½-inch-thick circle. Using a serrated knife, score the dough into 8 wedges (do not cut all the way through the dough). Sprinkle the brown sugar over the top. Bake for 18 to 20 minutes, or until the edges are golden brown. Remove from the oven and serve hot.

## BRAN AND RAISIN SCONES

MAKES: *8 scones*

1 cup all-purpose flour
2 teaspoons baking powder
3 tablespoons granulated sugar
½ teaspoon cinnamon
¼ teaspoon salt
⅓ cup chilled vegetable shortening
½ cup chopped raisins
2 large eggs, beaten
1 cup bran cereal

**1** Position the rack in the center of the oven and preheat to 400 degrees F. Lightly grease and flour a baking sheet.

**2** In a large bowl, blend together the flour, baking powder, sugar, cinnamon, and salt. Using a pastry blender or two knives scissor-fashion, cut in the shortening until the mixture forms coarse crumbs. Stir in the raisins. Add the eggs, stirring gently until the dough holds together. Stir in the cereal.

**3** Turn the dough out onto the prepared baking sheet and pat it into a ½-inch-thick circle. Using a serrated knife, score into 8 wedges (do not cut all the way through the dough). Bake for 18 to 20 minutes, or until the top is golden. Remove from the oven and serve hot.

3½ cups all-purpose flour
1 tablespoon baking powder
½ cup granulated sugar, plus more for sprinkling over the scones
Pinch salt
¾ cup chilled butter or margarine
½ cup raisins
1 large egg, beaten
½ cup milk
1 large egg white, beaten

**1** Position the rack in the center of the oven and preheat to 350 degrees F. Lightly grease and flour a baking sheet.

**2** In a large bowl, blend together the flour, baking powder, ½ cup sugar, and salt. Using a pastry blender or two knives scissor-fashion, cut in the butter until the mixture resembles coarse meal. Stir in the raisins. Add the egg and milk, stirring gently until the dough holds together.

**3** Turn the dough out onto the prepared baking sheet, and pat it into a ½-inch-thick circle. Using a serrated knife, score into 8 wedges (do not cut all the way through the dough). Brush with the beaten egg white and sprinkle with granulated sugar. Bake for 10 to 12 minutes, or until the top is golden brown. Remove from the oven and serve hot.

# BUCKINGHAM PALACE SCONES

MAKES: *8 scones*

2 cups all-purpose flour
¼ cup granulated sugar
1½ teaspoons baking powder
½ teaspoon baking soda
¼ teaspoon salt
¼ cup chilled butter or margarine, diced
⅓ cup finely chopped dried apricots
¼ cup buttermilk or sour milk
¼ cup apricot nectar
1 large egg

**1** Position the rack in the center of the oven and preheat to 400 degrees F. Lightly grease and flour a baking sheet.

**2** In a large bowl, blend together the flour, sugar, baking powder, baking soda, and salt. Using a pastry blender or two knives scissor-fashion, cut in the butter until the mixture resembles coarse meal. Stir in the apricots. In a small bowl, stir the buttermilk, apricot nectar, and egg until smooth. Combine the two mixtures, stirring gently until the dough holds together.

**3** Turn the dough out onto the prepared baking sheet and pat down to a ½-inch-thick circle. Using a serrated knife, score the dough into 8 wedges (do not cut all the way through the dough). Bake for 12 to 15 minutes, or until the top is golden brown. Remove from the oven and serve hot.

# BUTTERMILK– APRICOT SCONES

MAKES: *8 scones*

# BUTTERMILK–RAISIN–PEANUT SCONES

MAKES: *8 scones*

2 cups all-purpose flour
2½ teaspoons baking powder
½ teaspoon baking soda
1 tablespoon granulated sugar
½ teaspoon salt
½ cup butter or margarine, at room temperature
½ cup chopped raisins
½ cup chopped peanuts
¾ cup buttermilk or sour milk
1 large egg

**1** Position the rack in the center of the oven and preheat to 450 degrees F. Lightly grease and flour a baking sheet.

**2** In a large bowl, blend together the flour, baking powder, baking soda, sugar, and salt. Using a pastry blender or two knives scissor-fashion, cut in the butter until the mixture forms coarse crumbs. Stir in the raisins and peanuts. Add the buttermilk and egg, stirring gently until the dough holds together.

**3** Turn the dough out onto the prepared baking sheet and pat down a ½-inch-thick circle. Using a serrated knife, score into 8 wedges (do not cut all the way through the dough). Bake for 10 to 15 minutes, or until golden brown. Remove from the oven and serve hot.

# CAPE BRETON SCONES

MAKES: *16 scones*

2 cups all-purpose flour
1 tablespoon baking powder
¼ teaspoon baking soda
2 tablespoons granulated sugar, plus more for sprinkling over the scones
1 teaspoon salt
1 cup chopped raisins or currants
½ cup sour cream or yogurt
¼ cup canola oil
1 large egg, beaten
3 tablespoons milk, plus more for brushing the scones

**1** Position the rack in the center of the oven and preheat to 425 degrees F. Lightly grease and flour a baking sheet.

**2** In a large bowl, combine the flour, baking powder, baking soda, the 2 tablespoons of sugar, salt, raisins, sour cream, oil, egg, and the 3 tablespoons of milk and stir gently until the dough holds together.

**3** Turn the dough out onto a lightly floured surface and knead gently until no longer sticky. Divide into two equal parts and form each into a ball. Place the balls on the prepared baking sheet and pat them into a 6-inch circles. Using a serrated knife, score each into 8 wedges (do not cut all the way through the dough). Brush the tops with milk and sprinkle with granulated sugar. Bake for 10 to 12 minutes, or until the tops are golden brown. Remove from the oven and serve hot.

2½ cups all-purpose flour
2½ teaspoons baking powder
½ teaspoon baking soda
⅔ cup granulated sugar
¾ cup chilled butter or margarine
1 cup chopped fresh cranberries
2 teaspoons grated orange zest
1½ cups buttermilk

**1** Position the rack in the center of the oven and preheat to 400 degrees F. Lightly grease and flour a baking sheet.

**2** In a large bowl, blend together the flour, baking powder, baking soda, and sugar. Using a pastry blender or two knives scissor-fashion, cut in the butter until the mixture resembles coarse meal.

Stir in the cranberries and orange zest. Add the buttermilk and stir gently until the dough holds together.

**3** Turn the dough out onto a lightly floured surface and knead several times until the dough is no longer sticky. Divide into two equal pieces and roll each into a ball. Place the balls on the prepared baking sheet and pat each into a 6-inch circle. Using a serrated knife, score into 8 wedges (do not cut all the way through the dough). Bake for 12 to 15 minutes, or until the tops are golden brown. Remove from the oven and serve hot.

# CAPE COD CRANBERRY SCONES

MAKES: *16 scones*

---

2½ cups all-purpose flour
1 tablespoon baking powder
½ teaspoon salt
¾ cup chilled butter or margarine, diced
¼ cup fresh chopped parsley
2 teaspoons crushed dried dill
1 cup shredded Cheddar cheese
2 large eggs, beaten
½ cup half-and-half

**1** Position the rack in the center of the oven and preheat to 400 degrees F. Lightly grease and flour a baking sheet.

**2** In a large bowl, blend together the flour, baking powder, and salt. Using a pastry blender or

two knives scissor-fashion, cut in the butter until the mixture resembles coarse meal. Stir in the parsley, dill, and cheese. Add the eggs and half-and-half, stirring gently until the dough holds together.

**3** Turn the dough out onto a flour surface and divide into two equal pieces. Roll each piece into a ball. Place the balls on the prepared baking sheet and pat each into a ½-inch-thick circle. Using a serrated knife, score into 8 wedges (do not cut all the way through the dough). Bake for 15 to 20 minutes, or until a golden brown.

# CHEDDAR CHEESE-AND-DILL SCONES

MAKES: *8 scones*

# CHERRY SCONES

MAKES: *10 to 12 scones*

2 cups all-purpose flour
¼ cup graham flour
2 teaspoons baking powder
½ teaspoon baking soda
⅓ cup granulated sugar
½ teaspoon salt
⅓ cup chilled butter or margarine, diced
⅓ cup dried chopped cherries
2 large eggs
⅔ cup buttermilk
1 teaspoon Cherry-flavored brandy
1 tablespoon water

1 Position the rack in the center of the oven and preheat to 375 degrees F. Lightly grease and flour a baking sheet.

2 In a large bowl, blend together the two flours, baking powder, baking soda, sugar, and salt. Using a pastry blender or two knives scissor-fashion, cut in the butter until the mixture resembles coarse meal. Stir in the cherries. In a medium bowl, beat one of the eggs, the buttermilk, and brandy until smooth. Combine the two mixtures, stirring gently until the dough holds together.

3 Turn the dough out onto a lightly floured surface and knead several times. Pat down to a thickness of 1 inch and using a biscuit cutter, cut into 2-inch circles, reworking the scraps as you go. Place the circles ½-inch apart on the prepared baking sheet.

4 In a small bowl, whisk together the remaining egg with the water and use it to brush the scones. Bake for 15 to 18 minutes, or until golden brown. Remove from the oven and serve hot.

# CHOCOLATE BROWNIE SCONES

MAKES: *8 scones*

3 ounces unsweetened chocolate, chopped
2 cups all-purpose flour
2¼ teaspoons baking powder
½ cup granulated sugar
¼ teaspoon salt
⅓ cup chilled butter or margarine, diced
½ cup chopped walnuts
⅓ cup milk
½ cup packed brown sugar
1 large egg
1½ teaspoons vanilla extract

1 Position the rack in the center of the oven and preheat to 350 degrees F. Lightly grease and flour a baking sheet.

2 In the top of a double boiler set over simmering water, melt the chocolate, stirring occasionally, until smooth. Set aside to cool slightly.

3 In a large bowl, blend together the flour, baking powder, sugar, and salt. Using a pastry blender or two knives scissor-fashion, cut the butter into the mixture until it resembles coarse meal. Stir in the walnuts. In a small bowl, beat the milk, brown sugar, egg, and vanilla extract together until the sugar is dissolved. Stir in the melted chocolate. Combine the two mixtures, stirring gently until the dough holds together.

4 Turn the dough out onto a lightly floured surface and pat it into a 7-inch circle. Place the circle on the prepared baking sheet and use a serrated knife to score the dough into 8 wedges (do not cut all the way through the dough). Bake for 18 to 20 minutes, or until the top is a darker brown. Remove from the oven and serve hot.

2 cups all-purpose flour
2 teaspoons baking powder
⅓ cup granulated sugar
¼ teaspoon salt
½ cup chilled butter or margarine, diced
¾ cup semisweet chocolate chips
2 large eggs
¼ cup orange juice
2 teaspoons Triple Sec liqueur
½ teaspoon grated orange zest
Beaten egg white for brushing

**1** Position the rack in the center of the oven and preheat to 425 degrees F. Lightly grease and flour a baking sheet.

**2** In a large bowl, blend together the flour, baking powder, sugar, and salt. Using a pastry blender or two knives scissor-fashion, cut in the butter until the mixture resembles coarse meal. Stir in the chocolate chips. In a small bowl, whisk together the eggs, orange juice, liqueur, and orange zest until smooth. Combine the two mixtures, stirring gently until the dough holds together.

**3** Turn the dough out onto the prepared baking sheet and pat it into an 8-inch circle. Using a serrated knife, score the dough into 8 wedges (do not cut all the way through the dough). Bake for 18 to 20 minutes, or until the top is golden. Remove from the oven and serve hot.

# CHOCOLATE CHIP-AND-ORANGE SCONES

MAKES: *8 scones*

---

2 cups all-purpose flour
2½ teaspoons baking powder
½ teaspoon baking soda
½ teaspoon ground cinnamon
¼ teaspoon salt
½ cup chilled butter or margarine, diced
¾ cup semisweet chocolate chips
½ cup chopped toasted pecans
2 large eggs
½ cup buttermilk
½ cup packed light-brown sugar, plus more for sprinkling on the scones
½ teaspoon chocolate extract

**1** Position the rack in the center of the oven and preheat to 450 degrees F. Lightly grease and flour a baking sheet.

**2** In a large bowl, blend together the flour, baking powder, baking soda, cinnamon, and salt. Using a pastry blender or two knives scissor-fashion, cut the butter into the mixture until it resembles coarse meal. Stir in the chocolate chips and pecans. In a small bowl, beat the eggs, buttermilk, the ½ cup brown sugar, and the chocolate extract until smooth. Combine the two mixtures, stirring until the dough holds together.

**3** Turn the dough out onto a floured surface and knead a few times. Pat the dough out to a thickness of 1 inch. Using a biscuit cutter, cut into 2-inch circles, reworking the scraps as you go. Place the circles ½ inch apart on the prepared baking sheet. Sprinkle brown sugar over the tops and bake for 12 to 15 minutes, or until golden brown. Remove from the oven and serve hot.

# CHOCOLATE CHIP-PECAN SCONES

MAKES: *16 scones*

# CHOCOLATE–PEANUT BUTTER SCONES

MAKES: *10 to 12 scones*

2 cups all-purpose flour
2½ teaspoons baking powder
¼ teaspoon salt
¼ cup chilled butter or margarine, diced
½ cup unsalted chopped peanuts
1½ ounces bittersweet chocolate, grated
2 large eggs
¼ cup milk
½ cup firmly packed brown sugar
¾ cup creamy peanut butter
2 teaspoons vanilla extract
Chocolate syrup for drizzling

**1** Position the rack in the center of the oven and preheat to 375 degrees F. Lightly grease and flour a baking sheet.

**2** In a large bowl, blend together the flour, baking powder, and salt. Using a pastry blender or two knives scissor-fashion, cut in the butter until the mixture resembles coarse meal. Stir in the peanuts and chocolate. In a small bowl, beat the eggs, milk, brown sugar, peanut butter, and vanilla extract until smooth. Combine the two mixtures, stirring until the dough holds together.

**3** Turn the dough out onto a floured surface and pat down to a thickness of ½-inch. Using a biscuit cutter, cut the dough into 3-inch circles. Place the circles ½ inch apart on the prepared baking sheet. Bake for 17 to 19 minutes, or until golden. Remove from the oven, drizzle the tops of the scones with chocolate syrup, and serve hot.

# CORNMEAL SCONES

MAKES: *8 scones*

1½ cups all-purpose flour
¾ cup yellow cornmeal
2 teaspoons baking powder
¼ teaspoon salt
⅓ cup chilled butter or margarine, diced
1 large egg
½ cup milk
¼ cup packed light-brown sugar
½ teaspoon vanilla extract

**1** Position the rack in the center of the oven and preheat to 375 degrees F. Lightly grease and flour a baking sheet.

**2** In a large bowl, blend together the flour, cornmeal, baking powder, and salt. Using a pastry blender or two knives scissor-fashion, cut in the butter until the mixture resembles coarse meal. In a small bowl, beat the egg, milk, brown sugar, and vanilla extract until smooth. Combine the two mixtures, stirring gently until the dough holds together.

**3** Turn the dough out onto a floured surface and knead a few times before patting into an 8-inch circle. Place the circle on the prepared baking sheet. Using a serrated knife, score into 8 wedges (do not cut all the way through the dough). Bake for 15 to 18 minutes, or until golden brown. Remove from the oven and serve hot.

1 cup dried currants
3 tablespoons brandy
4 cups all-purpose flour
½ cup rice flour
2 teaspoons baking powder
½ teaspoon baking soda
¼ cup granulated sugar
1 cup chilled butter or margarine, diced
1 cup heavy cream

**1** In a cup, combine the currants and brandy and set aside to soak. In a large bowl, blend together the two flours, baking powder, baking soda, and sugar. Using a pastry blender or two knives scissor-fashion, cut the butter into the dry ingredients until the mixture resembles coarse meal. Add the currants and cream, stirring gently until the dough holds together.

**2** Gather the dough into a ball and wrap it in plastic wrap. Refrigerate until well chilled, about one hour.

**3** When ready to bake, position the rack in the center of the oven and preheat to 400 degrees F. Lightly grease and flour a baking sheet.

**4** Unwrap the dough and turn it out onto a floured surface. Roll the dough out to a thickness of ½-inch. Using a biscuit cutter, cut into 2-inch circles, reworking the scraps as you go. Place the circles 1 inch apart on the prepared baking sheet. Bake for 13 to 15 minutes, or until golden brown. Remove from the oven and serve hot.

## CURRANT AND BRANDY SCONES

**MAKES:** *10 to 12 scones*

---

½ cup dried cherries
2 tablespoons cherry-flavored brandy
3 tablespoons granulated sugar, plus more for sprinkling over the scones
2 cups all-purpose flour
1 tablespoon baking powder
6 tablespoons chilled butter or margarine, diced
¼ cup chopped almonds
1 large egg, beaten
⅓ cup light cream
Milk for brushing

**1** In a small bowl, combine the cherries, brandy, and the 3 tablespoons of sugar and stir until the sugar is dissolved. Set aside to soak for 30 minutes.

**2** When ready to bake, position the rack in the center of the oven and preheat to 400 degrees F. Lightly grease and flour a baking sheet.

**3** In a large bowl, blend together the flour and baking powder. Using a pastry blender or two knives scissor-fashion, cut in the butter until the mixture resembles coarse meal. Stir in the almonds. Add the egg, light cream, and cherry-brandy mixture and stir gently until the dough holds together.

**4** Turn the dough out onto a floured surface and knead a few times before rolling out to a thickness of ½-inch. Using a biscuit cutter, cut out 2-inch circles, reworking the scraps as you go. Place the circles 1 inch apart on the prepared baking sheet. Brush the tops with milk and sprinkle with sugar. Bake for 12 to 15 minutes, or until golden brown. Remove from the oven and serve hot.

## DRIED CHERRY SCONES

**MAKES:** *10 to 12 scones*

## ENGLISH CREAM SCONES

MAKES: *10 to 12 scones*

**2 cups all-purpose flour**
**1 tablespoon baking powder**
**4 teaspoons granulated sugar, plus more for sprinkling over the scones**
**½ teaspoon salt**
**¼ cup chilled butter or margarine, diced**
**2 large eggs, beaten**
**½ cup sweet cream**
**1 beaten egg white**

**1** Position the rack in the center of the oven and preheat to 375 degrees F. Lightly grease and flour a baking sheet.

**2** In a large bowl, blend together the flour, baking powder, the 4 teaspoons of sugar, and the salt. Using a pastry blender or two knives scissor-fashion, cut in the butter until the mixture resembles coarse meal. Add the egg and cream, stirring gently until the dough holds together.

**3** Turn the dough out onto a floured surface and knead several times before rolling out to a thickness of ½-inch. Using a biscuit cutter, cut the dough into 2-inch circles, reworking the scraps as you go. Place the circles 1 inch apart on the prepared baking sheet. Brush with the beaten egg white and sprinkle with sugar. Bake for 15 to 18 minutes, or until golden brown. Remove from the oven and serve hot.

## FRUIT SCONES

MAKES: *18 scones*

**2½ cups all-purpose flour**
**2 teaspoons baking powder**
**2 teaspoons baking soda**
**½ teaspoon salt**
**6 tablespoons chilled butter or margarine, diced**
**¼ cup golden raisins, plumped**
**¼ cup seedless raisins, plumped**
**1 large egg**
**½ cup granulated sugar**
**1 cup peach-flavored yogurt**
**Grated zest of ½ lemon**
**Milk for brushing tops**

**1** Position the rack in the center of the oven, and preheat to 425 degrees F. Lightly grease and flour a baking sheet.

**2** In a large bowl, blend together the flour, baking powder, baking soda, and salt. Using a pastry blender or two knives scissor-fashion, cut in the butter until the mixture resembles coarse meal. Stir in the two raisins. In a small bowl, beat the egg, sugar, yogurt, and lemon zest until smooth. Then combine the two mixtures, stirring gently until the dough holds together.

**3** Turn the dough out onto a floured surface and knead several time before rolling out to a thickness of ½-inch. Using a biscuit cutter, cut the dough into 2-inch circles, reworking the scraps as you go. Place the circles 1 inch apart on the prepared baking sheet. Brush the tops with milk and bake for 10 to 12 minutes, or until golden brown. Remove from the oven and serve hot.

1½ cups all-purpose flour
1¼ cups quick-cooking rolled oats
¼ cup granulated sugar
1 tablespoon baking powder
½ teaspoon ground nutmeg
¼ teaspoon salt
⅓ cup butter or margarine, at room temperature
1⅓ cups dried mixed fruits, diced
½ cup milk
1 large egg, beaten
Cinnamon sugar for sprinkling

**1** Position the rack in the center of the oven and preheat to 375 degrees F. Lightly grease and flour a baking sheet.

**2** In a large bowl, blend together the flour, oats, sugar, baking powder, nutmeg, and salt. Using a pastry blender or two knives scissor-fashion, cut in the butter until the mixture resembles coarse meal. Add the mixed fruit, milk, and egg, stirring gently until the dough holds together.

**3** Turn the dough out onto the prepared baking sheet and pat it into an 8-inch circle. Using a serrated knife, score the dough into 8 wedges (do not cut all the way through the dough). Sprinkle the top with the cinnamon sugar and bake for 20 to 25 minutes, or until lightly browned. Remove from the oven and serve hot.

# FRUITED OAT SCONES

MAKES: *8 scones*

---

**DOUGH**

2¾ cups all-purpose flour
3½ teaspoons baking powder
½ cup granulated sugar
½ teaspoon salt
6 tablespoons minced crystallized ginger
1⅔ cups heavy cream

**TOPPING**

¼ teaspoon ground ginger for sprinkling
6 tablespoons granulated sugar for sprinkling

**1** Position the rack in the center of the oven and preheat to 425 degrees F. Lightly grease and flour a baking sheet.

**2** To make the dough, in a large bowl, combine the flour, baking powder, sugar, salt, crystallized ginger, and cream and stir gently until the dough holds together.

**3** Turn the dough out onto a floured surface and knead several times before rolling out to a thickness of ½-inch. Using a biscuit cutter, cut the dough into 2-inch circles, reworking scraps as you go. Place the circles 1 inch apart on the prepared baking sheet.

**4** To make the topping, in a cup, combine the ground ginger and sugar. Sprinkle over the tops of the scones and bake for 10 to 15 minutes, or until golden brown. Remove from the oven and serve hot.

# GINGER SCONES

MAKES: *12 scones*

## HAZELNUT-AND-COCONUT SCONES

MAKES: *16 to 18 scones*

2 cups all-purpose flour
2 teaspoons baking powder
½ cup granulated sugar
½ teaspoon salt
⅓ cup butter or margarine, at room
  temperature
½ cup chopped hazelnuts
2 large eggs, beaten
½ cup coconut milk
1½ tablespoons rum
1 egg white, beaten, for brushing
Ground hazelnuts for topping

**1** Position the rack in the center of the oven and preheat to 350 degrees F. Lightly grease and flour a baking sheet.

**2** In a large bowl, blend together the flour, baking powder, sugar, and salt. Using a pastry blender or two knives scissor-fashion, cut in the butter until the mixture resembles coarse meal. Stir in the chopped hazelnuts. In a small bowl, beat the eggs, coconut milk, and rum together. Combine the two mixtures, stirring gently until the dough holds together.

**3** Turn the dough out onto a floured surface and knead several times before rolling out to a thickness of ½-inch. Using a biscuit cutter, cut the dough into 2-inch circles, reworking the scraps as you go. Place the circles 1 inch apart on the prepared baking sheet. Brush with the beaten egg white and sprinkle the ground hazelnuts over the top. Bake for 12 to 15 minutes, or until golden brown. Remove from the oven and serve hot.

## HAZELNUT-AND-CHOCOLATE CHIP SCONES

MAKES: *8 scones*

2 cups all-purpose flour
1½ teaspoons baking powder
½ teaspoon baking soda
¼ teaspoon salt
6 tablespoons chilled butter or
  margarine, diced
1 cup semisweet chocolate chips
½ cup toasted hazelnuts
1 large egg
½ cup buttermilk
⅓ cup packed dark-brown sugar
1½ teaspoons vanilla extract

**1** Position the rack in the center of the oven and preheat to 400 degrees F. Lightly grease and flour a baking sheet.

**2** In a large bowl, blend together the flour, baking powder, baking soda, and salt. Using a pastry blender or two knives scissor-fashion, cut in the butter until the mixture resembles coarse meal. Stir in the chocolate chips and hazelnuts. In a small bowl, beat the egg, buttermilk, brown sugar, and vanilla extract until smooth. Combine the two mixtures, stirring gently until the dough holds together.

**3** Turn the dough out onto the prepared baking sheet and pat it into an 8-inch circle. Using a serrated knife, score the dough into 8 wedges (do not cut all the way through the dough). Bake for 15 to 19 minutes, or until golden brown. Remove from the oven and serve hot.

1¾ cups all-purpose flour
1½ teaspoons baking powder
¼ teaspoon ground cinnamon
¼ cup hard candy, crushed to powder
⅓ cup chilled butter or margarine, diced
½ cup milk
1 large egg, beaten
¼ cup honey

**1** Position the rack in the center of the oven and preheat to 450 degrees F. Lightly grease and flour a baking sheet.

**2** In a large bowl, blend together the flour, baking powder, cinnamon, and crushed candy. Using a pastry blender or two knives scissor-fashion, cut in the butter until the mixture resembles coarse meal. Add the milk, egg, and honey, stirring gently until the dough holds together.

**3** Drop by tablespoonfuls, 1½-inches apart onto the prepared baking sheet and bake for 10 to 15 minutes, or until golden brown. Remove from the oven and serve hot.

# HONEY, CANDY, AND CINNAMON DROP SCONES

MAKES: *10 to 12 scones*

---

**DOUGH**

2 cups all-purpose flour
2 tablespoons baking powder
½ teaspoon baking soda
2 tablespoons granulated sugar
½ teaspoon salt
¼ cup chilled butter or margarine, diced
1 teaspoon grated lemon zest
1 tablespoon poppy seeds
⅔ cup buttermilk or sour milk
1 large egg, beaten

**TOPPING**

4 tablespoons granulated sugar
2 tablespoons lemon juice

**1** Position the rack in the center of the oven and preheat to 425 degrees F. Lightly grease and flour a baking sheet.

**2** To make the dough, in a large bowl, blend together the flour, baking powder, baking soda, sugar, and salt. Using a pastry blender or two knives scissor-fashion, cut in the butter until the mixture resembles coarse meal. Stir in the lemon zest and poppy seeds. Add the buttermilk and egg, stirring gently until the dough holds together.

**3** Turn the dough out onto the prepared baking pan and pat it into an 8-inch circle. Using a serrated knife, score the dough into 8 wedges (do not cut all the way through the dough). Bake for 12 to 15 minutes, or until golden brown.

**4** Meanwhile, make the topping: Combine the sugar and lemon juice and stir until the sugar is dissolved. As soon as the scones are removed from the oven, brush over the tops of the scones. Serve hot.

# LEMON–POPPY SEED SCONES

MAKES: *8 scones*

# LEMON SCONES

MAKES: *16 to 20 scones*

4 cups all-purpose flour
2 tablespoons baking powder
¼ cup granulated sugar
¼ teaspoon salt
½ cup chilled butter or margarine, diced
3 tablespoons grated lemon zest
2 large eggs, beaten
⅔ cup milk

**1** Position the rack in the center of the oven and preheat to 450 degrees F. Lightly grease and flour a baking sheet.

**2** In a large bowl, blend together the flour, baking powder, sugar, and salt. Using a pastry blender or two knives scissor-fashion, cut in the butter until the mixture resembles coarse meal. Stir in the zest. Add the eggs and milk, stirring gently until the dough holds together.

**3** Turn the dough out onto a floured surface and knead several times before rolling out to a thickness of ½-inch. Using a biscuit cutter, cut the dough into 2-inch circles, reworking the scraps as you go. Place the circles ½ inch apart on the prepared baking sheet. Bake for 12 to 15 minutes, or until golden brown. Remove from the oven and serve hot.

# OATMEAL AND CURRANT SCONES

MAKES: *6 to 8 scones*

1¾ cups whole-wheat flour
1½ teaspoons baking powder
¾ teaspoon baking soda
⅓ cup granulated sugar
½ teaspoon salt
¾ cup chilled butter or margarine, diced
1⅓ cups rolled oats
½ cup dried currants
1½ cups buttermilk or sour milk
1 large egg, beaten

**1** Position the rack in the center of the oven and preheat to 375 degrees F. Lightly grease and flour a baking sheet.

**2** In a large bowl, blend together the flour, baking powder, baking soda, sugar, and salt. Using a pastry blender or two knives scissor-fashion, cut in the butter until the mixture resembles coarse meal. Stir in the oats and currants. Add the buttermilk, stirring gently until the dough holds together.

**3** Turn the dough out onto a flour surface and pat to a thickness of 1-inch. Using a biscuit cutter, cut the dough into 3-inch circles, reworking the scraps as you go. Place the circles 3 inches apart on the prepared baking sheet. Brush with the beaten egg and bake for 25 to 30 minutes, or until golden brown. Remove from the oven and cool on a wire rack for about 5 to 7 minutes before serving warm.

2 cups all-purpose flour
1 tablespoon baking powder
¼ cup powdered sugar
½ teaspoon salt
¼ cup chilled butter or margarine
1 teaspoon grated orange zest
¾ cup heavy cream
1 large egg, beaten
½ cup finely chopped golden raisins

**1** Position the rack in the center of the oven and preheat to 350 degrees F. Lightly grease and flour the bottom of a 6-inch round baking pan.

**2** In a large bowl, blend together the flour, baking powder, sugar, and salt. Using a pastry blender or two knives scissor-fashion, cut in the butter until the mixture resembles coarse meal. Add the orange zest, cream, egg, and raisins and stir gently until the dough holds together.

**3** Turn the dough out into the prepared baking pan and pat it down. Using a serrated knife, score the dough into 8 wedges (do not cut all the way through). Bake for 20 to 25 minutes, or until a golden brown. Remove from the oven and cool on a wire rack for about 5 to 7 minutes before serving warm.

# OLD-FASHIONED ORANGE SCONES

MAKES: *8 scones*

2¼ cups all-purpose flour
1 teaspoon baking powder
½ cup granulated sugar
¼ cup poppy seeds
½ teaspoon salt
½ cup chilled butter or margarine, diced
1 teaspoon grated orange zest
1 large egg, beaten
½ cup fresh orange juice

**1** Position the rack in the center of the oven and preheat to 375 degrees F. Lightly grease and flour a baking sheet.

**2** In a large bowl, blend together the flour, baking powder, sugar, poppy seeds, and salt. Using a pastry blender or two knives scissor-fashion, cut in the butter until the mixture resembles coarse meal. Add the orange zest, egg, and orange juice and stir gently until the dough holds together.

**3** Turn the dough out onto the baking sheet and pat it down into a 9-inch circle. Using a serrated knife, score the dough into 8 wedges (do not cut all the way through the dough). Bake for 20 to 25 minutes, or until golden brown. Remove from the oven and cool on a wire rack for 5 to 7 minutes before serving warm.

# ORANGE-AND-POPPY SEED SCONES

MAKES: *8 scones*

## ORANGE–RAISIN SCONES

MAKES: *8 scones*

1¾ cups all-purpose flour
2½ teaspoons baking powder
3 tablespoons granulated sugar
½ teaspoon salt
5 tablespoons chilled butter or margarine, diced
2 tablespoons grated orange zest
½ cup raisins
1 large egg, beaten
6 tablespoons half-and-half

**1** Position the rack in the center of the oven and preheat to 400 degrees F. Lightly grease and flour a baking sheet.

**2** In a large bowl, blend together the flour, baking powder, sugar, and salt. Using a pastry blender or two knives scissor-fashion, cut in the butter until the mixture resembles coarse meal. Stir in the orange zest and raisins. Add the egg and half-and-half and stir gently until the dough holds together.

**3** Turn the dough out onto a floured surface and knead several times before placing on the prepared baking sheet. Pat it into a circle that is ½-inch thick. Using a serrated knife, score the dough into 8 wedges (do not cut all the way through the dough). Bake for 10 to 14 minutes, or until a golden brown. Remove from the oven and serve hot.

## ORANGE, WALNUT, AND CURRANT SCONES

MAKES: *8 scones*

½ cup crushed Rice Krispies™ cereal
2 cups Bisquick® baking mix
⅓ cup plus 1 tablespoon granulated sugar
¼ cup chopped walnuts
¼ cup currants
1 large egg, lightly beaten
1 teaspoon grated orange zest
⅓ cup skim milk
1 large egg white
1 tablespoon water

**1** Position the rack in the center of the oven and preheat to 375 degrees F. Lightly grease and flour a baking sheet.

**2** In a large bowl, combine the cereal, baking mix, ⅓ cup of the sugar, the walnuts, currants, egg, orange zest, and milk and stir gently until the dough holds together.

**3** Turn the dough out onto the prepared baking sheet and flatten into a 7- to 8-inch circle. Using a serrated knife, score the dough into 8 wedges (do not cut all the way through the dough).

**4** In a cup, whisk together the egg white and water until smooth and brush it over the top of the scone. Sprinkle with the remaining 1 tablespoon of granulated sugar. Bake for 10 to 13 minutes, or until lightly browned. Remove from the oven and cool on a wire rack for about 5 to 7 minutes before serving warm or cold.

2 cups all-purpose flour
2 teaspoons baking powder
Dash of ground cayenne pepper
¼ teaspoon salt
⅓ cup chilled butter or margarine, diced
3 tablespoons grated Parmesan cheese
1½ cups shredded Cheddar cheese
2 large eggs, beaten
⅓ cup milk

## PARMESAN AND CHEDDAR CHEESE SCONES

MAKES: *8 scones*

1  Position the rack in the center of the oven and preheat to 400 degrees F. Lightly grease and flour a baking sheet.

2  In a large bowl, blend together the flour, baking powder, cayenne, and salt. Using a pastry blender or two knives scissor-fashion, cut in the butter until the mixture resembles coarse meal. Stir in the Parmesan and Cheddar cheese. Add the eggs and milk, stirring gently until the dough holds together.

3  Turn the dough out onto the prepared baking sheet and pat it into an 8-inch circle. Using a serrated knife, score the dough into 8 wedges (do not cut all the way through the dough). Bake for 15 to 18 minutes, or until a golden brown. Remove from the oven and cool on a wire rack for 5 to 7 minutes before serving warm.

---

3 cups all-purpose flour
1 tablespoon baking powder
3 tablespoons poppy seeds, plus more for sprinkling over the scones
2 tablespoons granulated sugar
¼ teaspoon salt
½ cup chilled butter or margarine, diced
3 large eggs
1 cup plus 1 tablespoon milk

## POPPY SEED SCONES

MAKES: *18 to 20 scones*

1  Position the rack in the center of the oven and preheat to 450 degrees F. Lightly grease and flour two baking sheets.

2  In a large bowl, blend together the flour, baking powder, 3 tablespoons of the poppy seeds, the sugar, and salt. Using a pastry blender or two knives scissor-fashion, cut the butter into the mixture until it resembles coarse meal. In a small bowl, beat two of the eggs and 1 cup of the milk until smooth. Combine the two mixtures, stirring gently until the dough holds together.

3  Turn the dough out onto a floured surface and knead it several times before patting it out to a thickness of ½-inch. Using a biscuit cutter, cut the dough into 2-inch circles, reworking the scraps as you go. Place the circles on the prepared baking sheets.

4  In a cup, whisk together the remaining egg and 1 tablespoon of milk until smooth and brush it over the tops of the scones. Sprinkle with the poppy seeds and bake for 10 to 12 minutes, or until golden brown. Remove from the oven and cool on a wire rack for 5 to 7 minutes before serving warm or cold.

# POTATO-AND-BACON SCONES

MAKES: *6 to 8 scones*

1 cup cooked mashed potatoes (mashed without butter or milk)
1 large egg, beaten
¼ teaspoon salt
⅛ teaspoon ground black pepper
¼ cup all-purpose flour
5 strips crisply cooked bacon, crumbled
2 tablespoons bacon drippings, for coating the skillet

**1** In a large bowl, combine the potatoes, egg, salt, pepper, flour, and bacon and stir gently until the dough holds together.

**2** Coat the bottom of the skillet with bacon drippings and preheat over a medium heat. Using a ¼ cup measure, drop the dough into the hot skillet and fry the scones for 3 to 4 minutes on each side, or until golden brown. (You may have to work in batches.) Remove from the pan and drain on paper towels. Serve warm.

# PRUNE-AND-BRANDY SCONES

MAKES: *6 to 8 scones*

1 cup chopped, pitted, dried prunes
⅓ cup brandy
2 cups all-purpose flour
2 teaspoons baking powder
⅓ cup packed light-brown sugar
¼ teaspoon salt
⅓ cup chilled butter or margarine, diced
¼ cup chopped peanuts
3 ounces finely chopped semisweet chocolate
1 large egg
⅓ cup milk
1 teaspoon vanilla

**1** In a small saucepan set over medium heat, combine the prunes and brandy. Cook, stirring frequently, until the mixture boils. Remove from the heat and set aside.

**2** Position the rack in the center of the oven and preheat to 400 degrees F. Lightly grease and flour a baking sheet.

**3** In a large bowl, blend together the flour, baking powder, sugar, and salt. Using a pastry blender or two knives scissor-fashion, cut in the butter until the mixture resembles coarse meal. Stir in the peanuts and chocolate. In a medium bowl, combine the prune and brandy mixture, the egg, milk, and vanilla extract and stir until mixed. Combine with the dry ingredients, stirring gently until the dough holds together.

**4** Using a ⅓ cup measure, drop the dough 2 inches apart onto the prepared baking sheet and bake for 17 to 20 minutes, or until golden brown. Remove from the oven and cool on a wire rack for about 5 to 7 minutes before serving warm.

½ cup milk
1½ cups raisin bran cereal
2 cups all-purpose flour
2 teaspoons baking powder
½ cup packed dark-brown sugar
½ teaspoon salt
½ cup chilled butter or margarine, diced
⅔ cup chopped pecans
2 large eggs
1½ teaspoons vanilla extract

**1** Position the rack in the center of the oven and preheat to 375 degrees F. Lightly grease and flour a baking sheet.

**2** In a small bowl, blend together the milk and bran cereal and set aside for 10 minutes. Meanwhile, in a large bowl, blend together the flour, baking powder, sugar, and salt. Using a pastry blender or two knives scissor-fashion, cut in the butter until the mixture resembles coarse meal. To the bran mixture, add the eggs and vanilla extract and stir until smooth. Combine the wet and dry ingredients, stirring gently until the dough holds together.

**3** Turn the dough out onto the prepared baking sheet and pat down to a 9-inch circle. Using a serrated knife, score the dough into 8 wedges (do not cut all the way through the dough). Bake for 25 to 30 minutes, or until golden brown. Remove from the oven and cool on a wire rack for 5 to 7 minutes before serving warm or cold.

# RAISIN BRAN-AND-PECAN SCONES

MAKES: *8 scones*

---

3¼ cups all-purpose flour
1 tablespoon baking powder
5 tablespoons granulated sugar
1 teaspoon salt
6 tablespoons chilled butter or margarine, diced
1 cup golden raisins
1 cup milk

**1** Position the rack in the center of the oven and preheat to 425 degrees F. Lightly grease and flour a baking sheet.

**2** In a large bowl, blend together the flour, baking powder, sugar, and salt. Using a pastry blender or two knives scissor-fashion, cut in the butter until the mixture resembles coarse meal. Stir in the raisins. Add the milk and stir gently until the dough holds together.

**3** Turn the dough out onto a floured surface and knead several times before rolling it out to a thickness of ½-inch. Using a biscuit cutter, cut the dough into 2-inch circles, placing the circles 1½-inches apart on the prepared baking sheet. Bake for 8 to 10 minutes or until golden brown. Serve hot.

# RAISIN SCONES

MAKES: *16 to 18 scones*

# ROSEMARY SCONES

MAKES: *8 scones*

2¼ cups all-purpose flour
2 teaspoons baking powder
¼ teaspoon baking soda
1 teaspoon salt
½ cup cold butter or margarine, diced
1 teaspoon fresh minced rosemary
½ teaspoon grated lemon zest
⅓ cup buttermilk
1 large egg

**1** Position the rack in the center of the oven and preheat to 400 degrees F. Lightly grease and flour a baking sheet.

**2** In a large bowl, blend together the flour, baking powder, baking soda, and salt. Using a pastry blender or two knives scissor-fashion, cut in the butter until the mixture resembles coarse meal. Stir in the rosemary and lemon zest. In a small bowl, beat the buttermilk and egg until smooth. Combine the two mixtures, stirring gently until the dough holds together.

**3** Gather the dough into a ball and place it on the prepared baking sheet. Pat the dough into an 8-inch circle. Using a serrated knife, cut the circle into 8 wedges, cutting all the way through the dough. Separate the wedges slightly and bake for 13 to 15 minutes, or until the tops are lightly browned. Remove from the oven and serve hot.

# SCONES WITH ALMONDS, APRICOTS, AND CHOCOLATE CHIPS

MAKES: *8 to 10 scones*

2 cups all-purpose flour
⅓ cup granulated sugar
2 teaspoons baking powder
½ teaspoon salt
¼ cup chilled butter or margarine, diced
1 cup finely chopped almonds
1 cup dried apricots, diced
1 cup miniature chocolate chips
½ cup heavy cream or evaporated milk
1 large egg
1½ teaspoons almond extract

**1** Position the rack in the center of the oven and preheat to 375 degrees F. Lightly grease and flour a baking sheet.

**2** In a large bowl, blend together the flour, sugar, baking powder, and salt. Using a pastry blender or two knives scissor-fashion, cut in the butter until the mixture resembles coarse meal. Stir in the almonds, apricots, and chocolate chips. In a small bowl, beat the cream, egg, and almond extract until smooth. Combine the two mixtures, stirring gently until the dough holds together.

**3** Turn the dough out onto a floured surface and roll it out to a thickness of ½-inch. Using a biscuit cutter, cut the dough into 3-inch circles, reworking the scraps as you go. Place the circles 1 inch apart on the prepared baking sheet and bake for 15 to 20 minutes, or until golden brown. Remove from the oven and cool on a wire rack for 5 to 7 minutes before serving warm.

1½ cups all-purpose flour
1¼ cups old-fashioned rolled oats
1 tablespoon baking powder
1 teaspoon cream of tartar
¼ cup granulated sugar
½ teaspoon ground nutmeg
½ teaspoon salt
1 large egg, beaten
⅓ cup milk
⅔ cup melted butter or margarine
½ cup golden raisins

**1** Position the rack in the center of the oven and preheat to 450 degrees F. Lightly grease and flour a baking sheet.

**2** In a large bowl, combine the flour, oats, baking powder, cream of tartar, sugar, nutmeg, salt, egg, milk, butter, and raisins. Stir gently until the dough holds together.

**3** Gather the dough into a ball and transfer it to the prepared baking sheet. Pat the dough out into a ¾-inch-thick circle. Using a serrated knife, score into 8 wedges (do not cut all the way through) and bake for 10 to 12 minutes, or until golden brown. Remove from the oven and cool on a wire rack for 5 to 7 minutes before serving warm.

# SCOTTISH OAT SCONES

MAKES: *8 scones*

2 cups all-purpose flour
2 teaspoons baking powder
1 teaspoon baking soda
½ teaspoon salt
½ cup chilled butter or margarine, diced
3 large eggs
1 tablespoon honey
1 teaspoon sesame oil
⅓ cup buttermilk
Sesame seeds for topping

**1** Position the rack in the center of the oven and preheat to 425 degrees F. Lightly grease and flour a baking sheet.

**2** In a large bowl, blend together the flour, baking powder, baking soda, and salt. Using a pastry blender or two knives scissor-fashion, cut in the butter until the mixture resembles coarse meal. In a medium bowl, beat two of the eggs, the honey, oil, and buttermilk until smooth. Combine the two mixtures, stirring gently until the dough holds together.

**3** Turn the dough out onto a floured surface and pat it into a 1-inch-thick circle. Using a serrated knife, cut into 10 to 12 wedge shapes, cutting all the way through the dough. Separate the pieces slightly.

**4** In a cup, whisk the remaining egg until smooth and use it to brush the top of each scone. Sprinkle with sesame seeds and bake for 12 to 15 minutes, or until golden brown. Remove from the oven and serve hot.

# SESAME SCONES

MAKES: *10 to 12 scones*

## SOUR CREAM SCONES

MAKES: *6 scones*

1 cup all-purpose flour
1 teaspoon salt
6 tablespoons butter
½ cup sour cream
1 egg yolk
2 teaspoons milk

1  Position the rack in the center of the oven and preheat to 375 degrees F. Lightly grease and flour a baking sheet.

2  In a large bowl, blend together the flour and salt. Using a pastry blender or two knives scissor-fashion, cut in the butter until the mixture resembles coarse meal.

Add the sour cream, stirring gently until the dough holds together.

3  Turn the dough out onto a floured surface and roll out to a thickness of ½ inch. Using a biscuit cutter, cut the dough into 2-inch circles. Place the circles 1 inch apart on the prepared baking sheet.

4  In a cup, whisk together the egg yolk and milk and brush it over the tops of the scones. Bake for 12 to 15 minutes or until golden brown. Remove from the oven and cool on a wire rack for 5 to 7 minutes before serving warm.

## SPICY LEMON AND RAISIN SCONES

MAKES: *8 to 10 scones*

SCONES

2½ cups all-purpose flour
1 tablespoon baking powder
1 teaspoon ground cinnamon
¼ teaspoon ground allspice
¼ teaspoon ground cloves
¼ cup granulated sugar
½ teaspoon salt
¼ cup chilled butter, diced
½ cup raisins
2 tablespoons diced candied lemon peel
1½ cups milk

ICING

1¼ teaspoons milk
⅓ cup confectioners sugar

1  Position the rack in the center of the oven and preheat to 375 degrees F. Lightly grease and flour a baking sheet.

2  To make the scones, in a large bowl, blend together the flour, baking powder, cinnamon, allspice, cloves, sugar, and salt.

Using a pastry blender or two knives scissor-fashion, cut in the butter until the mixture resembles fine crumbs. Stir in the raisins and candied lemon. Add the milk and stir gently until the dough holds together.

3  Turn the dough out onto a floured surface and knead a few times before dividing the dough into 8 balls of equal size. Place the balls on the prepared baking sheet, leaving 1½-inches between them. Bake for 12 to 15 minutes, or until golden brown.

4  Meanwhile, make the icing: In a cup, combine the milk and powdered sugar and stir until smooth. When the scones are done, remove them from the oven and drizzle the icing over them. Cool the scones on a wire rack for 5 to 7 minutes before serving warm.

1 cup all-purpose flour
1 cup whole-wheat flour
1½ teaspoons baking powder
½ teaspoon baking soda
⅓ cup granulated sugar
½ teaspoon ground cinnamon
⅛ teaspoon ground ginger
Dash of ground cloves
Dash of ground nutmeg
¼ teaspoon salt
6 tablespoons chilled butter or
    margarine, diced
⅔ cup seedless raisins
1 large egg
½ cup buttermilk
1 teaspoon vanilla extract

1 Position the rack in the center of the oven and preheat to 400 degrees F. Lightly grease and flour a baking sheet.

2 In a large bowl, blend together the two flours, baking powder, baking soda, sugar, cinnamon, ginger, cloves, nutmeg, and salt. Using a pastry blender or two knives scissor-fashion, cut in the butter until the mixture resembles coarse meal. Stir in the raisins. In a small bowl, beat the egg, buttermilk, and vanilla extract until smooth. Combine the two mixtures, stirring gently until the dough holds together.

3 Turn the dough out onto the prepared baking sheet and pat it into an 8-inch circle. Using a serrated knife, score the dough into 8 wedges (do not cut all the way through the dough). Bake for 15 to 18 minutes, or until golden brown. Remove from the oven and cool on a wire rack for 5 to 7 minutes before serving warm or cooled.

## SPICY WHOLE-WHEAT SCONES

MAKES: *8 scones*

---

4 cups all-purpose flour
4 teaspoons baking powder
¼ teaspoon ground cayenne pepper
1 teaspoon salt
⅔ cup chilled vegetable shortening
½ teaspoon dried basil
¼ teaspoon dried thyme
1 cup grated Swiss cheese
1⅓ cups milk
1 teaspoon prepared Dijon mustard

1 Position the rack in the center of the oven and preheat to 425 degrees F. Lightly grease and flour a baking sheet.

2 In a large bowl, blend together the flour, baking powder, cayenne, and salt. Using a pastry blender or two knives scissor-fashion, cut in the shortening until the mixture resembles coarse meal. Stir in the basil, thyme, and cheese. Add the milk and mustard, stirring gently until the dough holds together.

3 Turn the dough out onto a lightly floured surface and knead a few times. Divide the dough into two equal pieces and roll each into a ball. Place the balls on the prepared baking sheet and pat each into a ½-inch-thick circle. Using a serrated knife, score the tops of each into 8 wedges (do not cut all the way through the dough). Bake for 15 to 20 minutes, or until golden brown. Remove from the oven and serve hot.

## SWISS CHEESE-AND-HERB SCONES

MAKES: *16 scones*

## TREACLE SCONES

MAKES: *8 scones*

1½ cups all-purpose flour
½ teaspoon baking soda
½ teaspoon cream of tartar
½ teaspoon ground cinnamon
½ teaspoon ground ginger
1 teaspoon granulated sugar
Pinch salt
3 tablespoons chilled butter or
   margarine, diced
1 tablespoon treacle or molasses
1 cup warm buttermilk or sour milk

**1** Position the rack in the center of the oven and preheat to 400 degrees F. Lightly grease and flour a baking sheet.

**2** In a large bowl, blend together the flour, baking soda, cream of tartar, cinnamon, ginger, sugar, and salt. Using a pastry blender or two knives scissor-fashion, cut the butter into the mixture until it resembles coarse meal. In a small bowl, combine the treacle and buttermilk and add it to the dry ingredients all at one time. Stir gently until the dough holds together.

**3** Turn the dough out onto a floured surface and knead several times before patting into a ½-inch circle. Place the circle on the prepared baking sheet and, using a serrated knife, score the top into 8 wedges (do not cut all the way through the dough). Bake for 10 to 15 minutes, or until golden brown. Remove from the oven and cool on a wire rack for 5 to 7 minutes before serving warm.

## WHOLE-WHEAT SCONES

MAKES: *4 scones*

1 cup whole-wheat flour
⅓ cup all-purpose flour
½ teaspoon baking powder
2 tablespoons wheat germ
2 tablespoons granulated sugar
¼ teaspoon salt
¼ cup chilled butter or margarine,
   diced
½ cup milk

**1** Position the rack in the center of the oven and preheat to 375 degrees F. Lightly grease and flour a baking sheet.

**2** In a large bowl, blend together the two flours, baking powder, wheat germ, sugar, and salt. Using a pastry blender or two knives scissor-fashion, cut in the butter until the mixture resembles coarse meal. Add the milk and stir gently until the dough holds together.

**3** Turn the dough out onto a floured surface and divide it into four equal pieces. Form each piece into a ball and place them on the prepared baking sheet. Pat each down into a 3-inch circle. Bake for 15 to 20 minutes, or until golden brown. Remove from the oven and cool on a wire rack for 5 to 7 minutes before serving warm or cooled.

# Chapter 11

# WAFFLES

Waffles are not just for breakfast anymore! The possibilities for creative additions to a waffle batter are vast. The restriction in variety comes because of the batter being prepared in a waffle iron—between a base and a cover. Therefore, whatever filling or flavoring is added cannot alter the shape, size, or look of the waffle drastically.

The best way to add a variation to the waffle is to come up with new and exciting toppings, sauces, and syrups. Waffles no longer have to be sweet, but may be served as an evening meal with a surprising savory and tasty topping. Aside from maple syrup, consider serving waffles with a cheese sauce, a salsa, or guacamole. Now that is creative!

# AMERICAN-STYLE CHEESE WAFFLES

MAKES: *8 to 10 waffles*

2 cups all-purpose flour
2 tablespoons granulated sugar
1 tablespoon baking powder
2 cups shredded American cheese
1 teaspoon salt
3 large eggs, separated
½ cup butter or margarine, melted
2 cups milk

**1** Preheat a waffle iron and oil as required.

**2** In a large bowl, combine the flour, sugar, baking powder, cheese, and salt. In a medium bowl, using a whisk or electric mixer on medium speed, beat the egg yolks and butter together until smooth. In a small bowl using an electric mixer on high speed, beat the egg whites until stiff but not dry. Beat the egg yolks with the milk. Combine the dry ingredients and the egg yolk mixture, blending until the dry ingredients are moistened and the batter is smooth. Fold in the egg whites.

**3** Pour ½ cup of the batter into the center of the waffle iron and bake according to the manufacturer's directions. Remove the waffle and continue until all the batter is used. Serve hot.

**SERVING SUGGESTION: Serve with apple butter on the side.**

# APPLE WAFFLES

MAKES: *4 waffles*

1½ cups all-purpose flour
1 teaspoon granulated sugar
1 tablespoon baking powder
1 large apple, peeled, cored and chopped fine
¼ teaspoon ground cinnamon
¼ teaspoon salt
2 large eggs
1 cup milk
¼ tablespoon butter, melted

**1** Preheat a waffle iron and oil as required.

**2** In a large bowl, using a fork or whisk, blend together the flour, sugar, baking powder, apple, cinnamon, and salt. In a small bowl, using an electric mixer on medium speed, beat the eggs until foamy. Beat in the milk and butter. Combine the two mixtures, blending until the dry ingredients are well moistened and the batter is smooth.

**3** Pour ½ cup of the batter onto the waffle iron and bake according to the manufacturer's instructions. Remove the waffle from the iron and continue until all the batter is used. Serve hot with a sprinkling of cinnamon sugar.

1¾ cups milk
½ cup finely chopped dried apricots
2 cups all-purpose flour
4 teaspoons baking powder
½ teaspoon salt
2 large eggs
½ cup butter or margarine, melted
2 tablespoons packed light-brown
  sugar

**1** In a small saucepan set over medium heat, warm the milk until bubbles form around the edges of the pan. Remove from the heat and stir in the apricots. Set aside.

**2** Preheat a waffle iron and oil as required.

**3** In a large bowl, combine the flour, baking powder, and salt. In a medium bowl, using a whisk or electric mixer on medium speed, beat the eggs until foamy. Beat in the butter, milk, and brown sugar. Fold in the apricots and milk. Combine the two mixtures, blending until the dry ingredients are moistened and the batter is smooth.

**4** Pour ½ cup of the batter into the center of the waffle iron and bake according to the manufacturer's directions. Remove the waffle and continue until all the batter is used. Serve hot.

**SERVING SUGGESTION: Serve with apple butter or chocolate syrup.**

# APRICOT WAFFLES

MAKES: *4 to 6 waffles*

# BACON WAFFLES

MAKES: *4 to 6 waffles*

1½ cups all-purpose flour
½ cup graham flour
1 tablespoon granulated sugar
1 tablespoon baking powder
½ cup crisply cooked crumbled
  bacon
¼ teaspoon salt
2 large eggs
2 cups milk
½ cup warmed bacon drippings

**1** Preheat a waffle iron and oil as required.

**2** In a large bowl, using a fork or whisk, blend together the two flours, sugar, baking powder, bacon, and salt. In a medium bowl, using a whisk or electric mixer on medium speed, beat the eggs until foamy. Beat in the milk and bacon drippings. Combine the two mixtures, blending until the dry ingredients are moistened and the batter is smooth.

**3** Pour ½ cup of the batter into the center of the waffle iron and bake according to the manufacturer's directions. Remove the waffle and continue until all the batter is used. Serve hot with whipped butter and maple syrup on the side.

# BANANA WAFFLES

MAKES: *6 waffles*

2 cups all-purpose flour
1 tablespoon granulated sugar
2¼ teaspoons baking powder
¾ teaspoon salt
3 large eggs
1½ cups milk
½ cup melted vegetable shortening
1 cup mashed bananas

**1** Preheat a waffle iron and oil as required.

**2** In a large bowl, combine the flour, sugar, baking powder, and salt. In a small bowl using an electric mixer on high speed, beat the egg whites until stiff but not dry.

**3** In a medium bowl, using a whisk or electric mixer on medium speed, beat the eggs until thick and light-colored. Beat in the milk, shortening, and bananas. Combine the dry ingredients with the egg yolk mixture, blending until the dry ingredients are moistened and the batter is smooth. Fold in the egg whites.

**4** Pour ½ cup of the batter into the center of the waffle iron and bake according to the manufacturer's directions. Remove the waffle and continue until all the batter is used. Serve hot.

**SERVING SUGGESTION: Serve with apple butter on the side.**

# BLUEBERRY WAFFLES

MAKES: *4 to 6 waffles*

2 cups all-purpose flour
4 teaspoons baking powder
¼ teaspoon ground nutmeg
½ teaspoon salt
2 large eggs
½ cup butter or margarine, melted
1¾ cups heavy cream
2 tablespoons granulated sugar
½ cup fresh or frozen, thawed and drained blueberries, finely chopped

**1** Preheat a waffle iron and oil as required.

**2** In a large bowl, combine the flour, baking powder, nutmeg, and salt. In a medium bowl, using a whisk or electric mixer on medium speed, beat the eggs until foamy. Beat in the butter. In a medium bowl, using a whisk or electric mixer on high speed, beat the cream and sugar together until a soft peak forms. Fold in the blueberries. Combine the egg and cream mixtures, blending until smooth. Stir in the dry ingredients, blending until the dry ingredients are moistened and the batter is smooth.

**3** Pour ½ cup of the batter into the center of the waffle iron and bake according to the manufacturer's directions. Remove the waffle and continue until all the batter is used. Serve hot.

**SERVING SUGGESTION: Serve with apple butter or chocolate syrup on the side.**

1 cup all-purpose flour
½ cup whole-wheat flour
½ cup bulgar wheat
1 tablespoon baking powder
½ teaspoon baking soda
1 teaspoon salt
2 large eggs
½ cup butter or margarine, melted
1¼ cups sour milk or buttermilk

**1** Preheat a waffle iron and oil as required.

**2** In a large bowl, combine the two flours, bulgar wheat, baking powder, baking soda, and salt. In a medium bowl, using a whisk or electric mixer on medium speed, beat the eggs thick and light-colored. Beat in the butter and milk. Combine the two mixtures, blending until the dry ingredients are moistened and the batter is smooth.

**3** Pour ½ cup of the batter into the center of the waffle iron and bake according to the manufacturer's directions. Remove the waffle and continue until all the batter is used. Serve hot.

**SERVING SUGGESTION: Serve with warm honey on the side.**

## BULGAR WHEAT WAFFLES

MAKES: *6 to 8 waffles*

---

2 cups all-purpose flour
4 teaspoons baking powder
½ teaspoon salt
2 large eggs
½ cup butter or margarine, melted
1¾ cups heavy cream
2 tablespoons granulated sugar
½ cup finely chopped dried cherries

**1** Preheat a waffle iron and oil as required.

**2** In a small bowl, combine the flour, baking powder, and salt. In a medium bowl, using a whisk or electric mixer on medium speed, beat the eggs until foamy. Beat in the butter. In a large bowl, using a whisk or electric mixer on high speed, beat the cream and sugar together until a soft peak forms. Fold in the cherries. Combine the egg and cream mixtures, blending until smooth. Blend in the dry ingredients, blending until the dry ingredients are moistened and the batter is smooth.

**3** Pour ½ cup of the batter into the center of the waffle iron and bake according to the manufacturer's directions. Remove the waffle and continue until all the batter is used. Serve hot.

**SERVING SUGGESTION: Serve with apple butter or chocolate syrup on the side.**

## CHERRY WAFFLES

MAKES: *4 to 6 waffles*

## COCOA WAFFLES

MAKES: *6 to 8 waffles*

2 cups all-purpose flour
½ cup granulated sugar
4 teaspoons baking powder
½ cup cocoa powder
¼ teaspoon salt
2 large eggs, separated
1½ cups milk
¼ cup melted vegetable shortening

**1** Preheat a waffle iron and oil as required.

**2** In a large bowl, combine the flour, sugar, baking powder, cocoa, and salt. In a medium bowl, using a whisk or electric mixer on medium speed, beat the egg yolks, milk, and shortening together until smooth. In a small bowl using an electric mixer on high speed, beat the egg whites until stiff but not dry. Combine the dry ingredients and the egg yolk mixture, blending until the dry ingredients are moistened and the batter is smooth. Fold in the egg whites.

**3** Pour ½ cup of the batter into the center of the waffle iron and bake according to the manufacturer's directions. Remove the waffle and continue until all the batter is used. Serve hot.

**SERVING SUGGESTION: Serve with a syrup of choice on the side.**

## CORNFLAKE WAFFLES

MAKES: *6 to 8 waffles*

1¼ cups all-purpose flour
2 tablespoons granulated sugar
2¼ teaspoons baking powder
1 cup cornflakes
½ teaspoon salt
3 large eggs, separated
1 cup milk
¼ cup melted vegetable shortening

**1** Preheat a waffle iron and oil as required.

**2** In a large bowl, combine the flour, sugar, baking powder, corn flakes, and salt. In a medium bowl, using a whisk or electric mixer on medium speed, beat the egg yolks, milk, and shortening until smooth. In a small bowl, using an electric mixer on high speed, beat the egg whites until stiff but not dry. Combine the dry ingredients and the egg yolk mixture, blending until the dry ingredients are moistened and the batter is smooth. Fold in the egg whites.

**3** Pour ½ cup of the batter into the center of the waffle iron and bake according to the manufacturer's directions. Remove the waffle and continue until all the batter is used. Serve hot with whipped fruit butter and syrup of choice on the side.

2 cups cornmeal
2 tablespoons vegetable shortening
3 cups water
2 teaspoons salt
4 large eggs
1 cup milk
1 cup buttermilk
2 cups all-purpose flour
1 teaspoon baking soda

1 In the top of a double boiler set over simmering water, combine the cornmeal, shortening, water, and salt. Cook, stirring frequently, for 8 to 10 minutes, or until the mixture is thick. Remove from the heat and cool for about 10 minutes.

2 Preheat a waffle iron and oil as required.

3 Transfer the cornmeal mixture to a large bowl. Using a whisk or an electric mixer on medium speed, beat in the eggs, one at a time, beating vigorously after each addition. Beat in the milk and buttermilk. Combine the flour and baking soda and stir it into the batter.

4 Pour ½ cup of the batter into the center of the waffle iron and bake according to the manufacturer's directions. Remove the waffle and continue until all the batter is used. Serve hot.

**SERVING SUGGESTION: Serve with a fruit compote and sweet whipped cream on the side.**

# CORNMEAL WAFFLES

MAKES: *10 to 12 waffles*

---

2 cups all-purpose flour
4 teaspoons baking powder
½ teaspoon salt
2 large eggs
½ cup butter or margarine, melted
1¾ cups heavy cream
2 tablespoons granulated sugar

1 Preheat a waffle iron and oil as required.

2 In a large bowl, combine the flour, baking powder, and salt. In a medium bowl, using a whisk or electric mixer on medium speed, beat the eggs until foamy. Beat in the butter. In a medium bowl, using a whisk or electric mixer on high speed, beat the cream

and sugar together until a soft peak forms. Combine the egg and cream mixtures, blending until smooth. Stir in the dry ingredients, blending until the dry ingredients are moistened and the batter is smooth.

3 Pour ½ cup of the batter into the center of the waffle iron and bake according to the manufacturer's directions. Remove the waffle and continue until all the batter is used. Serve hot.

**SERVING SUGGESTION: Serve with apple butter or chocolate syrup on the side.**

# CREAM WAFFLES

MAKES: *4 to 6 waffles*

## DATE WAFFLES

MAKES: *4 to 6 waffles*

1½ cups milk
¼ cup vegetable shortening
½ cup chopped, pitted dates
2 cups all-purpose flour
1 teaspoon granulated sugar
4 teaspoons baking powder
¼ teaspoon salt
2 large eggs

**1** In a medium saucepan set over medium heat, combine the milk, shortening, and dates. Cook, stirring frequently, until bubbles start to form around the edge of the pan. Remove from the heat.

**2** Preheat a waffle iron and oil as required.

**3** In a large bowl, combine the flour, sugar, baking powder, and salt. In a medium bowl, using a whisk or electric mixer on medium speed, beat the eggs until thick and light-colored. Continue beating and add the scalded milk mixture. Stir in the dry ingredients, blending until the dry ingredients are moistened and the batter is smooth.

**4** Pour ½ cup of the batter into the center of the waffle iron and bake according to the manufacturer's directions. Remove the waffle and continue until all the batter is used. Serve hot.

**SERVING SUGGESTION: Serve with whipped butter and grape jelly on the side.**

## DUTCH COCOA WAFFLES

MAKES: *4 to 6 servings*

2 cups all-purpose flour
2½ teaspoons baking powder
½ teaspoon baking soda
3 tablespoons Dutch-processed cocoa powder
¼ teaspoon salt
¼ cup granulated sugar
2 large eggs
¼ cup butter or margarine, melted
1¼ cups milk
1 teaspoon crème de cacao or chocolate extract

**1** Preheat a waffle iron and oil as required.

**2** In a large bowl, combine the flour, baking powder, baking soda, cocoa, and salt. In a medium bowl, using a whisk or electric mixer on medium speed, beat the sugar and eggs together until the sugar is dissolved. Beat in the butter, milk, and crème de cacao. Combine the two mixtures, blending until the dry ingredients are moistened and the batter is smooth.

**3** Pour ½ cup of the batter into the center of the waffle iron and bake according to the manufacturer's directions. Remove the waffle and continue until all the batter is used. Serve hot with Whipped Chocolate-Flavored Yogurt on the side.

3 cups all-purpose flour
4 teaspoons baking powder
1½ teaspoons ground ginger
1 teaspoon ground nutmeg
1 teaspoon salt
4 large eggs
⅔ cup packed light-brown sugar
1¼ cups milk
½ cup molasses
½ cup butter or margarine, melted
2 medium bananas, mashed
Ginger Cream (see recipe page 21)

**1** Preheat a waffle iron and oil as required.

**2** In a large bowl, combine the flour, baking powder, ginger, nutmeg, and salt. In a medium bowl, using a whisk or electric mixer on medium speed, beat the eggs and sugar together until the sugar is dissolved. Beat in the milk, molasses, butter, and bananas. Combine the two mixtures, blending until the dry ingredients are moistened.

**3** Pour ½ cup of the batter into the center of the waffle iron and bake according to the manufacturer's directions. Remove the waffle and continue until all the batter is used. Serve hot with Ginger Cream.

# GINGER-BANANA WAFFLES

MAKES: *8 to 10 waffles*

---

1¾ cups all-purpose flour
¼ cup corn flour
4 teaspoons baking powder
2 teaspoons finely chopped bell pepper
½ teaspoon salt
3 large eggs
1½ cups milk
5 tablespoons melted butter

**1** Preheat a waffle iron and oil as required.

**2** In a large bowl, combine the two flours, baking powder, bell pepper, and salt. In a medium bowl, using a whisk or electric mixer on medium speed, beat the eggs until thick and light-colored before beating in the milk and butter. Combine the two mixtures, blending until the dry ingredients are moistened and the batter is smooth.

**3** Pour ½ cup of the batter into the center of the waffle iron and bake according to the manufacturer's directions. Remove the waffle and continue until all the batter is used. Serve hot.

**SERVING SUGGESTION: Serve with whipped butter and syrup of choice on the side.**

# LOUISIANA WAFFLES

MAKES: *6 to 8 waffles*

## Pecan Waffles

Makes: *6 waffles*

1½ cups all-purpose flour
½ cup rice flour
1 tablespoon baking powder
2 teaspoons powdered sugar
½ teaspoon salt
3 large eggs
¼ cup canola oil
1½ cups milk
½ teaspoon vanilla extract

**1** Preheat a waffle iron and oil as required.

**2** In a large bowl, combine the two flours, baking powder, sugar, and salt. In a medium bowl, using a whisk or electric mixer on medium speed, beat the eggs until thick and light-colored. Beat in the oil, milk, and vanilla extract. Combine the two mixtures, blending until the dry ingredients are moistened and the batter is smooth.

**3** Pour ½ cup of the batter into the center of the waffle iron and bake according to the manufacturer's directions. Remove the waffle and continue until all the batter is used. Serve hot with whipped pecan butter on the side.

## Potato Waffles

Makes: *4 to 6 waffles*

1 cup all-purpose flour
2 teaspoons baking powder
½ teaspoon ground nutmeg
½ teaspoon salt
3 large eggs
1 tablespoon butter or margarine, melted
1 cup milk
2 cups mashed potatoes

**1** Preheat a waffle iron and oil as required.

**2** In a large bowl, combine the flour, baking powder, nutmeg, and salt. In a medium bowl, using a whisk or electric mixer on medium speed, beat the eggs until thick and light-colored. Beat in the butter, milk, and potatoes. Combine the two mixtures, blending until the dry ingredients are moistened and the batter is smooth.

**3** Pour ½ cup of the batter into the center of the waffle iron and bake according to the manufacturer's directions. Remove the waffle and continue until all the batter is used. Serve hot.

**Serving suggestion: Serve with whipped butter and syrup of choice on the side.**

## Rice–Buttermilk Waffles

Makes: *8 to 10 waffles*

2 cups all-purpose flour
1 teaspoon granulated sugar
1 tablespoon baking powder
½ teaspoon baking soda
½ teaspoon salt
3 large eggs, separated
6 tablespoons canola oil
2 cups buttermilk or sour milk
1 cup cooked rice

**1** Preheat a waffle iron and oil as required.

**2** In a large bowl, combine the flour, sugar, baking powder, baking soda, and salt. In a medium bowl, using a whisk or electric mixer on medium speed, beat the egg yolks, oil, and buttermilk together until smooth. Stir in the cooked rice. In a small bowl, using a whisk or an electric mixer on high speed, beat the egg whites stiff but not dry. Combine the dry mix with the egg yolk mix, blending until the dry ingredients are moistened and the batter is smooth. Fold in the egg whites.

**3** Pour ½ cup of the batter into the center of the waffle iron and bake according to the manufacturer's directions. Remove the waffle and continue until all the batter is used. Serve hot.

**Serving suggestion: Serve with apple butter on the side.**

1½ cups all-purpose flour
3 tablespoons granulated sugar
2 teaspoons baking powder
½ teaspoon salt
2 large eggs, separated
1¼ cups milk
¼ cup butter or margarine, melted
1 cup cooked Jasmine rice

**1** Preheat a waffle iron and oil as required.

**2** In a large bowl, combine the flour, sugar, baking powder, and salt. In a medium bowl, using a whisk or electric mixer on medium speed, beat the egg yolks, milk, and butter together until smooth. Stir in the cooked rice. In a small bowl, using an electric mixer on high speed, beat the egg whites stiff but not dry. Combine the dry mix with the egg yolk mix, blending until the dry ingredients are moistened and the batter is smooth. Fold in the egg whites.

**3** Pour ½ cup of the batter into the center of the waffle iron and bake according to the manufacturer's directions. Remove the waffle and continue until all the batter is used. Serve hot.

**SERVING SUGGESTION: Serve with apple butter on the side.**

# RICE WAFFLES

MAKES: *6 to 8 waffles*

2 cups all-purpose flour
1 tablespoon cornmeal
1 teaspoon baking soda
½ teaspoon salt
2 large eggs, separated
2 cups plain yogurt

**1** Preheat a waffle iron and oil as required.

**2** In a large bowl, combine the flour, cornmeal, baking soda, and salt. Make an indentation in the center of the dry mix and add the eggs and yogurt. Blend until the dry ingredients are moistened and the batter is smooth.

**3** Pour ½ cup of the batter into the center of the waffle iron and bake according to the manufacturer's directions. Remove the waffle and continue until all the batter is used. Serve hot.

**SERVING SUGGESTION: Serve with apple butter on the side.**

# SOUTH WEST SOUR CREAM WAFFLES

MAKES: *6 waffles*

## SWEET POTATO WAFFLES

MAKES: *6 waffles*

¾ cup all-purpose flour
1 tablespoon granulated sugar
2 teaspoons baking powder
Pinch ground cayenne
Pinch ground nutmeg
1 large egg, separated
1 cup mashed sweet potato
1 cup milk
¼ cup butter or margarine, melted

**1** Preheat a waffle iron and oil as required.

**2** In a large bowl, combine the flour, sugar, baking powder, cayenne, and nutmeg. In a medium bowl, using a whisk or electric mixer on medium speed, beat the egg until foamy. Beat in the potatoes. Beat in the milk and butter. Combine the two mixtures, blending until the dry ingredients are moistened and the batter is smooth.

**3** Pour ½ cup of the batter into the center of the waffle iron and bake according to the manufacturer's directions. Remove the waffle and continue until all the batter is used. Serve hot.

**SERVING SUGGESTION: Serve with apple butter on the side.**

## WHOLE-WHEAT WAFFLES

MAKES: *6 to 8 waffles*

1 cup all-purpose flour
1 cup whole-wheat flour
1 tablespoon baking powder
1 teaspoon salt
2 large eggs
½ cup butter or margarine, melted
1¼ cups milk

**1** Preheat a waffle iron and oil as required.

**2** In a large bowl, combine the two flours, baking powder, and salt. In a medium bowl, using a whisk or electric mixer on medium speed, beat the eggs until thick and light colored. Beat in the butter and milk. Combine the two mixtures, blending until the dry ingredients are moistened and the batter is smooth.

**3** Pour ½ cup of the batter into the center of the waffle iron and bake according to the manufacturer's directions. Remove the waffle and continue until all the batter is used. Serve hot.

**SERVING SUGGESTION: Serve with warm honey and powdered sugar on the side.**

# INGREDIENTS EQUIVALENCY CHARTS

## Bread Crumbs (includes cookie and cracker crumbs)

| | |
|---|---|
| 1 cup fresh bread crumbs | equals 2 ounces or 60 grams |
| 1 slice bread with crust | equals ½ cup bread crumbs, |
| 1 cup dried or toasted bread crumbs | equals 4 ounces or 110 grams |
| 1 pound of bread | equals 14 to 20 slices, or 454 grams |
| 1 cup saltine soda crackers crushed | equals 28 crackers |
| 1 cup graham cracker crumbs | equals 7 to 10 crumbled crackers, 4 ounces or 110 grams |
| 1⅓ cups graham cracker crumbs | equals 16 crumbled crackers, |
| 1 cup vanilla wafer crumbs | equals 30 wafers, 4 ounces, or 110 grams |
| 2 cups vanilla wafer crumbs | equals 8 ounces |
| 1⅔ cups chocolate wafer crumbs | equals 22 wafers |
| 1½ cups gingersnap crumbs | equals 20 snaps |
| 2 cups zwieback crumbs | equals 24 slices, 6 ounces |

## Dairy Products (includes cream, milk, sour cream, yogurt, and buttermilk)

### CHEESE

| | |
|---|---|
| 8 ounce package cream cheese | equals 1 cup or 16 tablespoons |
| 3 ounce package cream cheese | equals 6 tablespoons |
| 1 pound cheese | equals 4 cups grated cheese |

### CREAM

| | |
|---|---|
| ½ pint heavy cream | equals 1 cup or 2 cups whipped cream |
| 1 cup whipping cream | equals 2 to 2½ cups whipped cream |

### MILK

| | |
|---|---|
| 1 cup dry skim milk | equals 1 quart skim milk when mixed |
| 1 cup whole milk | equals 8 ounces weight |
| 1 cup heavy cream | equals 8⅜ ounces weight |
| One 6 ounce can evaporated milk | equals ⅔ cup evaporated milk |
| One 14½ ounce can evaporated milk | equals 1⅔ cups evaporated milk |
| One cup sweetened condensed milk | equals 10½ ounces weight |
| One 14 ounce can sweetened condensed milk | equals 1½ cups sweetened condensed milk |
| ⅓ cup evaporated milk | equals ⅓ cup dry milk plus 6 tablespoons water |

### SOUR CREAM

| | |
|---|---|
| One 8 ounce package sour cream | equals 1 cup sour cream |

# Eggs

| | |
|---|---|
| 1 large whole egg | equals 3 tablespoons, 2 ounces, or 60 grams |
| 1 cup large whole eggs | equals approx. 5 eggs |
| 1 large egg yolk | equals 1 generous tablespoon |
| 1 cup large egg yolks | equals approx. 12 egg yolks |
| 1 large egg white | equals 2 tablespoons, ⅛ cup |
| 2 large eggs | equals scant ½ cup, 3 medium eggs, or 180 grams |
| 1 cup large eggs | equals 4 to 5 large eggs |
| 1 cup eggs | equals 5 to 6 medium eggs |
| 1 cup egg yolks | equals 12 to 14 large egg yolks |
| 1 cup egg whites | equals 7 to 10 large egg whites |
| 1 large egg | equals 2 egg yolks in the recipe |
| 1 large fresh egg | equals ½ tablespoon dry plus 2½ tablespoons water |
| 3 large egg whites stiffly beaten | equals 3 cups meringue |

# Fats (includes butter, margarine, and vegetable shortening)

| | |
|---|---|
| ½ ounce butter | equals 1 tablespoon or ⅛ stick |
| 1 ounce butter | equals 2 tablespoons or ¼ stick |
| 2 ounces butter | equals 4 tablespoons or ½ stick |
| 1 pound butter | equals 2 cups, 4 sticks, 32 tablespoons, or 454 grams |
| ½ pound | equals 1 cup, 1 stick, 8 tablespoons, or 227 grams |
| ¼ pound | equals ½ cup, 1 stick, 4 tablespoons, or 113 grams |
| 1 cup butter or margarine | equals ⅞ cup of lard |
| 1 cup hydrogenated fat | equals 6⅔ ounces |
| 2 tablespoons | equals ¼ stick, 2 tablespoons, or 1 ounce |

# Dry Ingredients (includes arrowroot, baking powder, baking soda, cornmeal, cornstarch, cream of tartar, flour, and salt)

### ARROWROOT

| | |
|---|---|
| 1 teaspoon arrowroot | equals 1 teaspoon all-purpose flour or 1 teaspoon cornstarch |
| 1 tablespoon arrowroot | equals 3 tablespoons all-purpose flour or 2 tablespoons cornstarch |
| 1 tablespoon arrowroot | equals 1 tablespoon all-purpose flour plus 1 teaspoon cornstarch |

### BAKING POWDER & BAKING SODA

| | |
|---|---|
| 2 tablespoons baking powder or soda | equals 1 ounce |
| 1½ teaspoons | equals ¼ ounce |
| 1 tablespoon | equals 0.5 ounce |
| 1 teaspoon | equals 0.17 ounce |

### CORNMEAL

| | |
|---|---|
| 1 cup cornmeal | equals 3 to 4 ounces cornmeal |
| 1 cup uncooked cornmeal | equals 4 cups cooked cornmeal |

# Dry Ingredients (continued)

### CORNSTARCH

| | |
|---|---|
| 1 pound sifted cornstarch | equals 4 cups |
| 1 cup sifted cornstarch | equals 4 ounces |
| 1 ounce sifted cornstarch | equals 4 tablespoons, ¼ cup |
| 1 tablespoon sifted cornstarch | equals 0.29 ounce |
| 1 pound unsifted cornstarch | equals 3½ cups |
| 1 cup unsifted cornstarch | equals 4.5 ounces |
| 1 ounce unsifted cornstarch | equals 3½ tablespoons |
| 1 tablespoon unsifted cornstarch | equals 0.2 ounce |

### CREAM OF TARTAR

| | |
|---|---|
| 4 tablespoons | equals 1 ounce or 30 grams |
| 1 tablespoon | equals ¼ ounces or 7 grams |
| 1 teaspoon | equals 0.08 ounce |

### FLOUR

| | |
|---|---|
| 3 tablespoons all-purpose flour | equals ¼ cup |
| 6 tablespoons all-purpose flour | equals ⅓ cup |
| 9 tablespoons all-purpose flour | equals ½ cup |
| 12 tablespoons all-purpose flour | equals ⅔ cup |
| 15 tablespoons all-purpose flour | equals ¾ cup |
| 18 tablespoons all-purpose flour | equals 1 cup |
| 1 pound all-purpose flour | equals 4 cups |
| 1 cup bleached white all-purpose flour | equals 1 cup unbleached white all-purpose flour |
| 1 cup bleached all-purpose flour | equals 1 cup whole-wheat flour |
| 1 cup bleached all-purpose flour | equals ⅞ cup stone ground whole-wheat flour |
| 1 pound of sifted bread flour | equals 4 cups |
| 1 cup sifted bread flour | equals 4 ounces |
| 1 pound unsifted bread flour | equals 3½ cups |
| 1 cup unsifted bread flour | equals 4.75 ounces |
| 1 pound sifted cake flour | equals 4¼ cups |
| 1 cup sifted cake flour | equals 3.75 ounces |
| 1 pound unsifted cake flour | equals 3½ cups |
| 1 cup unsifted cake flour | equals 4.5 ounces |

### SALT

| | |
|---|---|
| 5 teaspoons salt | equals 1 ounce or 30 grams |
| 1¼ teaspoons | equals ¼ ounce or 7 grams |
| 1 teaspoon | equals 0.2 ounce |

# Fruits and Vegetables

**APPLES**

4 medium-size apples — equals 4 cups peeled and sliced
1 pound medium apples — equals 2 whole apples or 3 cups sliced apples

**APRICOTS**

1 pound dried apricots — equals 3 cups dried apricots

**BANANA**

1 pound banana — equals 3 medium or 1⅓ to 2 cups mashed

**BERRIES**

1 pint fresh berries — equals 1¾ cups of fresh berries

**CARROTS**

1 cup sliced — equals 2 medium-size carrots
1 cup shredded — equals 1½ medium-size carrots

**COCONUT**

1⅓ cups flaked coconut — equals 3½ ounces
1⅓ cups shredded coconut — equals 4 ounces or 115 grams

**CHERRIES**

1 pound candied cherries — equals 3 cups candied cherries

**DATES**

1 pound pitted dates — equals 2 to 2½ cups chopped dates

**FIGS**

1 pound whole figs — equals 2⅔ cups chopped figs

**LEMON**

1 medium-size lemon — equals 2 tablespoons lemon juice
1 medium-size lemon — equals 2 teaspoons lemon zest
1 teaspoon lemon juice — equals ½ teaspoon lemon extact

**LIME**

1 large-size lime — equals 2 tablespoons lime juice

**ORANGE**

1 medium-size orange — equals ⅓ cup orange juice
1 medium-size orange — equals 2 tablespoons orange zest

**POTATOES**

1 pound potatoes — equals 3 medium potatoes
1 pound new potatoes — equals 10 small new potatoes

**PRUNES**

1 pound unpitted prunes — equals 2¼ cups pitted prunes

# Fruits and Vegetables (continued)

### RAISINS

| | |
|---|---|
| 1 pound seedless raisins | equals 2¾ cups raisins |
| 1 pound seeded raisins | equals 3¼ cups raisins |

### STRAWBERRIES

| | |
|---|---|
| 1 quart fresh strawberries | equals 4 cups sliced |

# Gelatin

| | |
|---|---|
| 1 envelope unflavored gelatin | equals 1 scant tablespoon, enough to hard set 2 cups liquid |
| 3 tablespoons | equals 1 ounce or 30 grams |
| 2¼ teaspoons | equals ¼ ounce or 7 grams |
| 1 tablespoon | equals 0.33 ounce |
| 1 teaspoon | equals 0.11 ounce |

# Grains

### OATS

| | |
|---|---|
| 5 ounces rolled oats | equals 1 cup |
| 1 cup uncooked oats | equals 1¾ cups cooked |

### RICE

| | |
|---|---|
| 1 cup uncooked rice | equals 7½ ounces |
| 1 cup uncooked rice | equals 2 cups cooked rice |

# Nuts

### ALMONDS

| | |
|---|---|
| 1 pound almonds in shell | equals 1¼ cups nutmeat |
| 1 pound almonds shelled | equals 3 cups nutmeat or 454 grams |
| ¼ pound almonds shelled | equals 1 cup nutmeat |
| 1 pound slivered almonds | equals 5⅔ cups nutmeat or 454 grams |

### BRAZIL NUTS

| | |
|---|---|
| 1 pound Brazil nuts in shell | equals 1½ cups nutmeat |
| 1 pound Brazil nuts shelled | equals 3¼ cups nutmeat or 454 grams |

### CASHEWS

| | |
|---|---|
| 4½ ounces cashews, shelled | equals 1 cup nutmeat or 130 grams |

### CHESTNUTS

| | |
|---|---|
| 1 pound chestnuts, unshelled | equals 1½ cups nutmeat |

### HAZELNUTS

| | |
|---|---|
| 1 pound hazelnuts, unshelled | equals 1½ cups nutmeat |
| 1 pound hazelnuts, shelled | equals 3½ cups nutmeat |
| 4½ ounces hazelnuts, shelled | equals 1 cup nutmeat or 130 grams |

## Nuts (continued)

**MACADAMIA NUTS**

4 ounces macadamia nuts, shelled ........ equals 1 cup nutmeat or 110 grams

**PEANUTS**

1 pound peanuts, unshelled ........ equals 2 to 2½ cups nutmeat
1 pound peanuts, shelled ........ equals 3 cups nutmeat or 454 grams

**PECANS**

1 pound pecans, unshelled ........ equals 2¼ cups nutmeat
1 pound pecans, shelled ........ equals 4 cups nutmeat or 454 grams

**PISTACHIO NUTS**

5 ounces pistachio nuts, shelled ........ equals 1 cup nutmeat or 150 grams

**WALNUTS**

1 pound walnuts, unshelled ........ equals 2 cups nutmeat
1 pound walnuts, shelled ........ equals 4 cups nutmeat or 454 grams

## Sugar (includes granulated, brown, powdered sugar, and molasses)

**BROWN SUGAR**

1 pound firmly packed brown sugar ........ equals 2½ cups

**GRANULATED**

1 pound granulated sugar ........ equals 2¼ cups
1 cup granulated sugar ........ equals 7 ounces
1 cup granulated sugar ........ equals 1 cup packed brown sugar
1 cup granulated sugar ........ equals 1¾ cups confectioners sugar
1 tablespoon granulated sugar ........ equals 1 tablespoon maple sugar

**HONEY**

1 cup honey ........ equals 12 ounces

**MOLASSES**

11 ounces of molasses ........ equals 1 cups

**POWDERED**

1 pound sifted powdered sugar ........ equals 4 cups
1 cup sifted powdered sugar ........ equals 4 ounces
1 pound unsifted powdered sugar ........ equals 3½ cups
1 cup unsifted powdered sugar ........ equals 4.5 ounces

**SUBSTITUTE**

2 teaspoons sugar ........ equals 1 packet or ¼ teaspoon aspartame
1 tablespoon sugar ........ equals 1½ packets or ½ teaspoon aspartame
¼ cup sugar ........ equals 6 packets or 1¾ teaspoons aspartame
⅓ cup sugar ........ equals 8 packets or 2½ teaspoons aspartame
½ cup sugar ........ equals 12 packets or 3½ teaspoons aspartame
1 cup sugar ........ equals 24 packets or 7¼ teaspoons aspartame

# Equivalency Chart

**WEIGHT**

| | |
|---|---|
| ¼ oz. | 07 g |
| ½ oz. | 17 g |
| 1 oz. | 28 g |
| 2 oz. | 57 g |
| 5 oz. | 142 g |
| 8 oz. | 227 g |
| 12 oz. | 340 g |
| 16 oz. | 454 g |
| 32 oz. | 907 g |
| 64 oz. | 1.8 kg |

**VOLUME**

| | |
|---|---|
| ¼ tsp. | 1.25 ml |
| ½ tsp. | 2.5 ml |
| 1 tsp. | 5 ml |
| 1 tbl. | 15 ml |
| ¼ cup | 59 ml |
| ⅓ cup | 79 ml |
| ½ cup | 119 ml |
| ¾ cup | 177 ml |
| 1 cup | 237 ml |
| 1 pint (2 cups) | 473 ml |
| 1 quart (4 cups) | 946 ml |
| 1 gallon (4 quarts) | 3.78 litres |

**LENGTH**

| | |
|---|---|
| ¼ in. | 5 mm |
| ½ in. | 1 cm |
| ¾ in. | 2 cm |
| 1 in. | 2.5 cm |
| 2 in. | 5 cm |
| 4 in. | 10 cm |
| 1 foot (12 in.) | 30 cm |

**HEAT**

| | | |
|---|---|---|
| very cool | 250–275 F | 130–140 C |
| cool | 300 F | 150 C |
| warm | 325 F | 170 C |
| moderate | 350 F | 180 C |
| moderate hot | 375–400 F | 190–200 C |
| hot | 425 F | 220 C |
| very hot | 450–475 F | 230–250 C |